Principles of International Investment Law

Principles of International Investment Law

Third Edition

RUDOLF DOLZER
URSULA KRIEBAUM
and
CHRISTOPH SCHREUER

UNIVERSITY PRESS

Great Clarendon Street, Oxford, OX2 6DP,
United Kingdom

Oxford University Press is a department of the University of Oxford. It furthers the University's objective of excellence in research, scholarship, and education by publishing worldwide. Oxford is a registered trade mark of Oxford University Press in the UK and in certain other countries

First Edition published in 2008
Second Edition published in 2012
Third Edition published in 2022

Impression: 1

Published in the United States of America by Oxford University Press
198 Madison Avenue, New York, NY 10016, United States of America

British Library Cataloguing in Publication Data

Data available

Library of Congress Control Number: 2021946688

ISBN 978–0–19–285780–4 (hbk.)
ISBN 978–0–19–285781–1 (pbk.)

DOI: 10.1093/law/9780192857804.001.0001

Printed and bound in Great Britain by
Clays Ltd, Elcograf S.p.A.

Summary of Contents

Contents

Foreword to the Third Edition

Rudolf Dolzer conceived the idea and took the initiative for the preparation of this book. He was also the co-author of its first two editions. His death on 3 April 2020 was not only a terrible blow to his friends and colleagues but also affected the work on a further edition. Before the onset of this tragic development, together with Rudolf Dolzer we had taken the decision to add Ursula Kriebaum as a third author. This third edition still reflects Rudolf Dolzer's thinking in large measure and is dedicated to his memory.

In preparing this new edition, we have tried to remain faithful to the book's original idea, while updating and revising the manuscript substantially. These revisions reflect the rapidly developing case law, the evolving attitude of the European Union towards the protection of foreign investments, new developments affecting regional treaties in the field, as well as plans for a multilateral framework.

The dramatic increase in published decisions has necessitated relegating many case references into footnotes while discussing only the most important ones in the text. These case references, although substantially expanded, serve as illustrative examples and should not be taken as comprehensive statements of the existing case law.

We have tried to list some of the most important academic writings at the beginning of each chapter. Any in-depth discussion of specific questions will need to rely on specialized publications and tribunal practice.

In preparing this third edition, we have received help from several quarters. We owe particular thanks to Kilian Wagner who has been extremely helpful with substantive suggestions, has prepared the tables, and has helped with the proofreading. Vishesh Bhatia has prepared research notes for several chapters and has checked major parts of the manuscript. Additional help has come from Berta Boknik, Maria Förster, Nina Öllinger, Anushka Tanwar, Julia Hildebrandt, Isabella Hofmann, Michael Moffatt, Laura Winninger, and Markus Stemeseder. Special thanks to the professionals at Oxford University Press who have guided this volume to publication.

Ursula Kriebaum
Christoph Schreuer
September 2021

Foreword to the Third Edition

Table of Cases

INTERNATIONAL ARBITRATIONS

PCIJ/ICJ

EUROPEAN COURT OF HUMAN RIGHTS

COURT OF JUSTICE OF THE EUROPEAN UNION

Iran-US Claims Tribunal

INTERNATIONAL CRIMINAL TRIBUNAL FOR THE FORMER YUGOSLAVIA

WTO

NATIONAL COURTS

List of Abbreviations

AF	Additional Facility
AIG	American International Group
AJIL	American Journal of International Law
Arbitr Int	Arbitration International
ARSIWA	Articles on Responsibility of States for Internationally Wrongful Acts
ASEAN	Association of Southeast Asian Nations
ASIL Proceedings	Proceedings of the American Society of International Law
Austrian YB Int Arb	Austrian Yearbook on International Arbitration
BCDR	Bahrain Chamber for Dispute Resolution
BIT	Bilateral Investment Treaty
BLEU	Belgo-Luxembourg Economic Union
BOO	Build, Operate and Own
BOT	Build, Operate and Transfer
BYIL	British Year Book of International Law
CAFTA	Central American Free Trade Agreement
CETA	Comprehensive Economic and Trade Agreement (Canada-EU)
Chinese JIL	Chinese Journal of International Law
CIETAC	China International Economic and Trade Arbitration Commission
CJEU	Court of Justice of the European Union
Cornell Int'l LJ	Cornell International Law Journal
CPTPP	Comprehensive and Progressive Agreement for Trans-Pacific Partnership
DCF	Discounted Cash Flow
DFC	U.S. International Development Finance Corporation
DR-CAFTA	Dominican Republic CAFTA
DR Congo	Democratic Republic of the Congo
ECOWAS	Economic Community of West African States
ECT	Energy Charter Treaty
ECtHR	European Court of Human Rights
eg	*exempli gratia*—for example
EPIL	Encyclopedia of Public International Law
EU	European Union
EURIBOR	Euro Interbank Offered Rate
FCN	Friendship, Commerce, and Navigation
FET	Fair and Equitable Treatment
FIC	Foreign Investment Commission
FIPA	Foreign Investment Protection Agreement
FPS	Full Protection and Security

FSIA	Foreign Sovereign Immunities Act
FTA	Free Trade Agreement
FTC	Free Trade Commission
FYROM	Former Yugoslav Republic of Macedonia
GA	General Assembly
GATS	General Agreement on Trade in Services
GATT	General Agreement on Tariffs and Trade
Harvard ILJ	Harvard International Law Journal
HRLJ	Human Rights Law Journal
IBA	International Bar Association
ICC	International Chamber of Commerce
ICJ	International Court of Justice
ICJ Rep	International Court of Justice Reports
ICLQ	International & Comparative Law Quarterly
ICSID	International Centre for Settlement of Investment Disputes
ICSID Convention	Convention on the Settlement of Investment Disputes between States and Nationals of Other States
ICSID Rev	ICSID Review—Foreign Investment Law Journal
ICTY	International Criminal Tribunal for the former Yugoslavia
ILC	International Law Commission
ILM	International Legal Materials
ILR	International Law Reports
IMF	International Monetary Fund
Int'l Lawyer	The International Lawyer
Iran-US CTR	Iran-US Claims Tribunal Reports
JIDS	Journal of International Dispute Settlement
J Int Arb	Journal of International Arbitration
JWIT	Journal of World Investment & Trade
LCIA	London Court of International Arbitration
LIBOR	London Interbank Offered Rate
LPICT	Law and Practice of International Courts and Tribunals
LSA	Legal Stability Agreement
MAI	Multilateral Agreement on Investment
MERCOSUR	Mercado Común del Sur
MFN	Most-Favoured-Nation
MIGA	Multilateral Investment Guarantee Agency
MJDR	McGill Journal of Dispute Resolution
NAFTA	North American Free Trade Agreement
NGO	Non-Governmental Organization
NHA	National Highway Authority
NIA	Nevis Island Authority
NYU Environmental LJ	New York University Environmental Law Journal
NYU J Int'l L & Pol	New York University Journal of International Law and Politics
OECD	Organization for Economic Co-operation and Development
OHADA	Organisation for the Harmonisation of Business Law in Africa

OIC Agreement	Agreement on Promotion, Protection and Guarantee of Investments Among Member State of the Organisation of the Islamic Conference
OPIC	Overseas Private Investment Corporation
p	page
para	paragraph
PCA	Permanent Court of Arbitration
PCIJ	Permanent Court of International Justice
Recueil	Recueil des Cours de l'Académie de droit international (Collected Courses of the Hague Academy of International Law)
RIAA	Reports of International Arbitral Awards
SCA	Suez Canal Authority
SCC	[Arbitration Institute of the] Stockholm Chamber of Commerce
Stockholm Int Arb Rev	Stockholm International Arbitration Review
TDM	Transnational Dispute Management
TEC	Treaty Establishing the European Community
TFEU	Treaty on the Functioning of the European Union
TRIMS	Trade-Related Investment Measures
TTIP	Transatlantic Trade and Investment Partnership
UAE	United Arab Emirates
UN	United Nations
UNCITRAL	United Nations Commission on International Trade Law
UNCTAD	United Nations Conference on Trade and Development
UNESCO	United Nations Educational, Scientific and Cultural Organization
UNTS	United Nations Treaty Series
US	United States of America
USMCA	United States-Mexico-Canada Agreement
USSR	Union of Soviet Socialist Republics
VAT	value-added tax
VCLT	Vienna Convention on the Law of Treaties
WTO	World Trade Organization
YBILC	Yearbook of the International Law Commission

I

History, Sources, and Nature of International Investment Law

ADDITIONAL READING: PT Muchlinski, *Multinational Enterprises and the Law*, 2nd edn (2007); Z Douglas, *The International Law of Investment Claims* (2009); A Newcombe and L Paradell, *Law and Practice of Investment Treaties* (2009); SW Schill, *The Multilateralization of International Investment Law* (2009); KJ Vandevelde, *Bilateral Investment Treaties: History, Policy and Interpretation* (2010); J Alvarez, *The Public International Law Regime Governing International Investment* (2011); A Kulick, *Global Public Interest in International Investment Law* (2012); A Rigo Sureda, *Investment Treaty Arbitration* (2012); K Miles, *The Origins of International Investment Law: Empire, Environment and the Safeguarding of Capital* (2013); J Bonnitcha, *Substantive Protection under Investment Treaties* (2014); A Roberts, 'Triangular Treaties: The Extent and Limits of Investment Treaty Rights' (2015) 56 *Harvard ILJ* 353; D Collins, *An Introduction to International Investment Law* (2016); C Schreuer, 'The Development of International Law by ICSID Tribunals' (2016) 31 *ICSID Rev* 728; J Bonnitcha, LNS Poulsen, and M Waibel, *The Political Economy of the Investment Treaty Regime* (2017); J Hepburn, *Domestic Law in International Investment Arbitration* (2017); C McLachlan, L Shore, and M Weiniger, *International Investment Arbitration: Substantive Principles*, 2nd edn (2017); AR Parra, *The History of ICSID*, 2nd edn (2017); M Sasson, *Substantive Law in Investment Treaty Arbitration*, 2nd edn (2017); U Kriebaum, 'Evaluating Social Benefits and Costs of Investment Treaties: Depoliticization of Investment Disputes' (2018) 33 *ICSID Rev* 14; SW Schill et al, *International Investment Law and History* (2018); T St John, *The Rise of Investor–State Arbitration: Politics, Law and Unintended Consequences* (2018); F Ortino, *The Origin and Evolution of Investment Treaty Standards* (2019); B Sabahi, N Rubins, and D Wallace, *Investor–State Arbitration* (2019); P Dumberry, *A Guide to General Principles of Law in International Investment Arbitration* (2020); JW Salacuse, *The Law of Investment Treaties*, 3rd edn (2021).

1. The history of international investment law

(a) Early developments

In 1758, Emer de Vattel addressed the status of foreigners in his treatise *The Law of Nations*.[1] He explained that once a State admitted a foreigner to its territory, which it was not obliged to do, it had to protect him or her in the same manner as its own subjects.[2] In addition, the foreigner maintained the bond to the home State and his or her property remained part of the wealth of the home State. As a result, an injury to the property of a foreigner was an injury to the foreigner's home State which obtained the right to exercise protection over that property, known as diplomatic protection.[3]

In fact, States espoused the claims of their nationals throughout the eighteenth and nineteenth centuries, and the Permanent Court of International Justice formally recognized a State's right to do so.[4] States used economic, political, and military means to exercise diplomatic protection. This led to numerous inter-State conflicts and even military interventions referred to as gunboat diplomacy.[5]

Already the Jay Treaty of 1794[6] provided for mixed arbitration, that is, arbitration between States and individuals. A Commission created by this Treaty decided by majority vote and produced binding awards.[7] It served as model for future successful arbitrations.[8]

In 1818 Secretary of State John Adams emphatically highlighted the protection of alien property by the rules of international law in the context of a dispute concerning the Treaty of San Lorenzo of 1795:[9]

> There is no principle of the law of nations more firmly established than that which entitles the property of strangers within the jurisdiction of another country in friendship with their own to the protection of its sovereign by all efforts in his power.[10]

1 E de Vattel, *The Law of Nations*, J Chitty Translation, 1844, Book II, Chapter VIII.

2 Para 104.

3 Para 109.

4 *The Mavrommatis Palestine Concessions (Greece v United Kingdom)*, Judgment, 30 August 1924. PCIJ Ser A, No 12, at 12.

5 E Borchard, *Diplomatic Protection of Citizens Abroad* (1915).

6 Treaty of Amity, Commerce and Navigation between His Britannic Majesty and the United States of America, 19 November 1794.

7 Articles VI and VII.

8 JI Charney, 'Is International Law Threatened by Multiple International Tribunals?' (1998) 271 *Recueil* 101, 119.

9 Treaty of Friendship, Limits, and Navigation Between Spain and The United States, 27 October 1795.

10 Cited in JB Moore, *A Digest of International Law*, vol 4 (1906) 5.

Until the Communist Revolution in Russia in 1917, neither State practice nor the commentators of international law had reason to pay special attention to rules protecting foreign investment. Treaty practice in the nineteenth century protected alien property not on the basis of an autonomous standard, but by reference to the domestic laws of the host State. An illustration is found in Article 2(3) of the Treaty between Switzerland and the United States of 1850:

> In case of [...] expropriation for purposes of public utility, the citizens of one of the two countries, residing or established in the other, shall be placed on an equal footing with the citizens of the country in which they reside in respect to indemnities for damages they may have sustained.[11]

The implicit assumption was that each State would in its national laws protect private property and that the extension of the domestic scheme of protection would lead to sufficient guarantees for the alien investor.

In a famous study, first published in 1868, the Argentine jurist Carlos Calvo presented a new perspective of this paradigm. He asserted that the international rule should be understood as allowing the host State to reduce the protection of alien property together with reducing the guarantees for property held by nationals.[12] Calvo's view would have left room for all the vagaries of domestic law, allowing both strong guarantees, but also a complete lack of protection. In addition, Calvo argued that foreigners must assert their rights before domestic courts and that they have no right of diplomatic protection by their home State or access to international tribunals. The Calvo doctrine, as it became known, was conceived against the background of gunboat diplomacy by capital-exporting countries and other practices through which these countries imposed their view of international law on foreign governments.

In 1902, in reaction to an armed intervention by British, German, and Italian forces in Venezuela to enforce claims related to State-bonds held by their citizens, the foreign minister of Argentina, Luis María Drago, in a letter to the United States advanced a doctrine designed to prevent such events in the future. In 1907, the Drago–Porter Convention was adopted to prevent the use of force for the collection of debt,[13] and Calvo's radical attack on the protection of foreign citizens lost some of its justification.

On the international level, the Calvo doctrine remained at the margins of the debate, and the dominant position was that a State was bound by rules of international law, that were separate from national law. Therefore, treatment of foreigners in the

[11] Cited in R Wilson, *United States Commercial Treaties and International Law* (1960) 111.

[12] C Calvo, *Derecho Internacional Teórico y Práctico de Europa y América* (1868); C Calvo, *Le droit international—théorie et pratique*, vol 3 (1896) 138.

[13] W Benedek, 'Drago–Porter Convention' (1907) *EPIL* III 234.

same way as nationals was not necessarily sufficient. Elihu Root stated the prevalent position in 1910:

> There is a standard of justice, very simple, very fundamental, and of such general acceptance by all civilized countries as to form a part of the international law of the world. The condition upon which any country is entitled to measure the justice due from it to an alien by the justice which it accords to its own citizens is that its system of law and administration shall conform to this general standard. If any country's system of law and administration does not conform to that standard, although the people of the country may be content or compelled to live under it, no other country can be compelled to accept it as furnishing a satisfactory measure of treatment to its citizens.[14]

Nevertheless, the position proposed by Calvo was revived on a practical level in a dramatic fashion after the Russian revolution in 1917: The Soviet Union expropriated national enterprises without compensation and justified its uncompensated expropriation of alien property by relying on the national treatment standard. The ensuing dispute led, inter alia, to the Lena *Goldfields Arbitration* of 1930 in which case the Tribunal required the Soviet Union to pay compensation to the alien claimant, based upon the concept of unjust enrichment.[15]

A further attack upon the traditional standard of international law was mounted by Mexico in 1938 in the course of the nationalization of US interests in the Mexican agrarian and oil business. This dispute led to a forthright diplomatic exchange in which Secretary of State Cordell Hull wrote a now-famous letter to his Mexican counterpart. In this letter, he spelled out that the rules of international law allowed expropriation of foreign property, but required 'prompt, adequate and effective compensation'.[16] The Mexican position echoed the Calvo doctrine and foreshadowed harsh disputes between industrialized and developing countries in later decades of post-decolonization.

(b) The emergence of an international minimum standard

The Calvo doctrine, the Russian Revolution, and the Mexican position notwithstanding, what had emerged from the various international disputes about the status of aliens in general (not just in regard to foreign investment) was a widespread sense that the alien is protected against unacceptable measures of the host

[14] E Root, 'The Basis of Protection to Citizens Residing Abroad' (1910) 4 *AJIL* 517, 528.

[15] VV Veeder, 'The Lena Goldfields Arbitration: The Historical Roots of Three Ideas' (1998) 47 *ICLQ* 747; A Nussbaum, 'The Arbitration between the Lena Goldfields, Ltd. and the Soviet Government' (1950) 36 *Cornell Law Rev* 31.

[16] G Hackworth, *Digest of International Law*, vol 3 (1942), vol 5 (1943).

State by rules of international law which are independent of those of the host State. The sum of these rules eventually came to be known as the international minimum standard.[17] The fundamental reasons that prompted the evolution and recognition of these rules are reflected in general terms in a relatively modern decision of the European Court of Human Rights:

> Especially as regards a taking of property effected in the context of a social reform, there may well be good grounds for drawing a distinction between nationals and non-nationals as far as compensation is concerned. To begin with, non-nationals are more vulnerable to domestic legislation: unlike nationals, they will generally have played no part in the election or designation of its authors nor have been consulted on its adoption. Secondly, although a taking of property must always be effected in the public interest, different considerations may apply to nationals and non-nationals and there may well be legitimate reason for requiring nationals to bear a greater burden in the public interest than non-nationals.[18]

The minimum standard as it emerged historically, concerned the status of the alien in general, applying to such diverse areas as procedural rights in criminal law, rights before courts in general, rights in matters of civil law, and rights in regard to private property held by the foreigner. An early leading case on the subject matter, *Neer v Mexico*,[19] decided in 1926, was concerned with the duty of the host State Mexico to investigate appropriately the circumstances of the unaccounted death of a US national. The widow of the US national brought her claim for compensation before a Mixed Claims Commission. The Commission issued the following statement concerning a host State's responsibility for a violation of the minimum standard:

> the treatment of an alien, in order to constitute an international delinquency, should amount to an outrage, to bad faith, to willful neglect of duty, or to an insufficiency of governmental action so far short of international standards that every reasonable and impartial man would readily recognize its insufficiency.[20]

This statement of the standard did not relate to matters of property of the alien and was issued when matters of foreign investment and related issues such as economic growth, development, good governance, and an investment-friendly climate were

[17] E Borchard, *The Diplomatic Protection of Citizens Abroad* (1916); AH Roth, *The Minimum Standard of International Law Applied to Aliens* (1949).

[18] *James & others v United Kingdom*, ECtHR, Judgment, 21 February 1986, para 63; see also *Lemire v Ukraine*, Award, 28 March 2011, para 57.

[19] *Neer v Mexico*, 15 October 1926, 4 RIAA 60.

[20] At pp 61–62.

not yet high on the international agenda. Yet this case has resurfaced in decisions of investment tribunals.[21]

(c) Developments after the Second World War

The period between 1945 and 1990 saw major confrontations between the growing number of newly independent developing countries on the one hand and capital-exporting States on the other about the status of customary law governing foreign investment. The debates were often characterized by ideological positions, by an insistence on strict notions of sovereignty, and by the call for economic decolonization, including independence from centres of colonialism. A centrepiece of this debate was the call for 'Permanent Sovereignty over Natural Resources'.[22] Developing States asserted these positions in the United Nations General Assembly (GA), where they soon held, and still hold, the majority of votes.

In 1962, an early confrontation ended with a compromise: GA Resolution 1803 stated that in the case of expropriation, 'appropriate compensation' would have to be paid, thus explicitly confirming neither the Hull rule nor the Calvo doctrine. Remarkably, a consensus existed then that foreign investment agreements, concluded by a government, must be observed in good faith.[23]

The developing States decided to take the matter further and brought it to a culmination in 1974, again in the United Nations General Assembly. Encouraged by the success of the oil-producing countries in boycotting Western States, by sharp oil price increases, as well as by the then prevailing spirit of economic independence in Latin America, several resolutions were passed which called for a 'New International Economic Order'. One of its cornerstones was the aspiration to abolish the rules of international law governing the expropriation of alien property and to replace them by domestic rules as determined by national authorities:

> Each State has the right: … (c) To nationalize, expropriate or transfer ownership of foreign property, in which case appropriate compensation should be paid by the State adopting such measures, taking into account its relevant laws and regulations and all circumstances that the State considers pertinent. In any case where the question of compensation gives rise to a controversy, it shall be settled under

[21] See below VIII.1(f).

[22] See R Dolzer, 'Permanent Sovereignty over Natural Resources and Economic Decolonization' (1986) 7 *HRLJ* 217; K Gess 'Permanent Sovereignty over Natural Resources: An Analytical Review of the United Nations Declaration and its Genesis' (1964) 13 *ICLQ* 398; SM Schwebel 'The Story of the U.N.'s Declaration on Permanent Sovereignty over Natural Resources' (1963) 49 *ABA J* 463; C Brower and J Tepe 'The Charter of Economic Rights and Duties of States: A Reflection or Rejection of International Law?' (1975) 9 *The Int'l Lawyer* 295.

[23] UN GA Resolution 1803 (14 December 1962) para 8: 'Foreign investment agreements freely entered into by or between sovereign States shall be observed in good faith'.

> the domestic law of the nationalizing State and by its tribunals, unless it is freely and mutually agreed by all States concerned that other peaceful means be sought on the basis of the sovereign equality of States and in accordance with the principle of free choice of means.[24]

This confrontation led to insecurity about the customary international rules governing foreign investment. This phase lasted essentially until around 1990. At that time, it became clear that, together with the end of the Soviet Union, the socialist view of property had collapsed and that the call for economic independence had brought a major financial crisis, rather than more welfare upon the people of Latin America. From that time onwards, Latin American States started to conclude bilateral investment treaties (BITs) the spirit of which was at odds with the Calvo doctrine. The annual calls for 'permanent sovereignty' in the United Nations General Assembly came to an end.[25]

At the same time, international financial institutions revised their position on the role of private investment. The so-called Washington Consensus,[26] with its new emphasis on the private sector in the process of development, summarized the now dominant approach to development and its concomitant positive view of private foreign investment. In 1992, the new approach crystallized in the Preamble of the World Bank's Guidelines on the Treatment of Foreign Direct Investment. It recognizes:

> that a greater flow of foreign direct investment brings substantial benefits to bear on the world economy and on the economies of developing countries in particular, in terms of improving the long term efficiency of the host country through greater competition, transfer of capital, technology and managerial skills and enhancement of market access and in terms of the expansion of international trade.[27]

Within this new climate of international economic relations, the fight of previous decades against customary rules protecting foreign investment had abruptly become anachronistic and obsolete. The tide had turned, and the new theme for capital-importing States was not to oppose classical customary law but instead to attract additional foreign investment by granting more protection to foreign investment than required by traditional customary law, now on the basis of treaties. Five

[24] UN GA Resolution 3281 (12 December 1974) 'Charter of Economic Rights and Duties of States' Article 2.2(c).

[25] See T Wälde, 'A Requiem for the "New International Economic Order"—The Rise and Fall of Paradigms in International Economic Law and a Post-Mortem with Timeless Significance', in G Hafner et al (eds) *Liber Amicorum Professor Ignaz Seidl-Hohenveldern* (1998) 771.

[26] See VI.2 below.

[27] World Bank Group, 'Guidelines on the Treatment of Foreign Direct Investment', *Legal Framework for the Treatment of Foreign Investment: Volume II: Guidelines* (1992) 35.

decades after it was formulated, the Hull rule became a standard element of hundreds of new BITs as well as multilateral agreements, such as the Energy Charter Treaty (ECT), adopted in 1994 or the North American Free Trade Agreement (NAFTA), in which Mexico decided to join the United States and Canada, also adopted in 1994. Developing countries started to conclude investment treaties among themselves, and the characteristics of these treaties did not significantly deviate from those concluded with developed States.[28]

Since the early 1990s, the focus had shifted to the negotiation of new treaties on foreign investment, and to their application and interpretation. The elucidation of the state of customary law is no longer a central concern of academic commentators. However, the relevant issues have not disappeared. For instance, in the context of NAFTA, the three States parties decided that the standards of 'fair and equitable treatment' and of 'full protection and security' must be understood to require host States to observe customary law, and not a more demanding autonomous treaty-based standard.[29] In consequence, nearly forgotten arbitral decisions—mainly the *Neer* case of 1926—were unearthed. The importance of this award for the current state of customary law governing foreign investment has led to a debate on whether an old arbitral ruling addressing the duty to prosecute nationals suspected of a crime against a foreigner is the appropriate vantage point from which to develop contemporary rules governing foreign investment.[30]

(d) The evolution of investment protection treaties

The roots of modern treaty rules on foreign investment can be traced back to 1778 when the United States and France concluded their first commercial treaty,[31] followed in the nineteenth century by treaties between the United States and its European allies and subsequently the new Latin American States.[32] After 1919, the United States negotiated a series of agreements on Friendship, Commerce, and Navigation (FCN), followed by another series of treaties between 1945 and 1966.[33] These treaties mainly addressed trade issues, but most of them also contained rules requiring compensation in case of expropriation.

Rules on investment were never prominent or distinct in these FCN treaties, even though the pre-1945 treaties contained not just compensation clauses, but also provisions on the right to establish certain types of business in the partner

[28] See UNCTAD, Bilateral Investment Treaties 1995–2006: Trends in Investment Rulemaking (2007).

[29] See VIII.1(f) below.

[30] See VIII.1(f) below.

[31] KJ Vandevelde, *United States Investment Treaties: Policy and Practice* (1992) 14.

[32] R Wilson, *United States Commercial Treaties and International Law* (1960) 2.

[33] KJ Vandevelde, 'The Bilateral Investment Program of the United States' (1988) 21 *Cornell Int'l LJ* 201.

State. After 1945, trade matters were regulated in separate treaties, and FCN Treaties contained more detail on foreign investment.[34]

The era of modern BITs began in 1959 when Germany and Pakistan adopted a bilateral agreement, which entered into force in 1962. Germany had decided to pursue a programme of bilateral treaties to protect its companies' foreign investments made in accordance with the laws of the host State. Soon after Germany had launched its programme and successfully negotiated its first treaties, other European States followed suit: Switzerland concluded its first such treaty in 1961,[35] France in 1972.[36]

The early treaties did not provide for direct investor–State dispute settlement, but for the submission of disputes to the International Court of Justice or ad hoc State-to-State arbitration.[37] Starting with the treaty between Chad and Italy of 1969, BITs began offering arbitration between host States and foreign investors.

In 1977, the United States (US) State Department launched an initiative for the United States to join the European practice of concluding agreements dealing only with foreign investment, mainly to protect investments of nationals abroad.[38] Following a short period of political hesitation, caused by the fear of exporting jobs by way of promoting foreign investment, and a shift of responsibility from the State Department to the United States Trade Representative during that period, between 1982 and 2021 the United States concluded 47 BITs and 70 treaties with investment provisions, mainly with developing States.[39]

A similarly significant trend was the evolution of BIT practice by Asian States. China has concluded 124 BITs and 24 treaties with investment provisions.[40] India concluded its first BIT in 1994, but by 1999 had already entered into 26 BITs, and in 2021 was a party to 86 such treaties as well as 13 treaties with investment provisions. However, India terminated the majority of its investment treaties in order to

[34] JW Salacuse, 'Towards a Global Treaty on Foreign Investment: The Search for a Grand Bargain' in N Horn (ed) *Arbitrating Foreign Investment Disputes* (2004) 51, 56.

[35] Treaty between Switzerland and Tunisia, 2 December 1961; see N Huu-Tru, 'Le réseau suisse d'accords bilatéraux d'encouragement et de protection des investissements' (1988) 92 *Révue Générale de Droit International Public* 577.

[36] Treaty between France and Tunisia, 30 June 1972; see P Juillard, 'Le réseau francais des conventions bilatérales d'investissement: à la recherche d'un droit perdu?' (1987) 13 *Droit et Pratique du Commerce International* 9.

[37] Germany–Pakistan BIT (1959) Article 11.

[38] For an historical appraisal of the US BIT programme see KJ Vandevelde, 'The BIT Program: A Fifteen-Year Appraisal' (1992) 86 *ASIL Proceedings* 532.

[39] On the BIT practice of the United States, see KJ Vandevelde, *United States Investment Treaties: Policy and Practice* (1992); KJ Vandevelde, 'A Brief History of International Investment Agreements' (2005) 12(1) *University of California Davis J Int'l L & Pol'y* 157; SM Schwebel, 'The United States 2004 Model Bilateral Investment Treaty: An Exercise in the Regressive Development of International Law' in G Aksen et al (eds) *Liber Amicorum in Honour of Robert Briner* (2005) 815; K Gugdeon, 'United States Bilateral Investment Treaties' (1986) 4 *Int'l Tax and Business Law* 105; W Dodge, 'Investor–State Dispute Settlement Between Developed Countries: Reflections on the Australia–United States Free Trade Agreement' (2006) 39 *Vanderbilt J Transn'l Law* 1.

[40] On the evolution of China's attitude towards foreign investment, see D Chow, *The Legal System of the People's Republic of China in a Nutshell* (2003) 374 et seq.

modernize its treaty program after the adoption of the Indian Model BIT in 2016. The terminations will become effective over the next years. Japan has also decided to join the practice of other OECD (Organisation for Economic Co-operation and Development) countries and by 2021 had concluded 35 investment agreements and 22 treaties with investment provisions.

More and more developing States have negotiated BITs among themselves, altogether more than 770. China and Egypt are among the States with the largest number of BITs. A comparison of treaties concluded between developing countries does not reveal significant differences to agreements concluded with developed States.

One way to explain this trend is that countries with emerging markets increasingly see themselves as potential exporters of investments and wish to protect their nationals through investment agreements. While this explanation is correct, these treaties do illustrate the broader point that home States of investors, as well as host States, are willing to conclude treaties with guarantees and mechanisms that go beyond the rules of customary law and that the underlying concern is not peculiar to traditional Western liberal States with outgoing foreign investment. The general point seems to be that home States of investors, whatever their historical background, consider specially negotiated rules desirable and that host States are willing to offer guarantees to attract investments.

(e) The quest for a multilateral framework

The first efforts to establish a multilateral treaty for the protection of foreign property go back to the post-Second World War years. In 1957, Hermann Josef Abs, a German banker, called for a 'Magna Charta for the Protection of Foreign Property'[41] in the form of a global treaty. Such a treaty was meant to establish not just specific standards of protection but also a permanent arbitral tribunal charged with the application of the treaty and with the power to lay down economic sanctions against violating States, including non-signatories.

It soon became apparent that the time was not ripe for such an ambitious approach and Abs opted for a more modest multilateral initiative,[42] in cooperation with Sir Hartley Shawcross. These efforts culminated in the Abs–Shawcross Draft, which, together with other contributions such as a Swiss draft, in 1962 led to the first attempt of the OECD, the forum of the capital-exporting countries, to prepare a multilateral treaty.[43] A second draft was presented in 1967. However, these

[41] Speech given at the International Industrial Development Conference (San Francisco, 15 October 1957), (1957) *Recht der Internationalen Wirtschaft* 229.

[42] The drafts for a 'Convention on Investments Abroad' were published in (1959) *Recht der Internationalen Wirtschaft* 150.

[43] GA van Hecke, 'Le projet de convention de l'OCDE sur la protection des biens étrangers' (1964) 68 *Revue générale de droit international public* 641.

early attempts to create a multilateral framework remained unsuccessful. This was due mainly to the fact that the draft convention was meant to apply not only to OECD member States but to all countries. Also, the OECD efforts fell into a period of great divisions between capital-importing and capital-exporting countries concerning the content of recognized principles of foreign investment law. Eventually, the OECD contented itself with merely recommending its draft as a model for bilateral investment treaties by its member States.[44] This laid the groundwork for the future investment regime characterized by the absence of a universal treaty and the dominance of bilateral treaties.

In 1961, two years after the era of bilateral treaties had begun, the World Bank took the initiative to address the emerging international legal framework of foreign investment. It pointed to its mandate and to the link between economic development, international cooperation, and private international investment. It believed that the availability of impartial and independent dispute settlement by an international tribunal would lead to an improvement of a country's investment climate. This would lead to more foreign private investment in developing countries.[45] The debates then underway in the OECD and at the United Nations indicated that the state of opinion regarding substantive rules of customary law on foreign investment was deeply divided and that the prospect of reaching a global consensus was minimal.

In the World Bank, it was the then General Counsel, Aron Broches, who initiated and advanced the ensuing debates. Given the controversies within the United Nations, Broches properly concluded that, for the time being, the best contribution the Bank could make was to develop effective procedures for the impartial settlement of disputes without attempting to seek agreement on substantive standards. This approach seemed startling since logic would dictate that any system of dispute settlement would have to be based on a set of substantive rules which could be applied. But Broches argued that, from a pragmatic point of view, such an axiomatic approach was neither necessary nor promising.

At first sight, the Broches concept 'procedure before substance' seemed limited and modest. However, he designed what was to become, in 1965, the Convention on the Settlement of Investment Disputes between States and Nationals of Other States (ICSID Convention) establishing the International Centre for Settlement of Investment Disputes (ICSID). In retrospect, the creation of ICSID amounted to the boldest innovative step in the modern history of international cooperation concerning the role and protection of foreign investment.

The success of this concept became apparent when the ICSID Convention quickly entered into force in 1966 and especially when in subsequent decades more

[44] R Dolzer and M Stevens, *Bilateral Investment* Treaties (1995) 2.

[45] Note by the President to the Executive Directors of 28 December 1961, in *History of the ICSID Convention* vol II-1 (1968) 4–6.

and more investment treaties, bilateral and multilateral, referred to ICSID as a forum for dispute settlement. From the point of view of member States, one major advantage of the system was that investment disputes would become 'depoliticised' in the sense that it avoided confrontation between home State and host State.[46] For two decades, ICSID's caseload remained quite modest. But by the 1990s, ICSID had become the main forum for the settlement of investment disputes, and Broches' vision had become a reality.

Following its earlier efforts in the 1960s towards the creation of a multilateral investment treaty, the OECD decided in 1995 to launch a new initiative in this direction. These negotiations took place from 1995 to 1998 and built, to a considerable extent, on the substance of existing bilateral treaties. The last draft for a Multilateral Agreement on Investment (MAI), dated 22 April 1998,[47] indicates major areas of consensus and some points of disagreement. Although the draft shows that the negotiations had indeed progressed to a considerable extent, the discussions were halted in 1998. Several unrelated reasons had led to the breakdown.[48] The United States had never stood fully behind the initiative: domestic political support necessary for ratification seemed uncertain; in addition, the level of protection for foreign investment foreseen in the draft appeared unsatisfactory due to a number of compromises. In Europe, France decided in the latter stage of the negotiations that an agreement might not be compatible with its desire to protect French culture ('*exception culturelle*'). Non-governmental organizations (NGOs) argued that the debates within the OECD had been held without sufficient public information and input. Also, from the beginning, there was a debate as to whether the OECD, representing mainly capital-exporting countries, was the proper forum to negotiate a treaty meant to serve as a global instrument. In the end, these different aspects converged to undermine and halt support for the negotiations within the OECD.

In a partially overlapping effort, the World Trade Organization (WTO) had already placed the issue of a multilateral investment treaty on its agenda during a meeting in Singapore in 1996, in the middle of the OECD negotiations. The WTO Agreement of 1994 had embodied a first step of the trade organization into the field of foreign investment: the so-called TRIMS Agreement[49] was to regulate those

[46] I Shihata, 'Towards a Greater Depoliticization of Investment Disputes: the Roles of ICSID and MIGA' (1986) 1 *ICSID Rev* 1; U Kriebaum, 'Evaluating Social Benefits and Costs of Investment Treaties: Depoliticization of Investment Disputes' (2018) 33 *ICSID Rev* 14.

[47] Available at: <http://www1.oecd.org/daf/mai>.

[48] See the contributions to (1998) 31 (3) *Cornell Int'l LJ* (symposium edition). See also Société française de droit international (ed), *Un accord multilatéral sur l'investissement: d'un forum de négociation à l'autre?* (1999); UNCTAD, *Lessons from the MAI—UNCTAD Series on Issues in International Investment Agreements* (1999); EC Nieuwenhuys and MMTA Brus (eds), *Multilateral Regulation of Investment* (2001).

[49] Agreement on Trade-Related Investment Measures (TRIMS). See generally T Brewer and S Young, 'Investment Issues at the WTO: The Architecture of Rules and the Settlement of Disputes' (1998) 1 *Journal of International Economic Law* 457; M Koulen, 'Foreign Investment in the WTO' in EC Nieuwenhuys and MMTA Brus (eds) *Multilateral Regulation of Investment* (2001) 181.

aspects of foreign investment which led to direct negative consequences on a liberalized trade regime. In particular, this Agreement regulates issues of so-called performance requirements[50] imposed by the host State upon foreign investors and aims at reducing or eliminating laws which require that local products are used in the production process by foreign investors (local content requirements). The further development of the emerging investment agenda of the WTO was addressed but not decided in 1996. In 2004, six years after the end of the OECD initiative, the efforts within the WTO to include investment issues generally into the Organization's mandate also came to a halt.[51]

Even though developing countries had negotiated more than a thousand BITs, they were not prepared to accept a WTO-based multilateral investment treaty. They argued that a multilateral scheme might unduly narrow their regulatory space and that the effect of such a treaty would need to be studied in greater detail. Brazil and India in particular took this position. The support of the United States for a multilateral treaty was again limited, for reasons similar as within the OECD in 1998.

(f) Recent developments

Until the early 1990s, international investment law had not produced any significant case law.[52] In the meantime, this situation has changed dramatically. Both in the framework of the ICSID Convention and beyond, there is a veritable flood of cases that has produced and continues to produce an ever-growing case law in the field. To a large extent this dramatic increase of activity before arbitral tribunals was the direct consequence of the availability of investor–State arbitration based on a rapidly growing number of investment treaties. Inevitably, the large number of decisions produced by differently composed tribunals has led to concerns about consistency and coherence.[53]

The success of the system of investment arbitration has also led to weariness and criticism. Some countries have found themselves in the role of respondents more often than others and perceive the need to defend themselves repeatedly against claims by foreign investors as a serious burden. At the same time, there is

[50] See VI.6 below.

[51] Decision of the WTO General Council of 1 August 2004 on the Doha Agenda Work Program.

[52] In 1970, the International Court of Justice drew attention to the slow evolution of investment law: 'Considering the important developments of the last half-century, the growth of foreign investments and the expansion of the international activities of corporations, in particular of holding companies, which are often multinational, and considering the way in which the economic interests of States have proliferated, it may at first sight appear surprising that the evolution of the law has not gone further and that no generally accepted rules in the matter have crystallized on the international plane.' *Case concerning the Barcelona Traction, Light and Power Company (Belgium v Spain)*, Judgment, 5 February 1970, ICJ Reports (1970) 3, para 89.

[53] See II.1(f) below.

criticism that investment law in general and investment arbitration in particular restrict the freedom of States to take regulatory action. Therefore, enthusiasm for the current system is by no means undivided. In consequence, since November 2017, the United Nations Commission on International Trade Law (UNCITRAL) Working Group III has discussed numerous reform options. These include ad hoc tribunals, and standing multilateral mechanisms, a stand-alone review or appellate mechanism, a first instance and appeal investment court as well as a multilateral advisory centre.[54]

In 2009, under the Treaty of Lisbon, the European Union (EU) assumed exclusive competence for foreign direct investment. The precise scope of the competence became the subject of a controversial debate that was clarified by the Court of Justice of the European Union (CJEU) in an opinion on the Free Trade Agreement (FTA) between the EU and Singapore.[55] The outcome was that the EU has exclusive competence for foreign direct investment, and a shared competence for portfolio investment. Investor–State dispute settlement is also a competence shared between the EU and its member States. This has far-reaching potential consequences for the BITs to which member States of the EU are parties. Since roughly one-half of all BITs world-wide have at least one EU member State as a party, the future policy of the EU on investment is likely to have global repercussions. This raises questions as to both the status of BITs between member States (intra-EU BITs) and BITs of EU members with non-EU member States (extra-EU BITs).

With regard to intra-EU BITs, the European Commission wants all of these terminated and has worked actively to eliminate them. Some member States were opposed to these plans while others started terminating BITs with other EU members. The Commission received support from the CJEU which found in its *Achmea* Judgment[56] that intra-EU BITs would be incompatible with EU law. In the aftermath of *Achmea*, 23 member States signed a plurilateral treaty on 5 May 2020 to terminate their intra-EU BITs.[57] As of April 2021, less than half of the EU member States have ratified this treaty. It entered into force on 29 August 2020. Austria, Finland, and Sweden have committed themselves to terminate their intra-EU BITs bilaterally.

As for BITs with non-EU member States, EU law provides that these treaties may be maintained until a bilateral investment agreement between the EU and the same State enters into force. The European Commission wishes to gradually replace these BITs by new treaties to be negotiated by the Commission on behalf of the EU and its member States. The negotiations between the Commission and the United States on a Transatlantic Trade and Investment Partnership (TTIP) attracted much

[54] Available at: <https://uncitral.un.org/en/working_groups/3/investor-state>.

[55] CJEU Opinion 2/15, 16 May 2017.

[56] *Slovak Republic v Achmea*, Judgment, 6 March 2018, CJEU, Case C-284/16, ECLI:EU:C:2018:158.

[57] Agreement for the Termination of Bilateral Investment Treaties between the Member States of the European Union, 29 May 2020, OJ L 169/1-41.

public attention and provoked public fears and criticism about investment protection and arbitration. The treaties with Canada (the Comprehensive Economic and Trade Agreement, CETA), Viet Nam, and Singapore have been adopted but still await ratification by all EU member States. These treaties are mixed agreements, which means that both the EU and the individual member States would have to ratify them. They have a new dispute settlement system that the Commission intends to use as a model for future treaties.

The EU is currently negotiating investment agreements or investment chapters in FTAs with China, Chile, Indonesia, Philippines, Japan, and Mexico.

2. The sources of international investment law

Foreign investment law consists of general international law, of standards more specific to international economic law, and of distinct rules peculiar to the protection of investment. In addition, the law of the host State plays an important role. Depending upon the circumstances of an individual case, the interplay between relevant domestic rules of the host State and applicable rules of international law may become central to the analysis of a case.[58] The domestic rules on nationality may determine jurisdiction in a particular case. Other areas of domestic law that may become relevant in a particular case include property law, commercial law, labour law, zoning law, and tax law to name just a few.

Not only is the distinction between international law and domestic law becoming blurred by the modern regime of foreign investment law,[59] the classical separation between public and private law, as emphasized especially in Continental European legal orders, also cannot be maintained neatly in this field. The broader question whether international economic law allows for a useful distinction between private law and public law is particularly acute in foreign investment law. The rules governing contracts between an investor and a host State (see Chapter V) draw on both private and public law. In fact, these rules establish a link between domestic law and public international law. To some extent, the rules of domestic law are being confronted and superseded by rules of public international law, and in relevant international cases the decisions of arbitrators will turn on their understanding of domestic law, possibly accompanied by a process of review of domestic law under the international standards contained in treaties and in general international law.

[58] For more detail see XII.12 below.

[59] See F Orrego Vicuña, 'Of Contracts and Treaties in the Global Market' (2004) 8 *Max-Planck Yearbook of United Nations Law* 341.

What follows is a general survey of the most important sources of international investment law. More detailed discussion of the issues arising from these sources can be found in the relevant chapters of this book.

(a) The ICSID Convention

The Convention on the Settlement of Investment Disputes between States and Nationals of Other States (ICSID Convention) is a multilateral treaty. It provides a procedural framework for dispute settlement between host States and foreign investors through conciliation or arbitration.[60] The Convention does not contain substantive standards of protection for investments. Also, participation in the ICSID Convention does not amount to consent to arbitration. The process whereby consent to arbitration under the ICSID Convention is given by the host State and by the investor is described below.[61]

(b) Bilateral investment treaties

Bilateral investment treaties (BITs) are the most important source of contemporary international investment law. Some countries such as Germany, Switzerland, and China have each concluded well over 100 BITs with other countries. It is estimated that close to 3,000 BITs are in existence worldwide.

BITs provide guarantees for the investments of investors from one of the contracting States in the other contracting State. Traditionally, BITs are relatively short with no more than 12 to 14 articles. They typically consist of three parts.

The first part offers definitions, especially of the concepts of 'investor' and 'investment'.[62]

The second part consists of substantive standards for the protection of investments and investors. Typically, these contain: a provision on admission of investments; a guarantee of fair and equitable treatment (FET); a guarantee of full protection and security; a guarantee against arbitrary and discriminatory treatment; a guarantee of national treatment and a guarantee of most-favoured-nation treatment (MFN clause); guarantees in case of expropriation; and guarantees concerning the free transfer of payments. These various standards and guarantees are described in some detail in Chapters VI, VII, and VIII of this book.

The third part deals with dispute settlement. Most BITs contain two separate provisions on dispute settlement. One provides for arbitration in the event of

60 For details see XII.4(a) and XII.11 below.
61 See XII.7 below.
62 See Chapter III and Chapter IV below.

disputes between the host State and foreign investors (investor–State arbitration). Most BITs contain advance consent of the two States to international arbitration with investors from the other State party either before an ICSID tribunal or through some other form of arbitration. The other provision on dispute settlement in BITs provides for arbitration between the two States parties to the treaty (State–State arbitration). Whereas investor–State arbitration under BITs is very common, State–State arbitration has remained rare. The role of BITs in dispute settlement is described in Chapter XII.7(c).[63]

The classical BITs of past decades have addressed only issues of foreign investment. More recently, there is a trend to negotiate provisions on foreign investment in the context of wider agreements, often called free trade agreements (FTAs). As the name indicates, FTAs also address trade issues. This trend seems to have started with the agreement between Canada and the United States in 1989, which formed the basis for the NAFTA concluded in 1994 between these two States and Mexico. With the recent tendency to conclude bilateral or regional trade agreements in addition to the global rules of the WTO, States have tended to conclude broad agreements on economic cooperation regionally or bilaterally, instead of agreements specifically aimed at matters of trade or foreign investment. The number of these FTAs, covering also rules on foreign investment, has increased in recent years.[64] The European Commission is negotiating FTAs with third countries,[65] containing provisions on trade as well as on investment.

Some States have formulated model treaties for their own purpose.[66] In the early days of BITs, capital-exporting States would present their model to capital-importing States as a basis for negotiations. In the meantime, developing States have gradually developed their own preferences, sometimes with their own model drafts.[67] Investment treaties have been negotiated also between developing countries. Model treaties are revised from time to time to reflect changing circumstances and priorities.

As more and more treaties were concluded, and as the international discussion on the nature and the details of these treaties has progressed, including the contours and substance of individual clauses, any argument that host States have accepted investment obligations without proper knowledge of their scope and significance has become less convincing. Investment treaties are today seen as admission tickets to international investment markets.[68] Their limiting impact on the

[63] See XII.7(c) below.

[64] UNCTAD, *World Investment Report* (2020) 106.

[65] See I.1(f) above.

[66] C Brown, *Commentaries on Selected Model Investment Treaties* (2013). The United States has presented a new model treaty in 2012. The first US Model Treaty was adopted in 1981. See KJ Vandevelde, 'The BIT Program: A Fifteen-Year Appraisal', in *ASIL Proceedings* (1992) 532, 536.

[67] International Institute for Sustainable Development, *Survey on Developing Country Investment Treaty Negotiations* (2019).

[68] See I.3(d) below.

sovereignty of the host State, controversial as it may be in the individual case, is a necessary corollary to the objective of creating an investment-friendly climate.[69] Nevertheless, the attitude of some developing countries to investment treaties has changed significantly. They now scrutinize these treaties more carefully for potential costs. Some countries, such as India and South Africa, have withdrawn from some of their investment treaties.[70]

(c) Sectoral and regional treaties

The first multilateral treaty containing substantive rules on foreign investment is of a sectoral nature and not meant for universal membership. The Energy Charter Treaty (ECT) of 1994[71] essentially grew out of the desire of European States to co-operate closely with Russia and the new States in Eastern Europe and Central Asia in exploring and developing the energy sector, which is of crucial political, economic, and financial importance for both sides. Membership was open to all States committed to the establishment of closer cooperation and an appropriate international legal framework in the energy sector.

The ECT does not just deal with investments but covers a wide range of issues such as trade, transit, energy efficiency, and dispute settlement. The chapter on investment is largely patterned along the lines of BITs concluded by the member States of the EU. Its substantive standards are similar to those contained in BITs.[72] However, the treaty also contains some innovative features, such as special provisions concerning State entities and sub-national authorities,[73] and a 'best-efforts' clause concerning non-discrimination in the pre-establishment phase,[74] coupled with an expression of intent to transform it into a legally binding obligation in the future.[75]

The ECT entered into force in 1998. Fifty-two States and the EU are parties to the Treaty. The Russian Federation has signed it but announced that it does not intend to become a party.[76] Italy announced its withdrawal from the ECT in 2015.

[69] R Dolzer, 'The Impact of International Investment Treaties on Domestic Administrative Law' (2005) 37 *NYU J Int'l L & Pol* 953.

[70] J Bonnitcha, NS Poulsen, and M Waibel, *The Political Economy of the Investment Treaty Regime* (2017) 21, 226, 231.

[71] (1995) 34 ILM 360. See generally C Ribeiro (ed), *Investment Arbitration and the Energy Charter Treaty* (2006); T Wälde, 'Investment Arbitration under the Energy Charter Treaty' in N Horn (ed) *Arbitrating Foreign Investment Disputes* (2004) 193; R Happ, 'Dispute Settlement under the Energy Charter Treaty' (2002) 45 *German Yearbook of Int'l L* 331; T Wälde, 'International Energy Law' in JP Schneider and C Theobald (eds) *Handbuch zum Recht der Energiewirtschaft* (2003) 1129.

[72] ECT Article 10(1) and (3).

[73] ECT Articles 22 and 23.

[74] ECT Article 10(2).

[75] ECT Article 10(4).

[76] On 20 August 2009, Russia officially informed the Depository of the ECT that it did not intend to become a party.

Under the ECT, investors have the right to bring a suit before ICSID, before an arbitral tribunal established under the UNCITRAL arbitration rules, before the Arbitration Institute of the Stockholm Chamber of Commerce, or before the courts or administrative tribunals of the respondent State.[77] Between 2001 and 2020, 135 investment disputes were initiated under the framework of the ECT. Due to changes in their regulatory frameworks in the renewable energy sector, member States of the EU meanwhile outnumber other States as respondents in investment arbitrations under the ECT. While earlier cases mostly concerned investments in fossil fuels, these changes have created a spike in cases related to the renewable energy sector.

Along with the general developments concerning the content of investment treaties, the ECT is also undergoing a reform process.[78] Since the *Achmea* judgment of the CJEU[79] there is uncertainty concerning the future of intra-EU investment disputes under the ECT and the enforceability of awards resulting from these disputes.

The North American Free Trade Agreement (NAFTA) between Canada, Mexico, and the United States (1994)[80] was the most frequently invoked regional treaty. It addressed trade and investment. The Treaty aimed at the free movement and liberalization of goods, services, people, and investment. The famous Chapter Eleven of NAFTA specifically addressed the treatment of investments. The objective enunciated in Article 102 was to increase substantially investment opportunities in the territories of the parties.[81]

Chapter Eleven on investment amounted to an innovative bold scheme inasmuch as it tied Mexico as a developing country to its two northern developed neighbours against a history replete with conflict, especially in investment matters. In its substance, Chapter Eleven built upon the treaty practice of the United States, including the treaty with Canada concluded in 1989.

The substantive obligations under NAFTA covered traditional issues such as national treatment, MFN treatment, performance requirements, transfers, and possible denial of benefits to investors owned or controlled by investors of non-NAFTA States. In actual practice, the rules on expropriation (Article 1110) and on the 'Minimum Standard of Treatment' (Article 1105) have received most attention and have led to legal disputes and public controversies. The right of the investor to file a suit against the host State was limited to breaches of the treaty's substantive

[77] ECT Article 26.

[78] C Verburg, 'Modernizing the Energy Charter Treaty: An Opportunity to Enhance Legal Certainty in Investor–State Dispute Settlement' (2019) 20 *JWIT* 425.

[79] *Slovak Republic v Achmea*, Judgment, 6 March 2018, CJEU, Case C-284/16, ECLI:EU:C:2018:158.

[80] 32 (1993) ILM 605. At the time of writing, NAFTA is in the process of being replaced by the United States–Mexico–Canada Agreement (USMCA) but remains available for investors until June 2023.

[81] M Kinnear, A Bjorklund, and J Hannaford, *Investment Disputes under NAFTA* (2006); T Weiler (ed) *NAFTA Investment Law and Arbitration* (2004).

rules. The governing law was limited to the NAFTA itself and to applicable rules of international law (Article 1131(1)).

NAFTA's Chapter Eleven provided elaborate rules on dispute settlement. Article 1120 enabled an investor to bring a suit against the host State under the ICSID Convention. But for much of NAFTA's existence, only the United States was a Party to the ICSID Convention.[82] During that time, the ICSID Additional Facility was an important choice for investors.[83] The third possibility open to the investor was arbitration under the UNCITRAL Arbitration Rules.

The most remarkable feature of the dispute resolution scheme in NAFTA was the fact that, although it addressed both trade and investment, it recognized the right to bring a suit against a State only for an investor but not for a trader. This dualism is now established in State practice, some divergencies and concerns notwithstanding.

NAFTA is currently in the process of being replaced by the United States–Mexico–Canada Agreement (USMCA). It was signed in November 2018 and entered into force on 1 July 2020. The USMCA provides for investor–State arbitration only between nationals of Mexico and the United States and the respective other country. Disputes between Canadian and Mexican investors and the respective other country are subject to the investment arbitration provisions of the Comprehensive and Progressive Agreement for Trans-Pacific Partnership (CPTPP). Between Canada and the United States, the only avenue for dispute settlement is the USMCA's State–State dispute settlement mechanism. There is no investor–State arbitration between Canadian and US investors and the respective other country.

Chapter 14 of the USMCA offers the usual standards of protection but claims of investors against host States are more limited than under the NAFTA. They are restricted to national treatment and MFN, except with respect to establishment or acquisition, as well as to direct expropriation (Article 14.D.3.1) and to breaches of government contracts (Annex 14-E). No claims for violation of the FET standard and for indirect expropriation are foreseen. Therefore, the USMCA offers only limited protection.

Other regional treaties providing for investment protection include the Central American Free Trade Agreement (CAFTA) of 2004 that comprises the United States and five Central American countries. The DR–CAFTA added the Dominican Republic in the same year.

Regional agreements in Asia include the Treaty of the Eurasian Economic Union, the Eurasian Investment Agreement, and the Association of Southeast Asian Nations (ASEAN) Agreement for the Promotion and Protection of Investments.

[82] Canada became an ICSID Contracting State in 2013. Mexico in 2018.
[83] See XII.4(b) below.

Other regional treaties providing for investment arbitration comprise the Agreement on Promotion, Protection and Guarantee of Investments Among Member States of the Organisation of the Islamic Conference (OIC), and the Economic Community of West African States (ECOWAS).

Two investment protocols of MERCOSUR, dating from 1994, dealing with intra- and extra-MERCOSUR investments, were not in force as of April 2021. The Intra-MERCOSUR Cooperation and Facilitation Investment Protocol of 2017 (in force 2019) offers a low level of investment protection. It has a limiting definition of investment which, for example, explicitly excludes portfolio investment.[84] It does not offer protection against indirect expropriations[85] and explicitly excludes an obligation of the State to accord the investor fair and equitable treatment, full protection and security, and any protection in the pre-establishment phase.[86] It provides for corporate social responsibility obligations of investors[87] but does not offer investor–State arbitration.

A new trend is investment treaties of countries in different regions. The most important current example is the CPTPP which contains a Chapter 9 dealing with investment. The CPTPP incorporates by reference the substantive protection standards as well as the norms on investor–State arbitration of the 2016 Trans-Pacific Partnership (TPP) which never entered into force since the United States declared that it would not ratify it. It is inspired by the US Model BIT and contains the typical investment protection standards. Like in the US Model BIT, FET and full protection and security are only guaranteed in accordance with customary international law. Moreover, a mere breach of an investor's expectations resulting in loss or damage does not amount to a breach of FET. There is a detailed definition of what constitutes an indirect expropriation including an exception for *bona fide* regulations to advance public welfare objectives. Under the CPTPP, an investor may initiate investor–State arbitration on its own behalf and on behalf of an enterprise of the respondent that the claimant owns or controls directly or indirectly.

The CPTPP entered into force in 2018 among the first six countries that ratified the agreement: Canada, Australia, Japan, Mexico, New Zealand, and Singapore. In January 2019, it entered into force for Vietnam. Additional signatories are expected to ratify the CPTPP. In February 2021, the United Kingdom applied for accession.

84 Protocol for Cooperation and Facilitation for Investments Intra-MERCOSUR, Article 3.3.1(ii).
85 Article 6(6).
86 Article 4(3).
87 Article 14.

(d) Customary international law

Although treaties dominate international investment law, customary international law still plays an important role. The treaty-based rules have to be understood and interpreted, like all treaties, in the context of the general rules of international law. Article 31(3)(c) of the Vienna Convention on the Law of Treaties provides that together with the treaty's context 'any relevant rules of international law applicable in the relations between the parties' shall be taken into account.

Customary international law remains highly relevant in the practice of investment arbitration. Rules on attribution (Chapter X) and other areas of State responsibility as well as rules on damages illustrate the point. Other relevant areas of customary international law are the rules on expropriation, on denial of justice, and on the nationality of investors.

The growing case law on foreign investments has led to a situation in which some general rules of international law find their most frequent practical expression in foreign investment law. The consequence is that a full contemporary understanding of these rules requires knowledge of their interpretation and application in investment cases.

A basic doctrinal issue is the impact of the large number of bilateral investment treaties on the evolution of customary law.[88] This linkage between customary law and treaty law is particularly relevant for customary law rules regarding expropriation and compensation.[89]

(e) General principles of law

General principles of law in the sense of Article 38(1)(c) of the Statute of the International Court of Justice have received increasing attention in recent practice.[90] General principles of law acquire importance especially in the case of lacunae in the text of treaties and in the interpretation of individual terms and phrases. In *Merrill & Ring v Canada*,[91] the Tribunal said:

> The Tribunal must note that general principles of law also have a role to play in this discussion. Even if the Tribunal were to accept Canada's argument to the effect that good faith, the prohibition of arbitrariness, discrimination and other questions raised in this case are not stand-alone obligations under Article 1105(1)

[88] See VIII.1(f) below.

[89] S Schwebel, 'The Reshaping of the International Law of Foreign Investment by Concordant Bilateral Investment Treaties' in S Charnovitz et al (eds) *Law in the Service of Human Dignity—Essays in Honour of Florentino Feliciano* (2005) 241.

[90] See also XII.12(b) below.

[91] *Merrill & Ring v Canada*, Award, 31 March 2010.

> [of NAFTA] or international law, and might not be a part of customary law either, these concepts are to a large extent the expression of general principles of law and hence also a part of international law... no tribunal today could be asked to ignore these basic obligations of international law.[92]

Examples for general principles relied upon by tribunals include good faith,[93] *nemo auditur propriam turpitudinem allegans* (no-one can be heard, who invokes his own guilt),[94] estoppel,[95] *nullus commodum capere de sua injuria propria* (no advantage may be gained from one's own wrong),[96] *pacta sunt servanda*,[97] unjust enrichment,[98] *res judicata*,[99] and general principles of due process, including[100] the right to be heard.[101]

(f) Unilateral statements

The legal effect of unilateral statements and the conditions under which these may be considered binding has played a prominent role in some cases, especially in the context of the guarantee of FET.[102] Here, the principle of good faith is closely tied to the operation of the principle of estoppel. The International Court of Justice and its predecessor have recognized that unilateral declarations will be binding if the circumstances and the wording of statements of a representative of the State are such that the addressees are entitled to rely on them.[103] The International Law

[92] At para 187.

[93] *Sempra v Argentina*, Award, 28 September 2007, paras 290–299 (annulled on other grounds); *Phoenix v Czech Republic*, Award, 15 April 2009, paras 106–113, 142; *Cementownia v Turkey*, Award, 17 September 2009, paras 138–148; *Hamester v Ghana*, Award 18 June 2010, paras 123–124; *Renco v Peru*, Partial Award on Jurisdiction, 15 July 2016, para 175.

[94] *Rumeli v Kazakhstan*, Award, 29 July 2008, paras 310, 323; *Khan Resources v Mongolia*, Decision on Jurisdiction, 25 July 2012, para 383.

[95] *Chevron v Ecuador I*, Partial Award on the Merits, 30 March 2010, paras 334–353; *RSM v Grenada II*, Award, 10 December 2010, paras 7.1.1–7.1.3.

[96] *Occidental Petroleum v Ecuador*, Award, 5 October 2012, para 564.

[97] *Noble Ventures v Romania*, Award, 12 October 2005, para 51.

[98] *Strabag v Libya*, Award, 29 June 2020, paras 881, 899–900. See also C Binder, 'Unjust Enrichment as a General Principle of Law in Investment Arbitration' in A Gattini et al (eds) *General Principles of Law and International Investment Arbitration* (2018) 269.

[99] *Waste Management v Mexico II*, Decision on Mexico's Preliminary Objection concerning the Previous Proceedings, 26 June 2002, para 39; *Apotex v United States*, Award, 25 August 2014, para 7.11–7.66. See also P Janig and A Reinisch, 'General Principles and the Coherence of International Investment Law: of *Res Judicata, Lis Pendens* and the Value of Precedents' in M Andenas et al (eds) *General Principles and the Coherence of International Law* (2019) 247.

[100] *Amco v Indonesia*, Award, 20 November 1984, paras 199–201 and Decision on Annulment, 16 May 1986, paras 75–79.

[101] *Fraport v Philippines I*, Decision on Annulment, 23 December 2010, paras 197–208, 218–247; *Tulip v Turkey*, Decision on Annulment, 30 December 2015, paras 80–83, 145.

[102] See VIII.1 below.

[103] *Legal Status of Eastern Greenland (Denmark v Norway)*, Judgment, 5 April 1933, PCIJ Series A/B No 53, 22, 69; *Nuclear Tests Cases (Australia/New Zealand v France)*, Judgment, 20 December 1974, ICJ Reports (1974) 253, para 46.

Commission has adopted Guiding Principles applicable to unilateral declarations of States capable of creating legal obligations.[104]

Unilateral promises may exist also in the relationship between a host State and a foreign investor.[105] Arbitral tribunals have so held based on the principle of good faith. In *Waste Management v Mexico*,[106] the Tribunal found that in applying the FET standard, 'it is relevant that the treatment is in breach of representations made by the host State which were reasonably relied on by the claimant'.[107]

In *Total v Argentina*[108] the Tribunal said:

> Under international law, unilateral acts, statements and conduct by States may be the source of legal obligations which the intended beneficiaries or addressees, or possibly any member of the international community, can invoke. The legal basis of that binding character appears to be only in part related to the concept of legitimate expectations—being rather akin to the principle of 'estoppel'. Both concepts may lead to the same result, namely, that of rendering the content of a unilateral declaration binding on the State that is issuing it.[109]

Arbitral tribunals have discussed the interpretation of unilateral acts *inter alia* in the context of legislation by which a State consents to ICSID jurisdiction.[110]

(g) Case law

As explained in II.1(e),[111] tribunals are not bound by previous cases, but examine them and refer to them, frequently.

3. The nature of international investment law

International investment law does not fit easily into the traditional categories of law. It has public law aspects as well as private law aspects and therefore crosses the traditional divide made in some parts of the world separating private from public law. Also, it has international as well as national law aspects. In terms of actors, it is also peculiar in that it has private actors as well as State actors. This is an aspect

[104] A/CN.4/L.703.

[105] WM Reisman and MH Arsanjani, 'The Question of Unilateral Governmental Statements as Applicable Law in Investment Disputes' (2004) 19 *ICSID Rev* 328.

[106] *Waste Management v Mexico II*, Award, 30 April 2004.

[107] At para 98. See also below at VIII.1(g)bb.

[108] *Total v Argentina*, Decision on Liability, 27 December 2010.

[109] At para 131. Footnote omitted.

[110] See XII.7(b) below.

[111] See II.1(e) below.

international investment law shares with human rights law except that in investment law States and investors can sue and be sued, at least in theory, whereas in human rights law States are always in the position of the respondent. Therefore, the foundation of international investment law has rightly been described as hybrid and there is no unanimity on the individual's position in the system.[112]

The peculiar nature of investment law has its roots in a time when individuals were mere objects of international law and had no standing before international fora. The multitude of legal instruments that shaped its formation were adopted in response to the needs that had arisen at various points in time. Often, the instruments focused either on substance or on procedure since agreement on both was not achievable at the same time. Adaptations to the system were made when necessary. Some instruments were specifically adopted for international investment law purposes. Others were adopted primarily for commercial law purposes but were later used also in the context of investment law.

Over time, international investment law developed its distinctive features that share many commonalities but did not converge into a homogeneous system with one set of substantive standards and one set of procedure. Therefore, there is no one-size-fits-all model.

This chapter highlights certain aspects that are relevant for the nature of current international investment law.

(a) Investment law and trade law

Over time, the principles governing foreign investment have developed their own distinct features within the broader realm of international economic law. Today, it is a matter of semantics whether it is appropriate to speak of the existence of a separate category of 'principles of foreign investment law', given their strong links to international economic law in general. But there is no doubt that the international law of foreign investment has become a specialized area of the legal profession and that special courses are offered on the subject in universities worldwide. The common usage and parlance in international law has always been to single out and to designate distinct fields, such as the 'laws of war', or the 'law of the sea', whenever the body of rules in any one area has become extensive and dense enough to justify special attention and study.

The nature, structure, and purpose of international investment law make it inevitable that it stands out as structurally distinct in the broader realm of international law, especially in comparison to trade. The difference between the two

[112] Z Douglas, 'The Hybrid Foundation of Investment Treaty Arbitration' (2003) 74 *BYIL* 152; U Kriebaum, 'The Nature of Investment Disciplines' in Z Douglas et al (eds) *The Foundations of International Investment Law* (2014) 45.

fields excludes an assumption of methodological commonalities between foreign investment law and trade law. Whenever an analogy is proposed, or a solution is transferred from one area to the other, it must be examined in detail whether their different nature is amenable to an assumption of commonality. Often, upon more detailed analysis, a concept that appears to be in common turns out to have different shades and characteristics, in view of the peculiar business nature of long-term foreign investment projects.[113]

(b) Balancing duties and benefits

There have been speculations relating to the reciprocity of obligations in investment treaties, to the quid pro quo underlying these treaties, and to the mutual benefits arising from them. These concerns arise from a common perception that treaties on foreign investment place obligations solely on the host State without corresponding commitments on the part of the foreign investor.

These concerns reflect the assumption that all types of treaties are necessarily based on reciprocity and mutuality which must be reflected in the terms of the treaty. However, the very nature of the law of aliens, which is the origin of foreign investment law, indicates that the *raison d'être* of this field of law does not reflect the traditional themes of reciprocity and mutuality but instead sets standards for the unilateral conduct of the host State. Foreign investments take place in a setting that does not correspond to a transaction or to an agreement in which privileges are exchanged on a mutual basis by two parties. Notions of mutuality and reciprocity are not absent from the regime of investment treaties but they do not operate in the same manner as in a classical agreement. Instead, they are focused on the mutual benefits of host State and investor and on the complementarity of interests flowing from the long-term commitment of resources by the foreign investor under the territorial sovereignty of the host State.

In an investment treaty, the host State deliberately renounces an element of its sovereignty in return for a new opportunity: the chance to improve its attractiveness for new foreign investments which it would not be able to acquire in the absence of a treaty. This quid pro quo underlying the choice on the part of the host State is based on a policy judgment the nature of which escapes precise evaluation. It is based upon assumptions about the effect of the treaty that are uncertain.[114] As with every treaty, the acceptance of an investment treaty by a State and the determination of the desirable type and extent of obligations contained in it represent

[113] See VIII. 4(f) below.
[114] See I.3(d) below.

an exercise of the sovereign power to be made freely by each State in the light of its circumstances and preferences.[115]

Once the sovereign has committed itself to a treaty, the balancing of interests and aspirations is no longer subject to a unilateral decision. After the investment treaty is concluded, the investor is entitled to rely on the scheme accepted in the treaty by the host State as long as the treaty remains in force.

Investment treaties do not pit the interests and benefits of the host State against those of the investor. Instead, the motivation underlying such treaties assumes that the parties share a joint purpose. In this sense, it would be alien to the nature of an investment treaty to describe the interests of the host State and of the foreign investor as opposed to each other. The mode and spirit of investment treaties is to understand the two interests as complementary, held together by the joint purpose of implementing investments consistent with the business plan of the investor and the legal order of the host State.

(c) The investor's perspective: a long-term risk

Making a foreign investment is different in nature from engaging in a trade transaction. Whereas a trade deal typically consists of a one-time exchange of goods and money, an investment in a foreign country involves a long-term relationship between the investor and the host country. Often, the business plan of the investor is to sink substantial resources into the project at the outset of the investment, with the expectation of recouping this amount plus an acceptable rate of return during the subsequent period of investment, sometimes running up to 30 years or more.

A key feature in the design of such a foreign investment is to address in advance the risks inherent in such a long-term relationship, both from a business perspective and from the legal point of view. This involves identifying a business concept and a legal structure that is suitable to the implementation of the project and minimizes risks which may arise during the period of the investment. In many cases, this task is essential for the investor, as the money sunk into the project at the outset typically cannot be used subsequently elsewhere, because the machinery and installations of the project are specifically designed and tied to the particularities of the project and its location.

[115] See the statement made by the Permanent Court of International Justice in the *Wimbledon* case: 'The Court declines to see in the conclusion of any Treaty by which a State undertakes to perform or refrain from performing a particular act an abandonment of its sovereignty. No doubt any convention creating an obligation of this kind places a restriction upon the exercise of the sovereign rights of the State, in the sense that it requires them to be exercised in a certain way. But the right of entering into international engagements is an attribute of State sovereignty.' *Wimbledon* (*France v Germany*), Judgment, 17 August 1923, PCIJ Series A No 1, 25.

The dynamics in the relationship between the host State and the investor differ in nature before and after the investment has been made. Larger projects are typically not made under the general laws of the host country; instead, the host State and the foreign investor negotiate a deal—an investment agreement—which may adapt the general legal regime of the host country to the project-specific needs and preferences of both sides. During these negotiations, the investor will seek legal and other guarantees geared to the nature and the length of the project. Considerations will include bilateral or multilateral treaties concluded by the host State which will provide guarantees on the level of international law. If the host State is keen to attract the investment, the investor may be in the driver's seat during these negotiations.

The investor will normally bear the commercial risks inherent in possible changes in the market of the project, for example new competitors, price volatilities, exchange rates, or changes affecting the financial setting. In certain transactions, provision will be made for adaptation or renegotiation in the event of a change in the economic and financial context of the project. The political risks, that is, the risks inherent in a future intervention of the host State in the legal design of the project, will typically be addressed during these initial negotiations. Unless these risks are appropriately addressed in an applicable investment treaty, the investor may ask for assurances on a number of points, such as the applicable law, the tax regime, provisions dealing with inflation, a duty of the host State to buy a certain volume of the product (especially in the field of energy production), the future pricing of the investor's product or a customs regulation for materials needed for the product, and especially an agreement on future dispute settlement. These terms may be included in an investment contract between the investor and the host State.

Once negotiations are concluded and the investor's resources are sunk into the project, the dynamics of influence and power tend to shift in favour of the host State. The central political risk which henceforth arises for the foreign investor lies in a change of position of the host government that alters the balance of burdens, risks, and benefits which the two sides laid down when they negotiated the deal and which formed the basis of the investor's business plan and the legitimate expectations embodied in this plan. Such a change of position on the part of the host country becomes more likely with every subsequent change of government in the host State during the period of the investment.

(d) The host State's perspective: attracting foreign investment

It is reasonable to assume that the object and purpose of investment treaties is closely tied to the desirability of foreign investments, to the benefits for the host State and for the investor, to the conditions necessary for the promotion of foreign investment, and to the removal of obstacles which may stand in the way of allowing and channelling more foreign investment into host States. Thus, the purpose of investment treaties is to address the typical risks of a long-term investment project, and thereby to provide stability and predictability in the sense of an investment-friendly climate.

Under the rules of customary international law, no State is under an obligation to admit foreign investment in its territory, either generally or in any particular segment of its economy. While the right to exclude and to regulate foreign investment is an expression of State sovereignty, the power to conclude investment protection treaties with other States can also be seen as flowing from the same concept.

Once a host State has admitted a foreign investment, it must respect a minimum standard of customary international law.[116] Modern treaties on foreign investment go beyond this minimum standard of obligations that a host State owes foreign investors. Whether such treaties in general, or any particular version of them, are beneficial to the host State, remains a matter for each State to decide. Each State will weigh, or at least has the power to weigh, the economic and financial benefits of a treaty-based promotion of foreign investments against the burden of being bound to the standards of protection laid down in the treaty. Since investment decisions are based on a multitude of factors, it is difficult to undertake an objective assessment of the costs and benefits of treaties protecting foreign investments. Each State exercises its sovereign prerogative in determining its preferences and priorities when deciding whether to conclude an investment treaty.

There is an ongoing debate over the impact of foreign investment treaties on the promotion of foreign investment and its geographic distribution. Empirical studies on the relevance of investment protection treaties for an increase in foreign investment are contradictory.[117] Legal security in a host country for an investment project is one of several factors that will influence an investment decision, but the driving parameters are determined not by legal but by economic considerations. Therefore, an argument that international legal protection would in itself prompt an increased flow of foreign investment is unrealistic. On the other hand, globalization has led to fairly accurate real time information about economic and legal conditions around the globe, and the lack of legal stability surrounding a potential investment in a particular country may prevent a positive decision on the part of the investor. The perception of a sufficient degree of legal stability for a project and of a good investment climate in a State, will be one of several factors in the decision to make a new investment but will not by itself serve as the decisive incentive for

[116] See I.1(b) above and VIII.1(f) below.

[117] E Neumayr and L Spess, 'Do Bilateral Investment Treaties Increase Foreign Direct Investment to Developing Countries?' (2005) 33 *World Development* 1567; Z Elkins, A Guzman, and B Simmons, 'Competing for Capital: The Diffusion of Bilateral Investment Treaties, 1960–2000', *Berkeley Program in Law and Economics, Annual Papers* (2006); M Hallward-Driemeyer, 'Do Bilateral Investment Treaties Attract Foreign Investment?' *World Bank Policy Research Working Paper No 3121*; K Sauvant and L Sachs (eds), *The Effect of Treaties on Foreign Direct Investment* (2009); OECD Secretariat, *Societal Benefits and Costs of International Investment Agreements* (2018).

potential foreign investors.[118] Moreover, the perceived risk of investing in a particular country will determine the profit margin expected by the investor. High-risk investments may well be undertaken but will require a higher rate of return for the investor.

Another major advantage of treaties for the protection of investments, and of investment arbitration in particular, is that investment disputes become 'depoliticised'. This means that they remove the dispute from the foreign policy agenda of the investor's home State, thereby avoiding political confrontation between home State and host State.[119] In other words, the dispute is moved from the political inter-State arena into the judicial arena of investment arbitration. From the host State's perspective, facing an investor before an arbitral tribunal is a lesser evil compared to being exposed to the pressure of a powerful State or the European Commission.

(e) International investment law and sovereign regulation

The international law of foreign investment may be seen as a body of international rules of administrative law governing the relationship of the foreign investor and the host State.[120] The rules on foreign investment can reach far into segments of domestic law that traditionally belong to the '*domaine reservé*' of each host country. This has led to concerns not just about the preservation of national sovereignty but also about the democratic legitimacy of the process by which foreign investment law is developed and applied.

These concerns have been voiced not only by developing countries as recipients of foreign investments; the same observation has been made by segments of civil society in developed countries. In the United States, this was the case after it had become party to the NAFTA and a respondent in several cases.

In Europe, the discussion arose after the EU Commission had announced that it would negotiate an FTA with an investment chapter with the United States, known as TTIP. The debate spilled over into matters of investment protection and

[118] In 2006, the OECD adopted a Policy Framework for Investment that was updated in 2015. It has a focus on 12 policy areas which determine the degree to which a country is investment friendly: investment policy; investment promotion and facilitation; trade policy; competition policy; tax policy; corporate policy; policies for enabling responsible business conduct; developing human resources for investment; investment in infrastructure; financing investment; public governance; investment framework for green growth. See OECD, *Policy Framework for Investment* (2015).

[119] I Shihata, 'Towards a Greater Depoliticization of Investment Disputes: the Roles of ICSID and MIGA' in *The World Bank in A Changing World* (1991) 309: The *travaux préparatoires* to the ICSID Convention explicitly mention this goal: *History of the ICSID Convention* vol II-1 (1968) 236 at 242; C Schreuer, 'Investment Protection and International Relations' in A Reinisch and U Kriebaum (eds) *The Law of International Relations—Liber Amicorum Hanspeter Neuhold* (2007) 345; U Kriebaum, 'Evaluating Social Benefits and Costs of Investment Treaties: Depoliticization of Investment Disputes' (2018) 33 *ICSID Rev* 14. See also *Ecuador v United States*, Award, 29 September 2012, para 201.

[120] S Schill, *International Investment Law and Comparative Public Law* (2010).

arbitration in general. It had a strong influence on investment protection clauses in treaties negotiated by the EU. The debate led to the inclusion of an explicit right to regulate even though investment tribunals had never called that right into question. It also led to the concretization of certain protection standards like FET and to the inclusion of transparency provisions.[121] In addition, it triggered the move to change the dispute settlement system through the introduction of a court system either in addition to or instead of the current arbitration system.

A traditional understanding of sovereignty, detached from current international economic realities, may lead to the view that the international rules on foreign investment reach or even cross acceptable boundaries.[122] The rules on foreign investment touch upon domestic regulations as diverse as labour law, the organization of the judiciary, administrative principles, environmental law, health law, and, of course, rules governing property.

Modern trade law also affects domestic matters, but the impact of investment law on domestic law, and thus the potential concern for national sovereignty, is more severe. At the same time, economic literature has emphasized that openness of an economic system to foreign competition is among the factors that contribute to economic growth and to good governance in general. Thus, investment law embodies and represents economic globalization, with the potential advantages of economic efficiency and a higher standard of living, at the cost of a reduced legal power of national authorities to regulate areas that have an impact on foreign investment.[123] The current trend is a shift back towards national regulation, through the introduction of regulation exceptions, general exception clauses, and limiting language in clauses defining protection standards.[124]

(f) International investment law and good governance

The concept of good governance has increasingly influenced the international development agenda.[125] Earlier periods of development practice after 1945 had focused first on the significance of important individual projects and then on the role of macroeconomic policies. The new thinking, along with empirical studies, highlight the fact that all projects and policies depend in their implementation and,

[121] See also XII.11(j) below.

[122] In response to these concerns the United States has decided to opt for a treaty model that spells out definitions in great detail, so as to render arbitral decisions more predictable and to reduce the power of arbitrators. The EU follows this approach and has opted for closely defined standards, regulation exceptions, and a modified system of dispute settlement in the treaties it has negotiated.

[123] On the power of the host State to control multinational enterprises in general, see C Wallace, *The Multinational Enterprise and Legal Control—Host State Sovereignty in an Era of Economic Globalization* (2002).

[124] See eg CETA Articles 8.9, 28.3, 28.6, Annex 8-A (3).

[125] R Dolzer, M Herdegen, and B Vogel, *Good Governance* (2007).

indeed, in their conception and formulation, on a functioning State, especially on functioning institutions.

As a consequence, the concept of good governance has moved to the centre of international aid and poverty reduction policies. The first coherent formulation of the concept seems to be contained in a World Bank report written on the development challenges for Sub-Saharan Africa in 1989.[126] There is no single definition of good governance, but the core elements are expressed in working documents of the World Bank[127] and the International Monetary Fund.[128] The treaty between the European Community and African, Caribbean, and Pacific States adopted in 2000, the so-called Cotonou Agreement, offers the following definition:

> In the context of a political and institutional environment that upholds human rights, democratic principles and the rule of law, good governance is the transparent and accountable management of human, natural, economic and financial resources for the purposes of equitable and sustainable development. It entails clear decision-making procedures at the level of public authorities, transparent and accountable institutions, the primacy of law in the management and distribution of resources and capacity building for elaborating and implementing measures aiming in particular at preventing and combating corruption.[129]

The origin of the concept of good governance falls into the same period as the formulation of the Washington Consensus[130] and the beginning of the wave of investment treaties of the 1990s. The common core of the policies embodied in investment treaties, in the Washington Consensus, and the principle of good governance lies in the recognition that institutional effectiveness, the rule of law, and an appropriate degree of stability and predictability of policies form the governmental framework for domestic economic growth and for the willingness of foreign investors to enter the domestic market. Many investment protection standards as interpreted by arbitral tribunals contain typical rule of law requirements. Therefore, investment treaties provide for external constraints and disciplines which foster and reinforce values similar to the principle of good governance with its emphasis on domestic institutions and policies.

126 World Bank (ed), *Sub-Saharan Africa: From Crisis to Sustainable Growth* (1989).

127 World Bank (ed), *Governance: The World Bank's Experience* (1994) 12. See also S Killinger, *The World Bank's Non-Political Mandate* (2003).

128 IMF (ed), *Good Governance—The IMF's Role* (1997).

129 Cotonou Agreement, Article 9(3). See also P Hilpold, 'EU Development Cooperation at a Crossroad: The Cotonou Agreement of 23 June 2000 and the Principle of Good Governance' (2002) 7 *Eur Foreign Aff Rev* 53.

130 See I.1(c) above, VI.2 below.

(g) Obligations for investors

BITs give guarantees to investors but do not normally address obligations of investors, although many BITs provide that to be protected, investments must be in accordance with host State law.[131]

There is a debate on the inclusion in investment treaties of obligations of the foreign investor to observe certain human rights, environmental, or labour standards and on the possibility for host States to pursue counterclaims.[132] This would be in line with the idea of corporate responsibility reflected in the OECD Guidelines for Multinational Enterprises, adopted in 1976 and last updated in 2011, together with other efforts to promote voluntary initiatives for standards of corporate social responsibility.[133]

Within the United Nations, efforts to agree on non-binding rules broke down together with the negotiations on a multilateral treaty on foreign investment. An attempt to draw up a Code of Conduct on Transnational Corporations was made between 1977 and 1992 but was abandoned.[134]

The OECD Guidelines for Multinational Enterprises, which are part of the broader OECD Declaration on International Investment and Multinational Enterprises, constitute non-binding recommendations to multinational enterprises in areas such as employment, human rights, environment, the fight against bribery, science and technology, competition, taxation, information disclosure, and consumer interests. Within the administration of the adhering governments, so-called National Contact Points are charged with the promotion of the Guidelines and the handling of enquiries about their application. All OECD member countries as well as nine non-member States have so far adhered to the OECD Guidelines.

In 2003, a group of international banks launched an initiative for a framework addressing environmental and social risks in project financing.[135] The so-called Equator Principles are intended to apply to all project financings with total project capital costs of over US$10 million and require, *inter alia*, social and environmental assessment procedures and consultation, disclosure and monitoring mechanisms. For the applicable standards, the principles refer to various World

[131] See IV.8(c) below.

[132] H Mann et al, *IISD Model International Agreement on Investment for Sustainable Development* (2005); U Kriebaum, 'Privatizing Human Rights. The Interface between International Investment Protection and Human Rights' in A Reinisch and U Kriebaum (eds) *The Law of International Relations—Liber Amicorum Hanspeter Neuhold* (2007) 165.

[133] For a survey, see UNCTAD, *World Investment Report* (2011) 111. See also A Heinemann, 'Business Enterprises in Public International Law' in U Fastenrath et al (eds) *From Bilateralism to Community Interest: Essays in Honour of Judge Bruno Simma* (2011) 718.

[134] Draft UN Code of Conduct on Transnational Corporations (1984) 23 ILM 626.

[135] S Kass and J McCarroll, 'The Revised Equator Principles' (2006) *The New York LJ*, 1 September 2006; A Hardenbrook, 'The Equator Principles: The Private Financial Sector's Attempt at Environmental Responsibility' (2007) 40 *Vanderbilt J Transn'l L* 197.

Bank and International Finance Corporation (IFC) guidelines. Over 76 financial institutions have so far adopted the Equator Principles.

An effort to approach investment issues from the vantage point of human rights was made in the United Nations after 2000. The aim was to find a consensus on norms addressing responsibilities of transnational corporations.[136] In 2005, the United Nations named a Special Representative for human rights and transnational corporations and other business entities, tasked with 'identifying and clarifying standards of corporate responsibility and accountability with regard to human rights'. In 2011, the Special Representative prepared a Report on 'Guiding Principles on Business and Human Rights: Implementing the UN Protect, Respect and Remedy Framework'. It built on major research and extensive consultations with all relevant stakeholders. The Human Rights Council endorsed the Guiding Principles and established a Working Group on the issue of human rights and transnational corporations and other business enterprises to disseminate and implement them.[137] The Human Rights Council established an open-ended intergovernmental working group on transnational corporations and other business enterprises with respect to human rights in 2014.[138] It was mandated with elaborating an international legally binding instrument on transnational corporations and other business enterprises with respect to human rights. In 2020, the intergovernmental working group published a second revised draft. So far, no binding instrument has been adopted.

In 2019, a drafting team led by Judge Bruno Simma presented the Hague Rules on Business and Human Rights Arbitration.[139] One of the ideas of the Hague Rules is to close a remedial gap for individuals affected by business activities that impact their human rights. Under the Hague Rules, it is possible to resolve disputes in situations where more traditional remedies, such as judicial proceedings, are not available or not effective. This will often be the case in situations where foreign investments negatively affect the local population and where local legal remedies do not offer proper protection.

[136] D Weissbrodt and M Kruger, 'Norms on the Responsibilities of Transnational Corporations and Other Business Enterprises with Regard to Human Rights' (2003) 97 *AJIL* 901.

[137] Res A/HRC/RES/17/4.

[138] Res A/HRC/RES/26/9.

[139] Available at: <https://www.cilc.nl/cms/wp-content/uploads/2019/12/The-Hague-Rules-on-Business-and-Human-Rights-Arbitration_CILC-digital-version.pdf>.

II
Interpretation and Intertemporal Application of Investment Treaties

ADDITIONAL READING: N Gallus, *The Temporal Scope of Investment Protection Treaties* (2008); RK Gardiner, *Treaty Interpretation* (2008); A Roberts, 'Power and Persuasion in Investment Treaty Interpretation: the Dual Role of States' (2010) 104 *AJIL* 179; A Saldarriaga, 'Investment Awards and the Rules of Interpretation of the Vienna Convention' (2013) 28 *ICSID Rev* 197; JR Weeramantry, *Treaty Interpretation in Investment Arbitration* (2012); SA Alexandrov, 'Judge Brower and the Vienna Convention Rules of Treaty Interpretation' in DD Caron et al (eds) *Practicing Virtue: Inside International Arbitration* (2015) 434; A Reinisch, 'The Interpretation of International Investment Agreements' in M Bungenberg et al (eds) *International Investment Law* (2015) 372; N Rubins and B Love, 'Ratione Temporis' in M Bungenberg et al (eds) *International Investment Law* (2015) 481; H Ascensio, 'Article 31 of the Vienna Convention on the Law of Treaties and International Investment Law' (2016) 31 *ICSID Rev* 366; L Boisson de Chazournes, 'Rules of Interpretation and Investment Arbitration' in M Kinnear et al (eds) *Building International Investment Law* (2016) 12; N Gallus, 'Article 28 of the Vienna Convention on the Law of Treaties and Investment Treaty Decisions' (2016) 31 *ICSID Rev* 290; T Gazzini, *Interpretation of International Investment Treaties* (2016); EE Triantafilou, 'Contemporaneity and Evolutive Interpretation under the Vienna Convention on the Law of Treaties' (2017) 32 *ICSID Rev* 138; A Gattini, 'Jurisdiction *ratione temporis* in International Investment Arbitration' in A Gattini et al (eds) *General Principles of Law and International Investment Arbitration* (2018) 111.

1. The interpretation of investment treaties

As explained above (see I.2), investment law is shaped by a variety of treaties. In addition to bilateral treaties, mostly bilateral investment treaties (BITs) and free trade agreements (FTAs), there are regional treaties such as the Energy Charter Treaty (ECT), the North American Free Trade Agreement (NAFTA), the United States–Mexico–Canada Agreement (USMCA), the Comprehensive and Progressive Agreement for Trans-Pacific Partnership (CPTPP), the Dominican Republic–Central American Free Trade Agreement (DR–CAFTA), and the

Organisation of the Islamic Conference (OIC) Agreement. The Convention on the Settlement of Investment Disputes between States and Nationals of Other States (ICSID Convention), a multilateral treaty, is also frequently interpreted and applied.

(a) The general rule of treaty interpretation

Most tribunals, when interpreting treaties, start by invoking Article 31 of the Vienna Convention on the Law of Treaties (VCLT).[1] For instance, the Tribunal in *Siemens v Argentina*[2] said:

> Both parties have based their arguments on the interpretation of the Treaty in accordance with Article 31(1) of the Vienna Convention. This Article provides that a treaty be 'interpreted in good faith in accordance with the ordinary meaning to be given to the terms of the treaty in their context and in the light of its object and purpose.' The Tribunal will adhere to these rules of interpretation in considering the disputed provisions of the Treaty.[3]

Tribunals have recognized the validity of the rules on treaty interpretation in the VCLT as part of customary international law.[4] This means that these rules are of general application also in respect of treaties concluded before the VCLT's entry into force in 1980 and independently of whether all parties to a treaty have ratified the VCLT.

The reference to the ordinary meaning of the treaty's terms means that '[i]nterpretation must be based above all upon the text of the treaty'.[5] The use of dictionaries by tribunals[6] is a consequence of this textual approach. This approach

[1] Article 31(1) of the VCLT provides: 'A treaty shall be interpreted in good faith in accordance with the ordinary meaning to be given to the terms of the treaty in their context and in the light of its object and purpose.'

[2] *Siemens v Argentina*, Decision on Jurisdiction, 3 August 2004.

[3] At para 80.

[4] *Methanex v United States*, Final Award on Jurisdiction and Merits, 3 August 2005, IV, B, para 29; *Malaysian Historical Salvors v Malaysia*, Decision on Annulment, 16 April 2009, para 56; *BIVAC v Paraguay*, Decision on Jurisdiction, 29 May 2009, para 59; *Kiliç v Turkmenistan*, Decision on Article VII.2 of the Turkey–Turkmenistan Bilateral Investment Treaty, 7 May 2012, para 6.4; *Micula v Romania I*, Award, 11 December 2013, para 503; *Churchill Mining v Indonesia*, Decision on Jurisdiction, 24 February 2014, paras 95, 149; *Itisaluna v Iraq*, Award, 3 April 2020, para 61.

[5] *Territorial Dispute* (*Libya v Chad*), Judgment, 3 February 1994, ICJ Reports (1994) 6, 22, para 41. See also *Rizvi v Indonesia*, Award on Jurisdiction, 16 July 2013, para 64.

[6] *Vannessa v Venezuela*, Decision on Jurisdiction, 22 August 2008, sec 3.2.4; *Yukos v Russian Federation*, Interim Award on Jurisdiction and Admissibility, 30 November 2009, para 304; *Churchill Mining v Indonesia*, Decision on Jurisdiction, 24 February 2014, paras 163–164; *Orascom v Algeria*, Award, 31 May 2017, para 283; *Antin v Spain*, Award, 15 June 2018, para 518; *Almasryia v Kuwait*, Award under Rule 41(5), 1 November 2019, para 28; *Adamakopoulos v Cyprus*, Decision on Jurisdiction, 7 February 2020, para 293.

has also led to the rejection of assumed intentions of the parties to the treaty that were not clearly reflected in its text.[7] The Tribunal in *Wintershall v Argentina*[8] said:

> The carefully-worded formulation in Article 31 [of the VCLT] is based on the view that the text must be presumed to be the authentic expression of the intention of the parties. The starting point of all treaty-interpretation is the elucidation of the meaning of the text, not an independent investigation into the intention of the parties from other sources ....[9]

A treaty's object and purpose are among the primary guides for interpretation listed in Article 31 of the VCLT. Investment treaties often express their object and purpose in the preambles. These preambles highlight the positive role of foreign investment in general and the nexus between an investment-friendly climate and the flow of foreign investment.[10] A typical version of a preamble would read:

> The Government of X and the Government of Y; Desiring to create favourable conditions for greater investment by nationals and companies of one State in the territory of the other State; Recognising that the encouragement and reciprocal protection under international agreement of such investments will be conducive to the stimulation of individual business initiative and will increase prosperity in both States; Have agreed as follows ....[11]

Tribunals frequently interpret investment treaties in light of their object and purpose, often by looking at their preambles.[12] Often this has led to an interpretation

[7] *Methanex v United States*, Final Award on Jurisdiction and Merits, 3 August 2005, II, B, para 22; *El Paso v Argentina*, Award, 31 October 2011, para 590; *Al Warraq v Indonesia*, Award on Respondent's Preliminary Objections, 21 June 2012, para 81; *Garanti Koza v Turkmenistan*, Decision on the Objection to Jurisdiction for Lack of Consent, 3 July 2013, para 57; *ST-AD v Bulgaria*, Award on Jurisdiction, 18 July 2013, para 393; *Ping An v Belgium*, Award, 30 April 2015, para 166; *Belenergia v Italy*, Award, 6 August 2019, para 304.

[8] *Wintershall v Argentina*, Award, 8 December 2008.

[9] At para 78.

[10] R Dolzer and M Stevens, *Bilateral Investment Treaties* (1995) 20.

[11] See the preamble to the UK Model BIT 2008.

[12] *Lauder v Czech Republic*, Final Award, 3 September 2001, para 292; *Siemens v Argentina*, Decision on Jurisdiction, 3 August 2004, para 81; *CMS v Argentina*, Award, 12 May 2005, para 274; *Aguas del Tunari v Bolivia*, Decision on Jurisdiction, 21 October 2005, paras 153, 240–241, 247; *Continental Casualty v Argentina*, Decision on Jurisdiction, 22 February 2006, para 80; *Saluka v Czech Republic*, Partial Award, 17 March 2006, para 299; *Kardassopoulos v Georgia*, Decision on Jurisdiction, 6 July 2007, paras 178–181; *BG Group v Argentina*, Final Award, 24 December 2007, paras 132–134; *Société Générale v Dominican Republic*, Award on Preliminary Objections to Jurisdiction, 19 September 2008, paras 21, 29, 31–33, 103; *Hrvatska Elektroprivreda v Slovenia*, Decision on the Treaty Interpretation Issue, 12 June 2009, paras 177–179; *Lemire v Ukraine*, Decision on Jurisdiction and Liability, 14 January 2010, para 264; *Suez and InterAguas v Argentina*, Decision on Liability, 30 July 2010, para 198; *AFT v Slovakia*, Award, 5 March 2011, paras 236–237; *Daimler v Argentina*, Award, 22 August 2012, paras 254–260; *Tenaris v Venezuela I*, Award, 29 January 2016, para 153; *Valores Mundiales v Venezuela*, Award, 25 July 2017, para 538; *Wirtgen v Czech Republic*, Final Award, 11 October 2017, para 223; *Mera v Serbia*,

that is favourable to the investor.[13] But this development has also come under criticism. One Tribunal has warned against overextending the method of looking at the object and purpose.[14] Another Tribunal has denied the possibility to rely upon a preamble as a source creating legal rights or obligation.[15]

Closely related to object and purpose is the issue of a restrictive or effective interpretation of treaties. This issue has arisen particularly in the context of interpreting treaty provisions governing the jurisdiction of tribunals. Some tribunals seem to have favoured a restrictive interpretation of treaty provisions that limited the State's sovereignty.[16] Other tribunals have rejected a restrictive interpretation, at times favouring an interpretation that gives full effect to the rights of investors.[17] Most tribunals have distanced themselves from either approach, advocating a balanced approach to interpretation.[18]

A closer look at some of these decisions would indicate that the professed preference of tribunals for one or the other method of interpretation should not necessarily be taken at face value. A tribunal's avowed predilection for a particular approach to interpretation is not always reflected in the actual decision.[19] Ultimately, what matters is what the tribunal does, not what it says it is doing.

Under the established jurisprudence of investment tribunals, treaty language should be construed to have meaning and purpose (*effet utile*) and should not be read in a way that renders it redundant or superfluous.[20] In *AAPL v Sri Lanka*,[21] the Tribunal found:

Decision on Jurisdiction, 30 November 2018, paras 121–124; *Adamakopoulos v Cyprus*, Decision on Jurisdiction, 7 February 2020, paras 278–279.

[13] The Tribunal in *Amco v Indonesia*, interpreting the ICSID Convention, pointed out that investment protection was also in the longer-term interest of host States: 'to protect investments is to protect the general interest of development and of developing countries'. *Amco v Indonesia*, Decision on Jurisdiction, 25 September 1983, para 23. See also Award, 20 November 1984, para 249.

[14] *Plama v Bulgaria*, Decision on Jurisdiction, 8 February 2005, para 193.

[15] *İçkale v Turkmenistan*, Award, 8 March 2016, para 337.

[16] *SGS v Pakistan*, Decision on Jurisdiction, 6 August 2003, para 171; *Noble Ventures v Romania*, Award, 12 October 2005, para 55; *Tulip v Turkey*, Decision on Bifurcated Jurisdictional Issue, 5 March 2013, para 44.

[17] *Methanex v United States*, Preliminary Award on Jurisdiction and Admissibility, 7 August 2002, paras 103–105; *Aguas del Tunari v Bolivia*, Decision on Jurisdiction, 21 October 2005, para 91; *SGS v Philippines*, Decision on Jurisdiction, 29 January 2004, para 116; *Eureko v Poland*, Partial Award, 19 August 2005, para 248; *Suez and InterAguas v Argentina*, Decision on Jurisdiction, 16 May 2006, paras 59, 64; *ConocoPhillips v Venezuela*, Decision on Jurisdiction and Merits, 3 September 2013, para 309.

[18] See below XII.7(g).

[19] See eg *Noble Ventures v Romania*, Award, 12 October 2005, where the Tribunal, after subscribing to a 'restrictive interpretation' (at para 55), gave full effect to an umbrella clause (at paras 56–62). By contrast, in *El Paso v Argentina*, Decision on Jurisdiction, 27 April 2006, the Tribunal expresses a preference for a 'balanced interpretation' (at para 70) but then proceeds to interpret an umbrella clause very restrictively (at paras 70–86).

[20] *Eureko v Poland*, Partial Award, 19 August 2005, para 248; *CEMEX v Venezuela*, Decision on Jurisdiction, 30 December 2010, paras 104–107; *Sanum v Laos*, Award on Jurisdiction, 13 December 2013, para 335; *Rawat v Mauritius*, Award on Jurisdiction, 6 April 2018, para 182; *Krederi v Ukraine*, Award, 2 July 2018, para 273; *Vento v Mexico*, Award, 6 July 2020, para 183.

[21] *AAPL v Sri Lanka*, Final Award, 27 June 1990.

> Nothing is better settled, as a canon of interpretation in all systems of law, than that a clause must be so interpreted as to give it a meaning rather than so as to deprive it of meaning.[22]

The terms of a treaty are to be interpreted in their context. The context comprises the treaty's entire text including its preamble and annexes.[23] Under Article 31(2)(a) of the VCLT the context also includes any agreement relating to the treaty. Under Article 31(2)(b) the context includes also 'any instrument which was made by one or more parties in connexion with the conclusion of the treaty and accepted by the other parties as an instrument related to the treaty'.[24] In *Fraport v Philippines*,[25] the Tribunal interpreted the BIT between Germany and the Philippines with the help of the Philippines' Instrument of Ratification which was exchanged with Germany.[26]

(b) *Travaux préparatoires*

At times, tribunals also refer to the supplementary means of interpretation contained in Article 32 of the VCLT.[27] Article 32 treats the *travaux préparatoires* (preparatory work) to a treaty only as a supplementary means of interpretation to confirm the meaning resulting from the general rule of interpretation or if the application of Article 31 leaves the meaning ambiguous or obscure or leads to a result that is manifestly absurd or unreasonable.

The Tribunal in *Noble Ventures v Romania*,[28] after referring to the general rule of interpretation in Article 31 of the VCLT, said:

[22] At para 40.

[23] *Kiliç v Turkmenistan*, Award, 2 July 2013, paras 7.3.1–7.3.9.; *Eiser v Spain*, Award, 4 May 2017, paras 375–380; *Beijing Urban Construction v Yemen*, Decision on Jurisdiction, 31 May 2017, paras 78–87; *Mera v Serbia*, Decision on Jurisdiction, 30 November 2018, paras 56–57; *Eskosol v Italy*, Decision on Request for Immediate Termination, 7 May 2019, paras 81–102; *B-Mex v Mexico*, Partial Award, 19 July 2019, paras 101–113; *Glencore v Colombia*, Award, 27 August 2019, paras 1004–1009; *Manuel Garcia Armas v Venezuela*, Award on Jurisdiction, 13 December 2019, paras 709–723; *Itisaluna v Iraq*, Award, 3 April 2020, para 160; *Addiko v Croatia*, Decision on the EU *Acquis*, 12 June 2020, para 198; *Strabag v Libya*, Award, 29 June 2020, para 117.

[24] *Vattenfall v Germany II*, Decision on the *Achmea* Issue, 31 August 2018, paras 185–191.

[25] *Fraport v Philippines I*, Award, 16 August 2007.

[26] At paras 337–343. Inexplicably, the Decision on Annulment criticizes the Tribunal's use of the Instrument of Ratification: *Fraport v Philippines I*, Decision on Annulment, 23 December 2010, paras 98, 99, 107.

[27] Article 32 of the VCLT dealing with supplementary means of interpretation provides:
'Recourse may be had to supplementary means of interpretation, including the preparatory work of the treaty and the circumstances of its conclusion, in order to confirm the meaning resulting from the application of article 31, or to determine the meaning when the interpretation according to article 31:

(a) leaves the meaning ambiguous or obscure; or
(b) leads to a result which is manifestly absurd or unreasonable.'

[28] *Noble Ventures v Romania*, Award, 12 October 2005.

> recourse may be had to supplementary means of interpretation, including the preparatory work and the circumstances of its conclusion, only in order to confirm the meaning resulting from the application of the aforementioned methods of interpretation.[29]

In practice, resort to *travaux préparatoires* seems to be determined primarily by their availability. In *Malaysian Historical Salvors v Malaysia*,[30] the ad hoc Committee said:

> courts and tribunals interpreting treaties regularly review the *travaux préparatoires* whenever they are brought to their attention; it is mythological to pretend that they do so only when they first conclude that the term requiring interpretation is ambiguous or obscure.[31]

The drafting history of the ICSID Convention is well-documented, readily available, and easily accessible through an analytical index.[32] As a consequence, ICSID tribunals frequently resort to its *travaux préparatoires*. By contrast, the negotiating history of BITs is typically not or only poorly documented. Therefore, tribunals usually will not have access to these *travaux préparatoires*, even if they want to view them.[33]

The position with NAFTA occupies a middle ground. Initially, the documents illustrating the negotiating history were not available to the public. This led to complaints about an inequality of arms between a respondent State which had access to these materials and a claimant investor who did not. In July 2004, the NAFTA Free Trade Commission announced the release of the negotiating history of Chapter Eleven of NAFTA dealing with investment.[34]

The Tribunal in *Methanex v United States*[35] stressed the limited relevance of the negotiating history of the NAFTA in view of Article 32 of the VCLT:

29 At para 50.

30 *Malaysian Historical Salvors v Malaysia*, Decision on Annulment, 16 April 2009.

31 At para 57.

32 History of the ICSID Convention. Documents Concerning the Origin and the Formulation of the Convention on the Settlement of Investment Disputes between States and Nationals of Other States, Washington, DC 1968, reprinted 2001.

33 See *Aguas del Tunari v Bolivia*, Decision on Jurisdiction, 21 October 2005, para 274, where the Tribunal deplored the lack of insight to be gained from the sparse material provided by the parties. In *Perenco v Ecuador*, Decision on Jurisdiction, 30 June 2011, paras 92–95 the Tribunal asked the parties to try and obtain the *travaux préparatoires* to the France–Ecuador BIT on a particular point. In *Churchill Mining v Indonesia*, Decision on Jurisdiction, 24 February 2014, paras 208–230, after initial problems the *travaux préparatoires* were provided and heavily relied upon by the Tribunal to establish the meaning of a provision of the BIT concerning the consent to arbitration.

34 The documents are published at: <https://www.international.gc.ca/trade-agreements-accords-commerciaux/topics-domaines/disp-diff/trilateral_neg.aspx?lang=eng>. It is unclear whether the available documentation covers all existing documents.

35 *Methanex v United States*, Final Award, 3 August 2005.

> pursuant to Article 32, recourse may be had to supplementary means of interpretation only in the limited circumstances there specified. Other than that, the approach of the Vienna Convention is that the text of the treaty is deemed to be the authentic expression of the intentions of the parties; and its elucidation, rather than wide-ranging searches for the supposed intentions of the parties, is the proper object of interpretation.[36]

The Tribunal in *Blusun v Italy*, when discussing the existence of an alleged inherent disconnection clause for European Union (EU) member States in the Energy Charter Treaty, pointed out that it is not possible to rely on *travaux préparatoires* where the terms of the treaty are clear.[37]

(c) The relevance of other treaties

Article 32 of the VCLT also treats the circumstances of a treaty's conclusion as a supplementary means of interpretation. Some tribunals have looked at the prior and subsequent treaty practice of the parties to the treaty as a means of its interpretation.[38] In *KT Asia v Kazakhstan*,[39] the Tribunal said:

> Pursuant to Article 32 of the VCLT, supplementary means of interpretation can be used in particular to confirm the meaning resulting from the application of Article 31. These include treaties which one of the Contracting States entered into with third states if they deal with the same subject matter.[40]

In *Serafín García Armas v Venezuela*,[41] the Tribunal undertook a detailed examination of the treaty practice of Venezuela and Spain. It determined that out of 27 BITs of Venezuela that it examined, only three excluded dual nationals who also

[36] At II, B, para 22. Footnote omitted.

[37] *Blusun v Italy*, Award, 27 December 2016, para 280 (4); similar: *Garanti Koza v Turkmenistan*, Decision on the Objection to Jurisdiction for Lack of Consent, 3 July 2013, para 36.

[38] *Siemens v Argentina*, Decision on Jurisdiction, 3 August 2004, para 105; *Aguas del Tunari v Bolivia*, Decision on Jurisdiction, 21 October 2005, paras 289–314; *Berschader v Russian Federation*, Award, 21 April 2006, paras 145–147, 155, 203–204; *National Grid v Argentina*, Decision on Jurisdiction, 20 June 2006, para 85; *Kiliç v Turkmenistan*, Decision on Article VII.2 of the Turkey–Turkmenistan Bilateral Investment Treaty, 7 May 2012, paras 9.18–9.21; *Daimler v Argentina*, Award, 22 August 2012, paras 261–266, 273–274; *Agility v Pakistan*, Decision on Jurisdiction, 27 February 2013, paras 132–137; *ConocoPhillips* v *Venezuela*, Decision on Jurisdiction and Merits, 3 September 2013, paras 310–314, 316; *Metal-Tech v Uzbekistan*, Award, 4 October 2013, paras 159–161; *Churchill Mining v Indonesia*, Decision on Jurisdiction, 24 February 2014, paras 195–207; *UP and C.D v Hungary*, Decision on Jurisdiction, 3 March 2016, paras 169–172; *A11Y v Czech Republic*, Decision on Jurisdiction, 9 February 2017, paras 105–106; *Orascom v Algeria*, Award, 31 May 2017, para 303; *Wirtgen v Czech Republic*, Final Award, 11 October 2017, paras 230–234.

[39] *KT Asia v Kazakhstan*, Award, 17 October 2013.

[40] At para 122. Footnote omitted.

[41] *Serafín García Armas v Venezuela*, Decision on Jurisdiction, 15 December 2014.

possessed the host State's nationality. Out of 42 BITs of Spain, examined for this purpose, only one withheld the treaty's benefits from dual nationals possessing the host State's nationality. This treaty practice led the Tribunal to the conclusion that an exclusion of dual nationals who possessed the host State's nationality from the BIT's protection would have to be explicit and could hence not be assumed.[42]

Other tribunals have adopted a sceptical attitude towards an attempt to enlist third party treaties as an aid to interpreting treaties. They have denied the utility of resorting to other, often differently worded treaties to gauge the meaning of a treaty.[43]

In *Nova Scotia Power v Venezuela*,[44] the Tribunal said in response to an argument based on the prior treaty practice of both parties:

> The Tribunal does not find this argument persuasive. Whilst it is accepted that other tribunals have had recourse to prior treaty making practice, the Tribunal is not convinced that this avenue is open based on the interpretive framework provided for in the VCLT, and thus whether it is appropriate.[45]

(d) Interpretative statements

Some treaties provide for a consultation mechanism concerning their interpretation or application. The NAFTA[46] has a mechanism whereby the Free Trade Commission (FTC), a body composed of representatives of the three States parties, can adopt binding interpretations of the treaty.[47] The FTC has made use of this method in July 2001 when it interpreted the concepts of 'fair and equitable treatment' and 'full protection and security' under Article 1105 of the NAFTA.[48] NAFTA tribunals have accepted this interpretation as binding.[49] The

[42] At paras 176–181.

[43] *Nordzucker v Poland*, Partial Award, 10 December 2008, para 113 (vi); *Tza Yap Shum v Peru*, Decision on Jurisdiction and Competence, 19 June 2009, paras 109, 186; *Azurix v Argentina*, Decision on Annulment, 1 September 2009, para 128; *Mobil & Murphy v Canada*, Decision on Liability and on Principles of Quantum, 22 May 2012, paras 227–232; *Standard Chartered Bank v Tanzania*, Award, 2 November 2012, para 244; *Mobil v Argentina*, Decision on Jurisdiction and Liability, 10 April 2013, para 1038; *Beijing Urban Construction v Yemen*, Decision on Jurisdiction, 31 May 2017, para 97; *Valores Mundiales v Venezuela*, Award, 25 July 2017, para 199; *Doutremepuich v Mauritius*, Award on Jurisdiction, 23 August 2019, paras 231–235; *Adamakopoulos v Cyprus*, Decision on Jurisdiction, 7 February 2020, para 276.

[44] *Nova Scotia Power v Venezuela*, Award, 30 April 2014.

[45] At para 83.

[46] See I.2(c) above.

[47] NAFTA Article 2001(1): 'The Parties hereby establish the Free Trade Commission, comprising cabinet-level representatives of the Parties or their designees.' NAFTA Article 1131(2): 'An interpretation by the Commission of a provision of this Agreement shall be binding on a Tribunal established under this Section.'

[48] FTC Note of Interpretation of 31 July 2001. See VIII.1(f) below.

[49] *Mondev v United States*, Award, 11 October 2002, paras 100 et seq; *UPS v Canada*, Award on Jurisdiction, 22 November 2002, para 97; *ADF v United States*, Award, 9 January 2003, paras 175–178;

USMCA[50] has maintained this mechanism by establishing an FTC, composed of government representatives of each party, which has the power to issue interpretations of the provisions of the Agreement. Interpretations issued by the FTC are binding for tribunals established under Chapter 14 (Investment).[51] Other treaties provide for similar procedures for binding interpretations by the parties.[52]

In *Canadian Cattlemen v United States*,[53] the respondent relied on unilateral statements as well as on submissions in other cases of the three NAFTA Parties. But there was no formal interpretation by the FTC under Article 1131(2). The Tribunal found that there was no 'subsequent agreement' but held that there was 'subsequent practice' establishing the agreement of the NAFTA Parties on the issue. The Tribunal found that this 'subsequent practice' confirmed its own interpretation of the NAFTA.[54]

BITs do not normally have an institutional mechanism to obtain authentic interpretations of their meaning. But the United States Model BIT of 2012 provides for such a mechanism:

> ARTICLE 30(3)
> A joint decision of the Parties, each acting through its representative designated for purposes of this Article, declaring their interpretation of a provision of this Treaty shall be binding on a tribunal, and any decision or award issued by a tribunal must be consistent with that joint decision.

The BIT between the Czech Republic and the Netherlands provided for 'consultations' with a view to resolving any issue of interpretation and application of the treaty. The two States parties to that BIT have issued joint, non-binding statements which were taken into account by tribunals.[55]

Unilateral assertions of the disputing State Party on the meaning of a treaty provision, made in the process of ongoing proceedings, are of limited value. Such statements are likely to be perceived as self-serving and as determined by the desire to

Loewen v United States, Award, 26 June 2003, paras 124–128; *Waste Management v Mexico I*, Award, 30 April 2004, paras 90–91; *Methanex v United States*, Final Award, 3 August 2005, II, H, para 23; *Grand River v United States*, Award, 12 January 2011, paras 175–176; *Clayton/Bilcon v Canada*, Award on Jurisdiction and Liability, 17 March 2015, paras 429–430; see also *Mexico v Metalclad*, Judgment, Supreme Court of British Columbia, 2 May 2001, 5 ICSID Reports 236, paras 61–65.

[50] See I.2(c) above.
[51] USMCA Art 30.2 (2)(f).
[52] The ASEAN Comprehensive Investment Agreement (2009) Article 40(3) provides for binding interpretations through joint decisions of the Parties. CETA contains similar provisions: Articles 8.10.3 and 8.31.3.
[53] *Canadian Cattlemen v United States*, Award on Jurisdiction, 28 January 2008.
[54] At paras 181–189.
[55] *CME v The Czech Republic*, Final Award, 14 March 2003, paras 87–93, 437, 504; *Eastern Sugar v Czech Republic*, Partial Award, 27 March 2007, paras 193–197; *Invesmart v Czech Republic*, Award, 26 June 2009, para 195.

influence the tribunal's decision in favour of the State offering the interpretation.[56] The Tribunal in *Gas Natural v Argentina*,[57] said:

> We do not believe, however, that an argument made by a party in the context of an arbitration reflects practice establishing agreement between the parties to a treaty within the meaning of Article 31(3)(b) of the Vienna Convention on the Law of Treaties.[58]

Many treaties, especially those of the United States and Canada, provide for submissions of the non-disputing States parties to these treaties on issues of their interpretation. Non-disputing parties to the relevant treaties have, in fact, made submissions concerning the interpretation of these treaties in cases arising under the NAFTA[59] and under other treaties.[60]

Some tribunals have sought information from the investor's home State on certain aspects of the treaty's interpretation.[61] In *Renco v Peru*,[62] the Tribunal invited the government of the United States as a non-disputing party to the US–Peru Trade Promotion Agreement to comment on issues of its interpretation.[63] The Tribunal noted, however, that it was not bound by the resulting interpretation:

[56] *Telefónica v Argentina*, Decision on Jurisdiction, 25 May 2006, paras 109–114; *Daimler v Argentina*, Award, 22 August 2012, para 272; *Suez and Vivendi v Argentina*, Decision on Annulment, 5 May 2017, para 258; *Belenergia v Italy*, Award, 6 August 2019, para 308.

[57] *Gas Natural v Argentina*, Decision on Jurisdiction, 17 June 2005.

[58] At para 47, footnote 12.

[59] NAFTA Art 1128. *Canadian Cattlemen v United States*, Award on Jurisdiction, 28 January 2008, paras 106–109; *Merrill & Ring v Canada*, Award, 31 March 2010, paras 20–24; *Grand River v United States*, Award, 12 January 2011, para 59; *Mobil & Murphy v Canada*, Decision on Liability and Principles of Quantum, 22 May 2012, paras 25, 28, 31; *Apotex v United States*, Award, 25 August 2014, paras 1.27, 2.72–2.75; *Mesa Power v Canada*, Award, 24 March 2016, paras 195–204, 289–292, 491–494; *Mobil v Canada*, Decision on Jurisdiction and Admissibility, 13 July 2018, paras 28–30, 45–46, 121–122, 145; *Vento v Mexico*, Award, 6 July 2020, paras 37, 45, 53.

[60] *RDC v Guatemala*, Award, 29 June 2012, paras 12–17, 23, 25, 27, 207–211; *Al Tamimi v Oman*, Award, 3 November 2015, paras 32–33, 381; *Corona v Dominican Republic*, Award on the Respondent's Expedited Preliminary Objection, 31 May 2016, paras 25, 172–180, 245–247; *Pac Rim v El Salvador*, Award, 14 October 2016, para 1.36; *Spence v Costa Rica*, Interim Award, 25 October 2016, paras 153–161; *Bear Creek v Peru*, Award, 30 November 2017, paras 55–56, 90–91, 338–340; *Bridgestone v Panama*, Decision on Expedited Objections, 13 December 2017, paras 26, 28, 90–94, 151–152, 282–285; *Italba v Uruguay*, Award, 22 March 2019, paras 41, 48, 61–62; *Gran Colombia Gold v Colombia*, Decision on the Bifurcated Jurisdictional Issue, 23 November 2020, paras 119–125.

[61] *Aguas del Tunari v Bolivia*, Decision on Jurisdiction, 21 October 2005, paras 45–49, 249–263; *Eureko v Slovakia*, Award on Jurisdiction, Arbitrability and Suspension, 26 October 2010, paras 154–174; *Detroit Intl Bridge v Canada*, Award on Jurisdiction, 2 April 2015, paras 117–145. In *SGS v Pakistan*, Decision on Jurisdiction, 6 August 2003 the government of the claimant's nationality (Switzerland) took the unusual step of writing to ICSID to complain about an interpretation given by an ICSID tribunal stating that the Swiss authorities were wondering why the Tribunal had not found it necessary to enquire about their view of the meaning of the provision in the Pakistan–Switzerland BIT. See SA Alexandrov, 'Breaches of Contract and Breaches of Treaty' (2004) 5 *JWIT* 555, 570/71.

[62] *Renco v Peru*, Decision as to the Scope of Respondent's Preliminary Objections under Article 10.20.4, 18 December 2014.

[63] At para 29. See also para 69.

> The Tribunal credits the views of both State Contracting Parties with the highest respect. However, the Tribunal is not bound by the views of either party.
>
> Further, the Tribunal has taken note that the Free Trade Commission, established pursuant to the Treaty and authorized to issue binding interpretations as to the Treaty's provisions, has issued no interpretation of Article 10.20.4 to date.
>
> Under the circumstances, the proper interpretation of Article 10.20.4 and how it should be applied to the facts of this case are tasks which reside exclusively with this Tribunal.[64]

Joint declarations of the States parties on the proper interpretation of an investment treaty may appear efficient and look like a convenient method to settle questions of treaty interpretation. But if the question is relevant in pending proceedings, such an interpretation will give rise to serious concerns about the fairness of the procedure before the investor–State tribunal. Once a case is under way, a respondent State is motivated primarily by defensive concerns related to the pending dispute. Therefore, a mechanism whereby a party to a dispute can influence the outcome of judicial proceedings by issuing an official interpretation to the detriment of the other party, is questionable. This applies even where that party receives the support of the other treaty party or parties. In a situation of this kind, the respondent State becomes judge in its own cause and, if the interpretation is binding, the international tribunal will lose its power to decide independently.

(e) The authority of 'precedents'

Reliance on past decisions is a typical feature of an orderly decision process. Drawing on the experience of past decision-makers plays an important role in securing the necessary uniformity and stability of the law. A coherent case law strengthens the predictability of decisions and enhances their authority.

Tribunals routinely rely on previous decisions of other tribunals. Discussion of previous cases and of the interpretations adopted in them is a regular feature in almost every decision. At the same time, it is also well-established that tribunals in investment arbitration are not bound by precedents.[65]

Despite their reliance on case law, tribunals have pointed out repeatedly that they are not bound by previous decisions.[66] In *AES v*

[64] At paras 172–174. Footnote omitted.

[65] J Paulsson, 'The Role of Precedent in Investment Treaty Arbitration' in K Yannaca-Small (ed) *Arbitration under International Investment Agreements* (2018) 4.01.

[66] *Amco v Indonesia*, Decision on Jurisdiction, 25 September 1983, 1 ICSID Reports 395 and Decision on Annulment, 16 May 1986, para 44; *LETCO v Liberia*, Award, 31 March 1986, para 352; *Feldman v Mexico*, Award, 16 December 2002, para 107; *SGS v Philippines*, Decision on Jurisdiction, 29 January 2004, para 97; *Enron v Argentina*, Decision on Jurisdiction (Ancillary Claim), 2 August 2004, para 25; *Gas Natural v Argentina*, Decision on Jurisdiction, 17 June 2005, paras 36–52; *Bayindir v Pakistan*, Decision on Jurisdiction, 14 November 2005, para 76; *Romak v Uzbekistan*, Award, 26 November 2009,

Argentina,[67] the Tribunal entered into an extensive discussion of the value of previous decisions as 'precedents'. It said:

> each decision or award delivered by an ICSID Tribunal is only binding on the parties to the dispute settled by this decision or award. There is so far no rule of precedent in general international law; nor is there any within the specific ICSID system . . . .[68]

But the Tribunal also pointed to the value of previous decisions:

> Each tribunal remains sovereign and may retain, as it is confirmed by ICSID practice, a different solution for resolving the same problem; but decisions on jurisdiction dealing with the same or very similar issues may at least indicate some lines of reasoning of real interest; this Tribunal may consider them in order to compare its own position with those already adopted by its predecessors and, if it shares the views already expressed by one or more of these tribunals on a specific point of law, it is free to adopt the same solution.[69]

Having made these general statements, the Tribunal proceeded to examine and rely on previous decisions by other tribunals.[70]

The Tribunal in *Saipem v Bangladesh*[71] saw it as its duty to contribute to a harmonious development of the law. It said:

> The Tribunal considers that it is not bound by previous decisions. At the same time, it is of the opinion that it must pay due consideration to earlier decisions of international tribunals. It believes that, subject to compelling contrary grounds, it has a duty to adopt solutions established in a series of consistent cases. It also believes that, subject to the specifics of a given treaty and of the circumstances of the actual case, it has a duty to seek to contribute to the harmonious development of investment law and thereby to meet the legitimate expectations of the community of States and investors towards certainty of the rule of law.[72]

paras 170–171; *Abaclat v Argentina*, Decision on Jurisdiction, 4 August 2011, paras 292–293; *UP and C.D v Hungary*, Award, 9 October 2018, paras 288–289.

[67] *AES v Argentina*, Decision on Jurisdiction, 26 April 2005, paras 17–33.

[68] At para 23 footnote omitted.

[69] At para 30.

[70] At paras 51–59, 70, 73, 86, 89, 95–97.

[71] *Saipem v Bangladesh*, Decision on Jurisdiction, 21 March 2007.

[72] At para 67 footnotes omitted. Other tribunals have adopted the same or a similar formula: *Noble Energy v Ecuador*, Decision on Jurisdiction, 5 March 2008, para 50; *Duke Energy v Ecuador*, Award, 18 August 2008, paras 116–117; *Bayindir v Pakistan*, Award, 27 August 2009, para 145; *Austrian Airlines v Slovakia*, Final Award, 9 October 2009, paras 83–84; *Burlington v Ecuador*, Decision on Jurisdiction, 2

In some cases, tribunals did not follow earlier decisions. At times, they simply adopted a different solution without distancing themselves from earlier decisions. At other times, they referred to the earlier decision and pointed out that they were unconvinced by what another tribunal had said and that, therefore, their decision departed from it.[73]

(f) Towards a greater uniformity of interpretation

In international investment law, the interpretation of treaties takes place by tribunals whose composition varies from case to case. This makes it considerably more difficult to develop a consistent case law than in a permanent judicial institution. The divergence of interpretations on some issues has caused concern and has led to suggestions to improve the consistency of decisions.[74]

One perceived solution is the creation of an appeals mechanism that would open the possibility to review decisions, thereby increasing the chances of a consistent case law.[75] Some recent US treaties foresee this possibility in the form of an appellate body or similar mechanism. The United States Model BIT of 2012 contains the following provision in Article 28(10):

June 2010, paras 99–100; *Fakes v Turkey*, Award, 14 July 2010, para 96; *Suez and InterAgua v Argentina*, Decision on Liability, 30 July 2010, para 182; *Chemtura v Canada*, Award, 2 August 2010, paras 108–109; *Oostergetel v Slovakia*, Final Award, 23 April 2012, para 145; *Bosh v Ukraine*, Award, 25 October 2012, para 211; *Burlington v Ecuador*, Decision on Liability, 14 December 2012, para 187; *Metal-Tech v Uzbekistan*, Award, 4 October 2013, para 116; *KT Asia v Kazakhstan*, Award, 17 October 2013, para 83; *Levy and Gremcitel v Peru*, Award, 9 January 2015, para 76; *Mesa Power v Canada*, Award, 24 March 2016, para 222; *Vestey v Venezuela*, Award, 15 April 2016, para 113; *Churchill Mining v Indonesia*, Award, 6 December 2016, paras 252, 253; *Wirtgen v Czech Republic*, Final Award, 11 October 2017, para 181; *Lighthouse v Timor-Leste*, Award, 22 December 2017, para 111.

[73] *SGS v Philippines*, Decision on Jurisdiction, 29 January 2004, para 97; *Eureko v Poland*, Partial Award, 19 August 2005, paras 256–258; *El Paso Energy v Argentina*, Decision on Jurisdiction, 27 April 2006, paras 76–77; *Suez and InterAguas v Argentina*, Decision on Jurisdiction, 16 May 2006, para 64; *Plama v Bulgaria*, Decision on Jurisdiction, 8 February 2005, paras 216–221; *Wintershall v Argentina*, Award, 8 December 2008, paras 178, 194; *Tza Yap Shum v Peru*, Decision on Jurisdiction and Competence, 19 June 2009, para 173; *SGS v Paraguay*, Decision on Jurisdiction, 12 February 2010, paras 41–42; *Kiliç v Turkmenistan*, Decision on Article VII.2 of the Turkey–Turkmenistan Bilateral Investment Treaty, 7 May 2012, paras 9.9–9.13 and Award, 2 July 2013, para 6.3.4; *İçkale v Turkmenistan*, Award, 8 March 2016, paras 230, 244; *Orascom v Algeria*, Award, 31 May 2017, para 287; *Manuel García Armas v Venezuela*, Award on Jurisdiction, 13 December 2019, paras 726–733.

[74] M Waibel et al (eds), *The Backlash against Investment Arbitration* (2010); R Dolzer, 'Perspectives for Investment Arbitration: Consistency as a Policy Goal?' (2012) 3 *TDM*; A Reinisch, 'The Challenge of Fostering Greater Coherence in International Investment Law' in P Sauvé and R Echandi (eds) *Prospects in International Investment Law and Policy* (2013) 236; K Diel-Gligor, *Towards Consistency in International Investment Jurisprudence—A Preliminary Ruling System for ICSID Arbitration* (2017).

[75] See the Collection of Articles on an Appellate Body in ISDS in (2017) 32 *ICSID Rev* 457; AJ van den Berg, 'Appeal Mechanism for ISDS Awards: Interaction with the New York and ICSID Conventions'

> In the event that an appellate mechanism for reviewing awards rendered by investor–State dispute settlement tribunals is developed in the future under other institutional arrangements, the Parties shall consider whether awards rendered under Article 34 should be subject to that appellate mechanism.

It is doubtful whether separate appellate bodies established under different treaties would contribute to a coherent case law. A harmonizing effect will be achieved only if the institutional mechanism applies to all or at least many treaties. The creation of a multilateral appeals mechanism is currently under discussion. Its future establishment is anticipated in the DR–CAFTA[76] as well as in US FTAs with Singapore[77] and Chile[78] as well as in the Comprehensive Economic and Trade Agreement (CETA).[79]

ICSID at one point floated a draft that foresaw the creation of an appeals facility at ICSID,[80] but the idea was dropped as premature.

An appeals facility is not necessarily the best mechanism to achieve coherence and consistency in the interpretation of investment treaties. An appeal presupposes a decision that will be attacked for some alleged flaw. Rather than try to fix the damage after the fact through an appeal, it is more economical and effective to address the issue of inconsistency preventively.

A remarkably successful method, used elsewhere, to secure coherence and consistency is to allow for preliminary rulings while the original proceedings are still pending.[81] Under such a system a tribunal would suspend proceedings and request a ruling on a question of law from a body established for that purpose. A similar procedure is used very successfully in the framework of the EU to secure the uniform application of EU law by domestic courts.[82]

(2019) 34 *ICSID Rev* 156; C Schreuer and A de la Brena, 'Does ISDS Need an Appeals Mechanism' (2019) *Austrian YB on Int Arb* 493.

[76] DR–CAFTA Article 10.20(10).

[77] Singapore–US FTA (2004) Article 15.19(10).

[78] Chile–US FTA (2004) Article 10.19(10).

[79] CETA (2016) Article 8.29.

[80] ICSID Discussion Paper, Possible Improvements of the Framework for ICSID Arbitration, 22 October 2004.

[81] G Kaufmann-Kohler, 'Annulment of ICSID Awards in Contract and Treaty Arbitrations: Are there Differences?' in E Gaillard and Y Banifatemi (eds) *Annulment of ICSID Awards* (2004) 289; C Schreuer, 'Preliminary Rulings in Investment Arbitration' in KP Sauvant and M Chiswick-Patterson (eds) *Appeals Mechanism in International Investment Disputes* (2008) 207; K Diel-Gligor, *Towards Consistency in International Investment Jurisprudence—A Preliminary Ruling System for ICSID Arbitration* (2017).

[82] Article 267 (*ex* Article 234 TEC) of the Treaty on the Functioning of the European Union.

2. Application of investment treaties in time

(a) The date relevant to determine jurisdiction

It is an accepted principle of international adjudication, including in the International Court of Justice (ICJ),[83] that, in the absence of a treaty provision to the contrary, the relevant date to determine a court or tribunal's jurisdiction is the date of the institution of proceedings.[84] The Tribunal in *Vivendi v Argentina* (Resubmitted Case)[85] said:

> it is generally recognized that the determination of whether a party has standing in an international judicial forum, for purposes of jurisdiction to institute proceedings, is made by reference to the date on which such proceedings are deemed to have been instituted. ICSID Tribunals have consistently applied this Rule.[86]

Tribunals have applied this principle in many cases.[87] For instance, they have determined that for purposes of jurisdiction the decisive date for participation in the ICSID Convention, of the host State and of the investor's State of nationality, is the date of the institution of arbitration proceedings.[88] The same principle applies to the entry into force of BITs[89] and of other treaties relevant to jurisdiction.[90] Similarly, the sale of the investment or the assignment of the claim after the institution of proceedings did not affect the claimant's standing.[91]

[83] *Case Concerning Questions of Interpretation and Application of the 1971 Montreal Convention Arising from the Aerial Incident at Lockerbie (Libya v United States)*, Preliminary Objections, Judgment, 27 February 1998, ICJ Reports (1998) 9, paras 37–38; *Case Concerning the Arrest Warrant of 11 April 2000 (DR Congo v Belgium)*, Judgment, 14 February 2002, ICJ Reports (2002) 3, paras 26–28.

[84] C Schreuer, 'At What Time Must Jurisdiction Exist?' in DD Caron et al (eds) *Practising Virtue: Inside International Arbitration* (2016) 264.

[85] *Vivendi v Argentina*, Resubmitted Case: Decision on Jurisdiction, 14 November 2005.

[86] At para 60.

[87] *Bayindir v Pakistan*, Decision on Jurisdiction, 14 November 2005, paras 174–178; *EnCana v Ecuador*, Award, 3 February 2006, paras 123, 126, 132; *National Grid v Argentina*, Decision on Jurisdiction, 20 June 2006, paras 114–122; *Enron v Argentina*, Award, 22 May 2007, paras 196–198, 396; *Teinver v Argentina*, Decision on Jurisdiction, 21 December 2012, para 259; *Achmea v Slovak Republic II*, Award, 20 May 2014, paras 267–269; *Ampal-American v Egypt*, Decision on Jurisdiction, 1 February 2016, paras 167–168; *Magyar Farming v Hungary*, Award, 13 November 2019, paras 213–214; *Addiko v Croatia*, Decision on Alleged Incompatibility of the BIT with the EU *Acquis*, 12 June 2020, paras 217, 272–274; *Raiffeisen v Croatia*, Decision on Jurisdiction, 30 September 2020, paras 224–230.

[88] *Holiday Inns v Morocco*, Decision on Jurisdiction, 12 May 1974, unpublished. Described by P Lalive, 'The First "World Bank" Arbitration *(Holiday Inns* v. *Morocco)*—Some Legal Problems' (1980) 51 *BYIL* 123, 142–146; *Amco v Indonesia*, Decision on Jurisdiction, 25 September 1983, 1 ICSID Reports 403; *LETCO v Liberia*, Decision on Jurisdiction, 24 October 1984, 2 ICSID Reports 351; *Rompetrol v Romania*, Decision on Jurisdiction, 18 April 2008, para 79.

[89] *Tradex v Albania*, Decision on Jurisdiction, 24 December 1996, 5 ICSID Reports 58; *Goetz v Burundi*, Award, 10 February 1999, para 72.

[90] *Bayindir v Pakistan*, Decision on Jurisdiction, 14 November 2005, para 178.

[91] *CSOB v Slovakia*, Decision on Jurisdiction, 24 May 1999, para 31; *EnCana v Ecuador*, Award, 3 February 2006, paras 123–132; *El Paso v Argentina*, Decision on Jurisdiction, 27 April 2006, paras 117–136; *National Grid v Argentina*, Decision on Jurisdiction, 20 June 2006, paras 117–119; *Enron v*

This principle is mitigated by a practice to accept jurisdiction where requirements had not been satisfied fully at the time of the institution of proceedings, but were met subsequently.[92] Where these requirements concerned consultation periods to reach an amicable settlement or an attempt to seek redress before domestic courts for a certain period of time, some tribunals found that it made no sense to decline jurisdiction if the procedural requirements had been met in the meantime and the claimant could resubmit the claim immediately.[93]

(b) The timing of investments, events, and disputes

Investment treaties often contain specific provisions determining their temporal application. Many BITs provide that they shall be applicable to all investments whether made before or after their entry into force.[94] In other words, they protect also existing investments.[95] This should not lead to the conclusion that, in the absence of such a clause, treaties will apply only to 'new' investments.[96] Also, a provision that extends the treaty's protection to existing investments does not mean that acts committed before the treaty's entry into force are covered by its substantive provisions.[97]

Many BITs limit consent to arbitration to disputes arising after their entry into force. For instance, the Argentina–Spain BIT, after stating that it shall apply also to investments made before its entry into force, provides:

Argentina, Award, 22 May 2007, paras 196–198, 396; *Teinver v Argentina*, Decision on Jurisdiction, 21 December 2012, para 259.

[92] For practice in the Permanent Court of International Justice (PCIJ) and ICJ see: *Mavrommatis Palestine Concessions* case, Judgment No 2, 30 August 1924, PCIJ, Series A, No 2, 34; *Application of the Convention on the Prevention and Punishment of the Crime of Genocide* (*Bosnia and Herzegovina v Yugoslavia*) Preliminary Objections, Judgment, 11 July 1996, ICJ Reports (1996-II) 595, 614, para 26; *Application of the Convention on the Prevention and Punishment of the Crime of Genocide* (*Croatia v Serbia*), Preliminary Objections, Judgment, 18 November 2008, ICJ Reports (2008) 412, 441, paras 85, 87, 89.

[93] See XII.8(a) and (b) below.

[94] Argentina–Spain BIT Article II(2); BLEU–Egypt BIT Article 12; Ukraine–US BIT Article XII(3). See also ECT Article 1(6).

[95] *Genin v Estonia*, Award, 25 June 2001, para 326; *SGS v Pakistan*, Decision on Jurisdiction, 6 August 2003, para 153; *Generation Ukraine v Ukraine*, Award, 16 September 2003, para 11.1; *Pan American v Argentina*, Decision on Preliminary Objections, 27 July 2006, para 211; *OKO Pankki v Estonia*, Award, 19 November 2007, paras 184–186; *Chevron v Ecuador I*, Interim Award, 1 December 2008, paras 151–189; *H&H v Egypt*, Decision on Jurisdiction, 5 June 2012, paras 52–56.

[96] *Yaung Chi Oo v Myanmar*, Award, 31 March 2003, paras 69–75.

[97] *Tecmed v Mexico*, Award, 29 May 2003, paras 53–68; *SGS v Philippines*, Decision on Jurisdiction, 29 January 2004, para 166; *Kardassopoulos v Georgia*, Decision on Jurisdiction, 6 July 2007, paras 253–255; *Jan de Nul v Egypt*, Award, 6 November 2008, paras 128–141; *Bayindir v Pakistan*, Award, 27 August 2009, paras 131–132.

> However, this agreement shall not apply to disputes or claims originating before its entry into force.

Tribunals have interpreted phrases such as 'any dispute which may arise' or 'when a dispute arises' as referring to future disputes only.[98]

In some cases, tribunals grappled with the question at what time disputes had arisen.[99] The time of the dispute is not identical with the time of the events leading to the dispute. Inevitably, the detrimental acts must have occurred before the dispute. Therefore, the exclusion of disputes occurring before the treaty's entry into force cannot be read as excluding jurisdiction over events occurring before that date.[100]

In *Maffezini v Spain*[101] the respondent challenged the Tribunal's jurisdiction alleging that the dispute originated before the entry into force of the Argentina–Spain BIT. The Tribunal found that the events on which the parties disagreed began years before the BIT's entry into force. But this did not mean that a legal dispute existed at the time.[102] The Tribunal said:

> there tends to be a natural sequence of events that leads to a dispute. It begins with the expression of a disagreement and the statement of a difference of views. In time these events acquire a precise legal meaning through the formulation of legal claims, their discussion and eventual rejection or lack of response by the other party. The conflict of legal views and interests will only be present in the latter stage, even though the underlying facts predate them.[103]

On that basis, the Tribunal reached the conclusion that the dispute in its technical and legal sense had begun to take shape after the BIT's entry into force. It followed that the Tribunal was competent to consider the dispute.

[98] *Salini v Jordan*, Decision on Jurisdiction, 29 November 2004, para 170; *Impregilo v Pakistan*, Decision on Jurisdiction, 22 April 2005, paras 299–300; *ABCI v Tunisia*, Decision on Jurisdiction, 18 Feb 2011, paras 169–170; *Ping An v Belgium*, Award, 30 April 2015, paras 214–233.

[99] *Lucchetti v Peru*, Award, 7 February 2005, paras 48–59; *Helnan v Egypt*, Decision on Jurisdiction, 17 October 2006, paras 33–57; *Toto v Lebanon*, Decision on Jurisdiction, 11 September 2009, paras 88–90; *ATA v Jordan*, Award, 18 May 2010, paras 98–109, 115–120; *Venezuela Holding v Venezuela*, Award, 9 October 2014, paras 191–211; *Valores Mundiales v Venezuela*, Award, 25 July 2017, paras 231–244; *EuroGas v Slovakia*, Award, 18 August 2017, paras 427–461; *Gosling v Mauritius*, Award, 18 February 2020, paras 147–149.

[100] *Duke Energy v Peru*, Decision on Jurisdiction, 1 February 2006, paras 146–150 and Decision on Annulment, 1 March 2011, paras 111–113, 170–182; *Railroad Development v Guatemala*, Second Decision on Jurisdiction, 18 May 2010, paras 126–138; *Levy and Gremcitel v Peru*, Award, 9 January 2015, para 167; *Philip Morris v Australia*, Award on Jurisdiction and Admissibility, 17 December 2015, para 532. But see *Micula v Romania II*, Award, 5 March 2020, paras 294–300, where the Tribunal failed to make this distinction.

[101] *Maffezini v Spain*, Decision on Jurisdiction, 25 January 2000, paras 90–98.

[102] At paras 91–98.

[103] At para 96.

In *Jan de Nul v Egypt*,[104] the BIT between BLEU and Egypt of 2002 provided that it would not apply to disputes that had arisen prior to its entry into force. A dispute already existed when in 2002 that BIT replaced an earlier BIT of 1977. At that time, the dispute was pending before the Administrative Court of Ismaïlia, which eventually rendered an adverse decision in 2003, approximately one year after the new BIT's entry into force. The Tribunal accepted the claimants' contention that the dispute before it was different from the one that had been brought to the Egyptian court:

> while the dispute which gave rise to the proceedings before the Egyptian courts and authorities related to questions of contract interpretation and of Egyptian law, the dispute before this ICSID Tribunal deals with alleged violations of the two BITs....[105]

This conclusion was confirmed by the fact that the decision of the Ismaïlia Court was a major element of the complaint. The Tribunal said:

> The intervention of a new actor, the Ismaïlia Court, appears here as a decisive factor to determine whether the dispute is a new dispute. As the Claimants' case is directly based on the alleged wrongdoing of the Ismaïlia Court, the Tribunal considers that the original dispute has (re)crystallized into a new dispute when the Ismaïlia Court rendered its decision.[106]

It followed that the Tribunal had jurisdiction over the claim.

Jan de Nul also highlights the problems arising from consecutive BITs. A claim may be made under the later BIT for breaches of an earlier BIT where the dispute arises after the later BIT's entry into force. But if the dispute arises already before the later BIT's entry into force and the later BIT only foresees jurisdiction for future disputes, tribunals decline jurisdiction for disputes that had arisen before the later BIT's entry into force.[107]

(c) Applicable law and jurisdiction

In principle, a treaty does not apply to acts or events that occurred before its entry into force. This rule is expressed in Article 28 of the Vienna Convention on the Law of Treaties:

[104] *Jan de Nul v Egypt*, Decision on Jurisdiction, 16 June 2006.
[105] At para 117.
[106] At para 128.
[107] *Walter Bau v Thailand*, Award, 1 July 2009, paras 9.67–9.68; *Ping An v Belgium*, Award, 30 April 2015, paras 218, 224–231.

> *Article 28 Non-Retroactivity of Treaties*
> Unless a different intention appears from the treaty or is otherwise established, its provisions do not bind a party in relation to any act or fact which took place or any situation which ceased to exist before the date of the entry into force of the treaty with respect to that party.

This means that the substantive law in force at the time an act was performed is to be applied as the standard for the act's legality. This principle is reflected also in the International Law Commission's Articles on State Responsibility:

> *Article 13 International Obligation in Force for a State*
> An act of a State does not constitute a breach of an international obligation unless the State is bound by the obligation in question at the time the act occurs.[108]

International practice has adhered to this principle.[109] The Tribunal in *Impregilo v Pakistan*[110] said:

> Impregilo complains of a number of acts for which Pakistan is said to be responsible. The legality of such acts must be determined, in each case, according to the law applicable at the time of their performance.[111]

It follows that the legality of State action will be determined by reference to the law in force at the time of the action.

Treaties for the protection of investments contain substantive standards of protection as well as provisions on dispute settlement. A treaty's substantive standards will apply only to events that occurred after its entry into force.

A treaty's provisions on dispute settlement may endow investment tribunals with jurisdiction over events that took place before the treaty's entry into force. Many of these clauses refer to any dispute arising from an investment. Under provisions of this kind, what matters is that the dispute exists at the time proceedings are initiated. Even if jurisdiction is limited to disputes arising after the treaty's entry into force, these disputes may have their roots in events before that date. Therefore, the jurisdiction of a tribunal under a treaty may exist in respect of events that are not subject to the treaty's substantive standards. Of course, if the instrument expressing consent contains temporal limitations that exclude pre-existing disputes or past events,[112] these must be respected.

[108] International Law Commission, Articles on State Responsibility, 2001. See J Crawford, *The International Law Commission's Articles on State Responsibility* (2002) 131.

[109] *Island of Palmas* case, Award, 4 April 1928, 2 RIAA 829, 845; *Tradex v Albania*, Decision on Jurisdiction, 24 December 1996, 5 ICSID Reports 47 at 66.

[110] *Impregilo v Pakistan*, Decision on Jurisdiction, 22 April 2005.

[111] At para 311.

[112] See II.2(b).

A tribunal deciding on the legality of events that have taken place before the treaty's entry into force will apply substantive rules of international law that were in force prior to the treaty's entry into force but were contemporaneous to the acts or events in question.[113] This may be customary international law[114] or an earlier treaty that has since been terminated.[115] It follows that in some situations, a tribunal applies substantive rules of international law that are not contained in the treaty that is the basis of its jurisdiction.[116]

In *SGS v Philippines*,[117] the Tribunal distinguished the application *ratione temporis* of the BIT's jurisdictional provisions from the application of the BIT's substantive standards. It said:

> According to Article II of the BIT, it applies to investments 'made whether prior to or after the entry into force of the Agreement'. Article II does not, however, give the substantive provisions of the BIT any retrospective effect. The normal principle stated in Article 28 of the Vienna Convention on the Law of Treaties applies ... It may be noted that in international practice a rather different approach is taken to the application of treaties to procedural or jurisdictional clauses than to substantive obligations.[118]

Under some treaties, such as the NAFTA and the ECT, consent to arbitration is limited to claims arising from alleged breaches of the respective treaty.[119] Under these treaties, the date of the treaty's entry into force is also the date from which acts and events are covered by the consent.[120] A tribunal that is competent only for alleged violations of the treaty itself will not have jurisdiction over acts that occurred before the treaty's entry into force even if those acts were illegal under customary international law.[121]

[113] *Salini v Jordan*, Decision on Jurisdiction, 29 November 2004, paras 176–177; *Impregilo v Pakistan*, Decision on Jurisdiction, 22 April 2005, para 309; *Sistem Mühendislik v Kyrgyz Republic*, Decision on Jurisdiction, 13 September 2007, para 107; *Micula v Romania I*, Decision on Jurisdiction and Admissibility, 24 September 2008, paras 150–157; *Jan de Nul v Egypt*, Award, 6 November 2008, paras 128–141; *Chevron v Ecuador I*, Interim Award, 1 December 2008, paras 203, 209; *Nordzucker v Poland*, Partial Award (Jurisdiction), 10 December 2008, paras 101–111; *Pey Casado v Chile*, Decision on Annulment, 18 December 2012, paras 55–56, 159–168; *Ping An v Belgium*, Award, 30 April 2015, paras 186–233. But see: *Paushok v Mongolia*, Award on Jurisdiction and Liability, 28 April 2011, paras 428–471.

[114] *Chevron v Ecuador I*, Interim Award, 1 December 2008, paras 199, 201, 208–209.

[115] *Jan de Nul v Egypt*, Award, 6 November 2008, paras 132–141.

[116] C Schreuer, 'Jurisdiction and Applicable Law in Investment Treaty Arbitration' (2014) 1 *MJDR* 1.

[117] *SGS v Philippines*, Decision on Jurisdiction, 29 January 2004.

[118] At paras 166, 167.

[119] NAFTA Article 1116, ECT Article 26. Under the USMCA Article 14.D.3, jurisdiction is limited to certain substantive standards.

[120] *Tecmed v Mexico*, Award, 29 May 2003, paras 63–68; *SGS v Philippines*, Decision on Jurisdiction, 29 January 2004, paras 166–168.

[121] In *Generation Ukraine v Ukraine*, Award, 16 September 2003, paras 11.2, 11.3, 17.1 the Tribunal found that under the terms of the applicable BIT it was competent only for disputes arising from alleged breaches of the BIT itself. Therefore, there was no jurisdiction with regard to an expropriation that had occurred before the BIT's entry into force.

In some cases, tribunals found that the acts in question were of a continuing character, that is, they may have started before the treaty's entry into force but persisted thereafter.[122] The failure to pay sums due under a contract is an example of a continuing breach.[123] Another example is a continuing failure to grant permits.[124]

In *Mondev v United States*[125] the dispute had arisen already before NAFTA's entry into force. It was beyond doubt that NAFTA is not retrospective in effect. The Tribunal found that acts committed prior to NAFTA's entry into force might continue in effect after that date. It said:

> an act, initially committed before NAFTA entered into force, might in certain circumstances continue to be of relevance after NAFTA's entry into force, thereby becoming subject to NAFTA obligations... Thus events or conduct prior to the entry into force of an obligation for the respondent State may be relevant in determining whether the State has subsequently committed a breach of the obligation. But it must still be possible to point to conduct of the State after that date which is itself a breach.[126]

An alleged breach may arise through a series of acts or omissions that are spread over time.[127] Such a composite act will be deemed to have taken place at the point of completion, that is, when the last action or omission occurred.[128] Possible examples would be a creeping expropriation[129] or a violation of the principle of fair and equitable treatment that occurs through a combination of several acts.[130]

(d) Relevant dates under the ICSID Convention

The ICSID Convention entered into force on 14 October 1966, 30 days after the deposit of the twentieth ratification. It enters into force for individual States 30 days after the respective instrument of ratification has been deposited.[131]

[122] *Tecmed v Mexico*, Award, 29 May 2003, paras 63–68; *Impregilo v Pakistan*, Decision on Jurisdiction, 22 April 2005, paras 312–313; *OKO Pankki v Estonia*, Award, 19 November 2007, paras 194–196, 284; *Railroad Development v Guatemala*, Second Decision on Jurisdiction, 18 May 2010, paras 114–138; *Paushok v Mongolia*, Award on Jurisdiction and Liability, 28 April 2011, paras 491–500; *Mobil v Canada*, Decision on Jurisdiction and Admissibility, 13 July 2018, paras 112–120, 161–162, 173.

[123] *SGS v Philippines*, Decision on Jurisdiction, 29 January 2004, para 167.

[124] *Pac Rim v El Salvador*, Decision on Jurisdiction, 1 June 2012, paras 2.92–2.94.

[125] *Mondev v United States*, Award, 11 October 2002.

[126] At paras 58, 70.

[127] For detailed discussion see SA Alexandrov, 'The "Baby Boom" of Treaty-Based Arbitrations and the Jurisdiction of ICSID Tribunals: Shareholders as "Investors" and Jurisdiction *Ratione Temporis*' (2005) 4 *LPICT* 19, 52.

[128] ILC Articles on State Responsibility (2001) Article 15. See J Crawford, *The International Law Commission's Articles on State Responsibility* (2002) 141. See also Commentaries (7) and (8) at 143.

[129] See VII.3(i) below.

[130] See VIII.1(h) below.

[131] Article 68(2) of the ICSID Convention.

Article 25 of the ICSID Convention determines several dates that are critical to jurisdiction. The host State must be a party to the Convention on the date the proceedings are instituted. The same applies to the State of the investor's nationality: it must also be a party to the Convention by the time proceedings are instituted.

The temporal requirements for the investor's nationality are somewhat complex. For natural persons, under Article 25(2)(a), there are two different relevant dates: the investor must have the nationality of a State Party to the Convention both on the date of consent and on the date the request for arbitration is registered. In addition, the investor must not have the host State's nationality on either date. The latter provision concerns, in particular, dual or multiple nationals. As a practical matter, the date of consent and the date of the institution of proceedings will often coincide or, at least, be very close to each other. This is so whenever consent is based on a general offer in a treaty or in the host State's domestic legislation, which the investor accepts through the institution of proceedings.

For juridical persons, under Article 25(2)(b), the nationality requirement relates only to one date, the date of consent. On that date, the juridical person must have the nationality of a party to the Convention other than the host State. In practical terms, the date of consent will most often be that of the institution of proceedings also for juridical persons.

As explained below in more detail,[132] under Article 25(2)(b) of the Convention, the host State and the investor may agree to treat a locally incorporated company as a foreign investor because of its foreign control. That provision refers to the date of consent as the relevant date for the nationality of the host State but is silent on the date of the foreign control. Tribunals have generally favoured the date of consent also for purposes of control but have, at the same time, looked at subsequent changes up to the time of the institution of proceedings.[133] Some BITs and the ECT sensibly provide that the foreign control must exist before the dispute arises.[134]

The time of consent to ICSID's jurisdiction is the date by which both parties have agreed to arbitration. If the consent clause is contained in an offer by one party, its acceptance by the other party determines the time of consent. If the host State makes a general offer to consent to arbitration in its legislation or in a treaty, the time of consent will be determined by the investor's acceptance of the offer. The offer may be accepted simply by initiating the arbitration.

The date of consent is important for several purposes. Consent must exist at the time the proceedings are instituted.[135] Once consent is given it becomes

[132] Chapter III.4.

[133] *Amco v Indonesia*, Decision on Jurisdiction, 25 September 1983, 1 ICSID Reports 394; *Klöckner v Cameroon*, Award, 21 October 1983, 2 ICSID Reports 15–17; *SOABI v Senegal*, Decision on Jurisdiction, 1 August 1984, 2 ICSID Reports 183; *LETCO v Liberia*, Decision on Jurisdiction, 24 October 1984, 2 ICSID Reports 349, 351; *Vacuum Salt v Ghana*, Award, 16 February 1994, paras 35–54; *Vivendi v Argentina*, Resubmitted Case: Decision on Jurisdiction, 14 November 2005, paras 21, 42–44, 65, 95–97.

[134] ECT Article 26(7).

[135] See II.2(c) above.

irrevocable, that is, it can no longer be withdrawn unilaterally.[136] Other remedies become unavailable, in principle, from the date of consent and diplomatic protection is no longer permitted.[137] In addition, the Arbitration Rules in force at the time of consent will apply unless the parties agree otherwise.[138]

It is possible that consent to arbitration is expressed before other conditions for the jurisdiction of a tribunal are met. For instance, the parties may give their consent to ICSID arbitration before the Convention's ratification by the host State or by the investor's home State. In that case, the date of consent will be the date on which all the conditions have been met. If the host State or the investor's home State ratifies the Convention after the signature of a consent agreement, the time of consent will be the entry into force of the Convention for the respective State.[139]

The ICSID Convention provides for the withdrawal of States parties. Under Article 71 of the ICSID Convention, a Contracting State may denounce the Convention by written notice. Such a denunciation takes effect six months after receipt of the notice. Under Article 72 of the Convention, the denunciation does not affect rights or obligations arising out of consent to ICSID's jurisdiction given before the notice of denunciation. This provision has led to a lively debate as to whether the reference to consent in Article 72 means a perfected consent agreement or a mere offer of consent.[140] So far, three States, Bolivia, Ecuador, and Venezuela have withdrawn from the Convention.[141]

[136] ICSID Convention Article 25(1), last sentence. See XII.7(e) below.

[137] ICSID Convention Articles 26 and 27.

[138] ICSID Convention Article 44.

[139] See *Holiday Inns v Morocco*, Decision on Jurisdiction, 12 May 1974, P Lalive, 'The First "World Bank" Arbitration (*Holiday Inns* v. *Morocco*)—Some Legal Problems' (1980) 51 *BYIL* 123, 142, 143, 146; *Cable TV v St. Kitts and Nevis*, Award, 13 January 1997, paras 2.18, 4.09, 5.24; *Autopista v Venezuela*, Decision on Jurisdiction, 27 September 2001, paras 90, 91; *Generation Ukraine v Ukraine*, Award, 16 September 2003, paras 12.4–12.8.

[140] E Gaillard, 'The Denunciation of the ICSID Convention' (2007) 5 *TDM*; OM Garibaldi, 'On the Denunciation of the ICSID Convention' in C Binder et al (eds) *International Investment Law for the 21st Century* (2009) 251; K Rastegar, 'Denouncing ICSID' in C Binder et al (eds) *International Investment Law for the 21st Century* (2009) 278; C Schreuer, 'Denunciation of the ICSID Convention and Consent to Arbitration' in M Waibel et al (eds) *The Backlash against Investment Arbitration* (2010) 353; AR Parra, 'Participation in the ICSID Convention' (2013) 28 *ICSID Rev* 169; T Voon and AD Mitchell, 'Denunciation, Termination and Survival' (2016) 31 *ICSID Rev* 413.

[141] Bolivia effective 3 November 2007. Ecuador effective 7 January 2010. Venezuela effective 25 July 2012. Ecuador rejoined the ICSID Convention on 4 August 2021.

III
Investor

ADDITIONAL READING: R Wisner and R Gallus, 'Nationality Requirements in Investor–State Arbitration' (2004) 5 *JWIT* 927; A Sinclair, 'The Substance of Nationality Requirements in Investment Treaty Arbitration' (2005) 20 *ICSID Rev* 357; M Mendelson, 'Issues Relating to the Identity of the Investor' in AW Rovine (ed) *Contemporary Issues in International Arbitration and Mediation* (2010) 22; A Romanetti, 'Defining Investors' (2012) 29 *ICSID Rev* 231; AK Hoffmann, 'Denial of Benefits' in M Bungenberg et al (eds) *International Investment Law* (2015) 598; M Perkams, 'Protection for Legal Persons' in M Bungenberg et al (eds) *International Investment Law* (2015) 638; LF Reed and JE Davis, 'Who is a Protected Investor?' in M Bungenberg et al (eds) *International Investment Law* (2015) 614; S Jagusch et al, 'Restructuring Investments to Achieve Investment Treaty Protection' in M Kinnear et al (eds) *Building International Investment Law* (2016) 175; C Schreuer, 'Criteria to Determine Investor Nationality (Natural Persons)' in M Kinnear et al (eds) *Building International Investment Law* (2016) 153; P Tercier and N-H Tran Thang, 'Criteria to Determine Investor Nationality (Juridical Persons)' in M Kinnear et al (eds) *Building International Investment Law* (2016) 141; Y Kawabata et al, 'Covered Investors' in B Legum (ed) *The Investment Treaty Arbitration Review*, 3rd edn (2018) 14.

1. Private foreign investors

International investment law is designed to promote and protect the activities of private foreign investors. This does not necessarily exclude the protection of government-controlled entities as long as they act in a commercial rather than in a governmental capacity.[1] Even investors substantially owned by States will qualify.[2]

[1] A Broches, 'The Convention on the Settlement of Investment Disputes between States and Nationals of Other States' (1972-II) *Recueil* 331, 354–355; C Annacker, 'Protection and Admission of Sovereign Investment under Investment Treaties' (2010) 10 *Chinese JIL* 531; S Konrad, 'Protection of Investments Owned by States' in M Bungenberg et al (eds) *International Investment Law* (2015) 545; LN Skovgaard Poulsen, 'States as Foreign Investors' (2016) 31 *ICSID Rev* 12; R Mohtashami and F El-Hosseny, 'State-Owned Enterprises as Claimants before ICSID' (2016) 3 *BCDR Int'l Arb Rev* 371.

[2] *CSOB v Slovakia*, Decision on Jurisdiction, 24 May 1999, paras 16–27; *Rumeli Telekom v Kazakhstan*, Award, 29 July 2008, paras 324–329; *Flughafen Zürich v Venezuela*, Award, 18 November 2014, paras 271–286; *Beijing Urban Construction v Yemen*, Decision on Jurisdiction, 31 May 2017, paras 31–47; *Masdar v Spain*, Award, 16 May 2018, paras 155, 169–173; *Stadtwerke München v Spain*, Award, 2 December 2019, paras 133–134.

Exceptionally, investment treaties in their definitions of investors specifically exclude[3] or include[4] State-owned entities. Whether non-profit organizations may be regarded as investors is less clear and will depend on the nature of their activities.[5]

Investors are either individuals (natural persons) or companies (juridical persons). In the majority of cases the investor is a company but at times individuals also act as investors.[6] The investor's nationality determines the foreignness of the investment. The origin of the investment, in particular of the capital, is not decisive for the question of the existence of a foreign investment.[7]

The investor's nationality determines from which treaties it may benefit.[8] If the investor wishes to rely on a BIT, it must show that it has the nationality of one of the two States parties. If the investor wishes to rely on a regional treaty, such as the Energy Charter Treaty (ECT) or the United States–Mexico–Canada Agreement (USMCA), it must show that it has the nationality of one of the States parties to the treaty. If the investor wishes to rely on the ICSID Convention, it must show that it has the nationality of one of the States parties to the ICSID Convention.

The investor's nationality is relevant for two purposes. The substantive standards guaranteed in a treaty will only apply to the respective nationals.[9] In addition, the jurisdiction of an international tribunal is determined, *inter alia*, by the claimant's nationality.[10] In particular, if the host State's consent to jurisdiction is given through a treaty, it will apply only to nationals of a State that is a party to the treaty.

Traditionally, international practice on nationality issues has been shaped to a large extent by cases involving the diplomatic protection of individuals and companies by their States of nationality.[11] Whether the principles developed in that context can simply be transferred to situations where the investor has direct access

3 Panama–Germany BIT (1983) Article 1(4)(a); Panama–Switzerland BIT (1983) Article 8(b)(ii); Panama–United Kingdom BIT (1983) Article 1(d)(i).

4 Kuwait–Germany BIT (1994) Article 1(3)(b)(iii).

5 The MIGA Convention in Article 13(a)(iii) requires that an eligible investor operates on a commercial basis. The Argentina–Germany BIT includes legal persons 'whether or not organized for pecuniary gain'. Generally, see N Gallus and LE Peterson, 'International Investment Treaty Protection of NGOs' (2006) 22 *Arbitr Int* 527.

6 For this reason, it is most appropriate to refer to investors in general not as 'she' or 'he' but as 'it'.

7 See IV.6 below.

8 Exceptionally, the status of foreign investors may be extended to permanent residents. See NAFTA Article 201; ECT Article 1(7)(a)(i). Some treaties require domicile or economic activity in the State concerned in addition to nationality.

9 On the issue of rights conferred upon private investors through treaties see O Spiermann, 'Individual Rights, State Interests and the Power to Waive ICSID Jurisdiction under Bilateral Investment Treaties' (2004) 20 *Arbitr Int* 179, 183 et seq.

10 See XII.6(c) below.

11 *Nottebohm Case (Liechtenstein v Guatemala)*, Judgment, 6 April 1955, ICJ Reports (1955) 4; *Case Concerning the Barcelona Traction, Light and Power Company, Limited, (Belgium v Spain)*, Judgment, 5 February 1970, ICJ Reports (1970) 3. In *Diallo* (*Guinea v DR Congo*), Judgment, 24 May 2007, ICJ Reports (2007) 582 the International Court of Justice confirmed in para 61, that 'only the State of nationality may exercise diplomatic protection on behalf of the company when its rights are injured by a wrongful act of another State'.

to international arbitration is subject to doubt.[12] Applicable treaties as well as arbitral practice on investor protection have developed in a way that differs in several respects from the principles governing diplomatic protection.

2. Nationality of individuals

An individual's nationality is determined primarily by the law of the country whose nationality is at issue.[13] A certificate of nationality, issued by the competent authorities of a State, is strong evidence for the existence of the nationality of that State but is not necessarily conclusive.[14]

In *Soufraki v United Arab Emirates*,[15] the claimant had produced several Italian certificates of nationality. The Tribunal found that the claimant had lost that nationality as a consequence of the acquisition of Canadian nationality, a fact that was evidently unknown to the Italian authorities. As a Canadian national he was unable to rely on the BIT between Italy and the United Arab Emirates (UAE). Also, ICSID jurisdiction was unavailable since, at the time, Canada was not a party to the ICSID Convention. The Tribunal said:

> It is accepted in international law that nationality is within the domestic jurisdiction of the State, which settles, by its own legislation, the rules relating to the acquisition (and loss) of its nationality... But it is no less accepted that when, in international arbitral or judicial proceedings, the nationality of a person is challenged, the international tribunal is competent to pass upon that challenge... Where, as in the instant case, the jurisdiction of an international tribunal turns on an issue of nationality, the international tribunal is empowered, indeed bound, to decide that issue.[16]

Having found that the claimant did not have Italian nationality as a matter of Italian law, the Tribunal did not find it necessary to deal with the respondent's contention that in the absence of a genuine link this nationality would have been ineffective.[17]

In *Olguín v Paraguay*,[18] the claimant relied on the bilateral investment treaty (BIT) between Paraguay and Peru. The respondent objected that Olguín, in

[12] M Hirsch, *The Arbitration Mechanism of the International Centre for the Settlement of Investment Disputes* (1993) 76.

[13] *Pey Casado v Chile*, Award, 8 May 2008, paras 254–260.

[14] *Micula v Romania I*, Decision on Jurisdiction and Admissibility, 24 September 2008, paras 70–106; *Tza Yap Shum v Peru*, Decision on Jurisdiction and Competence, 19 June 2009, paras 42–77; *Arif v Moldova*, Award, 8 April 2013, paras 354–359; *Kim v Uzbekistan*, Decision on Jurisdiction, 8 March 2017, paras 5, 6, 206–236.

[15] *Soufraki v UAE*, Award, 7 July 2004.

[16] At para 55.

[17] At paras 42–46.

[18] *Olguín v Paraguay*, Award, 26 July 2001.

addition to his Peruvian nationality, also had US nationality and that he resided in the United States. The Tribunal found that the claimant held dual nationality and that both nationalities were effective. The fact that he had Peruvian nationality was enough, in the Tribunal's view, to afford him the protection of the BIT.[19]

Tribunals were generally unimpressed by arguments concerning the effectiveness of a nationality. In *Micula v Romania*[20] the Tribunal said:

> *Nottebohm* cannot be read to allow or require that a State disregard an individual's single nationality on the basis of the fact that this individual has not resided in the country of his nationality for a period of time.[21]

In *Fakes v Turkey*,[22] the claimant held both Netherlands and Jordanian nationalities and sought to rely on the BIT between the Netherlands and Turkey. The Tribunal rejected the respondent's argument concerning the lack of effectiveness of the Netherlands nationality. The Tribunal found the rules concerning a 'genuine link' as developed in the context of diplomatic protection inapplicable. But the Tribunal left open the possibility of applying an effective nationality test in exceptional circumstances such as a nationality of convenience or a nationality passed on over several generations without any ties to the country in question.[23]

Under the ICSID Convention, nationals of the host State will be excluded from international protection even if they also hold the nationality of another State. The ICSID Convention, in Article 25(2)(a), explicitly excludes dual nationals if one of their nationalities is that of the host State. Whether this negative nationality requirement should apply also in non-ICSID cases is not entirely clear. There is authority that host State nationality is not an obstacle to jurisdiction outside the ICSID context,[24] but there is also authority to the contrary[25] where the host State's nationality is dominant.[26] Exceptionally, a BIT may provide that an investor must not have the host State's nationality.[27]

In *Champion Trading v Egypt*,[28] three of the individual claimants had dual US and Egyptian nationality. The Tribunal was unimpressed by the argument that the Egyptian nationality was not effective.[29] It found that the ICSID

[19] At paras 60–62.
[20] *Micula v Romania I*, Decision on Jurisdiction and Admissibility, 24 September 2008.
[21] At para 103.
[22] *Fakes v Turkey*, Award, 14 July 2010.
[23] At paras 54–81.
[24] *Serafín García Armas v Venezuela*, Decision on Jurisdiction, 15 December 2014, paras 167–175.
[25] *Rawat v Mauritius*, Award on Jurisdiction, 6 April 2018, paras 166–184.
[26] *Manuel García Armas v Venezuela*, Award on Jurisdiction, 13 December 2019, paras 659–741.
[27] Canada–Venezuela BIT (1996) Article I(g).
[28] *Champion Trading v Egypt*, Decision on Jurisdiction, 21 October 2003.
[29] The claimants relied upon the *Nottebohm Case (Liechtenstein v Guatemala)*, Judgment, 6 April 1955, ICJ Reports (1955) 4 and upon a leading case before the Iran–US Claims Tribunal: *Decision in*

Convention had a clear and specific rule to the effect that any person who also has the nationality of the host State is excluded from bringing a claim under the Convention.[30]

On the other hand, a North American Free Trade Agreement (NAFTA) Tribunal found in *Feldman v Mexico*[31] that the claimant, being a citizen of the United States only, had standing although he had his permanent residence in the host State.[32] The Tribunal said:

> under general international law, citizenship rather than residence or any other geographic affiliation is the main connecting factor between a state and an individual.[33]

In *Siag v Egypt*,[34] the claimants' Italian nationality was uncontested. The Tribunal found that they had lost their previous Egyptian nationality as a matter of Egyptian law. The Tribunal held that the claimants' historic and continuing residence and business interests in Egypt were irrelevant. Since the claimants were not dual nationals, there was no room for a test of dominant or effective nationality.[35]

Under some treaties, the dominant and effective nationality shall be decisive in case of dual nationals.[36] In *Aven v Costa Rica*,[37] the claimant was a US and Italian national and brought his claim as a US citizen under the Dominican Republic–Central American Free Trade Agreement (DR–CAFTA). The respondent objected to the Tribunal's jurisdiction since the claimant, when dealing with the Costa Rican authorities, had presented himself as an Italian citizen.[38] The Tribunal held that the provision on dominant nationality in Article 10.28 DR–CAFTA only applies to cases where nationalities of two parties to the Treaty are at stake. Since the claimant was not a citizen of the host State, the dominant and effective test was not relevant.[39]

Case No. A/18 Concerning the Question of Jurisdiction over Claims of Persons with Dual Nationality, 5 Iran–US CTR 252, (1984) 23 ILM 489.

[30] At section 3.4.1.
[31] *Feldman v Mexico*, Decision on Jurisdiction, 6 December 2000.
[32] At paras 24–37.
[33] At para 30. See also the Award in the same case, 16 December 2002, para 48.
[34] *Siag v Egypt*, Decision on Jurisdiction, 11 April 2007.
[35] At paras 195–201.
[36] USMCA Article 14.1; DR–CAFTA Article 10.28: 'investor of a Party ... a natural person who is a dual national shall be deemed to be exclusively a national of the State of his or her dominant and effective nationality'.
[37] *Aven v Costa Rica*, Award, 18 September 2018.
[38] At para 211.
[39] At para 215. See also *Ballantine v Dominican Republic*, Final Award, 3 September 2019, paras 529–557.

3. Nationality of corporations

Nationality normally presupposes legal personality. Therefore, unincorporated entities and groupings will not, in general, enjoy legal protection,[40] although a treaty may provide otherwise.[41]

Corporate nationality is considerably more complex than that of individuals. Legal systems and treaties use a variety of criteria to determine whether a juridical person is a national or an investor of a particular State. Sometimes the same treaty adopts separate definitions of corporate nationality for each party.

The most commonly used criteria for corporate nationality are incorporation or the main seat of the business ('*siège social*'):

> According to international law and practice, there are different possible criteria to determine a juridical person's nationality. The most widely used is the place of incorporation or registered office. Alternatively, the place of the central administration or effective seat may also be taken into consideration.[42]

Many treaties follow one or the other of these criteria. Some stress incorporation. The Energy Charter Treaty's (ECT) definition of 'investor' includes 'a company or other organization organized in accordance with the law applicable in that Contracting Party'.[43] The BIT between Poland and the United Kingdom describes corporate investors as 'any corporations, firms, organisations and associations incorporated or constituted under the law in force in that Contracting Party'. The US Model BIT of 2012 describes an 'enterprise of a Party' as 'an enterprise constituted or organized under the law of a Party'.

In cases, in which the relevant treaties provided for incorporation as the relevant criterion, tribunals have refused to pierce the corporate veil and to look at the nationality of the company's owners.[44] In *Tokios Tokelės v Ukraine*,[45] the claimant

[40] *LESI DIPENTA v Algeria*, Award, 10 January 2005, paras 37–41; *Impregilo v Pakistan*, Decision on Jurisdiction, 22 April 2005, paras 131–139.

[41] The Argentina–Germany BIT in its definition of 'national' refers to 'any legal person and any commercial or other company or association with or without legal personality'. The BIT between China and Laos refers in its definition of 'investor' to 'economic entities established in accordance with the laws and regulations of each contracting State'. The Tribunal in *Sanum v Laos*, Award on Jurisdiction, 13 December 2013, para 307, held that the concept of an economic entity under Chinese law 'may include entities that are engaged in economic activities but without separate legal personality'.

[42] *Autopista v Venezuela*, Decision on Jurisdiction, 27 September 2001, para 107. See also *SOABI v Senegal*, Decision on Jurisdiction, 1 August 1984, para 29.

[43] Energy Charter Treaty, Article 1(7)(a)(ii).

[44] *AES v Argentina*, Decision on Jurisdiction, 26 April 2005, paras 75–80; *ADC v Hungary*, Award, 2 October 2006, paras 332–362; *Rompetrol v Romania*, Decision on Jurisdiction, 18 April 2008, paras 71, 75–110; *KT Asia v Kazakhstan*, Award, 17 October 2013, paras 113–144; *Gold Reserve v Venezuela*, Award, 22 September 2014, paras 250–252; *Pac Rim v El Salvador*, Award, 14 October 2016, para 5.58.

[45] *Tokios Tokelės v Ukraine*, Decision on Jurisdiction, 29 April 2004. See also *Wena Hotels v Egypt*, Decision on Jurisdiction, 29 June 1999, 6 ICSID Reports 74, 79–84.

was a business enterprise established under the laws of Lithuania. But nationals of the Ukraine owned 99 per cent of its shares. Article 1(2)(b) of the Lithuania–Ukraine BIT defines the term 'investor,' with respect to Lithuania, as 'any entity established in the territory of the Republic of Lithuania in conformity with its laws and regulations'. The respondent argued that the claimant was not a genuine entity of Lithuania because it was owned and controlled by Ukrainian nationals. However, the majority of the Tribunal concluded that the claimant was an 'investor' of Lithuania under the BIT and a 'national of another Contracting State' under Article 25 of the ICSID Convention.[46]

In *Saluka v Czech Republic*,[47] the claimant was a legal person incorporated under the laws of the Netherlands. The respondent objected that Saluka was merely a shell company controlled by its Japanese owners. Under the Czech–Netherlands BIT, the definition of 'investor' in Article 1(b)(ii) includes 'legal persons constituted under the laws of [the Netherlands]'.[48] The Tribunal said:

> The Tribunal has some sympathy for the argument that a company which has no real connection with a State party to a BIT, and which is in reality a mere shell company controlled by another company which is not constituted under the laws of that State, should not be entitled to invoke the provisions of that treaty.[49]

Nevertheless, it found that the claimant was a Dutch company. It said:

> The Tribunal cannot in effect impose upon the parties a definition of "investor" other than that which they themselves agreed. That agreed definition required only that the claimant-investor should be constituted under the laws of (in the present case) The Netherlands, and it is not open to the Tribunal to add other requirements which the parties could themselves have added but which they omitted to add.[50]

Other treaties refer to the entity's seat or principal seat of business. For instance, the Argentina–Germany BIT refers to 'company' as a legal person 'having its seat in the territory of one of the Contracting Parties'.[51]

[46] At paras 21–71. The decision was accompanied by a forcefully worded dissenting opinion by the Tribunal's President.

[47] *Saluka v Czech Republic*, Partial Award, 17 March 2006.

[48] At paras 1, 73, 183–186, 197.

[49] At para 240.

[50] At para 241.

[51] For cases dealing with the meaning of seat see: *AFT v Slovakia*, Award, 5 March 2011, paras 213–227; *Tenaris v Venezuela I*, Award, 29 January 2016, paras 134–154, 165–227; *CEAC v Montenegro*, Award, 26 July 2016, paras 143–211; *Orascom v Algeria*, Award, 31 May 2017, paras 257–315; *Mera v Serbia*, Decision on Jurisdiction, 30 November 2018, paras 84–97.

Some treaties combine incorporation with seat.[52] Article I(2) of the Association of Southeast Asian Nations (ASEAN) Agreement[53] provides:

> The term 'company' of a Contracting Party shall mean a corporation, partnership or other business association, incorporated or constituted under the laws in force in the territory of any Contracting Party wherein the place of effective management is situated.

This provision was applied in *Yaung Chi Oo v Myanmar*.[54] The claimant was incorporated in Singapore, a party to the Agreement. The Tribunal examined additionally whether it was also effectively managed from Singapore.[55]

Some treaties go beyond formal requirements such as incorporation or seat. They require a bond of economic substance between the corporate investor and the State whose nationality it claims.[56] Such an economic bond may consist of effective control over the corporation by nationals of the State. Alternatively, it may consist of genuine economic activity of the company in the State.[57]

Under some treaties a controlling interest of nationals in a company is sufficient to establish corporate nationality.[58] In the BIT between the Netherlands and Venezuela, the definition of 'nationals' in Article 1(b) covers not just legal persons incorporated in the respective State but alternatively legal persons not so incorporated but 'controlled, directly or indirectly' by nationals of that State. In *Mobil v Venezuela*[59] the investment had been made by the Netherlands holding company through its 100 per cent owned subsidiaries in the United States and the Bahamas. The respondent contended that the Netherlands company did not, in fact, exercise genuine control over its subsidiaries. The Tribunal rejected this argument stating:

> In the present case, Venezuela Holdings (Netherlands) owns 100 % of the share capital of its two American subsidiaries, which in turn own 100 % of the share capital of the two Bahamas subsidiaries. Thus the share capital of Venezuela Holdings (Netherlands) in those subsidiaries makes it possible for it to exercise

52 For instance, the BITs between Belgium and the Czech Republic, the BIT between Pakistan and Sweden and the BIT between Argentina and France. See *Total v Argentina*, Decision on Jurisdiction, 25 August 2006, para 57; *Alpha v Ukraine*, Award, 8 November 2010, paras 45–55, 333–345.

53 ASEAN Agreement for the Promotion and Protection of Investments, 15 December 1987, (1987) 27 ILM 612.

54 *Yaung Chi Oo v Myanmar*, Award, 31 March 2003.

55 At paras 46–52.

56 P Acconci, 'Determining the Internationally Relevant Link between a State and a Corporate Investor' (2004) 5 *JWIT* 139.

57 *Mabco v Kosovo*, Decision on Jurisdiction, 30 October 2020, para 395.

58 Eg the BIT between Moldova and the United States, see *Link-Trading v Moldova*, Final Award, 18 April 2002, para 54. BIT between Ecuador and France, see *Perenco v Ecuador*, Decision on Jurisdiction, 30 June 2011, para 49. BIT between Switzerland and Macedonia, see *Swisslion v Macedonia*, Award, 6 July 2012, paras 130–132.

59 *Mobil v Venezuela*, Decision on Jurisdiction, 10 June 2010.

> control on them. The Tribunal does not have to consider whether or not such control was exercised in fact.[60]

In *Guardian Fiduciary v FYROM*,[61] the BIT between the Netherlands and FYROM included in its definition of 'nationals':

> legal persons not constituted under the law of that Contracting State but controlled, directly or indirectly, by natural persons as defined in (I) or by legal persons as defined in (II).

The Tribunal declined jurisdiction because the claimant, a company incorporated in New Zealand, was not, in fact, controlled by a Dutch entity. The Tribunal found that despite a Dutch entity's indirect legal ownership of the claimant, the BIT did not apply since there was no evidence that the Dutch entity had exercised actual control over the claimant.[62] The situation was complicated by a split in legal and beneficial ownership. Only the legal ownership led to the Dutch entity whereas the beneficial ownership ultimately led to a Marshall Islands entity.

Some treaties combine seat with 'a predominant interest of an investor'.[63] The BIT between Iran and Switzerland combines all of the above elements. It grants investor status to a legal entity that is established under the law of the State in question and has its seat there, provided it also has real economic activities in that country. Alternatively, the same BIT grants investor status to a legal entity not incorporated in that State if it is effectively controlled by natural or juridical persons of the State.[64] The definition of corporate investors in that BIT is as follows:

> (b) legal entities, including companies, corporations, business associations and other organisations, which are established under the law of that Contracting Party and have their seat, together with real economic activities, in the territory of that same Contracting Party;
> (c) legal entities not established under the law of that Contracting Party but effectively controlled by natural persons as defined in (a) above or by legal entities as defined in (b) above.

The Convention Establishing the Multilateral Investment Guarantee Agency (MIGA Convention) requires incorporation and seat or, alternatively, control. Under Article 13(a)(ii) a juridical person will qualify as an 'eligible investor' if:

[60] At para 160. The Tribunal relied on a Protocol to the BIT which listed percentage of capital ownership as a relevant criterion for control.
[61] *Guardian Fiduciary v FYROM*, Award, 22 September 2015.
[62] At paras 126, 130–139.
[63] Eg the BIT between Lithuania and Sweden.
[64] Iran–Switzerland BIT, 1998, Article 1(1).

> such juridical person is incorporated and has its principal place of business in a member or the majority of its capital is owned by a member or members or nationals thereof, provided that such member is not the host country in any of the above cases;

In *Champion Trading v Egypt*,[65] the Tribunal applied the BIT between Egypt and the United States. That treaty, in its Article I(b), requires incorporation and control by nationals:

> (b) 'Company of a Party' means a company duly incorporated, constituted or otherwise duly organized under the applicable laws and regulations of a Party or its subdivisions in which (i) natural persons who are nationals of such Party... have a substantial interest.

The corporate claimant was incorporated in the United States but was owned by five individuals most of whom were dual Egyptian and US nationals. The Tribunal found that it had jurisdiction over the corporation since the BIT did not exclude dual nationals as controlling shareholders.[66]

In *Aguas del Tunari v Bolivia*,[67] the claimant was a legal person constituted under Bolivian law. It relied on the definition of 'national' in Article 1(b) of the Bolivia–Netherlands BIT which included legal persons incorporated in the host State but controlled by nationals of the other State. Aguas del Tunari argued that it was controlled by Netherlands corporations. Bolivia objected arguing that these Netherlands corporations were, in turn, controlled by a US corporation. The Tribunal found that the controlling Netherlands companies were more than just corporate shells set up to obtain jurisdiction over the dispute before it. Therefore, it found that the BIT's nationality requirements were fulfilled.[68]

4. A local company as a foreign investor

Host States often require that investments be made through locally incorporated companies. Normally, these local companies will not qualify as foreign investors and will hence not enjoy protection. But the ICSID Convention contains a specific provision to address the phenomenon of foreign investments made through corporations that are registered in the host State. Article 25(2)(b) of the ICSID Convention deals with juridical persons that are incorporated in the host State but

[65] *Champion Trading v Egypt*, Decision on Jurisdiction, 21 October 2003.
[66] At section 3.4.2.
[67] *Aguas del Tunari v Bolivia*, Decision on Jurisdiction, 21 October 2005.
[68] At paras 206–323.

are controlled by nationals of another State. These may be treated as foreign nationals on the basis of an agreement.

The relevant part of Article 25(2)(b) of the ICSID Convention provides:

> 'National of another Contracting State' means: ... any juridical person which had the nationality of the Contracting State party to the dispute on that date and which, because of foreign control, the parties have agreed should be treated as a national of another Contracting State for the purposes of this Convention.

Tribunals have applied a twofold test to establish whether the requirements under Article 25(2)(b) of the ICSID Convention are met. The test has a subjective and an objective element: There must be an agreement to treat the local company as a foreign investor (subjective element). This agreement alone is not enough. It must be supported by actual foreign control (objective element).[69] Control would have to be exercised by a national of a State that is a party to the ICSID Convention.[70]

The agreement between the host State and the investor required by Article 25(2)(b) may be contained in a contract between the host State and the investor. Tribunals have been flexible on the form of the necessary agreement: the insertion of an ICSID arbitration clause into a contract with the local company was accepted as implying an agreement to treat the local company as a foreign national. Otherwise, the ICSID clause would not have made any sense.[71]

Most contemporary investment arbitrations are instituted not on the basis of consent given in a contract between the host State and the investor but on the basis of an offer of consent contained in a treaty.[72] In that situation there is often no opportunity for the parties to agree to treat a particular locally incorporated company as a foreign national. Therefore, some treaties provide in general terms that companies constituted in one State but controlled by nationals of the other State shall be treated as nationals of the other State for purposes of Article 25(2)(b).[73] The provision in the treaty that a local company, because of foreign control, would be treated as a national of another Contracting State is part of the terms of the offer of consent to jurisdiction made by the host State. When the offer to submit disputes

[69] *Klöckner v Cameroon*, Award, 21 October 1983, 2 ICSID Reports 15–16; *SOABI v Senegal*, Decision on Jurisdiction, 1 August 1984, paras 28–46; *LETCO v Liberia*, Interim Award on Jurisdiction, 24 October 1984, 2 ICSID Reports 352; *Autopista v Venezuela*, Decision on Jurisdiction, 27 September 2001, paras 105–134; *Millicom v Senegal*, Decision on Jurisdiction, 16 July 2010, para 109; *National Gas v Egypt*, Award, 3 April 2014, paras 130–133.

[70] *SOABI v Senegal*, Decision on Jurisdiction, 1 August 1984, paras 32–33.

[71] *Klöckner v Cameroon*, Award, 21 October 1983, 2 ICSID Reports 16; *LETCO v Liberia*, Decision on Jurisdiction, 24 October 1984, 2 ICSID Reports 349–353; *Millicom v Senegal*, Decision on Jurisdiction, 16 July 2010, paras 110–114; *AHS Niger and Menzies v Niger*, Decision on Jurisdiction, 13 March 2013, paras 136–148.

[72] See XII.7(c)–(d) below.

[73] See eg Article 26(7) ECT. See also R Dolzer and M Stevens, *Bilateral Investment Treaties* (1995) 142.

to ICSID is accepted by the investor, that provision becomes part of the consent agreement between the parties to the dispute.

In *Micula v Romania*,[74] the relevant BIT between Romania and Sweden provided in Article 7(3):

> For the purpose of this Article and Article 25(2)(b) of the said Washington Convention, any legal person which is constituted in accordance with the legislation of one Contracting Party and which, before a dispute arises, is controlled by an investor of the other Contracting Party, shall be treated as a legal person of the other Contracting Party.

The three corporate claimants in that case were incorporated in Romania but were controlled by Swedish nationals. It followed that under Article 25(2)(b) of the ICSID Convention and Article 7(3) of the BIT the corporate claimants were to be treated as Swedish nationals.[75]

In addition to the agreement to treat the local company as a foreign investor, there must also be foreign control. Sometimes treaties specify what is to be understood by control. In *Quiborax v Bolivia*,[76] the relevant BIT between Chile and Bolivia provided in Article X(4) that majority ownership of shares shall trigger Article 25(2)(b) of the ICSID Convention:

> For purposes of this Article, any legal person created in accordance with the laws of one of the Contracting Parties, and whose shares are majority-owned by investors of the other Contracting Party, shall be regarded, in accordance with Article 25.2).b) of the [ICSID] Convention, as a legal person of the other Contracting Party.

The corporate claimant, NMM, had been created under Bolivian law but was majority owned (51 per cent of the shares) by Chilean nationals. Therefore, the Tribunal decided that NMM was allowed to act as claimant in the arbitration.[77]

In *Vacuum Salt v Ghana*,[78] the claimant was incorporated in Ghana. An agreement between the parties contained an ICSID clause. The Tribunal accepted that the ICSID clause implied an agreement to treat the claimant as a foreign national. But it found that it had to examine the existence of foreign control as a separate requirement:

[74] *Micula v Romania I*, Decision on Jurisdiction and Admissibility, 24 September 2008.
[75] At paras 107–116.
[76] *Quiborax v Bolivia*, Decision on Jurisdiction, 27 September 2012.
[77] At para 195.
[78] *Vacuum Salt v Ghana*, Award, 16 February 1994.

> the parties' agreement to treat Claimant as a foreign national 'because of foreign control' does not *ipso jure* confer jurisdiction. The reference in Article 25(2)(b) to 'foreign control' necessarily sets an objective Convention limit beyond which ICSID jurisdiction cannot exist ....[79]

An examination of the facts revealed that there was no foreign control. Therefore, the Tribunal declined jurisdiction.[80]

Majority share ownership will normally be sufficient to establish control.[81] There will, however, be no foreign control if a local company is owned by intermediary shell companies of another ICSID Contracting Party, that are ultimately owned by nationals or companies of the host State.[82] The same applies to control by a dual national who is a national of the host State.[83] Control by way of several layers of control culminating in ownership by a national of another Contracting State fulfils the requirement of Article 25(2)(b).[84]

In *Caratube v Kazakhstan*,[85] a case brought under the US–Kazakhstan BIT, the Tribunal required actual control over the local company despite the foreign investor's nominal ownership of 92 per cent of the shares in the investment:

> there is not sufficient evidence of exercise of actual control over CIOC by Devincci Hourani. In view of the above considerations, the Tribunal concludes that Claimant has not provided sufficient proof for control as required by Art. 25(2)(b) of the ICSID Convention. The Tribunal is not satisfied that a legal capacity to control a company, without evidence of an actual control, is enough in light of Devincci Hourani's characterisation of his purported investment in CIOC.[86]

In a second arbitration,[87] brought under a concession contract and the Kazakhstan Foreign Investment Law, the Tribunal stated that the 92 per cent share ownership created a presumption of foreign control that the respondent had been unable to rebut.[88]

Control over a juridical person is not a simple phenomenon. Participation in the company's capital stock or share ownership is not the only indicator of control.

[79] At para 36.

[80] At paras 35–55.

[81] *Levy and Gremcitel v Peru*, Award, 9 January 2015, para 171.

[82] *TSA Spectrum v Argentina*, Award, 19 December 2008, paras 147–162; *National Gas v Egypt*, Award, 3 April 2014, paras 133–149.

[83] *Burimi v Albania*, Award, 29 May 2013, para 121.

[84] *United Utilities v Estonia*, Award, 21 June 2019, paras 442–446; *Eyre and Montrose v Sri Lanka*, Award, 5 March 2020, para 266.

[85] *Caratube v Kazakhstan*, Award, 5 June 2012.

[86] At para 407.

[87] *Caratube and Hourani v Kazakhstan*, Award, 27 September 2017.

[88] At paras 470–473, 611, 622–623.

The existence of foreign control is a complex question requiring the examination of several factors such as equity participation, voting rights, and management.[89]

In *United Utilities v Estonia*,[90] the Tribunal had to determine whether the local company was controlled by a foreign investor who only held a minority stake. The Tribunal determined that the foreign investor had effective influence over operational control through its management and therefore controlled the local company.[91]

5. Nationality planning

The foregoing sections suggest that a prudent investor may organize its investment in a way that affords maximum protection under existing treaties. Most often this will be done by establishing a company in a State that has favourable treaty relations with the host State and accepts incorporation as a basis for corporate nationality. That company will then be used as a conduit for the investment. Nationality planning or 'treaty shopping' is not illegal or unethical as such.[92] But practice demonstrates that there are limits to it. In addition, States may regard corporate structuring for the purpose of obtaining advantages from treaties as undesirable and take appropriate measure against it.

In *Aguas del Tunari v Bolivia*,[93] the respondent asserted that the strategic changes in the corporate structure to obtain the protection of a BIT rose to the level of fraud and abuse of corporate form. The Tribunal accepted the 'migration' of the controlling company from one country to another and rejected this contention.[94] It said:

> It is not uncommon in practice, and—absent a particular limitation—not illegal to locate one's operations in a jurisdiction perceived to provide a beneficial regulatory and legal environment in terms, for examples, of taxation or the substantive law of the jurisdiction, including the availability of a BIT… The language of the definition of national in many BITs evidences that such national routing of

[89] *Vacuum Salt v Ghana*, Award, 16 February 1994, paras 43–53; *Aguas del Tunari v Bolivia*, Decision on Jurisdiction, 21 October 2005, paras 225–248, 264–323; *Vento v Mexico*, Award, 6 July 2020, paras 221–224; *Eskosol v Italy*, Award, 4 September 2020, paras 224–238.

[90] *United Utilities v Estonia*, Award, 21 June 2019.

[91] At paras 375–420.

[92] *Mobil v Venezuela*, Decision on Jurisdiction, 10 June 2010, para 204; *HICEE v Slovakia*, Partial Award, 23 May 2011, para 103; *Tidewater v Venezuela*, Decision on Jurisdiction, 8 February 2013, para 184; *Levy and Gremcitel v Peru*, Award, 9 January 2015, para 184; *MNSS v Montenegro*, Award, 4 May 2016, para 182; *Bridgestone v Panama*, Decision on Expedited Objections, 13 December 2017, para 161; *Mera v Serbia*, Decision on Jurisdiction, 30 November 2018, para 153.

[93] *Aguas del Tunari v Bolivia*, Decision on Jurisdiction, 21 October 2005.

[94] At paras 160–180.

> investments is entirely in keeping with the purpose of the instruments and the motivations of the state parties.[95]

Not every attempt at nationality planning will succeed. In *Banro v Congo*,[96] a transfer of the ownership of the investment was carried out from a company registered in a non-ICSID party, Canada,[97] to an affiliate company in the United States, a party to the ICSID Convention. The transfer was made after the dispute had arisen and only days before the institution of the arbitration proceedings. It served the obvious purpose to obtain access to ICSID. The Tribunal refused to accept jurisdiction under these circumstances.[98]

In *Phoenix v Czech Republic*,[99] there was originally a dispute between the Czech State and a Czech investor. Most of the incriminated facts had occurred and the dispute was in full swing when the Czech investor tried to acquire a seemingly convenient nationality by selling the investment to an Israeli company, Phoenix, which he had established especially for that purpose. Shortly after the transfer, Phoenix commenced ICSID arbitration, relying on the BIT between Israel and the Czech Republic. The Tribunal found that the claim constituted an abusive attempt to get access to the system of investment protection under the ICSID Convention. The claimant had made an investment not for the purpose of engaging in economic activity but for the sole purpose of bringing international litigation against the Czech Republic.[100]

In *Cementownia v Turkey*,[101] the claimant was a Polish company that claimed to have acquired shares of two Turkish companies. The alleged share transfers took place just 12 days before Turkey terminated concession agreements thereby, it was argued, violating its treaty obligations under the ECT. The Tribunal found that the entire share transaction between the Turkish company and the Polish claimant was fabricated and had never actually taken place.[102] The Tribunal added:

> Even if they did occur, the share transfers would not have been *bona fide* transactions, but rather attempts (in the face of government measures dating back some years about to culminate in the concessions' termination) to fabricate international jurisdiction where none should exist.[103]

95 At paras 330, 332.
96 *Banro v Congo*, Award, 1 September 2000.
97 Canada has since become a party to the ICSID Convention in 2013.
98 But see *Autopista v Venezuela*, Decision on Jurisdiction, 27 September 2001, paras 80–140. In that case the Respondent State had consented to the transfer of the shares from Mexican to US nationals. At the time, Mexico was not a party to the ICSID Convention.
99 *Phoenix v Czech Republic*, Award, 15 April 2009.
100 At paras 142–145. See also *Transglobal v Panama*, Award, 2 June 2016, paras 103, 118.
101 *Cementownia v Turkey*, Award, 17 September 2009.
102 At para 156.
103 At para 117.

In *Mobil v Venezuela*,[104] the investments had been made by Exxon Mobil through holding companies in Delaware and the Bahamas. After difficulties had arisen with the new Venezuelan government over royalties and income taxes,[105] Exxon Mobil restructured its investment by interposing a Netherlands holding company. Mobil informed the Venezuelan government of this step which did not raise any objection. As a consequence of the restructuring, the Delaware and Bahamian companies thereby became 100 per cent owned subsidiaries of the Dutch company.[106] After Mobil had completed its restructuring, Venezuela took nationalisation measures. Thereupon, Mobil instituted ICSID arbitration relying on the BIT between the Netherlands and Venezuela. Despite Venezuela's protestations, the Tribunal found that this form of corporate structuring was permissible. The Tribunal said:

> 204. ... the aim of the restructuring of their investments in Venezuela through a Dutch holding was to protect those investments against breaches of their rights by the Venezuelan authorities by gaining access to ICSID arbitration through the BIT. The Tribunal considers that this was a perfectly legitimate goal as far as it concerned future disputes.
> 205. With respect to pre-existing disputes, the situation is different and the Tribunal considers that to restructure investments only in order to gain jurisdiction under a BIT for such disputes would constitute, to take the words of the Phoenix Tribunal, 'an abusive manipulation of the system of international investment protection under the ICSID Convention and the BITs'.

Other cases confirm that prospective planning will be accepted by tribunals.[107] 'Prospective' means that the corporate arrangements were in place before the facts that led to the dispute occurred or at any rate before the dispute arose. On the other hand, where there was an existing or a foreseeable specific dispute, tribunals found it abusive and declined jurisdiction where an investor, who was not protected by an investment treaty, had restructured its investment in such a fashion as to obtain the protection of a treaty.[108]

[104] *Mobil v Venezuela*, Decision on Jurisdiction, 10 June 2010.

[105] At paras 200, 201.

[106] At paras 187–192. Under the BIT between the Netherlands and Venezuela not only companies incorporated in the Netherlands but also Companies controlled by Dutch incorporated companies are deemed to be nationals of the Netherlands.

[107] *Société Générale v Dominican Republic*, Award on Jurisdiction, 19 September 2008, paras 109–110; *Millicom v Senegal*, Decision on Jurisdiction, 16 July 2010, para 84; *ConocoPhillips v Venezuela*, Decision on Jurisdiction and Merits, 3 September 2013, paras 268–281; *Gold Reserve v Venezuela*, Award, 22 September 2014, paras 247–252, 270; *MNSS v Montenegro*, Award, 4 May 2016, paras 180–183; *Mera v Serbia*, Decision on Jurisdiction, 30 November 2018, paras 151–154.

[108] *Pac Rim v El Salvador*, Decision on Jurisdiction, 1 June 2012, para 2.99; *Tidewater v Venezuela*, Decision on Jurisdiction 8 February 2013, paras 146–148, 184, 194–196; *ST-AD v Bulgaria*, Award on Jurisdiction, 18 July 2013, paras 419, 423; *Levy and Gremcitel v Peru*, Award, 9 January 2015, paras 182, 185; *Philip Morris v Australia*, Award on Jurisdiction and Admissibility, 17 December 2015, paras 539, 545, 585.

6. Denial of benefits

States have devised methods to counteract strategies of investors that seek the protection of particular treaties by acquiring favourable nationalities. One such method is to require a bond of economic substance between the corporation and the State. This method is described above.[109] Another method is the insertion of a so-called denial of benefits clause into the treaty that provides consent to jurisdiction. Under such a clause, the States reserve the right to deny the benefits of the treaty to a company that is owned or controlled by nationals of a third country but is incorporated in a State Party to the treaty without having an economic connection to that State. The economic connection would consist of substantial business activities in the State of incorporation or ownership or control by a national of a State Party to the treaty.

Denial of benefits provisions of treaties show some variation.[110] Article I(2) of the Argentina–US BIT (1991) provides:

> Each Party reserves the right to deny to any company of the other Party the advantages of this Treaty if (a) nationals of any third country, or nationals of such Party, control such company and the company has no substantial business activities in the territory of the other Party, or (b) the company is controlled by nationals of a third country with which the denying Party does not maintain normal economic relations.

The ECT in Article 17(1) has the following denial of benefits clause:

> Each Contracting Party reserves the right to deny the advantages of this Part to: (1) a legal entity if citizens or nationals of a third state own or control such entity and if that entity has no substantial business activities in the Area of the Contracting Party in which it is organized....

The provision in the ECT is unusual in that it refers to a denial of the benefits of only the substantive standards contained in Part III and not to dispute settlement in Part V.

The most important questions raised by denial of benefits clauses are: is the denial of benefits an issue of jurisdiction, admissibility, or merits? When does the right have to be exercised by the host State? How does it have to be exercised and

[109] At III.3.

[110] NAFTA Article 1113; USMCA Article 14.14; United States Model BIT (2012) Article 17; Austria–Jordan BIT (2001) Article 10. Some treaties do not mention economic relations with a third country: Australia–Czech Republic BIT (1993) Article 2(2).

does the exercise operate retrospectively or only prospectively? The answers given by tribunals to these questions have not been uniform.

Tribunals operating under the ECT have decided that the denial of benefits clause is not an issue of jurisdiction. Since the clause in the ECT refers to a denial of substantive advantages but not to dispute settlement, tribunals have treated the denial of benefits as a merits issue[111] or a question of admissibility.[112] By contrast, tribunals operating under treaties containing denial of benefits clauses that were not restricted to substantive standards, found them to be an issue of jurisdiction.[113]

Tribunals have held that a denial of benefits clause does not operate automatically but had to be exercised actively.[114] An example for this approach can be found in *Plama v Bulgaria*.[115] The claimant was incorporated in Cyprus. After the arbitration proceedings had been instituted, Bulgaria sent a letter to ICSID purporting to exercise its right under the ECT's denial of benefits clause. Bulgaria argued that Plama had no substantial business activities in Cyprus and was controlled by nationals of States not parties to the ECT. The Tribunal found that the denial of benefits clause was drafted in permissive terms and did not operate automatically but required its actual exercise by the host State.[116]

The conditions for the denial of benefits must be met at the time of commencement of proceedings.[117] The burden of proof for the existence of the conditions for a denial of benefits is with the respondent State invoking it.[118] In *AMTO v Ukraine*,[119] the claimant was incorporated in Latvia, a party to the ECT. Ukraine objected to the Tribunal's jurisdiction based on the denial of benefits clause in Article 17(1) of the ECT. The Tribunal noted that the concept of a 'third state' under that provision meant a State that is not a Contracting Party to the ECT.[120] The burden of proof relating to the requirements of Article 17(1) of the ECT lay with the respondent State

[111] *Plama v Bulgaria*, Decision on Jurisdiction, 8 February 2005, paras 148–151; *Hulley v Russian Federation*, Interim Award on Jurisdiction and Admissibility, 30 November 2009, para 440; *Khan v Mongolia*, Decision on Jurisdiction, 25 July 2012, para 411; *Stati v Kazakhstan*, Award, 19 December 2013, para 745; see also: *Empresa Eléctrica v Ecuador*, Award, 2 June 2009, para 71, which is based on the US–Ecuador BIT.

[112] *Isolux v Spain*, Award, 12 July 2016, para 711.

[113] *Ulysseas v Ecuador*, Interim Award, 28 September 2010, para 172; *Pac Rim v El Salvador*, Decision on Jurisdictional Objections, 1 June 2012, para 4.4; *Guaracachi v Bolivia*, Award, 31 January 2014, paras 372–373; *Bridgestone v Panama*, Decision on Expedited Objections, 13 December 2017, para 288.

[114] *Hulley v Russian Federation*, Interim Award on Jurisdiction and Admissibility, 30 November 2009, para 455; *Khan v Mongolia*, Decision on Jurisdiction, 25 July 2012, para 419; *Stati v Kazakhstan*, Award, 19 December 2013, para 745.

[115] *Plama v Bulgaria*, Decision on Jurisdiction, 8 February 2005.

[116] At paras 157–158. See also in the same case: Award, 27 August 2008, paras 79–95.

[117] *Ulysseas v Ecuador*, Interim Award, 28 September 2010, para 174; *Ampal-American v Egypt*, Decision on Jurisdiction, 1 February 2016, paras 168, 171.

[118] *Ulysseas v Ecuador*, Interim Award, 28 September 2010, para 166; *Liman Caspian v Kazakhstan*, Award, 22 June 2010, para 164.

[119] *AMTO v Ukraine*, Final Award, 26 March 2008.

[120] At para 62. See also *Libananco v Turkey*, Award, 2 September 2011, paras 549–556.

invoking it.[121] In view of the Tribunal's finding that AMTO had a substantial business activity in Latvia there was no need to determine ownership and control.[122] The Tribunal said with respect to the requirement of 'substantial business activities' under Article 17(1) of the ECT:

> the purpose of Article 17(1) is to exclude from ECT protection investors which have adopted a nationality of convenience. Accordingly, 'substantial' in this context means 'of substance, and not merely of form'. It does not mean 'large', and the materiality not the magnitude of the business activity is the decisive question. In the present case, the Tribunal is satisfied that the Claimant has substantial business activity in Latvia, on the basis of its investment related activities conducted from premises in Latvia, and involving the employment of a small but permanent staff.[123]

Another disagreement concerns the time at which the State must exercise the right to deny benefits. The decision whether the denial has retrospective or only prospective effect is closely related to the answer to this question. Tribunals have indicated four different points in time for the exercise of a denial of benefits. The most investor-friendly tribunals decided that a host State must deny benefits already before the investor makes the investment since the investor needs to know beforehand whether the investment will be protected.[124] The Tribunal in *Plama v Bulgaria*[125] stated in this respect:

> The covered investor enjoys the advantages of Part III unless the host state exercises its right under Article 17(1) ECT; and a putative covered investor has legitimate expectations of such advantages until that right's exercise. A putative investor therefore requires reasonable notice before making any investment in the host state whether or not that host state has exercised its rights under Article 17(1) ECT.[126]

Other tribunals found that the host State could exercise its right to deny benefits until a dispute had arisen.[127] However, a number of tribunals, operating under BITs or the Central American Free Trade Agreement (CAFTA), found that it was

[121] At para 64. See also *Bridgestone v Panama*, Decision on Expedited Objections, 13 December 2017, para 289.

[122] At paras 67–70.

[123] At para 69. This position was adopted in *Masdar v Spain*, Award, 16 May 2018, paras 252–256 and in *9REN v Spain*, Award, 31 May 2019, para 181.

[124] *Khan v Mongolia*, Decision on Jurisdiction, 25 July 2012, paras 425–431.

[125] *Plama v Bulgaria*, Decision on Jurisdiction, 8 February 2005.

[126] At para 161.

[127] *Stati v Kazakhstan*, Award, 19 December 2013, para 745; *Isolux v Spain*, Award, 12 July 2016, para 715.

early enough to invoke the right to deny benefits once the benefits are claimed by the investor.[128] The Tribunal in *Ulysseas v Ecuador* stated as follows:

> The first question concerns whether there is a time-limit for the exercise by the State of the right to deny the BIT's advantages... Nothing in Article I(2) of the BIT excludes that the right to deny the BIT's advantages be exercised by the State at the time when such advantages are sought by the investor through a request for arbitration.[129]

The Tribunal in *Gran Colombia v Colombia*,[130] held that Article 814(2) of the Canada–Columbia FTA does not contain a temporal restriction for the invocation of the denial of benefits clause. It stated that the applicable deadline in cases governed by the ICSID Convention is the date when the respondent's counter-memorial is due. The Tribunal found that Colombia had complied with this condition since it had invoked the denial of benefits clause one day after receipt of the claimant's request for arbitration.[131]

The same disagreement among tribunals exists on whether the exercise of the denial of benefits merely has a prospective effect or also a retroactive effect. Tribunals under the ECT have opted for a prospective effect only.[132] The Tribunal in *Plama v Bulgaria*[133] said:

> the object and purpose of the ECT suggest that the right's exercise should not have retrospective effect. A putative investor, properly informed and advised of the potential effect of Article 17(1), could adjust its plans accordingly prior to making its investment. If, however, the right's exercise had retrospective effect, the consequences for the investor would be serious. The investor could not plan in the 'long term' for such an effect (if at all); and indeed such an unexercised right could lure putative investors with legitimate expectations only to have those expectations made retrospectively false at a much later date.[134]

[128] *Pac Rim v El Salvador*, Decision on Jurisdiction, 1 June 2012, para 4.85; *Guaracachi v Bolivia*, Award, 31 January 2014, para 376; *NextEra v Spain*, Decision on Jurisdiction, Liability and Quantum Principles, 12 March 2019, paras 262–271.

[129] *Ulysseas v Ecuador*, Interim Award, 28 September 2010, para 172. Footnote omitted.

[130] *Gran Colombia v Colombia*, Decision on the Bifurcated Jurisdictional Issue, 23 November 2020.

[131] At para 131.

[132] *Hulley v Russian Federation*, Interim Award on Jurisdiction and Admissibility, 30 November 2009, para 457; *Liman Caspian v Kazakhstan*, Award, 22 June 2010, para 225; *Khan v Mongolia*, Decision on Jurisdiction, 25 July 2012, paras 426–429; *Stati v Kazakhstan*, Award, 19 December 2013, para 745; *Isolux v Spain*, Award, 12 July 2016, para 715; *Masdar v Spain*, Award, 16 May 2018, paras 231–250. See also: *Ampal-American v Egypt*, Decision on Jurisdiction, 1 February 2016, para 170.

[133] *Plama v Bulgaria*, Decision on Jurisdiction, 8 February 2005.

[134] At para 162.

Tribunals opting for the retrospective effect of a denial of benefits clause have held that the offer of consent to arbitration was conditional and the conditions for consent were not fulfilled.[135] In *Guaracachi v Bolivia*,[136] the Tribunal said in this regard:

> Whenever a BIT includes a denial of benefits clause, the consent by the host State to arbitration itself is conditional and thus may be denied by it, provided that certain objective requirements concerning the investor are fulfilled. All investors are aware of the possibility of such a denial, such that no legitimate expectations are frustrated by that denial of benefits.[137]

7. An active investor?

Some tribunals have subscribed to the idea that the mere holding of assets that met the definition of an investment is not sufficient. Under this theory, passive ownership of an investment would not bestow the status of an investor.[138] Based on words such as 'made', 'by', 'of', and 'invested', some tribunals have found that the investor had to make some active contribution to be protected by the relevant treaty.[139]

In *Standard Chartered Bank v Tanzania*,[140] the UK claimant sought the benefits of a loan owed to a Hong Kong entity which it owned. The BIT between the United Kingdom and Tanzania referred to 'investments of [a UK company]', 'investments by investors', and 'investments made'. The Tribunal concluded that the BIT protected only investors that had made investments in some active way, rather than simple passive ownership.[141] It held:

> the Tribunal interprets the BIT to require an active relationship between the investor and the investment. To benefit from Article 8(1)'s arbitration provision, a claimant must demonstrate that the investment was made at the claimant's direction, that the claimant funded the investment or that the claimant controlled the investment in an active and direct manner. Passive ownership of shares in a company not controlled by the claimant where that company in turn owns the investment is not sufficient.

[135] *Ulysseas v Ecuador*, Interim Award, 28 September 2010, para 172; *Pac Rim v El Salvador*, Decision on Jurisdiction, 1 June 2012, para 4.90.

[136] *Guaracachi v Bolivia*, Award, 31 January 2014.

[137] At para 372.

[138] C Schreuer, 'The Active Investor' in E Bylander et al (eds) *Forward! Essays in Honour of Prof Dr Kaj Hobér* (2019) 237.

[139] *Caratube v Kazakhstan*, Award, 5 June 2012, paras 408–467.

[140] *Standard Chartered Bank v Tanzania*, Award, 2 November 2012, paras 206–232.

[141] At para 225.

> 231. The Tribunal is not persuaded that an 'investment of' a company or an individual implies only the abstract possession of shares in a company that holds title to some piece of property.
> 232. Rather, for an investment to be 'of' an investor in the present context, some activity of investing is needed, which implicates the claimant's control over the investment or an action of transferring something of value (money, know-how, contacts, or expertise) from one treaty-country to the other.[142]

In *KT Asia v Kazakhstan*,[143] the purported investment was a transfer between two foreign companies of shares in a Kazakh bank without any injection of a contribution of economic value. The two foreign companies belonged to the same individual. The Tribunal concluded that no investment had been made since there was neither any contribution nor any economic risk in this operation.[144] In particular, the Tribunal found:

> the Tribunal considers that KT Asia has made no contribution with respect to its alleged investment, nor is there any evidence on record that it had the intention or the ability to do so in the future. As a consequence, the Claimant has not demonstrated the existence of an investment under Article 25(1) of the ICSID Convention and under the BIT.[145]

In other cases, tribunals were either confronted with similar arguments[146] or seemed to support the idea that the role of an investor required more than ownership.[147]

A theory that requires an active contribution by each investor as a requirement for protection would require that every shareholder plays an active role in the investment. This would seriously undermine the position of shareholders as investors.[148] Moreover, this theory leads to the unsatisfactory result that a person who has not been involved in the making of an investment but acquires an existing investment does not enjoy the status of an investor.

A larger and weightier group of authorities suggest that the current owner of the assets is not required to have made an active contribution to qualify as an investor. To some extent, this debate hinges on the exact wording of the treaty in question. For instance, the ECT in its definition of investment in Article 1(6) does not refer

[142] At paras 230–232.
[143] *KT Asia v Kazakhstan*, Award, 17 October 2013.
[144] At paras 166–206.
[145] At para 206.
[146] *Gallo v Canada*, Award, 15 September 2011, para 145; *Mason v Korea*, Decision on Preliminary Objections, 22 December 2019, paras 197–203.
[147] *Quiborax v Bolivia*, Decision on Jurisdiction, 27 September 2012, paras 232–233; *OI European v Venezuela*, Award, 10 March 2015, paras 248–254; *Vestey v Venezuela*, Award, 15 April 2016, para 192.
[148] See IV.4(c) below.

to investments 'of' or 'by' an investor but refers to 'every kind of asset, owned or controlled directly or indirectly by an investor'.[149] This would clearly cover passive shareholding. Tribunals have found that investors who simply owned assets qualified as investors.[150]

Even without clear language to that effect, tribunals have held that mere ownership or control will be sufficient for the status of an investor. In *Levy v Peru*,[151] a father had transferred shares to his daughter free of charge. Peru argued that the resulting share ownership did not make the daughter an investor. The Tribunal disagreed:

> It is clear that the Claimant acquired her rights and shares free of charge. However, this does not mean that the persons from whom she acquired these shares and rights did not previously make very considerable investments of which ownership was transmitted to the Claimant by perfectly legitimate legal instruments.[152]

Other tribunals have similarly found that persons who passively held their investments qualified as investors.[153]

Similarly, the acquisition of assets in the context of corporate restructuring satisfies the condition of making an investment. This applies, for instance, when a company acquires another company that had previously been granted a concession. In *Gold Reserve v Venezuela*,[154] the Canada–Venezuela BIT referred to 'any enterprise . . . who makes the investment in the territory of Venezuela'. The Tribunal rejected the respondent's suggestion that the word 'makes' required some active step of the current owner.[155] The Tribunal concluded:

> there is no support in previous cases for contentions pertaining to a lack of investment as a result of (1) the parent company entering the structure after the concession had been granted; (2) the parent company being inserted as a result of an internal corporate restructure; or (3) the new parent company being incorporated in a jurisdiction with a BIT which has previously not been relevant.[156]

[149] On the other hand, Article 26(1) of the ECT, dealing with dispute settlement, speaks of an investment *of* an investor.

[150] *Saluka v Czech Republic*, Partial Award, 17 March 2006, para 211; *Phoenix v Czech Republic*, Award, 15 April 2009, para 119; *Veteran Petroleum v Russian Federation*, Interim Award on Jurisdiction and Admissibility, 30 November 2009, para 477; *Ryan v Poland*, Award, 24 November 2015, para 207; *Garanti Koza v Turkmenistan*, Award, 19 December 2016, paras 228–231; *Orascom v Algeria*, Award, 31 May 2017, para 384; *South American Silver v Bolivia*, Award, 22 November 2018, para 331; *Strabag v Libya*, Award, 29 June 2020, paras 118–119.

[151] *Levy v Peru*, Award, 26 February 2014.

[152] At para 148.

[153] *Mytilineos v Serbia and Montenegro*, Partial Award on Jurisdiction, 8 September 2006, paras 128–135; *von Pezold v Zimbabwe*, Award, 28 July 2015, paras 312–313; *Orascom v Algeria*, Award, 31 May 2017, para 384.

[154] *Gold Reserve v Venezuela*, Award, 22 September 2014.

[155] At paras 229–272.

[156] At para 270.

Tribunals have held that to become an investor it was sufficient to acquire an existing investment.[157] In *MNSS v Montenegro*,[158] the respondent disputed that the assignee of a loan could be regarded as an investor. It relied on several provisions of the Netherlands–Yugoslavia BIT all referring to an investment 'made'.[159] The Tribunal said:

> The fact that RCA was not an active investor because of the activity connotation of the expression 'making an investment', as argued by the Respondent, does not mean that an investor, once a loan is made or equity in a company is acquired, needs to make further investments or be particularly active in the management of the investment.[160]

It follows from these authorities that the preponderant view is that mere ownership or control of the investment will suffice to bestow the status of an investor. In other words, according to the majority view, it seems that an active contribution by the current owner of the assets is not required.

[157] *Flemingo v Poland*, Award, 12 August 2016, paras 321–324; *Kim v Uzbekistan*, Decision on Jurisdiction, 8 March 2017, paras 306–314; *Mera v Serbia*, Decision on Jurisdiction, 30 November 2018, paras 106–108.

[158] *MNSS v Montenegro*, Award, 4 May 2016.

[159] At para 126.

[160] At para 204.

IV

Investment

ADDITIONAL READING: R Dolzer, *Eigentum, Enteignung und Entschädigung im geltenden Völkerrecht* (1985); S Alexandrov, 'The "Baby Boom" of Treaty-Based Arbitrations and the Jurisdiction of ICSID Tribunals: Shareholders as "Investors" under Investment Treaties' (2005) 6 *JWIT* 387; R Dolzer, 'The Notion of Investment in Recent Practice' in S Charnovitz et al (eds) *Law in the Service of Human Dignity: Essays in Honour of Florentino Feliciano* (2005) 261; A Carlevaris, 'The Conformity of Investments with the Law of the Host State and the Jurisdiction of International Tribunals' (2008) 9 *JWIT* 35; N Rubins, 'The Notion of "Investment" in International Investment Arbitration' in N Horn (ed) *Arbitrating Foreign Investment Disputes* (2004) 283; U Kriebaum, *Eigentumsschutz im Völkerrecht* (2008); M Hwang, 'Recent Developments in Defining "Investment"' (2010) 24 *ICSID Rev* 2; U Kriebaum, 'Illegal Investments' (2010) 4 *Austrian YB Int Arb* 307; SW Schill, 'Illegal Investments in Investment Treaty Arbitration' (2012) 11 *LPICT* 281; Z Douglas, 'The Plea of Illegality in Investment Treaty Arbitration' (2014) 29 *ICSID Rev* 155; K Diel-Gligor and R Hennecke, 'Investment in Accordance with the Law' in M Bungenberg et al (eds) *International Investment Law* (2015) 566; E Gaillard and Y Banifatemi, 'The Long March towards a *Jurisprudence Constante* on the Notion of Investment' in M Kinnear et al (eds) *Building International Investment Law* (2015) 97; JA Bischoff and R Happ, 'The Notion of Investment' in M Bungenberg et al (eds) *International Investment Law* (2015) 495; C Knahr, 'The Territorial Nexus between an Investment and the Host State' in Bungenberg et al (eds) *International Investment Law* (2015) 590; K Yannaca-Small and D Katsikis, 'The Meaning of "Investment" in Investment Treaty Arbitration' in K Yannaca-Small (ed) *Arbitration under International Investment Agreements* (2018) 11.1; L Vanhonnaeker, *Shareholders' Claims for Reflective Loss in International Investment Law* (2020); S Klopschinski et al, *The Protection of Intellectual Property Rights under International Investment Law* (2021); SW Schill et al (eds), *Schreuer's Commentary on the ICSID Convention*, 3rd edn (2022) Article 25, paras 162–496; C Schreuer, 'The Unity of an Investment' (2021) 19 *ICSID Reports* 3; M Waibel, 'Subject-Matter Jurisdiction: the Notion of Investment'(2021) 19 *ICSID Reports* 25.

1. Terminology and concept

Economists distinguish between different types of investments: direct investments involve the transfer of funds, a longer-term project, the aim of regular income, the participation of the person transferring the funds, at least to some extent, in the management of the project, and a business risk. These elements distinguish foreign direct investment from a portfolio investment in which there is no element of personal management. Both types of investment differ from ordinary transactions for purposes of sales of goods or services and from short-term financial transactions.

Traditional treaties of friendship, commerce, and navigation (FCN), treaties to settle claims after hostilities, and human rights documents use the classical description 'property, rights, and interests'. By contrast, contemporary treaties use the modern term 'investment'.[1] This usage is now fully accepted. While the use of 'investment' is convenient, it also presents the challenge of defining the term to make it legally manageable and operational.

Treaties use the term 'investment' in three contexts. The first context is investment as object of protection *ratione materiae*. For example, Article 2 (2) of the UK Model BIT provides:

> **Investments** of nationals or companies of each Contracting Party shall ... be accorded fair and equitable treatment ...[2]

The second context is a reference in the formulas on consent to arbitration. For example, Article 10 of the German Model Treaty provides:

> (1) Disputes concerning **investments** between a Contracting State and an investor of the other contracting State should as far as possible be settled amicably between the parties to the dispute ...
> (2) If the dispute cannot be settled with ..., it shall, ... be submitted to arbitration.[3]

The third context is investment as a jurisdictional requirement under the ICSID Convention. Article 25 of the ICSID Convention provides:

[1] In French treaties: 'investissements'; in Spanish treaties: 'inversiones'; in German treaties: 'Kapitalanlagen'; in Austrian treaties: 'Investitionen'.

[2] UK Model BIT (2005) Article 2(2).

[3] German Model Treaty (2008) Article 10.

(1) The jurisdiction of the Centre shall extend to any legal dispute arising directly out of an **investment** . . . .

In practice, two conceptual approaches have been developed to give legal meaning to the term 'investment'. The first approach is to offer specific elaborate definitions in bilateral and multilateral treaties, usually at the beginning of the operative part. The second approach, adopted for example in the ICSID Convention, does not provide for a definition of 'investment' but leaves the interpretation and application of this term to the practice of States and tribunals.

In a particular situation, the first approach to establishing the meaning of 'investment' is to look at the definitions in investment treaties.[4] Since this leads to a definition by agreement, it is called the subjective approach. The second approach seeks to establish a general concept of the term 'investment'. Since this is independent of the parties' perspectives, it is called the objective approach. Tribunals often use this objective approach when interpreting the meaning of the term 'investment' in Article 25 of the ICSID Convention.[5]

Cases involving ICSID arbitration typically require two separate examinations of the existence of an 'investment': one under the instrument providing for consent to arbitration (BIT, national law, contract), the other under Article 25 of the ICSID Convention. This is often referred to as the double keyhole approach or double-barrelled test,[6] since the transaction at issue must fit both the definition of the consent instrument and the general concept applied to the ICSID Convention.

[4] *Gruslin v Malaysia II*, Award, 27 November 2000, para 13.6; *ATA v Jordan*, Award, 18 May 2010, para 111; *Al Tamimi v Oman*, Award, 3 November 2015, paras 275–280; *Garanti Koza v Turkmenistan*, Award, 19 December 2016, paras 235–242; *Tethyan Copper v Pakistan*, Decision on Jurisdiction and Liability, 10 November 2017, para 571.

[5] *CSOB v Slovakia*, Decision on Jurisdiction, 24 May 1999, para 68; *Salini v Morocco*, Decision on Jurisdiction, 16 July 2001, paras 44, 51–52; *Mihaly v Sri Lanka*, Award, 15 March 2002, paras 52, 58; *Joy Mining v Egypt*, Award on Jurisdiction, 6 August 2004, paras 42–50; *Jan de Nul v Egypt*, Decision on Jurisdiction, 16 June 2006, para 90; *Helnan v Egypt*, Decision on Jurisdiction, 17 October 2006, para 80; *Mitchell v DR Congo*, Decision on Annulment, 1 November 2006, para 31; *Fakes v Turkey*, Award, 14 July 2010, para 108; *El Paso v Argentina*, Award, 31 October 2011, para 142; *Quiborax v Bolivia*, Decision on Jurisdiction, 27 September 2012, paras 211–217; *Cortec v Kenya*, Award, 22 October 2018, para 255.

[6] *Aguas del Tunari v Bolivia*, Decision on Jurisdiction, 21 October 2005, para 278; *Malaysian Historical Salvors v Malaysia*, Award on Jurisdiction, 17 May 2007, para 55; *Malicorp v Egypt*, Award, 7 February 2011, para 107; *Phoenix v Czech Republic*, Award, 15 April 2009, para 74; *Ambiente Ufficio v Argentina*, Decision on Jurisdiction and Admissibility, 8 February 2013, para 438; *Kim v Uzbekistan*, Decision on Jurisdiction, 8 March 2017, para 242; *CMC v Mozambique*, Award, 24 October 2019, para 191.

2. Definitions of investment

(a) Investment contracts

A clause in an agreement by which the parties consent to submit disputes to investment arbitration under the ICSID Convention is a strong indication that they consider their transaction to be an investment. The classification of the proposed operation as an investment arises by necessary implication from the ICSID clause.[7] The contractual consent to ICSID arbitration will not, however, trigger an estoppel preventing the respondent from raising an objection to jurisdiction *ratione materiae*. Contracts cannot bring transactions or activities that would objectively not qualify as investments under the jurisdiction of ICSID.[8]

(b) Definitions in national laws

Some national laws contain offers of investment arbitration.[9] The United Nations Conference on Trade and Development (UNCTAD) currently lists 57 national laws that provide for consent to arbitration in investment disputes.[10] Twenty-six of these provide for ICSID Arbitration, 12 for UNCITRAL arbitration.[11]

Many of these national laws contain definitions of investment. Some are very terse like the definition in Article 3 of the Tanzanian Investment Act 1997:

> 'investment' means the creation or acquisition of new business assets and includes the expansion, restructuring or rehabilitation of an existing business enterprise;[12]

Some investment codes exclude certain economic activities from investment protection. For example, the investment Code of Congo, applicable in *Lahoud v DR Congo*, excludes: investments in mining, hydrocarbons, banking, insurance, production of arms and explosives, and commercial activities.[13]

[7] CF Amerasinghe, 'Submissions to the Jurisdiction of the International Centre for Settlement of Investment Disputes' (1973/74) 5 *J Marit Law Commer* 211, 223; A Broches, 'The Convention on the Settlement of Investment Disputes, Some Observations on Jurisdiction' (1966) 5 *Colum J Transnatl Law* 263, 268; H Golsong, 'A Guide to Procedural Issues in International Arbitration' (1984) 18 *Int'l Lawyer* 633, 634/5.

[8] *RSM v Grenada I*, Award, 13 March 2009, para 235; *RSM v Central African Republic*, Decision on Jurisdiction and Liability, 7 December 2010, para 48. See, however, *Caratube and Hourani v Kazakhstan*, Award, 27 September 2017, para 635.

[9] See XII.7(b) below. For a collection of national investment legislation see: Investment Laws of the World, loose-leaf collection (OUP, since 1973).

[10] <https://investmentpolicy.unctad.org/investment-laws>, accessed 16 July 2021.

[11] <https://investmentpolicy.unctad.org/investment-laws>, accessed 16 July 2021.

[12] Tanzania Investment Act, 1997 (1997), Act No 26 of 1997, Official Gazette No 40 Vol 78, Section 3.

[13] *Lahoud v DR Congo* Award, 7 February 2014, para 228.

Other definitions follow the pattern of modern BITs. Article 1 of the Law of Georgia on the Investment Activity Promotion and Guarantees (1996) provides:

> Article 1. Investments
>
> 1) Investments shall be deemed to be all types of property and intellectual valuables or rights invested and applied for gaining possible profit in the investment activity carried out in the territory of Georgia.
> 2) Such valuables or rights may be:
>   a. monetary assets, a share, stocks and other securities;
>   b. movable and immovable property—land, buildings, structures, equipment and other material valuables;
>   c. lease rights to land and the use of natural resources (including concession), patents, licenses, know-how, experience and other intellectual valuables;
>   d. other property or intellectual valuables or rights provided for by the law.[14]

In *Zhinvali v Georgia*, the Tribunal decided that development costs did not qualify as an investment under the Georgia Investment Law.[15]

The definitions and restrictions contained in national laws do not necessarily represent the general meaning of the term 'investment'. But they form part of the conditions of consent and must be respected in order to establish jurisdiction in a particular case.

(c) Definitions in treaties

The majority of cases in recent years have been brought under investment treaties.[16] Almost all of these treaties contain asset-based definitions of the term investment. Most of these definitions contain a general term (such as 'all assets') and several groups of illustrative categories. These lists contain traditional property rights but are not limited to them.

[14] Law of Georgia on the investment activity promotion and guarantees (1996), Law No 473-10, <https://investmentpolicy.unctad.org/investment-laws/laws/75/georgia-investment-law >, accessed 26 March 2021.

[15] *Zhinvali v Georgia*, Award, 24 January 2003, 10 ICSID Reports 3, paras 375–390, 406–419.

[16] In 76 per cent of the cases registered by ICSID, the basis of consent to establish jurisdiction was an investment protection treaty, of these, 60 per cent were based on BITs (ICSID Caseload-Statistics, Issue 2020-1).

Typical examples of multilateral treaties containing definitions of 'investment' are the Energy Charter Treaty (ECT), with its definition in Article 1(6),[17] the North American Free Trade Agreement (NAFTA), which defines 'investment' in Article 1139, and the United States–Mexico–Canada Agreement (USMCA) which contains a definition in Article 14.1.[18]

The definition of 'investment' in the BIT between Argentina and the United States is as follows:

> 'investment' means every kind of investment in the territory of one Party owned or controlled directly or indirectly by nationals or companies of the other Party, such as equity, debt, and service and investment contracts; and includes without limitation:
>
> (i) tangible and intangible property, including rights, such as mortgages, liens and pledges;
>
> (ii) a company or shares of stock or other interests in a company or interests in the assets thereof;
>
> (iii) a claim to money or a claim to performance having economic value and directly related to an investment;
>
> (iv) intellectual property which includes, inter alia, rights relating to: literary and artistic works, including sound recordings, inventions in all fields of human endeavour, industrial designs, semiconductor mask works, trade secrets, know-how, and confidential business information, and trademarks, service marks, and trade names;

[17] ECT, Article 1(6):

> 'Investment' means every kind of asset, owned or controlled directly or indirectly by an Investor and includes: (a) tangible and intangible, and movable and immovable, property, and any property rights such as leases, mortgages, liens, and pledges; (b) a company or business enterprise, or shares, stock, or other forms of equity participation in a company or business enterprise, and bonds and other debt of a company or business enterprise; (c) claims to money and claims to performance pursuant to contract having an economic value and associated with an Investment; (d) Intellectual Property; (e) Returns; (f) any right conferred by law or contract or by virtue of any licences and permits granted pursuant to law to undertake any Economic Activity in the Energy Sector.

[18] USMCA, Article 14.1:

> **investment** means every asset that an investor owns or controls, directly or indirectly, that has the characteristics of an investment, including such characteristics as the commitment of capital or other resources, the expectation of gain or profit, or the assumption of risk. An investment may include:
>
> (a) an enterprise; (b) shares, stock and other forms of equity participation in an enterprise; (c) bonds, debentures, other debt instruments, and loans; (d) futures, options, and other derivatives; (e) turnkey, construction, management, production, concession, revenue-sharing, and other similar contracts; (f) intellectual property rights; (g) licenses, authorizations, permits, and similar rights conferred pursuant to a Party's law; and (h) other tangible or

(v) and any right conferred by law or contract, and any licenses and permits pursuant to law;

The agreement between Canada and the European Union (the Comprehensive Economic and Trade Agreement, CETA)[19] defines 'investment' in its Article 8.1. The definition incorporates elements of the concept of investment as developed by tribunals interpreting Article 25 of the ICSID Convention. It describes these elements as 'characteristics of an investment':

> **investment means every kind of asset that an investor owns or controls, directly or indirectly, that** has the characteristics of an investment, which includes a certain duration and other characteristics such as the commitment of capital or other resources, the expectation of gain or profit, or the assumption of risk. Forms that an investment may take include:
> (a) an enterprise;
> (b) shares, stocks and other forms of equity participation in an enterprise;
> (c) bonds, debentures and other debt instruments of an enterprise;
> (d) a loan to an enterprise;
> (e) any other kind of interest in an enterprise;
> (f) an interest arising from:
> (i) a concession conferred pursuant to the law of a Party or under a contract, including to
> search for, cultivate, extract or exploit natural resources,
> (ii) a turnkey, construction, production or revenue-sharing contract; or
> (iii) other similar contracts;

intangible, movable or immovable property, and related property rights, such as liens, mortgages, pledges, and leases,
but investment does not mean:
(i) an order or judgment entered in a judicial or administrative action; (j) claims to money that arise solely from: (i) commercial contracts for the sale of goods or services by a natural person or enterprise in the territory of a Party to an enterprise in the territory of another Party, or (ii) the extension of credit in connection with a commercial contract referred to in subparagraph (j)(i) . . . .

[19] Comprehensive Economic and Trade Agreement (CETA) between Canada, the European Union, and its member States, signed 30 October 2016, not in force. Parts of the treaty are provisionally applied since 21 September 2017.

(g) intellectual property rights;
(h) other moveable property, tangible or intangible, or immovable property and related rights;
(i) claims to money or claims to performance under a contract.

For greater certainty, **claims to money does not include**:
(a) claims to money that arise solely from commercial contracts for the sale of goods or services by a natural person or enterprise in the territory of a Party to a natural person or enterprise in the territory of the other Party.
(b) the domestic financing of such contracts; or
(c) any order, judgment, or arbitral award related to sub-subparagraph (a) or (b).

Returns that are invested shall be treated as investments. Any alteration of the form in which assets are invested or reinvested does not affect their qualification as investment;

The matter will become more complicated if the definition itself contains a reference to the term 'investment', as is the case in the Argentina–US BIT or in the ECT.[20] In such circumstances, recourse to a general concept of 'investment' that goes beyond the treaty's definition may be necessary.

The definitions of investments in treaties frequently refer to rights governed by the host State's domestic laws. This applies to property rights, to contractual rights, and other rights granted by national law. The existence and extent of these rights constituting an investment depend upon the relevant national law.[21] In the individual case, the international tribunal will take the understanding of the law by the organs of the host State into account and may defer to this understanding. But the final decision is with the international tribunal.

Recurrent features in the definitions of the term 'investment' in investment treaties do not mean that they reflect a general definition. Rather, these definitions are part of the specific conditions of consent governing the relation between the disputing parties to individual disputes.

[20] ECT, Article 1(6)(c) refers to a 'contract having an economic value and associated with an Investment'. See in this respect *Petrobart v Kyrgyz Republic*, Award, 29 March 2005, p 72.

[21] *Suez and Vivendi v Argentina*, Decision on Liability, 30 July 2010, para 151; *Alpha v Ukraine*, Award, 8 November 2010, para 347; *Total v Argentina*, Decision on Liability, 27 December 2010, para 39; *Libananco v Turkey*, Award, 2 September 2011, para 112; *Quiborax v Bolivia*, Decision on Jurisdiction, 27 September 2012, paras 52, 115 et seq.; *Emmis v Hungary*, Award, 16 April 2014, para 48; *Philipp Morris v Uruquay*, Award, 8 July 2016, paras 177–178; *Gavrilovic v Croatia*, Award, 26 July 2018, para

3. A general concept of investment?

(a) 'Investment' in Article 25 of the ICSID Convention

Article 25 of the Convention serves as the jurisdictional gateway for access to ICSID, the most important form of investment arbitration.[22] Among the conditions for access to ICSID is the requirement that the dispute arises directly out of an investment. Yet, the ICSID Convention does not offer a definition or even a description of this basic term.

During the ICSID Convention's drafting there were extensive debates about the meaning of the term 'investment' and about possible definitions to be included in the Convention.[23] Suggestions to exclude insignificant claims by introducing a minimum limit, to require a certain duration of the investor's engagement, or to limit access to the Convention to certain types of transactions did not find entry into the Convention's text. Eventually, a compromise was reached, based on a suggestion by the United Kingdom, which resulted in the Convention's final version. The proposal was to limit ICSID's jurisdiction to 'investment disputes' without defining that notion. This was combined with a notification mechanism (now found in Article 25(4)) that allows States to declare what disputes they would not consider submitting to the Centre.

The Report of the Executive Directors, which is frequently cited on this point by arbitral tribunals, summarized the negotiations by way of concluding that the negotiators deliberately refrained from adopting any definition to leave room for an understanding by the parties:

> No attempt was made to define the term 'investment' given the essential requirement of consent by the parties, and the mechanism through which Contracting States can make known in advance, if they so desire, the classes of disputes which they would or would not consider submitting to the Centre (Article 25(4)).[24]

As is evident from the history of the Convention, this statement is incorrect since there had been a series of attempts to define the notion of investment which all failed. But it does reflect the fact that in the end a conscious decision was made not to define the term 'investment' and to leave the parties flexibility to decide which transactions they wished to submit.

432; *Italba v Uruguay*, Award, 22 March 2019, para 213; *Almasryia v Kuwait*, Award under Rule 41(5), 1 November 2019, paras 53–58.

[22] See below XII.5.

[23] For a detailed description see SW Schill et al (eds), *Schreuer's Commentary on the ICSID Convention* (2022) Article 25, paras 163–176.

[24] 1 ICSID Reports 28, para 27.

(b) The *Salini* test

Over time, tribunals operating under the ICSID Convention have developed criteria that they have found typical for the concept of an investment. The Tribunal in *Fedax v Venezuela*[25] listed five criteria as the basic features of an investment which it described as follows:

> The basic features of an investment have been described as involving a certain duration, a certain regularity of profit and return, assumption of risk, a substantial commitment and a significance for the host State's development.[26]

Among the five points in this approach, four have come to be widely considered, while regularity of profit was subsequently seldom considered relevant.[27]

The decision that has become most prominent in this context is *Salini v Morocco.*[28] It adopted four of these criteria. The Tribunal noted that the existence of an investment under the Convention was an objective condition of jurisdiction in addition to consent. It said:

> The doctrine generally considers that investment infers: contributions, a certain duration of performance of the contract and a participation in the risks of the transaction. In reading the Convention's preamble, one may add the contribution to the economic development of the host State of the investment as an additional condition.[29]

These four criteria for an investment have since become known as the 'Salini test.' They encompass:

- a (substantial) contribution;
- a certain duration of the operation;
- risk; and
- contribution to the host State's development.

[25] *Fedax v Venezuela*, Decision on Jurisdiction, 11 July 1997.

[26] At para 43. The Tribunal relied on C Schreuer, 'Commentary on the ICSID Convention' (1996) 11 *ICSID Rev* 372.

[27] But see: *Joy Mining v Egypt*, Award on Jurisdiction, 6 August 2004, para 53; *Helnan v Egypt*, Decision on Jurisdiction, 17 October 2006, para 77; *OKO Pankki v Estonia*, Award, 19 November 2007, para 203.

[28] *Salini v Morocco*, Decision on Jurisdiction, 16 July 2001.

[29] At para 52.

Tribunals have applied these criteria in numerous cases,[30] although the legal significance they attributed to them is not always clear. Tribunals have referred to them as basic features,[31] characteristics,[32] hallmarks,[33] indicative elements,[34] criteria,[35] and as representing an inherent meaning.[36] One tribunal tried to introduce two additional criteria.[37]

In tribunal practice, the first three of these criteria (contribution, duration, and risk) have been applied widely. The fourth criterion (contribution to host State development) has turned out to be controversial.

With regard to a *contribution*, tribunals have accepted a large variety of assets as investments. A contribution may be financial but may also consist of anything that has economic value such as know-how, management, equipment, material, personnel, labour, and services.[38] There is no minimum value, but purely symbolic contributions will not qualify.[39]

[30] *Bayindir v Pakistan*, Decision on Jurisdiction, 14 November 2005, paras 130–138; *Noble Energy v Ecuador*, Decision on Jurisdiction, 5 March 2008, paras 125–135; *Pey Casado v Chile*, Award, 8 May 2008, paras 231–232; *Toto v Lebanon*, Decision on Jurisdiction, 11 September 2009, paras 81–87; *Fakes v Turkey*, Award, 14 July 2010, paras 95–114; *Millicom v Senegal*, Decision on Jurisdiction, 16 July 2010, paras 80–81; *Alpha v Ukraine*, Award, 8 November 2010, paras 310–332; *Nations Energy v Panama*, Award, 24 November 2010, paras 442–455; *RSM v Central African Republic*, Award, 11 July 2011, paras 50–59; *Malicorp v Egypt*, Award, 7 February 2011, paras 106–114; *Meerapfel v Central African Republic*, Award, 12 May 2011, paras 175–186; *Quiborax v Bolivia*, Decision on Jurisdiction, 27 September 2012, paras 218–227; *Deutsche Bank v Sri Lanka*, Award, 31 October 2012, paras 293–307; *Electrabel v Hungary*, Decision on Jurisdiction, Applicable Law and Liability, 30 November 2012, paras 5.43–5.44; *Ambiente Ufficio v Argentina*, Decision on Jurisdiction and Admissibility, 8 February 2013, paras 475–487; *Niko Resources v Bangladesh*, Decision on Jurisdiction, 19 August 2013, para 352; *KT Asia v Kazakhstan*, Award, 17 October 2013, paras 161–173; *Flughafen Zürich v Venezuela*, Award, 18 November 2014, paras 244–258; *Mamidoil v Albania*, Award, 30 March 2015, paras 285–288; *Orascom v Algeria*, Award, 31 May 2017, para 370; *Karkey v Pakistan*, Award, 22 August 2017, paras 633, 636; *Koch v Venezuela*, Award, 30 October 2017, para 6.67; *Casinos Austria v Argentina*, Decision on Jurisdiction, 29 June 2018, paras 187–193; *Cortec v Kenya*, Award, 22 October 2018, para 300; *Standard Chartered Bank (Hong Kong) v Tanzania*, Award, 11 October 2019, paras 198–246; *CMC v Mozambique*, Award, 24 October 2019, paras 190–196.

[31] *Fedax v Venezuela*, Decision on Jurisdiction, 11 July 1997, para 43.

[32] *Helnan v Egypt*, Decision on Jurisdiction, 17 October 2006, para 77; *Mitchell v DR Congo*, Decision on Annulment, 1 November 2006, para 27; *RSM v Grenada I*, Award, 13 March 2009, para 240; *Pantechniki v Albania*, Award, 30 July 2009, para 36.

[33] *Malaysian Historical Salvors v Malaysia*, Award on Jurisdiction, 17 May 2007, para 106.

[34] *Jan de Nul v Egypt*, Decision on Jurisdiction, 16 June 2006, para 9.

[35] *Saipem v Bangladesh*, Decision on Jurisdiction, 21 March 2007, para 99; *Kardassopoulos v Georgia*, Decision on Jurisdiction, 6 July 2007, para 116.

[36] *Eyre and Montrose v Sri Lanka*, Award, 5 March 2020, para 293.

[37] *Phoenix v Czech Republic*, Award, 15 April 2009, para 114.

[38] *RFCC v Morocco*, Decision on Jurisdiction, 16 July 2001, para 61; *Bayindir v Pakistan*, Decision on Jurisdiction, 14 November 2005, para 131; *Malaysian Historical Salvors v Malaysia*, Award on Jurisdiction, 17 May 2007, para 109; *Sistem Mühendislik v Kyrgyz Republic*, Decision on Jurisdiction, 13 September 2007, para 86; *Toto v Lebanon*, Decision on Jurisdiction, 11 September 2009, para 86(a); *Deutsche Bank v Sri Lanka*, Award, 31 October 2012, para 297; *Flughafen Zürich v Venezuela*, Award, 18 November 2014, paras 248–249; *OI European v Venezuela*, Award, 10 March 2015, para 245; *A11Y v Czech Republic*, Award, 29 June 2018, paras 144–153; *Mason v Korea*, Decision on Respondent's Preliminary Objections, 22 December 2019, para 216.

[39] *Mihaly v Sri Lanka*, Award, 15 March 2002, para 51; *Mitchell v DR Congo*, Award, 9 February 2004, para 56 and Decision on Annulment, 1 November 2006, para 33; *Pantechniki v Albania*, Award, 30 July

A certain *duration* distinguishes an investment from a one-off transaction like a sale of goods. There is no clear limit for a minimum duration.[40] Some tribunals have suggested a minimum period of between one and five years.[41] In calculating the duration, tribunals take account also of the time taken for tender, work interruption, renegotiation, extension maintenance, and a contractor's guarantee.[42] What matters is the intended duration. An early termination does not affect the nature of the transaction as an investment.[43] Conversely, short-term transactions do not become investments due to an inadvertent delay in the sale of assets.[44]

Tribunals have accepted a wide range of *risks*, such as sovereign interference, unforeseen incidents, and commercial circumstances.[45] In some cases, the tribunals found that the very existence of the dispute before them was an evidence of risk.[46] In several cases, tribunals found that risk was inherent in any commercial activity.[47] Tribunals also found that the economic and political circumstances in the host State posed a relevant risk.[48]

Some tribunals have attempted to break down risk into various categories. Under this approach, commercial risk would have to be distinguished from the operational risk of an investment. The reason would be that commercial risk is not specific to an investment and can hence not be used to define the concept

2009, para 45; *Fakes v Turkey*, Award, 14 July 2010, para 112, fn 73; *Doutremepuich v Mauritius*, Award on Jurisdiction, 23 August 2019, para 126.

40 *Romak v Uzbekistan*, Award, 26 November 2009, para 225; *Deutsche Bank v Sri Lanka*, Award, 31 October 2012, para 303; *Doutremepuich v Mauritius*, Award on Jurisdiction, 23 August 2019, para 143.

41 *RFCC v Morocco*, Decision on Jurisdiction, 16 July 2001, para 62; *Salini v Morocco*, Decision on Jurisdiction, 16 July 2001, para 54; *Jan de Nul v Egypt*, Decision on Jurisdiction, 16 June 2006, paras 93–95; *Malaysian Historical Salvors v Malaysia*, Award on Jurisdiction, 17 May 2007, paras 110, 111.

42 *Bayindir v Pakistan*, Decision on Jurisdiction, 14 November 2005, para 133; *Jan de Nul v Egypt*, Decision on Jurisdiction, 16 June 2006, paras 94, 95; *LESI & ASTALDI v Algeria*, Decision on Jurisdiction, 12 July 2006, para 73(ii); *Saipem v Bangladesh*, Decision on Jurisdiction, 21 March 2007, paras 101, 102; *Toto v Lebanon*, Decision on Jurisdiction, 11 September 2009, para 86(c); *Deutsche Bank v Sri Lanka*, Award, 31 October 2012, para 304.

43 *ABCI v Tunisia*, Decision on Jurisdiction, 18 February 2011, para 62; *Mason v Korea*, Decision on Preliminary Objections, 22 December 2019, paras 226–248; *Adamakopoulos v Cyprus*, Decision on Jurisdiction, 7 February 2020, para 295.

44 *KT Asia v Kazakhstan*, Award, 17 October 2013, paras 207–216; *Kim v Uzbekistan*, Decision on Jurisdiction, 8 March 2017, paras 340–343.

45 *Salini v Morocco*, Decision on Jurisdiction, 16 July 2001, para 55; *Quiborax v Bolivia*, Decision on Jurisdiction, 27 September 2012, para 234; *Ambiente Ufficio v Argentina*, Decision on Jurisdiction and Admissibility, 8 February 2013, para 485.

46 *Fedax v Venezuela*, Decision on Jurisdiction, 11 July 1997, para 40; *Deutsche Bank v Sri Lanka*, Award, 31 October 2012, para 301.

47 *Salini v Morocco*, Decision on Jurisdiction, 16 July 2001, para 56; *Bayindir v Pakistan*, Decision on Jurisdiction, 14 November 2005, para 136; *Saipem v Bangladesh*, Decision on Jurisdiction, 21 March 2007, para 109; *RREEF v Spain*, Decision on Jurisdiction, 6 June 2016, para 158; *Krederi v Ukraine*, Award, 2 July 2018, para 238; *Gavrilovic v Croatia*, Award, 26 July 2018, para 215.

48 *Kardassopoulos v Georgia*, Decision on Jurisdiction, 6 July 2007, para 117; *Pey Casado v Chile*, Award, 8 May 2008, para 233 (c); *Meerapfel v Central African Republic*, Award, 12 May 2011, para 204; *Deutsche Bank v Sri Lanka*, Award, 31 October 2012, para 301.

of investment.[49] The better approach would be to look at the various forms of risk in combination and with some degree of flexibility. Any form of risk, commercial, operational, or sovereign, is part of the typical features of an investment even though not every type of risk will necessarily materialize in every investment.

Contribution to the host State's development has turned out to be the most controversial indicator of an investment. It is the only criterion that is expressed in the ICSID Convention's text through the Preamble's reference to economic development.[50] Many tribunals examined and confirmed the existence of such a contribution,[51] mostly without making a clear statement about its role as a criterion for the existence of an investment.[52]

In *Mitchell v DR Congo*, the Tribunal had found that the claimant's law firm in the Congo constituted an investment.[53] The ad hoc Committee annulled the Award since it considered that the law firm did not contribute to the host State's economic and social development.[54]

In *Malaysian Historical Salvors v Malaysia*, the Sole Arbitrator declined jurisdiction finding that there was no investment since the salvage of historical objects from an ancient shipwreck did not make a significant contribution to the host State's economy.[55] The Award was annulled because it had elevated the criterion of contribution to the host State's development into a jurisdictional condition and interpreted that condition as excluding small contributions and contributions of a cultural and historical nature.[56]

49 *Romak v Uzbekistan*, Award, 26 November 2009, paras 229–230; *Nova Scotia Power v Venezuela*, Award, 30 April 2014, paras 105–112; *Poštová banka v Greece*, Award, 9 April 2015, paras 367–370; *Doutremepuich v Mauritius*, Award on Jurisdiction, 23 August 2019, paras 145–147; *Standard Chartered Bank (Hong Kong) v Tanzania*, Award, 11 October 2019, paras 218–219; *Eyre and Montrose v Sri Lanka*, Award, 5 March 2020, paras 293–294.

50 *CSOB v Slovakia*, Decision on Jurisdiction, 24 May 1999, para 64; *Bayindir v Pakistan*, Decision on Jurisdiction, 14 November 2005, para 137.

51 *Fedax v Venezuela*, Decision on Jurisdiction, 11 July 1997, para 43; *Salini v Morocco*, Decision on Jurisdiction, 16 July 2001, para 57; *RFCC v Morocco*, Decision on Jurisdiction, 16 July 2001, paras 65, 66; *Helnan v Egypt*, Decision on Jurisdiction, 17 October 2006, para 77; *Saipem v Bangladesh*, Decision on Jurisdiction, 21 March 2007, paras 99–101; *Kardassopoulos v Georgia*, Decision on Jurisdiction, 6 July 2007, para 117; *OKO Pankki v Estonia*, Award, 19 November 2007, para 206; *Noble Energy v Ecuador*, Decision on Jurisdiction, 5 March 2008, paras 128, 132; *Millicom v Senegal*, Decision on Jurisdiction, 16 July 2010, paras 80–81; *Malicorp v Egypt*, Award, 7 February 2011, paras 109–112; *Meerapfel v Central African Republic*, Award, 12 May 2011, paras 179, 183, 206–209; *Convial Callao v Peru*, Final Award, 21 May 2013, paras 438; *Karkey v Pakistan*, Award, 22 August 2017, para 633; *Cortec v Kenya*, Award, 22 October 2018, para 300(c).

52 But see: *Toto v Lebanon*, Decision on Jurisdiction, 11 September 2009, para 86; *Standard Chartered Bank (Hong Kong) v Tanzania*, Award, 11 October 2019, para 220.

53 *Mitchell v DR Congo*, Award, 9 February 2004, paras 40–57.

54 *Mitchell v DR Congo*, Decision on Annulment, 1 November 2006, paras 39–48.

55 *Malaysian Historical Salvors v Malaysia*, Award on Jurisdiction, 17 May 2007, paras 44–146.

56 *Malaysian Historical Salvors v Malaysia*, Decision on Annulment, 16 April 2009, paras 64–80.

An increasing number of tribunals reject a contribution to the host State's development as an independent criterion for the existence of an investment.[57] Some have found that the contribution to the host State's development was a consequence of an investment rather than a precondition to its existence.[58]

Overall, the *Salini* test has had a mixed following.[59] It has been applied in numerous ICSID cases. Some tribunals have even applied it in non-ICSID cases.[60] Other tribunals have denied the relevance of the *Salini* test in non-ICSID proceedings.[61]

Some tribunals have explicitly distanced themselves from the *Salini* test. For instance, the Tribunal in *Biwater Gauff v Tanzania*[62] said:

> the Salini Test itself is problematic if, as some tribunals have found, the 'typical characteristics' of an investment as identified in that decision are elevated into a fixed and inflexible test, and if transactions are to be presumed excluded from the ICSID Convention unless each of the five criteria are satisfied. This risks the arbitrary exclusion of certain types of transaction from the scope of the Convention.[63]

The Annulment Committee in *Teinver v Argentina* found that a failure to apply the *Salini* test in itself cannot constitute a manifest excess of powers.[64] In a series of decisions, tribunals have described the *Salini* test as a misnomer,[65] as non-binding and non-exclusive,[66] as not absolute,[67] as not creating a limit,[68] and as not constituting jurisdictional requirements.[69]

[57] *LESI-DIPENTA v Algeria*, Award, 10 January 2005, para II 13(iv); *LESI & ASTALDI v Algeria*, Decision on Jurisdiction, 12 July 2006, para 72(iv); *Pey Casado v Chile*, Award, 8 May 2008, para 232; *Phoenix v Czech Republic*, Award, 15 April 2009, paras 85–86; *Alpha v Ukraine*, Award, 8 November 2010, para 312; *RSM v Central African Republic*, Award, 11 July 2011, paras 56–57; *Deutsche Bank v Sri Lanka*, Award, 31 October 2012, para 306; *Electrabel v Hungary*, Decision on Jurisdiction, Applicable Law and Liability, 30 November 2012, para 5.43; *Philip Morris v Uruguay*, Decision on Jurisdiction, 2 July 2013, paras 201, 207–208; *Houben v Burundi*, Award, 12 January 2016, para 112, fn 43; *İçkale v Turkmenistan*, Award, 8 March 2016, para 291; *Mabco v Kosovo*, Decision on Jurisdiction, 30 October 2020, paras 296, 301, 414.

[58] *Fakes v Turkey*, Award, 14 July 2010, para 111; *Quiborax v Bolivia*, Decision on Jurisdiction, 27 September 2012, paras 220–225; *KT Asia v Kazakhstan*, Award, 17 October 2013, paras 171–172.

[59] *Standard Chartered Bank (Hong Kong) v Tanzania*, Award, 11 October 2019, paras 198–200.

[60] *Romak v Uzbekistan*, Award (UNCITRAL), 26 November 2009, paras 190–208; *AFT v Slovakia*, Award (UNCITRAL), 5 March 2011, paras 239–246; *Nova Scotia Power v Venezuela*, Award (AF), 30 April 2014, paras 84–113; *MNSS v Montenegro*, Award (AF), 4 May 2016, paras 189–202.

[61] *White Industries v India*, Final Award (UNCITRAL), 30 November 2011, paras 7.4.8–7.4.19; *Guaracachi v Bolivia*, Award (UNCITRAL), 31 January 2014, para 364; *Flemingo v Poland*, Award (UNCITRAL), 12 August 2016, para 298; *Częścik v Cyprus*, Final Award (SCC), 11 February 2017, paras 192–195; *Anglia Auto v Czech Republic*, Final Award (SCC), 10 March 2017, para 150; *Strabag v Libya*, Award (AF), 29 June 2020, para 109.

[62] *Biwater Gauff v Tanzania*, Award, 24 July 2008, para 314.

[63] At para 314.

[64] *Teinver v Argentina*, Decision on Annulment, 29 May 2019, para 87.

[65] *Pantechniki v Albania*, Award, 30 July 2009, paras 36, 43.

[66] *Inmaris Perestroika v Ukraine*, Decision on Jurisdiction, 8 March 2010, para 131.

[67] *Malicorp v Egypt*, Award, 7 February 2011, para 109.

[68] *Abaclat v Argentina*, Decision on Jurisdiction and Admissibility, 4 August 2011, para 364.

[69] *Philip Morris v Uruguay*, Decision on Jurisdiction, 2 July 2013, para 206.

When tribunals have looked at the *Salini* criteria, they have at times emphasized that they are interdependent and should not be examined seriatim but in conjunction.[70] In *İçkale v Turkmenistan*[71] the Tribunal said:

> The Tribunal agrees that the three criteria identified by the Salini tribunal – contribution of capital, certain duration and assumption of risk – are not independent or free-standing criteria but interdependent in the sense that a commitment of capital to a business venture—'contribution' of capital—implies, in itself, a certain duration for the contribution in question and a risk of loss of the capital contributed.[72]

4. Types of investments

The concept of an investment covers a large variety of transactions. This diversity is reflected in the definitions contained in investment treaties.[73] The relevant cases show the wide range of economic sectors in which investments are made. They concern oil, gas, and mining; electric power and other energy; transportation; construction; finance; information and communication; water, sanitation, and flood protection; agriculture, fishing, and forestry; tourism; services and trade, as well as other industries.[74]

(a) Tangible assets

Property rights in tangibles is the most obvious form of investment. These properties will qualify as investments if they are destined for the pursuit of the investor's business activity. This will include movable as well as immovable property such as land, machinery, vehicles, office appliances, and other equipment.[75]

[70] *Salini v Morocco*, Decision on Jurisdiction, 16 July 2001, para 52; *Bayindir v Pakistan*, Decision on Jurisdiction, 14 November 2005, para 130; *Jan de Nul v Egypt*, Decision on Jurisdiction, 16 June 2006, para 91; *Malaysian Historical Salvors v Malaysia*, Award on Jurisdiction, 17 May 2007, paras 72; *Kardassopoulos v Georgia*, Decision on Jurisdiction, 6 July 2007, para 116; *Noble Energy v Ecuador*, Decision on Jurisdiction, 5 March 2008, para 128; *Meerapfel v Central African Republic*, Award, 12 May 2011, paras 184–186; *Caratube v Kazakhstan*, Award, 5 June 2012, para 409; *Adamakopoulos v Cyprus*, Decision on Jurisdiction, 7 February 2020, para 294.

[71] *İçkale v Turkmenistan*, Award, 8 March 2016.

[72] At para 290.

[73] See IV.2(c) above.

[74] The ICSID Caseload—Statistics, Issue 2020-1 (2020) 12.

[75] *Santa Elena v Costa Rica*, Award, 17 February 2000; *Middle East Cement v Egypt*, Award, 12 April 2002, paras 131–151; *Strabag v Libya*, Award, 29 June 2020, para 110.

(b) Contract rights

It is well established that rights arising from contracts between the investor and the government, or a governmental entity, may amount to an investment.[76] This includes concessions, licences, or permits, for example for the exploitation of natural resources, the operation of public utilities, or the implementation of other regulated business activities.[77] Contracts with private parties can also constitute an investment.[78]

Not every contract with the State, however, qualifies as an investment. There is a consistent practice to the effect that contracts that are not more than regular commercial transactions do not qualify as investments. A simple sale of goods or a transient commercial transaction is not an investment.[79]

(c) Shareholding

Shareholding is a frequently invoked form of investment. Many host States require that investments are made through locally incorporated companies whose shares the foreign investor holds in whole or in part. Shareholding is routinely mentioned in definitions of 'investment' in treaties[80] and has been routinely recognized by tribunals. The protection of shareholding is independent of and additional to the possible recognition of the local company as a foreign investor.[81] The protection of shareholdings

[76] *SPP v Egypt*, Award, 20 May 1992, paras 164, 165; *IBM v Ecuador*, Decision on Jurisdiction, 22 December 2003, paras 11–18; *Bayindir v Pakistan*, Decision on Jurisdiction, 14 November 2005, para 255; *Eureko v Poland*, Partial Award, 19 August 2005, para 241; *Inmaris Perestroika v Ukraine*, Decision on Jurisdiction, 8 March 2010, para 92.

[77] *Goetz v Burundi*, Award, 10 February 1999, para 124; *Tecmed v Mexico*, Award, 29 May 2003, para 91; *SGS v Pakistan*, Decision on Jurisdiction, 6 August 2003, para 135; *Azurix v Argentina*, Decision on Jurisdiction, 8 December 2003, para 62; *PSEG v Turkey*, Decision on Jurisdiction, 4 June 2004, para 104; *Telenor v Hungary*, Award, 13 September 2006, paras 61–62; *Malicorp v Egypt*, Award, 7 February 2011, paras 111–114; *Quiborax v Bolivia*, Decision on Jurisdiction, 27 September 2012, paras 228–237; *Flughafen Zürich v Venezuela*, Award, 18 November 2014, paras 238–258; *von Pezold v Zimbabwe*, Award, 28 July 2015, para 315.

[78] *Houben v Burundi*, Award, 12 January 2016, paras 127–130; *Devas v India*, Award on Jurisdiction and Merits, 25 July 2016, paras 199–210; *Adamakopoulos v Cyprus*, Decision on Jurisdiction, 7 February 2020, para 300; *Gosling v Mauritius*, Award, 18 February 2020, paras 130–135, 144–146, 166(i).

[79] *Joy Mining v Egypt*, Award on Jurisdiction, 6 August 2004, paras 55, 58; *Phoenix v Czech Republic*, Award, 15 April 2009, para 82; *Malaysian Historical Salvors v Malaysia*, Decision on Annulment, 16 April 2009, para 69; *Pantechniki v Albania*, Award, 30 July 2009, para 44; *Romak v Uzbekistan*, Award, 26 November 2009, para 211; *Global Trading v Ukraine*, Award, 1 December 2010, para 56; *GEA v Ukraine*, Award, 31 March 2011, paras 148–153; *Elsamex v Honduras*, Award, 16 November 2012, paras 253–283; *Ambiente Ufficio v Argentina*, Decision on Jurisdiction and Admissibility, 8 February 2013, para 470; *Philip Morris v Uruguay*, Decision on Jurisdiction, 2 July 2013, para 203; *Niko Resources v Bangladesh*, Decision on Jurisdiction, 19 August 2013, paras 358–359; *Nova Scotia Power v Venezuela*, Award, 30 April 2014, para 113; *Tenaris v Venezuela I*, Award, 29 January 2016, para 291; *Caratube and Hourani v Kazakhstan*, Award, 27 September 2017, para 635.

[80] See IV.2(c) above.

[81] See III.4 above and XII.6(c) below.

is not limited to majority or controlling shareholding but also covers minority shareholding.[82] The protection may extend to indirect shareholding and to the assets of the company whose shares the investor holds.[83]

(d) Financial instruments

Many cases involve financial instruments such as loans, bonds, treasury bills, and promissory notes. The funds may be put at the disposal of the host State or of a private party.[84] The financial transactions may be for the purpose of a particular project[85] or for the State's general budget.[86] Although financial instruments are a recognized form of investment, some tribunals have found that contingent liabilities such as bank guarantees or options did not qualify as investments.[87] On the other hand, a hedging agreement between a foreign bank and a national petroleum company, which had the objective of protecting the company against the impact of rising oil prices, qualified as an investment.[88]

(e) Intellectual property rights

Intellectual property rights, such as patents, trademarks, and designs are routinely listed in definitions of the term investment. Their potential as investment is beyond doubt,[89] although they have until now generated only limited case law.[90]

[82] See IV.9(c) below.

[83] See IV.9(e) below.

[84] *Sempra v Argentina*, Award, 28 September 2007, paras 214–216; *OKO Pankki v Estonia*, Award, 19 November 2007, paras 179–180, 208; *Daimler v Argentina*, Award, 22 August 2012, para 83; *Tulip v Turkey*, Award, 10 March 2014, paras 202–203; *Tenaris v Venezuela I*, Award, 29 January 2016, para 289; *MNSS v Montenegro*, Award, 4 May 2016, paras 196, 201; *Adamakopoulos v Cyprus*, Decision on Jurisdiction, 7 February 2020, paras 291–304. But see *Poštová banka v Greece*, Award, 9 April 2015, paras 248–350, 361–365, 370.

[85] *CSOB v Slovakia*, Decision on Jurisdiction, 24 May 1999, paras 76–91; *CDC v Seychelles*, Award, 17 December 2003, paras 6, 8, 18, 19, 21; *Alpha v Ukraine*, Award, 8 November 2010, paras 273–274, 322–323; *Standard Chartered Bank (Hong Kong) v Tanzania*, Award, 11 October 2019, paras 220, 251.

[86] *Fedax v Venezuela*, Decision on Jurisdiction, 11 July 1997, paras 18–43; *African Holding v DR Congo*, Award, 29 July 2008, paras 74–84; *Abaclat v Argentina*, Decision on Jurisdiction, 4 August 2011, paras 362–367; *Ambiente Ufficio v Argentina*, Decision on Jurisdiction and Admissibility, 8 February 2013, paras 441–471; *Alemanni v Argentina*, Decision on Jurisdiction and Admissibility, 17 November 2014, para 296.

[87] *PSEG v Turkey*, Decision on Jurisdiction, 4 June 2004, para 189; *Joy Mining v Egypt*, Award on Jurisdiction, 6 August 2004, paras 42–63, 78; *White Industries v India*, Final Award, 30 November 2011, paras 7.5.1–7.5.7, 12.2.1; *Deutsche Bank v Sri Lanka*, Award, 31 October 2012, paras 171–174, 245–246, 311; *Bosca v Lithuania*, Award, 17 May 2013, para 169; *ST-AD v Bulgaria*, Award on Jurisdiction, 18 July 2013, para 273.

[88] *Deutsche Bank v Sri Lanka*, Award, 31 October 2012, paras 283–312.

[89] S Klopschinski et al, *The Protection of Intellectual Property Rights under International Investment Law* (2021).

[90] *Philip Morris v Uruguay*, Award, 8 July 2016, paras 235–271; *Bridgestone v Panama*, Decision on Expedited Objections, 13 December 2017, paras 159–222.

(f) Arbitral awards

In some cases, tribunals found that claims arising from the non-performance of commercial arbitration awards gave rise to protected rights. They classified the awards either as investments or as reflecting rights arising from the investments.[91] In one case, the tribunal found that the right to arbitration amounted to a protected investment.[92]

5. The unity of an investment

Many investments are complex operations. They may consist of preparatory studies, licences, government permits, financing arrangements, real estate transactions, various contractual arrangements, and a variety of other legal dispositions. Each of these elements has its own legal existence but in economic terms they are united to serve a common purpose. Typically, investment tribunals have treated the various assets and activities that make up an investment as a unity. In most cases they have not dissected investments into their individual legal components but have treated them as an integral whole. In doing so, they have given precedence to economic realism over legal formalism.[93]

When determining the existence of an investment, tribunals have looked at a combination of elements that collectively made up the investment. In *Mytilineos v Serbia & Montenegro*,[94] the claimant had entered into a series of agreements with a 'socially owned company' under the law of Yugoslavia. The Respondent argued that there was no investment since these were ordinary commercial contracts. The Tribunal found that, in combination, the contracts amounted to an investment. It said:

> Even if one doubted whether the Agreements looked at in isolation would constitute investments by themselves, is seems clear that the combined effect of these agreements amounts to an investment... the combined effect of the Agreements is clearly more than an ordinary commercial transaction.[95]

[91] *Romak v Uzbekistan*, Award, 26 November 2009, para 211; *Saipem v Bangladesh*, Decision on Jurisdiction, 21 March 2007, paras 113–114, 127; *Frontier Petroleum v Czech Republic*, Final Award, 12 November 2010, para 231; *GEA v Ukraine*, Award, 31 March 2011, paras 144, 158–164, 227–237; *White Industries v India*, Final Award, 30 November 2011, paras 7.6.1–7.6.10; *Gavazzi v Romania*, Decision on Jurisdiction, Admissibility and Liability, 21 April 2015, paras 118–120; *Anglia Auto v Czech Republic*, Final Award, 10 March 2017, paras 151–154.

[92] *ATA v Jordan*, Award, 18 May 2010, paras 110–120.

[93] C Schreuer, 'The Unity of an Investment' (2021) 19 *ICSID Reports* 3.

[94] *Mytilineos v Serbia & Montenegro*, Partial Award on Jurisdiction, 8 September 2006.

[95] At paras 120, 125.

Other tribunals too found that several contracts had to be viewed in combination to establish the existence of an investment.[96]

Some cases involved a variety of assets and activities that combined to form an investment.[97] *Saipem v Bangladesh*[98] concerned the construction of a pipeline governed by a contract, retention money, warranty bonds as well as an ICC Arbitration Award in claimant's favour that had been nullified by the Respondent's Supreme Court. The Tribunal looked at the entire operation to establish the existence of an investment:

> [T]he Tribunal wishes to emphasize that for the purpose of determining whether there is an investment under Article 25 of the ICSID Convention, it will consider the entire operation. In the present case, the entire or overall operation includes the Contract, the construction itself, the Retention Money, the warranty and the related ICC Arbitration.[99]

Tribunals have also extended the protection of investments to assets and activities that were ancillary or incidental to the investment's core activity. In *Holiday Inns v Morocco*,[100] the agreement for the establishment and operation of hotels, providing for ICSID jurisdiction, had also foreseen financing by the government. The Respondent objected to the jurisdiction of ICSID over the separate loan contracts. The Tribunal emphasized the general unity of an investment operation to assert its jurisdiction also over the loan contracts. The Tribunal said:

> It is well known, and it is being particularly shown in the present case, that investment is accomplished by a number of juridical acts of all sorts. It would not be consonant either with economic reality or with the intention of the parties to consider each of these acts in complete isolation from the others. It is particularly important to ascertain which is the act which is the basis of the investment and which entails as measures of execution the other acts which have been concluded in order to carry it out.[101]

96 *ADC v Hungary*, Award, 2 October 2006, paras 325, 331; *Inmaris Perestroika v Ukraine*, Decision on Jurisdiction, 8 March 2010, para 92; *Arif v Moldova*, Award, 8 April 2013, para 367; *İçkale v Turkmenistan*, Award, 8 March 2016, para 293.

97 *OKO Pankki v Estonia*, Award, 19 November 2007, para 208; *White Industries v India*, Final Award, 30 November 2011, paras 7.4.19, 7.5.1, 7.6.8–7.6.10; *Electrabel v Hungary*, Decision on Jurisdiction, Applicable Law and Liability, 30 November 2012, para 5.44; *Ambiente Ufficio v Argentina*, Decision on Jurisdiction and Admissibility, 8 February 2013, paras 429, 432–434, 486; *A11Y v Czech Republic*, Award, 29 June 2018, para 107; *Unión Fenosa v Egypt*, Award, 31 August 2018, paras 6.66–6.68; *ICS v Argentina II*, Award on Jurisdiction, 8 July 2019, para 293. See also: *Joy Mining v Egypt*, Award on Jurisdiction, 6 August 2004, paras 42, 44–45, 47, 54; *Mitchell v DR Congo*, Award, 9 February 2004, para 55 and Decision on Annulment, 1 November 2006, paras 38–41; *Bear Creek v Peru*, Award, 30 November 2017, para 296.

98 *Saipem v Bangladesh*, Decision on Jurisdiction, 21 March 2007.

99 At para 110. Footnote omitted.

100 *Holiday Inns v Morocco*, Decision on Jurisdiction of 12 May 1974, 1 ICSID Reports 645.

101 At 680.

Other tribunals too have accepted that loan agreements were part of the overall investment they were designed to serve.[102] They applied the doctrine of the unity of the investment also to other activities incidental to the investment.[103]

In some cases, the unity of the investment led tribunals to conclude that consent to arbitration contained in some investment-related documents extended to legal relationships governed by other documents.[104]

The unity of the investment has also played a role in determining whether the investment had taken place in the host State's territory.[105] With respect to financial instruments they found that what mattered was the economic effect of the investment that was felt in the host State's territory.[106] Where the investment consisted of pre-shipment inspections, tribunals found that the services provided abroad were inseparable from the activity in the host State.[107]

In some cases, tribunals used the concept of the unity of the investment to extend the consequences of an illegality[108] to the entire investment. An illegality that tainted one aspect of the investment's formation had the consequence of withdrawing protection from the entire investment.[109]

In some cases, tribunals relied on the unity of the investment to determine whether an alleged expropriation had indeed amounted to a substantial deprivation.[110] They examined the impact of expropriatory measures on the investment as a whole and not upon its component parts.[111] On the other hand, some tribunals

[102] *CSOB v Slovakia*, Decision on Jurisdiction, 24 May 1999, para 72, but see Decision on Further and Partial Objection to Jurisdiction, 1 December 2000, paras 26–32; *Alpha v Ukraine*, Award, 8 November 2010, paras 272–273; *Tulip v Turkey*, Award, 10 March 2014, para 202; *MNSS v Montenegro*, Award, 4 May 2016, paras 201–202; *Tenaris v Venezuela I*, Award, 29 January 2016, para 289.

[103] *SOABI v Senegal*, Award, 25 February 1988, paras 8.01–8.23; *Enron v Argentina*, Decision on Jurisdiction, 14 January 2004, para 70; *H&H v Egypt*, Decision on Jurisdiction, 5 June 2012, para 42; *Niko Resources v Bangladesh*, Decision on Jurisdiction, 19 August 2013, paras 361, 371; *Mamidoil v Albania*, Award, 30 March 2015, para 288; *Magyar Farming v Hungary*, Award, 13 November 2019, paras 274–276.

[104] *Duke Energy v Peru*, Decision on Jurisdiction, 1 February 2006, paras 80–82, 89, 90, 92(2), 100, 102, 119–31; *Cambodia Power v Cambodia*, Decision on Jurisdiction, 22 March 2011, para 141.

[105] See IV.7 below.

[106] *Ambiente Ufficio v Argentina*, Decision on Jurisdiction and Admissibility, 8 February 2013, paras 500, 508.

[107] *SGS v Philippines*, Decision on Jurisdiction, 29 January 2004, paras 102, 112; *BIVAC v Paraguay*, Decision on Jurisdiction, 29 May 2009, para 103; *SGS v Paraguay*, Decision on Jurisdiction, 12 February 2010, paras 113, 115.

[108] See IV.8 below.

[109] *Fraport v Philippines I*, Award, 16 August 2007, paras 396–404 and Decision on Annulment, 23 December 2010, para 113; *Mamidoil v Albania*, Award, 30 March 2015, paras 366–367.

[110] See VII.3(c) below.

[111] *Feldman v Mexico*, Award, 16 December 2002, para 152; *Telenor v Hungary*, Award, 13 September 2006, paras 61–62, 65, 67, 79; *Merrill & Ring v Canada*, Award, 31 March 2010, para 144; *Grand River v United States*, Award, 12 January 2011, paras 155, 154; *Burlington v Ecuador*, Decision on Liability, 14 December 2012, paras 257, 260, 398, 470 530; *Electrabel v Hungary*, Decision on Jurisdiction, Applicable Law and Liability, 30 November 2012, para 6.58; *Philip Morris v Uruguay*, Award, 8 July 2016, para 283.

have recognized the possibility of partial expropriations[112] by looking at individual elements of investments to determine whether they had been expropriated.[113]

6. The origin of the investment

Only foreign investments are protected by international investment law. In some cases, respondents have argued that there was no foreign investment in the absence of fresh capital imported into the country because the investor had raised capital locally. A similar argument was that the investor had not used its own funds but had relied on funding from a third party.

The decisive criterion for the foreignness of an investment is the nationality of the investor. An investment is foreign if it is owned or controlled by a foreign investor. There is no additional requirement of foreignness for the investment in terms of the origin of capital.

The host State may impose the requirement that a certain amount of fresh capital in foreign currency must be imported into the country.[114] In the absence of such a requirement, investments made by foreign investors with local funds are to be treated in the same way as investments funded with imported capital.

Moreover, the benefits of foreign investments accrue to host States not merely through a transfer of capital. Know-how, technology, business experience, entrepreneurship, and intellectual property are non-monetary assets that are essential to investments and serve the local economy.

Tribunals have held consistently that the origin of the capital that goes into an investment is irrelevant for the investment's international nature.[115] In *Tokios*

[112] See VII.1(b) below.

[113] *Middle East Cement v Egypt*, Award, 12 April 2002, paras 107, 127, 138, 144, 163, 165; *Waste Management v Mexico II*, Award, 30 April 2004, paras 141, 175; *Eureko v Poland*, Partial Award, 19 August 2005, paras 239–241.

[114] *Amco v Indonesia*, Award, 20 November 1984, 1 ICSID Reports 413, 481–489.

[115] *Tradex v Albania*, Award, 29 April 1999, paras 105, 108–111; *Wena Hotels v Egypt*, Award, 8 December 2000, para 126 and Decision on Annulment, 28 January 2002, para 54; *Olguín v Paraguay*, Award, 26 July 2001, para 66, fn 9; *ADC v Hungary*, Award, 2 October 2006, paras 310–325, 342, 343, 346, 347, 355, 356, 358, 360; *Siag v Egypt*, Decision on Jurisdiction, 11 April 2007, paras 37–40, 62–66, 86, 100, 110, 122, 208–210; *Rompetrol v Romania*, Decision on Jurisdiction and Admissibility, 18 April 2008, paras 55–56, 71, 101, 110; *Yukos v Russian Federation*, Interim Award on Jurisdiction and Admissibility, 30 November 2009, paras 432–435; *Lemire v Ukraine*, Decision on Jurisdiction and Liability, 14 January 2010, paras 56–59; *Mobil v Venezuela*, Decision on Jurisdiction, 10 June 2010, para 198; *Paushok v Mongolia*, Award on Jurisdiction and Liability, 28 April 2011, para 205; *Caratube v Kazakhstan*, Award, 5 June 2012, para 355; *Arif v Moldova*, Award, 8 April 2013, para 383; *Urbaser v Argentina*, Decision on Jurisdiction, 19 December 2012, para 307; *OI European v Venezuela*, Award, 10 March 2015, para 242; *Gold Reserve v Venezuela*, Award, 22 September 2014, paras 261–262; *von Pezold v Zimbabwe*, Award, 28 July 2015, para 288; *RREEF v Spain*, Decision on Jurisdiction, 6 June 2016, para 158; *Eiser v Spain*, Award, 4 May 2017, para 228; *Masdar v Spain*, Award, 16 May 2018, paras 179–181, 190–191, 201–202; *A11Y v Czech Republic*, Award, 29 June 2018, paras 117–123, 137–142; *Gavrilovic v Croatia*, Award, 26 July 2018, paras 209, 216; *Cortec v Kenya*, Award, 22 October 2018, paras 269, 271; *Mera v Serbia*, Decision on Jurisdiction, 30 November 2018, para 170.

Tokelės v Ukraine,[116] the claimant had its registered seat in Lithuania. The respondent argued that there was no protected investment since the capital invested did not originate outside the Ukraine. The Tribunal's majority noted that neither the ICSID Convention nor the Ukraine–Lithuania BIT contained a requirement that capital used by a foreign investor should originate in its State of nationality or indeed originate outside the host State.[117] It rejected an 'origin-of-capital requirement' and said:

> The Respondent alleges that the Claimant has not proved that the capital used to invest in Ukraine originated from non-Ukrainian, sources, and, thus, the Claimant has not made a direct, or cross-border, investment. Even assuming, *arguendo*, that all of the capital used by the Claimant to invest in Ukraine had its ultimate origin in Ukraine, the resulting investment would not be outside the scope of the Convention. The Claimant made an investment for the purposes of the Convention when it decided to deploy capital under its control in the territory of Ukraine instead of investing it elsewhere. The origin of the capital is not relevant to the existence of an investment.[118]

In *Saipem v Bangladesh*, the claimant had entered into a contract to build a pipeline. The Respondent disputed the existence of an investment on the ground that the claimant had not put its own money into the project.[119] The Tribunal rejected this argument and said:

> it is true that the host State may impose a requirement that an amount of capital in foreign currency be imported into the country. However, in the absence of such a requirement, investments made by foreign investors from local funds or from loans raised in the host State are treated in the same manner as investments funded with imported capital. In other words, the origin of the funds is irrelevant.[120]

Therefore, unless specifically provided, the origin of the funds is irrelevant. Whether the investments were made from imported capital, from the investor's local funds, or from funds raised locally makes no difference. The decisive criterion for the existence of a foreign investment is the nationality of the investor.

[116] *Tokios Tokelės v Ukraine*, Decision on Jurisdiction, 29 April 2004.
[117] At paras 74–82.
[118] At para 80. But see also the reasoning to the contrary in the Dissenting Opinion by arbitrator Prosper Weil at paras 19, 20.
[119] *Saipem v Bangladesh*, Decision on Jurisdiction, 21 March 2007, para 103.
[120] At para 106. Footnote omitted.

An investment will be a foreign investment if it is owned or controlled by a foreign investor. There is no additional requirement of a foreign origin of the investment.

7. Investments in the host State's territory

Some treaties refer to investments 'in the territory' of the host State.[121] At times, respondents have argued that this requirement had not been met, since the would-be investor had not established a significant physical presence in the host State. The problem has arisen primarily in cases involving financial instruments, such as loans, and in cases involving pre-shipment inspection services.

(a) Financial instruments

In *Fedax v Venezuela* the investor had merely acquired promissory notes issued by the host country. The Tribunal rejected the respondent's argument that the claimant had not invested 'in the territory' of Venezuela:

> While it is true that in some kinds of investments ... such as the acquisition of interests in immovable property, companies and the like, a transfer of funds or value will be made into the territory of the host country, this does not necessarily happen in a number of types of investments, particularly those of a financial nature. It is a standard feature of many international financial transactions that the funds involved are not physically transferred to the territory of the beneficiary, but are put at its disposal elsewhere.[122]

In a similar way, tribunals found that the acquisition of government bonds met the territorial nexus requirement. *Abaclat v Argentina*,[123] concerned Argentinean government bonds held by Italian investors. The BIT between Argentina and Italy requires that the investment had to be made 'nel territorio dell'altra'. The Tribunal held that the requirement of territoriality had been met. The decisive element for purely financial investments was the place of the benefit. The Tribunal said:

[121] The ECT in Article 26(1) refers to investments 'in the Area' of a contracting party. NAFTA, Article 1101(1) speaks of 'investments in the territory'. The USMCA, Article 14.1 speaks of 'an investment in its territory'. The Argentina–United States BIT (1991) in Article I(1)(a) refers to 'every kind of investment in the territory'.

[122] *Fedax v Venezuela*, Decision on Jurisdiction, 11 July 1997, para 41. To the same effect: *CSOB v Slovakia*, Decision on Jurisdiction, 24 May 1999, paras 77, 78; *LESI & ASTALDI v Algeria*, Decision on Jurisdiction, 12 July 2006, para 73(i); *Renta 4 v Russian Federation*, Award on Preliminary Objections, 20 March 2009, para 144.

[123] *Abaclat v Argentina*, Decision on Jurisdiction and Admissibility, 4 August 2011.

> the determination of the place of the investment firstly depends on the nature of such investment. With regard to an investment of a purely financial nature, the relevant criteria cannot be the same as those applying to an investment consisting of business operations and/or involving manpower and property. With regard to investments of a purely financial nature, the relevant criteria should be where and/or for the benefit of whom the funds are ultimately used, and not the place where the funds were paid out or transferred.[124]

In other cases too, tribunals found that payments that had taken place outside the host State were sufficiently connected to its territory since they were made to its benefit.[125]

(b) Pre-shipment inspections

Some cases involved pre-shipment inspection services. These services are performed primarily in the country of origin of goods while information about cargo destined for the host country is transmitted there. Also in these cases, tribunals have found that the territorial nexus required by the applicable treaties was satisfied. This was so either in view of the investor's expenditures in the host State,[126] because a substantial and non-severable portion of the overall service was provided in the host State,[127] or in view of a local subsidiary and liaison office.[128]

These cases indicate that where the relevant treaty refers to investments in the territory of the host State, the performance of the relevant activities need not take place in the territory of the host State, at least not in its entirety. Neither is a physical transfer of assets into the host State's territory necessary. What matters is that the economic effect of the investment is felt in the host State's territory.

[124] At para 374. See also *Ambiente Ufficio v Argentina*, Decision on Jurisdiction and Admissibility, 8 February 2013, paras 328, 374–377, 404–409, 496–510.

[125] *Inmaris Perestroika v Ukraine*, Decision on Jurisdiction, 8 March 2010, paras 113–125; *Alpha v Ukraine*, Award, 8 November 2010, paras 275–285; *Deutsche Bank v Sri Lanka*, Award, 31 October 2012, paras 136–143, 221–229, 287–292; *Gold Reserve v Venezuela*, Award, 22 September 2014, paras 261–262; *Orascom v Algeria*, Award, 31 May 2017, para 382; *Adamakopoulos v Cyprus*, Decision on Jurisdiction, 7 February 2020, paras 300, 302–304.

[126] *SGS v Pakistan*, Decision on Jurisdiction, 6 August 2003, paras 46, 136.

[127] *SGS v Philippines*, Decision on Jurisdiction, 29 January 2004, paras 57, 70, 80–82, 89, 99–112; *SGS v Paraguay*, Decision on Jurisdiction, 12 February 2010, paras 109–117.

[128] *BIVAC v Paraguay*, Decision on Jurisdiction, 29 May 2009, paras 97–104. See also *Karkey v Pakistan*, Award, 22 August 2017, para 635.

(c) Transboundary harm

In some cases, tribunals dealt with claims for transboundary harm to investments located in the investors' home States. In *Canadian Cattlemen v United States*,[129] Canadian farmers claimed against the United States for alleged discrimination against their products in the US market. The Tribunal dismissed the claims ruling that the NAFTA protected only investments made in the territory of another State.[130]

In *Bayview v Mexico*,[131] the claimants, US nationals located in Texas, claimed for violation of their water rights by Mexico as a consequence of the diversion of water from a river. The Tribunal dismissed the claims finding that NAFTA only covers investments made by a national of one party in the territory of another NAFTA party. Here, the investment had been made by US citizens on the territory of the United States.[132]

8. Investment in accordance with host State law

In some cases, investment tribunals denied protection because the investment or the claimant's conduct in making it was illegal either under domestic law or under international legal rules or principles.[133] Most tribunals do not consider the legality of an investment as forming part of the notion of investment in the sense of Article 25(1) of the ICSID Convention.[134]

[129] *Canadian Cattlemen v United States*, Award on Jurisdiction, 28 January 2008.

[130] At para 111. See also *Grand River v United States*, Award, 12 January 2011, paras 87–89.

[131] *Bayview v Mexico*, Award, 19 June 2007.

[132] At para 113.

[133] For further discussion, see C Knahr, 'Investments "in Accordance with Host State Law"' in A Reinisch and C Knahr (eds) *International Investment Law in Context* (2008) 27; A Carlevaris, 'The Conformity of Investments with the Law of the Host State and the Jurisdiction of International Tribunals' (2008) 9 *JWIT* 35; U Kriebaum, 'Illegal Investments' (2010) 4 *Austrian YB Int'l Arb* 307; A Newcombe, 'Investor Misconduct: Jurisdiction, Admissibility, or Merits?' in C Brown and K Miles (eds) *Evolution in Investment Treaty Law and Arbitration* (2011) 187; SW Schill, 'Illegal Investments in Investment Treaty Arbitration' (2012) 11 *LPICT* 281; Z Douglas, 'The Plea of Illegality in Investment Treaty Arbitration' (2014) *ICSID Rev* 155; J Hepburn, 'In Accordance with *Which* Host State Laws?' (2014) 5 *JIDS* 531; T Obersteiner, '"In Accordance with Domestic Law" Clauses' (2014) 31 *J Int Arb* 265; K Diel-Gligor and R Hennecke, 'Investment in Accordance with the Law' in M Bungenberg et al (eds) *International Investment Law* (2015) 566; M Polckinghorne and S-M Volkmer, 'The Legality Requirement in Investment Arbitration' (2017) 34 *J Int Arb* 149; K Betz, *Proving Bribery, Fraud and Money Laundering in International Arbitration* (2017); AP Llamzon, *Corruption in International Investment Arbitration*, 2nd edn (2021).

[134] But see *Phoenix v Czech Republic*, Award, 15 April 2009, paras 100–116.

(a) Illegality in contract-based disputes

In contract-based disputes, tribunals have dealt with illegalities of investments at the merits stage and did not treat them as a matter of jurisdiction.[135] In *World Duty Free v Kenya*,[136] the Tribunal found that acts of bribery during the negotiation of the contract prevented the claimant from complaining about violations of the contract by the respondent State. It held that bribery was contrary to the international public order of most States and the applicable national laws and regulations. Therefore, it held that the contract was void. The Tribunal said:

> In light of domestic laws and international conventions relating to corruption, and in light of the decisions taken in this matter by courts and arbitral tribunals, this Tribunal is convinced that bribery is contrary to the international public policy of most, if not all, States or, to use another formula, to transnational public policy. Thus, claims based on contracts of corruption or on contracts obtained by corruption cannot be upheld by this Arbitral Tribunal.[137]

(b) Illegality in disputes based on domestic legislation

Some domestic laws regulating foreign investments condition protection, including access to arbitration, on the fulfilment of certain requirements. For instance, the Law on Foreign investments of Albania of 1993 imposes several conditions, including the prohibition to borrow money or take loans of any kind. In *Anglo-Adriatic v Albania*,[138] the claimant claimed a loan as part of its investment. The Tribunal held that the loan would not qualify as a protected investment since it had been made in breach of Albanian law. An illegal investment fell outside Albania's consent to arbitrate.[139]

(c) Illegality in treaty-based disputes

In treaty-based arbitrations, illegalities in the making of an investment can either have jurisdictional consequences or can deprive an investor of the substantive protection of the investment.

[135] *Niko Resources v Bangladesh*, Decision on Jurisdiction, 19 August 2013, paras 423–485 and Decision on the Corruption Claim, 25 February 2019, paras 568–597.
[136] *World Duty Free v Kenya*, Award, 4 October 2006.
[137] At para 157.
[138] *Anglo-Adriatic v Albania*, Award, 7 February 2019.
[139] At paras 281–296.

BITs frequently include the formula 'investments made in accordance with host State law' or similar formulae in their definitions of the term 'investment'.[140] In the presence of such a formula, an illegality in the making of the investment means that there is no investment for purposes of the BIT and consequently no consent to arbitrate.[141] The words 'in accordance with the laws ... ' relate to the laws on admission and establishment[142] and also to other rules of the domestic legal order, including those relating to corruption.[143] As a result, investments made in violation of domestic rules may be outside the protection of the relevant treaty, depending upon the nature and gravity of the violation.

Some host States have argued that the formula referring to host State law meant that the concept of 'investment', and hence the reach of protection under the treaty, had to be determined by reference to their own domestic law. Tribunals have rejected this approach. They have held that a reference to the host State's domestic law concerns not the definition of the term 'investment' but solely the legality of the investment.[144] The Tribunal in *Salini v Morocco*[145] stated in this respect:

> This provision [the required compliance with the laws and regulations of the host State] refers to the validity of the investment and not to its definition. More specifically, it seeks to prevent the Bilateral Treaty from protecting investments that should not be protected because they would be illegal.[146]

In *Fraport v Philippines*,[147] the Tribunal applied the BIT between Germany and the Philippines, which defines 'investment' as assets 'accepted in accordance with the respective laws and regulations of either Contracting State'. Furthermore,

140 According to the UNCTAD Investment Policy Hub, 1,647 out of 2,575 mapped treaties (BITs and treaties with investment chapters), that is 63 per cent of these treaties, contain an 'in accordance with host state laws' requirement.

141 *Fakes v Turkey*, Award, 14 July 2010, paras 115, 120, 121; *Fraport v Philippines II*, Award, 10 December 2014, para 467.

142 *PSEG v Turkey*, Decision on Jurisdiction, 4 June 2004, paras 109, 116–20; *Yaung Chi Oo v Myanmar*, Award, 31 March 2003, paras 53–62.

143 *Ampal-American v Egypt*, Decision on Jurisdiction, 1 February 2016, paras 301–311.

144 *Tokios Tokelės v Ukraine*, Decision on Jurisdiction, 29 April 2004, paras 83–86; *LESI-DIPENTA v Algeria*, Award, 10 January 2005, para 24(iii); *Plama v Bulgaria*, Decision on Jurisdiction, 8 February 2005, paras 126–31; *Gas Natural v Argentina*, Decision on Jurisdiction, 17 June 2005, paras 33, 34; *Aguas del Tunari v Bolivia*, Decision on Jurisdiction, 21 October 2005, paras 139–155; *Bayindir v Pakistan*, Decision on Jurisdiction, 14 November 2005, paras 105–10; *Saluka v Czech Republic*, Partial Award, 17 March 2006, paras 183, 202–21; *Inceysa v El Salvador*, Award, 2 August 2006, paras 190–207; *Saipem v Bangladesh*, Decision on Jurisdiction, 21 March 2007, paras 79–82, 120–124; *SGS v Paraguay*, Decision on Jurisdiction, 12 February 2010, paras 118–123; *Railroad Development v Guatemala*, Second Decision on Objections to Jurisdiction, 18 May 2010, para 140; *Convial Callao v Peru*, Final Award, 21 May 2013, paras 382–390.

145 *Salini v Morocco*, Decision on Jurisdiction, 16 July 2001.

146 At para 46.

147 *Fraport v Philippines I*, Award, 16 August 2007.

the treaty's provision on admission refers to 'investments in accordance with its Constitution, laws and regulations'.

Legislation in the Philippines contained restrictions on shareholding and management by foreigners in public utility enterprises. The Tribunal found that Fraport had circumvented this legislation by way of secret shareholder agreements. The Tribunal decided that, in view of the investor's conscious violation of the host State's law, it had no jurisdiction:

> Fraport knowingly and intentionally circumvented the ADL [ie domestic legislation] by means of secret shareholder agreements. As a consequence, it cannot claim to have made an investment 'in accordance with law'. Nor can it claim that high officials of the Respondent subsequently waived the legal requirements and validated Fraport's investment, for the Respondent's officials could not have known of the violation. Because there is no 'investment in accordance with law', the Tribunal lacks jurisdiction *ratione materiae*.[148]

The *Fraport* Award was annulled on the ground that the right to be heard had not been observed properly.[149] The Tribunal in the resubmitted case also found that it had no jurisdiction because of a lack of consent triggered by the illegality in the making of the investment. It stated:

> The illegality of the investment at the time it is made goes to the root of the host State's offer of arbitration under the treaty. As it has been held, '*States cannot be deemed to offer access to the ICSID dispute settlement mechanism to investments made in violation of their own law*'. Lack of jurisdiction is founded in this case on the absence of consent to arbitration by the State for failure to satisfy an essential condition of its offer of this method of dispute settlement.[150]

Sometimes, the requirement of compliance of the investment with domestic laws is not part of the definition of 'investment' but found in other parts of the treaty. This was the case in *Inceysa v El Salvador*.[151] The Tribunal had to apply the BIT between Spain and El Salvador, which did not refer to compliance with national laws in the definition of investment but within the provisions on admission and protection.

The Tribunal found that the claimant had presented false information in the bidding process that led to the award of the concession. The Tribunal referred to the principle of good faith, to international public policy, and to the rule that no one should benefit from his own wrongdoing. The Tribunal decided that El Salvador

[148] At para 401.
[149] *Fraport v Philippines I*, Decision on Annulment, 23 December 2010.
[150] *Fraport v Philippines II*, Award, 10 December 2014, para 467. Footnotes omitted. Italics original.
[151] *Inceysa v El Salvador*, Award, 2 August 2006.

had given its consent to ICSID jurisdiction on the condition that the claimant would act in accordance with the law:

> In conclusion, the Tribunal considers that, because Inceysa's investment was made in a manner that was clearly illegal, it is not included within the scope of consent expressed by Spain and the Republic of El Salvador in the BIT and, consequently, the disputes arising from it are not subject to the jurisdiction of the Centre. Therefore, this Arbitral Tribunal declares itself incompetent to hear the dispute brought before it.[152]

The Tribunal found that these considerations applied not just to the consent given under a treaty but also to the jurisdictional rules contained in domestic legislation.[153]

Even without an explicit reference to the host State's law in the governing treaty, an illegality on the part of the investor may deprive the tribunal of jurisdiction[154] or will deprive the investor of its substantive rights. In *Plama v Bulgaria*,[155] the claimant had misrepresented his resources and managerial capacities to the host State.[156] Although the ECT does not contain a clause requiring conformity with the laws of the host State, the Tribunal found that the claimant's conduct amounted to deliberate concealment and to fraud and that claimant could not invoke the ECT's substantive rights. The Tribunal pointed to the rule of law as a fundamental aim of the ECT and to the principle of good faith emanating from Bulgarian law and international law.[157]

(d) Illegality in making the investment

Tribunals have held in numerous cases that the legality requirement refers to the making of the investment. This means that the investment must be legal at its inception. The standard of legality does not relate to its conduct and management once it has been made.[158] In other words, an incidental violation of host State law

[152] At para 257.
[153] At para 258.
[154] *SAUR v Argentina*, Decision on Jurisdiction and Liability, 6 June 2012, paras 304–312; *Achmea v Slovak Republic*, Final Award, 7 December 2012, para 170. But see *Bear Creek v Peru*, Award, 30 November 2017, paras 320–324.
[155] *Plama v Bulgaria*, Award, 27 August 2008.
[156] At para 133.
[157] At paras 140–146.
[158] *Fraport v Philippines I*, Award, 16 August 2007, para 345; *Fraport v Philippines II*, Award, 10 December 2014, paras 331, 333; *Oostergetel v Slovak Republic*, Decision on Jurisdiction, 30 April 2010, paras 175–176, 183; *Fakes v Turkey*, Award, 14 July 2010, paras 115, 117, 119; *Khan Resources v Mongolia*, Decision on Jurisdiction, 25 July 2012, paras 381–385; *Quiborax v Bolivia*, Decision on Jurisdiction, 27 September 2012, paras 255, 266 and Award, 16 September 2015, para 129; *Urbaser v Argentina*, Decision on Jurisdiction, 19 December 2012, para 260; *Vannessa v Venezuela*, Award, 16

during the investment's lifetime will not lead to the withdrawal of protection under the BIT but may become relevant at the merits stage of the proceedings.

In *Hamester v Ghana*,[159] the Germany–Ghana BIT contained an express requirement of compliance with host State legislation.[160] The Tribunal held that an investment will not be protected if it has been created in violation of the national or international principles of good faith or of the host State's law, independently of the language of the BIT.[161] However, the jurisdictional consequences of that provision were limited to illegalities committed in the investment's making:

> The Tribunal considers that a distinction has to be drawn between (1) legality as at the *initiation* of the investment ('made') and (2) legality *during the performance* of the investment. Article 10 legislates for the scope of application of the BIT, but conditions this only by reference to legality at the initiation of the investment. Hence, only this issue bears upon this Tribunal's jurisdiction. Legality in the subsequent life or performance of the investment is not addressed in Article 10. It follows that this does not bear upon the scope of application of the BIT (and hence this Tribunal's jurisdiction)—albeit that it may well be relevant in the context of the substantive merits of a claim brought under the BIT. Thus, on the wording of this BIT, the legality of the creation of the investment is a jurisdictional issue; the legality of the investor's conduct during the life of the investment is a merits issue.[162]

Therefore, the principle of legality is relevant at the stage of the making of the investment but not at the subsequent stage of the investment's operation.

(e) The nature of the violated rules

Some tribunals have examined the rules allegedly violated by the investor. They found that the consequence of withdrawing legal protection from investments would be justified only if certain types of domestic legal rules were affected. This would be the case if the rules were specifically directed at the regulation of investments.[163] A violation of domestic rules of general application, such as tax legislation, will not make the investment illegal.

January 2013, para 167; *Metal-Tech v Uzbekistan*, Award, 4 October 2013, para 193; *Yukos v Russian Federation*, Final Award, 18 July 2014, paras 1349, 1354–1355; *von Pezold v Zimbabwe*, Award, 28 July 2015, para 420; *Oxus Gold v Uzbekistan*, Final Award, 17 December 2015, paras 706–710; *Kim v Uzbekistan*, Decision on Jurisdiction, 8 March 2017, paras 374, 377, 410.

159 *Hamester v Ghana*, Award, 18 June 2010.

160 At para 126.

161 At paras 123–124.

162 At para 127. Italics original.

163 *Achmea v Slovak Republic*, Final Award, 7 December 2012, para 172–173.

In *Fakes v Turkey*[164] the Tribunal drew a distinction between rules specifically directed at the regulation of investments and unrelated domestic rules. It said:

> the legality requirement contained therein concerns the question of the compliance with the host State's domestic laws governing the admission of investments in the host State... it would run counter to the object and purpose of investment protection treaties to deny substantive protection to those investments that would violate domestic laws that are unrelated to the very nature of investment regulation... unless specifically stated in the investment treaty under consideration, a host State should not be in a position to rely on its domestic legislation beyond the sphere of investment regime to escape its international undertakings vis-à-vis investments made in its territory.[165]

Another approach is to look at the fundamental nature of the affected rules of host State law.[166] In *Kim v Uzbekistan*,[167] the Tribunal found that the dominant tendency in practice was 'to state that the substantive scope of the legality requirement is limited to violations of fundamental laws of the Host State'.[168] On that basis, the Tribunal introduced a proportionality test to ascertain the significance of the obligation for the host State and the seriousness of the investor's conduct.[169]

(f) Severity of the violation

Not every minor infraction of host State law leads to a denial of investment protection. Minor errors by the investor or a failure to observe bureaucratic formalities are irrelevant in this context.[170] For instance, a failure to register companies at the appropriate time was held to be inconsequential for the protection of the investment.[171]

[164] *Fakes v Turkey*, Award, 14 July 2010.

[165] At para 119.

[166] *Desert Line v Yemen*, Award, 6 February 2008, para 104; *Rumeli v Kazakhstan*, Award, 29 July 2008, paras 168, 319; *Hochtief v Argentina*, Decision on Liability, 29 December 2014, para 199.

[167] *Kim v Uzbekistan*, Decision on Jurisdiction, 8 March 2017.

[168] At para 384.

[169] At paras 405–409.

[170] *Mytilineos v Serbia and Montenegro*, Partial Award on Jurisdiction, 8 September 2006, paras 137–157; *Desert Line v Yemen*, Award, 6 February 2008, paras 104–106; *Rumeli v Kazakhstan*, Award, 29 July 2008, para 319; *Inmaris Perestroika v Ukraine*, Decision on Jurisdiction, 8 March 2010, paras 144–145; *Quiborax v Bolivia*, Decision on Jurisdiction, 27 September 2012, para 266; *Vannessa v Venezuela*, Award, 16 January 2013, para 167; *Hochtief v Argentina*, Decision on Liability, 29 December 2014, para 199; *Alpha v Ukraine*, Award, 8 November 2010, para 297; *Mamidoil v Albania*, Award, 30 March 2015, paras 479–483, 489, 494; *Kim v Uzbekistan*, Decision on Jurisdiction, 8 March 2017, paras 390, 394; *Krederi v Ukraine*, Award, 2 July 2018, paras 344–370; *Cortec v Kenya*, Award, 22 October 2018, para 320.

[171] *Metalpar v Argentina*, Decision on Jurisdiction, 27 April 2006, para 84.

In *Tokios Tokelės v Ukraine*,[172] the respondent State argued that the name under which the claimant had registered its local subsidiary did not correspond to a recognized legal form under Ukrainian law. Furthermore, it had identified errors in the documents provided by the investor, including the absence of necessary signatures or notarizations. The Tribunal decided that these irregularities did not affect the protection of the investment under the bilateral treaty.[173] Furthermore, the governmental authorities of the respondent had registered the claimant's subsidiary as a valid enterprise. In light of these findings, the Tribunal concluded:

> Even if we were able to confirm the Respondent's allegations, which would require a searching examination of minute details of administrative procedures in Ukrainian law, to exclude an investment on the basis of such minor errors would be inconsistent with the object and purpose of the Treaty. In our view, the Respondent's registration of each of the Claimant's investments indicates that the 'investment' in question was made in accordance with the laws and regulations of Ukraine.[174]

(g) Toleration of illegality by the host State

If the host State has knowingly tolerated any alleged irregularities or illegalities, it cannot subsequently argue that the investment has lost its protection under the treaty.[175] In *Desert Line v Yemen*,[176] the Tribunal emphasized that a host State that had tolerated a legal setting for a certain time is estopped from insisting, against the investor, that the situation was unlawful from the beginning.[177]

In *Railroad Development v Guatemala*,[178] the claimant had not acquired its investment in the railroad business in accordance with the provisions of local law. However, the government was aware of the situation and did not object for years.

[172] *Tokios Tokelės v Ukraine*, Decision on Jurisdiction, 29 April 2004.
[173] At para 85.
[174] At para 86.
[175] *Swembalt v Latvia*, Decision by the Court of Arbitration, 23 October 2000, paras 34, 35; *Tokios Tokelės v Ukraine*, Decision on Jurisdiction, 29 April 2004, para 86; *Kardassopoulos v Georgia*, Decision on Jurisdiction, 6 July 2007, para 192; *Fraport v Philippines I*, Award, 16 August 2007, para 346; *Achmea v Slovak Republic*, Final Award, 7 December 2012, para 176; *Arif v Moldova*, Award, 8 April 2013, paras 374–384; *Stati v Kazakhstan*, Award, 19 December 2013, para 812; *Mamidoil v Albania*, Award, 30 March 2015, paras 466–478, 490–491; *von Pezold v Zimbabwe*, Award, 28 July 2015, para 411; *Philip Morris v Australia*, Award on Jurisdiction and Admissibility, 17 December 2015, para 522; *Rusoro v Venezuela*, Award, 22 August 2016, para 309, 314, 498; *Karkey v Pakistan*, Award, 22 August 2017, paras 627–628; *Gavrilović v Croatia*, Award, 26 July 2018, para 396; *Glencore v Colombia*, Award, 27 August 2019, para 858; *Gosling v Mauritius*, Award, 18 February 2020, para 124.
[176] *Desert Line v Yemen*, Award, 6 February 2008.
[177] At paras 97–123.
[178] *Railroad Development v Guatemala*, Second Decision on Jurisdiction, 18 May 2010.

The Tribunal held that principles of fairness precluded the respondent from raising an objection to the Tribunal's jurisdiction.[179]

(h) Illegalities committed by the host State

Illegalities on the part of State organs will not play out against the investor[180] unless the investor triggered them by its own actions, like for example corruption. In *Kardassopoulos v Georgia*,[181] the host State argued that the Joint Venture Agreement with the claimant was void *ab initio* because the State entities that had signed it had acted *ultra vires*. The Tribunal found that the claim submitted was nevertheless protected under the BIT, primarily due to assurances given to the investor.[182]

A systematic and wilful failure of State organs to apply the host State's law to the investor's detriment, may amount to a violation of the fair and equitable treatment standard.[183]

9. Indirect investments

An indirect investment is an investment that the investor holds through one or more intermediate companies. Typically, the investor will hold shares in a company which, in turn, owns the investment. The Tribunal in *RREEF v Spain*[184] described an indirect investment in the following terms:

> The very concept of an indirect investor and an indirect investment contains within it the concept that there will be a chain of ownership and control that involve more than one entity. Otherwise, there could be no investment that is indirectly owned or controlled. The very concept of indirect ownership or control presupposes that there is interposed between a claimant that is an indirect owner or controller and the investment one or more other owners and controllers through which the claimant owns or controls the investment.[185]

[179] At paras 145–147.
[180] *Karkey v Pakistan*, Award, 22 August 2017, paras 624–628.
[181] *Kardassopoulos v Georgia*, Decision on Jurisdiction, 6 July 2007.
[182] At paras 171–194. See also *Inmaris Perestroika v Ukraine*, Decision on Jurisdiction, 8 March 2010, para 139; *Alpha v Ukraine*, Award, 8 November 2010, para 299. But see: *Anderson v Costa Rica*, Award, 19 May 2010, paras 28, 51–61.
[183] See VIII.1(g)ff below.
[184] *RREEF v Spain*, Decision on Jurisdiction, 6 June 2016.
[185] At para 142.

(a) Customary international law

Customary international law does not look favourably upon the protection of assets owned indirectly by way of an interposed company. In the *Barcelona Traction* case,[186] the International Court of Justice (ICJ) held that Belgium, the State of nationality of the majority shareholders of a company incorporated in Canada, was unable to exercise diplomatic protection against Spain for damage caused to the company. As the ICJ recognized, its judgment was of limited authority in the context of investment treaty arbitration. In an allusion to international investment law, the ICJ acknowledged that its decision was based on customary international law and that treaties may provide otherwise.[187]

In *Diallo v DR Congo*,[188] the ICJ held similarly that the State of nationality of the shareholder (Guinea) was unable to exercise diplomatic protection for damage sustained by the claimant's company against the State in which the company was incorporated (Democratic Republic of Congo). Again, the ICJ pointed out that its decision was based on customary international law. It noted that in contemporary international law the protection of shareholders is governed by bilateral and multilateral treaties and by contracts between States and foreign investors.[189]

Therefore, under customary international law, the State of nationality of shareholders is not entitled to exercise diplomatic protection. As pointed out by the ICJ, this rule does not apply in cases governed by a system of investment treaties. This fact has been noted by investment tribunals.[190] In *Teinver v Argentina*,[191] the Tribunal said:

> *Barcelona Traction* and *Diallo* do not solidify any general principle of international law on shareholder rights that should be applied to the present dispute. Indeed, the Court has taken pains in both *Barcelona Traction* and *Diallo* to distinguish these cases from the situation in which an investment treaty regime would apply.[192]

[186] *Barcelona Traction, Light and Power Co, Ltd (Belgium v Spain)*, Judgment, 5 February 1970, ICJ Reports (1970) 4.

[187] At paras 89–90.

[188] *Diallo case (Guinea v DR Congo)*, Judgment, 24 May 2007, ICJ Reports (2007) 582.

[189] At paras 88–90.

[190] *Telefónica v Argentina*, Decision on Jurisdiction, 25 May 2006, para 83; *Daimler v Argentina*, Award, 22 August 2012, para 90.

[191] *Teinver v Argentina*, Decision on Jurisdiction, 21 December 2012.

[192] At para 221. See also *Gosling v Mauritius*, Award, 18 February 2020, paras 138–139.

(b) Shareholding as a form of investment

Most investment treaties list shareholding or participation in companies as a form of investment that enjoys protection.[193] In this way, even if the affected company does not meet the nationality requirements under the relevant treaty there will be a remedy if the shareholder or controller does. Interest in assets by way of shareholding in or control over companies is referred to as indirect investment.

Respondent States have argued that an investment in assets through shareholding in an intermediary company would be an indirect investment that was outside the tribunals' jurisdiction.[194] Tribunals have consistently rejected this argument and have held that indirect investment through shareholding is a form of investment that was covered by the respective BITs.[195]

In *Genin v Estonia*,[196] the claimants, US nationals, were the principal shareholders of EIB, a financial institution incorporated under the law of Estonia. The BIT between Estonia and the United States in its definition of 'investment' includes 'a company or shares of stock or other interests in a company or interests in the assets thereof'. The Tribunal rejected the respondent's argument that the claim did not relate to an 'investment' as understood in the BIT:

> The term 'investment' as defined in Article I(a)(ii) of the BIT clearly embraces the investment of Claimants in EIB. The transaction at issue in the present case, namely the Claimants' ownership interest in EIB, is an investment in 'shares of

[193] See IV.2(c) above.

[194] For general discussion see SA Alexandrov, 'The "Baby Boom" of Treaty-based Arbitrations and the Jurisdiction of ICSID Tribunals: Shareholders as "Investors" and Jurisdiction *Ratione Temporis*' (2005) 4 *LPICT* 19; C Schreuer, 'Shareholder Protection in International Investment Law' in P-M Dupuy et al (eds) *Festschrift für Christian Tomuschat* (2006) 601; D Gaukrodger, 'Investment Treaties and Shareholder Claims: Analysis of Treaty Practice', OECD Working Papers on International Investment, 2014/03 (2014).

[195] *Vivendi v Argentina*, Resubmitted Case: Decision on Jurisdiction, 14 November 2005, paras 88–94 and Appendix 1 listing 18 cases to this effect. In addition, see: *IBM v Ecuador*, Decision on Jurisdiction and Competence, 22 December 2003, paras 44, 48; *Continental Casualty v Argentina*, Decision on Jurisdiction, 22 February 2006, paras 51–54, 76–89; *Suez and InterAguas v Argentina*, Decision on Jurisdiction, 16 May 2006, paras 46–51; *National Grid v Argentina*, Decision on Jurisdiction, 20 June 2006, para 165 and Award, 3 November 2008, para 126; *Pan American v Argentina*, Decision on Preliminary Objections, 27 July 2006, paras 209–222; *Suez and Vivendi v Argentina*, Decision on Jurisdiction, 3 August 2006, paras 46–51; *Telenor v Hungary*, Award, 13 September 2006, paras 19, 27, 60; *Parkerings v Lithuania*, Award, 11 September 2007, paras 250–254; *Yukos v Russian Federation*, Interim Award on Jurisdiction and Admissibility, 30 November 2009, paras 430–435; *Lemire v Ukraine*, Award, 28 March 2011, paras 34–39; *Paushok v Mongolia*, Award on Jurisdiction and Liability, 28 April 2011, para 202; *Meerapfel v Central African Republic*, Award, 12 May 2011, paras 195, 216–222; *Impregilo v Argentina*, Award, 21 June 2011, paras 110–40, 238–46, 271; *Achmea v Slovakia*, Final Award, 7 December 2012, paras 157–161; *Teco v Guatemala*, Award, 19 December 2013, paras 438–439; *Hochtief v Argentina*, Decision on Liability, 29 December 2014, paras 150–181, 302–307; *Awdi v Romania*, Award, 2 March 2015, para 194; *Busta v Czech Republic*, Final Award, 10 March 2017, para 191.

[196] *Genin v Estonia*, Award, 25 June 2001.

stock or other interests in a company' that was 'owned or controlled, directly or indirectly' by Claimants.[197]

(c) Minority shareholding

The acceptance of shareholding as a protected investment includes minority shareholding.[198] In *CMS v Argentina*,[199] the claimant owned 29.42 per cent of TGN, a company incorporated in Argentina. The definition of 'investment' in the Argentina–US BIT includes 'a company or shares of stock or other interests in a company or interests in the assets thereof'. Argentina argued that CMS, as a minority shareholder in TGN, could not claim for any indirect damage resulting from its participation in the Argentinian company.[200] The Tribunal rejected this argument.[201] It said:

> The Tribunal therefore finds no bar in current international law to the concept of allowing claims by shareholders independently from those of the corporation concerned, not even if those shareholders are minority or non-controlling shareholders.[202] ... There is indeed no requirement that an investment, in order to qualify, must necessarily be made by shareholders controlling a company or owning the majority of its shares.[203]

(d) Indirect shareholding

Tribunals have also accepted indirect shareholding, that is, shareholding by way of intermediate companies, as investments. In some of these cases, the definition of 'investments' in the applicable BITs contained references to direct or indirect

[197] At para 324.

[198] *LANCO v Argentina*, Decision on Jurisdiction, 8 December 1998, para 10; *Vivendi v Argentina*, Resubmitted Case: Decision on Jurisdiction, 14 November 2005, paras 88–90; *Enron v Argentina*, Decision on Jurisdiction, 14 January 2004, paras 39, 44, 49; *Enron v Argentina*, Decision on Jurisdiction (Ancillary Claim), 2 August 2004, paras 21, 22, 29, 39; *LG&E v Argentina*, Decision on Jurisdiction, 30 April 2004, paras 50–63; *Sempra v Argentina*, Decision on Jurisdiction, 11 May 2005, paras 92–94; *El Paso v Argentina*, Decision on Jurisdiction, 27 April 2006, para 138 and Award, 31 October 2011, paras 206–213; *Metalpar v Argentina*, Decision on Jurisdiction, 27 April 2006, para 68; *CMS v Argentina*, Decision on Annulment, 25 September 2007, paras 58–76; *Phoenix v Czech Republic*, Award, 15 April 2009, paras 121–123; *Walter Bau v Thailand*, Award, 1 July 2009, paras 12.31–12.32; *Hochtief v Argentina*, Decision on Jurisdiction, 24 October 2011, paras 112–119; *Levy v Peru*, Award, 26 February 2014, para 144; *Adamakopoulos v Cyprus*, Decision on Jurisdiction, 7 February 2020, paras 286–288.

[199] *CMS v Argentina*, Decision on Jurisdiction, 17 July 2003.

[200] At paras 36, 37.

[201] At paras 47–65.

[202] At para 48.

[203] At para 51. See also *CMS v Argentina*, Decision on Annulment, 25 September 2007, para 73.

investments.[204] In other cases the applicable BITs did not contain such references.[205] The existence or absence of references to direct or indirect investments does not appear to have made a decisive difference to the tribunals' decisions. Investments made by way of intermediate corporations were invariably accepted as investments covered by the respective BITs. The intermediate companies may be registered in the investor's home State, in the host State, or in a third State.

One form of indirect shareholding is an investment through a company registered in the investor's home State which is not itself a claimant.[206] This constellation has rarely led to difficulties.

Investments through companies established in the host State are common.[207] Many States require that foreign investments are made through locally established companies. In *Paushok v Mongolia*,[208] the claimant was the 100 per cent owner of GEM, a company incorporated in Mongolia. The respondent contested the existence of an investment. The Tribunal pointed out that the relevant BIT's definition of 'investment' included shares and said:

> Claimants' investment are the shares of GEM, a company incorporated under Mongolian law as required by that country in order to engage into the mining business and, through ownership of those shares, Claimants are entitled to make claims concerning alleged Treaty breaches resulting from actions affecting the assets of GEM.[209]

[204] *Azurix v Argentina*, Decision on Jurisdiction, 8 December 2003, paras 63–74; *Enron v Argentina*, Decision on Jurisdiction, 14 January 2004, paras 42–57 and Decision on Annulment, 30 July 2010, paras 115–127; *Waste Management v Mexico II*, Award, 30 April 2004, paras 77–85; *Camuzzi v Argentina*, Decision on Jurisdiction, 11 May 2005, para 32; *Noble Energy v Ecuador*, Decision on Jurisdiction, 5 March 2008, paras 70–83; *Société Générale v Dominican Republic*, Decision on Jurisdiction, 19 September 2008, paras 16, 51; *Arif v Moldova*, Award, 8 April 2013, para 379.

[205] *Siemens v Argentina*, Decision on Jurisdiction, 3 August 2004, paras 138–144; *Gas Natural v Argentina*, Decision on Jurisdiction, 17 June 2005, paras 32–35; *Kardassopoulos v Georgia*, Decision on Jurisdiction, 6 July 2007, paras 121–124; *Tza Yap Shum v Peru*, Decision on Jurisdiction, 19 June 2009, paras 80, 91–111; *Inmaris Perestroika v Ukraine*, Decision on Jurisdiction, 8 March 2010, paras 109–112; *Mobil v Venezuela*, Decision on Jurisdiction, 10 June 2010, paras 162–166; *CEMEX v Venezuela*, Decision on Jurisdiction, 30 December 2010, paras 141–158; *Urbaser v Argentina*, Decision on Jurisdiction, 19 December 2012, paras 235–254; *Teinver v Argentina*, Decision on Jurisdiction, 21 December 2012, paras 229–235; *Adamakopoulos v Cyprus*, Decision on Jurisdiction, 7 February 2020, paras 273–285.

[206] *Siemens v Argentina*, Decision on Jurisdiction, 3 August 2004, paras 123–134, 137, 142; *Berschader v Russian Federation*, Award, 21 April 2006, paras 47, 127, 138, 143; *Teinver v Argentina*, Decision on Jurisdiction, 21 December 2012, paras 4, 207, 229–232; *Awdi v Romania*, Award, 2 March 2015, para 201.

[207] *Enron v Argentina*, Decision on Jurisdiction, 14 January 2004, paras 50–57; *Total v Argentina*, Decision on Jurisdiction, 25 August 2006, para 76; *BG Group v Argentina*, Final Award, 24 December 2007, para 205; *Urbaser v Argentina*, Decision on Jurisdiction, 19 December 2012, paras 29, 235–254; *Krederi v Ukraine*, Award, 2 July 2018, para 245; *Casinos Austria v Argentina*, Decision on Jurisdiction, 29 June 2018, paras 49, 186.

[208] *Paushok v Mongolia*, Award on Jurisdiction and Liability, 28 April 2011.

[209] At para 202.

Some cases involve indirect investment made by way of companies in a third State, that is, a State that is neither the host State nor the investor's home State. Practice dealing with investments by way of third country companies shows a general acceptance also of this form of indirect investment.[210]

In *Noble Energy v Ecuador*,[211] the claimant indirectly owned the local company through two levels of intermediaries registered in the Cayman Islands and in Delaware respectively. Ecuador contended that Noble Energy could not bring the claim because it did not make the investment itself and because the ICSID Convention did not allow a 'grandparent company' to bring a claim.[212] The Tribunal said:

> The Tribunal concurs with previous tribunals that have held that an indirect shareholder can bring a claim under the ICSID Convention and under a BIT in respect of a direct and an indirect investment. Failing any contrary wording, the BIT and the ICSID Convention encompass actions of indirect shareholders for their damages.[213]

The Tribunal also addressed the question how far indirect ownership may be traced to still qualify for treaty purposes. It noted that there may well be a cut-off point somewhere. But it found:

> the cut-off point, whatever it may be, is not reached with two intermediate layers. The relationship between the investment and the direct shareholder, on the one hand, and the indirect shareholder, on the other, is not too remote.[214]

It followed that Noble Energy had standing under the ICSID Convention and the BIT as indirect owner of the local company.[215]

[210] *Sedelmayer v Russian Federation*, Award, 7 July 1998, sections 4.1., 2.1.1, 2.1.4, and 2.1.5; *Lauder v Czech Republic*, Award, 3 September 2001, paras 77, 120, 153, 154; *Kardassopoulos v Georgia*, Decision on Jurisdiction, 6 July 2007, paras 123–124; *Tza Yap Shum v Peru*, Decision on Jurisdiction, 19 June 2009, para 106; *Al Warraq v Indonesia*, Final Award, 15 December 2014, paras 511, 517; *Eyre and Montrose v Sri Lanka*, Award, 5 March 2020, paras 264–266.

[211] *Noble Energy v Ecuador*, Decision on Jurisdiction, 5 March 2008.

[212] At para 71.

[213] At para 77.

[214] At para 82. See also *Enron v Argentina*, Decision on Jurisdiction, 14 January 2004, paras 50–56; *Kim v Uzbekistan*, Decision on Jurisdiction, 8 March 2017, para 320: 'The Tribunal concludes that there is no basis—in the BIT or in the authorities to which the Parties make reference—to read a "remoteness" test into the definition of "investor".'

[215] *Noble Energy v Ecuador*, Decision on Jurisdiction, 5 March 2008, para 83.

(e) The nature of the protected rights

Indirect investors are protected not only against action that affects their ownership rights in the shares. Their protection extends to the company's economic value and its assets. In other words, rights derived from the shares are also protected. Those derivative rights are primarily the right to participate in the operation and economic success of the company. It follows that adverse action by the host State, in violation of treaty standards affecting the company's economic position, gives rise to rights by the company's shareholders and controllers. Investment tribunals have upheld this principle in numerous cases.[216]

In *Continental Casualty v Argentina*,[217] the Tribunal relied on a definition of 'investment' in the Argentina–US BIT that included 'a company or shares of stock or other interests in a company or interests in the assets thereof.' The Tribunal summarized these rights in the following terms:

> the treaty protection is not limited to the free enjoyment of the shares, that is the exercise of the rights inherent to the position as a shareholder, specifically a controlling or sole shareholder. It also extends to the standards of protection spelled out in the BIT with regard to the operation of the local company that represents the investment.[218]

The principle that shareholders may complain of State actions that adversely affect the economic position of the companies whose shares they hold, is reflected in Article 13(3) of the Energy Charter Treaty dealing with expropriation:

> For the avoidance of doubt, Expropriation shall include situations where a Contracting Party expropriates the assets of a company or enterprise in its Area

[216] *CMS v Argentina*, Decision on Jurisdiction, 17 July 2003, paras 59, 66–69 and Decision on Annulment, 25 September 2007, paras 58–76; *Azurix v Argentina*, Decision on Jurisdiction, 8 December 2003, paras 69, 73 and Decision on Annulment, 1 September 2009, paras 57–62, 76–80, 86–130; *Enron v Argentina*, Decision on Jurisdiction, 14 January 2004, paras 35, 43–49, 58–60 and Decision on Jurisdiction (Ancillary Claim), 2 August 2004, paras 17, 34–35; *Siemens v Argentina*, Decision on Jurisdiction, 3 August 2004, paras 125, 136–150; *GAMI v Mexico*, Award, 15 November 2004, paras 26–33; *Camuzzi v Argentina*, Decision on Jurisdiction, 11 May 2005, paras 45–67; *Sempra Energy v Argentina*, Decision on Jurisdiction, 11 May 2005, paras 73–79; *Bogdanov v Moldova*, Award, 22 September 2005, para 5.1; *Continental Casualty v Argentina*, Decision on Jurisdiction, 22 February 2006, para 79; *Telefónica v Argentina*, Decision on Jurisdiction, 25 May 2006, paras 68–83; *Total v Argentina*, Decision on Jurisdiction, 25 August 2006, para 74; *Azurix v Argentina*, Decision on Annulment, 1 September 2009, para 108; *RosInvest v Russian Federation*, Final Award, 12 September 2010, paras 605–609, 625; *Daimler v Argentina*, Award, 22 August 2012, paras 82–93; *Arif v Moldova*, Award, 8 April 2013, para 380; *Bogdanov v Moldova III*, Final Award, 16 April 2013, paras 167–168; *ST-AD v Bulgaria*, Award on Jurisdiction, 18 July 2013, paras 278–285; *Hochtief v Argentina*, Decision on Liability, 29 December 2014, paras 150–181, 302–307; *von Pezold v Zimbabwe*, Award, 28 July 2015, paras 321, 326; *Alghanim v Jordan*, Award, 14 December 2017, paras 118–121; *Mera v Serbia*, Decision on Jurisdiction, 30 November 2018, paras 130, 135; *Anglo American v Venezuela*, Award, 18 January 2019, paras 208–213; *Strabag v Libya*, Award, 29 June 2020, paras 125–136; *Bridgestone v Panama*, Award, 14 August 2020, paras 172–174.

[217] *Continental Casualty v Argentina*, Decision on Jurisdiction, 22 February 2006.

[218] At para 79.

in which an Investor of another Contracting Party has an Investment, including through the ownership of shares.

Some tribunals have expressed the view that the rights of indirect investors do not go beyond what could be derived from their shareholding.[219] In *Poštová banka v Greece*,[220] the Tribunal said:

> a shareholder of a company incorporated in the host State may assert claims based on measures taken against such company's assets that impair the value of the claimant's shares. However, such claimant has no standing to pursue claims directly over the assets of the local company, as it has no legal right to such assets.[221]

It follows that, based on treaty provisions listing participation in companies as a form of investment, shareholding in a company enjoys protection. Thus, even if the affected company does not meet the nationality requirements under the relevant treaty, there will be a remedy if the shareholder does. This is particularly relevant where, as is frequently the case, the company has the nationality of the host State and does not qualify as a foreign investor. In this situation, the company in question is not treated as the investor but as the investment.

Shareholder protection extends not only to ownership in the shares but also to the economic value of the shareholding. The tribunals' case law is, however, split concerning the question whether the protection covers the assets of the company only to the extent that the value of the investor's shares is affected. The difference between the adherents of a direct right to damages for adverse action against the investment and the adherents of an indirect right via the value of the participation in the investment is of limited practical significance. It represents different ways of describing the legal foundation of the investor's claim. It may have some influence on the calculation of damages at the quantum stage. But it does not affect the fundamental question of the investor's *ius standi*, that is, its right to present a claim.

Practical problems can arise where claims are pursued in parallel, especially by different shareholders or groups of shareholders. In addition, the affected company itself may pursue certain remedies while a group of its shareholders may pursue different ones. The situation becomes even more complex where indirect shareholding through intermediaries is combined with minority shareholding. In such a case, shareholders and companies at different levels may pursue conflicting or competing litigation strategies that may be difficult to reconcile and coordinate.

[219] *BG Group v Argentina*, Final Award, 24 December 2007, paras 214–217; *El Paso v Argentina*, Award, 31 October 2011, paras 177–214; *ST-AD v Bulgaria*, Award on Jurisdiction, 18 July 2013, paras 268–285; *Enkev Beheer v Poland*, First Partial Award, 29 April 2014, paras 310, 313; *Casinos Austria v Argentina*, Decision on Jurisdiction, 29 June 2018, paras 184, 185.

[220] *Poštová banka v Greece*, Award, 9 April 2015.

[221] At para 245.

V

Investment Contracts

ADDITIONAL READING: A El-Kosheri and T Riad, 'The Law Governing a New Generation of Petroleum Agreements' (1986) 1 *ICSID Rev* 257; RD Bishop, 'International Arbitration of Petroleum Disputes: The Development of a *Lex Petrolea*?' (1998) 23 *YB Commercial Arb* 1131; E Smith et al, *International Petroleum Transactions* (2003); I Alvik, *Contracting with Sovereignty: State Contracts and International Arbitration* (2011); P Dumberry, 'International Investment Contracts' in T Gazzini and E de Brabandere (eds) *International Investment Law* (2012) 215; S Frank, 'Stabilisation Clauses and Foreign Direct Investment' (2015) 16 *JWIT* 88; A von Walter, 'Investor–State Contracts in the Context of International Investment Law' in M Bungenberg et al (eds) *International Investment Law* (2015) 80; R Dolzer, *Petroleum Contracts and International Law* (2018); J Gjuzi, *Stabilization Clauses in International Investment Law* (2018).

Large-scale investments may last for decades. They involve interests of the investor, as well as public interests of the host State. General legislation of the host country may not sufficiently address the nature of the project and the kind of interests concerned. The legal setting of an investment may need to be adjusted to its specifics and complexities by way of an investment contract. In practice, especially the legal regime of oil and gas projects by multinational companies has been determined in large part by investment contracts.

1. Types of investment contracts

The investment contract will reflect the bargaining power of both sides under the circumstances of the individual project. Not surprisingly, no general pattern applicable to all situations has emerged in practice. Even within individual sectors of the economy, typical agreements have evolved significantly over the past decades.

In the decades before 1945, investment agreements (concessions) typically covered large areas of land, transferred title of the oil reserves to the investor, and did not contain an obligation of the investor to explore or produce oil. Under these agreements, the host country would receive a bonus for the concession as such and royalties for barrels actually produced.

A second generation of agreements emerged in the 1960s and 1970s. These reflected the new power of oil-producing countries, their desire to control their resources,[1] and their aspiration to develop the necessary skills and technologies within their own borders. Often, State-owned companies were set up for the purpose of concluding and supervising agreements with foreign investors. Areas with potential reserves were more restricted and closely defined, and the title to oil and gas remained with the host country. The risks inherent in a failure to find suitable oil or gas were shifted to the foreign investor who was, however, allowed to recover exploration costs in cases where commercially usable reserves were found. Once oil or gas was produced, the product was divided between the two parties to the investment agreement under a negotiated formula, often subject to a gradual decrease of the rights of the investor. These arrangements were set out in so-called production-sharing or profit-sharing agreements.

Increasingly, host countries tended to restrict the role of the foreign investor to the provision of technical expertise and services. Exploration, however, remained in the hands of the investor at its own risk. While this type of agreement seems preferable at first sight for the host country, especially if non-exporting, it also places the burden of financing on the host country and therefore has not been relied upon by all countries.

Beyond the area of energy exploration and production, projects creating utilities and infrastructure blossomed, especially in the era of privatization in the early 1990s. Typical arrangements often relied on the concept of 'build, operate, own' (BOO), placing all major risks and benefits on the investor. Sometimes, the entire project was to be transferred to the host country after a certain period—'build, operate, transfer' (BOT). Joint venture arrangements with companies of the host State have their own advantages for the foreign investor, but they have sometimes also led to disappointments. Projects for construction usually follow a special pattern.

In addition to the allocation of rights, tasks, risks, and responsibilities, investment contracts had to lay down the ground rules on which the parties agreed. These rules included, in particular, the law applicable to the project and the choice of a forum for dispute resolution. Specific provisions concerning *force majeure*, good faith, and changed circumstances were often included. From a legal perspective, the most complex and difficult questions often concerned the inclusion of clauses regulating the conduct of the parties in the event of political changes in the host country and in the event of changes in the economic equilibrium between the host State and the investor.

The parties to investment contracts vary. Not all investment contracts are directly between the State and the foreign investor.[2] Some are between a State entity and the investor or between the State and a local subsidiary of the investor. There are also contracts between State entities and local subsidiaries.[3]

[1] On the concept of 'Permanent Sovereignty over National Resources' and UN GA Res Nos 1803, 14 December 1962, and 3281, 12 December 1974, see I.1(c) above.

[2] See VIII.6(d) below.

[3] *Azurix v Argentina*, Award, 14 July 2006, para 52.

In *Duke Energy v Ecuador*[4] the Tribunal held that, in order to be protected by a bilateral investment treaty (BIT), an investment agreement must be entered into by the host State and the foreign investor, and not by a State-owned entity or a local company established by the investor.[5] In *Burlington v Ecuador*,[6] the Tribunal had to answer the question whether an agreement between the host State and a subsidiary of the claimant incorporated in a third State amounted to an 'investment agreement' between the host State and the claimant. The provision on tax matters in the US–Ecuador BIT covered these cases only if they arose under an 'investment agreement' between the host State and a national of the other party. In a split decision, following earlier jurisprudence, the Tribunal found that such an agreement was not an 'investment agreement' within the meaning of the US–Ecuador BIT.[7]

2. Applicable law

The determination of the law applicable to the contract and the agreement on dispute resolution are often the most sensitive legal issues. The host State will view both areas from the vantage point of protecting its national sovereignty. The investor's priority will be the choice of a legal order that provides a stable and predictable legal environment and the choice of a forum for dispute resolution that will preclude bias or political influence against the investor.

Depending upon the bargaining power and the negotiating skill of the parties, a number of possible choices have emerged for the applicable law.[8] These range from a choice of the law of the host State to an exclusive choice of international law. Between these extremes, general principles of law, usage in the industry, and, more seldom, rules of natural justice or of equity have been chosen. Often, a combination of national law and international rules as applicable law has been negotiated as a compromise.

The matter will also be determined by the position of international law in the domestic order of the host State. If international law is applicable under the host State's law, the investor will find it less difficult to accept a reference to domestic law alone. However, such rules in a constitution or in legislative provisions are subject to unilateral change on the part of the host country without a right to object on the part of the investor.

Choice of law clauses may be in need of interpretation in various ways. The meaning of clauses referring to general principles of law or to the usage of trade may not be self-evident. The reference to the rules or principles of international

4 *Duke Energy v Ecuador*, Award, 18 August 2008.
5 At paras 182 et seq.
6 *Burlington v Ecuador*, Decision on Jurisdiction, 2 June 2010.
7 At para 234.
8 See also XII.12(a) below.

law also raises issues of interpretation, as will be seen in the context of the understanding of Article 42 of the ICSID Convention.[9]

Any reference in a choice of law clause to two different legal orders or principles will, in the event of conflict or diversity between them, pose the question of the hierarchy or selection of the legal order for the individual issue concerned.

Even in the presence of a choice of a domestic law in the contract, customary international law remains applicable unless the parties exclude it expressly. Therefore, normally customary international law applies in the context of an investment arbitration as a minimum standard.[10]

Tribunals have taken divergent approaches in cases in which no applicable law clause was included in a contract and which did not provide for ICSID arbitration. While in older cases tribunals have opted for not applying host State law,[11] in more recent cases they applied host State law (together with international law) when it was relevant to a particular issue under consideration.[12]

3. Dispute settlement

Many investment contracts provide for arbitration.[13] The intended effect of these clauses is to exclude the jurisdiction of national courts. Older contracts often provided for ad hoc arbitration, that is, arbitration without an institutional framework.[14] More recently, it has become customary to provide for arbitration within the framework of an arbitration institution.[15] Often ICSID is chosen for this purpose,[16] but other forms of arbitration are also known.[17] ICSID has developed

[9] For choice of law in ICSID arbitrations see XII.12 below.

[10] SW Schill et al (eds), *Schreuer's Commentary on the ICSID Convention*, 3rd edn (2022) Article 42, paras 157–170; see also *Cambodia Power v Cambodia*, Decision on Jursidiction, 22 March 2011, paras 331–334; *Caratube and Hourani v Kazakhstan*, Award, 27 September 2017, paras 288–290, 415.

[11] *In the Matter of an Arbitration between Petroleum Development (Trucial Coast) and the Sheikh of Abu Dhabi*, Award, September 1951, 18 ILR 144 at 149; *Ruler of Qatar v International Marine Oil Company*, Award, June 1953, 20 ILR 534 at 544, 545; *Sapphire v NIOC*, Award, 15 March 1963, 35 ILR 136, at 176–177.

[12] *Aminoil v Kuwait*, Award, 24 March 1982, (1982) 21 ILM 976, at 1000, para 6; *Wintershall v Qatar*, Award, 5 February 1988 and 31 May 1988, (1989) 28 ILM 795, at 802.

[13] See also XII.7(a) below.

[14] *Texaco v Libya*, Award, 19 January 1977, 53 ILR 389; *LIAMCO v Libya*, Award, 12 April 1977, 62 ILR 141; *British Petroleum v Libya*, Award, 10 October 1973, 53 ILR 297.

[15] See below XII.4.

[16] *Holiday Inns v Morocco*, Decision on Jurisdiction, 12 May 1974, (1993) 1 ICSID Reports 650; *Amco v Indonesia*, Decision on Jurisdiction, 25 September 1983, para 10; *Noble Energy v Ecuador*, Decision on Jurisdiction, 5 March 2008, paras 22–23, 54–55, 150; *Duke Energy v Ecuador*, Award, 18 August 2008, paras 62, 120; *Aguaytia v Peru*, Award, 11 December 2008, paras 66–67; *Cambodia Power v Cambodia*, Decision on Jurisdiction, 22 March 2011, paras 11–14; *Perenco v Ecuador*, Decision on Jurisdiction, 30 June 2011, paras 125–147; *Niko Resources v Bangladesh*, Decision on Jurisdiction, 19 August 2013, paras 45, 88–90; *Caratube and Hourani v Kazakhstan*, Award, 27 September 2017, para 626.

[17] *SPP v Egypt*, ICC Award, 11 March 1983, 3 ICSID Reports 46; *SGS v Pakistan*, Decision on Jurisdiction, 6 August 2003, para 15; *Joy Mining v Egypt*, Award on Jurisdiction, 6 August 2004, paras

a set of Model Clauses to facilitate the drafting of consent clauses in investment contracts.[18]

Contractual consent to arbitration within the framework of an arbitral institution does not prevent the parties from shaping their consent and to determine the modalities of their arbitration agreement. Typically, investment agreements refer to 'any dispute' or to 'all disputes' under the respective agreements.[19] But there are also clauses circumscribing the tribunal's jurisdiction more narrowly.[20]

Some investment contracts contain clauses that refer disputes arising from the application of these contracts to the host States' domestic courts. In the presence of investment treaties providing for international arbitration, these domestic forum selection clauses have led to complex disputes about the respective jurisdiction of the domestic courts and international tribunals.[21]

4. Stabilization clauses

Investment agreements are negotiated by the investor and the host State to allow for special rules between the two parties, separate from the general legislation of the host State. For the investor, a key concern will invariably be to safeguard the stability of the agreement. Applicable treaties between the host State and the investor's home State may provide for rules designed to ensure or to promote stable contractual relations for their citizens, such as umbrella clauses or a provision on fair and equitable treatment. However, such rules will not always be in place,[22] or they may not be as specific as desired by the investor. Against this background, a practice of including stabilization clauses[23] in State–investor agreements has developed. No single specific wording for such clauses has emerged, and different types with different functions and scope have been drafted. In consequence, the significance and interpretation of each such clause will have to be assessed in the light of its specific wording.

Unsurprisingly, investors have sought to negotiate stabilization clauses in particular with States whose political and legal regime has in the past been subject to frequent changes or volatility. The governments of these States may have reason to

92–93; *Saipem v Bangladesh*, Decision on Jurisdiction and Recommendation on Provisional Measures, 21 March 2007, para 10; *ATA v Jordan*, Award, 18 May 2010, para 33.

18 ICSID Model Clauses, Doc. ICSID/5/Rev 2 of 1993. Reproduced in 4 ICSID Reports 357.
19 *World Duty Free v Kenya*, Award, 4 October 2006, para 6.
20 *Perenco v Ecuador*, Decision on Jurisdiction, 30 June 2011, para 108.
21 See below XII.10.
22 P Cameron, *International Energy Investment Law, The Pursuit of Stability* (2010) 233 et seq.
23 The Tribunal in *Amoco v Iran*, Award, 14 July 1987, 15 Iran–US CTR 189, 239, observed that the term 'stabilization clause' normally refers to 'contract language which freezes the provisions of a national system of law chosen as the law of the contract as of the date of the contract in order to prevent the application to the contract of any future alterations of this system'.

agree to such clauses because they wish to attract foreign investment and because stability serves to facilitate this goal. For the host country, a stabilization clause may be more attractive than a treaty, which requires lengthy international negotiations and ratification processes. Some States have introduced specific legislation authorizing the executive branch to conclude Legal Stability Agreements (LSAs).[24]

A stabilization clause in its strictest sense would require the host State not to alter its general legal regime for the area covered by the contract. Typically, however, the investor's concern will be limited to the stability of the individual agreement it has concluded with the host State. Thus, stabilization in the form of an intangibility (or inviolability) clause will provide that changes in the law of the host State will not apply to the investment contract. It is not uncommon for the contract to limit the scope of the stabilization clause to specific areas, such as tax law. Another version consists of so-called freezing clauses. These will choose the law of the host State as it stands at a specified time, typically the time of the contract's entry into force, as the applicable law.[25]

A doctrinal issue that arises for stabilization clauses in general is whether they bind the host State or whether, because of its sovereignty, a State may change a stabilization clause. International tribunals have ruled that stabilization clauses are valid and have legal effect.[26]

In *AGIP v Congo*,[27] the Tribunal had to deal with a stabilization clause that ensured that changes of domestic law by the Congo would not affect certain parts of the contract with AGIP pertaining to the status of the protected company. When the Congo later nationalized the company, the Tribunal examined the compatibility of the nationalization decree with the stabilization clause from the viewpoint of international law (to which the contract explicitly referred). The Tribunal ruled:

> These stabilization clauses, which were freely entered into by the Government, do not affect the principle of its legislative and regulatory sovereignty since it retains both with respect to those, whether nationals of foreigners, with whom the Government has not entered into such undertakings, and that, in the present case, they are limited to rendering the modifications to the legislative regulatory provisions provided for the Agreement, unopposable to the other contracting party. ... It suffices to concentrate the examination of the compatibility of the nationalization with international law on the stabilization clauses.

[24] *Duke Energy v Peru*, Award, 18 August 2008, paras 201–228.

[25] In *Noble Energy v Ecuador*, Decision on Jurisdiction, 5 March 2008, para 12, the Investment Agreement guaranteed 'full legal stability of the legal framework in force'. In *Duke Energy v Peru*, Award, 18 August 2008, para 227, the Tribunal found that not only the law but also its interpretation was frozen.

[26] *MINE v Guinea*, Decision on Annulment, 14 December 1989, paras 6.33, 6.36; *CMS v Argentina*, Award, 12 May 2005, para 151; *Aguaytia v Peru*, Award, 11 December 2008, paras 89, 95.

[27] *AGIP v Congo*, Award, 30 November 1979, 1 ICSID Reports 306.

> It is indeed in connection with these clauses that the principles of international law are used to complete the rules of Congolese law. The reference made to international law suffices to demonstrate the irregular nature, from the point of view of this law of the acts of nationalization carried out in the present case. It follows that the Government is obliged to compensate AGIP for the damage suffered by it as a result of the nationalization ....[28]

In *LETCO v Liberia*,[29] the Tribunal explained:

> This clause, commonly referred to as a 'Stabilization Clause', is commonly found in long-term development contracts and ... is meant to avoid the arbitrary actions of the contracting government. This clause must be respected, especially in this type of agreement. Otherwise, the contracting State may easily avoid its contractual obligations by legislation.[30]

In *Aminoil v Kuwait*,[31] the Tribunal concluded that a typical stabilization clause should not be presumed to imply that a State lost the right to expropriate a contract running for a period of 60 years. The Tribunal came to the conclusion that the main effect of a stabilization clause would lie in the calculation of the amount of compensation, provoking a sharp dissent from Arbitrator Fitzmaurice.

The majority ruling in *Amoco v Iran*[32] also took the view that a typical stabilization clause in a contract should not be understood as a renunciation on the part of the host State of its right to expropriate a concession.

None of the cases discussed here had to apply an umbrella clause in an investment treaty, which is designed to protect an investor against violation of a contractual arrangement.

The mostly unarticulated premise of these cases is that a State has the power to bind itself, and that the respect for the principle *pacta sunt servanda* as well as the principle of good faith will forestall an attempt to ignore the contractual bond. Tribunals have differed in their views whether a violation of the stabilization clause will require specific performance of the contract[33] or whether the aggrieved party merely has a right to be compensated for its loss.[34]

Special questions will arise if the stabilization clause is in a contract that does not bind the host State and the foreign investor directly. This applies where a stabilization clause is included in a contract between an entity created by the State, such as

[28] At paras 86–88.
[29] *LETCO v Liberia*, Award, 31 March 1989.
[30] 2 ICSID Reports 368.
[31] *Aminoil v Kuwait*, Final Award, 24 March 1982.
[32] *Amoco v Iran*, Award, 14 July 1987, 15 Iran–US CTR 189.
[33] *Texaco v Libya*, Award, 19 January 1977.
[34] *LIAMCO v Libya*, Award, 12 April 1977, with an explicit recognition of *pacta sunt servanda*.

a national company, and a foreign investor. Here, it will be relevant whether the national company has been given the power to bind the State, or whether the foreign investor may rely on such a commitment on other grounds, such as good faith. If the stabilization clause is contained in a contract between the State and the foreign investor's local subsidiary, the foreign investor may be unable to rely on it.[35]

In the oil and gas business, stabilization is frequently achieved by means other than a stabilization clause in the conventional sense. One technique is that investment agreements provide that the national oil company, being the investor's contractual partner, will pay the tax for the foreign investor and that this will continue to be the case in the event of a future change of domestic tax law.

Concerning the scope of stabilization clauses States have to be mindful not to compromise other international obligations stemming from areas such as human rights, labour law or environmental law.[36]

5. Renegotiation and adaptation

As an alternative to preserving the stability of a contract, the more recent trend is to agree on renegotiation clauses.[37] These clauses may focus on economic equilibrium rather than on legal stability. The following clause was, for instance, adopted in 1994 in the Model Exploration and Production Sharing Agreement of the Sheikdom of Qatar:

> **Art 34.12 Equilibrium of the Agreement**
> Whereas the financial position of the Contractor has been based, under the Agreement, on the laws and regulations in force at the Effective Date, it is agreed that, if any future law, decree or regulation affects Contractor's financial position, and in particular if the customs duties exceed ... percent during the term of the Agreement, both parties shall enter into negotiations, in good faith, in order to reach an equitable solution that maintains the economic equilibrium of this Agreement. Failing to reach agreement on such equitable solution, the matter may be referred by either Party to arbitration pursuant to Article 31.[38]

[35] *Total v Argentina*, Decision on Liability, 27 December 2010, para 101.

[36] Principles for Responsible Contracts, Integrating the Management of Human Rights Risks into State–Investor Contract Negotiations, United Nations, Human Rights, Office of the High Commissioner, 2015.

[37] See also W Peter, *Arbitration and Renegotiation of International Investment Agreements* (1995); A Kolo and T Wälde, 'Renegotiation and Contract Adaptation in International Investment Projects' (2000) 1 *JWIT* 5, 7; J Salacuse, 'Renegotiating International Business Transactions' (2001) 35 *Int'l Lawyer* 1507; J Gotanda, 'Renegotiation and Adaptation Clauses in Investment Contracts' (2003) 36 *Vanderbilt J Transn'l L* 1461; S Kröll, 'The Renegotiation and Adaptation in Investment Contracts' in N Horn (ed) *Arbitrating Foreign Investment Disputes* (2004) 425; M Besch, 'Typical Questions Arising within Negotiations' in M Bungenberg et al (eds) *International Investment Law* (2015) 93.

[38] The clause is reproduced by P Bernardini, 'The Renegotiation of Investment Contracts' (1998) 13 *ICSID Rev* 411, 416; for similar clauses and their significance, see also K Berger, 'Renegotiation and

Difficulties will arise if the circumstances triggering the right to renegotiate are not described in sufficient detail in the investment contract. Beyond the triggering clause, the parties have various choices for structuring the actual process of appropriate renegotiation. The adjustment of a contract based on automatically applicable criteria is rarely foreseen. Typically, renegotiation clauses rely on open-ended criteria. Sometimes no criteria for the process of renegotiation are included.

Obviously, renegotiation clauses provide for more flexibility than a stabilization clause, but their practicability and usefulness are questionable. The concept of an 'economic equilibrium' remains to be defined in legal terms. Moreover, a duty to renegotiate relies on the continued goodwill of both parties during a dispute. The clause may therefore not prove helpful in the context of a dispute. Thus, it is far from clear whether a duty to renegotiate will serve the practical needs of a long-term investment.

6. Relationship to investment treaties

Cases involving investment contracts frequently arise in combination with claims that are based on investment treaties. Therefore, it is often not possible to separate 'contract cases' from 'treaty cases'.

For instance, stabilization clauses in contracts have legal effects in the context of the protection standards in investment treaties. Where investors argue that legislative changes in the host State violate their rights, tribunals may take stabilization clauses in contracts into consideration when deciding on the existence of legitimate expectations to the stability of the host State's legal order. Tribunals have considered the existence or non-existence of stabilization clauses in their findings on fair and equitable treatment and indirect expropriation[39] as well as in the calculation of damages.[40] Explicit undertakings by the host State made in contracts are a strong basis for legitimate expectations, which play a central role in the fair and equitable treatment standard.[41]

Umbrella clauses contained in investment treaties put contractual assurances that the investor has received from the host State under the treaty's protective

Adaptation of International Investment Contracts: The Role of Contract Drafters and Arbitrators' (2003) 36 *Vanderbilt J Transn'l L* 1347.

[39] *AES v Hungary*, Award, 23 September 2010, para 9.3.25; *Paushok v Mongolia*, Award on Jurisdiction and Liability, 28 April 2011, paras 226–233, 302, 410 et seq, 476; *Micula v Romania I*, Award, 11 December 2013, para 666; *Charanne v Spain*, Final Award, 21 January 2016, paras 489–490, 503; *Sun Reserve v Italy*, Final Award, 25 March 2020, para 702.

[40] *Kardassopoulos v Georgia*, Award, 3 March 2010, paras 477–485.

[41] See VIII.1(g)dd below.

umbrella. In consequence, a breach of contract may amount to a breach of treaty, leading to the State's international responsibility.[42]

In many cases, treaty claims and contract claims arise side by side in one and the same case. This has led to complex questions concerning the jurisdiction of international tribunals.[43]

[42] See VIII.6 below.
[43] See XII.10 below.

VI
Admission and Establishment

ADDITIONAL READING: P Juillard, 'Freedom of Establishment, Freedom of Capital Movements, and Freedom of Investment' (2000) 15 *ICSID Rev* 322; T Pollan, *Legal Framework for the Admission of FDI* (2006); I Gomez-Palacio and P Muchlinski, 'Admission and Establishment' in P Muchlinski et al (eds) *The Oxford Handbook of International Investment Law* (2008) 227; J Ma, 'International Investment and National Security Review' (2019) 52 *Vanderbilt J Transn'l L* 899; A Genest, *Performance Requirement Prohibitions in International Investment Law* (2019).

1. The right to control admission and establishment

From the perspective of general international law, States are in no way compelled to admit foreign investments. The economic dimension of territorial sovereignty leaves it to each government to decide whether to close the national economy to foreign investors or to open it up, fully or with respect to certain sectors. This includes the right to determine the modalities for the admission and establishment of foreign investors. Among the national considerations speaking against a full liberalization is the concern that weak domestic industries may be 'crowded out', and the social effects of rapid economic change. In addition, there are moral, health, and environmental concerns and a growing agenda of national security.[1]

Views differ on whether it is useful to conclude treaties providing for guarantees towards liberalization or whether the flexibility inherent in domestic legislation subject to continuous review provides more benefits for the host State's national economy. In any event, governments negotiating investment treaties must be aware that binding commitments on admission and establishment create lasting obligations, even when economic circumstances change.

[1] See also the General Agreement on Trade in Services (GATS) Article XIV; the General Agreement on Tariffs and Trade (GATT) Article XX.

2. The move towards economic liberalism

In the late 1980s, there was a growing international consensus that economic liberalism promised more growth and innovation than economic protectionism within closed national or regional borders. A now famous paper by J Williamson provided a list of conditions for successful economic growth, which eventually came to be known as the 'Washington Consensus'.[2] The 1980s were considered, from a development perspective, as the 'lost decade' in Latin America and Africa. It had led to more poverty, economic stagnation, and fiscal disorder, mainly due to inward-looking, non-competitive economic policies and a lack of domestic reforms. The comparison of empirical economic data between countries with growth (mainly in Asia) and stagnant regions, pointed to economic liberalization and domestic reforms as the main driving forces of growth. The lack of support for Third World countries from the Soviet Union and its eventual collapse lent further support to this movement. Ultimately, the retreat of 'bureaucrats in business' and the move toward privatization was prompted in developing countries by the reality of insufficient goods and services for the population, by fiscal disorder, and by the compelling need for foreign capital and technology.

The Washington Consensus had a strong influence on international economic policies, even though it has also become clear that economic reforms need to be complemented by social and environmental policies. In current practice, the Washington Consensus is reinforced by competition among capital-importing States for foreign investment. Nevertheless, national policies are far from uniform in this area, and even liberal countries, such as the United States, have by no means totally opened up their economies. The global trends in national policy developments do not point into one direction. Whereas most developing countries have, since 2000, introduced measures with the aim of liberalizing the regime of foreign investment, others, mainly developed countries, have adopted new regulations and restrictions.[3] In recent years, the amount of foreign investment that goes into traditional capital-exporting States has increased and some of these States have become respondents in investor–State disputes. In reaction to this development, certain European States have to some extent reversed their liberalization and deregulation policies and reintroduced regulatory approaches to address public welfare concerns.[4] For example, they have adopted and expanded investment-screening

[2] Originally, the 'Consensus' was nothing more than a research paper by John Williamson at the Washington-based Peterson Institute for International Economics. For its history, see J Williamson, 'From Reform Agenda to Damaged Brand Name—A Short History of the Washington Consensus and Suggestions for What to do Next' (2003) *Finance Dev* 10.

[3] For details, see United Nations Conference on Trade and Development (UNCTAD), *World Investment Report 2011* (2011) 94, *World Investment Report 2020* (2020) 97.

[4] See eg the adoption of EU Regulation 2019/452 establishing a framework for the screening of foreign direct investments into the Union.

mechanisms in order to assess potentially negative implications for the host State.[5] The coronavirus pandemic has led to tightened foreign investment screening mechanisms to protect health care and other strategic industries.[6] At the same time, some States have extended standards for the international protection of investments to the pre-establishment phase.[7]

3. Investment promotion

The title of many bilateral investment treaties refers to investment promotion.[8] This is in line with the object of these treaties to increase economic cooperation between the treaty parties. The BIT between Australia and India provides for example in its Article 3(1):

> Each Contracting Party shall encourage and promote favourable conditions for investors of the other Contracting Party to make investments in its territory.

The case law on such provisions is scarce. In *White Industries Australia v India*,[9] the claimant contended that India had, among several treaty guarantees, also failed to observe the above investment promotion provision. Claimants argued that India would be under an obligation:

> (a) to create a suitable governance framework for supervising the action of state-owned corporations, including Coal India, in their dealings with foreign investors;
> (b) to ensure that its arbitration laws are administered in line with India's New York Convention obligations; and
> (c) to take steps to reduce the backlog of cases in its courts, given the prospect that such backlog must necessarily have significant effect on domestic and international businesses, including investors, as defined under the BIT.[10]

[5] UNCTAD, *World Investment Report 2020* (2020) 98 f; J Ma, 'International Investment and National Security Review' (2019) 52 *Vanderbilt J Transn'l L* 899.

[6] UNCTAD, *World Investment Report 2020* (2020) xi, 92, 98.

[7] UNCTAD, *World Investment Report 2015* (2015) 110.

[8] See eg Agreement Between the Federal Republic of Germany and the Federation of Malaya Concerning the Promotion and Reciprocal Protection of Investments (1960); Agreement between the Government of Australia and the Government of the Republic of India on the Promotion and Protection of Investments (1999); Convenio entre el Gobierno de la República del Perú y el Gobierno de la República de Cuba sobre la Promoción y Protección Recíproca de Inversiones (2000); Agreement for the Promotion and Reciprocal Protection of Investment between the Government of the Republic of Austria and the Government of the Republic of Kazakhstan (2012); Agreement between Japan and Georgia for the Liberalisation, Promotion and Protection of Investment (2021).

[9] *White Industries Australia v India*, Final Award, 30 November 2011.

[10] At para 9.2.1.

The Tribunal found that there was agreement among commentators that investment promotion provisions like Article 3(1) of the Australia–India BIT 'do not give rise to substantive rights'.[11] It considered the clause far too general to create an enforceable substantive right of the investor.[12]

In *Nordzucker v Poland*,[13] the claimant had made an investment by acquiring two sugar enterprises but had failed in its efforts to acquire two additional enterprises. The dispute related to the acquisition of the additional enterprises. The German–Polish BIT contained an obligation to promote, as far as possible, investments and to admit them in accordance with its laws and to treat these investments fairly and equitably. The Tribunal held that in this context the term 'investment' had to be understood as covering also intended investments about to be made.[14] The Tribunal concluded that Poland's handling of the sales procedure had violated the claimant's right to be treated fairly and equitably.[15]

4. The right to admission and the right of establishment

The right of admission of foreign investments has been distinguished from the right of establishment.[16] Admission concerns the right of entry of the investment in principle, whereas establishment pertains to the conditions under which the investor is allowed to carry out its business during the period of the investment. For an investor with a short-term business, the right of establishment is less important than for one who plans a longer business presence in the host State.

Typical issues of admission concern the definition of relevant economic sectors and geographic regions, the requirement of registration or of a licence, and the legal structure of an admissible investment (eg the type and seat of corporation, joint venture, restrictions of ownership). In contrast, the right of establishment deals with issues such as expansion of the investment, payment of taxes, or transfer of funds. An overlap may exist in important areas such as capital or performance requirements. The distinction between admission and establishment may be important for treaties that allow for the right of admission but contain no regulation concerning establishment.

In the absence of a treaty, the host State is free to shape the conditions for admission and establishment in its national legislation. Some investment laws, such

[11] At para 9.2.7.

[12] At para 9.1.12. The Tribunal in *Stadtwerke München v Spain*, Award, 2 December 2019, para 196, relied on this reasoning.

[13] *Nordzucker v Poland*, Partial Award, 10 December 2008.

[14] At paras 179, 182–185, 208, 212, 216–217.

[15] *Nordzucker v Poland*, Second Partial Award, 28 January 2009, paras 77, 95.

[16] I Shihata, 'Recent Trends Relating to Entry of Foreign Direct Investment' (1994) 9 *ICSID Rev* 47; Juillard uses the terms 'freedom of investment' and 'freedom of establishment': P Juillard, 'Freedom of Establishment, Freedom of Capital Movements, and Freedom of Investment' (2000) 15 *ICSID Rev* 322.

as the one in Timor-Leste, require an approval of the investment. The non-observance of this provision led to a denial of jurisdiction in *Lighthouse v Timor-Leste* and the exclusion of the investment from the protection of the investment law.[17]

5. Treaty models of admission

The policy decision of the host State whether to grant a right of admission is fundamental for all parties to investment treaties. On this point, there are basic differences in the regulatory approach of existing investment treaties.[18] In balancing their interest to attract investments with their desire to control the entry of foreign investments to protect particular domestic interests, States have followed basically two models: the admission clause model and the right of establishment model.[19] The first one provides only for post-establishment protection. The second one grants to a certain extent some rights in the pre-establishment phase of an investment.

(a) The admission clause model

Investment treaties of European countries generally do not grant a right of admission but limit themselves to standards and guarantees for those investments that the host State has unilaterally decided to admit. A typical clause of this kind reads: 'Each Contracting State shall in its territory promote as far as possible investments by investors of the other Contracting State and admit such investments in accordance with its legislation.'[20]

An admission clause of this type means that the host State is under no obligation to admit an investment or revise its domestic laws of admission. A possible consequence is that under these laws investors receive treatment less favourable than nationals of third States or nationals of the host State. Also, the host State remains free to change its laws on admission after the investment treaty has entered into force.

Treaties that refer to admission according to the domestic laws of the host State, accept the conditions for admission contained in these laws. Notification and registration requirements and various types of approval mechanisms, including

[17] *Lighthouse v Timor-Leste*, Award, 22 December 2017, paras 322–323, 333–334.

[18] T Pollan, *Legal Framework for the Admission of FDI* (2006); JW Salacuse, *The Law of Investment Treaties*, 3rd edn (2021) 252; B Sabahi et al, *Investor-State Arbitration*, 2nd edn (2019) 336.

[19] UNCTAD, Bilateral Investment Treaties 1995–2006: Trends in Investment Rule Making (2007) 23.

[20] German Model Treaty of 2005, Article 2(1). On the clause 'accepted in accordance with the respective laws and regulations of either Contracting State', see *Fraport v Philippines I*, Award, 16 August 2007, para 335 (subsequently annulled on different grounds) and *Fraport v Philippines II*, Award, 10 December 2014, paras 322–333. See also IV.8 above.

case-by-case screening, will have to be observed in accordance with the specific laws of each host State.[21]

(b) The right of establishment model

The most common technique to grant a right of establishment is to rely on the standard of national treatment[22] and on a most-favoured-nation clause.[23] The principles of national and most-favoured-nation (MFN) treatment are simply extended to admission, combined with positive or negative lists.

The United States, followed by Canada and Japan, in their investment treaties have pursued this model which differs from that of European States. These three States have negotiated treaty provisions which, to some extent, grant a right of establishment. Under these provisions, a right of establishment, albeit limited in scope, is typically based on a national treatment clause. National treatment is not limited to existing investments but extends to establishment.

For instance, the 2004 and 2012 US Model BITs provide in their respective Articles 3 section 1:

> Each Party shall accord to investors of the other Party treatment no less favorable than that it accords, in like circumstances, to its own investors with respect to the establishment, acquisition, expansion, management, conduct, operation, and sale or other disposition of investments in its territory.

This extension is combined with a broader definition of investors that also covers activities pre-dating the establishment.[24] However, the liberalizations in the US Model BIT is not without limits. A rule on exceptions is laid down in Article 14 section 2 of the US Model BITs:

> Articles 3 [National Treatment], 4 [Most-Favoured-Nation Treatment], 8 [Performance Requirements], and 9 [Senior Management and Boards of Directors] do not apply to any measure that a Party adopts or maintains with respect to sectors, subsectors, or activities, as set out in its Schedule to Annex II.

[21] See Article 2(1) Bahrain–Thailand BIT: 'The benefits of this Agreement shall apply to the investments by the investors of one Contracting Party in the territory of the other Contracting Party which is **specifically approved in writing** by the competent authority in accordance with the laws and regulations of the latter Contracting Party.' (Emphasis added).

[22] On national treatment see VIII.4 below.

[23] On MFN treatment see VIII.5 below.

[24] Article 1 (Definitions) US Model BIT: '"investor of a Party" means a Party or state enterprise thereof, or a national or an enterprise of a Party, that attempts to make, is making, or has made an investment in the territory of the other Party".

In practice, no State grants unlimited access to foreign investments. Two basic approaches are available to articulate limitations in treaties containing a right of establishment. One approach is to identify all sectors that are open to the investors of the other party (positive list). The other is to identify all sectors that are closed to them (negative list). Exceptions may apply to certain categories of investors and of investments. Some treaties provide that exceptions to be made in the future—that is, after the treaty's entry into force—must not have the effect of placing the nationals of the other State in a less favourable position. However, other treaties specifically allow the adoption of measures that are more restrictive than those existing at the time of the signature of the treaty.

Investment chapters in Free Trade Agreements generally seek to provide for a closer economic relationship between the Contracting States and therefore also incorporate the right to establishment model.[25] The recent treaty practice of the European Union, as exemplified by the Comprehensive Economic and Trade Agreement (CETA), is in line with this approach, notwithstanding the exclusion of certain sectors and industries.[26] Moreover, the CETA also reduces investment barriers such as joint venture requirements or ownership and control caps.[27] At the same time, a trend has evolved to exclude disputes on questions of admission and establishment from dispute settlement mechanisms.[28]

If the treaty provides for a right of establishment and the domestic rules are inconsistent with this right, an international tribunal will decide on the basis of the host State's international obligation. Tribunals have addressed the consequences of non-compliance with admission regulations and the right of the investor to invoke a dispute settlement provision.[29]

Some treaties explicitly exclude national decisions made in the process of screening investments that prevent or restrict an investment, from the scope of the treaty or from the dispute settlement mechanism.[30] This is not necessarily restricted to treaties offering pre-establishment protection.[31]

[25] Comprehensive and Progressive Agreement for Trans-Pacific Partnership (CPTPP) Article 9.4 (national treatment), Article 9.5 (MFN); United States–Mexico–Canada Agreement (USMCA) Article 14.4 (national treatment), Article 14.5 (MFN); NAFTA Article 1102 (national treatment), Article 1103 (MFN).

[26] Comprehensive Economic and Trade Agreement between Canada and the European Union and its Member States (CETA) Article 8.6 (national treatment), Article 8.7 (MFN).

[27] CETA, Article 8.4 (Market Access).

[28] CETA Article 8.18(1)(a); USMCA Annex Article 14.D.3(1)(a)(i)(A) and (b)(i)(A).

[29] See IV.8 above.

[30] Canada Model BIT, Annex IV excludes decisions following a review under the Investment Canada Act.

[31] Mexico–Germany BIT, Article 20 (Exclusions): 'The dispute settlement provisions of this Section shall not apply to the resolutions adopted by a Contracting State, which for national security reasons, prohibit or restrict the acquisitions of an investment in its territory, owned or controlled by its nationals, by nationals or companies of the other Contracting State, according to the legislation of the relevant Contracting State.'

A promotion or admission provision may contain exceptions for measures in the public interest like security or public health.[32] As the Tribunal in *Philipp Morris v Uruguay* noted, such a provision is only concerned with admission and not suited to carve out such measures adopted after the establishment of an investment from the scope of protection of a BIT.[33]

Global Telecom v Canada[34] dealt with a national security review decision preventing the expansion of an investment. The applicable BIT distinguished between a national treatment guarantee for the establishment of investments[35] and the obligation to grant national treatment after establishment.[36] While the former excluded national decisions from dispute settlement,[37] the latter contained exceptions to certain sectors. The Tribunal applied a narrow understanding of the term 'acquisition' and held that the mere conversion of shares to gain control was not excluded from dispute settlement.[38] Canada additionally objected to the Tribunal's jurisdiction on the national treatment claim due to an exclusion of the service sector[39] comprising telecommunication services,[40] which the Tribunal accepted.[41]

The Energy Charter Treaty (ECT), rather than providing for a right to establishment, in Article 10(2) requires States to 'endeavour to accord to Investors' national treatment and MFN treatment in the making of investments. Exceptions to non-discriminatory treatment (national treatment and MFN) in the making of investments are to be limited to a minimum and are to be progressively removed.[42]

[32] See eg Uruguay–Switzerland BIT Article 2(1): 'Each Contracting Party shall in its territory promote as far as possible investments by investors of the other Contracting Party and admit such investments in accordance with its laws. The Contracting Parties recognize each other's right not to allow economic activities for reasons of public security and order, public health or morality, as well as activities which by law are reserved to their own investors.'

[33] *Philip Morris v Uruguay*, Decision on Jurisdiction, 2 July 2013, paras 167–174.

[34] *Global Telecom v Canada*, Award, 27 March 2020.

[35] Canada–Egypt BIT, Article II(3): 'Each Contracting Party shall permit establishment of a new business enterprise or acquisition of an existing business enterprise or a share of such enterprise by investors or prospective investors of the other contracting Party on a basis no less favourable than that which, in like circumstances, it permits such acquisition or establishment by: (a) its own investors or prospective investors; or (b) investors or prospective investors of any third state.'

[36] Article IV(1).

[37] Article II(4):

> (a) Decisions by either Contracting Party, pursuant to measures not inconsistent with this Agreement, as to whether or not to permit an acquisition shall not be subject to the provisions of Articles XIII or XV of this Agreement,
> (b) Decisions by either Contracting Party not to permit establishment of a new business enterprise or acquisition of an existing business enterprise or a share of such enterprise by investors or prospective investors shall not be subject to provisions of Article XIII of this Agreement.

[38] *Global Telecom v Canada*, Award, 27 March 2020, paras 324–34.

[39] Canada–Egypt BIT, Article IV(2)(d) and Annex(1).

[40] *Global Telecom v Canada*, Award, 27 March 2020, paras 341–51. See, however, the Dissenting Opinion by arbitrator Gary Born.

[41] At paras 363–69, 380.

[42] ECT Article 10(5).

Furthermore, States can voluntarily commit themselves not to introduce new restrictions in this field.[43] So far, these provisions have not led to case law.

A more recent trend is to incorporate objectives such as sustainable development, environmental protection, or provisions against corruption into investment treaties. These treaties include these objectives either in an investment promotion provision, the preamble, or in a separate clause containing corporate social responsibility standards.[44] In some treaties, States undertake to refrain from lowering environmental, social, or labour standards to attract foreign investment.[45] Most of these provisions, however, do not contain binding commitments.

6. Performance requirements

Another possibility to protect the domestic market when admitting foreign investments is to oblige the investor to conduct its business in a prescribed manner ('performance requirements'). Most BITs do not deal with performance requirements, but BITs concluded by the United States and Canada typically prohibit them. Article 1106 of the North American Free Trade Agreement (NAFTA) and Article 14.10 of its successor treaty, the United States–Mexico–Canada Agreement (USMCA), also contain a list of prohibited performance requirements similar to the US Model BITs.

Performance requirements are imposed upon foreign investors. Examples are the compulsion to use local materials, the duty to export a certain quantity of products, and the obligation to hire local personnel. These practices are deemed undesirable, since they are inconsistent with the principle of liberal markets.[46] A typical older clause prohibiting performance requirements is found in the BIT between the United States and Cameroon:

> Neither Party shall impose performance requirements as a condition of establishment, expansion or maintenance of investments owned by nationals or companies of the other Party, which require or enforce commitments to export goods produced, or which specify that goods or services must be purchased locally, or which impose any other similar requirements.[47]

The 2004 and 2012 US Model BITs, Article 8, address the issue in more detail:

[43] ECT Article 10(6).
[44] Netherlands Model BIT 2019, Article 3(4)
[45] Norway Model BIT 2015, Article 11.
[46] A Genest, *Performance Requirement Prohibitions in International Investment Law* (2019).
[47] US–Cameroon BIT (1986), Article II Section 6.

> Neither Party may, in connection with the establishment, acquisition, expansion, management, conduct, operation, or sale or other disposition of an investment of an investor of a Party or of a non-Party in its territory, impose or enforce any requirement or enforce any commitment or undertaking: (a) to export a given level or percentage of goods or services; (b) to achieve a given level or percentage of domestic content; (c) to purchase, use, or accord a preference to goods produced in its territory, or to purchase goods from persons in its territory; (d) to relate in any way the volume or value of imports to the volume or value of exports or to the amount of foreign exchange inflows associated with such investment; (e) to restrict sales of goods or services in its territory that such investment produces or supplies by relating such sales in any way to the volume or value of its exports or foreign exchange earnings; (f) to transfer a particular technology, a production process, or other proprietary knowledge to a person in its territory; or (g) to supply exclusively from the territory of the Party the goods that such investment produces or the services that it supplies to a specific regional market or to the world market.

More recently, variations of clauses prohibiting performance requirements have appeared and more States have included provisions on performance requirements, influenced by the US Model BITs.[48]

Despite the distinction between trade and investment, performance requirements are also addressed in the World Trade Organization (WTO) context in the framework of the Agreement on Trade-Related Investment Measures (TRIMs, 1994). An Annex to that agreement contains an illustrative list of prohibited performance requirements:

> 1. TRIMs that are inconsistent with the obligation of national treatment... include those... which require: (a) the purchase or use by an enterprise of products of domestic origin or from any domestic source, whether specified in terms of particular products, in terms of volume or value of products, or in terms of a proportion of volume or value of its local production; or (b) that an enterprise's purchases or use of imported products be limited to an amount related to the volume or value of local products that it exports.
> 2. TRIMs that are inconsistent with the obligation of general elimination of quantitative restrictions ... include those which ... restrict: (a) the importation by an enterprise of products used in or related to its local production, generally or to an amount related to the volume or value of local production that it exports; (b) the importation by an enterprise of products used in or related to its local production by restricting its access to foreign exchange to an

48 A Genest, *Performance Requirement Prohibitions in International Investment Law* (2019) 30 et seq.

amount related to the foreign exchange inflows attributable to the enterprise; or (c) the exportation or sale for export by an enterprise of products, whether specified in terms of particular products, in terms of volume or value of products, or in terms of a proportion of volume or value of its local production.

A concurrent challenge of these measures before the WTO disputes settlement system and before investment tribunals would lead to issues of competing jurisdiction and consistency.[49] Furthermore, performance requirements that apply only to foreign investors would raise questions under the national treatment standard.

Some treaties contain clauses concerning the hiring and presence of non-local personnel to manage the investment in the host country. They provide that applications by such persons shall receive 'sympathetic consideration'[50] or that quotas or numerical restrictions will not be allowed in that context.[51] Some treaties recognize the investor's right to appoint key technical and managerial personnel, subject to the host State's law.[52]

In arbitral practice, claims concerning breaches of prohibitions of performance requirements have so far been scarce and merely of secondary importance.[53] In *Mobil & Murphy v Canada*,[54] the investor based its claim of a violation of Article 1106(1)(c) NAFTA mainly on the requirement to spend large sums on local research and development. Canada argued that research and development activities were neither 'services' pursuant to Article 1106 nor was there an element of compulsion. The Tribunal interpreted the term 'services' broadly as including research and development and found that the requirement clearly imposed a legal obligation on the claimant.[55]

7. The inception of an investment

In some cases, the question arises whether claimants have actually made an investment or have merely engaged in activity preparatory to an investment. The existence of an investment is of crucial importance since most investment treaties, national investment legislation as well as the ICSID Convention require an investment as a condition for a tribunal's jurisdiction *ratione materiae*.[56]

[49] An investor will presumably have a right to invoke the TRIMs Agreement before an investment tribunal if both State Parties concerned are members of the WTO. This will be the case if a BIT refers to other existing international obligations that could be invoked by the investor.

[50] See Protocol to the Treaty between Germany and Bosnia & Herzegovina of 18 October 2001, para 3(c).

[51] United States–Nicaragua BIT (1995) Article VII.

[52] Australia–Egypt BIT (2001) Article 5.

[53] A Genest, *Performance Requirement Prohibitions in International Investment Law* (2019) 6 et seq.

[54] *Mobil & Murphy v Canada*, Decision on Liability and on Principles of Quantum, 22 May 2012.

[55] At paras 172–246.

[56] See XII.5(d) below

(a) Pre-investment activities

In some cases, tribunals found that the claimants' activities had not progressed beyond mere preparatory steps and that hence there was no investment. For instance, in *Mihaly v Sri Lanka*,[57] the parties had engaged in extensive negotiations on the construction and operation of a power station. They had exchanged various documents but never reached the stage of signing a contract. After the negotiations had failed, the claimant sought to recover its development costs. The Tribunal rejected the claim in the absence of an investment. It found that the documents did not contain any binding obligations and said:

> Ultimately, there was never any contract entered into between the Claimant and the Respondent for the building, ownership and operation of the power station... The Tribunal is consequently unable to accept as a valid denomination of 'investment', the unilateral or internal characterization of certain expenditures by the Claimant in preparation for a project of investment.[58]

Also in other cases, tribunals found that unsuccessful negotiations in preparation for an investment did not amount to an actual investment.[59] This applied even where non-binding preparatory documents expressing the parties' intentions had been signed.[60] Winning a tender did not amount to an investment in the absence of a resulting operating agreement.[61] In the absence of 'substantive commitments and arrangements ... involving specific commitments and financial costs', there was no investment.[62]

In these cases, claimants had not only failed to reach a definitive agreement that had a commercial value. They also had never reached the stage of actual investment operations. In view of the purely preparatory nature of their efforts, which had never reached the stage of a binding contract or any actual investment activity, the tribunals denied the existence of an investment.

Some investment treaties explicitly include pre-investment activities within their ambit of protection. This is achieved through a wide interpretation of the term 'investor of a Party', which includes an investor that 'attempts to make, is making

[57] *Mihaly v Sri Lanka*, Award, 15 March 2002.

[58] At paras 47, 61.

[59] *Zhinvali v Georgia*, Award, 24 January 2003, 10 ICSID Reports 3, paras 377, 388, 410, 415, 417.

[60] *ST-AD v Bulgaria*, Award on Jurisdiction, 18 July 2013, para 273; *Nagel v Czech Republic*, Final Award, 9 September 2003, paras 320, 328–329; *Generation Ukraine v Ukraine*, Award, 16 September 2003, para 18.9; *Doutremepuich v Mauritius*, Award on Jurisdiction, 23 August 2019, paras 149–155; *Gosling v Mauritius*, Award, 18 February 2020, paras 99, 144–146, 230–242.

[61] *F-W Oil Interests v Trinidad and Tobago*, Award, 3 March 2006, paras 125, 142, 183; *Axos v Kosovo*, Award, 3 May 2018, paras 133–245.

[62] *Eyre and Montrose v Sri Lanka*, Award, 5 March 2020, paras 301–303.

or has made an investment'.[63] In *Mason v Korea*,[64] the Tribunal found that this definition extended the treaty's temporal scope of application to the pre-investment phase. It meant that 'an investor is already protected by the FTA if it is still in the process of making an investment'.[65]

(b) The existence of investment activities

In other cases, tribunals found that activities had actually reached the stage of being investments. In these cases, the investor had entered into a binding contract or had, in fact, contributed assets to the investment.

In *PSEG v Turkey*,[66] the parties had signed a concession contract for a power plant, but the project was not carried out. The respondent argued that there was no investment since the project had never moved beyond the drawing board and essential terms were still missing from the contract.[67] The Tribunal noted that the concession contract existed, was valid and legally binding. Therefore, there was jurisdiction based on an investment made in the form of a concession contract.[68] The Tribunal said:

> A contract is a contract. The Concession Contract exists, is valid and is legally binding. This conclusion is sufficient to establish that the Tribunal has jurisdiction on the basis of an investment having been made in the form of a Concession Contract.[69]

In other cases too, the parties had reached the stage of signing binding agreements or concessions. Tribunals found that these amounted to investments.[70] Where a successful tender was followed by a concession contract, there was an investment.[71] Also the acquisition of rights to supplement an existing investment was covered.[72] Where the investor had put substantial assets into a project, it had made an investment.[73]

[63] See US–Korea FTA, 2019, Article 11.28: 'investor of a Party means a Party or state enterprise thereof, or a national or an enterprise of a Party, that *attempts to make*, is making, or has made an investment in the territory of the other Party'. The US–Morocco FTA, 2004, Article 10.27 refers to an investor 'that *concretely attempts to make*, . . .' (italics added).

[64] *Mason v Korea*, Decision on Preliminary Objections, 22 December 2019.

[65] At para 210.

[66] *PSEG v Turkey*, Decision on Jurisdiction, 4 June 2004.

[67] At paras 66–73.

[68] At paras 79–104.

[69] At para 104.

[70] *RSM v Grenada I*, Award, 13 March 2009, paras 253–257; *Devas v India*, Award on Jurisdiction and Merits, 25 July 2016, paras 5, 196–210; *Bear Creek v Peru*, Award, 30 November 2017, paras 295–298.

[71] *Malicorp v Egypt*, Award, 7 February 2011, paras 113–114; *Bosca v Lithuania*, Award, 17 May 2013, paras 164–168.

[72] *Lemire v Ukraine*, Decision on Jurisdiction and Liability, 14 January 2010, paras 86, 89–90.

[73] *Blusun v Italy*, Award, 27 December 2016, para 269.

Therefore, an investment will exist once an agreement materializes, even if it does not ultimately lead to actual economic activity. The decisive criterion is that the agreement contains binding commitments and has financial value. An investment also exists if the relevant activity, in the form of economically significant steps, has actually commenced.

VII
Expropriation

ADDITIONAL READING: GC Christie, 'What Constitutes a Taking of Property under International Law' (1962) 38 *BYIL* 307; R Dolzer, 'New Foundations of the Law of Expropriation of Alien Property' (1981) 75 *AJIL* 553; R Higgins, 'The Taking of Foreign Property by the State' (1982) 176 *Recueil* 259; R Dolzer, 'Indirect Expropriation of Alien Property' (1986) 1 *ICSID Rev* 41; WM Reisman and RD Sloane, 'Indirect Expropriation and its Valuation in the BIT Generation' (2003) 74 *BYIL* 115; Y Fortier and SL Drymer, 'Indirect Expropriation in the Law of International Investment' (2004) 19 *ICSID Rev* 293; A Newcombe, 'The Boundaries of Regulatory Expropriation in International Law' (2005) 20 *ICSID Rev* 1; CH Schreuer, 'The Concept of Expropriation under the ECT and other Investment Protection Treaties' in C Ribeiro (ed) *Investment Arbitration and the Energy Charter Treaty* (2006) 108; V Heiskanen, 'The Doctrine of Indirect Expropriation in Light of the Practice of the Iran–United States Claims Tribunal' (2007) 8 *JWIT* 215; U Kriebaum, 'Partial Expropriation' (2007) 8 *JWIT* 69; U Kriebaum, 'Regulatory Takings' (2007) 8 *JWIT* 717; A Siwy, 'Indirect Expropriation and the Legitimate Expectations of the Investor' in C Klausegger et al (eds) *Austrian Arb YB* (2007) 355; A Hoffmann, 'Indirect Expropriation' in A Reinisch (ed) *Standards of Investment Protection* (2008) 151; A Reinisch, 'Expropriation' in P Muchlinski et al (eds) *The Oxford Handbook of International Investment Law* (2008) 407; U Kriebaum, 'Expropriation' in M Bungenberg et al (eds) *International Investment Law* (2015) 959; SR Ratner, 'Compensation for Expropriations in a World of Investment Treaties' (2017) 111 *AJIL* 7; HG Gharavi, 'Discord Over Judicial Expropriation' (2018) 33 *ICSID Rev* 349; A Rajput, *Regulatory Freedom and Indirect Expropriation in Investment Arbitration* (2018); C Titi, 'Police Powers Doctrine and International Investment Law in A Gattini et al (eds) *General Principles of Law and International Investment Arbitration* (2018) 323; JM Cox, *Expropriation in Investment Treaty Arbitration* (2019); A Reinisch and C Schreuer, *International Protection of Investments* (2020) 1–250.

The rules of international law governing the expropriation of alien property have long been of central concern to foreigners in general and to foreign investors in particular. Expropriation is the most severe form of interference with property. All expectations of the investor are destroyed in case the investment is taken without adequate compensation.

Consistent with the notion of territorial sovereignty, the classical rules of international law have accepted the host State's right to expropriate alien property. Customary international law placed certain limitations on the host State's right to take alien property. But even modern investment treaties respect the right to expropriate in principle. Treaty law typically addresses only the conditions and consequences of an expropriation, leaving the right to expropriate as such unaffected. The legality of an expropriation depends on whether these conditions have been met.[1]

1. The object of an expropriation

Most contemporary treaties, in their provisions dealing with expropriation, refer to 'investments'. Similarly, the jurisdiction of arbitral tribunals is typically restricted to disputes arising from 'investments'. Therefore, it is 'investments', as defined in these treaties, that are protected.

As described in Chapter IV, an investment is typically a complex operation consisting of a multitude of tangible and intangible assets. The definitions of 'investments' in treaties, include various intangible rights such as mortgages, shares, claims to money, intellectual property rights, and contracts.[2] Practice shows that claims for expropriations relate to a variety of assets, tangible and intangible, and even to arbitral awards. Among intangible assets, the expropriation of contract rights has played an important role in practice.

(a) Expropriation of contract rights

'The taking away or destruction of rights acquired, transmitted, and defined by a contract is as much a wrong, entitling the sufferer to redress, as the taking away or destruction of tangible property.' This principle, stated in 1903 by a member of the US–Venezuela Mixed Claims Commission in the *Rudloff* case,[3] was followed in 1922 by the Permanent Court of Arbitration in the *Norwegian Shipowners* case[4] and also by the Permanent Court of International Justice (PCIJ) in 1926 in the

[1] See VII.4 below.

[2] See IV.2(c) and IV.4 above.

[3] American–Venezuelan Mixed Claims Commission, *Rudloff Case*, Decision on Merits, 1 January 1903, 9 RIAA 255.

[4] Permanent Court of Arbitration, *Norwegian Shipowners' Claim* (*Norway v USA*), Award, 13 October 1922, (1948) 1 RIAA 307. The arbitrators held that by requisitioning ships that were to be built for Norwegian citizens, the government of the United States had expropriated the underlying construction contracts.

Chorzow Factory case.[5] Cases decided in investment arbitrations[6] and by the Iran–United States Claims Tribunal[7] have confirmed this position.

The Tribunal in *SPP v Egypt*[8] examined whether measures by Egypt affecting rights under a contract to build hotels may amount to an expropriation. The Tribunal said:

> 164. Nor can the Tribunal accept the argument that the term 'expropriation' applies only to *jus in rem*. The Respondent's cancellation of the project had the effect of taking certain important rights and interests of the Claimants... Clearly, those rights and interests were of a contractual rather than *in rem* nature. However, there is considerable authority for the proposition that contract rights are entitled to the protection of international law and that the taking of such rights involves an obligation to make compensation therefore.
> 165. Moreover, it has long been recognized that contractual rights may be indirectly expropriated.[9]

In the modern investment context, many investment decisions are accompanied and protected by specific investment agreements with the host State, often covering matters such as taxation, customs regulations, the right and duty to sell at a certain price to the host State, or pricing issues. As set out in more detail in Chapter V, these agreements form the legal and financial foundations of the investment, and the business decisions based upon them may collapse in their absence. Thus, it is understandable that practically all investment treaties state that contracts are covered by the term 'investment'.[10] In turn, provisions dealing with expropriation in these treaties refer to 'investments'. It follows that contracts are protected against expropriation.

The Tribunal in *Tokios Tokelės v Ukraine* stated that all business operations associated with the physical property of the investors are covered by the term 'investment', including contractual rights.[11]

[5] *Case Concerning Certain German Interests in Polish Upper Silesia*, 1926 PCIJ Series A, No 7, 3.

[6] See *Wena Hotels v Egypt*, Award, 8 December 2000, para 98; *CME v Czech Republic*, Partial Award, 13 September 2001, paras 591–609; *Impregilo v Pakistan*, Decision on Jurisdiction, 22 April 2005, para 274; *Eureko v Poland*, Partial Award, 19 August 2005, para 241; *Bayindir v Pakistan*, Decision on Jurisdiction, 14 November 2005, para 255 and Award, 27 August 2009, para 456; *Azurix v Argentina*, Award, 14 July 2006, para 314; *Vivendi v Argentina*, Resubmitted Case: Award, 20 August 2007, para 7.5.4.; *Deutsche Bank v Sri Lanka*, Award, 31 October 2012, para 506; *Flemingo v Poland*, Award, 12 August 2016, paras 592–594; *Karkey v Pakistan*, Award, 22 August 2017, para 646.

[7] Article IV-2 of the Treaty of Amity between Iran and the USA (1955) protects not only 'property' but also 'interests in property'. According to the Tribunal in *Phillips Petroleum*, the term 'interest in property' was 'included at the insistence of the United States for the stated purpose of ensuring that contract rights in the petroleum industry would be protected by the treaty in the same way as would the older type of property represented by a petroleum concession' (*Phillips Petroleum Company v Iran*, Award, 29 June 1989, 21 Iran–US CTR 79, para 105). See also *Amoco v Iran*, Partial Award, 14 July 1987, 15 Iran–US CTR 189, para 108.

[8] *SPP v Egypt*, Award, 20 May 1992.

[9] At paras 164–165.

[10] See eg Article 1(6)(f) of the Energy Charter: 'any right conferred by law or contract'. See also Article 1139 of the NAFTA and Article 14.1 USMCA.

[11] *Tokios Tokelės v Ukraine*, Decision on Jurisdiction, 29 April 2004, paras 92–93.

The Tribunal in *Siemens v Argentina*,[12] applying the bilateral investment treaty (BIT) between Argentina and Germany, said:

> The Contract falls under the definition of 'investments' under the Treaty and Article 4(2) refers to expropriation or nationalization of investments. Therefore, the State parties recognized that an investment in terms of the Treaty may be expropriated. There is nothing unusual in this regard. There is a long judicial practice that recognizes that expropriation is not limited to tangible property.[13]

(b) Partial expropriation

The doctrine of the unity of the investment[14] would appear to militate against admitting the possibility of an expropriation of only a part of the investment. In addition, the requirement of a substantial or total deprivation of the investment for the existence of an expropriation[15] would make a partial expropriation unlikely.[16]

The Tribunal in *Electrabel v Hungary*[17] rejected the idea of a partial expropriation of the investment. It said:

> If it were possible so easily to parse an investment into several constituent parts each forming a separate investment (as Electrabel here contends), it would render meaningless that tribunal's approach to indirect expropriation based on 'radical deprivation' and 'deprivation of any real substance' as being similar in effect to a direct expropriation or nationalisation. It would also mean, absurdly, that an investor could always meet the test for indirect expropriation by slicing its investment as finely as the particular circumstances required, without that investment as a whole ever meeting that same test... it is clear that both in applying the wording of Article 13(1) ECT and under international law, the test for expropriation is applied to the relevant investment as a whole, even if different parts may separately qualify as investments for jurisdictional purposes. Here the investment held by Electrabel as a whole was its aggregate collection of interests in Dunamenti; it was thus one integral investment; and in the context of expropriation it was not a series of separate, individual investments.[18]

12 *Siemens v Argentina*, Award, 6 February 2007.
13 At para 267. The Tribunal relied on the *Norwegian Shipowners* and *Chorzow Factory* cases.
14 See IV.5 above.
15 See VII.3(c) below.
16 In this sense: *Grand River v United States*, Award, 12 January 2011, paras 146–148, 155.
17 *Electrabel v Hungary*, Decision on Jurisdiction, Applicable Law and Liability, 30 November 2012.
18 At paras 6.57–6.58. See also *Burlington v Ecuador*, Decision on Liability, 14 December 2012, paras 258–261, 398, 470–471.

Nevertheless, some tribunals have accepted the possibility of an expropriation of particular rights that formed part of an overall business operation.[19] In *Middle East Cement v Egypt*,[20] the investor had, *inter alia*, obtained an import licence for cement and had operated a ship. Egypt subsequently took measures that prevented the investor from operating its licence and seized and auctioned the ship. The investor asserted a series of rights in respect of which it alleged expropriation. These included the import licence and ownership of the ship. The Tribunal looked at these claims separately and determined in respect of each of them whether an expropriation had taken place. It found that the licence qualified as an investment and that the measures that prevented the exercise of the rights under it amounted to an expropriation.[21] The Tribunal examined separately whether an expropriation of the ship had occurred and gave an affirmative answer.[22] Several other claims of expropriation in respect of other rights were also examined but denied for a variety of reasons.[23] Therefore, *Middle East Cement* demonstrates that it is possible to expropriate specific rights enjoyed by the investor separately regardless of the control over the overall investment.

In *Eureko v Poland*,[24] the investor had acquired a minority share in a privatized insurance company. A related agreement granted the investor the right to acquire further shares thereby gaining majority control of the company. The right to acquire the additional shares was subsequently withdrawn by the State. The original investment remained unaffected. The Tribunal found that the right to acquire further shares constituted 'assets', which were separately capable of expropriation.[25] It follows from this decision that even where control over the basic investment remains unaffected, the taking of specific rights that are related to the basic investment may amount to an expropriation.

In *Ampal-American v Egypt*,[26] the Tribunal considered whether Egypt's revocation of a licence to participate in a tax-free zone amounted to an expropriation, although this interference did not destroy the entire project.[27] The Tribunal confirmed that the licence was an investment in its own right and that the revocation therefore was a direct and total taking of a discrete investment protected by the Treaty.[28]

What counts for the tribunals that admit a partial expropriation claim is that the right concerned by the expropriatory measure could have been an investment

[19] *Waste Management v Mexico II*, Award, 30 April 2004, para 141; *EnCana v Ecuador*, Award, 3 February 2006, paras 172–183; *Philip Morris v Uruguay*, Award, 8 July 2016, paras 280–283.

[20] *Middle East Cement v Egypt*, Award, 12 April 2002.

[21] At paras 101, 105, 107, 127.

[22] At paras 138, 144.

[23] At paras 152–156, 163–165.

[24] *Eureko v Poland*, Partial Award, 19 August 2005.

[25] At paras 239–241.

[26] *Ampal-American v Egypt*, Decision on Liability and Heads of Loss, 21 February 2017

[27] At para 179.

[28] At paras 180, 187.

by itself and would have enjoyed protection independent from the rest of the investment.[29]

2. Expropriation as an act of government

It is uncontested that expropriation requires an act of the State in its official capacity. Typically, expropriations occur through legislative acts and through measures taken by the State's administration, often in combination. Some cases even involve action or inaction of the host State's courts that are said to be expropriatory.[30]

The need for an act of an official nature is particularly evident in the treatment of claims based on contract. As pointed out above,[31] contracts can be assets that are susceptible to expropriation. But not every failure by a government to perform a contract will amount to an expropriation even if the violation leads to a loss of rights under the contract. A simple breach of contract at the hands of the State is not an expropriation.[32] Tribunals have found that the decisive factor is whether the State has acted in an official, governmental capacity.[33]

In *RFCC v Morocco*, the Tribunal differentiated between the mere exercise of a contractual right and an action by the host State 'in public capacity' and placed emphasis on whether or not a law or a governmental decree had been passed or a judgment executed.[34]

Other tribunals have held similarly that mere breaches of contract or defects in its performance would not amount to an expropriation. What was needed was an act of public authority.[35] In *Siemens v*

[29] U Kriebaum, 'Partial Expropriation' (2007) 8 *JWIT* 69.

[30] *Noble Ventures v Romania*, Award, 12 October 2005, paras 211–216; *Saipem v Bangladesh*, Decision on Jurisdiction and Recommendation on Provisional Measures, 21 March 2007, paras 131–133 and Award, 30 June 2009, paras 129, 132; *Swisslion v Macedonia*, Award, 6 July 2012, paras 312–321; *Tatneft v Ukraine*, Award on the Merits, 29 July 2014, paras 459–481; *İçkale v Turkmenistan*, Award, 8 March 2016, paras 371–376; *MNSS v Montenegro*, Award, 4 May 2016, para 370; *Garanti Koza v Turkmenistan*, Award, 19 December 2016, para 365; *Anglia Auto v Czech Republic*, Final Award, 10 March 2017, paras 290–303; *Eli Lilly v Canada*, Final Award, 16 March 2017, para 221; *Teinver v Argentina*, Award, 21 July 2017, paras 954–959; *Krederi v Ukraine*, Award, 2 July 2018, paras 690–716; *Standard Chartered Bank (Hong Kong) v Tanzania*, Award, 11 October 2019, paras 279, 380; *Staur Eiendom v Latvia*, Award, 28 February 2020, paras 511–514; *Interocean v Nigeria*, Award, 6 October 2020, paras 310–315.

[31] See VII.1(a) above.

[32] For detailed discussion, see SM Schwebel, 'On Whether the Breach by a State of a Contract with an Alien is a Breach of International Law' in *International Law at the Time of its Codification, Essays in Honour of Roberto Ago, III* (1987) 401.

[33] See also American Law Institute, *Restatement (Third) of the Foreign Relations Law of the United States*, vol 2 (1986) 201: 'a state is responsible for such a repudiation or breach only ... if it is akin to an expropriation in that the contract is repudiated or breached for governmental rather than commercial reasons'.

[34] *RFCC v Morocco*, Award, 22 December 2003, paras 60–62, 65–69, 85–89.

[35] *Azinian v Mexico*, Award, 1 November 1999, paras 87, 90, 99–100; *Impregilo v Pakistan*, Decision on Jurisdiction, 22 April 2005, paras 260, 274, 281; *Bayindir v Pakistan*, Decision on Jurisdiction, 14 November 2005, para 257 and Award, 27 August 2009, paras 444–445, 458, 461; *Azurix v Argentina*, Award, 14 July 2006, para 315; *Parkerings v Lithuania*, Award, 11 September 2007, paras 440–447;

Argentina,[36] the Tribunal, in discussing expropriation, found that a State Party to a contract would breach the applicable treaty only if its behaviour went beyond that which an ordinary contracting party could adopt.[37] The Tribunal said:

> for the State to incur international responsibility it must act as such, it must use its public authority. The actions of the State have to be based on its 'superior governmental power'. It is not a matter of being disappointed in the performance of the State in the execution of a contract but rather of interference in the contract execution through governmental action.[38]

Specifically, tribunals have held that a failure to pay a debt under a contract does not amount to an expropriation.[39] *Waste Management v Mexico II*[40] concerned a concession for waste disposal. The Tribunal found that the mere non-payment by the city of Acapulco of amounts due under the concession agreement did not amount to an expropriation.[41] It found that the State's failure to pay bills, did not amount to an 'outright repudiation of the transaction', and did not purport to terminate the contract. Only a decree or executive act or an exercise of legislative public authority could amount to an expropriation. The Tribunal said:

> The mere non-performance of a contractual obligation is not to be equated with a taking of property, nor (unless accompanied by other elements) is it tantamount to expropriation. Any private party can fail to perform its contracts, whereas nationalization and expropriation are inherently governmental acts[42] ... The Tribunal concludes that it is one thing to expropriate a right under a contract and another to fail to comply with the contract. Non-compliance by a government with contractual obligations is not the same thing as, or equivalent or tantamount to, an expropriation.[43]

Biwater Gauff v Tanzania, Award, 24 July 2008, paras 458, 489, 492; *Saipem v Bangladesh*, Award, 30 June 2009, para 131; *Al-Bahloul v Tajikistan*, Partial Award on Jurisdiction and Liability, 2 September 2009, para 281; *Suez and Vivendi v* Argentina, Decision on Liability, 30 July 2010, para 154; *Inmaris Perestroika v Ukraine*, Award, 1 March 2012, para 301; *Vannessa v Venezuela*, Award, 16 January 2013, paras 209–214; *Convial Callao v Peru*, Final Award, 21 May 2013, para 504; *Tulip v Turkey*, Award, 10 March 2014, paras 417–418; *OI European v Venezuela*, Award, 10 March 2015, para 356; *Crystallex v Venezuela*, Award, 4 April 2016, paras 683–708; *Caratube v Kazakhstan*, Award, 27 September 2017, paras 908, 935; *Gosling v Mauritius*, Award, 18 February 2020, paras 273–277.

[36] *Siemens v Argentina*, Award, 6 February 2007.
[37] At para 248.
[38] At para 253.
[39] *SGS v Philippines*, Decision on Jurisdiction, 29 January 2004, para 161.
[40] *Waste Management v Mexico II*, Award, 30 April 2004.
[41] At paras 159–174.
[42] At para 174.
[43] At para 175.

While these considerations are clearly helpful, they do not exhaust the subject matter. Indeed, the *Waste Management II* Tribunal itself recognized, without elaboration, that 'one could envisage conduct tantamount to an expropriation which consisted of acts and omissions not specifically or exclusively governmental'.[44] An analysis designed to cover all acts of expropriation cannot focus exclusively on the existence of formal governmental acts. It must also contemplate other relevant factors, such as the exercise of contractual rights as a mere pretext to conceal an expropriatory measure.[45]

3. Indirect expropriation

The difference between a direct or formal expropriation and an indirect expropriation turns on whether the legal title of the owner is affected by the measure in question. Today direct expropriations have become rare.[46] Most States are reluctant to jeopardize their investment climate by taking the drastic and conspicuous step of an open taking of foreign property. An official act that takes the title of the foreign investor's property will attract negative publicity and is likely to do lasting damage to the State's reputation as a venue for foreign investments.

In consequence, indirect expropriations have gained in importance. An indirect expropriation leaves the title untouched but deprives the investor of the possibility to utilize the investment in a meaningful way. A typical feature of an indirect expropriation is that the State will deny the existence of an expropriation and will not contemplate the payment of compensation.

(a) Broad formulae

The contours of the definition of an indirect expropriation are not precisely drawn. This is so, even under new investment protection treaties that attempt to define indirect investment.[47] An increasing number of arbitral cases and a growing body of literature on the subject have shed some light on the issue but the debate goes on. Some tribunals have interpreted the concept of indirect expropriation

[44] At para 175.

[45] *Alpha v Ukraine*, Award, 8 November 2010, para 412; *Gold Reserve v Venezuela*, Award, 22 September 2014, paras 663–667; *Vigotop v Hungary*, Award, 1 October 2014, paras 331, 634.

[46] But occasionally States still resort to direct expropriations, see eg *Santa Elena v Costa Rica*, Final Award, 17 February 2000, para 17; *Funnekotter v Zimbabwe*, Award, 22 April 2009, paras 55, 90; *Siag v Egypt*, Award, 1 June 2009, para 427; *von Pezold v Zimbabwe*, Award, 28 July 2015, para 494; *Quiborax v Bolivia*, Award, 16 September 2015, paras 200–234; *Rusoro Mining v Venezuela*, Award, 22 August 2016, paras 377, 379; *Gavrilovic v Croatia*, Award, 26 July 2018, paras 922, 933.

[47] See eg Annex B to the 2004 and 2012 US Model BIT.

narrowly and have preferred to find a violation of the standard of fair and equitable treatment.[48]

The concept of indirect expropriation as such was clearly recognized in the early case law of arbitral tribunals and of the Permanent Court of International Justice in the 1920s and 1930s.[49] Today it is generally accepted that certain types of measures affecting foreign property will be considered an expropriation, and require compensation, even though the owner retains the formal title. What was and remains contentious is the line between non-compensable regulatory and other governmental activity and measures amounting to indirect, compensable expropriation. The issue is equally important to the host State, which may wish to broaden the range of non-compensable activities and to the foreign investor who will argue in favour of a broad understanding of the concept of indirect takings.

Bilateral and multilateral treaties and draft treaties typically contain a reference to indirect expropriation or to measures tantamount to expropriation. The Abs–Shawcross Draft Convention on Investment Abroad (1959) referred to 'measures against nationals of another Party to deprive them directly or indirectly of their property'. Essentially, the same wording appears in the 1967 OECD Draft Convention on the Protection of Foreign Property. The Draft United Nations Code of Conduct on Transnational Corporations referred to '[a]ny such taking of property whether direct or indirect'. The 1992 World Bank Guidelines on the Treatment of Foreign Direct Investment speak of expropriation or 'measures which have similar effects'. Similarly, the 1998 OECD Draft for a Multilateral Agreement on Investment refers to 'measures having equivalent effect'. The 1994 Energy Charter Treaty (ECT) similarly refers to 'a measure or measures having effect equivalent to nationalization or expropriation'. Another variation is contained in the NAFTA of 1992, which speaks of 'a measure tantamount to nationalization or expropriation'. The USMCA of 2020 speaks of 'measures equivalent to expropriation or nationalization'.

Most current bilateral investment treaties contain similar language. The French Model Treaty states: 'Neither Contracting Party shall take any measures of expropriation or nationalization or any other measures having the effect of dispossession, direct or indirect, of nationals or companies of the other Contracting Party of their investments.'[50] According to the 2008 German Model Treaty '[i]nvestments by investors of either Contracting State shall not directly or indirectly be expropriated, nationalized or subjected to any other measure the effects of which would be tantamount to expropriation or nationalization'.[51] The 2008 Model Treaty used by the United Kingdom provides that '[i]nvestments of nationals or companies of

[48] See eg *Saluka v Czech Republic*, Partial Award, 17 March 2006, paras 276, 407.

[49] See *Norwegian Shipowners' Claims*, 13 October 1922 (1948) 1 RIAA 307; *Case concerning certain German interests in Polish Upper Silesia*, 25 May 1926, PCIJ Series A, No 7 (1926) 3.

[50] Article 6(2) of the French Model Treaty.

[51] Article 4(2) of the German Model Treaty.

either Contracting Party shall not be nationalized, expropriated or subjected to measures having effect equivalent to nationalization or expropriation'.[52]

The 2004 and 2012 US Model BITs approach the issue in greater detail. After stating in Article 6(1) that '[n]either Party may expropriate or nationalize a covered investment either directly or indirectly through measures equivalent to expropriation or nationalization',[53] a special Annex B named 'Expropriation' adds:

> (a) The determination of whether an action or series of actions by a Party, in a specific fact situation, constitutes an indirect expropriation, requires a case-by-case, fact-based inquiry that considers, among other factors:
> (i) the economic impact of the government action, although the fact that an action or series of actions by a Party has an adverse effect on the economic value of an investment, standing alone, does not establish that an indirect expropriation has occurred;
> (ii) the extent to which the government action interferes with distinct, reasonable investment-backed expectations; and
> (iii) the character of the government action.
> (b) Except in rare circumstances, non-discriminatory regulatory actions by a Party that are designed and applied to protect legitimate public welfare objectives, such as public health, safety, and the environment, do not constitute indirect expropriations.[54]

Among the broader formulae proposed in general studies and drafts, some have received special attention in the decisions of arbitral tribunals and in academic writings. Professors Sohn and Baxter included in their 1961 Draft Convention on the International Responsibility of States for Injuries to Aliens, a version that contains specific categories of indirect takings:

> A taking of property includes not only an outright taking of property but also any such unreasonable interference with the use, enjoyment, or disposal of property as to justify an inference that the owner thereof will not be able to use, enjoy, or dispose of the property within a reasonable period of time after the inception of such interference.[55]

The 1986 Restatement (Third) of the Foreign Relations Law of the United States (§ 712) is much shorter and in its text only speaks of a 'taking'. Comment (g) refers

[52] Article 5(1) of the UK Model Treaty.
[53] See Article 6(1) of the US Model Treaties.
[54] Annex B, Article 4 of the 2004 and 2012 US Model Treaties.
[55] LB Sohn and RR Baxter, 'Responsibility of States for Injuries to the Economic Interests of Aliens' (1961) 55 *AJIL* 545, 553 (Article 10(3)(a)).

to actions 'that have the effect of "taking" the property, in whole or in large part, outright or in stages ("creeping expropriation")'.

A United Nations Conference on Trade and Development (UNCTAD) study, prepared in 2000, uses different language and considers that 'measures short of physical takings may amount to takings in that they result in the effective loss of management, use or control, or a significant depreciation of the value, of the assets of a foreign investor'.[56]

In an early influential article Gordon Christie reviewed the then existing case law and pointed to certain recognized groups and categories of indirect takings, without an attempt to present a general formula.[57] Judge Rosalyn Higgins, in her 1982 Hague Lectures, questioned the usefulness of a distinction between non-compensable *bona fide* governmental regulation and 'taking' for a public purpose:

> Is this distinction intellectually viable? Is not the State in both cases (that is, either by a taking for a public purpose, or by regulating) purporting to act in the common good? And in each case has the owner of the property not suffered loss? Under international law standards, a regulation that amounted (by virtue of its scope and effect) to a taking, would need to be 'for a public purpose' (in the sense of a general, rather than for a private, interest). And just compensation would be due.[58]

It has been argued elsewhere that the international law of expropriation has essentially grown out of, and mirrored, the parallel domestic laws.[59] As a consequence of this linkage, it appears plausible that measures that are, under the rules of the main domestic laws, normally considered regulatory without requiring compensation, will not require compensation under international law either.

The importance of the effect of a measure for the question of whether an expropriation has occurred was highlighted by Reisman and Sloane:

> tribunals have increasingly accepted that expropriation must be analyzed in consequential rather than in formal terms. What matters is the effect of governmental conduct—whether malfeasance, misfeasance, or nonfeasance, or some combination of the three—on foreign property rights or control over an investment, not whether the state promulgates a formal decree or otherwise expressly proclaims its intent to expropriate. For purposes of state responsibility and the obligation to

[56] UNCTAD, *Series on Issues in International Investment Agreements: 'Taking of Property'* (2000) 4.

[57] GC Christie, 'What Constitutes a Taking of Property under International Law?' (1962) 38 *BYIL* 307.

[58] R Higgins, 'The Taking of Property by the State: Recent Developments in International Law' (1982-III) 176 *Recueil* 259, 331.

[59] R Dolzer, 'Indirect Expropriation of Alien Property' (1986) 1 *ICSID Rev* 41.

make adequate reparation, international law does not distinguish indirect from direct expropriations.[60]

In recent jurisprudence, the formula most often found is that the existence of an expropriation requires a 'substantial deprivation' of an investment.[61]

The oscillating understanding of this approach may be illustrated in the light of relevant jurisprudence.

(b) Some illustrative cases

Cases decided by tribunals demonstrate the variety of scenarios in which the question of indirect expropriation may come up. Tribunals have had to adapt their focus of inquiry to these different circumstances. An emphasis on different aspects of the law must not necessarily be construed as an expression of inconsistency. Often, the facts of a case simply highlight only one specific factor and the neglect of other possible factors does not result from oversight but from their irrelevance to the specific circumstances. A short survey of cases may indicate the diversity of factual bases and of the reasoning of tribunals.

The *Oscar Chinn* case[62] illustrates that the prohibition of uncompensated expropriation is no insurance against changes in the business environment. It concerned the interests of a British shipping business in the Congo. In the aftermath of the economic crisis of 1929, the Belgian government had intervened in the shipping business on the Congo River by reducing the prices charged by Mr Chinn's only competitor, the partly State-owned company, *UNATRA*. The government had also granted corresponding subsidies to *UNATRA* in order to keep the transport system on the Congo River viable. This made the business of Oscar Chinn economically unsustainable. The PCIJ concluded that there was no taking. It said:

> The Court ... is unable to see in his [Mr. Chinn's] original position—which was characterized by the possession of customers and the possibility of making a profit—anything in the nature of a genuine vested right. Favourable business conditions and good-will are transient circumstances, subject to inevitable changes; ... No enterprise ... can escape from the chances and hazards resulting from general economic conditions.[63]

[60] WM Reisman and RD Sloane, 'Indirect Expropriation and its Valuation in the BIT Generation' (2003) 74 *BYIL* 115, 121. Footnotes omitted.

[61] See eg *Société Générale v Dominican Republic*, Award, 19 September 2008, para 64; *Alpha v Ukraine*, Award, 8 November 2010, para 408; *Bosh v Ukraine*, Award, 25 October 2012, para 218; *Enkev Beheer v Poland*, First Partial Award, 29 April 2014, para 344; *UP and C.D v Hungary*, Award, 9 October 2018, paras 333, 335, 354; *Casinos Austria v Argentina*, Decision on Jurisdiction, 29 June 2018, para 228.

[62] *Oscar Chinn Case* (*UK v Belgium*), Judgment, 12 December 1934, PCIJ Series A/B, No 63 (1934) 4.

[63] At 27.

The arbitration in *Revere Copper v OPIC*[64] concerned a dispute arising from the insurance by the US Overseas Private Investment Corporation (OPIC)[65] of an investment made by the US claimant in Jamaica. This case illustrates how a State measure that does not interfere with the title to the property (a mining lease) and does not take away the property of the plant or the facilities of an investor, nevertheless makes it impossible to control the investment economically and, therefore, can be an indirect expropriation.

Revere Copper had made substantial investments in the Jamaican bauxite mining sector. An agreement concluded in 1967 between RJA, the investor's local subsidiary, and the Jamaican government fixed the taxes and royalties that were to be paid by RJA for a period of 25 years and provided that no further taxes or financial burdens would be imposed on RJA by the Jamaican authorities. However, in 1972, the newly elected Jamaican government announced a far-reaching reform of the bauxite sector and, in 1974, increased the royalties to be paid by RJA so drastically that RJA ceased operating in 1975.

Revere Copper then sought recovery under its OPIC insurance contract, alleging that the measures adopted by the Jamaican government amounted to an expropriation of its investment. The General Terms and Conditions of the OPIC contract defined 'expropriatory action' *inter alia*, as: 'any action which … for a period of one year directly results in preventing … the Foreign Enterprise from exercising effective control over the use or disposition of substantial portion of its property or from constructing the project or operating the same'. Although there had been no interference with Revere's physical property, the majority of the Tribunal found that the repudiation of the guarantees given to Revere amounted to an action that had resulted in preventing the foreign enterprise from exercising effective control over the use or disposition of a substantial portion of its property:

> OPIC argues that RJA still has all the rights and property that it had before the events of 1974: it is in possession of the plant and other facilities; it has its Mining Lease; it can operate as it did before. This may be true in a formal sense but … we do not regard RJA's 'control' of the use and operation of its properties as any longer 'effective' in view of the destruction by Government actions of its contract rights.[66]

The arbitral Tribunal came to this conclusion by emphasizing that 'control in a large industrial enterprise … is exercised by a continuous stream of decisions' and that without the repudiated agreement between RJA and Jamaica, '[t]here is no way in which rational decisions can be made'.[67]

64 *Revere Copper v OPIC*, Award, 24 August 1978, 56 ILR 258.
65 On investment insurance see Chapter XI below.
66 At 291–292.
67 At 292.

Metalclad v Mexico[68] illustrates that the effect of a measure is more important than the form. In *Metalclad*, a US company had been granted a permit for the development and operation of a hazardous waste landfill by the Mexican federal government. Subsequently, the local municipal authorities refused to grant the necessary construction permit and the regional government declared the land in question a national area for the protection of cactuses. The arbitral Tribunal found a violation of the North American Free Trade Agreement (NAFTA) Article 1110, which provides that '[n]o Party may directly or indirectly nationalize or expropriate an investment of an investor of another Party in its territory or take a measure tantamount to nationalization or expropriation of such an investment'. An often-repeated passage in the Tribunal's Award reads:

> Thus, expropriation under NAFTA includes not only open, deliberate and acknowledged takings of property, such as outright seizure or formal or obligatory transfer of title in favour of the host State, but also covert or incidental interference with the use of property which has the effect of depriving the owner, in whole or in significant part, of the use or reasonably-to-be-expected economic benefit of property even if not necessarily to the obvious benefit of the host State.[69]

Middle East Cement v Egypt[70] shows that the withdrawal of a licence can also amount to an expropriation. The case concerned the revocation of a free zone licence through the prohibition of import of cement into Egyptian territory. The prohibition resulted in paralysis of the investor's business, which essentially consisted of importing, storing, and dispatching cement within Egypt. The Tribunal found that the import prohibition resulted in an indirect taking of the claimant's investment:

> When measures are taken by a State the effect of which is to deprive the investor of the use and benefit of his investment even though he may retain nominal ownership of the respective rights being the investment, the measures are often referred to as a 'creeping' or 'indirect' expropriation or, as in the BIT, as measures 'the effect of which is tantamount to expropriation.' As a matter of fact, the investor is deprived by such measures of parts of the value of his investment. This is the case here, and, therefore, it is the Tribunal's view that such a taking amounted to an expropriation within the meaning of Art. 4 of the BIT and that, accordingly, Respondent is liable to pay compensation therefor.[71]

68 *Metalclad v Mexico*, Award, 30 August 2000.
69 At para 103.
70 *Middle East Cement v Egypt*, Award, 12 April 2002.
71 At para 107.

Fireman's Fund v Mexico[72] illustrates that the expropriation clause of investment treaties is no insurance against business risk. The case involved an expropriation claim under NAFTA Chapter XIV, devoted to cross-border investment in financial services. That Chapter allows an expropriation claim under Article 1110 NAFTA but does not allow claims pertaining to a violation of the minimum standard or the rule on national treatment. The US claimant submitted that its investment in a Mexican financial institution was expropriated by a series of actions of the Mexican government.[73] The bank in which claimant had invested was in a delicate financial situation, and the claimant argued that the Mexican government had taken steps which permanently deprived it of the value of the investment. The Tribunal summarized the law of expropriation as follows:

> NAFTA does not give a definition for the word 'expropriation.' In some ten cases in which Article 1110(1) of the NAFTA was considered to date, the definitions appear to vary. Considering those cases and customary international law in general, the present Tribunal retains the following elements.
>
> (a) Expropriation requires a taking (which may include destruction) by a government-type authority of an investment by an investor covered by the NAFTA.
> (b) The covered investment may include intangible as well as tangible property.
> (c) The taking must be a substantially complete deprivation of the economic use and enjoyment of the rights to the property, or of identifiable distinct parts thereof (i.e., it approaches total impairment).
> (d) The taking must be permanent, and not ephemeral or temporary.
> (e) The taking usually involves a transfer of ownership to another person (frequently the government authority concerned), but that need not necessarily be so in certain cases (e.g., total destruction of an investment due to measures by a government authority without transfer of rights).
> (f) The effects of the host State's measures are dispositive, not the underlying intent, for determining whether there is expropriation.
> (g) The taking may be *de jure* or *de facto*.
> (h) The taking may be 'direct' or 'indirect.'
> (i) The taking may have the form of a single measure or a series of related or unrelated measures over a period of time (the so-called 'creeping' expropriation).
> (j) To distinguish between a compensable expropriation and a non-compensable regulation by a host State, the following factors (usually in combination) may be taken into account: whether the measure is within the

[72] *Fireman's Fund v Mexico*, Award, 17 July 2006.
[73] At para 185.

recognized police powers of the host State; the (public) purpose and effect of the measure; whether the measure is discriminatory; the proportionality between the means employed and the aim sought to be realized and the bona fide nature of the measure.

(k) The investor's reasonable 'investment-backed expectations' may be a relevant factor whether (indirect) expropriation has occurred.[74]

In the end, the Tribunal considered that the actual cause of the problems faced by the investor was that its investment had been risky and that the business risks involved had materialized. It found that Mexico had discriminated against the investor and possibly had acted in an unfair manner, but that it had no jurisdiction in these respects under NAFTA's rules on financial services.[75]

Vivendi v Argentina[76] is an example for a case where a combination of several State measures, not interfering with the physical control of the investor's assets, can nevertheless lead to an expropriation. The case concerned a concession for a water and sewage business. The claimants alleged that Argentina had unilaterally modified tariffs, had used its power of oversight to confront the claimants with unjustified accusations, had used the media to generate hostility towards claimants, had incited claimants' customers not to pay, and had forced claimants to renegotiate the concession.

The Tribunal agreed with the claimants that Argentina's measures went beyond a partial deprivation,[77] left the concession without value, and held that they amounted to a creeping expropriation. The Tribunal rejected Argentina's defence that claimants' control of their physical assets excluded an expropriation.[78] It pointed to the effects of Argentina's destructive acts[79] and emphasized that the pursuit of a public purpose does not immunize a governmental measure from a claim of expropriation.[80]

Biwater Gauff v Tanzania[81] concerned a claim for expropriation surrounding the peculiar circumstances of a termination of a lease contract in the water and sewage business. The Tribunal confirmed that the contract was an investment,[82] that an expropriation claim must be determined in the light of the effect of the measures (not necessarily of an economic nature),[83] and recognized that all relevant acts of a government affecting the property must be considered cumulatively.[84] The Tribunal

[74] At para 176.
[75] At paras 203, 217–218.
[76] *Vivendi v Argentina*, Resubmitted Case: Award, 20 August 2007.
[77] At para 7.5.11.
[78] At para 7.5.18.
[79] At para 7.5.20.
[80] At para 7.5.21.
[81] *Biwater Gauff v Tanzania*, Award, 24 July 2008.
[82] At para 453.
[83] At para 455.
[84] At para 456.

also found that an exercise of *puissance publique* was necessary for a finding of expropriation, but not a denial of justice.[85] According to this decision, an indirect expropriation had to be assumed in case of 'a substantial deprivation of rights for at least a meaningful period of time'.[86]

In the event, the Tribunal found that the formal termination of the lease by Tanzania was of an ordinary contractual nature and therefore could not amount to an expropriation. However, a series of acts preceding the termination did violate the treaty rule on expropriation: an inflammatory press conference by a Minister, the withdrawal of a value-added tax (VAT) exemption, the forceful occupation of claimants' facilities, the usurpation of the claimants' management rights and the deportation of senior staff amounted to an indirect expropriation. The Tribunal examined arbitral jurisprudence and found that occupation and seizure, takeover of management, and the deportation of management personnel in themselves led to this conclusion.

In the end, however, claimants received no compensation; already before the government's interventions, the company had significant liabilities, its contract was about to be terminated, and a willing buyer would not have paid any money to acquire the company.

Suez and InterAgua v Argentina[87] concerned Argentina's treatment of claimant's right to operate, for 30 years, a water and sewage system and to receive corresponding revenues based on a tariff regime for that period. Claimants submitted that regulatory measures by Argentina and also its refusal to adjust the tariffs amounted to an expropriation. On both counts, the Tribunal rejected the claim, pointing to claimant's ongoing control of its operations.[88]

As regards the regulatory measures in particular, the Tribunal relied on the opaque concept of an 'overt taking'[89] which, in its view, did not exist despite a series of measures affecting the right to withdraw cash from bank accounts, new taxes, currency measures resulting in a deprivation of the local Peso, and the abandonment of an index-based scheme of tariff adjustment. In principle, at least, the Tribunal recognized that an examination of a taking must be targeted at the effects, not at the intention of a measure.[90] In general, an indirect expropriation presupposed 'a substantial, permanent deprivation of the claimant's investments or the enjoyment of those investments' economic benefits'. Under the circumstances, the termination of the underlying concession contract by Argentina was deemed contractual in nature and did not involve the exercise of Argentina's sovereign power; as a consequence, the measure was not expropriatory in nature.[91]

[85] At para 458.
[86] At para 463.
[87] *Suez and InterAgua v Argentina*, Decision on Liability, 30 July 2010.
[88] At paras 117 et seq.
[89] At para 125.
[90] At para 122.
[91] At para 143.

In *Alpha v Ukraine*[92] the Austrian claimant had entered into an agreement with a State enterprise concerning the renovation and operation of a hotel in the Ukraine. After a while, regular payments due to the claimant under the agreement were stopped amidst political and criminal turmoil. It turned out that the State had, for non-political reasons, halted the payments to the claimant.[93] As a result of the non-payment, the economic value of the rights held by the claimant was largely wiped out. The Tribunal questioned the relevance of the distinction between 'sovereign' and 'commercial' actions to the question whether Ukraine's actions had expropriated the claimant's investment. It concluded that the State's actions amounted to an indirect expropriation. The decision illustrates that the issue of non-payment of debt resists generalization. Depending upon the circumstances, non-payment may amount to an expropriation.

These cases illustrate that indirect expropriations can arise out of very diverse factual situations and take very different forms. Tribunals have considered various factors when they decided whether in a particular case an expropriation had occurred. What all these awards have in common is that a substantial interference through a sovereign act over a significant period of time is always a requirement of an indirect expropriation.

(c) Severity of the deprivation

The effect of the State measure(s) upon the economic benefit and value as well as upon the control over the investment is the key question in determining whether an expropriation has occurred. Whenever the effect is not substantial, tribunals decide that there was no expropriation.[94] Whenever the effect is substantial and lasts for a significant period of time, there is a prima facie assumption that a taking of the property has occurred.[95]

Tribunals have accordingly based their decisions primarily on economic considerations. An indirect expropriation was seen to exist if the measure constituted a deprivation of the economic use and enjoyment, 'as if the rights related thereto—such as the income or benefits . . . had ceased to exist', or when 'the use or enjoyment of benefits related thereto is exacted or interfered with to a similar extent'.[96] Other formulae and phrases have also been used.[97]

[92] *Alpha v Ukraine*, Award, 8 November 2010.

[93] At para 412.

[94] See eg *SD Myers v Canada*, First Partial Award, 13 November 2000, paras 283–284; *Azurix v Argentina*, Award, 14 July 2006, para 322; *Glamis Gold v United States*, Award, 8 June 2009, para 536; *Roussalis v Romania*, Award, 7 December 2011, paras 354–358; *Allard v Barbados*, Award, 27 June 2016, paras 263–266.

[95] See eg *Norwegian Shipowners' Claims*, 13 October 1922, 1 RIAA 307.

[96] *Tecmed v Mexico*, Award, 29 May 2003, paras 115–116.

[97] See Y Fortier and S L Drymer, 'Indirect Expropriation in the Law of International Investment: I Know It When I See It, or *Caveat Investor*' (2004) 19 *ICSID Rev* 293, 305:

In *RFCC v Morocco*,[98] the Tribunal stated that an indirect expropriation exists in case the measures have 'substantial effects of an intensity that reduces and/or removes the legitimate benefits related with the use of the rights targeted by the measure to an extent that they render their further possession useless'.[99]

Other decisions have in various wordings and degrees also emphasized the significance of the severity of the measure.[100] In *CMS v Argentina*,[101] the Tribunal found that no indirect expropriation had occurred when Argentina unilaterally suspended a previously agreed tariff adjustment scheme for the gas transport sector in the context of its economic and financial crisis. The US company CMS had argued, *inter alia*, that the suspension of the tariff adjustment formula amounted to an indirect expropriation of its investment in the Argentine gas transport sector. The Tribunal rejected this argument even though it admitted that the measures had an important effect on the claimant's business:

> The essential question is therefore to establish whether the enjoyment of the property has been effectively neutralized. The standard that a number of tribunals have applied in recent cases where indirect expropriation has been contended is that of substantial deprivation... the investor is in control of the investment; the Government does not manage the day-to-day operations of the company; and the investor has full ownership and control of the investment.[102]

'the required level of interference with such rights—has been variously described as: (1) *unreasonable*; (2) an interference that renders rights so *useless that they must be deemed to have been expropriated*; (3) an interference that deprives the investor of *fundamental rights of ownership*; (4) an interference that makes rights *practically useless*; (5) an interference *sufficiently restrictive* to warrant a conclusion that the property has been 'taken'; (6) and interference that deprives, in whole or in significant part, the *use or reasonably-to-be-expected economic benefit* of the property; (7) an interference that *radically deprives* the economical use and enjoyment of an investment, as if the rights related thereto had ceased to exist; (8) an interference that makes *any form of exploitation of the property disappear* ...; (9) an interference such that the property can no longer be put to *reasonable use*.'

See also U Kriebaum, 'Expropriation' in M Bungenberg et al (eds) *International Investment Law* (2015) 959, at 984, 985; JM Cox, *Expropriation in Investment Treaty Arbitration* (2019) 169.

[98] *RFCC v Morocco*, Award, 22 December 2003.

[99] At para 69 (original in French: 'avoir des effets substantiels d'une intensité certaine qui réduisent et/ou font disparaître les bénéfices légitimement attendus de l'exploitation des droits objets de ladite mesure à un point tel qu'ils rendent la détention de ces droits inutile'). See also *LESI & ASTALDI v Algeria*, Award, 12 November 2008, para 132; *Bayindir v Pakistan*, Award, 27 August 2009, para 459.

[100] *Pope & Talbot v Canada*, Interim Award, 26 June 2000, para 102; *Metalclad v Mexico*, Award, 30 August 2000, para 103; *Tecmed v Mexico*, Award, 29 May 2003, paras 102, 115; *Bayindir v Pakistan*, Decision on Jurisdiction, 14 November 2005, para 255; *Vivendi v Argentina*, Resubmitted Case: Award, 20 August 2007, para 7.5.34; *Biwater Gauff v Tanzania*, Award, 24 July 2008, paras 452, 463; *Plama v Bulgaria*, Award, 27 August 2008, para 193; *AES v Hungary*, Award, 23 September 2010, para 14.3.1; *Bosh v Ukraine*, Award, 25 October 2012, para 218; *Enkev Beheer v Poland*, First Partial Award, 29 April 2014, para 344; *Venezuela Holdings v Venezuela*, Award, 9 October 2014, para 286; *Belokon v Kyrgyz Republic*, Award, 24 October 2014, para 206; *Allard v Barbados*, Award, 27 June 2016, para 263; *Isolux v Spain*, Award, 17 July 2016, para 839; *Busta v Czech Republic*, Final Award, 10 March 2017, para 389; *Valores Mundiales v Venezuela*, Award, 25 July 2017, paras 389–394; *Casinos Austria v Argentina*, Decision on Jurisdiction, 29 June 2018, para 228; *InfraRed v Spain*, Award, 2 August 2019, paras 504, 505.

[101] *CMS v Argentina*, Award, 12 May 2005.

[102] At paras 262, 263.

In *Telenor v Hungary*,[103] the investor held a telecom concession. It was affected by a special levy on all telecommunications service providers. The Tribunal held that to constitute an expropriation, the conduct complained of must have a major adverse impact on the economic value of the investment.[104] The Tribunal said:

> the interference with the investor's rights must be such as substantially to deprive the investor of the economic value, use or enjoyment of its investment.[105] . . In considering whether measures taken by government constitute expropriation the determinative factors are the intensity and duration of the economic deprivation suffered by the investor as the result of them.[106]

In the event, the Tribunal found that the special levy amounted to a very limited sum and fell below the threshold of the standard defining an indirect expropriation.[107]

The Tribunal in *Electrabel v Hungary*[108] summarizes the required effect of the measures as follows:

> In short, the Tribunal considers that the accumulated mass of international legal materials, comprising both arbitral decisions and doctrinal writings, describe for both direct and indirect expropriation, consistently albeit in different terms, the requirement under international law for the investor to establish the substantial, radical, severe, devastating or fundamental deprivation of its rights or the virtual annihilation, effective neutralisation or factual destruction of its investment, its value or enjoyment.[109]

(d) Duration of a measure

Closely related to the severity of the interference is the duration of a governmental measure affecting the interests of a foreign investor. The Iran–United States Claims Tribunal has ruled that the appointment of a temporary manager by the host State against the will of the foreign investor will constitute a taking if the consequential deprivation is not 'merely ephemeral'.[110]

[103] *Telenor v Hungary*, Award, 13 September 2006.
[104] At para 64.
[105] At para 65.
[106] At para 70. Footnote omitted.
[107] At para 79.
[108] *Electrabel v Hungary*, Decision on Jurisdiction, Applicable Law and Liability, 30 November 2012.
[109] At para 6.62.
[110] See *Tippetts v TAMS-AFFA*, Award, 22 June 1984, 6 Iran–US CTR 219, 225; *Phelps Dodge v Iran*, Award, 19 March 1986, 10 Iran–US CTR 121, 130; *Saghi v Iran*, Award, 22 January 1993, 29 Iran–US CTR 44 et seq.

Investment tribunals have also laid emphasis on the duration of the measure in question.[111] In *SD Myers v Canada*,[112] the Tribunal said:

> An expropriation usually amounts to a lasting removal of the ability of an owner to make use of its economic rights although it may be that, in some contexts and circumstances, it would be appropriate to view a deprivation as amounting to an expropriation, even if it were partial or temporary.[113]

The Tribunal found that the measure had lasted for 18 months only and that this limited effect did not amount to an expropriation.[114]

In *Wena Hotels v Egypt*,[115] the Tribunal found that the seizure of the investor's hotel lasting for nearly a year was not 'ephemeral' but amounted to an expropriation.[116] In its subsequent Decision on Interpretation[117] the *Wena* Tribunal said:

> It is true that the Original Tribunal did not explicitly state that such expropriation totally and permanently deprived Wena of its fundamental rights of ownership. However, in assessing the weight of the actions described above, there was no doubt in the Tribunal's mind that the deprivation of Wena's fundamental rights of ownership was so profound that the expropriation was indeed a total and permanent one.[118]

LG&E v Argentina also ruled that the duration of the measure had to be taken into account.[119] The Tribunal found that, as a rule, only an interference that is permanent will lead to an expropriation:

> Similarly, one must consider the duration of the measure as it relates to the degree of interference with the investor's ownership rights. Generally, the expropriation must be permanent, that is to say, it cannot have a temporary nature, unless the investment's successful development depends on the realization of certain activities at specific moments that may not endure variations.[120]

[111] *Tecmed v Mexico*, Award, 29 May 2003, at para 116; *Generation Ukraine v Ukraine*, Award, 16 September 2003, para 20.32; *RFCC v Morocco*, Award, 22 December 2003, para 68; *Azurix v Argentina*, Award, 14 July 2006, para 313; *Unglaube v Costa Rica*, Award, 16 May 2012, paras 226, 234; *Achmea v Slovak Republic*, Final Award, 7 December 2012, paras 289, 292; *Olin v Libya*, Final Award, 25 May 2018, para 165; *Gavrilovic v Croatia*, Award, 26 July 2018, para 922.

[112] *SD Myers v Canada*, First Partial Award, 13 November 2000.

[113] At para 283.

[114] At para 287.

[115] *Wena Hotels v Egypt*, Award, 8 December 2000.

[116] At para 99.

[117] *Wena Hotels v Egypt*, Decision on Interpretation, 31 October 2005.

[118] At para 120.

[119] *LG&E v Argentina*, Decision on Liability, 3 October 2006.

[120] At para 193.

The Tribunal concluded:

> Thus, the effect of the Argentine State's actions has not been permanent on the value of the Claimants' shares, and Claimants' investment has not ceased to exist. Without a permanent, severe deprivation of LG&E's rights with regard to its investment, or almost complete deprivation of the value of LG&E's investment, the Tribunal concludes that these circumstances do not constitute expropriation.[121]

What is important is the effect over time and not the intended duration of a measure. Therefore, measures that were originally intended to be permanent but are reversed after a short period will not amount to an expropriation. Conversely, even temporary measures that have an equivalent effect to a permanent loss will be considered expropriatory.[122]

(e) Loss of control

Several awards suggest that continued control of an enterprise by the investor militates against a finding that an indirect expropriation has occurred. The requirement of a total or substantial deprivation has led these tribunals to deny the existence of an expropriation where the investor had retained control over the overall investment even though it had been deprived of specific rights.[123]

Azurix v Argentina[124] concerned breaches of a water concession by a province of Argentina. The Tribunal, although finding other breaches of the BIT, including fair and equitable treatment, denied the existence of an indirect expropriation, since the investor had retained control over the enterprise:

> the impact on the investment attributable to the Province's actions was not to the extent required to find that, in the aggregate, these actions amounted to an expropriation; Azurix did not lose the attributes of ownership, at all times continued to control ABA and its ownership of 90% of the shares was unaffected. No doubt the

121 At para 200.

122 *RFCC v Morocco*, Award, 22 December 2003, para 68; *Achmea* (formerly *Eureko*) *v Slovakia*, Final Award, 7 December 2012, paras 289, 292; *Unglaube v Costa Rica*, Award, 16 May 2012, paras 226, 227, 234; *Olin v Libya*, Final Award, 25 May 2018, para 165.

123 *Feldman v Mexico*, Award, 16 December 2002, paras 142, 152; *Nykomb v Latvia*, Award, 16 December 2003, para 4.3.1; *Occidental Exploration v Ecuador*, Final Award, 1 July 2004, para 89; *CMS v Argentina*, Award, 12 May 2005, paras 263, 264; *Enron v Argentina*, Award, 22 May 2007, para 245; *PSEG v Turkey*, Award, 19 January 2007, para 278; *Sempra v Argentina*, Award 28 September 2007, para 285; *Archer Daniels Midland v Mexico*, Award, 21 November 2007, paras 242, 244; *AES v Hungary*, Award, 23 September 2010, para 14.3.2; *El Paso v Argentina*, Award, 31 October 2011, paras 245, 248–249; *Mobil v Argentina*, Decision on Jurisdiction and Liability, 10 April 2013, para 843; *Cervin v Costa Rica*, Decision on Jurisdiction, 15 December 2014, para 333.

124 *Azurix v Argentina*, Award, 14 July 2006.

> management of ABA was affected by the Province's actions, but not sufficiently for the Tribunal to find that Azurix's investment was expropriated.[125]

Similarly, in *LG&E v Argentina*,[126] the host State had violated the terms of concessions for the distribution of gas. The Tribunal, although finding that other standards had been violated, denied the existence of an expropriation in view of the investor's continuing control:

> Ownership or enjoyment can be said to be 'neutralized' where a party no longer is in control of the investment, or where it cannot direct the day-to-day operations of the investment... Interference with the investment's ability to carry on its business is not satisfied where the investment continues to operate, even if profits are diminished.[127]

Biwater Gauff v Tanzania,[128] another case dealing with a water concession, is an example for an expropriation through a forceful takeover of management control by the State. The Tribunal noted that effective loss of management, use or control may trigger an expropriation:

> The Treaty encompasses ... also de facto or indirect expropriations which do not involve actual takings of title but nonetheless result in the effective loss of management, use or control, or a significant depreciation of the value, of the assets of a foreign investor.[129]

The Tribunal qualified the physical occupation and the takeover of management control as an expropriation.[130]

In *Saint-Gobain v Venezuela*,[131] the Tribunal found a de facto takeover of the investment by the Venezuelan State oil firm PDVSA, and a subsequent formal expropriation by decree. The plant was overrun by local union members shortly after a televised speech in which President Chavez had identified the investment as an impending target for expropriation. The Tribunal saw no conduct attributable to

[125] At para 322.
[126] *LG&E v Argentina*, Decision on Liability, 3 October 2006.
[127] At paras 188, 191. Footnotes omitted.
[128] *Biwater Gauff v Tanzania*, Award, 24 July 2008.
[129] At para 452.
[130] At paras 503, 510. The Tribunal cited a series of cases of the Iran–US Claims Tribunal in which a usurpation of management had led to the finding of an expropriation: *Sedco v National Iranian Oil Company*, Award, 24 October 1985, 9 Iran–US CTR 248, 278; *Tippetts v TAMS-AFFA*, Award, 22 June 1984, 6 Iran–US CTR 219, 225; *Starrett Housing v Iran*, Award, 19 September 1983, 4 Iran–US CTR 122, 154–155; *ITT Industries v Iran*, Award, 26 May 1983, 2 Iran–US CTR 348, 351–352; *Phelps Dodge v Iran*, Award, 19 March 1986, 10 Iran–US CTR 121, 130–131.
[131] *Saint-Gobain v Venezuela*, Decision on Liability and the Principles of Quantum, 30 December 2016.

Venezuela in the takeover itself.[132] However, shortly after the takeover, Venezuela had adopted the private conduct as its own, fulfilling the test in Article 11 of the International Law Commission (ILC) Articles on State Responsibility.[133] PDVSA had taken advantage of the situation to install itself at the plant. It carried out direct instructions from the government to prepare the plant for transfer to State control.[134] The Tribunal held that Saint-Gobain had not abandoned the plant but had in fact tried to regain control, writing letters, and filing requests for 'judicial inspection'.[135] It found that an expropriation had occurred because of the de facto loss of control already before the formal expropriation.[136]

Control is obviously an important aspect in the analysis of a taking.[137] However, the continued exercise of control by the investor is not necessarily the decisive criterion. The issue becomes obvious when a host State substantially deprives the investor of the value of the investment leaving the investor with the control of an entity that does not amount to much more than the shell of the former investment.

This illustrates the significance of a test which includes criteria other than control, such as economic use and benefit. Any attempt to define an indirect expropriation on the basis of one factor alone will not lead to a satisfactory result in all cases. In particular, an approach that looks exclusively at control over the overall investment is unable to contemplate the expropriation of specific rights enjoyed by the investor.

(f) Effect or intention?

As the Tribunal in *Azurix* pointed out, there is disagreement in the case law of arbitral tribunals whether only the effect or also the purpose of a measure matters:

> Whether to consider only the effect of measures tantamount to expropriation or consider both the effect and purpose of the measures is a point on which not only the parties disagree but also arbitral tribunals.[138]

In some cases, tribunals found that what mattered for an indirect expropriation was only the effect of the measure and that any intention to expropriate was not

132 At para 454.

133 At paras 455–456. ILC Articles on State Responsibility Article 11: '*Conduct acknowledged and adopted by a State as its own* Conduct which is not attributable to a State under the preceding articles shall nevertheless be considered an act of that State under international law if and to the extent that the State acknowledges and adopts the conduct in question as its own.'

134 At para 464.

135 At para 475.

136 At para 477.

137 See also: *El Paso v Argentina*, Award, 31 October 2011, para 248; *Enkev Beheer v Poland*, First Partial Award, 29 April 2014, para 344.

138 *Azurix v Argentina*, Award, 14 July 2006, para 309.

decisive.[139] In *Tecmed v Mexico*,[140] the Tribunal held that there had been an indirect expropriation. After explaining the concept of indirect or de facto expropriation, the Tribunal said: 'The government's intention is less important than the effects of the measures on the owner of the assets or on the benefits arising from such assets affected by the measures; and the form of the deprivation measure is less important than its actual effects.'[141]

In *Siemens v Argentina*,[142] the Tribunal found support in the applicable BIT for its finding that what mattered for the existence of an expropriation was the effect of the measures and not the government's intention. The Argentina–Germany BIT, like many other BITs, refers to indirect expropriation in terms of a 'measure the effects of which would be tantamount to expropriation'. The Tribunal said: 'The Treaty refers to measures that have the effect of an expropriation; it does not refer to the intent of the State to expropriate.'[143]

Authority for the 'sole effect doctrine' also comes from the practice of the Iran–US Claims Tribunal. In *Starrett Housing v Iran*,[144] the Tribunal said:

> it is recognized in international law that measures taken by a State can interfere with property rights to such an extent that these rights are rendered so useless that they must be deemed to have been expropriated, even though the State does not purport to have expropriated them and the legal title to the property formally remains with the original owner.[145]

The Tribunal in *Saipem v Bangladesh* also very clearly opted for the sole effect doctrine when it stated:

> As a matter of principle, case law considers that there is expropriation if the deprivation is substantial, as it is in the present case....[146]

Despite the strong authority for the sole effect doctrine, there are indications that the host State's intentions are not entirely irrelevant. If there is evidence of an

[139] *Biloune v Ghana*, Award on Jurisdiction and Liability, 27 October 1989, 95 ILR 183, 209; *Azurix v Argentina*, Award, 14 July 2006, at para 310; *Chemtura v Canada*, Award, 2 August 2010, para 242.

[140] *Tecmed v Mexico*, Award, 29 May 2003, cited in *Plama v Bulgaria*, Award, 27 August 2008, para 192.

[141] At para 116. Footnote omitted.

[142] *Siemens v Argentina*, Award, 6 February 2007.

[143] At para 270.

[144] *Starrett Housing v Iran*, Award, 19 December 1983, 4 Iran–US CTR 122, 154–155, cited in *Plama v Bulgaria*, Award, 27 August 2008, para 191.

[145] At p 154. See also *Tippetts v TAMS-AFFA*, Award, 22 June 1984, 6 Iran–US CTR 219, 225–226; *Phillips Petroleum v Iran*, Award, 29 June 1989, 21 Iran–US CTR 79, 115, para 97; *Ebrahimi v Iran*, Award, 12 October 1994, 30 Iran–US CTR 170, 189–190, para 72.

[146] *Saipem v Bangladesh*, Award, 30 June 2009, paras 133–134.

intentional deprivation this will weigh heavily in favour of showing that an expropriation has occurred.[147]

In addition, some decisions, especially in the context of regulatory measures, display a differentiated approach to the relevance of intent. They take account of the context of the measure, including the purpose pursued by the host State.[148] *Sea-Land Service v Iran*[149] seems to fall into this category. Upon review of the case law, Fortier[150] has concluded that an approach balancing different factors seems to be dominant. This is certainly true for the jurisprudence of the European Court of Human Rights (ECtHR).[151] Also, the 2004 and 2012 US Model BITs, in their description of indirect expropriation, refer not only to the economic impact of the government action but also to the design to protect legitimate public welfare objectives.[152] What is uncontroversial is that the mere ex-post facto explanation by the host State of its intention will in itself carry no decisive weight.[153]

Indeed, one tribunal has pointed out that a proper analysis of an expropriation claim must go beyond the technical consideration of the formalities and 'look at the real interests involved and the purpose and effect of the government measure'.[154]

(g) Legitimate expectations

Objective legitimate expectations play a key role in the interpretation of the fair and equitable treatment standard.[155] But they have also found entry into the law governing indirect expropriations. This theme has also found expression in various forms in domestic laws. In fact, it is arguable that the protection of legitimate expectations is part of the general principles of law.

The general nature of the concept of legitimate expectations makes it difficult to draw mechanical conclusions from it but it may be employed usefully in a number of settings. Legitimate expectations may be created not only by explicit undertakings on the part of the host State in contracts but also by undertakings of a more general kind. In particular, the legal framework provided by the host State will be

[147] *Vivendi v Argentina*, Resubmitted Case: Award, 20 August 2007, para 7.5.20; *Rumeli v Kazakhstan*, Award, 29 July 2008, para 700; *Bayindir v Pakistan*, Award, 27 August 2009, para 459; *Gemplus v Mexico*, Award, 16 June 2010, paras 8–23; *E energija v Latvia*, Award, 22 December 2017, para 1079.

[148] See also VII.3(h) below.

[149] *Sea-Land Service v Iran*, Award, 20 June 1984, 6 Iran–US CTR 149, 166.

[150] Y Fortier and SL Drymer, 'Indirect Expropriation in the Law of International Investment: I Know It When I See It, or Caveat Investor' (2004) 19 *ICSID Rev* 293.

[151] See *Sporrong&Lönnroth v Sweden*, Judgment of 23 September 1982, ECtHR Series A/52, paras 69–74.

[152] US Model BITs 2004 and 2012, Annex B, para 4.

[153] *Norwegian Shipowners' Claims* (1922) 1 RIAA 307; R Dolzer, 'Indirect Expropriations: New Developments?' (2003) 11 *NYU Environmental LJ* 64, 91.

[154] *SD Myers v Canada*, First Partial Award, 13 November 2000, para 285.

[155] See VIII.1(g)bb below. For the requirement of objective legitimate expectations see eg *ECE v Czech Republic*, Award, 19 September 2013, para 4.813.

an important source of expectations on the part of the investor. What matters for the investor's expectations is the state of the law of the host country at the time of the investment. If the law was transparent and did not violate minimum standards, an investor will not convince a tribunal that the proper application of that law has led to an expropriation. What matters are the rights acquired by the investor at the time of the investment.

Not every change in the host State's legal system affecting foreign property will violate legitimate expectations. No such violation will occur if the change remains within the boundaries of normal adjustments customary in the host State and accepted in other States. Such changes are predictable for a prudent investor at the time of the investment. For instance, the Tribunal in *Methanex v United States*[156] found that certain new environmental regulations in California had been foreseeable for the Canadian investor. Apart from specific commitments that were not honoured subsequently, the investor had no legitimate expectations that the environmental regulation would not be changed.[157]

Tribunals have relied on the legitimate expectations of investors in a number of cases relating to indirect expropriation. In *Revere Copper v OPIC*,[158] the host State had given explicit contractual assurances not to increase taxes and royalties. The Tribunal said:

> We regard these principles as particularly applicable where the question is, as here, whether actions taken by a government contrary to and damaging to the economic interests of aliens are in conflict with undertakings and assurances given in good faith to such aliens as an inducement to their making the investments affected by the action.[159]

In *Metalclad v Mexico*,[160] the investor had acted in reliance on assurances to the effect that he had all necessary permits. Nevertheless, the project was foiled by a refusal of the municipality to grant a construction permit. The Tribunal put much emphasis on the expectations created by the government's assurances:

> These measures, taken together with the representations of the Mexican federal government, on which Metalclad relied, and the absence of a timely, orderly or substantive basis for the denial by the Municipality of the local construction permit, amount to an indirect expropriation.[161]

[156] *Methanex v United States*, Final Award on Jurisdiction and Merits, 3 August 2005.
[157] At IV, D, para 10.
[158] *Revere Copper v OPIC*, Award, 24 August 1978, 56 ILR 258.
[159] At 271.
[160] *Metalclad v Mexico*, Award, 30 August 2000.
[161] At para 107.

In a similar way, in *Tecmed v Mexico*[162] the Tribunal, in determining that the investment had been expropriated, found:

> upon making its investment, the Claimant had legitimate reasons to believe that the operation of the Landfill would extend over the long term... the Claimant's expectation was that of a long-term investment relying on the recovery of its investment and the estimated return through the operation of the Landfill during its entire useful life.[163]

In *Thunderbird v Mexico*,[164] the Tribunal gave a general definition of legitimate expectations:

> Having considered recent investment case law and the good faith principle of international customary law, the concept of 'legitimate expectations' relates, within the context of the NAFTA framework, to a situation where a Contracting Party's conduct creates reasonable and justifiable expectations on the part of an investor (or investment) to act in reliance on said conduct, such that a failure by the NAFTA Party to honour those expectations could cause the investor (or investment) to suffer damages.[165]

On the basis of this definition, the Tribunal reached the conclusion that the investor's continued operation of gaming facilities in Mexico was not based on a legitimate expectation.[166]

In *Azurix v Argentina*,[167] the Tribunal discussed the issue of legitimate expectations at some length.[168] It held that expectations 'are not necessarily based on a contract but on assurances explicit or implicit, or on representations made by the State which the investor took into account in making the investment'.[169]

On that basis it found that Argentina had created 'reasonable expectations' that it had not fulfilled.[170] The Tribunal held, however, that no indirect expropriation had taken place, since the investor had continued to exercise control over the investment.[171]

The Tribunal in *Grand River v United States*[172] also required a specific assurance for the existence of a legitimate expectation. It explained that in the event of an

[162] *Tecmed v Mexico*, Award, 29 May 2003.
[163] At para 149.
[164] *Thunderbird v Mexico*, Award, 26 January 2006.
[165] At para 147. Footnote omitted.
[166] At para 208.
[167] *Azurix v Argentina*, Award, 14 July 2006.
[168] At paras 316–322.
[169] At para 318.
[170] See paras 316 et seq.
[171] At para 322.
[172] *Grand River v United States*, Award, 12 January 2011.

unsettled situation in domestic law and an absence of specific assurances made to an investor, the investor would not have had a legitimate expectation:

> The Tribunal understands the concept of reasonable or legitimate expectations in the NAFTA context to correspond with those expectations upon which an investor is entitled to rely as a result of representations or conduct by a state party. As the tribunal in *Thunderbird Gaming* explained, the "concept of 'legitimate expectations' relates … to a situation where a Contracting Party's conduct creates reasonable and justifiable expectations on the part of an investor (or investment) to act in reliance on said conduct, such that a failure by the NAFTA Party to honour those expectations could cause the investor (or investment) to suffer damages." The question of reasonable expectations, therefore, is not equivalent to whether or not an investor is ultimately right on a contested legal proposition that would favor the investor.
>
> … Ordinarily, reasonable or legitimate expectations of the kind protected by NAFTA are those that arise through targeted representations or assurances made explicitly or implicitly by a state party.[173]

Therefore, a regulatory interference with an investment that is of the necessary severity and frustrates a government assurance amounts to an expropriation. On the other hand, a breach of explicit assurances is, of course, not always a requirement for the existence of an expropriation.

To be 'legitimate' expectations must be objective. In this context, the Tribunal in *ECE v Czech Republic* applied a standard of reasonableness.[174] Therefore, the specificity of the assurance (stabilization clause, contract, specific government programme) as well as the regulatory environment (highly regulated field or not) will be relevant factors in the assessment of the legitimacy of an expectation.

(h) Regulatory measures

A question of prime importance both for the host State and for the foreign investor is the role of general regulatory measures of the host country under the rules of indirect expropriation. Emphasis on the host State's sovereignty supports the argument that the investor should not expect compensation for a measure of general application. One way to identify a taking may indeed be to clarify whether or not the measure in question was taken in the exercise of functions that are generally

[173] At paras 140–141.
[174] *ECE v Czech Republic*, Award, 19 September 2013, para 4.813.

considered part of the government's powers to regulate the general welfare.[175] This approach calls for the comparison of domestic legal orders.[176]

In the United States, governmental regulatory powers are referred to as 'police power'. While it is debatable whether the term 'police power' is appropriate in the modern regulatory context, some investment tribunals have relied on it,[177] as did the US Restatement of Foreign Relations Law.[178] The US Model BIT of 2012 contains an explicit exception from the definition of expropriation for 'regulatory actions by a Party that are designed and applied to protect legitimate public welfare objectives'.[179]

The Iran–United States Claims Tribunal ruled in *Too v Greater Modesto Insurance Associates*:[180]

> A state is not responsible for loss of property or for other economic disadvantage resulting from *bona fide* general taxation or any other action that is commonly accepted as within the police power of States, provided it is not discriminatory and is not designed to cause the alien to abandon the property to the State or to sell it at a distress price.

In *Feldman v Mexico*,[181] the Tribunal stated the position as follows:

> the ways in which governmental authorities may force a company out of business, or significantly reduce the economic benefits of its business, are many. In the past, confiscatory taxation, denial of access to infrastructure or necessary raw materials, imposition of unreasonable regulatory regimes, among others, have been considered to be expropriatory actions. At the same time, governments must be free to act in the broader public interest through protection of the environment, new or modified tax regimes, the granting or withdrawal of government subsidies, reductions or increases in tariff levels, imposition of zoning restrictions and the like. Reasonable governmental regulation of this type cannot be achieved

[175] *Telenor v Hungary*, Award, 13 September 2006, at para 78; *Philip Morris v Uruguay*, Award, 8 July 2016, paras 291–307; *A11Y v Czech Republic*, Award, 29 June 2018, paras 211–217; *Marfin v Cyprus*, Award, 26 July 2018, para 826.

[176] R Dolzer, 'Indirect Expropriation of Alien Property' (1986) 1 *ICSID Rev* 41.

[177] See eg *Tecmed v Mexico*, Award, 29 May 2003, paras 115, 119.

[178] American Law Institute, *Restatement (Third) of the Foreign Relations Law of the United States*, vol 1 (1987), Section 712, Comment (g):

> a state is not responsible for loss of property or for other economic disadvantage resulting from *bona fide* general taxation, regulation, forfeiture for crime, or other action of the kind that is commonly accepted as within the police power of the states, if not discriminatory.

[179] See VII.3(a) above.

[180] *Too v Greater Modesto Insurance Associates*, Award, 29 December 1989, 23 Iran–US CTR 378, 387, para 26. See also *SEDCO v NIOC*, Award, 24 October 1985, 9 Iran–US CTR 248, 275.

[181] *Feldman v Mexico*, Award, 16 December 2002.

> if any business that is adversely affected may seek compensation, and it is safe to say that customary international law recognizes this.[182]

Similarly, the Tribunal in *SD Myers v Canada*[183] held:

> The general body of precedent usually does not treat regulatory action as amounting to expropriation. Regulatory conduct by public authorities is unlikely to be the subject of legitimate complaint under Article 1110 of the NAFTA, although the Tribunal does not rule out that possibility.[184]

In *Methanex v USA*,[185] the arbitral Tribunal found that a Californian ban of the gasoline additive MTBE did not constitute an expropriation because the measure was adopted for a public purpose, was not discriminatory, and because no specific commitments had been given to the foreign investor:

> In the Tribunal's view, Methanex is correct that an intentionally discriminatory regulation against a foreign investor fulfils a key requirement for establishing expropriation. But as a matter of general international law, a non-discriminatory regulation for a public purpose, which is enacted in accordance with due process and, which affects, inter alios, a foreign investor or investment is not deemed expropriatory and compensable unless specific commitments had been given by the regulating government to the then putative foreign investor contemplating investment that the government would refrain from such regulation.[186]

Similarly, in *Saluka v Czech Republic*,[187] the Tribunal said:

> In the opinion of the Tribunal, the principle that a State does not commit an expropriation and is thus not liable to pay compensation to a dispossessed alien investor when it adopts general regulations that are 'commonly accepted as within the police power of States' forms part of customary international law today. There is ample case law in support of this proposition.[188]

The Award in *Continental Casualty v Argentina*[189] refers to

[182] At para 103.
[183] *SD Myers v Canada*, First Partial Award, 13 November 2000.
[184] At para 281.
[185] *Methanex v USA*, Final Award on Jurisdiction and Merits, 3 August 2005.
[186] At IV, D, para 7.
[187] *Saluka v Czech Republic*, Partial Award, 17 March 2006.
[188] At para 262, citing *Methanex v United States.*
[189] *Continental Casualty v Argentina*, Award, 5 September 2008.

> limitations to the use of property in the public interest that fall within typical government regulations of property entailing mostly inevitable limitations imposed in order to ensure the rights of others or of the general public (being ultimately beneficial also to the property affected). These restrictions do not impede the basic, typical use of a given asset and do not impose an unreasonable burden on the owner as compared with other similar situated property owners. These restrictions are not therefore considered a form of expropriation and do not require indemnification, provided however that they do not affect property in an intolerable, discriminatory or disproportionate manner.[190]

On the other hand, general regulatory rules and the measures based on them are subject to the same standards of protection that have been developed for all other instances. In the words of the decision of *Pope & Talbot v Canada*, 'a blanket exception for regulatory measures would create a gaping loophole' in the international rules protecting foreigners.[191]

In *Santa Elena v Costa Rica*,[192] the Tribunal found that the fact that measures were taken for the purpose of environmental protection did not affect their nature as an expropriation. Therefore, the obligation to pay compensation remained. The Tribunal said:

> Expropriatory environmental measures—no matter how laudable and beneficial to society as a whole—are in this respect, similar to any other expropriatory measures that a state may take in order to implement its policies: where property is expropriated, even for environmental purposes, whether domestic or international, the state's obligation to pay compensation remains.[193]

In *ADC v Hungary*,[194] the claimants argued that their investment in an airport project was expropriated by measures which deprived them of their rights to operate two airport terminals and to benefit from associated future business opportunities. The Tribunal accepted the claim of indirect expropriation and rejected Hungary's argument based on its right to regulate. The Tribunal said:

> 423. The Tribunal cannot accept the Respondent's position that the actions taken by it against the Claimants were merely an exercise of its rights under international law to regulate its domestic economic and legal affairs. It is the Tribunal's understanding of the basic international law principles that while a sovereign State possesses the inherent right to regulate its domestic affairs, the exercise of

[190] At para 276. Footnotes omitted.
[191] *Pope & Talbot v Canada*, Interim Award, 26 June 2000, para 99.
[192] *Santa Elena v Costa Rica*, Final Award, 17 February 2000.
[193] At para 72. Quoted with approval in *Azurix v Argentina*, Award, 14 July 2006, para 309.
[194] *ADC v Hungary*, Award, 2 October 2006.

> such right is not unlimited and must have its boundaries. As rightly pointed out by the Claimants, the rule of law, which includes treaty obligations, provides such boundaries. Therefore, when a State enters into a bilateral investment treaty like the one in this case, it becomes bound by it and the investment-protection obligations it undertook therein must be honoured rather than be ignored by a later argument of the State's right to regulate.
>
> 424. The related point made by the Respondent that by investing in a host State, the investor assumes the '*risk*' associated with the State's regulatory regime is equally unacceptable to the Tribunal. It is one thing to say that an investor shall conduct its business in compliance with the host State's domestic laws and regulations. It is quite another to imply that the investor must also be ready to accept whatever the host State decides to do to it. In the present case, had the Claimants ever envisaged the risk of any possible depriving measures, the Tribunal believes that they took that risk with the legitimate and reasonable expectation that they would receive fair treatment and just compensation and not otherwise.[195]

In addition, the Tribunal made the rare finding that the host State had failed to demonstrate that its measures were in the public interest[196] and that, moreover, the taking had not taken place under due process of law.[197]

Some decisions have sought to find a balance between the host State's right to act in the public interest and the protection of the investor's rights by requiring that regulatory measures must be proportionate.[198] The Tribunal in *Azurix*[199] held that the issue was whether legitimate measures serving a public purpose should give rise to a compensation claim. It found the criterion of *bona fide* regulation within the accepted police powers of the State insufficient and contradictory. The Tribunal said about this argument:

> According to it, the BIT would require that investments not be expropriated except for a public purpose and that there be compensation if such expropriation takes place and, at the same time, regulatory measures that may be tantamount to expropriation would not give rise to a claim for compensation if taken for a public purpose.[200]

[195] At paras 423, 424.

[196] At para 433.

[197] At paras 434–440.

[198] See *Tecmed v Mexico*, Award, 29 May 2003, para 122; *Fireman's Fund v Mexico*, Award, 17 July 2006, para 176(j); *Deutsche Bank v Sri Lanka*, Award, 31 October 2012, para 522; *Mobil v Argentina*, Decision on Jurisdiction and Liability, 10 April 2013, paras 818, 820; *Novenergia II v Spain*, Final Award, 15 February 2018, paras 732–737. For a proposal to balance investor and host state rights that goes beyond current arbitral practice, see U Kriebaum, 'Regulatory Takings: Balancing the Interests of the Investor and the State' (2007) 8 *JWIT* 717.

[199] *Azurix v Argentina*, Award, 14 July 2006.

[200] At para 311.

The *Azurix* Tribunal approvingly quoted the ECtHR,[201] which had found that in addition to a legitimate aim in the public interest there had to be 'a reasonable relationship of proportionality between the means employed and the aim sought to be realized'. This proportionality would be lacking if the person concerned 'bears an individual and excessive burden'.[202]

The Tribunal in *LG&E v Argentina*[203] adopted a similar balancing test. It said:

> In order to establish whether State measures constitute expropriation under Article IV(1) of the Bilateral Treaty, the Tribunal must balance two competing interests: the degree of the measure's interference with the right of ownership and the power of the State to adopt its policies... With respect to the power of the State to adopt its policies, it can generally be said that the State has the right to adopt measures having a social or general welfare purpose. In such a case, the measure must be accepted without any imposition of liability, except in cases where the State's action is obviously disproportionate to the need being addressed. The proportionality to be used when making use of this right was recognized in *Tecmed*, which observed that 'whether such actions or measures are proportional to the public interest presumably protected thereby and the protection legally granted to investments, taking into account that the significance of such impact, has a key role upon deciding the proportionality.'[204]

The Tribunal in *Marfin v Cyprus*[205] also applied a balancing approach. The Tribunal first assessed whether the measure deprived the investors of the economic enjoyment of their rights.[206] In a next step it stated several criteria, among them proportionality, to assess whether an expropriation had occurred:

> The Tribunal considers that the economic harm consequent to the non-discriminatory application of generally applicable regulations adopted in order to protect the public welfare do not constitute a compensable taking, provided that the measure was taken in good faith, complied with due process and was proportionate to the aim sought to be achieved.[207]

The Tribunal found that the treaty's expropriation provision must be interpreted in accordance with Article 31(3)(c) of the Vienna Convention on the Law of Treaties.[208] It considered customary international law relevant in the context of

201 *James v United Kingdom*, Judgment, 21 February 1986, ECtHR, Series A/98, paras 50 and 63.
202 *Azurix v Argentina*, Award, 14 July 2006, para 311.
203 *LG&E v Argentina*, Decision on Liability, 3 October 2006.
204 At paras 189, 195. Footnote omitted.
205 *Marfin v Cyprus*, Award, 26 July 2018.
206 At para 823.
207 At para 826.
208 Article 31(3)(c) VCLT: '3. There shall be taken into account, together with the context: ... (c) any relevant rules of international law applicable in the relations between the parties.'

this article and held that a normal exercise of the regulatory power will not lead to a compensable taking.[209] For that purpose the measures must be 'taken *bona fide* for the purpose of protecting the public welfare, must be non-discriminatory and proportionate'.[210]

The Tribunal in *PL Holdings v Poland*[211] further refined the balancing test. It found that the measure, a forced sale of shares, amounted to an indirect expropriation.[212] For that purpose it assessed whether the measures ordered by the authorities were proportionate to the public purpose they sought to achieve.[213] The Tribunal found that the 'principle [of proportionality] is understood in largely similar terms across jurisdictions'.[214] It indicated a number of criteria that had to be fulfilled to satisfy the principle:

> [A] measure must
> (a) be one that is *suitable* by nature for achieving a legitimate public purpose,
> (b) be *necessary* for achieving that purpose in that no less burdensome measure would suffice, and
> (c) *not be excessive* in that its advantages are outweighed by its disadvantages.[215]

(i) Creeping expropriation

The rules on the protection of foreign investment must not be circumvented by way of splitting up a measure amounting to an indirect expropriation into a series of discrete steps which, taken together, have the same effect on the foreign owner. Article 15 of the ILC's Articles on State Responsibility (2001) recognizes that a breach of international law may occur through a series of actions or omissions defined in aggregate as wrongful.[216]

[209] At paras 827–828. For the same approach see eg *Philipp Morris v Uruguay*, Award, 8 July 2016, para 290.
[210] At para 829.
[211] *PL Holdings v Poland*, Partial Award, 28 June 2017.
[212] At paras 320–323.
[213] At para 354.
[214] At para 355.
[215] At para 355. Emphases added.
[216] Articles on Responsibility of States for Internationally Wrongful Acts:
Article 15 *Breach consisting of a composite* act

1. The breach of an international obligation by a State through a series of actions or omissions defined in aggregate as wrongful occurs when the action or omission occurs which, taken with the other actions or omissions, is sufficient to constitute the wrongful act.
2. In such a case, the breach extends over the entire period starting with the first of the actions or omissions of the series and lasts for as long as these actions or omissions are repeated and remain not in conformity with the international obligation.

Therefore, it has long been accepted that an expropriation may occur 'outright or in stages'.[217] Thus, the term 'creeping expropriation' describes a taking through a series of acts.[218] A study by UNCTAD has referred in this context to 'a slow and incremental encroachment on one or more of the ownership rights of a foreign investor that diminishes the value of its investment'.[219]

Practice has recognized the phenomenon of creeping expropriation.[220] The Tribunal in *Generation Ukraine v Ukraine*[221] explained creeping expropriation as follows:

> Creeping expropriation is a form of indirect expropriation with a distinctive temporal quality in the sense that it encapsulates the situation whereby a series of acts attributable to the State *over a period of time* culminate in the expropriatory taking of such property... A plea of creeping expropriation must proceed on the basis that the investment existed at a particular point in time and that subsequent acts attributable to the State have eroded the investor's rights to its investment to an extent that is violative of the relevant international standard of protection against expropriation.[222]

The decision in *Tradex v Albania*[223] emphasized the cumulative effect of the measures in question:

> While the ... Award has come to the conclusion that none of the single decisions and events alleged by Tradex to constitute an expropriation can indeed be qualified by the Tribunal as expropriation, it might still be possible that, and the Tribunal, therefore, has to examine and evaluate hereafter whether the combination of the decisions and events can be qualified as expropriation of Tradex' foreign investment in a long, step-by-step process by Albania.[224]

[217] See American Law Institute, *Restatement (Third) of the Foreign Relations Law of the United States*, vol 1 (1987) § 712; GC Christie, 'What Constitutes a Taking of Property under International Law?' (1962) 38 *BYIL* 307.

[218] The term 'creeping expropriation' has occasionally also been used interchangeably with term 'indirect expropriation'.

[219] UNCTAD, *Series on Issues in International Investment Agreements: 'Taking of Property'* (2000) 11.

[220] *Biloune v Ghana*, Award on Jurisdiction and Liability, 27 October 1989, 95 ILR 183, 209; *Santa Elena v Costa Rica*, Final Award, 17 February 2000, para 76; *Azurix v Argentina*, Award, 14 July 2006, para 313; *Telenor v Hungary*, Award, 13 September 2006, para 63; *Rumeli v Kazakhstan*, Award, 29 July 2008, paras 700, 708; *Meerapfel v Central African Republic*, Award, 12 May 2011, para 316; *Burlington v Ecuador*, Decision on Liability, 14 December 2012, para 538; *Crystallex v Venezuela*, Award, 4 April 2016, paras 668–671; *Valores Mundiales v Venezuela*, Award, 25 July 2017, para 398.

[221] *Generation Ukraine v Ukraine*, Award, 16 September 2003.

[222] At paras 20.22, 20.26. Italics original.

[223] *Tradex v Albania*, Award, 29 April 1999.

[224] At para 191.

In the end, the Tribunal found that a combined evaluation of the events did not amount to an expropriation.[225]

In *Siemens v Argentina*,[226] the host State had taken a series of adverse measures, including postponements and suspensions of the investor's profitable activities, fruitless renegotiations, and ultimately the cancellation of the project. The Tribunal found that this had amounted to an expropriation and described creeping expropriation in the following terms:

> By definition, creeping expropriation refers to a process, to steps that eventually have the effect of an expropriation. If the process stops before it reaches that point, then expropriation would not occur. This does not necessarily mean that no adverse effects would have occurred. Obviously, each step must have an adverse effect but by itself may not be significant or considered an illegal act. The last step in a creeping expropriation that tilts the balance is similar to the straw that breaks the camel's back. The preceding straws may not have had a perceptible effect but are part of the process that led to the break.[227]

Professor Reisman and RD Sloane have rightly pointed out that the issue must sometimes be seen in retrospective:

> Discrete acts, analyzed in isolation rather than in the context of the overall flow of events, may, whether legal or not in themselves, seem innocuous vis-à-vis a potential expropriation. Some may not be expropriatory in themselves. Only, in retrospect will it become evident that those acts comprised part of an accretion of deleterious acts and omissions, which in the aggregate expropriated the foreign investor's property rights... Because of their gradual and cumulative nature, creeping expropriations also render it problematic, perhaps even arbitrary, to identify a single interference (or failure to act where a duty requires it) as the 'moment of expropriation'.[228]

4. The legality of an expropriation

It is generally accepted that the legality of a measure of expropriation is conditioned on three (or four) requirements. These requirements are explicitly stated in

[225] At para 203.
[226] *Siemens v Argentina*, Award, 6 February 2007.
[227] At para 263.
[228] WM Reisman and RD Sloane, 'Indirect Expropriation and its Valuation in the BIT Generation' (2003) 74 *BYIL* 115, 123.

most treaties. They are also regarded as part of customary international law. These requirements must be fulfilled cumulatively:[229]

- The measure must serve a *public purpose*. In most cases the existence of a public purpose is difficult to contest, and tribunals have often left host States with a large measure of discretion in this regard.[230]
- The measure must *not* be *discriminatory*. Most relevant cases concerned discrimination based on nationality.[231] But tribunals have also addressed other instances of discrimination.[232]
- Some treaties explicitly require that the procedure of expropriation must follow principles of *due process*.[233] Due process is an expression of the minimum standard under customary international law and of the requirement of fair and equitable treatment. Therefore, it is not clear whether such a clause adds an independent requirement for the legality of the expropriation. Tribunals have occasionally held an expropriation to be illegal for lack of due process.[234]
- The expropriatory measure must be accompanied by prompt, adequate, and effective *compensation*.

Of these requirements for the legality of an expropriation, the existence and measure of compensation has been by far the most controversial one. In the 1960s and 1970s, the rules of customary law on compensation were at the centre of a heated debate on expropriation.[235] They were discussed in the broader context

[229] *Bogdanov v Moldova*, Arbitral Award, 22 September 2005, para 4.2.5; *Siag v Egypt*, Award, 1 June 2009, para 428; *Al Tamimi v Oman*, Award, 3 November 2015, para 347; *Vestey v Venezuela*, Award, 15 April 2016, para 250.

[230] *SPP v Egypt*, Award, 20 May 1992, para 158; *Santa Elena v Costa Rica*, Final Award, 17 February 2000, para 71; *ADC v Hungary*, Award, 2 October 2006, paras 429–433; *Siemens v Argentina*, Award, 6 February 2007, para 273; *Siag v Egypt*, Award, 1 June 2009, paras 431–433; *Kardassopoulos v Georgia*, Award, 3 March 2010, paras 391–392; *von Pezold v Zimbabwe*, Award 28 July 2015, para 502; *Copper Mesa v Ecuador*, Award, 15 March 2016, para 6.64; *Vestey v Venezuela*, Award, 15 April 2016, paras 294, 296; *Devas v India*, Award on Jurisdiction and Merits, 25 July 2016, para 413; *Rusoro v Venezuela*, Award, 22 August 2016, para 385; *Teinver v Argentina*, Award, 21 July 2017, paras 984, 985; *UP and C.D v Hungary*, Award, 9 October 2018, paras 414–415.

[231] *Eureko v Poland*, Partial Award, 19 August 2005, paras 241–243; *ADC v Hungary*, Award, 2 October 2006, paras 441–443; *Tatneft v Ukraine*, Award on the Merits, 29 July 2014, para 469; *Rusoro v Venezuela*, Award, 22 August 2016, paras 394–397; *Olin v Libya*, Final Award, 25 May 2018, paras 173–174, 200–218; *UP and C.D v Hungary*, Award, 9 October 2018, para 417.

[232] *von Pezold v Zimbabwe*, Award 28 July 2015, para 501.

[233] Article 6(1)(d) of the 2004 and 2012 US Model BITs.

[234] *ADC v Hungary*, Award, 2 October 2006, paras 435–440; *Siag v Egypt*, Award, 1 June 2009, paras 440–442; *Kardassopoulos v Georgia*, Award, 3 March 2010, paras 397–404; *Deutsche Bank v Sri Lanka*, Award, 31 October 2012, para 523; *Yukos v Russia*, Final Award, 18 July 2014, para 1583; *OI European v Venezuela*, Award, 10 March 2015, para 392; *von Pezold v Zimbabwe*, Award 28 July 2015, para 499; *Quiborax v Bolivia*, Award, 16 September 2015, paras 221–227; *Crystallex v Venezuela*, Award, 4 April 2016, paras 713–714; *Vestey v Venezuela*, Award, 15 April 2016, para 309; *Bear Creek v Peru*, Award, 30 November 2017, paras 446–447.

[235] See I.1(c) above.

of economic decolonization, the notion of 'Permanent Sovereignty over Natural Resources', and of the call for a 'New International Economic Order'. These debates are reflected in a series of Resolutions of the UN General Assembly which culminated in the demand that any disputes about compensation for expropriation should be settled under the domestic law and by the domestic court of the expropriating State.[236]

Today, nearly all expropriation cases before tribunals follow the treaty-based standard of compensation in accordance with the fair market value.[237] In the terminology of the earlier decades this means 'full' or 'adequate' compensation. However, this does not mean that the amount of compensation is easy to determine. Especially in cases of foreign enterprises operating under complex contractual agreements, the task of valuation requires close cooperation of valuation experts and the legal profession.

Various methods may be employed to determine market value. In the case of a going concern that has already produced income, the discounted cash flow method will often be a relevant yardstick, rather than book value or replacement value. Where there is no reliable indicator of profitability, the liquidation value will be the more appropriate measure.

An issue that has never been resolved entirely concerns the consequences of an illegal expropriation. In the case of an indirect expropriation, illegality is the rule since there will be no compensation,[238] although a delay in the payment of compensation will not render the expropriation unlawful.[239]

According to one school of thought, the measure of damages for an illegal expropriation is no different from compensation for a lawful taking.[240] The better view is that an illegal expropriation will fall under the general rules of State responsibility. In case of an illegal act the damages should, as far as possible, restore the situation that would have existed had the illegal act not been committed.[241] By contrast, compensation for a lawful expropriation should represent the market

[236] UN GA Resolution on Permanent Sovereignty over Natural Resources, GA Res. 1803 (XVII) 1962; UN GA Resolution on Permanent Sovereignty over Natural Resources, UNGA Res. 3171 (XXVIII) 1973; UN GA Resolution on a Charter of Economic Rights and Duties of States, UNGA Res. 3281 (XXIX) 1974.

[237] For a decision based on customary international law see *Santa Elena v Costa Rica*, Final Award, 17 February 2000, para 73.

[238] *Siemens v Argentina*, Award, 6 February 2007, para 273; *Kardassopoulos v Georgia*, Award, 3 March 2010, para 408; *Gemplus v Mexico*, Award, 16 June 2010, paras 8–25; *Burlington v Ecuador*, Decision on Liability, 14 December 2012, paras 543–545; *Guaracachi v Bolivia*, Award, 31 January 2014, para 441; *Crystallex v Venezuela*, Award, 4 April 2016, para 717; *Olin v Libya*, Final Award, 25 May 2018, paras 175–181; *Gavrilovic v Croatia*, Award, 26 July 2018, para 949; *UP and C.D v Hungary*, Award, 9 October 2018, para 411.

[239] *ConocoPhillips v Venezuela*, Decision on Jurisdiction and Merits, 3 September 2013, para 362; *Venezuela Holdings v Venezuela*, Award, 9 October 2014, para 301; *Tidewater v Venezuela*, Award, 13 March 2015, paras 122–146.

[240] *Gemplus v Mexico*, Award, 16 June 2010, paras 15–53, 16–16; *Guaracachi v Bolivia*, Award, 31 January 2014, para 443; *Tenaris v Venezuela I*, Award, 29 January 2016, paras 512 et seq.

[241] Article 31 ILC Articles on State Responsibility.

value at the time of the taking.[242] The result of these two methods can be markedly different.[243] The issue of compensation and damages is discussed in more detail below in the chapter on the settlement of investment disputes.[244]

The requirement of 'prompt' compensation means 'without undue delay'.[245] The requirement of 'effective' compensation means that payment is to be made in a convertible currency.

242 *SPP v Egypt*, Award, 20 May 1992, para 183; *ADC v Hungary*, Award, 2 October 2006, paras 479–499; *Siemens v Argentina*, Award, 6 February 2007, para 352; *Kardassopoulos v Georgia*, Award, 3 March 2010, para 502–517; *ConocoPhillips v Venezuela*, Decision on Jurisdiction and Merits, 3 September 2013, para 342; *Venezuela Holding v Venezuela*, Award, 9 October 2014, para 307; *Saint-Gobain v Venezuela*, Decision on Liability and the Principles of Quantum, 30 December 2016, paras 596–602; *Magyar Farming v Hungary*, Award, 13 November 2019, paras 368–372.

243 I Marboe, 'Compensation and Damages in International Law, The Limits of "Fair Market Value"' (2006) 7 *JWIT* 723.

244 See XII.13(c) below.

245 *Siag v Egypt*, Award, 1 June 2009, paras 434–435; *OI European v Venezuela*, Award, 10 March 2015, para 425; *Saint-Gobain v Venezuela*, Decision on Liability and the Principles of Quantum, 30 December 2016, paras 417–425.

VIII
Standards of Protection

1. Fair and equitable treatment

ADDITIONAL READING: S Vasciannie, 'The Fair and Equitable Treatment Standard in International Investment Law and Practice' (1999) 70 *BYIL* 99; J Paulsson, *Denial of Justice in International Law* (2005); C Schreuer, 'Fair and Equitable Treatment in Arbitral Practice' (2005) 6 *JWIT* 357; I Tudor, *The Fair and Equitable Treatment Standard in the International Law of Foreign Investment* (2008); SW Schill, 'Fair and Equitable Treatment, the Rule of Law, and Comparative Public Law' in SW Schill (ed) *International Investment Law and Comparative Public Law* (2010) 151; R Kläger, *'Fair and Equitable Treatment' in International Investment Law* (2011); A Diehl, *The Core Standard of International Investment Protection: Fair and Equitable Treatment* (2012); R Dolzer, 'Fair and Equitable Treatment: Today's Contours' (2013) 12 *Santa Clara Journal of Int'l Law* 7; M Paparinskis, *The International Minimum Standard and Fair and Equitable Treatment* (2013); M Potestà, 'Legitimate Expectations in Investment Treaty Law' (2013) 28 *ICSID Rev* 88; M Jacob and SW Schill, 'Fair and Equitable Treatment: Content, Practice, Method' in M Bungenberg et al (eds) *International Investment Law* (2015) 700; P Dumberry, *Fair and Equitable Treatment: Its Interaction with the Minimum Standard and Its Customary Status* (2018); FM Palombino, *Fair and Equitable Treatment and the Fabric of General Principles* (2018); K Yannaca-Small, 'Fair and Equitable Treatment: Have its Contours Fully Evolved?' in K Yannaca-Small (ed) *Arbitration under International Investment Agreements* (2018) 20.01; A Reinisch and C Schreuer, *International Protection of Investments* (2020) 251.

(a) Introduction

Most BITs and other investment treaties provide for fair and equitable treatment (FET) of foreign investments. This concept is the most frequently invoked standard in investment disputes. It is also the standard with the highest practical relevance: a major part of successful claims pursued in international arbitration are based on a violation of the FET standard.

Some tribunals have pointed to the vagueness and lack of definition of the FET standard.[1] The European Parliament has deplored the use of vague language in this

[1] *CMS v Argentina*, Award, 12 May 2005, para 273; *Sempra v Argentina*, Award, 28 September 2007, para 296; *Rumeli v Kazakhstan*, Award, 29 July 2008, para 610; *Suez and InterAgua v Argentina*, Decision

context.[2] In fact, the lack of precision may be a virtue rather than a shortcoming. In actual practice it is impossible to anticipate in the abstract the range of possible types of infringements upon the investor's legal position. The principle of FET allows for independent and objective third-party determination of this type of behaviour on the basis of a flexible standard.[3] Therefore, it is not devoid of independent legal content. Like other broad principles of law, it is susceptible of specification through judicial practice.[4] As Prosper Weil wrote in the year 2000:

> The standard of 'fair and equitable treatment' is certainly no less operative than was the standard of 'due process of law', and it will be for future practice, jurisprudence and commentary to impart specific content to it.[5]

Investment tribunals have since given detailed content to the meaning of the standard. They have applied it to a broad range of circumstances and have given it meaning through their practice. The evolution of this practice is traced in some detail below.

Although 'fair and equitable' may be reminiscent of the extra-legal concepts of fairness and equity, it should not be confused with decision *ex aequo et bono*.[6] The Tribunal in *ADF v United States* pointed out that the requirement to accord FET does not allow a tribunal to adopt its own idiosyncratic standard but 'must be disciplined by being based upon State practice and judicial or arbitral case law or other sources of customary or general international law'.[7]

FET is an expression of the rule of law that is enshrined in major legal systems. Stephan Schill has pointed out that 'fair and equitable treatment can be understood as embodying the rule of law as a standard that the legal systems of host States have to embrace in their treatment of foreign investors'.[8] Several tribunals agree

on Liability, 30 July 2010, paras 196, 202; *Total v Argentina*, Decision on Liability, 27 December 2010, paras 106–109; *Mamidoil v Albania*, Award, 30 March 2015, paras 599–601; *Flemingo v Poland*, Award, 12 August 2016, para 530; *Urbaser v Argentina*, Award, 8 December 2016, paras 611–612.

[2] European Parliament Resolution of 6 April 2011 on the Future European International Investment Policy, Preamble, para G.

[3] S Vasciannie, 'The Fair and Equitable Treatment Standard in International Investment Law and Practice' (1999) 70 *BYIL* 99, 100, 104, 145.

[4] *Saluka v Czech Republic*, Partial Award, 17 March 2006, para 284: 'Even though Article 3 obviously leaves room for judgment and appreciation by the Tribunal, it does not set out totally subjective standards.'

[5] P Weil, 'The State, the Foreign Investor, and International Law: The No Longer Stormy Relationship of a *Ménage À Trois*' (2000) 15 *ICSID Rev* 401, 415.

[6] See C Schreuer, 'Decisions Ex Aequo et Bono under the ICSID Convention' (1996) 11 *ICSID Rev* 37.

[7] *ADF v United States*, Award, 9 January 2003, para 184. See also *Mondev v United States*, Award, 11 October 2002, para 119; *Saluka v Czech Republic*, Partial Award, 17 March 2006, paras 282–284; *Enron v Argentina*, Award, 22 May 2007, paras 256–257; *MCI v Ecuador*, Award, 31 July 2007, para 370; *Total v Argentina*, Decision on Liability, 27 December 2010, paras 108–109; *Micula v Romania I*, Award, 11 December 2013, para 507.

[8] SW Schill, 'Fair and Equitable Treatment, the Rule of Law, and Comparative Public Law' in SW Schill (ed) *International Investment Law and Comparative Public Law* (2010) 151.

that FET is a general principle of law that may be identified by way of a comparative public law analysis.[9]

The FET standard does not depend on how a host State treats its own nationals or the nationals of a third State. It is an absolute standard that has its reference point in international law.[10] FET is also an absolute standard in the sense that it does not depend on domestic law.[11]

(b) History

The concept of FET is not new but has appeared in international documents for some time. Some of these documents were non-binding, others entered into force as multilateral or bilateral treaties.[12] The origin of the clause seems to date back to the treaty practice of the United States in the period of Treaties on Friendship, Commerce and Navigation (FCN).[13] For instance, Article I (1) of the 1954 Treaty between Germany and the United States reads: 'Each Party shall at all times accord fair and equitable treatment to the nationals and companies of the other Party and to their property, enterprises and other interests.'[14]

A reference to a 'just and equitable treatment' standard appeared in Article 11(2) of the Havana Charter for an International Trade Organization of 1948.[15] The Abs–Shawcross Draft Convention on Investment Abroad of 1959 in its Article I referred to 'fair and equitable treatment to the property of the nationals of the other Parties',[16] and the subsequent Organisation for Economic Co-operation and Development (OECD) Draft Convention on the Protection of Foreign Property of 1967 in its Article 1 contained similar language.[17]

[9] *Petrobart v Kyrgyz Republic*, Arbitral Award, 29 March 2005, p 75; *Thunderbird v Mexico*, Arbitral Award, 26 January 2006, Separate Opinion Thomas Wälde, 1 December 2005, paras 27–30; *Enron v Argentina*, Award, 22 May 2007, para 257; *AMTO v Ukraine*, Final Award, 26 March 2008, para 87; *Merrill & Ring v Canada*, Award, 31 March 2010, para 187; *Total v Argentina*, Decision on Liability, 27 December 2010, para 111; *Toto v Lebanon*, Award, 7 June 2012, paras 166, 193; *Philip Morris v Uruguay*, Concurring and Dissenting Opinion Gary Born, 8 July 2016, paras 40–42; *Casinos Austria v Argentina*, Decision on Jurisdiction, 29 June 2018, paras 242–243.

[10] *Garanti Koza v Turkmenistan*, Award, 19 December 2016, para 380; *CME v Czech Republic*, Partial Award, 13 September 2001, para 611; *ADF v United States*, Award, 9 January 2003, para 178.

[11] *Genin v Estonia*, Award, 25 June 2001, para 367; *El Paso v Argentina*, Award, 31 October 2011, para 337.

[12] See especially UNCTAD Series on issues in international investment agreements, Fair and Equitable Treatment (1999) 3/4, 7–9, 25–28, 31/32; S Vasciannie, 'The Fair and Equitable Treatment Standard in International Investment Law and Practice' (1999) 70 *BYIL* 99, 100/111, 107.

[13] See RR Wilson, *United States Commercial Treaties and International Law* (1960) 113, 120.

[14] Treaty of Friendship, Commerce and Navigation, 29 October 1954, US–FR Germany, 273 UNTS 4. See also Treaty of Amity, Economic Relations, and Consular Rights, 15 August 1955, US–Iran, 284 UNTS 110, 114.

[15] UNCTAD, 1 *International Investment Instruments: A Compendium* (1996) 4. The Havana Charter never entered into force.

[16] UNCTAD, 5 *International Investment Instruments: A Compendium* (2001) 395. The Draft Convention represented a private initiative by H Abs and Lord Shawcross.

[17] OECD Draft Convention on the Protection of Foreign Property (1967), (1968) 7 ILM 117, 119.

The draft for a United Nations Code of Conduct on Transnational Corporations in its 1983 version provided that transnational corporations should receive FET.[18] The Guidelines on the Treatment of Foreign Direct Investment adopted by the Development Committee of the Board of Governors of the International Monetary Fund and the World Bank in 1992 in their Section III dealing with 'Treatment' provided that '2. Each State will extend to investments established in its territory by nationals of any other State fair and equitable treatment according to the standards recommended in these Guidelines'.[19]

The OECD Draft Negotiating Text for a Multilateral Agreement on Investment (MAI) of 1998 contained the following text in its section on investment protection:

> 1.1. Each Contracting Party shall accord to investments in its territory of investors of another Contracting Party fair and equitable treatment and full and constant protection and security. In no case shall a Contracting Party accord treatment less favourable than that required by international law.[20]

Since the mid-1960, FET clauses regularly appear in bilateral investment treaties (BITs). In some BITs, FET only appears in the preambles and does not form a self-standing treatment standard. FET provisions are included also in the investment chapters of most of the new post-2000 generation of expanded free trade agreements (FTAs).

The concept of FET has also found entry into multilateral treaties. For instance, the Convention Establishing the Multilateral Investment Guarantee Agency (MIGA) of 1985 in its Article 12 requires the availability of FET as a precondition for extending insurance cover.

The North American Free Trade Agreement (NAFTA) of 1994[21] contained the FET principle in its Article 1105, paragraph 1. The United States–Mexico–Canada Agreement (USMCA) promises FET in Article 14.6 (1).

The Energy Charter Treaty (ECT) of 1994 contains elaborate language around the requirement of FET in its Article 10(1):

> Each Contracting Party shall, in accordance with the provisions of this Treaty, encourage and create stable, equitable, favourable and transparent conditions for Investors of other Contracting Parties to make investments in its area. Such

[18] UNCTAD, 1 *International Investment Instruments: A Compendium* (1996) 172.

[19] Guidelines on the Treatment of Foreign Direct Investment, (1992) 7 *ICSID Rev* 297, 300.

[20] UNCTAD, 4 *International Investment Instruments: A Compendium* (2001) 148.

[21] The North American Free Trade Agreement (NAFTA) was a trilateral treaty between Canada, Mexico and the United States that existed from 1994 to 2020. The NAFTA was replaced by the USMCA on 1 July 2020. But NAFTA's Chapter 11, dealing with investments including investment arbitration, remains available to investors from all three countries should they choose to use it for three years after that date. See also I.2(c) above.

> conditions shall include a commitment to accord at all times to Investments of Investors of other Contracting Parties fair and equitable treatment.

The FTAs negotiated by the EU Commission in the 2010s, *inter alia*, with Canada, Singapore, Vietnam, and Mexico, contain FET clauses, though often in a modified, limited version.

(c) Textual variations

The use of the term 'fair and equitable' is fairly uniform. Some treaties refer to 'just and equitable', 'just and fair', or 'equitable and reasonable' These variations do not appear to reflect a difference in meaning and have been treated as synonymous.[22]

The two concepts of 'fair' and of 'equitable' are not to be taken as distinct elements to be applied separately. The general assumption is that 'fair and equitable' represent a single, unified standard.

Many treaties offer the FET standard together with other standards, often in the same sentence. In particular, FET and full protection and security (FPS)[23] are often listed together. Some FET provisions refer to international law.[24] For instance, the USMCA promises 'treatment in accordance with customary international law, including fair and equitable treatment and full protection and security'.[25] Some BITs refer to FET in accordance with the 'principles of international law'[26] or provide that treatment shall in no case be less favourable than that required by international law.[27] Some treaties contain clarifications that FET does not go beyond the customary international minimum standard.[28]

More recently, some BITs offer substantive detail on the meaning of FET. For instance, the US Model BIT of 2012, after a general reference to FET, states:

> 'fair and equitable treatment' includes the obligation not to deny justice in criminal, civil, or administrative adjudicatory proceedings in accordance with the principle of due process embodied in the principal legal systems of the world....

22 *Parkerings v Lithuania*, Award, 11 September 2007, paras 271–278; *Total v Argentina*, Decision on Liability, 27 December 2010, para 106; *OKO Pankki v Estonia*, Award, 19 November 2007, paras 214–215; *Bosca v Lithuania*, Award, 17 May 2013, para 196.

23 For the FPS standard see VIII.2 below.

24 For the relationship between FET and customary international law see VIII.1(f) below.

25 Article 14.6 (1) USMCA. See also 1105 (1) NAFTA.

26 Article 3 Argentina–France BIT (1991).

27 Article II(2) Argentina–US BIT (1991).

28 Article 5 US Model BIT 2012.

A restrictive description of FET is found in recent treaties negotiated by the European Union (EU). For instance, the CETA, after promising FET in general terms, offers the following definition:

> A Party breaches the obligation of fair and equitable treatment referenced in paragraph 1 if a measure or series of measures constitutes:
> (a) denial of justice in criminal, civil or administrative proceedings;
> (b) fundamental breach of due process, including a fundamental breach of transparency, in judicial and administrative proceedings;
> (c) manifest arbitrariness;
> (d) targeted discrimination on manifestly wrongful grounds, such as gender, race or religious belief;
> (e) abusive treatment of investors, such as coercion, duress and harassment; or
> (f) a breach of any further elements of the fair and equitable treatment obligation adopted by the Parties in accordance with paragraph 3 of this Article.[29]

(d) Definitions of fair and equitable treatment

In some cases, the tribunals have tried to give a more specific meaning to the FET standard by formulating general definitions or descriptions.[30]

Genin v Estonia[31] concerned the withdrawal of a banking licence. The Tribunal stated that acts violating the fair and equitable standard:

> would include acts showing a wilful neglect of duty, an insufficiency of action falling far below international standards, or even subjective bad faith.[32]

The most comprehensive definition has been set forth in *Tecmed v Mexico*.[33] The case concerned the withdrawal of a licence for a landfill for hazardous waste. The Tribunal found that it had to interpret the concept of FET autonomously, taking into account its text according to its ordinary meaning, international law, and the good faith principle. The intention behind the concept was to strengthen the

[29] Article 8.10 (2) CETA. See U Kriebaum, 'FET and Expropriation in the Comprehensive Economic Trade Agreement between the European Union and Canada' (2016) 1 *TDM*.

[30] Tribunals have made frequent use of these definitions in subsequent cases. At times, they have presented surveys of such definitions: *Biwater Gauff v Tanzania*, Award, 24 July 2008, paras 596–600; *Total v Argentina*, Decision on Liability, 27 December 2010, para 110; *El Paso v Argentina*, Award, 31 October 2011, paras 341–347.

[31] *Genin v Estonia*, Award, 25 June 2001, (2002) 17 *ICSID Rev* 395.

[32] At para 367. Footnote omitted. Since there were ample grounds for the action taken by the Estonian authorities, the Tribunal did not find that a violation of the fair and equitable standard had occurred.

[33] *Tecmed v Mexico*, Award, 29 May 2003.

security and trust of foreign investors thereby maximizing the use of economic resources. This goal was expressed in the Preamble.[34] The Tribunal defined FET in the following terms:

> The Arbitral Tribunal considers that this provision of the Agreement, in light of the good faith principle established by international law, requires the Contracting Parties to provide to international investments treatment that does not affect the basic expectations that were taken into account by the foreign investor to make the investment. The foreign investor expects the host State to act in a consistent manner, free from ambiguity and totally transparently in its relations with the foreign investor, so that it may know beforehand any and all rules and regulations that will govern its investments, as well as the goals of the relevant policies and administrative practices or directives, to be able to plan its investment and comply with such regulations... The foreign investor also expects the host State to act consistently, i.e. without arbitrarily revoking any preexisting decisions or permits issued by the State that were relied upon by the investor to assume its commitments as well as to plan and launch its commercial and business activities. The investor also expects the State to use the legal instruments that govern the actions of the investor or the investment in conformity with the function usually assigned to such instruments, and not to deprive the investor of its investment without the required compensation.[35]

In *MTD v Chile*,[36] the Tribunal applied a provision in the BIT between Chile and Malaysia requiring that '[i]nvestments of investors of either Contracting Party shall at all times be accorded fair and equitable treatment'.[37] In doing so, the Tribunal agreed with a legal opinion by Judge Schwebel that FET encompassed such fundamental standards as good faith, due process, non-discrimination, and proportionality. The Tribunal relied on the standard as defined in *Tecmed*[38] and emphasized a duty to adopt a proactive behaviour in favour of the investor. It said:

> fair and equitable treatment should be understood to be treatment in an even-handed and just manner, conducive to fostering the promotion of foreign investment. Its terms are framed as a pro-active statement—'to promote', 'to create', 'to stimulate'—rather than prescriptions for a passive behavior of the State or avoidance of prejudicial conduct to the investors.[39]

[34] At paras 155, 156. See also *Azurix v Argentina*, Award, 14 July 2006, para 360; *MTD v Chile*, Award, 25 May 2004, paras 112, 113.

[35] At para 154.

[36] *MTD v Chile*, Award, 25 May 2004.

[37] At para 107.

[38] At paras 114–115.

[39] At para 113.

On the basis of this standard the Tribunal found that Chile had violated the FET standard.

The ad hoc Committee in *MTD v Chile*[40] upheld the Award but criticized the reliance on the *Tecmed* standard:

> the *TECMED* Tribunal's apparent reliance on the foreign investor's expectations as the source of the host State's obligations (such as the obligation to compensate for expropriation) is questionable. The obligations of the host State towards foreign investors derive from the terms of the applicable investment treaty and not from any set of expectations investors may have or claim to have.[41]

Saluka v Czech Republic[42] concerned the takeover of an ailing bank, in which the claimants had invested, by a competitor that had received financial assistance from the State for the purpose of the takeover. The bank that was the object of the takeover had not received similar aid when the claimants attempted to negotiate the conditions to keep the bank viable. The Tribunal found that there was a violation of FET and described the requirements of the FET standard in terms of consistency, transparency, and reasonableness:

> A foreign investor whose interests are protected under the Treaty is entitled to expect that the [host state] will not act in a way that is manifestly inconsistent, non-transparent, unreasonable (*i.e.* unrelated to some rational policy), or discriminatory (*i.e.* based on unjustifiable distinctions).[43]

The NAFTA case, *Waste Management v Mexico*,[44] arose from a failed concession for the disposal of waste that involved a number of grievances, including the municipality's failure to pay its bills, failure to honour exclusivity of services, difficulties with a line of credit agreement, and proceedings before Mexican courts. The Tribunal summarized its position on the FET standard in Article 1105 of the NAFTA in the following terms:

> the minimum standard of treatment of fair and equitable treatment is infringed by conduct attributable to the State and harmful to the claimant if the conduct is arbitrary, grossly unfair, unjust or idiosyncratic, is discriminatory and exposes the claimant to sectional or racial prejudice, or involves a lack of due process leading to an outcome which offends judicial propriety—as might be the case with a manifest failure of natural justice in judicial proceedings or a complete

[40] *MTD v Chile*, Decision on Annulment, 21 March 2007.
[41] At para 67.
[42] *Saluka v Czech Republic*, Partial Award, 17 March 2006.
[43] At para 309.
[44] *Waste Management v Mexico II*, Award, 30 April 2004.

> lack of transparency and candour in an administrative process. In applying this standard it is relevant that the treatment is in breach of representations made by the host State which were reasonably relied on by the claimant.[45]

Other tribunals have adopted similar broad definitions.[46]

In some cases, tribunals have resorted to enumerating typical elements that amount to a violation of the FET standard.[47] The Tribunal in *Micula v Romania I*,[48] relying on this book's first edition, listed the following elements:

> According to Dolzer and Schreuer, tribunal practice shows that the concepts of transparency, stability and the protection of the investor's legitimate expectations play a central role in defining the FET standard, and so does compliance with contractual obligations, procedural propriety and due process, action in good faith and freedom from coercion and harassment.[49]

In *Philip Morris v Uruguay*,[50] the Tribunal gave the following definition of FET:

> Based on investment tribunals' decisions, typical fact situations have led a leading commentator to identify the following principles as covered by the FET standard: transparency and the protection of the investor's legitimate expectations; freedom from coercion and harassment; procedural propriety and due process, and good faith. In a number of investment cases tribunals have tried to give a more definite meaning to the FET standard by identifying forms of State conduct that are contrary to fairness and equity.[51]

The Tribunal in *Glencore v Colombia*[52] listed the following factors as amounting to violations of the FET standard:

> The threshold of propriety required by FET must be determined by the tribunal in light of all the relevant circumstances of the case. To this end, the tribunal must

[45] At 98. On the facts of the case, the Tribunal found that this standard had not been violated. At para 140.

[46] *LG&E v Argentina*, Decision on Liability, 3 October 2006, para 131; *Siag v Egypt*, Award, 1 June 2009, para 450; *Invesmart v Czech Republic*, Award, 26 June 2009, para 200; *Cargill v Mexico*, Award, 18 September 2009, para 296; *Inmaris Perestroika v Ukraine*, Award, 1 March 2012, para 265; *Marfin v Cyprus*, Award, 26 July 2018, para 1211; *SolEs Badajoz v Spain*, Award, 31 July 2019, para 308; *Gosling v Mauritius*, Award, 18 February 2020, paras 244–246.

[47] *Rumeli v Kazakhstan*, Award, 29 July 2008, para 609; *Biwater Gauff v Tanzania*, Award, 24 July 2008, para 602.

[48] *Micula v Romania I*, Award, 11 December 2013.

[49] At para 519.

[50] *Philip Morris v Uruguay*, Award, 8 July 2016.

[51] At para 320.

[52] *Glencore v Colombia*, Award, 27 August 2019.

carefully analyse and take into consideration all the relevant facts, among them the following factors:
—whether the host State has engaged in harassment, coercion, abuse of power, or other bad-faith conduct against the investor;
—whether the State made specific representations to the investor before the investment was made and then acted contrary to such representations;
—whether the State has respected the principles of due process, consistency, and transparency when adopting the measures at issue;
—whether the State has failed to offer a stable and predictable legal framework, in breach of the investor's legitimate expectations.[53]

Other tribunals have offered similar lists of actions by the host State as contrary to FET.[54]

(e) Relationship of FET to other standards

At times it has been suggested that the FET standard is merely an overarching principle that embraces the other standards of treatment typically found in investment treaties.[55] While it is undeniable that there is some interaction and overlap with other standards, it is widely accepted that FET is an autonomous standard.[56] In most cases, tribunals have distinguished FET from other standards and have examined separately whether there has been a violation of the respective standards.[57]

Claimants alleging an expropriation have sometimes also claimed a violation of the FET standard. In view of the high threshold for expropriation claims, especially

[53] At para 1310. Footnotes omitted.

[54] *Ares v Georgia*, Award, 28 February 2008, para 9.3.7; *Biwater Gauff v Tanzania*, Award, 24 July 2008, para 602; *Rumeli v Kazakhstan*, Award, 29 July 2008, para 609; *Siag v Egypt*, Award, 1 June 2009, para 450; *Invesmart v Czech Republic*, Award, 26 June 2009, para 200; *Bayindir v Pakistan*, Award, 27 August 2009, para 178; *Lemire v Ukraine*, Decision on Jurisdiction and Liability, 14 January 2010, para 284; *Paushok v Mongolia*, Award on Jurisdiction and Liability, 28 April 2011, para 253; *Deutsche Bank v Sri Lanka*, Award, 31 October 2012, para 420; *Electrabel v Hungary*, Decision on Jurisdiction, Applicable Law and Liability, 30 November 2012, para 7.74; *Tatneft v Ukraine*, Award, 29 July 2014, para 394; *Rusoro v Venezuela*, Award, 22 August 2016, para 524; *Krederi v Ukraine*, Award, 2 July 2018, paras 437–440; *Stadtwerke München v Spain*, Award, 2 December 2019, para 256.

[55] *Noble Ventures v Romania*, Award, 12 October 2005, para 182; *Lemire v Ukraine*, Decision on Jurisdiction and Liability, 14 January 2010, paras 259, 385; *Impregilo v Argentina*, Award, 21 June 2011, paras 333–334.

[56] I Tudor, *The Fair and Equitable Treatment Standard in International Law of Foreign Investment* (2008) 182; C Schreuer, 'Fair and Equitable Treatment (FET): Interactions with Other Standards' in G Coop and C Ribeiro (eds) *Investment Protection and the Energy Charter Treaty* (2008) 63.

[57] *Azurix v Argentina*, Award, 14 July 2006, paras 407–408; *LG&E v Argentina*, Decision on Liability, 3 October 2006, paras 162, 163; *PSEG v Turkey*, Award, 19 January 2007, para 239; *Plama v Bulgaria*, Award, 27 August 2008, paras 161–163, 183–184; *El Paso v Argentina*, Award, 31 October 2011, paras 226, 228–231; *Mobil v Argentina*, Decision on Jurisdiction and Liability, 10 April 2013, paras 810–813.

the requirement to prove a substantial or total deprivation, this seemed a promising fallback position.[58] Tribunals have repeatedly insisted on the separate nature of expropriation and FET.[59]

There is some confusion about the relationship of FET to the FPS standard.[60] Some tribunals seem to think that FPS was covered by the concept of FET and that there was no need to examine the facts separately under the two standards.[61] Other tribunals have held that the two standards are distinct and should be treated separately.[62] The Tribunal in *Frontier Petroleum v Czech Republic*[63] explained the difference between FPS and FET in the following terms:

> full protection and security obliges the host state to provide a legal framework that grants security and protects the investment against adverse action by private persons as well as state organs, whereas fair and equitable treatment consists mainly of an obligation on the host state's part to desist from behaviour that is unfair and inequitable.[64]

The relationship of FET to the standard that prohibits arbitrary or discriminatory treatment[65] is particularly relevant in the context of NAFTA and the USMCA, which contain clauses on FET but no explicit prohibition of arbitrary treatment.[66] The same applies to the recently negotiated treaties of the EU such as the CETA. Some NAFTA tribunals have found that arbitrary treatment violates the requirement of FET.[67] Tribunals applying BITs have also sometimes merged the two standards.[68]

[58] *Sempra v Argentina*, Award, 28 September 2007, paras 300–301; *PSEG v Turkey*, Award, 19 January 2007, para 238; *Malicorp v Egypt*, Award, 7 February 2011, para 124; *Valores Mundiales v Venezuela*, Award, 25 July 2017, paras 523–527; *Saint-Gobain v Venezuela*, Decision on Liability and Principles of Quantum, 30 December 2016, paras 503–504.

[59] *Nations Energy v Panama*, Award, 24 November 2010, paras 682 et seq; *Tidewater v Venezuela*, Award, 13 March 2015, para 150; *Venezuela Holdings v Venezuela*, Award, 9 October 2014, para 276.

[60] See VIII.2(a) below.

[61] *Occidental Exploration v Ecuador*, Final Award, 1 July 2004, para 187; *Azurix v Argentina*, Award, 14 July 2006, para 408; *Impregilo v Argentina*, Award, 21 June 2011, para 334; *Roussalis v Romania*, Award, 7 December 2011, para 321; *Tatneft v Ukraine*, Award, 29 July 2014, para 427.

[62] *El Paso v Argentina*, Award, 31 October 2011, paras 228–231; *Oostergetel v Slovak Republic*, Final Award, 23 April 2012, para 226; *Ulysseas v Ecuador*, Final Award, 12 June 2012, para 271–272; *Arif v Moldova*, Award, 8 April 2013, para 505; *Mamidoil v Albania*, Award, 30 March 2015, paras 819–820.

[63] *Frontier Petroleum v Czech Republic*, Final Award, 12 November 2010.

[64] At para 296.

[65] See VIII.3 below.

[66] NAFTA Article 1105; USMCA 14.6.(1).

[67] *SD Myers v Canada*, First Partial Award, 13 November 2000, para 263; *Mondev v United States*, Award, 11 October 2002, para 127; *Waste Management v Mexico II*, Award, 30 April 2004, para 98; *Eli Lilly v Canada*, Final Award, 16 March 2017, para 418.

[68] See *CMS v Argentina*, Award, 12 May 2005, para 290; *Impregilo v Pakistan*, Decision on Jurisdiction, 22 April 2005, para 264 et seq; *MTD v Chile*, Award, 25 May 2004, para 196; *Noble Ventures v Romania*, Award, 12 October 2005, para 182; *Saluka v Czech Republic*, Partial Award, 17 March 2006, para 460; *PSEG v Turkey*, Award, 19 January 2007, para 261; *MCI v Ecuador*, Award, 31 July 2007, paras 366–367, 371; *Rumeli v Kazakhstan*, Award, 29 July 2008, paras 679–681; *Lemire v Ukraine*, Decision on Jurisdiction and Liability, 14 January 2010, paras 259, 356–357, 418; *AES v Kazakhstan*, Award, 1 November 2013, para 329; *Quiborax v Bolivia*, Award, 16 September 2015, para 292; *Oxus v Uzbekistan*,

Tribunals applying the FET standards have examined whether measures taken by the host State were reasonable,[69] proportionate,[70] and non-discriminatory.[71]

Other tribunals have examined compliance with the standards of FET and unreasonable or discriminatory treatment separately.[72] Although there is often no explicit discussion of the relationship of the two concepts, their sequential and separate treatment in awards indicates that the tribunals regarded them as distinct standards.

The Tribunal in *Duke Energy v Ecuador*[73] had to interpret a provision in the Ecuador–US BIT that afforded protection against impairment by arbitrary or discriminatory measures. The respondent argued that this was part of the FET standard. The Tribunal disagreed and said:

> In view of the structure of the provisions of the BIT, the Tribunal has difficulty following Ecuador's argument that there is only one concept of fair and equitable treatment which encompasses a non-impairment notion. The Tribunal will thus make a separate determination to decide whether the contested measures were arbitrary . . . [74]

Final Award, 17 December 2015, paras 323, 785; *Philip Morris v Uruguay*, Award, 8 July 2016, para 445; *Devas v India*, Award on Jurisdiction and Merits, 25 July 2016, para 480; *Antaris v Czech Republic*, Award, 2 May 2018, para 360; *Greentech v Spain*, Final Award, 14 November 2018, para 412; *Urbaser v Argentina*, Award, 8 December 2016, paras 1080, 1081; *Eskosol v Italy*, Award, 4 September 2020, paras 487–488.

[69] *Saluka v Czech Republic*, Partial Award, 17 March 2006, para 309; *Biwater Gauff v Tanzania*, Award, 24 July 2008, para 692; *Cargill v Mexico*, Award, 18 September 2009, paras 291–293; *Unglaube v Costa Rica*, Award, 16 May 2012, paras 246–247; *Philip Morris v Uruguay*, Award, 8 July 2016, paras 410, 418–420; *RREEF v Spain*, Decision on Responsibility and on the Principles of Quantum, 30 November 2018, paras 463–464; *Belenergia v Italy*, Award, 6 August 2019, paras 601–606; *Watkins v Spain*, Award, 21 January 2020, 595–603.

[70] *Tecmed v Mexico*, Award, 29 May 2003, paras 122, 149; *Total v Argentina*, Decision on Liability, 27 December 2010, para 123; *Occidental Petroleum v Ecuador*, Award, 5 October 2012, paras 402–452; *AES v Kazakhstan*, Award, 1 November 2013, paras 403–412; *Electrabel v Hungary*, Award, 25 November 2015, paras 165–166, 179; *Charanne v Spain*, Award, 21 January 2016, paras 514–540; *Marfin v Cyprus*, Award, 26 July 2018, para 1213; *Stadtwerke München v Spain*, Award, 2 December 2019, para 354; *BayWa v Spain*, Decision on Jurisdiction, Liability and Directions on Quantum, 2 December 2019, paras 497–515; *RWE v Spain*, Decision on Jurisdiction, Liability, and Certain Issues of Quantum, 30 December 2019, paras 550–600; *Eskosol v Italy*, Award, 4 September 2020, paras 384–415.

[71] *Eureko v Poland*, Partial Award, 19 August 2005, para 233; *Biwater Gauff v Tanzania*, Award, 24 July 2008, para 602; *Tatneft v Ukraine*, Award on the Merits, 29 July 2014, para 408.

[72] *Occidental Exploration v Ecuador*, Final Award, 1 July 2004, paras 159–166; *Lauder v Czech Republic*, Award, 3 September 2001, paras 214–288; *Genin v Estonia*, Award, 25 June 2001, paras 368–371; *Noble Ventures v Romania*, Award, 12 October 2005, paras 175–180; *Azurix v Argentina*, Award, 14 July 2006, paras 385–393; *LG&E v Argentina*, Decision on Liability, 3 October 2006, paras 162–163; *Siemens v Argentina*, Award, 6 February 2007, paras 310–321; *BG Group v Argentina*, Final Award, 24 December 2007, para 342; *Biwater Gauff v Tanzania*, Award, 24 July 2008, paras 586–676; *Plama v Bulgaria*, Award, 27 August 2008, para 184; *El Paso v Argentina*, Award, 31 October 2011, para 231; *Arif v Moldova*, Award, 8 April 2013, para 515; *Valores Mundiales v Venezuela*, Award, 25 July 2017, para 609; *Krederi v Ukraine*, Award, 2 July 2018, paras 670–672.

[73] *Duke Energy v Ecuador*, Award, 18 August 2008, paras 367–383.

[74] At para 377.

Tribunals have also emphasized the independence of the FET standard from the national treatment standard.[75] There is no doubt that the FET standard is meant as a rule of international law and is not determined by the laws of the host State. The FET standard may be violated even if the foreign investor receives the same treatment as investors of the host State's nationality.[76] In the same way, an investor may have been treated unfairly and inequitably even if it is unable to benefit from a most-favoured-nation (MFN) clause because it cannot show that investors of other nationalities have received better treatment.

In *Flemingo v Poland*,[77] the Tribunal rejected an argument that would have reduced FET to MFN and national treatment. The Tribunal said:

> Respondent is not correct when it argues that 'fair and equitable treatment' boils down to treating foreign investors the same way as domestic and other foreign investors ... Equal treatment with domestic and other foreign entities is another specific standard ... It is not because the host State would treat all investors – domestic as well as foreign – in the same way that such treatment could not be unfair or inequitable.[78]

Despite a tendency of some tribunals to merge the FET standard with other standards of protection, there are weighty arguments in favour of treating them as conceptually separate. There is no good reason why treaty drafters would use different terms when they mean one and the same thing. It is also difficult to see why one standard should be part of the other when the text of the treaties lists them sequentially without indicating that one is merely an emanation of the other. Of course, there may be considerable overlap and a particular set of facts may well violate both FET and another standard, but this is no reason not to examine claims based on different standards separately.

(f) Fair and equitable treatment and customary international law

Considerable debate has surrounded the question of whether the FET standard merely reflects the international minimum standard, as contained in customary international law,[79] or offers an autonomous standard that is additional to general

[75] *Genin v Estonia*, Award, 25 June 2001, para 367; *SD Myers v Canada*, First Partial Award, 13 November 2000, para 259; *CME v Czech Republic*, Partial Award, 13 September 2001, para 611; *UPS v Canada*, Award on Jurisdiction, 22 November 2002, para 80; *El Paso v Argentina*, Award, 31 October 2011, para 337.

[76] On a possible violation of the FET standard through the host State's failure to apply its own law see VIII.1(g)ff below.

[77] *Flemingo v Poland*, Award, 12 August 2016.

[78] At para 531.

[79] See I.1(b) above.

international law. As a matter of textual interpretation, it seems implausible that a treaty would refer to a well-known concept like the 'minimum standard of treatment in customary international law' by using the expression 'fair and equitable treatment'. If the parties to a treaty want to refer to customary international law, one would assume that they will refer to it as such rather than using a different term.[80]

Commentators have expressed the view that FET constitutes an independent treaty standard that goes beyond a mere restatement of customary international law.[81] Prominent among the supporters of an independent concept of fair and equitable treatment is *FA Mann*. Writing about British BITs in 1981 he said:

> It is submitted that nothing is gained by introducing the conception of a minimum standard and, more than this, it is positively misleading to introduce it. The terms 'fair and equitable treatment' envisage conduct which goes far beyond the minimum standard and afford protection to a greater extent and according to a much more objective standard than any previously employed form of words. A tribunal would not be concerned with a minimum, maximum or average standard. It will have to decide whether in all circumstances the conduct in issue is fair and equitable or unfair and inequitable. No standard defined by other words is likely to be material. The terms are to be understood and applied independently and autonomously.[82]

The contrary opinion has also been expressed. The Notes and Comments to the OECD Draft Convention on the Protection of Foreign Property of 1967 indicate that the FET standard is set by customary international law.[83]

The European Parliament, in a resolution adopted in 2011, stated that in investment agreements to be concluded by the EU, FET should be 'defined on the basis of the level of treatment established by international customary law'.[84] The CETA does not, however, contain such a definition. Instead, it contains a definition based on some of the typical elements of FET developed by tribunal practice.[85]

[80] *Biwater Gauff v Tanzania*, Award, 24 July 2008, para 591; *Deutsche Bank v Sri Lanka*, Award, 31 October 2012, para 418.

[81] R Dolzer and M Stevens, *Bilateral Investment Treaties* (1995) 60; PT Muchlinski, *Multinational Enterprises and the Law* (1999) 626; UNCTAD Series on issues in international investment agreements, Fair and Equitable Treatment (1999) 13, 17, 37–40, 53, 61; S Vasciannie, 'The Fair and Equitable Treatment Standard in International Investment Law and Practice' (1999) 70 *BYIL* 99, 104/105, 139; I Tudor, *The Fair and Equitable Treatment Standard in International Law of Foreign Investment* (2008) 54.

[82] FA Mann, 'British Treaties for the Promotion and Protection of Investments' (1981) 52 *BYIL* 241, 244.

[83] (1968) 7 ILM 118, 120. See also a comment by the Swiss Foreign Office of 1979 in (1980) 36 *Annuaire suisse de droit international* 178.

[84] European Parliament Resolution of 6 April 2011 on the Future European International Investment Policy, para 19.

[85] Article 8.10 (2) CETA.

The starting point for an examination of the relationship to customary international law must be the exact wording of the treaty clauses providing for FET. These clauses provide in varying degrees for a linkage with customary international law. Some treaties simply prescribe 'fair and equitable treatment' without a reference to customary international law. German, Dutch, Swedish, and Swiss BITs generally follow this pattern.

Some treaties state that FET is to be afforded 'in accordance with international law'.[86] The French Model Treaty provides that the States parties 'shall extend fair and equitable treatment in accordance with the principles of International Law'. Some treaties state that FET must in no case provide for less protection than the rules of international law. Yet another version lists FET in addition to the rules of international law.

Other clauses dealing with FET treat the standard as an element of the general rules of international law. Article 1105 of NAFTA treats FET as part of international law. That provision reads as follows:

> **Article 1105: Minimum Standard of Treatment**
> 1. Each Party shall accord to investments of investors of another Party treatment in accordance with international law, including fair and equitable treatment and full protection and security.

This provision has been the subject of an official interpretation by the NAFTA Free Trade Commission (FTC), a body composed of representatives of the three States parties with the power to adopt binding interpretations.[87] The FTC interpretation stated that Article 1105(1) reflects the customary international law minimum standard and does not require treatment in addition to or beyond that which is required by customary international law.[88] NAFTA tribunals have accepted the FTC interpretation.[89]

The subsequent treaty practice of the United States[90] and of Canada[91] has followed the FTC interpretation. The US Model BITs of 2004 and 2012 offer the

[86] *Koch v Venezuela*, Award, 30 October 2017, para 8.44.
[87] Article 1131 (2) NAFTA.
[88] FTC Note of Interpretation of 31 July 2001.
[89] *Pope & Talbot v Canada*, Award on Damages, 31 May 2002, paras 17–69; *Mondev v United States*, Award, 11 October 2002, paras 100 et seq; *UPS v Canada*, Award on Jurisdiction, 22 November 2002, para 97; *ADF v United States*, Award, 9 January 2003, paras 175–178; *Loewen v United States*, Award, 26 June 2003, paras 124–128; *Waste Management v Mexico II*, Award, 30 April 2004, paras 90–91; *Methanex v United States*, Final Award on Jurisdiction and Merits, 3 August 2005, IV, C, paras 17–24; *Thunderbird v Mexico*, Award, 26 January 2006, paras 192, 193; *Glamis Gold v United States*, Award, 8 June 2009, para 599; *Chemtura v Canada*, Award, 2 August 2010, para 121; *Grand River v United States*, Award, 12 January 2011, paras 173–176, 214; *Mesa Power v Canada*, Award, 24 March 2016, para 503; *Vento v Mexico*, Award, 6 July 2020, paras 276–284. See also *Mexico v Metalclad*, Review by British Columbia Supreme Court, 2 May 2001, 5 ICSID Reports (2002) 236, paras 61–65.
[90] See Article 10.4, Chile–United States FTA of 2003; Article 5, United States–Uruguay BIT of 2004.
[91] Article 5, Canada Model FIPA.

clarification that FET does not go beyond the standard afforded by the minimum standard of treatment under customary international law.[92]

This practice was carried over into the USMCA. It provides for 'treatment in accordance with customary international law, including fair and equitable treatment and full protection and security' and adds the following explanation:

> For greater certainty, paragraph 1 prescribes the customary international law minimum standard of treatment of aliens as the standard of treatment to be afforded to covered investments. The concepts of 'fair and equitable treatment' and 'full protection and security' do not require treatment in addition to or beyond that which is required by that standard, and do not create additional substantive rights.[93]

The authority of this practice, equating FET with the international minimum standard under customary international law, is of limited relevance for the interpretation of other treaties. Arbitral tribunals applying treaties that do not contain statements about the relationship of FET to customary international law have tended to interpret the relevant provisions autonomously based on their respective wording.[94] Even in cases where the applicable provisions on FET did refer to international law, tribunals have given these provisions independent meaning.[95] Some of these tribunals have, however, found that FET does not differ from the international minimum standard required by international law.[96]

In *Azurix v Argentina*,[97] the Tribunal had to interpret Article II(2) of the Argentina–US BIT guaranteeing FET and full protection and security. The

[92] Article 5(2), US Model BIT 2012.

[93] Article 14.6 (2), USMCA.

[94] *MTD v Chile*, Award, 25 May 2004, paras 110–112; *Occidental Exploration v Ecuador*, Final Award, 1 July 2004, paras 188–190; *Saluka v Czech Republic*, Partial Award, 17 March 2006, paras 286–295; *Enron v Argentina*, Award, 22 May 2007, para 258; *Sempra v Argentina*, Award, 28 September 2007, para 302; *OKO Pankki v Estonia*, Award, 19 November 2007, paras 217–230; *Ares v Georgia*, Award, 26 February 2008, para 9.3.3; *Continental Casualty v Argentina*, Award, 5 September 2008, para 254; *National Grid v Argentina*, Award, 3 November 2008, paras 167–173; *Bayindir v Pakistan*, Award, 27 August 2009, para 164; *Total v Argentina*, Decision on Liability, 27 December 2010, paras 125–127; *Inmaris Perestroika v Ukraine*, Award, 1 March 2012, para 265; *Cervin v Costa Rica*, Award, 7 March 2017, paras 452 et seq; *Valores Mundiales v Venezuela*, Award, 25 July 2017, para 530; *Belenergia v Italy*, Award, 6 August 2019, para 568.

[95] *Tecmed v Mexico*, Award, 29 May 2003, para 155; *Enron v Argentina*, Award, 22 May 2007, para 258; *Sempra v Argentina*, Award, 28 September 2007, para 302; *Cargill v Poland*, Final Award, 29 February 2008, para 453; *Continental Casualty v Argentina*, Award, 5 September 2008, para 254; *Lemire v Ukraine*, Decision on Jurisdiction and Liability, 14 January 2010, paras 247–255; *Liman Caspian v Kazakhstan*, Award, 22 June 2010, para 263; *Total v Argentina*, Decision on Liability, 27 December 2010, paras 125–127; *Perenco v Ecuador*, Decision on Remaining Issues of Jurisdiction and on Liability, 12 September 2014, para 557; *Crystallex v Venezuela*, Award, 4 April 2016, paras 530–538.

[96] *Occidental Exploration v Ecuador*, Final Award, 1 July 2004, paras 189–190; *CMS v Argentina*, Award, 12 May 2005, paras 282–284; *AMTO v Ukraine*, Final Award, 26 March 2008, para 74; *Biwater Gauff v Tanzania*, Award, 24 July 2008, para 592; *Rumeli v Kazakhstan*, Award, 29 July 2008, para 611; *Duke Energy v Ecuador*, Award, 18 August 2008, paras 332–337; *El Paso v Argentina*, Award, 31 October 2011, paras 331–337; *Unión Fenosa v Egypt*, Award, 31 August 2018, para 9.51.

[97] *Azurix v Argentina*, Award, 14 July 2006.

provision adds that investments shall 'in no case be accorded treatment less than that required by international law'. The Tribunal said:

> The clause, as drafted, permits to interpret fair and equitable treatment and full protection and security as higher standards than required by international law. The purpose of the third sentence is to set a floor, not a ceiling, in order to avoid a possible interpretation of these standards below what is required by international law.[98]

In *Vivendi v Argentina*,[99] the applicable BIT provided for 'fair and equitable treatment according to the principles of international law'. The Tribunal found that there was no basis for the view that FET was limited to the international minimum standard and that such an interpretation would run counter to the text's ordinary meaning.[100] The Tribunal said:

> Article 3 refers to fair and equitable treatment *in conformity* with the principles of international law, and not to the minimum standard of treatment... The Tribunal sees no basis for equating principles of international law with the minimum standard of treatment. First, the reference to principles of international law supports a broader reading that invites consideration of a wider range of international law principles than the minimum standard alone. Second, the wording of Article 3 requires that the fair and equitable treatment *conform* to the principles of international law, but the requirement for conformity can just as readily set a floor as a ceiling on the Treaty's fair and equitable treatment standard.[101]

There are growing doubts about the relevance of this debate.[102] Tribunals have indicated that the difference between the treaty standard of FET and the customary minimum standard 'when applied to the specific facts of a case, may well be more apparent than real'.[103] The Tribunal in *El Paso v Argentina* has pointed out that the discussion was somewhat futile, seeing that the content of the international minimum standard is 'as little defined as the BIT's FET standard'.[104]

[98] At para 361.
[99] *Vivendi v Argentina*, Resubmitted Case: Award, 20 August 2007.
[100] At para 7.4.5.
[101] At paras 7.4.6, 7.4.7. Italics original. Footnote omitted.
[102] See SW Schill, 'Fair and Equitable Treatment, the Rule of Law, and Comparative Public Law' in SW Schill (ed) *International Investment Law and Comparative Public Law* (2010) 152.
[103] *Saluka v Czech Republic*, Partial Award, 17 March 2006, para 291. See also *Azurix v Argentina*, Award, 14 July 2006, para 361, 364; *Rumeli v Kazakhstan*, Award, 29 July 2008, para 611; *Impregilo v Argentina*, Award, 21 June 2011, paras 287–289; *ECE v Czech Republic*, Award, 19 September 2013, para 4.754; *Murphy v Ecuador II*, Partial Final Award, 6 May 2016, para 206; *Rusoro v Venezuela*, Award, 22 August 2016, para 520; *Gosling v Mauritius*, Award, 18 February 2020, para 243.
[104] *El Paso v Argentina*, Award, 31 October 2011, para 335. See also *MNSS v Montenegro*, Award, 4 May 2016, para 326; *Devas v India*, Award on Jurisdiction and Merits, 25 July 2016, para 456.

Depending on the specific wording of a particular treaty, FET may well overlap with or even be identical to the minimum standard required by international law. The fact that the host State has breached a rule of international law may be evidence of a violation of the fair and equitable standard,[105] but this is not the only conceivable form of its breach.

The emphasis on linkages between FET and customary international law is unlikely to restrain the evolution of the FET standard. On the contrary, this may well have the effect of accelerating the development of customary law through the rapidly expanding practice on FET clauses in treaties.[106] The Tribunal in *Chemtura v Canada*[107] said in this respect:

> the Tribunal notes that it is not disputed that the scope of Article 1105 of NAFTA must be determined by reference to customary international law. Such determination cannot overlook the evolution of customary international law, nor the impact of BITs on this evolution... in determining the standard of treatment set by Article 1105 of NAFTA, the Tribunal has taken into account the evolution of international customary law as a result *inter alia* of the conclusion of numerous BITs providing for fair and equitable treatment.[108]

The Tribunal in *Merrill & Ring v Canada* went one step further and stated that FET had become part of customary international law:

> A requirement that aliens be treated fairly and equitably in relation to business, trade and investment is the outcome of this changing reality and as such it has become sufficiently part of widespread and consistent practice so as to demonstrate that it is reflected today in customary international law as *opinio juris*.[109]

A related question is the substance of the international minimum standard for the treatment of foreigners under customary international law.[110] The historical starting point for this debate is often seen in the *Neer* case of 1926.[111] The case did not concern an investment but the murder of a US citizen in Mexico. The charge

[105] *SD Myers v Canada*, First Partial Award, 13 November 2000, para 264: 'the fact that a host Party has breached a rule of international law that is specifically designed to protect investors will tend to weigh heavily in favour of finding a breach of Article 1105'.

[106] R Dolzer and A von Walter, 'Fair and Equitable Treatment and Customary Law—Lines of Jurisprudence' in F Ortino et al (eds) *Investment Treaty Law: Current Issues* (2007) 99; I Tudor, *The Fair and Equitable Treatment Standard in International Law of Foreign Investment* (2008) 83.

[107] *Chemtura v Canada*, Award, 2 August 2010.

[108] At paras 121, 236.

[109] *Merrill & Ring v Canada*, Award, 31 March 2010, para 210.

[110] See I.1(b) above.

[111] *Neer v Mexico*, Opinion, United States–Mexico General Claims Commission, 15 October 1926, (1927) 21 *AJIL* 555; 4 RIAA 60.

was that the Mexican authorities had shown a lack of diligence in investigating and prosecuting the crime. The Commission said:

> the treatment of an alien, in order to constitute an international delinquency, should amount to an outrage, to bad faith, to wilful neglect of duty, or to an insufficiency of governmental action so far short of international standards that every reasonable and impartial man would readily recognize its insufficiency.[112]

The Commission found that the facts did not show such a lack of diligence as would render Mexico liable and dismissed the claim.

Respondent States in investment cases have frequently invoked *Neer*. Although some tribunals have relied on *Neer*,[113] most investment tribunals have rejected the high threshold for a violation of international law formulated there and have pointed out that the international minimum standard was an evolving concept.[114] The NAFTA Tribunal, in *Merrill & Ring*, clearly distanced itself from any undifferentiated reliance on *Neer*:

> the Tribunal finds that the applicable minimum standard of treatment of investors is found in customary international law and that, except for cases of safety and due process, today's minimum standard is broader than that defined in the *Neer* case and its progeny.[115]

Similarly, in *ADF v United States*,[116] the Tribunal found:

> that the customary international law referred to in Article 1105(1) [of NAFTA] is not 'frozen in time' and that the minimum standard of treatment does evolve.... what customary international law projects is not a static photograph of the

[112] At 556.

[113] *Glamis Gold v United States*, Award, 8 June 2009, paras 598–627; *Cargill v Mexico*, Award, 18 September 2009, paras 272–288.

[114] *Pope & Talbot v Canada*, Award on the Merits, 10 April 2001, para 118; *Pope & Talbot v Canada*, Award in respect of Damages, 31 May 2002, paras 63, 64; *Mondev v United States*, Award, 11 October 2002, paras 116, 123, 125, 127; *GAMI v Mexico*, Award, 15 November 2004, para 95; *Eureko v Poland*, Partial Award, 19 August 2005, para 234; *Thunderbird v Mexico*, Award, 26 January 2006, para 194; *Azurix v Argentina*, Award, 14 July 2006, paras 365–368; *LG&E v Argentina*, Decision on Liability, 3 October 2006, para 123; *Vivendi v Argentina*, Resubmitted Case: Award, 20 August 2007, para 7.4.7., note 325; *Merrill & Ring v Canada*, Award, 31 March 2010, paras 195–213; *Ulysseas v Ecuador*, Final Award, 12 June 2012, para 245; *Railroad Development v Guatemala*, Award, 29 June 2012, para 218; *Gold Reserve v Venezuela*, Award, 22 September 2014, para 567; *von Pezold v Zimbabwe*, Award, 28 July 2015, para 546; *Tatneft v Ukraine*, Award on the Merits, 29 July 2014, para 392; *Philip Morris v Uruguay*, Award, 8 July 2016, para 319; *Devas v India*, Award on Jurisdiction and Merits, 25 July 2016, para 457; *Mesa Power v Canada*, Award, 24 March 2016, paras 495–500; *Crystallex v Venezuela*, Award, 4 April 2016, paras 534–536; *Urbaser v Argentina*, Award, 8 December 2016, para 605; *Anglo American v Venezuela*, Award, 18 January 2019, para 442.

[115] *Merrill & Ring v Canada*, Award, 31 March 2010, para 213.

[116] *ADF v United States*, Award, 9 January 2003.

minimum standard of treatment of aliens as it stood in 1927 when the Award in the *Neer* case was rendered. For both customary international law and the minimum standard of treatment of aliens it incorporates, are constantly in a process of development.[117]

(g) Specific applications of the fair and equitable treatment standard

Broad definitions or descriptions are not the only way to gauge the meaning of a concept such as FET. Another method is to identify typical factual situations to which this principle has been applied.[118] The practice of tribunals shows several principles that fall under the standard of FET. The cases discussed below demonstrate that stability, transparency, and the investor's legitimate expectations play a central role in the understanding of the FET standard. Other contexts in which the standard has been applied concern compliance with contractual obligations, procedural propriety, action in good faith, freedom from coercion and harassment, and observance of the host State's law.

aa. Stability and consistency

Predictability is a cornerstone of investment protection. The idea is to reduce political risk by making investments more calculable. This applies not only to the stability of the legal framework under which the investor operates but also to the uniform application of legal rules. Whereas stability primarily relates to the quality of the host State's legal framework, consistency refers to the application of these legal rules by the administrative and judicial organs of the host State.

Some treaties link stability to FET[119] or list stability side by side with FET.[120] But even without an explicit reference to stability, tribunals have regarded it as an essential element of FET. The Tribunal in *Total v Argentina*[121] expressed the importance of stability in the following terms:

> stability, predictability and consistency of legislation and regulation are important for investors in order to plan their investments, especially if their business plans extend over a number of years. Competent authorities of States entering into BITs

[117] At para 179.

[118] See also K Yannaca-Small, 'Fair and Equitable Treatment Standard' in K Yannaca-Small (ed) *Arbitration under International Investment Agreements* (2010) 393; SW Schill, 'Fair and Equitable Treatment, the Rule of Law, and Comparative Public Law' in SW Schill (ed) *International Investment Law and Comparative Public Law* (2010) 159.

[119] See Preamble Argentina–US BIT (1991): 'Agreeing that fair and equitable treatment of investment is desirable in order to maintain a stable framework for investment.'

[120] Article 10(1) ECT.

[121] *Total v Argentina*, Decision on Liability, 27 December 2010.

> in order to promote foreign investment in their economy should be aware of the importance for the investors that a legal environment favourable to the carrying out of their business activities be maintained.[122]

Tribunals have found that the investor may rely on the legal framework under which it makes the investment.[123] The Tribunal in *Eiser v Spain*[124] held that the stability element of FET can be breached through regulatory changes. The tribunal said:

> fair and equitable treatment does protect investors from a fundamental change to the regulatory regime in a manner that does not take account of the circumstances of existing investments made in reliance on the prior regime.[125]

Numerous other tribunals have referred to the importance of stability of the host State's legal framework in the application of the FET standard.[126]

The investor's right to stability, however, is not absolute. Tribunals have stressed that the host State's right to regulate domestic matters in the public interest has to be taken into consideration. Therefore, the need for stability does not mean that the host State is deprived of every opportunity to adapt its legal system to changed circumstances.[127] The Tribunal in *EDF v Romania*[128] said in this respect:

> The idea that legitimate expectations, and therefore FET, imply the stability of the legal and business framework, may not be correct if stated in an overly-broad and unqualified formulation. The FET might then mean the virtual freezing of the legal regulation of economic activities, in contrast with the State's normal regulatory power and the evolutionary character of economic life. Except where specific

[122] At para 114.

[123] See also the decision in *Tecmed v Mexico*, Award, 29 May 2003, para 154, quoted at VIII.1(d) above.

[124] *Eiser v Spain*, Award, 4 May 2017.

[125] At para 363. See also para 382.

[126] *Occidental Exploration v Ecuador*, Final Award, 1 July 2004, paras 183–184; *CMS v Argentina*, Award, 12 May 2005, para 274–276; *LG&E v Argentina*, Decision on Liability, 3 October 2006, para 124; *Sempra v Argentina*, Award, 28 September 2007, para 300; *BG Group v Argentina*, Final Award, 24 December 2007, para 307; *Bayindir v Pakistan*, Decision on Jurisdiction, 14 November 2005, para 239; *Plama v Bulgaria*, Award, 27 August 2008, para 173; *Merrill & Ring v Canada*, Award, 31 March 2010, para 232; *Unglaube v Costa Rica*, Award, 16 May 2012, para 248.

[127] *Parkerings v Lithuania*, Award, 11 September 2007, paras 332–338; *BG Group v Argentina*, Final Award, 24 December 2007, para 298; *Plama v Bulgaria*, Award, 27 August 2008, para 219; *Continental Casualty v Argentina*, Award, 5 September 2008, paras 258; *AES v Hungary*, Award, 23 September 2010, paras 9.3.27–9.3.35; *Paushok v Mongolia*, Award on Jurisdiction and Liability, 28 April 2011, para 302; *Impregilo v Argentina*, Award, 21 June 2011, paras 290–291; *Ulysseas v Ecuador*, Final Award, 12 June 2012, paras 240– 256; *TECO v Guatemala*, Award, 19 December 2013, para 629; *Mobil & Murphy v Canada*, Decision on Liability and on Principles of Quantum, 22 May 2012, para 153; *Levy v Peru*, Award, 26 February 2014, para 319; *Mamidoil v Albania*, Award, 30 March 2015, paras 614, 617; *Teinver v Argentina*, Award, 21 July 2017, para 668.

[128] *EDF v Romania*, Award, 8 October 2009.

> promises or representations are made by the State to the investor, the latter may not rely on a bilateral investment treaty as a kind of insurance policy against the risk of any changes in the host State's legal and economic framework. Such expectation would be neither legitimate nor reasonable.[129]

Therefore, investors are not protected against every unfavourable change in the law but only against fundamental changes of the regulatory framework under which they operate. What matters is whether measures exceed normal regulatory powers and fundamentally modify the regulatory framework for the investment beyond an acceptable margin of change.[130] In the words of the Tribunal in *RREEF v Spain*:[131]

> Stability is not an absolute concept; absent a clear stabilization clause, it does not equate with immutability... However, the obligation to create a stable environment certainly excludes any unpredictable radical transformation in the conditions of the investments.[132]

In deciding between the investor's right to stability and the State's right to regulate, tribunals have balanced the investor's legitimate expectations against the State's duty to act in the public interest.[133]

For a foreign investor it is important not only that the law displays a certain degree of stability but also that the law is applied by the courts and administrative agencies coherently and consistently and hence in a predictable fashion. Contradictory and inconsistent action by State authorities undermines the ability of the investor to plan effectively.

Tribunals have found that inconsistent behaviour of the host State's organs may amount to a violation of the FET standard.[134] In *MTD v*

[129] At para 217.

[130] *El Paso v Argentina*, Award, 31 October 2011, para 402; *Toto v Lebanon*, Award, 7 June 2012, para 244; *Charanne v Spain*, Award, 21 January 2016, para 517; *Philip Morris v Uruguay*, Award, 8 July 2016, para 423; *Eiser v Spain*, Award, 4 May 2017, para 363; *Novenergia II v Spain*, Final Award, 15 February 2018, para 656; *Masdar v Spain*, Award, 16 May 2018, para 484; *Antin v Spain*, Award, 15 June 2018, para 531; *Foresight v Spain*, Final Award, 14 November 2018, paras 359, 397–398; *RWE v Spain*, Decision on Jurisdiction, Liability and Certain Issues of Quantum, 30 December 2019, paras 610–612.

[131] *RREEF v Spain*, Decision on Responsibility and on the Principles of Quantum, 30 November 2018.

[132] At para 315.

[133] *Saluka v Czech Republic*, Partial Award, 17 March 2006, para 306; *Plama v Bulgaria*, Award, 27 August 2008, para 177; *Lemire v Ukraine*, Decision on Jurisdiction and Liability, 14 January 2010, para 273; *Total v Argentina*, Decision on Liability, 27 December 2010, paras 123–124, 162, 309, 429; *El Paso v Argentina*, Award, 31 October 2011, para 358; *EDF v Argentina*, Award, 11 June 2012, para 1005; *Electrabel v Hungary*, Decision on Jurisdiction, Applicable Law and Liability, 30 November 2012, para 7.77; *Arif v Moldova*, Award, 8 April 2013, para 537; *Micula v Romania I*, Award, 11 December 2013, para 529; *Perenco v Ecuador*, Decision on Remaining Issues of Jurisdiction and on Liability, 12 September 2014, para 560; *Urbaser v Argentina*, Award, 8 December 2016, paras 622–623; *Antaris v Czech Republic*, Award, 2 May 2018, para 360(9); *Greentech v Italy*, Final Award, 23 December 2018, para 454; *Stadtwerke München v Spain*, Award, 2 December 2019, para 264.

[134] *Lauder v Czech Republic*, Final Award, 3 September 2001, para 290; *EnCana v Ecuador*, Award, 3 February 2006, para 158; *PSEG v Turkey*, Award, 19 January 2007, para 249; *Binder v Czech Republic*, Final Award, 15 July 2011, para 446; *Arif v Moldova*, Award, 8 April 2013, para 547(b); *Crystallex v*

Chile,[135] the Foreign Investment Commission (FIC), a Chilean government body, had signed a contract approving the investment. After the investors had invested into the project, they were informed that the land they had acquired for the project would not be re-zoned on the grounds that it would be inconvenient and contrary to Chilean law. The Tribunal found that approval of a project in a location gave the investor a prima facie expectation that the project was feasible. The Tribunal emphasized:

> the inconsistency of action between two arms of the same Government vis-à-vis the same investor even when the legal framework of the country provides for a mechanism to coordinate... Chile also has an obligation to act coherently and apply its policies consistently, independently of how diligent an investor is. Under international law ... the State of Chile needs to be considered by the Tribunal as a unit... approval of an investment by the FIC for a project that is against the urban policy of the Government is a breach of the obligation to treat an investor fairly and equitably.[136]

bb. Legitimate expectations

The investor's legitimate expectations are a central concept in the application of the FET standard. It may be described as the protection of reliance on the position taken by a public authority. The concept of legitimate expectations is not a creation of international law but stems from a variety of legal systems[137] and is based on a general principle of law.

Tribunals have pointed to the dominant role of legitimate expectations for FET in international investment law.[138] The investor's legitimate expectations are based on the host State's legal framework and on any undertakings and representations made explicitly or implicitly by the host State.[139] The regulatory framework on

Venezuela, Award, 4 April 2016, para 579; *Garanti Koza v Turkmenistan*, Award, 19 December 2016, paras 381–382; *Olin v Libya*, Final Award, 25 May 2018, para 347; *Glencore v Colombia*, Award, 27 August 2019, paras 1419–1420.

135 *MTD v Chile*, Award, 25 May 2004.

136 At paras 163, 165, 166.

137 *Thunderbird v Mexico*, Arbitral Award, 26 January 2006, Separate Opinion Thomas Wälde, 1 December 2005, paras 27–30; *Total v Argentina*, Decision on Liability, 27 December 2010, para 128–130.

138 *Saluka v Czech Republic*, Partial Award, 17 March 2006, para 302; *Invesmart v Czech Republic*, Award, 26 June 2009, para 202; *EDF v Romania*, Award, 8 October 2009, para 216; *Impregilo v Argentina*, Award, 21 June 2011, para 285; *El Paso v Argentina*, Award, 31 October 2011, para 348; *Electrabel v Hungary*, Decision on Jurisdiction, Applicable Law and Liability, 30 November 2012, para 7.75; *Mobil v Argentina*, Decision on Jurisdiction and Liability, 10 April 2013, para 927; *Novenergia II v Spain*, Final Award, 15 February 2018, para 648.

139 For early discussions of the relevance of the concept of legitimate expectations in foreign investment law, see R Dolzer 'New Foundations of the Law of Expropriation of Alien Property' (1981) 75 *AJIL* 553.

which the investor is entitled to rely consists of legislation and treaties as well as of assurances contained in decrees, licences, and similar executive statements.[140] Explicit representations and specific assurances play a central role in the creation of legitimate expectations.[141] Explicit undertakings and representations made by the host State are the strongest basis for legitimate expectations.[142] In the renewable energy cases against Spain, tribunals have increasingly looked for the existence of explicit assurances on the part of the host State.[143]

A reversal of assurances by the host State that have led to legitimate expectations will be contrary to good faith and violate the FET principle.[144] Mere political statements, however, will not create legitimate expectations.[145]

Despite the reference to 'expectations', the test is not subjective or psychological but depends on objective facts. Legitimate expectations are what a prudent investor would have anticipated. Tribunals discussing legitimate expectations do not look for the assumptions or wishes of investors but rely on the objective circumstances created by the host State, on its legal framework, and on any specific commitments made by it. It is these objectively verifiable facts that make expectations legitimate,

[140] *CMS v Argentina*, Award, 12 May 2005, para 275; *LG&E v Argentina*, Decision on Liability, 3 October 2006, para 133; *PSEG v Turkey*, Award, 19 January 2007, para 250; *Sempra v Argentina*, Award, 28 September 2007, para 303; *BG Group v Argentina*, Final Award, 24 December 2007, para 310; *National Grid v Argentina*, Award, 3 November 2008, paras 177–179; *Novenergia II v Spain*, Final Award, 15 February 2018, paras 662–667, 681, 697; *Antin v Spain*, Award, 15 June 2018, paras 532, 552. But see *Blusun v Italy*, Award, 27 December 2016, paras 371–372; *Antaris v Czech Republic*, Award, 2 May 2018, para 360(6).

[141] Article 8.10 of the CETA contains the following specification of the FET standard: '4. When applying the above fair and equitable treatment obligation, a Tribunal may take into account whether a Party made a specific representation to an investor to induce a covered investment, that created a legitimate expectation, and upon which the investor relied in deciding to make or maintain the covered investment, but that the Party subsequently frustrated.'

[142] *Eureko v Poland*, Partial Award, 19 August 2005, paras 231–234; *Parkerings v Lithuania*, Award, 11 September 2007, para 331; *OKO Pankki v Estonia*, Award, 19 November 2007, para 247; *Duke Energy v Ecuador*, Award, 18 August 2008, paras 359–364; *EDF v Romania*, Award, 8 October 2009, para 217; *Total v Argentina*, Decision on Liability, 27 December 2010, paras 117, 119–120, 131; *White Industries v India*, Final Award, 30 November 2011, para 10.3.7; *Saint-Gobain v Venezuela*, Decision on Liability and the Principles of Quantum, 30 December 2016, para 531, 535; *Unión Fenosa v Egypt*, Award, 31 August 2018, para 9.83; *Greentech v Italy*, Final Award, 23 December 2018, paras 452–453; *United Utilities v Estonia*, Award, 21 June 2019, paras 576–578; *Micula v Romania II*, Award, 5 March 2020, paras 361–362.

[143] *Charanne v Spain*, Award, 21 January 2016, paras 493, 499; *Masdar v Spain*, Award, 16 May 2018, paras 520–521; *RREEF v Spain*, Decision on Responsibility and on the Principles of Quantum, 30 November 2018, paras 320–321; *Cube v Spain*, Decision on Jurisdiction, Liability and Partial Decision on Quantum, 19 February 2019, paras 388, 397; *NextEra v Spain*, Decision on Jurisdiction, Liability and Quantum Principles, 12 March 2019, paras 587–596; *9REN v Spain*, Award, 31 May 2019, paras 292–299; *SolEs Badajoz v Spain*, Award, 31 July 2019, para 313; *InfraRed v Spain*, Award, 2 August 2019, paras 366–367, 406–436; *RWE v Spain*, Decision on Jurisdiction, Liability, and Certain Issues of Quantum, 30 December 2019, paras 453–462, 535–549; *Watkins v Spain*, Award, 21 January 2020, paras 495, 533.

[144] *Tecmed v Mexico*, Award, 29 May 2003, para 154; *Siag v Egypt*, Award, 1 June 2009, para 450; *Charanne v Spain*, Award, 21 January 2016, para 486; *Devas v India*, Award on Jurisdiction and Merits, 25 July 2016, paras 465–470.

[145] *Continental Casualty v Argentina*, Award, 5 September 2008, para 261; *El Paso v Argentina*, Award, 31 October 2011, paras 378, 395; *Mamidoil v Albania*, Award, 30 March 2015, para 643.

justified, or reasonable. These objective circumstances have a dual function: they are the origin of legitimate expectations and the evidence for them.

The Tribunal in *Suez and InterAguas v Argentina*[146] summarized this point as follows:

> When an investor undertakes an investment, a host government through its laws, regulations, declared policies, and statements creates in the investor certain expectations about the nature of the treatment that it may anticipate from the host State. The resulting reasonable and legitimate expectations are important factors that influence initial investment decisions and afterwards the manner in which the investment is to be managed.[147]
>
> ... one must not look single-mindedly at the Claimants' subjective expectations. The Tribunal must rather examine them from an objective and reasonable point of view.[148]

Numerous other tribunals have also stressed the objective nature of legitimate expectations.[149]

At the same time, investors are under an obligation to perform a proper due diligence, that is, to inform themselves of the legal environment and general economic and political conditions in the host State before investing.[150] The investor's legitimate expectations will be reduced if there is general instability of political conditions in the country concerned.[151] Despite the host State's obligations 'it is the responsibility of the investor to assure itself that it is properly advised, particularly when investing abroad in an unfamiliar environment'.[152] The Tribunal in *Invesmart v Czech*

146 *Suez and InterAguas v Argentina*, Decision on Liability, 30 July 2010.

147 At para 203.

148 At para 209.

149 *Saluka v Czech Republic*, Partial Award, 17 March 2006, para 304; *Glamis Gold v United States*, Award, 8 June 2009, paras 621, 627, 799; *Invesmart v Czech Republic*, Award, 26 June 2009, para 255; *El Paso v Argentina*, Award, 31 October 2011, paras 356, 358, 364; *Arif v Moldova*, Award, 8 April 2013, para 532; *Perenco v Ecuador*, Decision on Remaining Issues of Jurisdiction and on Liability, 12 September 2014, para 560; *Charanne v Spain*, Award, 21 January 2016, para 495; *Isolux v Spain*, Award, 12 July 2016, para 777; *Urbaser v Argentina*, Award, 8 December 2016, para 613; *Antin v Spain*, Award, 15 June 2018, para 538; *RREEF v Spain*, Decision on Responsibility and Principles of Quantum, 30 November 2018, paras 261, 380.

150 *Parkerings v Lithuania*, Award, 11 September 2007, para 333; *Lemire v Ukraine*, Decision on Jurisdiction and Liability, 14 January 2010, para 285; *Anderson v Costa Rica*, Award, 19 May 2010, para 58; *Isolux v Spain*, Award, 12 July 2016, para 781; *E energija v Latvia*, Award, 22 December 2017, para 837; *Novenergia II v Spain*, Final Award, 15 February 2018, para 679; *Antaris v Czech Republic*, Award, 2 May 2018, paras 432, 435; *Gavrilović v Croatia*, Award, 26 July 2018, para 986; *Zelena v Serbia*, Award, 9 November 2018, paras 98, 377; *Cube v Spain*, Decision on Jurisdiction, Liability and Partial Decision on Quantum, 19 February 2019, paras 394–396, 405–406; *SolEs Badajoz v Spain*, Award, 31 July 2019, paras 330–331; *OperaFund v Spain*, Award, 6 September 2019, paras 486–487.

151 *Bayindir v Pakistan*, Award, 27 August 2009, paras 192–197. See also U Kriebaum, 'The Relevance of Economic and Political Conditions for the Protection under Investment Treaties' (2011) 10 *LPICT* 383.

152 *MTD v Chile*, Award, 25 May 2004, para 164.

Republic[153] described this obligation as follows:

> the due diligence performed when the investor made its investment plays an important role in evaluating its expectation. A putative investor, especially one making an investment in a highly regulated sector such as financial services, as in the instant case, has the burden of performing its own due diligence in vetting the investment within the context of the operative legal regime.[154]

In most of these cases, tribunals seem to have presumed reliance on the host State's regulatory framework and have not examined the investor's due diligence in any detail.[155] Therefore, a lack of due diligence seems relevant only if sufficient due diligence would have led to different expectations.

The investor must convince the tribunal that in making the investment it relied on the host State's representations.[156] Therefore, the relevant time for the examination of legitimate expectations is the making of the investment. Tribunals have emphasized that the legitimate expectations of the investor will be grounded in the legal order of the host State as it stands at the time when the investor acquires the investment.[157] Tribunals have stressed that the legal framework as it existed at that time was decisive for any legitimate expectations.[158] In *National Grid v Argentina*,[159] the Tribunal said:

> this standard protects the reasonable expectations of the investor at the time it made the investment and which were based on representations, commitments or specific conditions offered by the State concerned. Thus, treatment by the State should 'not affect the basic expectations that were taken into account by the foreign investor to make the investment.'[160]

[153] *Invesmart v Czech Republic*, Award, 26 June 2009.

[154] At para 254.

[155] An exception to this observation is *RWE v Spain*, Decision on Jurisdiction, Liability, and Certain Issues of Quantum, 30 December 2019, paras 494, 497, 504–506.

[156] *Antaris v Czech Republic*, Award, 2 May 2018, para 360(3); *Olin v Libya*, Final Award, 25 May 2018, para 307.

[157] C Schreuer and U Kriebaum, 'At What Time Must Legitimate Expectations Exist?' in J Werner and AH Ali (eds) *A Liber Amicorum: Thomas Wälde. Law Beyond Conventional Thought* (2009) 265.

[158] *LG&E v Argentina*, Decision on Liability, 3 October 2006, para 130; *Enron v Argentina*, Award, 22 May 2007, para 262; *BG Group v Argentina*, Final Award, 24 December 2007, paras 297–298; *Duke Energy v Ecuador*, Award, 18 August 2008, paras 340, 365; *Jan de Nul v Egypt*, Award, 6 November 2008, para 265; *Bayindir v Pakistan*, Award, 27 August 2009, paras 190, 191; *EDF v Romania*, Award, 8 October 2009, para 219; *AES v Hungary*, Award, 23 September 2010, paras 9.3.8–9.3.18; *Frontier Petroleum v Czech Republic*, Final Award, 12 November 2010, paras 287–288, 468; *Micula v Romania I*, Award, 11 December 2013, para 722; *United Utilities v Estonia*, Award, 21 June 2019, paras 606–608; *SolEs Badajoz v Spain*, Award, 31 July 2019, paras 312, 418; *RWE v Spain*, Decision on Jurisdiction, Liability and Certain Issues of Quantum, 30 December 2019, paras 482–490.

[159] *National Grid v Argentina*, Award, 3 November 2008.

[160] At para 173. Footnote omitted.

The stability of the legal framework existing at the time of the investment will be especially affected by retroactive legislation. Several tribunals have found that a violation of legitimate expectations will be compounded by retroactive measures.[161] *ATA v Jordan*[162] concerned the extinguishment of the claimant's right to arbitration. The retroactivity of the underlying Jordanian legislation constituted the ground for the breach of the FET standard. The Tribunal held:

> The retroactive effect of the Jordanian Arbitration Law, which extinguished a valid right to arbitration deprived an investor such as the Claimant of a valuable asset in violation of the Treaty's investment protections.[163]

cc. Transparency

Transparency is closely related to the protection of the investor's legitimate expectations. Transparency means that the legal framework for the investor's operations is readily apparent and that any decisions affecting the investor can be traced to that legal framework.[164] Some treaties contain specific references to transparency.[165] Tribunals have, however, found that the obligation to provide a transparent regulatory framework was part of the FET standard.[166]

In *Metalclad v Mexico*,[167] the issue of transparency played a central role. The federal government of Mexico and the state government had issued construction and operating permits for the investor's landfill project. The investor was assured that it had all the permits it needed but the municipality refused to grant a construction

[161] *Total v Argentina*, Decision on Liability, 27 December 2010, para 129; *Novenergia II v Spain*, Final Award, 15 February 2018, para 697; *Casinos Austria v Argentina*, Decision on Jurisdiction, 29 June 2018, para 244; *RREEF v Spain*, Decision on Responsibility and on the Principles of Quantum, 30 November 2018, paras 328–330; *Cavalum v Spain*, Decision on Jurisdiction, Liability and Directions of Quantum, 31 August 2020, paras 417, 633–637.

[162] *ATA v Jordan*, Award, 18 May 2010.

[163] At para 126. See also para 128.

[164] *Frontier Petroleum v Czech Republic*, Final Award, 12 November 2010, para 285; *Micula v Romania I*, Award, 11 December 2013, para 530.

[165] ECT Art 10(1). See *Electrabel v Hungary*, Decision on Jurisdiction, Applicable Law and Liability, 30 November 2012, para 7.79; *RREEF v Spain*, Decision on Responsibility and on the Principles of Quantum, 30 November 2018, paras 415–416; *Greentech v Italy*, Final Award, 23 December 2018, paras 457–458; *Stadtwerke München v Spain*, Award, 2 December 2019, paras 309–315.

[166] *Maffezini v Spain*, Award, 13 November 2000, para 83; *LG&E v Argentina*, Decision on Liability, 3 October 2006, para 131; *Cargill v Poland*, Final Award, 29 February 2008, para 511, 515, 517; *Plama v Bulgaria*, Award, 27 August 2008, para 178; *Nordzucker v Poland*, Second Partial Award, 28 January 2009, paras 14, 84, 95; *Lemire v Ukraine*, Decision on Jurisdiction and Liability, 14 January 2010, para 418; *Levy v Peru*, Award, 26 February 2014, paras 322, 327–328; *Gold Reserve v Venezuela*, Award, 22 September 2014, para 570; *Crystallex v Venezuela*, Award, 4 April 2016, para 579; *Bear Creek v Peru*, Award, 30 November 2017, para 523; *Olin v Libya*, Final Award, 25 May 2018, para 320; *InfraRed v Spain*, Award, 2 August 2019, paras 372, 468–475; *CMC v Mozambique*, Award, 24 October 2019, paras 421–424; *Watkins v Spain*, Award, 21 January 2020, paras 590–594; *Eskosol v Italy*, Award, 4 September 2020, paras 416–422. But see *Cargill v Mexico*, Award, 18 September 2009, para 294.

[167] *Metalclad v Mexico*, Award, 30 August 2000. See also T Weiler, 'Good Faith and Regulatory Transparency: The Story of Metalclad v. Mexico' in T Weiler (ed) *International Investment Law and Arbitration: Leading Cases* (2005) 701.

permit. The claimant complained about a lack of transparency surrounding the process. In interpreting the concept of transparency, the Tribunal said:

> The Tribunal understands this to include the idea that all relevant legal requirements for the purpose of initiating, completing and successfully operating investments made, or intended to be made, under the Agreement should be capable of being readily known to all affected investors of another Party. There should be no room for doubt or uncertainty on such matters. Once the authorities of the central government of any Party . . . become aware of any scope for misunderstanding or confusion in this connection, it is their duty to ensure that the correct position is promptly determined and clearly stated so that investors can proceed with all appropriate expedition in the confident belief that they are acting in accordance with all relevant laws.[168]

The Tribunal held that the investor was entitled to rely on the representations of the federal officials.[169] It concluded that the acts of the State and the municipality were in violation of the FET standard. The Tribunal said:

> Mexico failed to ensure a transparent and predictable framework for Metalclad's business planning and investment. The totality of these circumstances demonstrates a lack of orderly process and timely disposition in relation to an investor of a Party acting in the expectation that it would be treated fairly and justly in accordance with the NAFTA.[170]

In *Tecmed v Mexico*,[171] the dispute concerned the replacement of an unlimited licence by a licence of limited duration for the operation of a landfill. The Tribunal applied a provision in the BIT between Mexico and Spain guaranteeing FET. The Tribunal found that this provision required transparency and protection of the investor's basic expectations. The Tribunal explained that:

> The foreign investor expects the host State to act in a consistent manner, free from ambiguity and totally transparently in its relation with the foreign investor, so that it may know beforehand any and all rules and regulations that will govern its investments, as well as the goals of the relevant policies and administrative practices or directives, to be able to plan its investment and comply with such regulations.[172]

[168] At para 76.

[169] At para 89.

[170] At para 99. The Award was set aside in part by the Supreme Court of British Columbia on grounds that were peculiar to NAFTA.

[171] *Tecmed v Mexico*, Award, 29 May 2003.

[172] At para 154.

The Tribunal concluded that the investor's fair expectations were frustrated by the contradiction and uncertainty in Mexico's behaviour which was

> characterized by its ambiguity and uncertainty which are prejudicial to the investor in terms of its advance assessment of the legal situation surrounding its investment and the planning of its business activity and its adjustment to preserve its rights.[173]

In *MTD v Chile*,[174] the respondent had signed an investment contract for the construction of a planned community with the country's Foreign Investment Commission. The project failed because it turned out to be inconsistent with zoning regulations. The Tribunal found that the guarantee of FET in the BIT between Chile and Malaysia had been violated by what it described as 'the inconsistency of action between two arms of the same Government *vis-à-vis* the same investor'.[175] It went on to state that while it was the investor's duty to inform itself of the country's law and policy in principle, Chile also had an obligation to act coherently and apply its policies consistently.[176]

The duty of transparency, however, has its limits.[177] In *Micula v Romania I*,[178] the Tribunal warned of a standard of transparency that would be inappropriate and unrealistic. After referring to the statements on transparency in *Metalclad* and in *Tecmed*, it said:

> Whether a state has been unfair and inequitable by failing to be transparent with respect to its laws and regulations, or being ambiguous and inconsistent in their application, must be assessed in light of all of the factual circumstances surrounding such conduct. For example, it would be unrealistic to require Romania to be totally transparent with the general public in the context of diplomatic negotiations. The question before the Tribunal is thus not whether Romania has failed to make full disclosure of or grant full access to sensitive information; it is whether, in the event that Romania failed to do so, Romania acted unfairly and inequitably with respect to the Claimants.[179]

dd. Compliance with contractual obligations

Closely related to the issue of legitimate expectations is the question of the observance of obligations arising from contracts. Contractual agreements are the

[173] At para 172.
[174] *MTD v Chile*, Award, 25 May 2004.
[175] At para 163.
[176] At paras 165–166. Chile failed in its attempt to have this Award annulled: *MTD v Chile*, Decision on Annulment, 21 March 2007.
[177] See also *Al Tamimi v Oman*, Award, 3 November 2015, para 399.
[178] *Micula v Romania I*, Award, 11 December 2013.
[179] At para 533.

classical instrument in most, if not all, legal systems for the creation of legal stability and predictability. Therefore, *pacta sunt servanda* would seem to be an obvious application of the stability requirement that is so prominent in the FET standard. The connection between this aspect of FET and the umbrella clause[180] is evident.

In several cases dealing with the protection of the investors' legitimate expectations, these expectations were actually based on contractual arrangements with the host State. It does not, however, follow that every breach of a contract by a host State or one of its entities automatically amounts to a violation of the FET standard.

Some tribunals seemed to take the view that a failure to observe contractual obligations on the part of a government would be contrary to the FET standard.[181] The Tribunal in *Mondev v United States*[182] found it clear that the protection of FET under Article 1105(1) NAFTA extended to contract claims. The Tribunal said:

> a governmental prerogative to violate investment contracts would appear to be inconsistent with the principles embodied in Article 1105 and with contemporary standards of national and international law concerning governmental liability for contractual performance.[183]

Similarly, in *SGS v Paraguay*,[184] a case involving unpaid invoices for pre-shipment inspections, the Tribunal spoke of a 'baseline expectation of contractual compliance'. It said:

> a State's non-payment under a contract is, in the view of the Tribunal, capable of giving rise to a breach of a fair and equitable treatment requirement, such as, perhaps, where the non-payment amounts to a repudiation of the contract, frustration of its economic purpose, or substantial deprivation of its value.[185]

Some tribunals found that the existence of a contract created legitimate expectations that were protected by the FET standard.[186]

Most tribunals, however, have adopted a more restrictive approach. They have found that a simple breach of contract by a State would not trigger a violation of

180 See VIII.6 below.

181 Tentatively: *SGS v Philippines*, Decision on Jurisdiction, 29 January 2004, para 162; *Noble Ventures v Romania*, Award, 12 October 2005, para 182; *SGS v Paraguay*, Decision on Jurisdiction, 12 February 2010, paras 144–151; *Teinver v Argentina*, Award, 21 July 2017, paras 849–851, 854–857.

182 *Mondev v United States*, Award, 11 October 2002.

183 At para 134.

184 *SGS v Paraguay*, Decision on Jurisdiction, 12 February 2010.

185 At para 146.

186 *Continental Casualty v Argentina*, Award, 5 September 2008, para 261; *Suez and Vivendi v Argentina*, Decision on Liability, 30 July 2010, para 231; *Tulip v Turkey*, Award, 10 March 2014, para 404; *Perenco v Ecuador*, Decision on Remaining Issues of Jurisdiction and Liability, 12 September 2014, paras 562–563.

the FET standard.[187] Rather, 'a breach of FET requires conduct in the exercise of sovereign powers'.[188] Only a termination of the contract, brought about through the employment of sovereign prerogative, would lead to a violation of the FET standard.[189] The same would apply to government interference with a contract between the investor and a State entity.[190]

In *Waste Management*,[191] one of the claims concerned the failure of the City of Acapulco to make payments under a concession agreement.[192] The Tribunal did not find that this amounted to a violation of FET. It said:

> even the persistent non-payment of debts by a municipality is not to be equated with a violation of Article 1105, provided that it does not amount to an outright and unjustified repudiation of the transaction and provided that some remedy is open to the creditor to address the problem.[193]

The view that a simple breach of contract is insufficient to amount to a breach of the FET standard is clearly prevalent. But this seemingly simple test leads to further questions. The distinction between sovereign and commercial acts, which is accepted in the field of State immunity, is of unclear validity in the field of State responsibility. Also, even if the underlying relationship and the breach are clearly commercial, the motives of a government for a certain act may still be governmental.

ee. Procedural propriety and due process

Some treaties offer a separate provision guaranteeing effective means for the assertion of rights under domestic law.[194] But the bulk of the case law dealing with due process rests on the FET standard.

[187] *GAMI v Mexico*, Final Award, 15 November 2004, para 101; *Parkerings v Lithuania*, Award, 11 September 2007, paras 344–345; *Biwater Gauff v Tanzania*, Award, 24 July 2008, para 636; *Duke Energy v Ecuador*, Award, 18 August 2008, paras 342–345, 354; *Glamis Gold v United States*, Award, 8 June 2009, para 620; *EDF v Romania*, Award, 8 October 2009, paras 238–260; *Hamester v Ghana*, Award, 18 June 2010, paras 333–338; *Hochtief v Argentina*, Decision on Liability, 29 December 2014, para 216; *MNSS v Montenegro*, Award, 4 May 2016, para 328; *Urbaser v Argentina*, Award, 8 December 2016, paras 606–607; *United Utilities v Estonia*, Award, 21 June 2019, paras 581–587.

[188] *RFCC v Morocco*, Award, 22 December 2003, paras 33–34, 51; *Bayindir v Pakistan*, Award, 27 August 2009, paras 180, 377; *Burlington v Ecuador*, Decision on Jurisdiction, 2 June 2010, para 204; *Toto v Lebanon*, Award, 7 June 2012, para 162; *BIVAC v Paraguay*, Further Decision on Objections to Jurisdiction, 9 October 2012, paras 246–247; *E energija v Latvia*, Award, 22 December 2017, para 838; *Glencore v Colombia*, Award, 27 August 2019, paras 1373–1378.

[189] *Rumeli v Kazakhstan*, Award, 29 July 2008, para 615.

[190] *Alpha v Ukraine*, Award, 8 November 2010, para 422.

[191] *Waste Management v Mexico II*, Award, 30 April 2004.

[192] At paras 108–117.

[193] At para 115. This part of the decision is cited with approval in *GAMI v Mexico*, Award, 15 November 2004, para 101.

[194] See VIII.7 below.

Fair procedure is an elementary requirement of the rule of law and a vital element of FET. Therefore, a host State is under the obligation to establish a judicial system that allows the effective exercise of the substantive rights granted to foreign investors. This does not necessarily mean that all governmental actions must be subject to judicial review. The contours of this requirement may be outlined with the help of a comparative analysis[195] and by resort to international human rights instruments.[196] Under international law, it is beyond doubt that the acts of domestic courts are attributable to the State for purposes of State responsibility.[197]

Fair procedure includes the traditional international law concept of denial of justice.[198] The Tribunal in *Azinian v Mexico*[199] gave the following description of a denial of justice:

> A denial of justice could be pleaded if the relevant courts refuse to entertain a suit, if they subject it to undue delay, or if they administer justice in a seriously inadequate way... There is a fourth type of denial of justice, namely the clear and malicious misapplication of the law.[200]

Unlike other aspects of investment protection,[201] it is generally accepted that a claim for denial of justice is conditioned on a prior exhaustion of local remedies.[202]

The US Model BIT of 2012 as well as the USMCA specifically clarify that the FET standard covers protection from denial of justice and guarantees due process. They provide that:

[195] *Total v Argentina*, Decision on Liability, 27 December 2010, para 111.

[196] *Rompetrol v Romania*, Award, 6 May 2013, paras 89(c), 168–172; *Al-Warraq v Indonesia*, Final Award, 15 December 2014, paras 556–621; *Chevron v Ecuador II*, Second Partial Award on Track II, 30 August 2018, para 8.57–8.58.

[197] See X.2(a) below.

[198] *RosInvest v Russia*, Final Award, 12 September 2010, para 279; *Binder v Czech Republic*, Final Award, 15 July 2011, para 448; *Oostergetel v Slovakia*, Final Award, 23 April 2012, para 273; *Arif v Moldova*, Award, 8 April 2013, para 442; *Philip Morris v Uruguay*, Award, 8 July 2016, paras 498–501; *Olin v Libya*, Final Award, 25 May 2018, paras 348–349, 352; *Krederi v Ukraine*, Award, 2 July 2018, paras 441–450; *Chevron v Ecuador II*, Second Partial Award on Track II, 30 August 2018, paras 8.23–8.42; *United Utilities v Estonia*, Award, 21 June 2019, paras 868–870. Generally, on denial of justice see J Paulsson, *Denial of Justice in International Law* (2005).

[199] *Azinian v Mexico*, Award, 1 November 1999.

[200] At paras 102, 103. See also *Iberdrola v Guatemala*, Award, 17 August 2012, para 432.

[201] *AES v Argentina*, Decision on Jurisdiction, 26 April 2005, para 69; *Mytilineos v Serbia & Montenegro*, Partial Award on Jurisdiction, 8 September 2006, paras 221–222.

[202] *Jan de Nul v Egypt*, Award, 6 November 2008, paras 255–261; *Chevron v Ecuador I*, Interim Award, 1 December 2008, paras 233, 235; *Pantechniki v Albania*, Award, 30 July 2009, paras 96, 102; *Toto v Lebanon*, Decision on Jurisdiction, 11 September 2009, para 164; *Frontier Petroleum v Czech Republic*, Final Award, 12 November 2010, para 293; *Lemire v Ukraine*, Decision on Jurisdiction and Liability, 14 January 2010, paras 274–281; *Flughafen Zürich v Venezuela*, Award, 18 November 2014, paras 642–643; *Corona v Dominican Republic*, Award, 31 May 2016, para 248; *Bear Creek v Peru*, Award, 30 November 2017, para 205; *Krederi v Ukraine*, Award, 2 July 2018, paras 473–485; *Marfin v Cyprus*, Award, 26 July 2018, para 1272.

> 'fair and equitable treatment' includes the obligation not to deny justice in criminal, civil, or administrative adjudicatory proceedings in accordance with the principle of due process embodied in the principal legal systems of the world ....[203]

Tribunals have held that lack of a fair procedure, or serious procedural shortcomings, were important elements in a finding of a violation of the FET standard[204] but that 'the standard for a finding of procedural impropriety is a high one under the FET'.[205] The relevant cases relate to access to the courts, undue delays, fair procedure, and the right to be heard in judicial or administrative proceedings.

Access to the courts is a basic aspect of due process. In *Siemens v Argentina*,[206] the Tribunal found a breach of FET as a result of 'the denial of access to the administrative file for purposes of filing the appeal'.[207] Tribunals have held that the unjustified refusal of an access to justice was a denial of justice and hence a violation of the FET standard.[208]

In some cases, the claimants had complained about the length of judicial proceedings in domestic courts which, in some cases, had taken many years. The tribunals, while critical of delays, did not find that these amounted to a violation to the FET standard.[209] They cited special circumstances relating to the complexity of the issues[210] or to the political situation in the country concerned.[211] Only rarely did delays in domestic proceedings lead to a finding of a violation of FET.[212]

203 Article 5(2)(a) US Model BIT 2012; Article 14.6(2)(a) USMCA. The CETA in Article 8.10(2) provides: 'A Party breaches the obligation of fair and equitable treatment referenced in paragraph 1 if a measure or series of measures constitutes: (a) denial of justice in criminal, civil or administrative proceedings; (b) fundamental breach of due process, including a fundamental breach of transparency, in judicial and administrative proceedings ....'

204 *Frontier Petroleum v Czech Republic*, Final Award, 12 November 2010, para 292; *Apotex v United States*, Award, 25 August 2014, paras 9.16–9.65; *Bear Creek v Peru*, Award, 30 November 2017, para 205; *Krederi v Ukraine*, Award, 2 July 2018, para 436; *Glencore v Colombia*, Award, 27 August 2019, paras 1318–1319.

205 *Belenergia v Italy*, Award, 6 August 2019, para 609. See also *Krederi v Ukraine*, Award, 2 July 2018, paras 442–448, 631.

206 *Siemens v Argentina*, Award, 6 February 2007. See also *Azinian v Mexico*, Award, 1 November 1999, para 102.

207 At para 308.

208 *AMTO v Ukraine*, Final Award, 26 March 2008, para 75; *Iberdrola v Guatemala*, Award, 17 August 2012, para 432; *Dan Cake v Hungary*, Decision on Jurisdiction and Liability, 24 August 2015, paras 143–154; *Krederi v Ukraine*, Award, 2 July 2018, paras 451–454.

209 *Roussalis v Romania*, Award, 7 December 2011, paras 602–604; *Vannessa Ventures v Venezuela*, Award, 16 January 2013, paras 226–227; *Krederi v Ukraine*, Award, 2 July 2018, paras 455–460.

210 *Jan de Nul v Egypt*, Award, 6 November 2008, paras 202–204; *White Industries v India*, Final Award, 30 November 2011, paras 10.4.10–10.4.24; *Oostergetel v Slovakia*, Final Award, 23 April 2012, para 290.

211 *Toto v Lebanon*, Decision on Jurisdiction, 11 September 2009, para 165; *Olin v Libya*, Final Award, 25 May 2018, para 350.

212 *Pey Casado v Chile*, Award, 8 May 2008, paras 659–660; *Chevron v Ecuador I*, Partial Award on the Merits, 30 March 2010, para 250; *Valores Mundiales v Venezuela*, Award, 25 July 2017, para 583.

Findings that proceedings lacked procedural fairness often concerned the right to be heard.[213] In *Metalclad v Mexico*,[214] the municipality had refused to grant a construction permit. The Tribunal found that there had been a violation of the FET guarantee in Article 1105 of the NAFTA. An element in this finding was a lack of procedural propriety, specifically a failure to hear the investor:

> Moreover, the permit was denied at a meeting of the Municipal Town Council of which Metalclad received no notice, to which it received no invitation, and at which it was given no opportunity to appear.[215]

In *Middle East Cement v Egypt*,[216] one of the complaints concerned the seizure and auction of the claimant's ship without a proper notification to the owner. The Tribunal applied provisions promising FET and full protection and security in the BIT between Greece and Egypt. It found that a matter as important as the seizure and auctioning of a ship of the claimant should have been notified by a direct communication. Therefore, it found that the procedure applied did not meet the requirements of the FET and full protection and security standards.[217]

In some cases, tribunals found serious defects in the adjudicative process.[218] *Loewen v United States*[219] concerned the propriety of court proceedings in a Mississippi state court against a Canadian undertaker. The trial in Mississippi exhibited a gross failure to afford due process and to protect the investor from prejudice on account of his nationality. The Tribunal found that the conduct of the trial was so flawed that it constituted a miscarriage of justice.[220] As to Article 1105 of the NAFTA, the Tribunal also recognized the significance of due process:

> Manifest injustice in the sense of a lack of due process leading to an outcome which offends a sense of judicial propriety is enough,[221] ... the whole trial and its resultant verdict were clearly improper and discreditable and cannot be squared with minimum standards of international law and fair and equitable treatment.[222]

[213] *Tecmed v Mexico*, Award, 29 May 2003, para 162; *Al-Bahloul v Tajikistan*, Partial Award on Jurisdiction and Liability, 2 September 2009, para 221; *Gold Reserve v Venezuela*, Award, 22 September 2014, para 600; *Clayton/Bilcon v Canada*, Award on Jurisdiction and Liability, 17 March 2015, paras 543, 594; *Krederi v Ukraine*, Award, 2 July 2018, paras 595–596.

[214] *Metalclad v Mexico*, Award, 30 August 2000.

[215] At para 91.

[216] *Middle East Cement v Egypt*, Award, 12 April 2002.

[217] At para 143.

[218] *Krederi v Ukraine*, Award, 2 July 2018, paras 461–467.

[219] *Loewen v United States*, Award, 26 June 2003.

[220] At para 54.

[221] At para 132.

[222] At para 137.

Other cases in which tribunals found a lack of fair procedure concerned the intervention of the executive in court proceedings,[223] the secret awarding of licences without the possibility of judicial review[224] bias on the part of a court,[225] and the corruption of a judge. In *Chevron v Ecuador II*,[226] the Tribunal found that a domestic judge had allowed the plaintiffs in national court proceedings against the foreign investor to write his judgment in exchange for a bribe and that this amounted to a violation of the FET standard. The Tribunal said:

> the Tribunal has found that Judge Zambrano acted corruptly, in return for a bribe promised to him by certain of the Lago Agrio Plaintiffs' representatives. Judge Zambrano's collusive conduct in the 'ghostwriting' of the Lago Agrio Judgment was not authorised under Ecuadorian law. Nor was it under judicial standards long established under international law. He was far from acting as an independent or impartial judge deciding the Lago Agrio Litigation fairly between the parties, under minimum standards for judicial conduct long recognized under international law.[227]

The Tribunal added that this situation remained unremedied by the appellate courts.[228]

For a finding of procedural unfairness, the investor must be directly affected by the lack of independence or impartiality in court proceedings. The identification of a general lack of independence and impartiality in the judicial system is not enough for a finding of a denial of justice in a particular case.[229]

Denial of justice is traditionally associated with the administration of justice by domestic courts.[230] This includes criminal proceedings against the investor.[231] But investment tribunals have accepted that the procedural guarantees inherent in the FET standard extend to the activities of the host State's administrative authorities.[232] On the other hand, the requirement to afford a fair procedure on the basis of the FET standard does not extend to a State entity's management of its contractual relationship with the investor.[233]

223 *Petrobart v Kyrgyzstan*, Arbitral Award, 29 March 2005, p 75.

224 *Lemire v Ukraine*, Decision on Jurisdiction and Liability, 14 January 2010, para 418.

225 *Flughafen Zürich v Venezuela*, Award, 18 November 2014, para 707.

226 *Chevron v Ecuador II*, Second Partial Award on Track II, 30 August 2018.

227 At para 8.56. Footnote omitted.

228 At para 8.60.

229 *Vannessa Ventures v Venezuela*, Award, 16 January 2013, para 228.

230 *Grand River v United States*, Award, 12 January 2011, paras 222–236.

231 *Tokios Tokelės v Ukraine*, Award, 26 July 2007, para 133; *Rompetrol v Romania*, Award, 6 May 2013, paras 278–279; *Al-Warraq v Indonesia*, Final Award, 15 December 2014, para 621.

232 *Genin v Estonia*, Award, 25 June 2001, para 364; *Rumeli v Kazakhstan*, Award, 29 July 2008, paras 615, 617–618, 623; *Chemtura v Canada*, Award, 2 August 2010, paras 211–224; *AES v Hungary*, Award, 23 September 2010, paras 9.3.36–9.3.73; *Frontier Petroleum v Czech Republic*, Final Award, 12 November 2010, para 292; *Bosh v Ukraine*, Award, 25 October 2012, paras 145, 214; *TECO v Guatemala*, Award, 19 December 2013, paras 454–465; *Corona v Dominican Republic*, Award, 31 May 2016, para 248.

233 *Bayindir v Pakistan*, Award, 27 August 2009, paras 343–348.

In *Thunderbird v Mexico*,[234] the Tribunal held that the standards of due process and procedural fairness applicable in administrative proceedings are lower than in a judicial process. In the particular case, it found no violation of the FET standard, explaining that the claimant had been given a full opportunity to be heard and to present evidence and that the proceedings were subject to a judicial review by the courts.[235]

An investment tribunal will not act as a court of appeal and will not decide whether the decision of a domestic court was in error or whether another view of the law would have been preferable. Nevertheless, there is a line between an ordinary error and a gross miscarriage of justice, which no longer may be considered as an exercise of the rule of law. This line will be crossed when it is impossible for a third party to recognize how an impartial judge could have reached the result in question. Proof of bad faith may be relevant but is not required in such a case. Therefore, allegations of violations of substantive due process through manifestly wrong or unjust decisions must overcome a high threshold and have rarely succeeded.[236] In *Pantechniki v Albania*,[237] the Tribunal said in this respect:

> The general rule is that 'mere error in the interpretation of the national law does not *per se* involve responsibility.' Wrongful application of the law may nonetheless provide 'elements of proof of a denial of justice.' But that requires an extreme test: the error must be of a kind which no 'competent judge could reasonably have made.' Such a finding would mean that the state had not provided even a minimally adequate justice system.[238]

ff. Application of domestic law

Although an error in the application of the law will not normally amount to a treaty violation, there is authority to the effect that a systematic and wilful failure to apply the host State's law on the part of State organs may amount to a violation of the FET standard.

In *Gami v Mexico*,[239] the claimant had alleged that the host State's failure to enforce its own sugar regime violated the FET standard under the NAFTA. The Tribunal said:

234 *Thunderbird v Mexico*, Award, 26 January 2006.

235 At paras 197–201.

236 *Mondev v United States*, Award, 11 October 2002, para 127; *Ares v Georgia*, Award, 26 February 2008, paras 9.3.41–9.3.42; *AMTO v Ukraine*, Final Award, 26 March 2008, para 80; *Oostergetel v Slovakia*, Final Award, 23 April 2012, para 273; *Iberdrola v Guatemala*, Award, 17 August 2012, para 432; *Arif v Moldova*, Award, 8 April 2013, paras 442, 445; *Krederi v Ukraine*, Award, 2 July 2018, paras 468–472, 486–490, 584, 612, 629; *Marfin v Cyprus*, Award, 26 July 2018, para 1272.

237 *Pantechniki v Albania*, Award, 30 July 2009.

238 At para 94. Footnotes omitted.

239 *GAMI v Mexico*, Final Award, 15 November 2004.

> a government's failure to implement or abide by its own law in a manner adversely affecting a foreign investor may but will not necessarily lead to a violation of Article 1105.[240]

Other tribunals have found similarly that 'deliberate and sustained illegality in the treatment of a protected investment could, in appropriate circumstances, be suggestive of a failure to meet the applicable standards of fair and equitable treatment'.[241] Investors are entitled to expect that the host State will comply with its laws and regulations.[242]

In *Siag v Egypt*,[243] the claimants had obtained a series of judicial rulings in their favour by Egyptian courts, but the government failed to comply with these rulings. The Tribunal found that Egypt's actions constituted a denial of justice and a violation of the FET standard.[244]

In *Gavrilović v Croatia*,[245] the Tribunal confirmed the principle that, although an error by the host State in the application of its law will not necessarily give rise to a treaty violation, a State's failure to apply its law may amount to a violation of the FET standard. The Tribunal said:

> An erroneous application of the law by a State may be sufficient to implicate treaty standards where it is established that there was a blatant disregard of the applicable law, a clear and malicious misapplication of the law, or a complete lack of candor or good faith in the application of the law. The error of law must be of such a nature as to give rise to justified concerns as to the judicial propriety of the outcome....[246]

The clearest endorsement of the principle that a State's failure to enforce its own legislation amounts to a violation of the FET principle came from the Tribunal in *Zelena v Serbia*.[247] The case arose from the operation of an animal-rendering facility and the government's failure to enforce legislation on the handling of

[240] At para 91.

[241] *Rompetrol v Romania*, 6 May 2013, Award, para 177; see also *Lemire v Ukraine*, Decision on Jurisdiction and Liability, 14 January 2010, para 385; *Lemire v Ukraine*, Award, 28 March 2011, para 43; *TECO v Guatemala*, Award, 19 December 2013, para 458; *Clayton/Bilcon v Canada*, Award on Jurisdiction and Liability, 17 March 2015, para 602; *Dan Cake v Hungary*, Decision on Jurisdiction and Liability, 24 August 2015, para 145.

[242] *Tenaris v Venezuela I*, Award, 29 January 2016, paras 490–496; *Teinver v Argentina*, Award, 21 July 2017, para 679; *RREEF v Spain*, Decision on Responsibility and Principles of Quantum, 30 November 2018, para 287.

[243] *Siag v Egypt*, Award, 1 June 2009.

[244] At paras 451–455.

[245] *Gavrilović v Croatia*, Award, 26 July 2018.

[246] At para 878. Footnotes omitted.

[247] *Zelena v Serbia*, Award, 9 November 2018 (unpublished).

hazardous material also against the claimant's competitors. The Tribunal summarized its analysis as follows:

> In sum, as regards the implementation and enforcement of the Serbian ABP legislation by the Respondent, the Tribunal concludes that it was reasonable and legitimate for the Claimants to rely on a reasonable level of implementation and enforcement of the Serbian ABP legislation within a reasonable time and that these legitimate expectations were frustrated by the Respondent's conduct. Thus, the Respondent has breached its obligation, under Article 3(1) of the BIT, to accord fair and equitable treatment to the Claimants' investment.[248]

Micula v Romania II[249] arose from the government's alleged failure to enforce its tax legislation against illegal producers of alcohol thereby tolerating a black market which made the claimants' business unviable. The Tribunal, relying on *GAMI* and *Zelena*, said:

> The Tribunal agrees that there may be circumstances in which a failure to enforce laws could amount to a denial of legitimate expectations and hence a breach of the obligation to provide fair and equitable treatment.[250]

The Tribunal noted that the parties' experts had estimated the rate of untaxed spirits at 90 per cent (Claimant) and 55–80 per cent (Respondent).[251] Nevertheless, it found that Romania had engaged in serious and visible efforts to enforce its taxation laws relating to alcohol and dismissed the claim.[252]

gg. Freedom from coercion and harassment

Freedom from coercion and harassment is part of FET.[253] Tribunals have found that harassment, threats, and coercion directed at the investor were in violation of the FET standard.[254]

In *Pope & Talbot v Canada*,[255] SLD, a government regulatory authority, had launched a 'verification review' against the investor that was confrontational and

[248] At para 267.
[249] *Micula v Romania II*, Award, 5 March 2020.
[250] At para 367.
[251] At para 409.
[252] At paras 368–372.
[253] Article 8.10(2) of the CETA includes the following clarifying language on the meaning of FET: '(e) abusive treatment of investors, such as coercion, duress and harassment'.
[254] *Al-Bahloul v Tajikistan*, Partial Award on Jurisdiction and Liability, 2 September 2009, para 221; *Total v Argentina*, Decision on Liability, 27 December 2010, paras 129, 338; *Mobil v Argentina*, Decision on Jurisdiction and Liability, 10 April 2013, paras 938–940; *Stati v Kazakhstan*, Award, 19 December 2013, para 1095; *Tatneft v Ukraine*, Award on the Merits, 29 July 2014, paras 396–397; *Burlington v Ecuador*, Decision on Reconsideration and Award, 7 February 2017, paras 171–172; *Olin v Libya*, Final Award, 25 May 2018, paras 326–345.
[255] *Pope & Talbot v Canada*, Award on the Merits, 10 April 2001, paras 156–181.

aggressive. The Tribunal held that this investigation was 'more like combat than cooperative regulation'.[256] It found that these actions by the regulatory authority were 'threats and misrepresentation', 'burdensome and confrontational', and hence a violation of the FET standard.[257]

In *Tecmed v Mexico*,[258] an unlimited licence for the operation of a landfill had been replaced by a licence of limited duration. The Tribunal applied a provision in the BIT between Mexico and Spain guaranteeing FET according to international law. The Tribunal found that the denial of the permit's renewal was designed to force the investor to relocate to another site, bearing the costs and the risks of a new business. The Tribunal said:

> Under such circumstances, such pressure involves forms of coercion that may be considered inconsistent with the fair and equitable treatment to be given to international investments under Article 4(1) of the Agreement and objectionable from the perspective of international law.[259]

Desert Line v Yemen[260] concerned contracts for road construction. A dispute about outstanding payments involved armed threats by the State and the arrest of some of the investor's personnel. A local arbitration resulted in an award in the claimant's favour who was, however, subsequently forced to accept a substantially reduced amount in a settlement agreement. The Tribunal found that the settlement agreement had been imposed upon the claimant under threats and physical attacks. It said:

> the subjection of the Claimant's employees, family members, and equipment to arrest and armed interference, as well as the subsequent peremptory 'advice' that it was 'in [his] interest' to accept that the amount awarded be amputated by half, falls well short of minimum standards of international law and cannot be the result of an authentic fair and equitable negotiation.[261]

In the resulting award, the Tribunal took the unusual step of awarding not just damages for the violation of the FET standard but additionally awarded moral damages in the amount of US$1 million.

In other cases, tribunals found that the investors' allegations of coercion and harassment had not been proven. These included complaints of a campaign to

[256] At para 181.
[257] *Pope & Talbot v Canada*, Award in respect of Damages, 31 May 2002, paras 67–69.
[258] *Tecmed v Mexico*, Award, 29 May 2003.
[259] At para 163. Footnote omitted. See, however, *Mamidoil v Albania*, Award, 30 March 2015, paras 742–749.
[260] *Desert Line v Yemen*, Award, 6 February 2008, paras 151–194.
[261] At para 179.

punish the investor for publishing material critical to the regime,[262] of cumbersome inspections,[263] of coercion in contract renegotiation,[264] and of criminal prosecution.[265]

hh. Good faith

Good faith is a general principle of law and one of the foundations of international law in general and of foreign investment law in particular.[266] Arbitral tribunals have confirmed that good faith is inherent in FET.[267] It is 'the common guiding beacon' to the obligation under BITs, it is 'at the heart of the concept of FET' and 'permeates the whole approach' to investor protection.[268] The Tribunal in *Tecmed v Mexico*,[269] interpreting a BIT provision on FET, said:

> The Arbitral Tribunal finds that the commitment of fair and equitable treatment ... is an expression and part of the *bona fide* principle recognized in international law ....[270]

The FET standard in general and the obligation to act in good faith in particular includes the obligation not to purposefully inflict damage upon an investment.[271] The Tribunal in *Waste Management v Mexico*[272] found that the obligation to act in good faith was a basic obligation under the FET standard as contained in Article 1105 of the NAFTA. In particular, a deliberate conspiracy by government authorities to defeat the investment would violate this principle:

> The Tribunal has no doubt that a deliberate conspiracy—that is to say, a conscious combination of various agencies of government without justification to defeat the purposes of an investment agreement—would constitute a breach of Article 1105(1). A basic obligation of the State under Article 1105(1) is to act in good faith and form, and not deliberately to set out to destroy or frustrate the investment by improper means.[273]

[262] *Tokios Tokelės v Ukraine*, Award, 26 July 2007, paras 123–137.

[263] *AMTO v Ukraine*, Final Award, 26 March 2008, para 96; *Helnan v Egypt*, Award, 3 July 2008, paras 138–146; *Levy v Peru*, Award, 26 February 2014, para 382.

[264] *Ampal-American v Egypt*, Decision on Liability and Heads of Loss, 21 February 2017, paras 194–216; *CMC v Mozambique*, Award, 24 October 2019, paras 425–427.

[265] *Levy v Peru*, Award, 26 February 2014, para 386; *OI European v Venezuela*, Award, 10 March 2015, paras 537–548; *Quiborax v Bolivia*, Award, 16 September 2015, paras 305–306, 563–572; *Al Tamimi v Oman*, Award, 3 November 2015, paras 432–447; *Krederi v Ukraine*, Award, 2 July 2018, paras 637–640.

[266] *Merrill & Ring v Canada*, Award, 31 March 2010, para 187; *Devas v India*, Award on Jurisdiction and Merits, 25 July 2016, para 467; *Bear Creek v Peru*, Award, 30 November 2017, paras 524, 527.

[267] *Genin v Estonia*, Award, 25 June 2001, para 367; *Siag v Egypt*, Award, 1 June 2009, para 450.

[268] *Sempra v Argentina*, Award, 28 September 2007, paras 297–299.

[269] *Tecmed v Mexico*, Award, 29 May 2003.

[270] At para 153, quoting I Brownlie, *Principles of Public International Law* (1989) 19.

[271] *Vivendi v Argentina*, Resubmitted Case: Award, 20 August 2007, para 7.4.39.

[272] *Waste Management v Mexico II*, Award, 30 April 2004.

[273] At para 138.

In *Bayindir v Pakistan*,[274] the investor claimed that its expulsion was based on local favouritism and on bad faith since the reasons given by the Government did not correspond to its actual motivation.[275] The Tribunal in its Decision on Jurisdiction found that 'the allegedly unfair motives of expulsion, if proven, are capable of founding a fair and equitable treatment claim under the BIT'.[276]

In *Saluka v Czech Republic*,[277] the Tribunal described the central role of the requirement of good faith in FET as follows:

> A foreign investor protected by the Treaty may in any case properly expect that the Czech Republic implements its policies *bona fide* by conduct that is, as far as it affects the investors' investment, reasonably justifiable by public policies and that such conduct does not manifestly violate the requirements of consistency, transparency, even-handedness and non-discrimination.[278]

In *Frontier Petroleum v Czech Republic*,[279] the Tribunal gave the following description of violations of the good faith principle:

> Bad faith action by the host state includes the use of legal instruments for purposes other than those for which they were created. It also includes a conspiracy by state organs to inflict damage upon or to defeat the investment, the termination of the investment for reasons other than the one put forth by the government, and expulsion of an investment based on local favouritism. Reliance by a government on its internal structures to excuse non-compliance with contractual obligations would also be contrary to good faith.[280]

It follows from these authorities that action in bad faith against the investor would be a violation of FET. Bad faith action by the host State includes the use of legal instruments for purposes other than those for which they were created.[281] It also includes a conspiracy by State organs to inflict damage upon or to defeat the investment.

Allegations of bad faith require a high standard of proof and will often fail.[282]

[274] *Bayindir v Pakistan*, Decision on Jurisdiction, 14 November 2005.
[275] At paras 242, 243.
[276] At para 250.
[277] *Saluka v Czech Republic*, Partial Award, 17 March 2006.
[278] At para 307.
[279] *Frontier Petroleum v Czech Republic*, Final Award, 12 November 2010.
[280] At para 300. Footnotes omitted.
[281] *Flemingo v Poland*, Award, 12 August 2016, paras 554–560.
[282] *Nordzucker v Poland*, Second Partial Award, 18 January 2009, paras 92–95; *Chemtura v Canada*, Award, 2 August 2010, paras 143–148, 158, 184; *Oostergetel v Slovakia*, Final Award, 23 April 2012, paras 300–301; *Micula v Romania I*, Award, 11 December 2013, para 836; *Gosling v Mauritius*, Award, 18 February 2020, para 250; *Micula v Romania II*, Award, 5 March 2020, para 378.

A related but different question is whether every violation of the standard of FET requires bad faith. Put differently, is it a valid defence for the host State to argue that, although its actions may have caused harm to the investor, these actions were taken *bona fide* and hence could not have violated the FET standard? Arbitral practice clearly indicates that the FET standard may be violated, even if no *mala fides* is involved.[283] For instance, the Tribunal in *Mondev v United States*[284] said:

> To the modern eye, what is unfair or inequitable need not equate with the outrageous or the egregious. In particular, a State may treat foreign investment unfairly and inequitably without necessarily acting in bad faith.[285]

Similarly, the Tribunal in *Mobil v Argentina*[286] held:

> Although action in bad faith is a violation of fair and equitable treatment, a violation of the standard can be found even if there is a mere objective disregard of the rights enjoyed by the investor under the FET standard. Thus such a violation does not require bad faith on the part of the State. This has been stated in several ICSID awards.[287]

The Tribunal in *El Paso v Argentina*[288] said that 'a violation can be found even if there is a mere objective disregard of the rights enjoyed by the investor under the FET standard, and that such a violation does not require subjective bad faith on the part of the State'.[289] Other tribunals have consistently adopted the same approach.[290]

[283] The only contrary indication would be a dictum in *Genin v Estonia*, Award, 25 June 2001, para 371: 'any procedural irregularity that may have been present would have to amount to bad faith, a willful disregard of due process of law or an extreme insufficiency of action'. However, this passage does not relate to fair and equitable treatment but to the standard of arbitrary and discriminatory measures in Article II (3)(b) of the Estonia–United States BIT.

[284] *Mondev v United States*, Award, 11 October 2002.

[285] At para 116. Quoted with approval in *Crystallex v Venezuela*, Award, 4 April 2016, para 543.

[286] *Mobil v Argentina*, Decision on Jurisdiction and Liability, 10 April 2013.

[287] At para 934.

[288] *El Paso v Argentina*, Award, 31 October 2011.

[289] At para 372.

[290] *Tecmed v Mexico*, Award, 29 May 2003, para 153; *Occidental Exploration v Ecuador*, Final Award, 1 July 2004, para 186; *Loewen v United States*, Award, 26 June 2003, para 132; *CMS v Argentina*, Award, 12 May 2005, para 280; *Azurix v Argentina*, Award, 14 July 2006, para 372; *LG&E v Argentina*, Decision on Liability, 3 October 2006, para 129; *PSEG v Turkey*, Award, 19 January 2007, paras 245–246; *Siemens v Argentina*, Award, 6 February 2007, paras 299–300; *Enron v Argentina*, Award, 22 May 2007, para 263; *Biwater Gauff v Tanzania*, Award, 24 July 2008, para 602; *Duke Energy v Ecuador*, Award, 18 August 2008, para 341; *National Grid v Argentina*, Award, 3 November 2008, para 173; *Jan de Nul v Egypt*, Award, 6 November 2008, para 185; *Invesmart v Czech Republic*, Award, 26 June 2009, paras 419–422; *Bayindir v Pakistan*, Award, 27 August 2009, para 181; *Lemire v Ukraine*, Decision on Jurisdiction and Liability, 14 January 2010, para 249; *RSM v Grenada II*, Award, 10 December 2010, para 7.2.24; *Deutsche Bank v Sri Lanka*, Award, 31 October 2012, para 420; *Micula v Romania I*, Award, 11 December 2013, para 524; *E energija v Latvia*, Award, 22 December 2017, para 839.

Therefore, good faith is indeed a central element of FET. A showing of bad faith on the part of the host State would almost certainly amount to a violation of FET. At the same time, absence of bad faith is not a guarantee of compliance with the FET standard. There is ample authority that good faith is inherent in FET but also that the FET standard may be violated even without bad faith.

(h) Composite acts

Adverse action by the host State need not take place through a single event but may occur through several acts and may be scattered over time. The phenomenon of composite acts is well-known in the law of State responsibility and has found expression in the International Law Commission's (ILC) Articles on State Responsibility in the following terms:

> **Article 15**
> ***Breach consisting of a composite act***
> 1. The breach of an international obligation by a State through a series of actions or omissions defined in aggregate as wrongful occurs when the action or omission occurs which, taken with the other actions or omissions, is sufficient to constitute the wrongful act.
> 2. In such a case, the breach extends over the entire period starting with the first of the actions or omissions of the series and lasts for as long as these actions or omissions are repeated and remain not in conformity with the international obligation.

In international investment law, creeping expropriation is well-recognized.[291] The incremental infringement of investor rights is not, however, limited to expropriation but is frequently discussed in the context of FET. In examining the State's behaviour for compliance with the FET standard, tribunals have not just looked at individual occurrences but have looked at the overall cumulative impact of the measures.[292] As succinctly stated by the Tribunal in *RosInvest v Russia*:

[291] See VII.3(i) above.

[292] *Tecmed v Mexico*, Award, 29 May 2003, para 62; *Trans-Global v Jordan*, Decision under Rule 41(5), 12 May 2008, paras 108–117; *Chevron v Ecuador I*, Interim Award, 1 December 2008, paras 296–301; *Lemire v Ukraine*, Decision on Jurisdiction and Liability, 14 January 2010, para 316; *Suez and InterAgua v Argentina*, Decision on Liability, 30 July 2010, paras 217, 227; *Pac Rim v El Salvador*, Decision on Jurisdiction, 1 June 2012, para 2.71; *Swisslion v Macedonia*, Award, 6 July 2012, paras 275–277, 291;

> an assessment of whether Respondent breached the IPPA can only be effectively conducted if the conduct as a whole is reviewed, rather than isolated measures or aspects.[293]

The Tribunal in *El Paso v Argentina*[294] adopted the concept of a composite act from Article 15 of the ILC Articles and pointed to the parallel phenomenon of creeping expropriation.[295] It said:

> Although they may be seen in isolation as reasonable measures to cope with a difficult economic situation, the measures examined can be viewed as cumulative steps which individually do not qualify as violations of FET, ... but which amount to a violation if their cumulative effect is considered... A *creeping violation of the FET standard* could thus be described as a process extending over time and comprising a succession or an accumulation of measures which, taken separately, would not breach that standard but, when taken together, do lead to such a result.[296]

Some tribunals found that that the individual acts leading to a violation of FET had to be linked by a pattern or purpose. In *Rompetrol v Romania*,[297] the Tribunal said:

> the cumulative effect of a succession of impugned actions by the State of the investment can together amount to a failure to accord fair and equitable treatment even where the individual actions, taken on their own, would not surmount the threshold for a Treaty breach. But this would only be so where the actions in question disclosed some link of underlying pattern or purpose between them; a mere scattered collection of disjointed harms would not be enough.[298]

Tatneft v Ukraine, Award on the Merits, 29 July 2014, paras 327–332, 412–413, 462; *Perenco v Ecuador*, Decision on Remaining Issues of Jurisdiction and on Liability, 12 September 2014, paras 606, 607; *Flemingo v Poland* Award, 12 August 2016, para 536; *E energija v Latvia*, Award, 22 December 2017, paras 1060–1066; *Gavrilović v Croatia*, Award, 26 July 2018, para 1134; *NextEra v Spain*, Decision on Jurisdiction, Liability and Quantum Principles, 12 March 2019, para 598.

293 *RosInvest v Russia*, Final Award, 12 September 2010, para 599, see also para 621. The IPPA is the Agreement between the Government of the United Kingdom and the Government of the USSR for the Promotion and Reciprocal Protection of Investments of 1989.

294 *El Paso v Argentina*, Award, 31 October 2011.

295 At paras 516, 518.

296 At paras 515, 518. Italics original.

297 *Rompetrol v Romania*, Award, 6 May 2013.

298 At para 271. See also para 278. See also *Stati v Kazakhstan*, Award, 19 December 2013, para 1095; *Gold Reserve v Venezuela*, Award, 22 September 2014, para 566. By contrast, in *Blusun v Italy*, Award, 27 December 2016, at para 362 the Tribunal found that a violation of FET could occur through a series of measures 'taken without plan or coordination'.

Where part of the series of acts occurred before the date of the treaty's entry into force, the resulting obligations will be applied only to the acts that have taken place after that date.[299]

(i) Conclusion

As demonstrated, tribunals have applied the FET standard to typical fact situations and have now developed considerable case law in this area. The categories outlined above by no means exhaust the possibilities of the FET standard. With the progression of arbitral practice tribunals are likely to further develop these categories and add new ones.

At the same time, there is a trend in modern investment treaties to restrict the impact of the FET standard. The US Model BITs of 2004 and 2012 specify that the protection offered by FET does not go beyond the international minimum standard under customary international law. The USMCA contains an explanation to the same effect.[300] The Comprehensive and Progressive Agreement for Trans-Pacific Partnership (CPTPP), in addition to restricting FET to customary international law, states that a mere breach of an investor's expectation resulting in loss or damage does not amount to a breach of FET.[301] The CETA contains an exhaustive definition of FET.[302] In addition, the CETA contains a far-reaching exception for regulatory measures.[303]

2. Full protection and security

ADDITIONAL READING: HE Zeitler, 'The Guarantee of "Full Protection and Security" in Investment Treaties Regarding Harm Caused by Private Actors' (2005) *Stockholm Intl Arb Rev* 1; G Cordero Moss, 'Full Protection and Security' in A Reinisch (ed) *Standards of Investment Protection* (2008) 131; C Schreuer, 'Full Protection and Security' (2010) 1 *Journal of International Dispute Settlement* 353; HE Zeitler, 'Full Protection and Security' in SW Schill (ed) *International Investment Law and Comparative Public Law* (2010) 183; RA Lorz, 'Protection and Security' in M Bungenberg et al (eds) *International Investment Law* (2015) 764; S Alexandrov, 'The Evolution of the Full Protection and Security Standard' in M

[299] *Société Générale v Dominican Republic*, Award on Preliminary Objections to Jurisdiction, 19 September 2008, paras 91–92; *Walter Bau v Thailand*, Award, 1 July 2009, paras 12.43, 13.1(f).

[300] See VIII.1(f) above.

[301] CPTPP Article 9.6(4).

[302] CETA Article 8.10. See VIII.1(c) above.

[303] CETA Article 8.9. See also CETA Articles 28.3 and 28.6.

Kinnear et al (eds) *Building International Investment Law* (2016) 319; A Reinisch and C Schreuer, *International Protection of Investments* (2020) 536.

(a) Concept

At first sight, the traditional notion of full protection and security (FPS) is amorphous and not readily amenable to operational applicability. However, as with other standards contained in BITs, arbitral jurisprudence has gradually refined the understanding of the term.

FPS is a standard feature in most BITs. It has also found entry into multilateral investment treaties, such as the ECT (Article 10(1)), NAFTA (Article 1105(1)), and the USMCA (Article 14.6 (1)).

Treaty practice has relied on different formulations and patterns. Whereas the traditional version (found in a series of US FCN treaties going back to the nineteenth century)[304] relies on the classical version of a guarantee which provides for 'full protection and security', other treaties have omitted the word 'full'. Another variation promises 'protection in accordance with fair and equitable treatment'. A simple approach is restricted to the granting of 'protection' (and not security), and yet another wording relies on the promise of 'legal security'. Other phrases and combinations will also be found. Overall, these variations seem to have played a limited role in the practice of tribunals.[305] The two elements 'protection' and 'security' are part of a unitary concept. There is no indication that they should be interpreted and applied separately. 'Protection' denotes the host State's obligation to take the necessary measures, whereas 'security' indicates the condition to which the investor is entitled.

The FPS standard has been applied chiefly to three settings. In some earlier cases, acts of insurgents or rioting groups had harmed the foreign investment. In a second group of cases, government forces like police authorities or military units were involved. More recent cases have addressed governmental regulatory acts that disturb the legal stability surrounding the investor's business.

The breadth of the clause raises issues of delimitation in relation to other treaty standards, like FET or the umbrella clause. Especially when it comes to the protection against the application of laws affecting the security and protection of the investment, the standard may acquire special importance if the treaty does not contain other clauses with a broad scope.

304 See K Vandevelde, *Bilateral Investment Treaties, History, Policy, and Interpretation* (2010) 243.

305 *Parkerings v Lithuania*, Award, 11 September 2007, para 354. But see the discussion of the significance of the word 'full' in *AAPL v Sri Lanka*, Final Award, 27 June 1990, para 50; *Azurix v Argentina*, Award, 14 July 2006, para 408; *Suez and InterAgua v Argentina*, Decision on Liability, 30 July 2010, paras 162, 169.

Some tribunals have interpreted the standard of full protection and security in conjunction with FET.[306] Other tribunals have found that the two standards were separate.[307] As a matter of treaty interpretation, it appears unconvincing to assume that two standards listed separately in the same document have the same meaning and need not be examined independently.[308] This does not apply where the treaty links the two standards, for instance by providing that one is an expression of the other or should be interpreted in accordance with the other.

In *Frontier Petroleum v Czech Republic*,[309] the Tribunal described the difference between the FPS and the FET standards as follows:

> full protection and security obliges the host state to provide a legal framework that grants security and protects the investment against adverse action by private persons as well as state organs, whereas fair and equitable treatment consists mainly of an obligation on the host state's part to desist from behaviour that is unfair and inequitable.[310]

(b) The standard of liability

FPS is an absolute standard, which means that its content does not depend upon the level of treatment given to nationals or to other foreign investors. However, there is broad consensus that the standard does not provide absolute protection against physical or legal infringement. The host State is not placed under an obligation of strict liability to prevent such violations. Rather, it is generally accepted that the host State will have to exercise 'due diligence' and will have to take such measures to protect the foreign investment as are reasonable under the circumstances.[311] At

306 *Wena Hotels v Egypt*, Award, 8 December 2000, paras 84–95; *Occidental Exploration v Ecuador*, Final Award, 1 July 2004, para 187; *PSEG v Turkey*, Award, 19 January 2007, paras 257–259; *National Grid v Argentina*, Award, 3 November 2008, paras 187 and 189; *Vannessa v Venezuela*, Award, 16 January 2013, paras 216–232; *Rompetrol v Romania*, Award, 6 May 2013, para 197; *OI European v Venezuela*, Award, 10 March 2015, para 576; *Rusoro v Venezuela*, Award, 22 August 2016, para 548.

307 *Azurix v Argentina*, Award, 14 July 2006, para 407; *Jan de Nul v Egypt*, Award, 6 November 2008, para 269; *Suez and InterAgua v Argentina*, Decision on Liability, 30 July 2010, para 166; *Ulysseas v Ecuador*, Final Award, 12 June 2012, para 272; *Mamidoil v Albania*, Award, 30 March 2015, paras 819–820; *OperaFund v Spain*, Award, 6 September 2019, para 576; *BayWa v Spain*, Decision on Jurisdiction, Liability and Directions on Quantum, 2 December 2019, para 529.

308 *Krederi v Ukraine*, Award, 2 July 2018, para 650.

309 *Frontier Petroleum v Czech Republic*, Final Award, 12 November 2010.

310 At para 296. See also *Gemplus v Mexico*, Award, 16 June 2010, paras 9–11; *Krederi v Ukraine*, Award, 2 July 2018, para 651.

311 *Elettronica Sicula SpA (ELSI) (United States v Italy)*, Judgment, 20 July 1989, ICJ Rep (1989) 15, para 108; *AAPL v Sri Lanka*, Final Award, 27 June 1990, para 53; *Tecmed v Mexico*, Award, 29 May 2003, para 177; *Noble Ventures v Romania*, Award, 12 October 2005, para 164; *Saluka v Czech Republic*, Partial Award, 17 March 2006, para 484; *Biwater Gauff v Tanzania*, Award, 24 July 2008, paras 725–726; *Suez and InterAgua v Argentina*, Decision on Liability, 30 July 2010, para 158; *Frontier Petroleum v Czech*

the same time, the standard would be eviscerated and downgraded to a meaningless requirement if it were assumed – as was the case in *LESI v Algeria*[312]—that it accords no more protection than clauses on national treatment or MFN treatment.

The level of a host State's economic development, the availability of appropriate resources, the existence of an armed conflict, and other political as well as economic circumstances may have an impact on its ability to provide full protection and security. It is under debate to what extent these economic and social conditions should be taken into account when assessing a State's compliance with the full protection and security standard.[313]

In *Pantechniki v Albania*,[314] the investor sought to recover losses sustained during the widespread civil strife that prevailed in Albania in 1997. The sole arbitrator addressed the level of development of Albania in the context of the full protection and security standard. He distinguished FPS from denial of justice which should not depend on a host State's level of development. Protection against physical violence emanating from private persons would depend on the State's resources. The arbitrator concluded that the Albanian authorities had been powerless in the face of major social unrest and held that there had been no violation of the FPS standard because of the general situation prevailing in the country. He added that the assessment might have been different had the police refused to intervene.[315]

The FPS standard will not be violated through a reasonable exercise of a State's right to regulate.[316] But recognition of a State's police powers does not as such afford a valid defence against an alleged violation of the FPS standard. In exercising its sovereign right to regulate the State must remain within the boundaries of international law.[317]

Republic, Final Award, 12 November 2010, paras 269–270; *Paushok v Mongolia*, Award on Jurisdiction and Liability, 28 April 2011, paras 324–325; *Vannessa v Venezuela*, Award, 16 January 2013, para 223; *Mamidoil v Albania*, Award, 30 March 2015, para 821; *von Pezold v Zimbabwe*, Award, 28 July 2015, para 596; *MNSS v Montenegro*, Award, 4 May 2016, para 351; *Ampal-American v Egypt*, Decision on Liability and Heads of Loss, 21 February 2017, para 241; *Strabag v Libya*, Award, 29 June 2020, para 335; *Eskosol v Italy*, Award, 4 September 2020, paras 479–482.

[312] *LESI & ASTALDI v Algeria*, Award, 12 November 2008, para 174; the BIT applicable in that case required 'protection et securité constantes, pleines et entières.'

[313] N Gallus, 'The Influence of the Host State's Level of Development on International Investment Treaty Standards of Protection' (2005) 6 *JWIT* 711; U Kriebaum, 'The Relevance of Economic and Political Conditions for the Protection under Investment Treaties' (2011) 10 *LPICT* 383. See also *AAPL v Sri Lanka*, Final Award, 27 June 1990, para 77; *Mamidoil v Albania*, Award, 30 March 2015, para 824; *Strabag v Libya*, Award, 29 June 2020, paras 234–236, 344–345.

[314] *Pantechniki v Albania*, Award, 30 July 2009.

[315] At paras 71–84.

[316] *AES v Hungary*, Award 23 September 2010, para 13.3.2; *Belenergia v Italy*, Award, 6 August 2019, paras 620–623.

[317] *Suez and InterAgua v Argentina*, Decision on Liability, 30 July 2010, paras 148-150; *Marfin v Cyprus*, Award, 26 July 2018, para 1324.

(c) Protection against physical violence and harassment

The duty to grant physical protection and security may operate in relation to encroachments by State organs[318] or in relation to private acts.[319] A minority of tribunals considers that protection under the standard is limited to violence emanating from third parties.[320] The host State's responsibility may be incurred by its failure to prevent the resulting damage or its failure to punish the perpetrators.[321]

Violence by State organs was under review in *AAPL v Sri Lanka*.[322] Security forces had destroyed the investment in the course of a counter-insurgency operation. The Tribunal reviewed all circumstances and held that these actions were unwarranted and excessive.

In *AMT v Zaire*,[323] the host country was held liable under a protection and security clause in the applicable BIT after incidents of looting by elements of the armed forces.

In *Eureko v Poland*,[324] there was an allegation of harassment of the investor's senior representatives. The Tribunal found that there was no violation of the standard, since there was no evidence that the State had authorized or instigated these acts. However, the position might have been different had such actions occurred repeatedly without protective measures on the part of the State.

Tenaris v Venezuela[325] involved labour unrest and accusations of collusion or lack of protection on the part of State organs. The Tribunal accepted that the State's obligation is not limited to physical protection from third parties but also extends to actions of State organs. On the facts it decided that no violation of the standard had occurred.

Other cases concerned private violence.[326] In the *ELSI* case,[327] a Chamber of the International Court of Justice (ICJ) applied a provision in an FCN Treaty that granted 'the most constant protection and security'. One charge by the claimants was that the Italian authorities had allowed workers to occupy the factory.

318 *Parkerings v Lithuania*, Award, 11 September 2007, para 355; *Biwater Gauff v Tanzania*, Award, 24 July 2008, para 730; *Frontier Petroleum v Czech Republic*, Final Award, 12 November 2010, para 261; *Tenaris v Venezuela I*, Award, 29 January 2016, para 439; *Krederi v Ukraine*, Award, 2 July 2018, para 656.

319 *Pantechniki v Albania*, Award, 30 July 2009, paras 77 et seq; *Ampal-American v Egypt*, Decision on Liability and Heads of Loss, 21 February 2017, para 290.

320 *El Paso v Argentina*, Award, 31 October 2011, para 522; *Mobil v Argentina*, Decision on Jurisdiction and Liability, 10 April 2013, para 1004.

321 *Parkerings v Lithuania*, Award, 11 September 2007, para 355.

322 *AAPL v Sri Lanka*, Final Award, 27 June 1990, paras 45 et seq, 78 et seq.

323 *AMT v Zaire*, Award, 21 February 1997, paras 6.02 et seq. See also *Saluka v Czech Republic*, Partial Award, 17 March 2006, para 483.

324 *Eureko v Poland*, Partial Award, 19 August 2005, paras 236–237.

325 *Tenaris v Venezuela I*, Award, 29 January 2016, paras 439, 443.

326 See also *Eastern Sugar v Czech Republic*, Partial Award, 27 March 2007, para 203; *Pantechniki v Albania*, Award, 30 July 2009, paras 77 et seq; *Toto v Lebanon*, Award, 7 June 2012, para 229; *OI European Group v Venezuela*, Award, 10 March 2015, para 580.

327 *Elettronica Sicula SpA (ELSI) (United States v Italy)*, Judgment, 20 July 1989, ICJ Reports (1989) 15.

The Court found that the response of the Italian authorities had been adequate under the circumstances.[328] The Court stated that '[t]he reference in Article V to the provision of "constant protection and security" cannot be construed as the giving of a warranty that property shall never in any circumstances be occupied or disturbed'.[329]

In *Wena Hotels v Egypt*,[330] the Tribunal found Egypt liable under the FPS standard because employees of a State entity had seized the hotel in question and because the police authorities had been aware of the seizure and had not acted to protect the investor before or after the invasive action.

In *Tecmed v Mexico*,[331] the claimant alleged that the Mexican authorities had not acted efficiently against 'social demonstrations' and disturbances at the site of the landfill under dispute. The Tribunal applied a treaty provision guaranteeing 'full protection and security to the investments . . . in accordance with International Law'. It found that there was not sufficient evidence to prove that the Mexican authorities had encouraged, fostered, or contributed to the actions in question and that there was no evidence that the authorities had not reacted reasonably.[332]

Similarly, *Noble Ventures v Romania*[333] involved demonstrations and protests by employees. The relevant treaty provision stipulated that the '[i]nvestment shall . . . enjoy full protection and security'. The Tribunal rejected the claim, finding that it was difficult to identify any specific failure on the part of Romania to exercise due diligence in protecting the claimant.[334]

In *Ampal-American v Egypt* the Tribunal decided that a failure by the Egyptian authorities to protect claimant's investment against terrorist attacks was a violation of the FPS standard.[335]

(d) Legal protection

There is authority to the effect that the principle of full protection and security reaches beyond physical violence and requires legal protection for the investor.[336]

[328] At paras 105–108.
[329] At para 108.
[330] *Wena Hotels v Egypt*, Award, 8 December 2000, para 84.
[331] *Tecmed v Mexico*, Award, 29 May 2003.
[332] At paras 175–177.
[333] *Noble Ventures v Romania*, Award, 12 October 2005.
[334] At paras 164–166.
[335] *Ampal-American v Egypt*, Decision on Liability and Heads of Loss, 21 February 2017, para 290.
[336] *CSOB v Slovakia*, Award, 29 December 2004, para 170; *Ares v Georgia*, Award, 26 February 2008, para 10.3.4; *National Grid v Argentina*, Award, 3 November 2008, paras 187–190; *Frontier Petroleum v Czech Republic*, Final Award, 12 November 2010, paras 260–273; *Total v Argentina*, Decision on Liability, 27 December 2010, para 343; *Unglaube v Costa Rica*, Award 16 May 2012, para 283; *Vannessa v Venezuela*, Award, 16 January 2013, para 223; *Levy v Peru*, Award, 26 February 2014, para 406; *Anglo American v Venezuela*, Award, 18 January 2019, para 482.

Some treaties explicitly provide for 'full protection and legal security'.[337] An explicit reference to legal security leaves no doubt that FPS extends to the protection of legal rights.[338] But even the usual formula 'full protection and security' was held by tribunals to include the protection of investor's rights through a functioning legal system.[339]

In the *ELSI* case,[340] the guarantee of 'the most constant protection and security' was also the basis for a complaint concerning the time taken (16 months) for a decision on an appeal against an order requisitioning the factory. The ICJ's Chamber examined this argument and found that the time taken, though undoubtedly long, did not violate the treaty standard in view of other procedural safeguards under Italian law.[341]

In *CME v Czech Republic*,[342] a regulatory authority had created a legal situation that enabled the investor's local partner to terminate the contract on which the investment depended. The Tribunal said that '[t]he host State is obligated to ensure that neither by amendment of its laws nor by actions of its administrative bodies is the agreed and approved security and protection of the foreign investor's investment withdrawn or devalued'.[343]

In the parallel case *Lauder v Czech Republic*,[344] the Tribunal, however, denied a violation of the standard, based on a different assessment of the same facts. It reached the result that the only duty of the host State under the 'protection and security' clause had been to grant the investor access to its judicial system.

In *Azurix v Argentina*,[345] the Tribunal confirmed that 'full protection and security may be breached even if no physical violence or damage occurs':[346]

> The cases referred to above show that full protection and security was understood to go beyond protection and security ensured by the police. It is not only a matter of physical security; the stability afforded by a secure investment environment is as important from an investor's point of view. The Tribunal is aware that in recent free trade agreements signed by the United States, for instance, with Uruguay, full protection and security is understood to be limited to the level of police

[337] Germany–Argentina BIT (1991) Article 4(1): 'plena protección y seguridad jurídica'.

[338] *Siemens v Argentina*, Award, 6 February 2007, para 303; *Paushok v Mongolia*, Award on Jurisdiction and Liability, 28 April 2011, para 326; *Tatneft v Ukraine*, Award on the Merits, 29 July 2014, para 425.

[339] *Frontier Petroleum v Czech Republic*, Final Award, 12 November 2010, paras 263, 273; *Electrabel v Hungary*, Decision on Jurisdiction, Applicable Law and Liability, 30 November 2012, para 7.146; *Krederi v Ukraine*, Award, 2 July 2018, para 652.

[340] *Elettronica Sicula SpA (ELSI) (United States of America v Italy)*, Judgment, 20 July 1989, ICJ Reports (1989) 15.

[341] At para 109.

[342] *CME v Czech Republic*, Partial Award, 13 September 2001.

[343] At para 613.

[344] *Lauder v Czech Republic*, Final Award, 3 September 2001, para 314.

[345] *Azurix v Argentina*, Award, 14 July 2006.

[346] At para 406.

> protection required under customary international law. However, when the terms 'protection and security' are qualified by 'full' and no other adjective or explanation, they extend, in their ordinary meaning, the content of this standard beyond physical security.[347]

In *Siemens v Argentina*,[348] the Tribunal derived additional authority for the proposition that FPS goes beyond physical security and extends to legal protection from the fact that the applicable BIT's definition of investment applied also to intangible assets:

> As a general matter and based on the definition of investment, which includes tangible and intangible assets, the Tribunal considers that the obligation to provide full protection and security is wider than 'physical' protection and security. It is difficult to understand how the physical security of an intangible asset would be achieved.[349]

In *Vivendi v Argentina*,[350] the Tribunal had to apply a clause requiring 'full protection and security in accordance with the principle of fair and equitable treatment'. The Tribunal found that the scope of that provision was not limited to safeguarding 'physical possession or the legally protected terms of operation of the investment'.[351]

Sempra v Argentina[352] recognized that the standard had traditionally developed in the context of the physical protection of the investment, but that exceptionally a broader interpretation would be possible.

In *Biwater Gauff v Tanzania*,[353] the Tribunal confirmed that the guarantee of 'full security' extends to legal protection:

> The Arbitral Tribunal adheres to the *Azurix* holding that when the terms 'protection' and 'security' are qualified by 'full', the content of the standard may extend to matters other than physical security. It implies a State's guarantee of stability in a secure environment, both physical, commercial and legal.[354]

The investor may have to take active legal steps to obtain the investment's protection. In *GEA v Ukraine*,[355] the claimant argued that the host State should have

347 At para 408.
348 *Siemens v Argentina*, Award, 6 February 2007.
349 At para 303.
350 *Vivendi v Argentina*, Resubmitted Case: Award, 20 August 2007.
351 At para 7.4.15. Cited approvingly in *AES v Hungary*, Award, 23 September 2010, para 13.3.2.
352 *Sempra v Argentina*, Award, 28 September 2007, para 323.
353 *Biwater Gauff v Tanzania*, Award, 24 July 2008.
354 At para 729.
355 *GEA v Ukraine*, Award, 31 March 2011, para 247.

initiated proceedings to inquire into a theft of its property. The Tribunal rejected the claim because the claimant itself had never brought a criminal complaint.

Therefore, there is substantial authority for the proposition that the FPS standard goes beyond physical security and extends to a measure of legal security. On the other hand, a considerable number of tribunals have denied that 'full protection and security' offers a guarantee of legal protection and found that the FPS standard should be confined to physical protection and security.[356]

In *Suez and InterAgua v Argentina*,[357] the Tribunal found that FPS did not extend to an obligation to maintain a stable and secure legal and commercial environment.[358] The Tribunal found that an overly extensive interpretation of FPS would result in an undesirable overlap with other standards of protection.[359] A textual and historical interpretation led the Tribunal to reject the concept of legal security.[360]

(e) Relationship to customary international law

It is undeniable that the full protection and security standard has its origins in customary international law. This is illustrated by the *Amco v Indonesia*[361] case which was not decided on the basis of a BIT but in the framework of customary international law. The Tribunal found that under international law 'a State has a duty to protect aliens and their investment against unlawful acts'.[362]

Some treaty provisions on protection and security tie the standard to general international law ('full protection and security in accordance with international law'), parallel to the practice on FET. Other treaties refer to protection and security and to treatment in accordance with international law as separate standards, suggesting that the two are not identical.

The question remains whether an unqualified reference to 'full protection and security' provides an autonomous treaty standard or merely serves to incorporate customary law. To clarify the issue for purposes of the NAFTA, the three parties stated in a Note of Interpretation that the provision on FPS (together with FET) in Article 1105(1) embodies customary law.[363] In other words, the NAFTA parties

356 *Saluka v Czech Republic*, Partial Award, 17 March 2006, para 484; *BG Group v Argentina*, Final Award, 24 December 2007, paras 323–328; *Rumeli v Kazakhstan*, Award, 29 July 2008, para 668; *Liman Caspian v Kazakhstan*, Award, 22 June 2010, para 289; *EDF v Argentina*, Award, 11 June 2012, para 1109; *Gold Reserve v Venezuela*, Award, 22 September 2014, paras 622–623; *Crystallex v Venezuela*, Award, 4 April 2016, para 632; *Olin v Libya*, Final Award, 25 May 2018, paras 365–366; *OperaFund v Spain*, Award, 6 September 2019, para 576.

357 *Suez and InterAgua v Argentina*, Decision on Liability, 30 July 2010, paras 158–173.

358 At para 170.

359 At para 168.

360 At para 171.

361 *Amco v Indonesia*, Award, 20 November 1984.

362 At para 172.

363 NAFTA Free Trade Commission, Interpretative Note of 31 July 2001, quoted in *Mondev v USA*, Award, 11 October 2002, para 101.

assumed that the standard reflects the requirements of the international minimum standard as applied to aliens.[364] The subsequent BIT practice of the United States and Canada has followed this interpretation. Article 14.6 of the USMCA explicitly links the full protection and security standard to the level of protection under customary international law.

In the *ELSI* case, the ICJ suggested that the standard 'may go further' than general international law,[365] even though the clause in the relevant treaty contained a reference to international law ('full protection and security required by international law'). Some tribunals have regarded FPS as a standard that is independent of customary international law.[366] Other tribunals have expressed the view that FPS is no more than the traditional obligation to protect aliens under customary international law.[367]

3. Arbitrary or discriminatory measures

ADDITIONAL READING: V Heiskanen, 'Arbitrary and Unreasonable Measures' in A Reinisch (ed) *Standards of Investment Protection* (2008) 87; F Ortino, 'Non-Discriminatory Treatment in Investment Disputes' in P-M Dupuy et al (eds) *Human Rights in International Investment Law and Arbitration* (2009) 344; C Schreuer, 'Protection against Arbitrary or Discriminatory Measures' in C Rogers et al (eds) *The Future of Investment Arbitration* (2009) 183; P Dumberry, 'The Prohibition against Arbitrary Conduct and the Fair and Equitable Treatment Standard under NAFTA Article 1105' (2014) 15 *JWIT* 117; C Titi, 'Full Protection and Security, Arbitrary or Discriminatory Treatment and the Invisible EU Model BIT' (2014) 15 *JWIT* 534; U Kriebaum, 'Arbitrary/Unreasonable or Discriminatory Measures' in M Bungenberg et al (eds) *International Investment Law* (2015) 790; V Lowe, 'Arbitrary and Discriminatory Treatment' in M Kinnear et al (eds) *Building International Investment Law* (2016) 307; A Reinisch and C Schreuer, *International Protection of Investments* (2020) 813.

(a) Introduction

By definition, every State oriented at the rule of law will outlaw arbitrary action, and foreign investors properly expect that host States will follow this standard.

[364] See I.1(c) and VIII.1(f) above.

[365] *Elettronica Sicula SpA (ELSI) (US v Italy)*, Judgment, 20 July 1989, ICJ Reports (1989) 15, para 111.

[366] *Azurix v Argentina*, Award, 14 July 2006, para 361; *Frontier Petroleum v Czech Republic*, Final Award, 12 November 2010, para 268; *Crystallex v Venezuela*, Award, 4 April 2016, para 632.

[367] *Occidental Exploration v Ecuador*, Final Award, 1 July 2004, para 190; *Noble Ventures v Romania*, Award, 12 October 2005, para 164; *El Paso v Argentina*, Award, 31 October 2011, para 522.

The traditional understanding of the international minimum standard for the treatment of foreigners under customary international law prohibits arbitrary action.[368] It follows that the treaty standard against arbitrariness is also reflected in customary international law. This does not, however, mean that the treaty term is necessarily restricted to the traditional concept as developed in customary international law.

Measures differentiating between foreign investors and nationals or among foreign investors do not violate the minimum standard under traditional international law.[369] But the host State may promise non-discrimination through a pertinent treaty provision. A guarantee against discrimination may be given through the prohibition of arbitrary or discriminatory treatment or through clauses granting national treatment[370] and MFN treatment[371] to foreign investors.

Protection against discriminatory treatment is a relative standard, similar to the national treatment and MFN treatment standards. Its content depends upon the level of treatment given to a national or other foreign investor in a similar situation. On the other hand, protection against arbitrary treatment is an absolute standard comparable to the FET standard. This is also evident in the debate on the relationship of the arbitrary and discriminatory standard to the FET standard.[372]

(b) Textual variations

In treaty practice, the rule against arbitrariness is typically combined with the prohibition of discrimination ('shall not impair investments by arbitrary or discriminatory measures'). The separate listing of the two standards, separated by the word 'or', suggests that each must be accorded its own significance and scope.[373]

Some treaties do not use the term 'arbitrary' but refer to 'unjustified or discriminatory action' or to 'unreasonable or discriminatory action'. It would be difficult to identify a difference between 'arbitrary' and 'unjustified' or 'unreasonable' action and, presumably, the terms are interchangeable. The Tribunal in *National Grid v Argentina*,[374] said in response to an argument by the claimant that the concepts were different:

[368] A Verdross, 'Les règles internationales concernant le traitement des étrangers' (1931-III) 37 *Recueil* 323, 358; Restatement (Third) of the Foreign Relations Law of the United States (1986) 2: 196.

[369] *Genin v Estonia*, Award, 25 June 2001, para 368.

[370] See VIII.4 below.

[371] See VIII.5 below.

[372] See VIII.1(e) above.

[373] In this sense: *Azurix v Argentina*, Award, 14 July 2006, para 391; *Siag v Egypt*, Award, 1 June 2009, para 457; *AES v Hungary*, Award, 23 September 2010, para 10.3.2.

[374] *National Grid v Argentina*, Award, 3 November 2008.

> It is the view of the Tribunal that the plain meaning of the terms 'unreasonable' and 'arbitrary' is substantially the same in the sense of something done capriciously, without reason.[375]

The Tribunal in *Urbaser v Argentina*[376] though seems to have tried to distinguish between the terms 'unjustified' and 'unlawful' when it stated that the applicable BIT clause did

> not use the term 'unlawful' but instead the word 'unjustified,' which can imply possible justifications by reference to grounds other than legal ones, in particular in case of measures justified by reasons based on equity or good faith.[377]

(c) The meaning of 'arbitrary'

Tribunals have adopted different approaches to establishing the meaning of 'arbitrary' and its application to a specific case. One reading of the clause simply refers to the ordinary meaning and seeks to extrapolate this meaning from general legal dictionaries. Some tribunals have consulted *Black's Law Dictionary*, according to which 'arbitrary' means 'depending on individual discretion' or action 'founded on prejudice or preference rather than on reason of fact'.[378]

The Tribunal in *Azurix v Argentina*[379] gave the following definition of 'arbitrary' based on its ordinary meaning in accordance with Article 31 of the Vienna Convention on the Law of Treaties (VCLT):

> In its ordinary meaning, 'arbitrary' means 'derived from mere opinion', 'capricious', 'unrestrained', 'despotic.' Black's Law Dictionary defines the term, *inter alia*, as 'done capriciously or at pleasure', 'not done or acting according to reason or judgment', 'depending on the will alone.'[380]

Tribunals have applied the concept of 'arbitrary' to the following categories of measures:

[375] At para 197.
[376] *Urbaser v Argentina*, Award, 8 December 2016.
[377] At para 1089.
[378] *Lauder v Czech Republic*, Final Award, 3 September 2001, para 221, cited with approval in *Occidental Exploration v Ecuador*, Final Award, 1 July 2004, para 162 and in *CMS v Argentina*, Award, 12 May 2005, para 291; *Azurix v Argentina*, Award, 14 July 2006, para 392. See also *Siemens v Argentina*, Award, 6 February 2007, para 318; *Plama v Bulgaria*, Award, 27 August 2008, para 184; *El Paso v Argentina*, Award, 31 October 2011, para 319.
[379] *Azurix v Argentina*, Award, 14 July 2006.
[380] At para 392. In identical terms: *Siemens v Argentina*, Award, 6 February 2007, para 318.

- a measure that inflicts damage on the investor without serving any apparent legitimate purpose. The decisive criterion for the determination of the unreasonable or arbitrary nature of a measure harming the investor would be whether it can be justified in terms of rational reasons that are related to the facts. Arbitrariness would be absent if the measure is a reasonable and proportionate reaction to objectively verifiable circumstances;
- a measure that is not based on legal standards but on discretion, prejudice, or personal preference;
- a measure taken for reasons that are different from those put forward by the decision maker. This applies, in particular, where a public interest is put forward as a pretext to take measures that are designed to harm the investor;
- a measure taken in wilful disregard of due process and proper procedure.

Tribunals have adopted these categories to establish the existence of arbitrary action by the host State.[381]

aa. Rational decision-making

In a considerable number of cases, tribunals have examined whether the measure alleged to be unreasonable or arbitrary was the result of a rational decision-making process.[382] Tribunals were not satisfied with the host State's unilateral assertion of public interest or public purpose. Rather, they went into an independent examination of the public interest postulated by the State. This examination involved two elements:

[381] *EDF v Romania*, Award, 8 October 2009, para 303; *Lemire v Ukraine*, Decision on Jurisdiction and Liability, 14 January 2010, para 262; *SAUR v Argentine Republic*, Decision on Jurisdiction and Liability, 6 June 2012, para 488; *Toto v Lebanon*, Award, 7 June 2012, para 157; *TRACO v Poland*, First Partial Award, 5 September 2012, para 224; *OI European v Venezuela*, Award, 10 March 2015, paras 494, 519; *Teinver v Argentina*, Award, 21 July 2017, footnote 1116; *Krederi v Ukraine*, Award, 2 July 2018, paras 669, 672; *Glencore v Colombia*, Award, 27 August 2019, para 1449; *RWE v Spain*, Decision on Jurisdiction, Liability and certain issues of Quantum, 30 December 2019, para 647.

[382] *Lauder v Czech Republic*, Award, 3 September 2001, paras 222, 230, 232; *Occidental Exploration v Ecuador*, Award, 1 July 2004, para 163; *LG&E v Argentina*, Decision on Liability, 3 October 2006, paras 158, 162; *Enron v Argentina*, Award, 22 May 2007, para 281; *Sempra v Argentina*, Award, 28 September 2007, para 318; *Cargill v Poland*, Final Award, 29 February 2008, paras 524–528; *Biwater Gauff v Tanzania*, Award, 24 July 2008, para 709; *Al-Bahloul v Tajikistan*, Partial Award on Jurisdiction and Liability, 2 September 2009, para 251; *El Paso v Argentina*, Award, 31 October 2011, para 322; *Mobil v Argentina*, Decision on Jurisdiction and Liability, 10 April 2013, paras 872–878; *Mamidoil v Albania*, Award, 30 March 2015, paras 791, 795; *Philip Morris v Uruguay*, Award, 8 July 2016, paras 389–420; *Isolux v Spain*, Award, 12 July 2016, paras 820–825; *Antaris v Czech Republic*, Award, 2 May 2018, paras 360, 443, 444; *Greentech v Italy*, Award, 23 December 2018, para 462; *SolEs Badajoz v Spain*, Award, 31 July 2019, para 326; *Glencore v Colombia*, Award, 27 August 2019, paras 1453–1454, 1457; *RWE v Spain*, Decision on Jurisdiction, Liability and Certain Issues of Quantum, 30 December 2019, paras 644–645; *Watkins v Spain*, Award, 21 January 2020, para 604.

1. The examination of the existence of a genuine public purpose.
2. The examination of the existence of a reasonable relationship between the aims pursued by the State and the effectiveness of the measures taken.

The Tribunal in *Saluka v Czech Republic*[383] emphasized the need for a rational process of decision in the following terms:

> The standard of 'reasonableness' therefore requires, in this context as well, a showing that the State's conduct bears a reasonable relationship to some rational policy....[384]

Similarly, the Tribunal in *Plama v Bulgaria*[385] explained arbitrariness in terms of an absence of reason or fact:

> Unreasonable or arbitrary measures—as they are sometimes referred to in other investment instruments—are those which are not founded in reason or fact but on caprice, prejudice or personal preference.[386]

In *Invesmart v Czech Republic*,[387] the Tribunal held that the requirement of reasonableness was satisfied provided the measure was based on reasonable policy considerations. It was not for the Tribunal to second-guess the merits of the policy considerations in question. The Tribunal said:

> The Czech Republic can be held to have acted reasonably so long as, in the Tribunal's view, it did so out of some reasonable policy consideration, as opposed to conduct that was motivated by the intention to deprive an investor of the value of its investment.
>
> Whilst the merits of this decision may be questioned, this is not a matter for this Tribunal. It is clear that the Czech Republic acted in the interests of legitimate policy concerns....[388]

In *AES v Hungary*,[389] the Tribunal went one step further. It undertook a detailed analysis of the concept of 'unreasonable and discriminatory measures'. In doing so, the Tribunal found that a rational policy pursued by the State was not enough. The measure taken also had to be suitable in objective terms:

[383] *Saluka v Czech Republic*, Partial Award, 17 March 2006.
[384] At para 460. Quoted with approval in *Biwater Gauff v Tanzania*, Award, 24 July 2008, para 693.
[385] *Plama v Bulgaria*, Award, 27 August 2008.
[386] At para 184.
[387] *Invesmart v Czech Republic*, Award, 26 June 2009, paras 452–463.
[388] At paras 460, 462.
[389] *AES v Hungary*, Award, 23 September 2010.

> 10.3.7 There are two elements that require to be analyzed to determine whether a state's act was unreasonable: the existence of a rational policy; and the reasonableness of the act of the state in relation to the policy.
> 10.3.8 A rational policy is taken by a state following a logical (good sense) explanation and with the aim of addressing a public interest matter.
> 10.3.9 Nevertheless, a rational policy is not enough to justify all the measures taken by a state in its name. A challenged measure must also be reasonable. That is, there needs to be an appropriate correlation between the state's public policy objective and the measure adopted to achieve it. This has to do with the nature of the measure and the way it is implemented.

The Tribunal proceeded to examine separately whether the State had pursued a rational policy and whether there was a reasonable correlation between the State's policy objective and the measures adopted to achieve it.[390]

In *Micula v Romania I*,[391] the Tribunal found that the concept 'reasonable' required the examination of two elements: the existence of a rational policy and an appropriate relation of the act in question to that policy. The Tribunal said:

> With respect to the meaning of the term 'unreasonable', both Parties appear to agree that 'unreasonable' means lacking in justification or not grounded in reason (i.e., arbitrary), or not enacted in pursuit of legitimate objectives ... The Respondent also proposes the formulation used by the *Saluka* tribunal: for a state's conduct to be reasonable, it must 'bear a reasonable relationship to rational policies [...]'. Although the definition is rather circular, the Tribunal finds it appropriate, with the specification made by the *AES* tribunal, namely that the determination of whether the state's conduct is reasonable requires the analysis of two elements: 'the existence of a rational policy; and the reasonableness of the act of the state in relation to the policy' (*AES v. Hungary*, ¶ 10.3.7). As noted by the *AES* tribunal, a policy is rational when the state adopts it 'following a logical (good sense) explanation and with the aim of addressing a public interest matter' (*Id.*, ¶ 10.3.8), and an action is reasonable when there is 'an appropriate correlation between the state's public policy objective and the measure adopted to achieve it' (*Id.*, ¶ 10.3.9). In other words, for a state's conduct to be reasonable, it is not sufficient that it be related to a rational policy; it is also necessary that, in the implementation of that policy, the state's acts have been appropriately tailored to the pursuit of that rational policy with due regard for the consequences imposed on investors.[392]

390 At paras 10.3.1–10.3.36.
391 *Micula v Romania I*, Award, 11 December 2013.
392 At para 525.

The Tribunal in *Electrabel v Hungary*[393] followed the approach developed in these cases. It said:

> *Standard for 'Arbitrariness'*: As already indicated above, this Tribunal agrees with the *Saluka*, *AES*, and *Micula* tribunals in that a measure will not be arbitrary if it is reasonably related to a rational policy. As the *AES* tribunal emphasised, this requires two elements: 'the existence of a rational policy; and the reasonableness of the act of the state in relation to the policy. A rational policy is taken by a state following a logical (good sense) explanation and with the aim of addressing a public interest matter. Nevertheless, a rational policy is not enough to justify all the measures taken by a state in its name. A challenged measure must also be reasonable. That is, there needs to be an appropriate correlation between the state's public policy objective and the measure adopted to achieve it. This has to do with the nature of the measure and the way it is implemented.' In the Tribunal's view, this includes the requirement that the impact of the measure on the investor be proportional to the policy objective sought. The relevance of the proportionality of the measure has been increasingly addressed by investment tribunals and other international tribunals, including the ECtHR. The test for proportionality has been developed from certain municipal administrative laws, and requires the measure to be suitable to achieve a legitimate policy objective, necessary for that objective, and not excessive considering the relative weight of each interest involved.[394]

bb. Rule of law

Another approach to interpreting 'arbitrary', 'unjustified', or 'unreasonable' is to examine whether measures are based on legal standards or on discretion. The ICJ gave an often-cited definition of the term 'arbitrary' in the *ELSI* case.[395] It said:

> Arbitrariness is not so much something opposed to a rule of law, as something opposed to the rule of law.[396]

In *Lauder v Czech Republic*,[397] the Tribunal found that the Czech Republic had taken a discriminatory and arbitrary measure. It said:

[393] *Electrabel v Hungary*, Award, 25 November 2015.
[394] At para 179. Footnotes omitted.
[395] *Elettronica Sicula SpA (ELSI) (United States v Italy)*, International Court of Justice, Judgment, 20 July 1989, ICJ Reports (1989) 15.
[396] At para 128.
[397] *Lauder v Czech Republic*, Final Award, 3 September 2001.

> The measure was arbitrary because it was not founded on reason or fact, nor on the law which expressly accepted '*applications from companies with foreign equity participation*' . . ., but on mere fear reflecting national preference.[398]

In *Lemire v Ukraine*,[399] the Tribunal related violations of the local law to arbitrary or discriminatory measures in the following way:

> Although not every violation of domestic law necessarily translates into an arbitrary or discriminatory measure under international law and a violation of the FET standard, in the Tribunal's view a blatant disregard of applicable tender rules, distorting fair competition among tender participants, does.[400]

In *Crystallex v Venezuela*,[401] the Tribunal described arbitrary action in terms of an absence of legal standards, discretion, prejudice, or personal preference:

> In the Tribunal's eyes, a measure is for instance arbitrary if it is not based on legal standards but on excess of discretion, prejudice or personal preference, and taken for reasons that are different from those put forward by the decision maker.[402]

In *Cervin v Costa Rica*,[403] the Tribunal defined arbitrary conduct as conduct that is not governed by law, justice, or reason but is based only on 'capriciousness'. In *Valores Mundiales v Venezuela*,[404] the Tribunal found that certain measures taken by Venezuela lacked any foundation in Venezuelan law and were hence arbitrary for purposes of the BIT with Spain.

Other tribunals too have found that action that was unlawful under local law was contrary to the treaty requirement not to take unreasonable or discriminatory measures.[405] It follows that illegality under the local law is a relevant factor to determine whether actions taken by the State are unjustified.

cc. Adverse intention

In some cases, tribunals examined the existence of an adverse intention on the part of the host State when interpreting the concept of arbitrary/unreasonable.[406] In

398 At para 232. Italics original.
399 *Lemire v* Ukraine, Decision on Jurisdiction and Liability, 14 January 2010.
400 At para 385.
401 *Crystallex v Venezuela*, Award, 4 April 2016.
402 At para 578.
403 *Cervin v Costa Rica*, Award, 7 March 2017, para 523.
404 *Valores Mundiales v Venezuela*, Award, 25 July 2017, paras 605–619.
405 *Saluka v Czech Republic*, Partial Award, 17 March 2006, paras 467, 470; *El Paso v Argentina*, Award, 31 October 2011, para 323; *TECO v Guatemala*, Award, 19 December 2013, para 621; *Olin v Libya*, Final Award, 25 May 2018, para 376.
406 *Enron v Argentina*, Award, 22 May 2007, para 281.

CME v Czech Republic,[407] the Media Council, a regulatory authority, had created a legal situation that enabled the investor's local partner to terminate the contract on which the investment depended. The Tribunal looked at the Media Council's intention to determine that this was in violation of the BIT's provision on 'unreasonable or discriminatory measures'. The Tribunal said:

> On the face of it, the Media Council's actions and inactions in 1996 and 1999 were unreasonable as the clear intention of the 1996 actions was to deprive the foreign investor of the exclusive use of the Licence under the MOA and the clear intention of the 1999 actions and inactions was [to] collude with the foreign investor's Czech business partner to deprive the foreign investor of its investment. The behaviour of the Media Council also smacks of discrimination against the foreign investor.[408]

The intention to deprive the investor of its investment under the pretext of a decision based on law was the decisive criterion for the application of this standard.

In *Biwater Gauff v Tanzania*,[409] the Tribunal, applying the BIT's prohibition of unreasonable or discriminatory measures, diagnosed an adverse intention in the following terms:

> In each case, the Republic's actions were abusive and unreasonable. There is no evidence supporting the Republic's asserted justifications for the seizure and deportation, which were instead parts of a concerted campaign against BGT and City Water.[410]

In *Teinver v Argentina* the Tribunal found that a series of abusive and artificial justifications were crucial for its finding of unjustified measures.[411]

On the other hand, there are some decisions in which tribunals indicated that they did not believe that an adverse intention or bad faith were essential for a violation of the prohibition of arbitrary or discriminatory treatment.[412]

dd. Due process

Another group of decisions have linked the concept of 'arbitrary' to violations of procedural propriety and due process.[413] In the *ELSI*

[407] *CME v Czech Republic*, Partial Award, 13 September 2001.
[408] At para 612.
[409] *Biwater Gauff v Tanzania*, Award, 24 July 2008.
[410] At para 709.
[411] *Teinver v Argentina*, Award, 21 July 2017, para 925.
[412] *Occidental Exploration v Ecuador*, Final Award, 1 July 2004, Dispositif, para 5, para 163; *Azurix v Argentina*, Award, 14 July 2006, para 392; *Siemens v Argentina*, Award, 6 February 2007, para 318.
[413] *Inmaris Perestroika v Ukraine*, Award, 1 March 2012, para 282; *Roussalis v Romania*, Award, 7 December 2011, paras 358–359; *OI European Group v Venezuela*, Award, 10 March 2015, para 494.

case,[414] the ICJ, when describing the concept of 'arbitrary or discriminatory measures', also referred to procedural aspects:

> a wilful disregard of due process of law, an act which shocks, or at least surprises, a sense of juridical propriety.[415]

Investment tribunals have followed the lead of the ICJ in *ELSI*.[416] The *Azurix* Tribunal said:

> The Tribunal finds that the definition in *ELSI* is close to the ordinary meaning of arbitrary since it emphasizes the element of willful disregard of the law.[417]

The Tribunal in *Genin v Estonia*[418] gave a restrictive description of the term 'arbitrary'. It made the following statement about the issue of arbitrariness arising from procedural irregularity:

> in order to amount to a violation of the BIT, any procedural irregularity that may have been present would have to amount to bad faith, a willful disregard of due process of law or an extreme insufficiency of action.[419]

Other tribunals have adopted a less demanding standard for arbitrariness through procedural shortcomings. In *Lemire v Ukraine*[420] the Tribunal said:

> the President's 'Instruction' amounted to interference with the independent and impartial decision of the National Council in favour of two of Claimant's competitors ... and thus amounts to an '*arbitrary or discriminatory measure*' within the meaning of Article II.3 (b) of the BIT.[421]

In *Alghanim v Jordan*,[422] the Tribunal described arbitrariness flowing from a violation of due process of law in the following terms:

[414] *Elettronica Sicula SpA (ELSI) (United States of America v Italy)*, Judgment, 20 July 1989, ICJ Reports (1989) 15.

[415] At para 128. The Court found on the facts of the case, that the temporary requisitioning of the industrial plant had not violated this standard.

[416] See also *Duke Energy* v *Ecuador*, Award, 18 August 2008, para 378; *E energija v Latvia*, Award, 22 December 2017, para 841.

[417] *Azurix v Argentina*, Award, 14 July 2006, para 392. In the same sense: *Siemens v Argentina*, Award, 6 February 2007, para 318.

[418] *Genin v Estonia*, Award, 25 June 2001.

[419] At para 371, quoting the ICJ in *ELSI*. The Tribunal found that on the facts of the case before it the standard had not been violated.

[420] *Lemire v Ukraine*, Decision on Jurisdiction and Liability, 14 January 2010.

[421] At para 356. Italics original. See also para 418.

[422] *Alghanim v Jordan*, Award, 14 December 2017.

> The protection from arbitrary measures requires the Tribunal to assess whether the investment has been subject to 'a wilful disregard of due process of law', not whether the act is 'opposed to a rule of law'. This necessarily entails consideration of the whole process of law to which the investment was subjected.[423]

(d) The meaning of 'discriminatory'

The Tribunal in *Plama v Bulgaria*[424] gave the following general definition of discrimination:

> With regard to discrimination, it corresponds to the negative formulation of the principle of equality of treatment. It entails like persons being treated in a different manner in similar circumstances without reasonable or justifiable grounds.[425]

Discrimination can take several forms. It can be based on race, religion, political affiliation, disability, and other criteria. In the context of the treatment of foreign investment, the most frequent problem is discrimination based on nationality. Consequently, most of the practice dealing with discrimination focuses on nationality. Discrimination based on nationality is addressed in investment treaties by way of two specific standards: national treatment and MFN treatment.[426] But this does not mean that the issue of discrimination is necessarily restricted to nationality.

In *Ulysseas v Ecuador*,[427] the respondent had contended that the only standard for discriminatory treatment was nationality.[428] The Tribunal rejected this argument and said:

> In the Tribunal's view, for a measure to be discriminatory it is sufficient that, objectively, two similar situations are treated differently. As stated by the ICSID tribunal in *Goetz v. Burundi*, '*discrimination supposes a differential treatment applied to people who are in similar situations*'. As such, discrimination may well disregard nationality and relate to a foreign investor being treated differently from another investor whether national or foreign in a similar situation.[429]

[423] At para 309.
[424] *Plama v Bulgaria*, Award, 27 August 2008.
[425] At para 184.
[426] These standards are dealt with in VIII.4 and VIII.5.
[427] *Ulysseas v Ecuador*, Final Award, 12 June 2012.
[428] At para 292.
[429] At para 293. Italics original. Footnote omitted.

In *von Pezold v Zimbabwe*,[430] the Tribunal found that the measures taken by Zimbabwe regarding the expropriation of certain farms were discriminatory as they were directed against claimants based on their skin colour.

A finding of discrimination is independent of a violation of domestic law. In fact, domestic law may be the cause for a violation of the international standard. In *Lauder v Czech Republic*,[431] the applicable BIT offered protection against 'arbitrary and discriminatory measures.' The Tribunal said:

> For a measure to be discriminatory, it does not need to violate domestic law, since domestic law can contain a provision that is discriminatory towards foreign investment, or can lack a provision prohibiting the discrimination of foreign investment.[432]

Practice dealing with discrimination has concentrated on two key issues. One concerns the basis of comparison for the alleged discrimination. The other concerns the question whether discriminatory intent is a requirement for a finding of discrimination or whether the fact of unequal treatment is sufficient.

aa. The basis of comparison

The basis of comparison is a crucial question in applying provisions dealing with non-discrimination.[433] As held by the Tribunal in *Metalpar v Argentina*:

> [t]reating different categories of subjects differently is not unequal treatment. The principle of equality only applies between equal subjects, not between unequal subjects.[434]

If the investor is entitled to non-discrimination what group must be looked at for comparison? Only businesses engaged in exactly the same activity? Or also businesses engaged in similar activity? Or businesses engaged in any economic activity?[435]

In some cases, the issue of the basis of comparison never arose since the tribunals were able to pinpoint unjustifiable differential treatment among businesses

[430] *von Pezold v Zimbabwe*, Award, 28 July 2015, para 501.

[431] *Lauder v Czech Republic*, Final Award, 3 September 2001.

[432] At para 220.

[433] *Goetz v Burundi*, Award, 10 February 1999, para 121; *Electrabel v Hungary*, Award, 25 November 2015, para 175.

[434] *Metalpar v Argentina*, Award on the Merits, 6 June 2008, para 162.

[435] NAFTA tribunals have dealt with a similar question when interpreting the provision of Article 1102 of the NAFTA on national treatment. See *SD Myers v Canada*, Partial Award, 13 November 2000, para 250; *Pope & Talbot v Canada*, Award on the Merits of Phase 2, 10 April 2001, paras 45–63, 68–69, 78; *Methanex v United States*, Final Award on Jurisdiction and Merits, 3 August 2005, IV, B, paras 17–19, 25–37; *Feldman v Mexico*, Award, 16 December 2002, para 171.

within the same area of activity.[436] In *Occidental v Ecuador*,[437] the Tribunal rejected a narrow comparison that would have looked only at the same economic sector or activity.[438] In *Enron v Argentina*,[439] the Tribunal looked at the question whether there had been 'any capricious, irrational or absurd differentiation' in the treatment of different sectors of the economy.[440]

In some cases, tribunals found that it was not possible to compare different sectors of the economy and to establish discrimination on that basis.[441] The Tribunal in *BG Group v Argentina* found that gas distributors and other public service providers such as electricity distributors were not in like circumstances.[442]

In *El Paso v Argentina*,[443] the claimant had complained about differences in treatment between the hydrocarbons sector and the banking sector. The Tribunal said:

> It is this Tribunal's view that a differential treatment based on the existence of a different factual and legal situation does not breach the BIT's standard. Here the Tribunal is in line with the approach of other tribunals already cited and finds itself in agreement with the tribunal in *Enron*, which found no discrimination between the different sectors of the economy, although they were indeed treated differently, as there was no 'capricious, irrational or absurd differentiation in the treatment accorded to the Claimant as compared to other entities or sectors.'[444]

bb. Discriminatory intent

Tribunals generally favour an objective approach that looks at the discriminatory consequences of a particular measure and not at any discriminatory intent.[445] The Tribunal in *Siemens v Argentina*[446] said:

[436] *Nykomb v Latvia*, Arbitral Award, 16 December 2003, Section 4.3.2; *Saluka v Czech Republic*, Partial Award, 17 March 2006, paras 313–347, 466; *Lemire v Ukraine*, Decision on Jurisdiction and Liability, 14 January 2010, paras 384–385.

[437] *Occidental Exploration v Ecuador*, Final Award, 1 July 2004.

[438] At paras 167–176. The Tribunal added that it found the practice concerning 'like products' developed within GATT/WTO not specifically pertinent, paras 174–176.

[439] *Enron v Argentina*, Award, 22 May 2007.

[440] At para 282. See also *Sempra v Argentina*, Award, 28 September 2007, para 319.

[441] *CMS v Argentina*, Award, 12 May 2005, para 293; *Metalpar v Argentina*, Award on the Merits, 6 June 2008, paras 161–164; *National Grid v Argentina*, Award, 3 November 2008, paras 201–202; *El Paso v Argentina*, Award, 31 October 2011, paras 309–315.

[442] *BG Group v Argentina*, Final Award, 24 December 2007, para 357.

[443] *El Paso v Argentina*, Award, 31 October 2011, paras 305–316.

[444] At para 315. Footnote omitted.

[445] *SD Myers v Canada*, Partial Award, 13 November 2000, paras 252–254; *Feldman v Mexico*, Award, 16 December 2002, para 184; *Occidental Exploration v Ecuador*, Final Award, 1 July 2004, para 177; *Eastern Sugar v Czech Republic*, Partial Award, 27 March 2007, para 338; *Cargill v Poland*, Final Award, 29 February 2008, para 522; *El Paso v Argentina*, Award, 31 October 2011, para 305; *Unglaube v Costa Rica*, Award, 16 May 2012, para 263; *Ulysseas v Ecuador*, Final Award, 12 June 2012, para 293; *Electrabel v Hungary*, Decision on Jurisdiction, Applicable Law and Liability, 30 November 2012, para 7.152.

[446] *Siemens v Argentina*, Award, 6 February 2007.

> The Tribunal concurs that intent is not decisive or essential for a finding of discrimination, and that the impact of the measure on the investment would be the determining factor to ascertain whether it had resulted in non-discriminatory treatment.[447]

However, there are cases that indicate that discriminatory intent is relevant. In some cases, the Tribunals also looked at the question whether measures had been taken in view of the investors' foreign nationality.[448] In *LG&E v Argentina*,[449] the Tribunal held that either discriminatory intent or discriminatory effect would suffice. In the end, it relied on the effect of the acts in question. The Tribunal said:

> In the context of investment treaties, and the obligation thereunder not to discriminate against foreign investors, a measure is considered discriminatory if the intent of the measure is to discriminate or if the measure has a discriminatory effect.[450]

Therefore, the primary criterion for discrimination under a treaty clause protecting the investor against arbitrary or discriminatory treatment is whether the investor has, in fact, been treated less favourably than other investors, especially based on nationality. Despite some cases pointing to discriminatory intent, the preponderant view is that discrimination need not be based on an intention to discriminate. *De facto* discrimination is enough.

4. National treatment

ADDITIONAL READING: AK Bjorklund, 'National Treatment' in A Reinisch (ed) *Standards of Investment Protection* (2009) 29; A Kamperman Sanders (ed) *The Principle of National Treatment in International Economic Law* (2014); A Reinisch, 'National Treatment' in M Bungenberg et al (eds) *International Investment Law* (2015) 846; RE Vinuesa, 'National Treatment, Principle' in R Wolfrum (ed) *International Economic Law—The Max Planck Encyclopedia of Public International Law* (2015) 664; J Kurtz, 'National Treatment' in J Kurtz (ed) *The WTO and International Investment Law* (2016) 79; AK Bjorklund, 'The National Treatment Obligation' in K Yannaca-Small (ed) *Arbitration under International Investment*

447 At para 321.

448 *Lauder v Czech Republic*, Final Award, 3 September 2001, para 231. In *Methanex v United States*, Final Award on Jurisdiction and Merits, 3 August 2005, the Tribunal is unclear on this point: see IV, B, para 1 and para 12; *Noble Ventures v Romania*, Award, 12 October 2005, para 180; *Lemire v Ukraine*, Decision on Jurisdiction and Liability, 14 January 2010, para 356; *Urbaser v Argentina*, Award, 8 December 2016, para 1088.

449 *LG&E v Argentina*, Decision on Liability, 3 October 2006.

450 At para 146. Footnote omitted.

Agreements (2018) 21.01; A Reinisch and C Schreuer, *International Protection of Investments* (2020) 587.

(a) General meaning

Clauses on national treatment are part of the standard repertoire of investment treaties. They appear in BITs as well as in multilateral treaties like the ECT (Article 10(3)), the NAFTA (Article 1102), and the USMCA (Article 14.4). Most of the relevant practice deals with the national treatment clause of NAFTA which provides in Article 1102(1):

> Each Party shall accord to investors of another Party treatment no less favorable than that it accords, in like circumstances, to its own investors with respect to the establishment, acquisition, expansion, management, conduct, operation, and sale or other disposition of investments.

National treatment clauses are an expression of the non-discrimination principle. Under customary international law there is no obligation to treat nationals and foreigners alike.[451] National treatment clauses are meant to provide a level playing field between foreign investors and their local competitors and to prevent protectionist measures by host States in favour of national investors. They oblige host States to make no negative differentiation between foreign and national investors when enacting and applying their rules and regulations and thus to promote the position of the foreign investor to the level accorded to nationals.[452] The standard is therefore contingent, relative, or comparative. The required treatment of foreign investors depends on treatment accorded to national investors.

The purpose of national treatment clauses in investment treaties differs fundamentally from the concept of 'national treatment' as it became known a few decades ago, as part of the proposed 'New International Economic Order'.[453] That concept was intended to limit, as far as possible, any rights a foreign investor could derive from international law.

Most national treatment clauses apply once a business is established (post-entry national treatment). This covers both regulatory and contractual matters.[454] Some investment treaties, especially those concluded by the United States and Canada,[455]

[451] *Methanex v United States*, Final Award on Jurisdiction and Merits, 3 August 2005, IV, C, para 25.

[452] *Thunderbird v Mexico*, Arbitral Award, 26 January 2006, para 175; *Champion Trading v Egypt*, Award, 27 October 2006, para 125; *Parkerings v Lithuania*, Award, 11 September 2007, para 367; *Archer Daniels Midland v Mexico*, Award, 21 November 2007, para 193; *Bayindir v Pakistan*, Award, 27 August 2009, para 387.

[453] See I.1(c) above.

[454] *Bayindir v Pakistan*, Award, 27 August 2009, para 388.

[455] The CETA text includes a pre-entry national treatment requirement which is however not arbitrable (Article 8.6. CETA in combination with Article 8.18 CETA).

also offer a right of access to a national market based on national treatment (pre-entry national treatment).[456]

The relative homogeneity of national treatment clauses in BITs does not mean that the standard is easy to apply. Although the basic clause is generally the same, the practical implications differ due to exemptions of certain business sectors. More importantly, even the basic guarantee contained in the national treatment standard itself is not always clear. Only few tribunals have found breaches of this standard and even where they did, they usually failed to discuss the exact meaning of the concept. It is generally agreed that the application of national treatment clauses is fact specific.[457] Like the concept of FET,[458] the national treatment standard resists abstract definition and a consistent approach to its interpretation is difficult to make out.

There is a certain overlap of the national treatment standard with the non-discrimination obligation under the FET standard[459] and the prohibition of arbitrary or discriminatory measures[460] contained in many investment protection treaties.

In examining whether the national treatment standard has been respected, tribunals typically take three steps.[461] First, the tribunal will determine whether the foreign investor and the domestic investor are placed in a comparable setting, in 'a like situation' or in 'like circumstances'. Second, it must determine whether the treatment accorded to the foreign investor was at least as favourable as the treatment accorded to domestic investors. Third, in the case of treatment that is less favourable, it must determine whether the differentiation was justified. Behind these seemingly simple parameters of the clause, lie complex issues that are not fully answered by existing case law.

(b) The basis of comparison: like circumstances

National treatment clauses typically do not contain an indication how to decide on the comparator. US treaties traditionally specify that the clause will apply in 'like situations'.[462] In recent years, US treaty practice has changed to 'in like

456 See VI.5(b) above. See also *ADF v United States*, Award, 9 January 2003, para 153.

457 The Appellate Body of the WTO has observed that the 'concept of "likeness" is a relative one that evokes the image of an accordion'; *Japan—Taxes on Alcoholic Beverages II*, WT/DS8, -10, -11/AB/R (4 October 1996), at H.1.(a).

458 See VIII.1(d) above.

459 See VIII.1(e) above.

460 See VIII.3(d) above.

461 *Methanex v United States*, Final Award, 3 August 2005, IV, B, para 13; *UPS v Canada*, Award on the Merits, 24 May 2007, para 83; *Archer Daniels Midland v Mexico*, Award, 21 November 2007, para 196; *Bayindir v Pakistan*, Award, 27 August 2009, para 399; *Olin v Libya*, Award, 25 May 2018, para 204. In *Gavrilović v Croatia*, Award, 26 July 2018, para 1191 the Tribunal focused on only two of the elements. It analysed whether: (i) the Claimants and [a host State national] were in like circumstances; and (ii) the Claimants were accorded less favourable treatment than [the host state national].

462 See the 1984 US Model BIT Article II.1.

circumstances'.[463] The NAFTA (Article 1102) and the USMCA (Article 14.4) refer to 'in like circumstances'. The CETA (Article 8.6) refers to 'in like situations'.

Finding a suitable basis of comparison has turned out to be difficult.[464] Some tribunals have pointed out that this analysis was fact-specific.[465] Some investment tribunals have taken the view that in order to determine whether a foreign investor and a local comparator were in 'like circumstances' or 'like situations' they had to assess whether they operated in the same economic sector.[466] For instance, the Tribunal in *SD Myers v Canada*[467] emphasized the relevance of the 'economic' or 'business' sector for the determination of likeness:

> The concept of 'like circumstances' invites an examination of whether a non-national investor complaining of less favorable treatment is in the same 'sector' as the national investor. The Tribunal takes the view that the word 'sector' has a wide connotation that includes the concepts of 'economic sector' and 'business sector'.[468]

Similarly, in *Feldman v Mexico*, 'in like circumstances' was interpreted to refer to the same business: the export of cigarettes.[469] By contrast, the Tribunal in *Occidental v Ecuador* referred to local producers in general, 'and this cannot be done by addressing exclusively the sector in which that particular activity is undertaken'.[470] It considered the measure 'VAT refund' rather than the particular economic activity of the investor for the establishment of the relevant comparator.

A fact-specific assessment of 'like circumstances' must look beyond business sectors and include the business and regulatory environment surrounding the activity in question.[471] This approach was taken in *Merrill & Ring v Canada*.[472] The Tribunal said:

> NAFTA tribunals have, on a number of occasions, considered various factors in assessing whether investors are 'in like circumstances' ... The environment, trade, the nature of services and functions, and public policy considerations are

[463] See the 2004 and 2012 US Model BITs Article 3.

[464] *Bogdanov v Moldova III*, Final Award, 16 April 2013, para 218.

[465] *Bayindir v Pakistan*, Award, 27 August 2009, para 389; *Apotex v United States*, Award, 25 August 2014, para 8.15; *Vento v Mexico*, Award, 6 July 2020, para 240.

[466] *Pope & Talbot v Canada*, Award on the Merits of Phase 2, 10 April 2001, para 78; *ADF v United States*, Award, 9 January 2003, para 156; *Champion Trading v Egypt*, Award, 27 October 2006, para 130; *Archer Daniels Midland v Mexico*, Award, 21 November 2007, paras 198–201; *Olin v Libya*, Award, 25 May 2018, paras 205–208.

[467] *SD Myers v Canada*, Partial Award, 13 November 2000.

[468] At para 250.

[469] *Feldman v Mexico*, Award, 16 December 2002, para 171.

[470] *Occidental Exploration v Ecuador*, Final Award, 1 July 2004, para 173.

[471] *Grand River v United States*, Award, 12 January 2011, para 166; *Railroad Development v Guatemala*, Award, 29 June 2012, para 153; *Levy v Peru*, Award, 26 February 2014, paras 396–401.

[472] *Merrill & Ring v Canada*, Award, 31 March 2010.

> found among such factors. This also explains why it is not enough on occasions to undertake the comparison solely in the same sector of economic activity and it might be necessary, as in *Occidental*, to consider whole sectors of the economy and business.[473]

Instead of focusing on business sectors, the Tribunal decided 'that the proper comparison is between investors which are subject to the same regulatory measures under the same jurisdictional authority'.[474]

The Tribunal in *Apotex v United States*[475] noted that the parties accepted that both the business sector and the regulatory regime were relevant. It said:

> it is appropriate in the identification of comparators which are in 'like circumstances' to look at, *inter alia*, whether those which are said to be comparators: (i) are in the same economic of business sector; (ii) have invested in, or are businesses that compete with the investor or its investments in terms of goods or services; or (iii) are subject to a comparable legal regime or regulatory requirements, as the Claimants and their investments.[476]

In *Clayton/Bilcon v Canada*, the Tribunal found that the comparison cases concerning environmental impact assessments invoked by the investor where 'sufficiently similar' to use them for a comparison with the treatment that the claimant's investment had received.[477] The application of a 'less favourable evaluation standard' to the foreign investor led to a finding of a violation.[478]

Therefore, the overall legal context in which a measure is placed must also be considered when 'like circumstances' are identified.

(c) Less favourable treatment

The application of a national treatment clause presupposes some type of 'treatment' by the host State. This indicates that what is required is not a theoretical distinction but actual behaviour.[479] The Tribunal in *Daimler v Argentina*[480] stated:

473 At para 88.
474 At para 89.
475 *Apotex v United States*, Award, 25 August 2014.
476 At para 8.15.
477 *Clayton/Bilcon v Canada*, Award on Jurisdiction and Liability, 17 March 2015, para 695.
478 At para 705.
479 *SD Myers v Canada*, Partial Award, 13 November 2000, para 254; *Merrill & Ring v Canada*, Award, 31 March 2010, paras 79–80.
480 *Daimler v Argentina*, Award, 22 August 2012.

> beyond dispute is that 'treatment' deals with the actual behavior of the Host States towards a foreign private investment as measured against the international obligations binding upon the State on the basis of treaty law and general international law.[481]

Under most national treatment clauses, the treatment of foreign investors must be 'no less favourable' than that of their domestic counterparts. This leaves the possibility that national law may be more favourable for the foreign investor. Hence, a positive differentiation remains permissible and will even be obligatory if the minimum standard under international law is higher than the one applied to nationals.

Several questions arise with regard to the existence of a differentiation. Must the host State give a foreign investor the most favourable treatment given to any national comparator, or treatment no less favourable than the average domestic investor or even only the least favourably treated domestic investor?[482] Most investment protection treaties do not address this question and the case law of tribunals also does not provide a general answer. NAFTA tribunals have accepted that it is enough to prove that the foreign investor was treated less favourably than a single domestic investor who was in like circumstances.[483]

Some tribunals have distinguished between *de jure* and *de facto* discrimination, sometimes also referred to as direct and indirect discrimination.[484] The difference between the two is usually the degree to which the discriminatory treatment is evident. *De jure* or direct discrimination refers to discriminatory treatment that is openly linked to (foreign) nationality, whereas *de facto* or indirect discrimination indicates treatment that disadvantages foreign investors as a matter of fact even though it may be neutral on its face.

In *Archer Daniels Midland v Mexico*,[485] the Tribunal endorsed this view and defined these two forms of discrimination as follows:

> The national treatment obligation under Article 1102 is an application of the general prohibition of discrimination based on nationality, including both *de jure* and *de facto* discrimination. The former refers to measures that on their face treat entities differently, whereas the latter includes measures which are neutral on their face but which result in differential treatment.[486]

[481] At para 218. See also *Apotex v United States*, Award, 25 August 2014, paras 8.11–8.14.

[482] *Feldman v Mexico*, Award, 16 December 2002, para 185. See also AK Bjorklund, 'National Treatment' in A Reinisch (ed) *Standards of Investment Protection* (2009) 29, 54.

[483] *Pope & Talbot v Canada*, Award of the Merits of Phase 2, 10 April 2001, para 41; *Archer Daniels Midland v Mexico*, Award, 21 November 2007, para 205.

[484] *ADF v United States*, Award, 9 January 2003, para 157; *Parkerings v Lithuania*, Award, 11 September 2007, para 368; *Corn Products v Mexico*, Decision on Responsibility, 15 January 2008, para 115; *Casinos Austria v Argentina*, Decision on Jurisdiction, 29 June 2018, para 249.

[485] *Archer Daniels Midland v Mexico*, Award, 21 November 2007.

[486] At para 193.

The same view was expressed by the Tribunal in *Alpha v Ukraine*:[487]

> Such discrimination could arise *de jure* if there is a government measure such as a law or regulation that explicitly discriminates between domestic and foreign investors, or *de facto* if the measure is not explicitly or inherently discriminatory but discriminates between domestic and foreign investors in the way in which it is applied.[488]

The references to 'national treatment' and to 'investors of the other Contracting State' indicate that these clauses prohibit discrimination based on nationality. This leaves open the question whether they apply to differentiations that are not nationality-based but are still unjustifiable on rational grounds.[489] The Tribunal in *Feldman v Mexico*[490] seemed to think that it was sufficient to produce proof of discrimination and not necessary to show discrimination based on nationality. The Tribunal said:

> it is not self-evident, as the Respondent argues, that any departure from national treatment must be *explicitly* shown to be a result of the investor's nationality. There is no such language in Article 1102. Rather, Article 1102 by its terms suggests that it is sufficient to show less favorable treatment for the foreign investor than for domestic investors in like circumstances... For practical as well as legal reasons, the Tribunal is prepared to assume that the differential treatment is a result of the Claimant's nationality, at least in the absence of any evidence to the contrary.[491]

Similarly, the Tribunal in *Thunderbird v Mexico*[492] indicated that it was not necessary for the claimant to show separately that the discrimination was motivated by nationality. The fact of less favourable treatment was enough. The Tribunal said:

> It is not expected from Thunderbird that it show *separately* that the less favourable treatment was motivated because of nationality. The text of Article 1102 of the NAFTA does not require such showing. Rather, the text contemplates the case where a foreign investor is treated less favourably than a national investor. That case is to be proven by a foreign investor, and, additionally, the reason why there was a less favourable treatment.[493]

[487] *Alpha v Ukraine*, Award, 8 November 2010.

[488] At para 426.

[489] *Pope & Talbot v Canada*, Award on the Merits of Phase 2, 10 April 2001, para 79; *Occidental Exploration v Ecuador*, Final Award, 1 July 2004, para 177; *Merrill & Ring v Canada*, Award, 31 March 2010, para 94.

[490] *Feldman v Mexico*, Award, 16 December 2002.

[491] At para 181. Italics original.

[492] *Thunderbird v Mexico*, Arbitral Award, 26 January 2006.

[493] At para 177. Underlining original.

On the other hand, a purely incidental differentiation resulting from misguided policy decisions does not suffice to show discrimination.[494] Also, a differentiation need not violate domestic law to be contrary to the national treatment standard. The Tribunal in *Lauder v Czech Republic*[495] said in this respect:

> For a measure to be discriminatory, it does not need to violate domestic law, since domestic law can contain a provision that is discriminatory towards foreign investment, or can lack a provision prohibiting the discrimination of foreign investment.[496]

(d) Is there a justification for the differentiation?

The third part of an investigation into an alleged violation of a national treatment clause pertains to the justification for a differentiating measure. Although most investment treaties do not explicitly say so, it is widely accepted that differentiations are justifiable if rational grounds are shown. However, a precise definition of these grounds has remained elusive. Furthermore, the case law is not uniform on whether the pursuit of some rational policy by the government to justify the differential treatment is sufficient[497] or whether the State must use the least interfering means with investor rights if there are several alternative ways to achieve its policy goals.[498]

Some tribunals have merged the justification test with their analysis of whether the foreign investor was in 'like circumstances' with the domestic comparator.[499] This conflates the question whether two entities are comparable for the purpose of the national treatment standard with the question whether a difference in treatment is justified by a rational government policy. For reasons of clarity, judicial rigour, and transparency it is better to keep the three steps of analysis (like circumstances, less favourable treatment, justification) apart. This allows States and investors to anticipate more effectively which differentiations are accepted as justified by tribunals.

National policies in favour of the domestic public interest can, under certain circumstances, constitute a rational ground for according less than national treatment. However, which specific grounds may be argued in this regard is unclear.[500]

494 *GAMI v Mexico*, Final Award, 15 November 2004, para 114.

495 *Lauder v Czech Republic*, Final Award, 3 September 2001.

496 At para 220.

497 *GAMI v Mexico*, Final Award, 15 November 2004, para 114.

498 *SD Myers v Canada*, Partial Award, 13 November 2000, para 221.

499 *SD Myers v Canada*, Partial Award, 13 November 2000, para 250; *Pope & Talbot v Canada*, Award on Merits of Phase 2, 10 April 2001, para 78; *Feldman v Mexico*, Award, 16 December 2002, para 170; *Apotex v United States*, Award, 25 August 2014, para 8.55.

500 See already the PCIJ in the *Oscar Chinn Case (UK v Belgium)*, Judgment, 12 December 1934, PCIJ, Series A/B, No 63.

Tribunals have accepted a variety of circumstances as legitimizing differential treatment. In *SD Myers v Canada*, the Tribunal seems to have assumed that subsidies are allowed to promote national policies.[501] In *GAMI v Mexico*, the Tribunal found that the solvency of an important local industry, in this case sugar, was a legitimate policy goal.[502] In *ADF v United States*, the Tribunal found no violation of the national treatment standard in a US requirement to use locally produced steel for government projects, if it was applied equally to national and foreign contractors.[503]

In *Clayton/Bilcon v Canada*, the respondent had applied different environmental impact tests to comparable projects. The Tribunal found that the host State must pursue a reasonable and non-discriminatory policy and decided that there was no rational government policy for applying the different standards.[504]

In *Rusoro v Venezuela*,[505] the Tribunal decided that it was justified to differentiate between small-scale miners and large mining companies. It did not, however, distinguish between the 'in like circumstances' test and the 'justification' analysis and stated:

> The Bolivarian Republic has adopted an official policy, differentiating between small scale, traditional miners and large mining companies and offering additional support and less stringent requirements to small miners. Thus Rusoro (and other large miners) and small scale miners are not 'in like circumstances', and the difference in treatment is justified by valid policy reasons.
>
> The Tribunal finds that the distinct treatment given to small scale miners in the 2010 Measures does not result in a breach of Art. IV.1 of the BIT.[506]

One factor in deciding on the legality of differential treatment might be whether the policy in the specific case is lawful under other relevant rules of international law. Some States promote domestic entities based on cultural policies by way of subsidies.[507] The UNESCO Convention on the Protection and Promotion of the Diversity of Cultural Expressions, may justify such a differentiation.[508]

In *Thunderbird v Mexico*, the Tribunal held in an *obiter dictum* that no claim to national treatment could be made if the conduct of the investor was illegal under national law, in this case gambling. This applied even if that national law was not

[501] *SD Myers v Canada*, Partial Award, 13 November 2000, para 255: 'CANADA's right to source all government requirements and to grant subsidies to the Canadian industry are but two examples of legitimate alternative measures.'

[502] *GAMI v Mexico*, Final Award, 15 November 2004, para 114.

[503] *ADF v United States*, Award, 9 January 2003, paras 156–158.

[504] *Clayton/Bilcon v Canada*, Award on Jurisdiction and Liability, 17 March 2015, paras 724–725.

[505] *Rusoro v Venezuela*, Award, 22 August 2016.

[506] At paras 563, 564.

[507] See *UPS v Canada*, Award on the Merits, 24 May 2007, para 156.

[508] Article 20 of the Convention on the Protection and Promotion of the Diversity of Cultural Expressions, 20 October 2005.

uniformly enforced.[509] Hence, no 'equality in injustice' can be claimed by a foreign investor under this standard.

(e) The relevance of discriminatory intent

Most tribunals do not require proof of discriminatory intent for the finding of a violation of a national treatment provision. The Tribunal in *SD Myers v Canada*[510] looked at the practical impact of a government measure rather than for any intent on the part of the host government to favour its national and said:

> Intent is important, but protectionist intent is not necessarily decisive on its own. The existence of an intent to favour nationals over non-nationals would not give rise to a breach of [Article] 1102 of the NAFTA if the measure in question were to produce no adverse effect on the non-national complainant. The word 'treatment' suggests that practical impact is required to produce a breach of Article 1102, not merely a motive or intent that is in violation of Chapter 11.[511]

Other tribunals have similarly held that an intent to discriminate was not decisive and that what mattered was the impact or result of the measure.[512]

On the other hand, there are some tribunals whose findings concerning the requirement of intent are ambiguous. The Tribunal in *Genin v Estonia* seemed to require a discriminatory intent as a necessary prerequisite for a finding of discrimination.[513] *Methanex v United States* also includes language that may be understood to require evidence of intent to discriminate.[514] The same is true for *Electrabel v Hungary*.[515]

[509] *Thunderbird v Mexico*, Arbitral Award, 26 January 2006, para 183.

[510] *SD Myers v Canada*, Partial Award, 13 November 2000.

[511] At para 254.

[512] *Feldman v Mexico*, Award, 16 December 2002, para 181; *RFCC v Morocco*, Award, 22 December 2003, para 74; *Occidental Exploration v Ecuador*, Final Award, 1 July 2004, para 177; *Siemens v Argentina*, Award, 6 February 2007, para 321; *Parkerings v Lithuania*, Award, 11 September 2007, para 368; *Corn Products v Mexico*, Decision on Responsibility, 15 January 2008, para 138; *Cargill v Poland*, Final Award, 29 February 2008, para 345; *Bayindir v Pakistan*, Award, 27 August 2009, para 390; *Clayton/Bilcon v Canada*, Award on Jurisdiction and Liability, 17 March 2015, para 719.

[513] *Genin v Estonia*, Award, 25 June 2001, para 369.

[514] *Methanex v United States*, Final Award, 3 August 2005, IV, B, para 12: 'In order to sustain its claim under Article 1102(3), Methanex must demonstrate, cumulatively, that California intended to favour domestic investors by discriminating against foreign investors and that Methanex and the domestic investor supposedly being favored by California are in like circumstances.' But in para 1 of the same chapter the Tribunal says: 'an affirmative finding under NAFTA Article 1102 … does not require the demonstration of the malign intent alleged by Methanex.'

[515] *Electrabel v Hungary*, Decision on Jurisdiction, Applicable Law and Liability, 30 November 2012, para 7.163: 'There is no factual evidence that any relevant conduct by MVM, HEO or the Hungarian Government (including its ministers) was ever motivated by national or other discrimination within the terms of Article 10(7) ECT.'

(f) The relevance of WTO case law

On the significance of World Trade Organization (WTO) law and its jurisprudence for the interpretation of investment treaties, earlier NAFTA decisions in *SD Myers*,[516] *Pope & Talbot*,[517] and *Feldman*[518] seemed to assume that the relevant WTO jurisprudence was indeed suitable to guide tribunals. Meanwhile, the tide seems to have turned against relying on WTO jurisprudence in the interpretation and application of the national treatment standard in investment treaties.

The departure from the original approach started in 2004 when the Tribunal in *Occidental Exploration v Ecuador*[519] rejected the argument that WTO jurisprudence should be applied to the BIT between Ecuador and the United States. It noted that the WTO is concerned with 'like products', but the BIT addressed 'like situations', and added that the WTO policies concerning competitive and substitutable goods could not be treated in the same way as the BIT policies concerning 'like situations'.[520]

The decisive turnaround came with the *Methanex* ruling and its detailed clause-by-clause analysis of the various parts of the NAFTA as compared to the language in WTO law.[521] The Tribunal pointed out that the NAFTA rules use different language in different parts. In part, the language is the same as that used in the WTO, but not so in Chapter Eleven dealing with foreign investment. The conclusion in *Methanex* was that the NAFTA parties were aware of the difference in language, and that in Chapter Eleven of the NAFTA the parties deliberately referred to 'like circumstances' as opposed to 'like goods'. Thus, the *Methanex* Tribunal ruled that 'like circumstances' in the context of a foreign investment cannot be considered to be identical with the concept of 'like goods' and that, therefore, the NAFTA investment provisions had to be interpreted autonomously, independent from trade law considerations.[522]

Other tribunals have adopted the same approach and have refused to transfer GATT/WTO law concerning 'like products' to investment law concerning 'like circumstances'.[523] Nevertheless, *Corn Products v Mexico*[524] suggests that the

[516] *SD Myers v Canada*, Partial Award, 13 November 2000, paras 244–247.

[517] *Pope & Talbot v Canada*, Award on Merits, 10 April 2001, paras 45–63, 68–69.

[518] *Feldman v Mexico*, Award, 16 December 2002, para 165.

[519] *Occidental Exploration v Ecuador*, Final Award, 1 July 2004.

[520] At paras 153–155, 174–176. At para 175 the Tribunal found that the purpose of national treatment was rather the opposite of that under GATT/WTO: 'it [the national treatment] is to avoid exporters being placed at a disadvantage in foreign markets because of the indirect taxes paid in the country of origin, while in GATT/WTO the purpose is to avoid imported products being affected by a distortion of competition with similar domestic products because of taxes and other regulations in the country of destination'.

[521] *Methanex v United States*, Final Award, 3 August 2005, IV, B, paras 25–37.

[522] At paras 35, 37.

[523] *Bayindir v Pakistan*, Award, 27 August 2009, para 389; *Cargill v Mexico*, Award, 18 September 2009, para 193; *Merrill & Ring v Canada*, Award, 31 March 2010, paras 86–87; *Clayton/Bilcon v Canada*, Award on Jurisdiction and Liability, 17 March 2015, para 692.

[524] *Corn Products v Mexico*, Decision on Responsibility, 15 January 2008, para 122.

determination of a 'like product' under the GATT rules and the investment provision of Article 1102 of the NAFTA are closely linked. Similarly, the Tribunal in *Cargill v Poland* referred to WTO case law to argue that there is no precise and final definition of 'like'.[525]

Therefore, although there is no complete departure from GATT/WTO law, there is a clear trend in the case law of investment tribunals to interpret 'like circumstances' or 'like situations' autonomously.

(g) Burden of proof

In general, tribunals have imposed upon the claimant the burden of proving the existence of like circumstances and of discrimination.[526] On the other hand, respondents had to prove their affirmative defences, notably the existence of a justification for the differentiation.[527]

5. Most-favoured-nation treatment

ADDITIONAL READING: P Acconci, 'Most-Favoured Nation Treatment and International Law on Foreign Investment' in P Muchlinski et al (eds) *The Oxford Handbook of International Investment Law* (2008) 363; W Ben Hamida, 'MFN Clauses and Procedural Rights' in T Weiler (ed) *Investment Treaty Arbitration and International Law*, vol 1 (2008) 231; AR Ziegler, 'Most-Favoured-Nation (MFN) Treatment' in A Reinisch (ed) *Standards of Investment Protection* (2008) 59; K Hobér, 'MFN Clauses and Dispute Resolution in Investment Treaties' in C Binder et al (eds) *International Investment Law for the 21st Century* (2009) 31; SW Schill, *The Multilateralization of International Investment Law* (2009); GS Tawil, 'Most Favoured Nation Clauses and Jurisdictional Clauses in Investment Treaty Arbitration' in C Binder et al (eds) *International Investment Law for the 21st Century* (2009) 9; Z Douglas, 'The MFN Clause in Investment Arbitration' (2011) 2 *JIDS* 97; M Paparinskis, 'MFN Clauses and International Dispute Settlement' (2011) 26 *ICSID Rev* 14; C Greenwood, 'Reflections on "Most Favoured Nation"

[525] *Cargill v Poland*, Final Award, 5 March 2008, para 311.

[526] *ADF v United States*, Award, 9 January 2003, para 157; *Tecmed v Mexico*, Award, 29 May 2003, para 181; *Thunderbird v Mexico*, Arbitral Award, 26 January 2006, para 176; *UPS v Canada*, Award on the Merits, 24 May 2007, para 84; *Alpha v Ukraine*, Award, 8 November 2010, para 428; *Total v Argentina*, Decision on Liability, 27 December 2010, para 212; *Anglo American v Venezuela*, Award, 18 January 2019, paras 495–501.

[527] *Feldman v Mexico*, Award, 16 December 2002, para 177; *Nykomb v Latvia*, Arbitral Award, 16 December 2003, p 34; *Apotex v United States*, Award, 25 August 2014, paras 8.6–8.10; *Clayton/Bilcon v Canada*, Award on Jurisdiction and Liability, 17 March 2015, paras 717–724; *Al Tamimi v Oman*, Award, 3 November 2015, para 457; *Mercer v Canada*, Award, 6 March 2018, paras 7.15–7.16; *Olin v Libya*, Award, 25 May 2018, paras 203, 217.

Clauses in Bilateral Investment Treaties' in DD Caron et al (eds) *Practising Virtue: Inside International Arbitration* (2015) 556; A Reinisch, 'Most Favoured Nation Treatment' in M Bungenberg et al (eds) *International Investment Law* (2015) 807; C Titi, 'Most-Favoured-Nation Treatment' (2016) 33 *J Int Arb* 425; S Batifort and JB Heath, 'The New Debate on the Interpretation of MFN Clauses in Investment Treaties' (2017) 111 *AJIL* 873; P Dumberry, 'The Importation of the FET Standard through MFN Clauses' (2017) 32 *ICSID Rev* 116; NJ Calamita and E Zelazna, 'Most-Favoured-Nation Clauses and the Centrality and Limits of General Principles' in A Gattini et al (eds) *General Principles of Law and International Investment Arbitration* (2018) 398; A Cohen Smutny et al, 'The MFN Clause and its Evolving Boundaries', in K Yannaca-Small (ed) *Arbitration under International Investment Agreements* (2018) Ch 23; A Reinisch and C Schreuer, *International Protection of Investments* (2020) 680.

(a) Introduction

Customary international law does not require equal treatment of investors of different nationalities. To remedy inequalities, almost all BITs and most other treaties for the protection of investments contain most-favoured-nation (MFN) clauses. The idea of an MFN clause is to avoid discrimination by ensuring that the State Parties to the treaty treat each other and their nationals at least as favourably as they treat third States and their nationals. The more favourable treatment of other States and their nationals may result from mere practice or from treaty obligations. In international investment law, most cases involving MFN clauses concern situations in which an investor invokes benefits granted in treaties of the host State with third States ('third party treaties').

An MFN clause contained in a treaty (called the 'basic treaty'), will extend the better treatment granted to a third State or its nationals to a beneficiary of the MFN clause. This means not only that discrimination based on nationality in comparison to nationals of third States is prohibited. It also means that the beneficiary of the MFN clause is entitled to rely on treaties that the host State has concluded with third States and that would not be applicable otherwise.

MFN clauses have a multilateralizing effect. MFN treatment ensures that investors automatically receive the most favourable treatment extended by a host State to any third-State investor. The purpose of MFN clauses in investment treaties is the creation of a level playing field for investors by avoiding distortion of competition through differentiated treatment.[528] In *National Grid v Argentina*,[529] the Tribunal expressed this aim in the following terms:

[528] *Telefónica v Argentina*, Decision on Jurisdiction, 25 May 2006, para 98: 'An MFN clause is aimed at ensuring equality of treatment to the beneficiaries in respect of its subject matter at the most advantageous level.'

[529] *National Grid v Argentina*, Decision on Jurisdiction, 20 June 2006.

> The MFN clause is an important element to ensure that foreign investors are treated on a basis of parity with other foreign investors ... when they invest abroad.[530]

An MFN clause creates a standard that is relative and dynamic. This means that its effect depends on the treaty relations of the host State which may develop over time. If the host State does not grant any relevant benefit to a third State and its nationals, the clause will be without practical significance. However, as soon as the host State does confer a relevant benefit to a third State and its investors, that benefit is automatically extended to the beneficiary of the MFN clause.

The traditional significance of MFN treatment in economic relations has led to the inclusion of MFN clauses in international economic treaties for centuries. It is the core standard for the liberalization of international trade. Article I of the GATT, which contains a general MFN clause, is the cornerstones of the entire regime.

(b) The *ejusdem generis* rule

The application of an MFN clause is subject to the *ejusdem generis* rule. The *ejusdem generis* rule states that benefits from a generally worded MFN clause will accrue only within the subject-matter covered by the basic treaty.[531] If the matters covered by the basic treaty and the matters invoked in the third-party treaty are *ejusdem generis* (of the same kind), the MFN clause will apply. If the benefit to be derived from the third-party treaty relates to issues different from the subject-matter of the basic treaty, the MFN clause will not apply. Therefore, an MFN clause in an investment treaty will not attract provisions from a consular or an extradition treaty.

The Commentary to the International Law Commission's Report on The Most-Favoured-Nation Clause of 1978 describes the *ejusdem generis* rule in the following terms:

> a clause conferring most-favoured-nation rights in respect of a certain matter, or class of matter, can attract the rights conferred by other treaties ... only in regard to the same matter or class of matter.[532]

The 'same subject-matter' requirement of the *ejusdem generis* rule is satisfied if both treaties relate to the protection of foreign investments. The Tribunal in *Maffezini v Spain*[533] described the *ejusdem generis* principle as follows:

[530] At para 92.

[531] For a detailed exposition of this principle see the work of the International Law Commission on this topic at YBILC 1978 II, 27.

[532] Article 9(1) of the ILC Draft Articles on Most-Favoured-Nation Clauses (1978).

[533] *Maffezini v Spain*, Decision on Jurisdiction, 25 January 2000.

> if a third-party treaty contains provisions for the settlement of disputes that are more favorable to the protection of the investor's rights and interests than those in the basic treaty, such provisions may be extended to the beneficiary of the most favored nation clause as they are fully compatible with the *ejusdem generis* principle. Of course, the third-party treaty has to relate to the same subject matter as the basic treaty, be it the protection of foreign investments or the promotion of trade, since the dispute settlement provisions will operate in the context of these matters;[534]

(c) The scope of MFN clauses

The application of an MFN clause presupposes the applicability of the treaty containing it. To be applicable, BITs and other investment treaties require the existence of an admitted investor and a covered investment. Therefore, an MFN clause cannot be used to expand the category of 'investor' and 'investment' as defined in the treaty.[535]

The Tribunal in *Metal-Tech v Uzbekistan*[536] said in this respect:

> As a general matter, the Tribunal notes that, ordinarily, an MFN clause cannot be used to import a more favorable definition of investment contained in another BIT. The reason is that the defined terms 'investments' and 'investors' are used in the MFN clause itself, so that the treatment assured to investments and investors by Article 3 necessarily refers to investments and investors as defined in Article 1 of the BIT. In other words, one must fall within the scope of the treaty, which is in particular circumscribed by the definition of investment and investors, to be entitled to invoke the treaty protections, of which MFN treatment forms part. Or, in fewer words, one must be under the treaty to claim *through* the treaty.[537]

An MFN clause is not a rule of interpretation. It does not just come into play where the wording of the basic treaty leaves room for doubt. An MFN clause endows its beneficiary with rights that are additional to the rights contained in the basic treaty.

[534] At para 56. See also *Suez and InterAgua v Argentina*, Decision on Jurisdiction, 16 May 2006, para 57.

[535] *Berschader v Russia*, Award, 21 April 2006, para 188; *Société Générale v Dominican Republic*, Award on Preliminary Objections to Jurisdiction, 19 September 2008, paras 40–41; *HICEE v Slovakia*, Partial Award, 23 May 2011, paras 148–149; *Vannessa v Venezuela*, Award, 16 January 2013, para 133; *Rizvi v Indonesia*, Award on Jurisdiction, 16 July 2013, paras 200–228; *ST-AD v Bulgaria*, Award on Jurisdiction, 18 July 2013, para 397; *Nova Scotia Power v Venezuela*, Award, 30 April 2014, para 150; *Krederi v Ukraine*, Award, 2 July 2018, para 295; *Itisaluna v Iraq*, Award, 3 April 2020, para 150.

[536] *Metal-Tech v Uzbekistan*, Award, 4 October 2013, paras 132–163.

[537] At para 145. Italics original.

Whoever is entitled to rely on an MFN clause will be granted rights accruing from a third-party treaty even if these rights go beyond the basic treaty.

The final report of the ILC Study Group on the Most-Favoured-Nation clause described the function of an MFN clause as follows:

> this is at the very core of what MFN is about: it seeks to provide something better than what the beneficiary would otherwise receive under the basic treaty. On that basis, it would seem inevitable that if the basic treaty provides for a certain kind of treatment, the consequence of the application of an MFN clause is that the treaty provision in the basic treaty would be overridden.[538]

Opponents of a wide application of MFN clauses point out that investment treaties are the result of specific negotiations. The application of MFN clauses may lead to the replacement of the negotiated substance of these treaties. Under such circumstances, the question arises whether and to what extent the MFN rule is meant to alter specific arrangements and to import a regime from another treaty.

The rules of interpretation laid down in the VCLT apply also to MFN clauses.[539] Thus, the primary task is to identify the ordinary meaning of the clause in its context and in the light of the treaty's object and purpose.

A focus on the intention of the parties that would be reflected in the basic treaty's substantive provisions is unconvincing. The intentions of the parties are relevant to the extent that they find expression in the treaty's text.[540] The treaty's text includes the MFN clause and there is no good reason why the parties' intention should be reflected in the basic treaty's substantive provisions rather than in its MFN clause.

(d) Variations of MFN clauses

The wording of MFN clauses varies, and each clause must be interpreted and applied on its own terms.[541] In many treaties, the MFN clause is combined with a national treatment clause. For instance, the ECT provides:

[538] International Law Commission, Final report of the Study Group on the Most-Favoured-Nation clause, Doc A/CN.4/L.852, 29 May 2015, para 115.

[539] *National Grid v Argentina*, Decision on Jurisdiction, 20 June 2006, para 80.

[540] *Garanti Koza v Turkmenistan*, Decision on the Objection to Jurisdiction for Lack of Consent, 3 July 2013, para 57: 'The best indication of the intentions of the State parties to the U.K.–Turkmenistan BIT is the text of the treaty they signed.' See also *Wintershall v Argentina*, Award, 8 December 2008, paras 78, 88; *El Paso v Argentina*, Award, 31 October 2011, para 590.

[541] *Tza Yap Shum v Peru*, Decision on Jurisdiction and Competence, 19 June 2009, para 198: 'Each MFN clause is a world in itself, which demands an individualised interpretation to determine its scope of application.'

> Each Contracting Party shall accord to Investments in its Area of Investors of other Contracting Parties, and their related activities including management, maintenance, use, enjoyment or disposal, treatment no less favourable than that which it accords to Investments of its own Investors or of the Investors of any other Contracting Party or any third state and their related activities including management, maintenance, use, enjoyment or disposal, whichever is the most favourable.[542]

Other versions of MFN clauses do not refer to the same 'treatment', but to 'all matters subject to this agreement'.[543] Some MFN clauses are restricted to a specific standard like FET.[544] Some MFN clauses, like those in many BITs of the United Kingdom, list the Articles to which MFN treatment is meant to apply.[545]

Many MFN clauses contain exceptions. Typical exceptions relate to regional economic integration organisations and to tax agreements.[546] Some tribunals have concluded that, under the principle *expressio unius est exclusio alterius*, this means that all matters not falling under an exception must be covered by the MFN clause. The presence of a defined list of exceptions means that other unlisted issues are not excluded.[547]

The application of MFN clauses to dispute settlement is highly contested.[548] Some treaties specify that their MFN clauses exclude[549] or include[550] dispute settlement.

Most MFN clauses relate only to the post-establishment phase. Some treaties, however, especially those of the United States and Canada, extend MFN treatment to the pre-establishment (pre-entry) phase, by including the word 'establishment' among the matters covered by the MFN clause.[551]

542 ECT Article 10(7).

543 See eg Spain–Argentina BIT (1991) Article IV(2).

544 See *Paushok v Mongolia*, Award on Jurisdiction and Liability, 28 April 2011, para 570.

545 United Kingdom Model Investment Promotion and Protection Agreement (IPPA 2008) Article 3(3).

546 Argentina–Germany BIT (1991) Article 3(4).

547 *MTD v Chile*, Award, 25 May 2004, para 104; *Siemens v Argentina*, Decision on Jurisdiction, 3 August 2004, para 85; *Gas Natural v Argentina*, Decision on Jurisdiction, 17 June 2005, para 30; *Suez and InterAgua v Argentina*, Decision on Jurisdiction, 16 May 2006, para 56; *National Grid v Argentina*, Decision on Jurisdiction, 20 June 2006, para 82; *RosInvest v Russian Federation*, Award on Jurisdiction, 5 October 2007, para 135; *Hochtief v Argentina*, Decision on Jurisdiction, 24 October 2011, para 74.

548 See XII.9 below.

549 See CETA, Article 8.7.(4).

550 Austrian Model BIT Article 3(3); Austria–Kazakhstan BIT (2010) Article 3(3).

551 See VI.5(b) above.

(e) MFN and substantive rights

Although the application of MFN clauses to dispute settlement is highly controversial, it is widely accepted that investors may rely on MFN clauses to claim a better substantive treatment accorded by a host State to investors of third States.[552] There is ample practice to demonstrate that tribunals have allowed the importation, by operation of an MFN clause, of substantive standards of protection not contained in the basic treaty.[553] The Tribunal in *Berschader v Russian Federation*[554] found that:

> [i]t is universally agreed that the very essence of an MFN provision in a BIT is to afford to investors all material protection provided by subsequent treaties....[555]

Not all treaties offer all the typical standards of treatment like compensation for expropriation, FET, FPS, national treatment, protection against arbitrary or discriminatory measures, umbrella clauses, and transfer clauses. Where some of these substantive standards were missing in the basic treaty or were expressed in narrower terms, claimants have successfully resorted to MFN clauses in the respective treaties to rely on the wider protection in other treaties.

For instance, where the assurance of FET was missing from the basic treaty, tribunals have imported it with the help of an MFN clause.[556] In *ATA v Jordan*,[557] the Tribunal permitted the claimant to invoke a breach of FET although the applicable Jordan–Turkey BIT did not contain such a clause. The Tribunal noted:

> by virtue of Article II(2) of the Treaty (the 'MFN' clause), the Respondent has assumed the obligation to accord to the Claimant's investment fair and equitable treatment (see the UK–Jordan BIT) and treatment no less favourable than that required by international law (see the Spain–Jordan BIT).[558]

Other standards of treatment, not contained in the basic treaty, were also made applicable with the help of an MFN clause.[559] In *Tatneft v Ukraine*,[560] the Tribunal

[552] See, however, CETA, Article 8.7 which seems to exclude the use of the MFN clause to import substantive standards from other treaties.

[553] DD Caron and E Shirlow, 'Most-Favored-Nation Treatment: Substantive Protection' in M Kinnear et al (eds) *Building International Investment Law* (2016) 399, 400; P Dumberry, 'The Importation of the FET Standard through MFN Clauses: An Empirical Study of BITs' (2017) 32 *ICSID Rev* 116.

[554] *Berschader v Russian Federation*, Award, 21 April 2006.

[555] At para 179.

[556] *Bayindir v Pakistan*, Award, 27 August 2009, paras 155, 157; *Rumeli v Kazakhstan*, Award, 29 July 2008, para 575; *LESI & ASTALDI v Algeria*, Award, 12 November 2008, para 151; *Paushok v Mongolia*, Award, 28 April 2011, paras 242, 246, 254, 307, 562–572; *Al-Warraq v Indonesia*, Final Award, 15 December 2014, paras 541, 555.

[557] *ATA v Jordan*, Award, 18 May 2010.

[558] At para 125, footnote 16.

[559] *Micula v Romania II*, Award, 5 March 2020, paras 439–443, 446.

[560] *Tatneft v Ukraine*, Award, 29 July 2014.

permitted the importation not only of FET but also of the full protection and security standard by way of an MFN clause.[561] In *Devas v India*,[562] the Tribunal affirmed 'the possibility of importing the full protection and security clause of a third-party treaty'.[563]

MFN clauses have also been invoked in the context of defining the standard of compensation for expropriation. In *CME v Czech Republic*,[564] the applicable BIT provided for 'just compensation' representing the 'genuine value of the investment affected'. In its award, the Tribunal relied on the MFN clause to rule that the compensation should represent the 'fair market value' of the investment:

> The determination of compensation under the Treaty between the Netherlands and the Czech Republic on basis of the 'fair market value' finds further support in the 'most favored nation' provision of Art. 3(5) of the Treaty … The bilateral investment treaty between the United States of America and the Czech Republic provides that compensation shall be equivalent to the fair market value of the expropriated investment immediately before the expropriatory action was taken … The Czech Republic therefore is obligated to provide no less than 'fair market value' to Claimant in respect of its investment, should (in contrast to this Tribunal's opinion) 'just compensation' representing the 'genuine value' be interpreted to be less than 'fair market value.'[565]

There is also case authority to support the importation of an umbrella clause, that is absent in the basic treaty, by way of an MFN clause.[566] In *Arif v Moldova*,[567] the Tribunal accepted that an umbrella clause was one of the 'substantive obligations' to which the MFN clause applied. The Tribunal stated:

> Both Parties agree that an MFN clause applies to substantive obligations. The MFN clause in Article 4 is broadly drafted and does not restrict its application to any particular kind of substantive obligation under the BIT. Therefore, the Tribunal finds that the MFN clause of the BIT can import an 'umbrella' clause (which is substantive in nature), from either the Moldova–UK or Moldova–USA BIT, thereby extending the more favourable standard of protection granted by the 'umbrella' clause in either one of these BIT's into the BIT at hand. Respondent's

561 At para 365.
562 *Devas v India*, Award on Jurisdiction and Merits, 25 July 2016.
563 At para 496.
564 *CME v Czech Republic*, Final Award, 14 March 2003.
565 At para 500.
566 *Abaclat v Argentina*, Decision on Jurisdiction and Admissibility, 4 August 2011, para 317; *EDF v Argentina*, Award, 11 June 2012, para 937; *EDF v Argentina*, Decision on Annulment, 5 February 2016, para 237; *Consutel v Algeria*, Final Award, 3 February 2020, paras 356–359.
567 *Arif v Moldova*, Award, 8 April 2013.

> arguments to the contrary are rejected. The Tribunal therefore has jurisdiction over Claimant's 'specific commitments' claim via the MFN clause of Article 4.[568]

A seemingly innocuous reference in the MFN clause to all matters covered by the basic treaty may serve to exclude the importation of additional standards. In *Teinver v Argentina*,[569] the Spain–Argentina BIT contained an MFN clause that was subject to the limiting words 'in all matters governed by this Agreement'. The Tribunal held that this phrase amounted to a limitation to matters already governed by the BIT which excluded the importation of new standards from a more favourable treaty. The Tribunal said:

> In the Tribunal's view, in interpreting the scope of the MFN Clause contained in Article IV(2) of the Treaty, meaning must be given to the critical words '[i]n all matters governed by this Agreement'. According to Claimants, this language should be interpreted as referring generally to the protection of foreign investors. This interpretation is too broad and disregards the reference to all 'matters' governed by the Treaty. In the Tribunal's view, the plain and ordinary meaning of this language is to refer to the various rights or forms of protection contained in the individual provisions of the Treaty.[570]

In some cases, tribunals declined to apply an MFN clause because they found that the claimants were not in 'like circumstances' or in a 'similar situation'.[571]

6. The umbrella clause

ADDITIONAL READING: S Alexandrov, 'Breaches of Contract and Breaches of Treaty' (2004) 5 *JWIT* 555; A Sinclair, 'The Origins of the Umbrella Clause in the International Law of Investment Protection' (2004) 4 *Arbitration International* 411; T Wälde, 'The "Umbrella" Clause in Investment Arbitration' (2005) 6 *JWIT* 183; N Gallus, 'An Umbrella just for Two?' (2008) 24 *Arbitration International* 157; MC Gritón Salias, 'Do Umbrella Clauses Apply to Unilateral Undertakings?' in C Binder et al (eds) *International Investment Law for the 21st Century* (2009) 490; SW Schill, 'Umbrella Clauses as Public Law Concepts in Comparative Perspective' in SW Schill (ed) *International Investment Law and Comparative Public Law* (2010) 317; T Gazzini and A Tanzi, 'Handle with Care: Umbrella Clauses and MFN Treatment in Investment Arbitration' (2013) 14 *JWIT* 978; S Hamamoto, 'Parties to the

[568] At para 396.
[569] *Teinver v Argentina*, Award, 21 July 2017.
[570] At para 884.
[571] *Parkerings v Lithuania*, Award, 11 September 2007, paras 369, 396; *İçkale v Turkmenistan*, Award, 8 March 2016, paras 328–329; *Vento v Mexico*, Award, 6 July 2020, paras 240–265.

"Obligations" in the Obligations Observance ("Umbrella") Clause' (2015) 30 *ICSID Rev* 449; A Sinclair, 'Umbrella Clauses' in M Bungenberg et al (eds) *International Investment Law* (2015) 887; ME Footer, 'Umbrella Clauses and Widely-Formulated Arbitration Clauses' (2017) 16 *LPICT* 87; K Yannaca-Small, 'The Umbrella Clause' in K Yannaca-Small (ed) *Arbitration under International Investment Agreements*, 2nd edn (2018) 16.01; A Reinisch and C Schreuer, *International Protection of Investments* (2020) 855.

(a) Meaning and origin

An umbrella clause is a provision in an investment protection treaty that guarantees the observance of obligations assumed by the host State vis-à-vis the investor. These clauses are referred to as 'umbrella clauses' because they bring contractual and other commitments under the treaty's protective umbrella. At times, they are also referred to as 'observance of undertakings clauses'. The most contentious issue in relation to clauses of this kind is whether, and in what circumstances, they place contracts between the host State and the investor under the treaty's protection.

A typical umbrella clause is Article 2(2) of the British Model Treaty:

> Each Contracting Party shall observe any obligation it may have entered into with regard to investments of nationals or companies of the other Contracting Party.

The German Model Treaty contains a similar clause in Article 8(2). Many, but by no means all, BITs contain clauses of this kind. The ECT offers such a clause in Article 10(1),[572] but the NAFTA and its successor treaty the USMCA as well as the CETA and the texts of other investment Chapters in FTAs negotiated by the EU do not contain an umbrella clause.

The wording of umbrella clauses in investment treaties is not uniform. A general discussion must allow for the variation in language of these clauses and the resulting differences in interpretation. Some treaties follow the British model quoted above, whereas other treaties use more detailed wording. The investment protection treaty concluded between France and Hong Kong in 1995 states in Article III:

> Without prejudice to the provisions of this Agreement, each Contracting Party shall observe any particular obligation it may have entered into with regard to investments of investors of the other Contracting Party, including provisions more favourable than those of this Agreement.

[572] ECT Article 10(1), last sentence: 'Each Contracting Party shall observe any obligation it has entered into with an Investor or an Investment of an Investor of any other Contracting Party.'

A provision that addresses the future legal order of the host State is not an umbrella clause properly speaking:

> Each Contracting Party shall create and maintain in its territory a legal framework apt to guarantee to investors the continuity of legal treatment, including the compliance, in good faith, of all undertakings assumed with regard to each specific investor.[573]

Umbrella clauses are by no means of recent vintage. They arose in the context of the post-1945 controversies on whether State contracts were subject to the host State's domestic laws[574] or undertakings on the level of international law.[575] At that time, projects for large-scale foreign investments prompted the question whether guarantees given under the domestic law of the host State provided sufficient legal stability to justify the required expenditures for such projects.

As early as 1953, Sir Elihu Lauterpacht proposed an 'umbrella treaty' between Iran and the United Kingdom in the context of the Anglo-Iranian Oil Company dispute. He suggested that the contractual settlement between the Anglo-Iranian Oil Company and the National Iranian Oil Company and/or the Iranian Government should provide that a breach of the consortium agreement would also qualify simultaneously as a breach of treaty obligations between the United Kingdom and Iran.[576]

The BIT between Germany and Pakistan of 1959—the first modern investment treaty—already contained a clause of this kind. In 1959, the German government informed the German Parliament about the effect of an umbrella clause:

> The violation of such an obligation [of an investment agreement] accordingly will also amount to a violation of the international legal obligation contained in the present Treaty.[577]

[573] Italy–Jordan BIT (1996) Article 2(4). See *Salini v Jordan*, Decision on Jurisdiction, 29 November 2004, para 126.

[574] In 1929, the PCIJ ruled in the *Serbian Loans* case that '[a]ny contract which is not a contract between States in their capacity as subjects of international law is based on the municipal law of some country'. PCIJ, Judgment, 12 July 1929, No 14, Series A, No 20, 41; see also *Noble Ventures v Romania*, Award, 12 October 2005, para 53: 'The Tribunal recalls the well established rule of general international law that in normal circumstances *per se* a breach of a contract by the State does not give rise to direct international responsibility on the part of the State.'

[575] FA Mann, 'State Contracts and State Responsibility' (1960) 54 *AJIL* 572; R Jennings, 'State Contracts in International Law' (1961) 37 *BYIL* 156; S Schwebel, 'International Protection of Contractual Agreements' (1959) 53 *ASIL Proceedings* 273; A Verdross, 'Protection of Private Property under Quasi-International Agreements' (1959) 6 *Nederlands Tijdschrift voor Internationaal Recht* 355; C Hyde, 'Economic Development Agreements' (1962-I) 105 *Recueil* 267.

[576] A Sinclair, 'The Origins of the Umbrella Clause in the International Law of Investment Protection' (2004) 4 *Arbitr Int* 411, 415; Y Chernykh, 'The Gust of the Wind: The Unknown Role of Sir Elihu Lauterpacht in the Drafting of the Abs–Shawcross Draft Convention' in SW Schill et al (eds) *International Investment Law and History* (2018) 262.

[577] Translation by the authors. For the original German text, see J Alenfeld, *Die Investitionsförderungsverträge der Bundesrepublik Deutschland* (1971) 97, note 180.

Contract claims may be put under the protection of a treaty and be referred to international adjudication. Jennings and Watts make this point in *Oppenheim's International Law* in the following words:

> It is doubtful whether a breach by a state of its contractual obligations with aliens constitutes *per se* a breach of an international obligation, unless there is some such additional element as denial of justice, or expropriation, or breach of treaty, in which case it is that additional element which will constitute the basis for the state's international responsibility. However, either by virtue of a term in the contract itself or of an agreement between the state and the alien, or by virtue of an agreement between the state allegedly in breach of its contractual obligations and the state of which the alien is a national, disputes as to compliance with the terms of contracts may be referred to an internationally composed tribunal, applying, at least in part, international law.[578]

Umbrella clauses in treaties were seen as a bridge between private contractual arrangements, the domestic law of the host State, and public international law, allowing for more investor security. One effect of these clauses is to blur the distinction between investment arbitration and commercial arbitration.

Only in exceptional circumstances will breaches of contracts by States amount to expropriations.[579] Similarly, not every breach of contract is a violation of the FET standard.[580] Therefore, an umbrella clause is designed to close an important gap. An umbrella clause in a treaty protects a contract that an investor has entered into with the host State and is an expression of the maxim *pacta sunt servanda*. It follows that in the presence of an umbrella clause, a breach by the host country of an investment contract with the foreign investor constitutes a violation of the treaty and the investor can raise it in international arbitration. The existence, the content and a violation of the underlying obligation have to be established by reference to its proper law.[581]

Until 2003, the umbrella clause received little attention in academic discussion or arbitral practice, although treaties often contained such clauses. The few authors who drew attention to the clause essentially shared the view of the purpose of the clause as a means to elevate violations of investment contracts to the level of international law.[582] However, the arbitral decision in *SGS v Pakistan* in

578 R Jennings and A Watts, *Oppenheim's International Law*, vol 1 (9th ed 1996) 927. Footnotes omitted.

579 See VII.2 above.

580 See VIII.1(g)dd above.

581 *SGS v Philippines*, Decision on Jurisdiction, 29 January 2004, para 126; *Burlington v Ecuador*, Decision on Liability, 14 December 2012, para 214; *Micula v Romania I*, Award, 11 December 2013, para 418.

582 P Weil, 'Problèmes relatifs aux contrats passés entre un État et un particulier' (1969) 128 *Recueil* 130; FA Mann, 'British Treaties for the Promotion and Protection of Investments' (1981) 52 *BYIL* 241, 246; R Dolzer and M Stevens, *Bilateral Investment Treaties* (1995) 81; I Shihata, 'Applicable Law in

2003,[583] which departed fundamentally from the conventional understanding of the clause, put an end to this phase of unanimity. Ever since this ruling, the purpose, meaning, and scope of the clause have caused controversy leading to divergent lines of jurisprudence. The positions of tribunals and academic writers reach from elevating any breach of a promise by a host State to a treaty breach, to denying any effect to the clause, plus a number of intermediate positions. These intermediate positions would limit violations of the umbrella clause to contractual commitments, to commitments undertaken by the host State in its sovereign capacity, or to breaches committed in the exercise of sovereign authority.

(b) Effective application of umbrella clauses

One line of decisions gives full effect to umbrella clauses. This practice is best represented by *Noble Ventures v Romania*[584] where the Tribunal had to interpret and apply the following clause in Article II(2)(c) of the BIT between the United States and Romania: 'Each party shall observe any obligation it may have entered into with regard to investments.' The US claimant argued, *inter alia*, that Romania had breached the umbrella clause by failing to abide by its contractual obligation to renegotiate the debts of a formerly State-owned company acquired by the investor. The Tribunal insisted on the specificity of each umbrella clause, distinguishing earlier cases on this basis. The ruling emphasized that the wording obviously referred to investment contracts.[585] Consistent with Article 31 of the VCLT, it emphasized the object and purpose of investment treaties.[586] The Tribunal said:

> two States may include in a bilateral investment treaty a provision to the effect that, in the interest of achieving the objects and goals of the treaty, the host State may incur international responsibility by reason of a breach of its contractual obligations towards the private investor of the other Party, the breach of contract being thus 'internationalized', i.e. assimilated to a breach of the treaty.[587]

International Arbitration: Specific Aspects in the case of the Involvement of State Parties' in I Shihata and D Wolfensohn (eds) *The World Bank in a Changing World—Selected Essays and Lectures* (II 1995) 601; C Schreuer, 'Travelling the BIT-Route—Of Waiting Periods, Umbrella Clauses and Forks in the Road' (2004) 5 *JWIT* 231, 250; SW Schill, 'Enabling Private Ordering: Function, Scope and Effect of Umbrella Clauses in International Investment Treaties' (2009) 10 *Minnesota JIL* 1, 2.

583 *SGS v Pakistan*, Decision on Jurisdiction, 6 August 2003.
584 *Noble Ventures v Romania*, Award, 12 October 2005.
585 At para 51.
586 At para 52.
587 At para 54. See also para 85.

> ... [I]n including Art. II(2)(c) in the BIT, the Parties had as their aim to equate contractual obligations governed by municipal law to international treaty obligations as established in the BIT.
>
> By reason therefore of the inclusion of Art. II(2)(c) in the BIT, the Tribunal therefore considers the Claimant's claims of breach of contract on the basis that any such breach constitutes a breach of the BIT.[588]

In the event, the Tribunal found that Romania had not violated its contractual obligation, and the Tribunal left open the question whether the wide scope of an umbrella clause had to be narrowed in some way.[589]

The *Noble Ventures* Tribunal was not the first one to accord a broad or full scope to the clause. In *SGS v Philippines*,[590] the Tribunal, in its Decision on Jurisdiction, also ruled that in the presence of an umbrella clause in the Philippines–Swiss BIT, a violation of an investment agreement will lead to a violation of the investment treaty: 'Article X(2) [the umbrella clause] means what it says.'[591] The Tribunal stated:

> Article X(2) makes it a breach of the BIT for the host State to fail to observe binding commitments, including contractual commitments, which it has assumed with regard to specific investments. But it does not convert the issue of the *extent* or *content* of such obligations into an issue of international law. That issue (in the present case, the issue of how much is payable for services provided under the CISS Agreement) is still governed by the investment agreement.[592]

However, *SGS v Philippines* did not carry this approach to its logical conclusion. Instead, the Tribunal assumed that, due to the existence of a forum selection clause in favour of the courts of the host State, the Philippine courts were to rule on the obligations contained in the investment contract.[593]

In *Eureko v Poland*,[594] the Tribunal had to rule on the umbrella clause in Article 3.5 of the treaty between the Netherlands and Poland. The Tribunal considered the ordinary meaning, the context of the clause, and the maxim of *effet utile*. It concluded that breaches by Poland of its obligations under contracts could be breaches

588 At paras 61, 62.
589 At para 61.
590 *SGS v Philippines*, Decision on Jurisdiction, 29 January 2004.
591 At para 119.
592 At para 128. Italics original.
593 At para 155. Other tribunals have followed this approach: *BIVAC v Paraguay*, Decision on Jurisdiction, 29 May 2009, paras 141–161; *Bosh v Ukraine*, Award, 25 October 2012, paras 251–258. But see *SGS v Paraguay*, Award, 10 February 2012, para 107.
594 *Eureko v Poland*, Partial Award, 19 August 2005.

of the BIT's umbrella clause, even if these breaches did not violate the BIT's other standards.[595] The Tribunal said:

> The plain meaning—the 'ordinary meaning'—of a provision prescribing that a State 'shall observe any obligation it may have entered into' with regard to certain foreign investment is not obscure. The phrase, 'shall observe' is imperative and categorical. 'Any' obligations is capacious; it means not only obligations of a certain type, but 'any'—that is to say, all—obligations entered into with regard to investments of investors of the other Contracting Party.... The context of Article 3.5 [the umbrella clause] is a Treaty whose object and purpose is 'the encouragement and reciprocal protection of investment', a treaty which contains specific provisions designed to accomplish that end, of which Article 3.5 is one. It is a cardinal rule of the interpretation of treaties that each and every operative clause of a treaty is to be interpreted as meaningful rather than meaningless.[596]

In the event, the Tribunal found that Poland had violated its obligations arising from a privatization scheme vis-à-vis the investor.

In *SGS v Paraguay* the claim was for unpaid bills under a contract between the investor and the State for the pre-shipment inspection of goods. The BIT between Switzerland and Paraguay provided in Article 11 that '[e]ither Contracting Party shall constantly guarantee the observance of the commitments it has entered into with respect to the investments of the investors of the other Contracting Party'. The Tribunal rejected a restrictive interpretation of this umbrella clause based either on the nature of the contract or on the nature of its breach. It said:

> Article 11 does not exclude commercial contracts of the State from its scope. Likewise, Article 11 does not state that its constant guarantee of observance of such commitments may be breached only through actions that a commercial counterparty cannot take, through abuses of state power, or through exertions of undue government influence.[597]
>
> ... Article 11 requires the 'observance' of commitments. Also as a matter of the ordinary meaning of the term, a failure to meet one's obligations under a contract is clearly a failure to 'observe' one's commitments. There is nothing in Article 11 that states or implies that a government will only fail to observe its commitments if it abuses its sovereign authority.[598]

[595] At para 250. For a critical review see Z *Douglas*, 'Nothing if not Critical for Investment Treaty Arbitration: *Occidental, Eureko* and *Methanex*' (2006) 22 *Arbitr Int* 27.

[596] At paras 246 and 248.

[597] *SGS v Paraguay*, Decision on Jurisdiction, 12 February 2010, para 168.

[598] *SGS v Paraguay*, Award, 10 February 2012, para 91.

In other decisions, tribunals similarly gave full effect to umbrella clauses and confirmed that, by virtue of such a clause, failure by the host State to meet obligations assumed in relation to investments amounted to a breach of the treaty.[599] This ensured that investors were able to enforce host State promises through investment arbitration irrespective of the chosen law.

(c) Restrictive application of umbrella clauses

In a series of other cases, tribunals have imposed various limitations upon the application of umbrella clauses.[600] In *SGS v Pakistan*,[601] the Swiss claimant had concluded a contract with Pakistan on pre-shipment inspection services with a forum selection clause for Pakistani courts. When Pakistan unilaterally terminated the contract, the claimant started ICSID proceedings under the BIT between Pakistan and Switzerland. The BIT contained the following clause: 'Either Contracting Party shall constantly guarantee the observance of the commitments it has entered into with respect to the investments of the investors of the other Contracting Party.'

The Tribunal refused to give effect to the umbrella clause and found that the proper mode of interpretation was a restrictive one (*in dubio mitius*).[602] The Tribunal made no reference to the modes of interpretation laid down in Article 31 of the VCLT which does not embrace this maxim. In the light of this interpretative approach, the Tribunal concluded that any other understanding would have a far-reaching impact on the sovereignty of the host State which could not be presumed in the absence of a clear expression of a corresponding will by the parties.[603]

The Tribunal presented four arguments in support of its position. First, the conventional view would also cover non-contractual obligations arising under the laws of the host State, including the smallest types of commitments, and would lead to a flood of lawsuits before international tribunals.[604] Secondly, the conventional view would make other guarantees contained in investment treaties superfluous because even a violation of a small obligation would allow a lawsuit.[605] Thirdly, the Tribunal considered that the location of the umbrella clause not with the substantive guarantees but towards the end of the treaty, spoke against a far-reaching

[599] *LG&E v Argentina*, Decision on Liability, 3 October 2006, paras 164–175; *Siemens v Argentina*, Award, 6 February 2007, paras 196–206; *Plama v Bulgaria*, Award, 27 August 2008, paras 185–187; *Duke Energy v Ecuador*, Award, 18 August 2008, paras 314–325; *AMTO v Ukraine*, Award, 26 March 2008, paras 109–112; *Garanti Koza v Turkmenistan*, Award, 19 December 2016, para 247.

[600] For a critical evaluation see SW Schill, 'Umbrella Clauses as Public Law Concepts in Comparative Perspective' in SW Schill (ed) *International Investment Law and Comparative Public Law* (2010) 317.

[601] *SGS v Pakistan*, Decision on Jurisdiction, 6 August 2003.

[602] At para 171.

[603] At paras 167–168.

[604] At paras 166, 168.

[605] At para 168.

obligation.[606] And fourthly, it pointed out that the forum selection in investment agreements would, under the conventional view, not be binding for the investor whereas the host State would be bound to honour such clauses.[607] The Tribunal did not refer to the distinction between 'commercial acts' and 'sovereign acts'.

The Tribunal denied that its position would deprive an umbrella clause of its meaning. It pointed out that the clause would be relevant in the context of the implementation of the investment treaty in the domestic legal order or if the host State failed to participate in international proceedings to which it had agreed earlier.[608]

This decision was widely criticized.[609] The sharpest criticism came from the Tribunal in *SGS v Philippines*,[610] but commentators also pointed to weaknesses of the decision.[611] The most vulnerable aspect of the decision is the lack of an attempt to ground the method of interpretation in the accepted canons embodied in Article 31 of the VCLT.

For a while it seemed as if *SGS v Pakistan* would remain an isolated decision. But the decision has also found a measure of support.[612] In 2006, two nearly identical decisions (*El Paso v Argentina* and *Pan American v Argentina*) explicitly supported the first and the second argument set forth in *SGS v Pakistan* (flood of lawsuits, overreach because of wider scope than other treaty guarantees).[613] But unlike *SGS v Pakistan*, the Tribunals then introduced the distinction between the State as a merchant and the State as a sovereign. They concluded, with a broad brush, that investment arbitration will cover only disputes concerning investment agreements or State contracts in which the State is involved 'as a sovereign' but not mere commercial contracts.[614] The Tribunal in *El Paso* sought to establish a balance between the interests of the host State and those of the investor:

[606] At para 169.

[607] At para 168.

[608] At para 172.

[609] The government of Switzerland took the unusual step of expressing its disapproval and concern over the decision in a letter of 1 October 2003 to the Deputy Secretary-General of ICSID.

[610] *SGS v Philippines*, Decision on Jurisdiction, 29 January 2004, para 125: 'Not only are the reasons given by the Tribunal in *SGS v. Pakistan* unconvincing: the Tribunal failed to give any clear meaning to the "umbrella clause".' See also *Eureko v Poland*, Partial Award, 19 August 2005, para 257.

[611] SA Alexandrov, 'Breaches of Contract and Breaches of Treaty, The Jurisdiction of Treaty-based Arbitration Tribunals to Decide Breach of Contract Claims in *SGS v. Pakistan and SGS v. Philippines*' (2004) 5 *JWIT* 555, 569; C Schreuer 'Travelling the BIT-Route—Of Waiting Periods, Umbrella Clauses and Forks in the Road' (2004) 5 *JWIT* 231, 253; 253; T Wälde, 'The "Umbrella Clause" in Investment Arbitration—A Comment on Original Intentions and Recent Cases' (2005) 6 *JWIT* 183, 225; E Gaillard, *La jurisprudence du CIRDI* (2004) 834; SW Schill, 'Enabling Private Ordering: Function, Scope and Effect of Umbrella Clauses in International Investment Treaties' (2009) 10 *Minnesota JIL* 1, 84.

[612] See eg *Toto v Lebanon*, Decision on Jurisdiction, 11 September 2009, paras 187–202.

[613] *El Paso v Argentina*, Decision on Jurisdiction, 27 April 2006, paras 72–74; *Pan American v Argentina*, Decision on Preliminary Objections, 27 July 2006, paras 101–103.

[614] *El Paso v Argentina*, Decision on Jurisdiction, 27 April 2006, paras 77 et seq; *Pan American v Argentina*, Decision on Preliminary Objections, 27 July 2006, para 108; in *Salini v Jordan*, Decision on Jurisdiction, 29 November 2004, para 155, the Tribunal had stated categorically: 'Only the State, in the exercise of its sovereign authority (*puissance publique*), and not as a contracting party, has assumed obligations under the bilateral agreement.'

> This Tribunal considers that a balanced interpretation is needed, taking into account both State sovereignty and the State's responsibility to create an adapted and evolutionary framework for the development of economic activities, and the necessity to protect foreign investment and its continuing flow.[615]

Thus, the decisions in *El Paso* and in *Pan American* did not restrict the scope of the umbrella clause as drastically as *SGS v Pakistan*. They accepted that obligations in investment agreements are covered by the clause to the extent that they bind the State in its sovereign capacity. Essentially, the two decisions seem to echo the French concept of *contrat administratif*.[616]

The distinction between different types of investment agreements was rejected by other tribunals.[617] In *Siemens v Argentina*[618] the Tribunal stated:

> The Tribunal does not subscribe to the view of the Respondent that investment agreements should be distinguished from concession agreements of an administrative nature. Such distinction has no basis in Article 7(2) of the Treaty which refers to 'any obligations', or in the definition of 'investment' in the Treaty. Any agreement related to an investment that qualifies as such under the Treaty would be part of the obligations covered under the umbrella clause.[619]

Another approach to limiting the effect of the umbrella clause does not look at the nature of the affected contract but at the nature or magnitude of its violation. The Tribunal in *CMS v Argentina*[620] referred to the distinction between governmental and commercial action and the significance of the interference with the contract:

> the Tribunal believes the Respondent is correct in arguing that not all contract breaches result in breaches of the treaty. The standard of protection of the treaty will be engaged only when there is a specific breach of treaty rights and obligations or a violation of contract rights protected under the treaty. Purely commercial aspects of a contract might not be protected by the treaty in some situations, but the protection is likely to be available when there is significant interference by governments or public agencies with the rights of the investor.[621]

615 *El Paso v Argentina*, Decision on Jurisdiction, 27 April 2006, para 70.

616 This is contrary to the position taken by arbitrator René-Jean Dupuy in *Texaco v Libya*, Award, 19 January 1977, (1979) 53 ILR, 389, para 72 who had held that the theory of administrative contracts had no place in international law. See also *ARAMCO v Saudi Arabia*, Award, 23 August 1958, (1963) 27 ILR, 117, 164.

617 *ICS v Argentina II*, Award on Jurisdiction, 8 July 2019, paras 343–346; *Strabag v Libya*, Award, 29 June 2020, paras 164–165.

618 *Siemens v Argentina*, Award, 6 February 2007.

619 At para 206.

620 *CMS v Argentina*, Award, 12 May 2005.

621 At para 299.

Similarly, in *Sempra v Argentina*[622] the Tribunal held that ordinary commercial breaches of a contract would not violate the umbrella clause in the Argentina–US BIT. Only a breach in the exercise of a sovereign State function or power but not the conduct of an ordinary contract party could amount to a breach of the umbrella clause. In the particular case, the Tribunal found that the sweeping changes that Argentina had introduced were no ordinary contractual breaches but had been brought about in exercise of the State's public function. Therefore, it concluded that the breaches of the obligations in question resulted in a breach of the umbrella clause.[623]

Other tribunals have rejected such an approach. For example, the Tribunal in *Burlington v Ecuador* explicitly stated that to require a sovereign act for a breach of the umbrella clause has no basis in the treaty's text:

> Second, Ecuador alleges that Burlington's claims do not involve the exercise of sovereign power. This requirement, however, has no support in the text of the umbrella clause of the Treaty. Moreover, while different views have been expressed on this matter, in line with other decisions such as for instance *Duke Energy*, the Tribunal considers that umbrella clauses may apply even if no exercise of sovereign power is involved (*Duke Energy*, ¶ 320).[624]

The distinction between 'treaty claims' and 'contract claims', introduced by the *Vivendi* Annulment Committee and subsequently often relied upon by tribunals,[625] does not facilitate the understanding of the umbrella clause. The crucial point is that certain (or all) types of violations of contracts between the State and the investor will, in the presence of an umbrella clause, amount to a violation of the investment treaty.

States entering into an investment treaty are free to fashion its scope and the guarantees granted therein. If the parties choose to extend the scope of the treaty to cover, to some extent, operations previously deemed 'commercial' or 'contractual' in nature, conventional terminology cannot stand in the way of the parties' intentions. For this reason, any attempt to confine the scope of the umbrella clause by reference to abstract concepts such as 'sovereign acts', 'commercial acts', or '*contrats*

[622] *Sempra v Argentina*, Award, 28 September 2007.

[623] At paras 305–314.

[624] *Burlington v Ecuador*, Decision on Jurisdiction, 2 June 2010, para 190. See also *SGS v Paraguay*, Decision on Jurisdiction, 12 February 2010, para 168; *SGS v Paraguay*, Award, 10 February 2012, para 91.

[625] *Vivendi v Argentina*, Decision on Annulment, 3 July 2002, paras 98–101: 'In a case where the essential basis of a claim brought before an international tribunal is a breach of contract, the tribunal will give effect to any valid choice of forum clause in the contract... On the other hand, where "the fundamental basis of the claim" is a treaty laying down an independent standard by which the conduct of the parties is to be judged, the existence of an exclusive jurisdiction clause in a contract between the claimant and the respondent state cannot operate as a bar to the application of the treaty standard.' Generally, on the distinction between treaty claims and contract claims see XII.10 below.

administratifs' are unconvincing. References to categories of a specific domestic legal order have no place within the canon of interpretation laid down in Article 31 of the VCLT. Furthermore, as a historical perspective shows, the function of these clauses is to make State promises in connection with investments enforceable. This function depends neither on the form (sovereign or commercial) in which the promises are made nor on the form in which a State breaks the promise. The umbrella clause does not change the substance of the obligation nor the law applicable to it but merely makes it enforceable under international law.

(d) Umbrella clauses and privity of contract

In principle, contracts to which an umbrella clause is to apply would be between the disputing parties, that is, a State and a foreign investor. But in some cases, the disputing parties and the parties to the contract on which the investor relies for purposes of the umbrella clause are not identical. On the host State's side, the party to the contract may be a State entity or a territorial subdivision rather than the State itself. On the investor's side, the party to the contract may not be the foreign investor itself but its subsidiary in the host State. In these situations, the question arises whether an umbrella clause will protect a contract that is not directly between the host State and the investor.[626]

In some cases, tribunals found that contracts concluded by State entities were attributable to the State. *Noble Ventures v Romania*[627] concerned a contract between the claimant and the Romanian 'State Ownership Fund', a separate legal entity. The Tribunal reached the conclusion that the contractual conduct of the Fund had to be attributed to the Romanian government in view of the grant of governmental power to the Fund. The Tribunal found that, for purposes of attribution, the distinction between commercial acts and sovereign acts had no relevance.[628] It followed that the umbrella clause was applicable to the contract. The Tribunal said:

> where the acts of a governmental agency are to be attributed to the State for the purposes of applying an umbrella clause, such as Art. II(2)(c) of the BIT, breaches of a contract into which the State has entered are capable of constituting a breach of international law *by virtue of the breach of the umbrella clause.*[629]

In *Strabag v Libya*,[630] the investor had contracted with several State entities. The Tribunal applied Article 8(1) of the Austria–Libya BIT which provided that '[e]ach

[626] N Gallus, 'An Umbrella just for Two? BIT Obligations Observance Clauses and the Parties to a Contract' (2008) 24 *Arbitr Int* 157.
[627] *Noble Ventures v Romania*, Award, 12 October 2005.
[628] At para 82.
[629] At para 85. Emphasis original.
[630] *Strabag v Libya*, Award, 29 June 2020.

Contracting Party shall observe any obligation it may have entered into with regard to specific investments by investors of the other Contracting Party'. The Tribunal found that the matter required a more searching analysis than asking who the formal parties to the contracts were. The Tribunal examined the nature of the entities and of the contracts, and the manner in which the contracts were concluded and implemented. It noted that the entities performed State functions and that the contracts involved significant public projects. Moreover, the entities acted at the direction of Libyan State organs and were dependent on funding provided by State organs. All of this led the Tribunal to the conclusion that, for purposes of the umbrella clause, Libya had entered into the contracts.[631]

In other decisions, tribunals found that the umbrella clause was inapplicable where the State had not contracted in its own name.[632] In *Impregilo v Pakistan*,[633] the contracts had been concluded not by Pakistan directly but by the Pakistan Water and Power Development Authority. The claimant wanted to benefit from an umbrella clause in a third country BIT by way of an MFN clause contained in the BIT between Italy and Pakistan. The Tribunal found that contracts concluded by a separate entity of Pakistan would not be protected by an umbrella clause.[634]

A similar problem arises on the investor's side when it operates through a local subsidiary that enters into a contract. The question is whether the foreign investor may rely on the umbrella clause in relation to a contract to which it is not a party. The ECT in Article 10(1) gives an affirmative answer to this question by referring to 'any obligations it has entered into with an Investor *or an Investment of an Investor*'.[635]

Most BITs do not contain a clarification of this kind. The practice of tribunals is divided on whether foreign investors are entitled to the protection of umbrella clauses for claims arising from contracts of their local subsidiaries. Some tribunals have allowed claims of this nature.

In *Continental Casualty v Argentina*,[636] the investor's local subsidiary, CNA, had entered into a number of contracts with Argentina. The claimant invoked the umbrella clause in respect of these contracts[637] and the Tribunal left no doubt

[631] At paras 167–188.

[632] *Azurix v Argentina*, Award, 14 July 2006, paras 52, 384; *AMTO v Ukraine*, Award, 26 March 2008, paras 109–112; *EDF v Romania*, Award, 8 October 2009, paras 317, 318; *Hamester v Ghana*, Award, 18 June 2010, paras 339–350; *Bosh v Ukraine*, Award, 25 October 2012, paras 242–249; *Oxus v Uzbekistan*, Final Award, 17 December 2015, para 854; *Gavrilović v Croatia*, Award, 26 July 2018, para 1159; *Staur Eiendom v Latvia*, Award, 28 February 2020, paras 515–519.

[633] *Impregilo v Pakistan*, Decision on Jurisdiction, 22 April 2005.

[634] At para 223.

[635] Emphasis added. The Reader's Guide to the ECT offers the following explanation: 'This provision covers any contract that a host country has concluded with a subsidiary of the foreign investor in the host country, or a contract between the host country and the parent company of the subsidiary.' See also *AMTO v Ukraine*, Award, 26 March 2008, para 110.

[636] *Continental Casualty v Argentina*, Award, 5 September 2008.

[637] At para 288.

that the umbrella clause covered contracts concluded by the investor's subsidiary. The Tribunal stated, with respect to obligations covered by the umbrella clause in Article II(2)(c) of the Argentina–US BIT:

> provided that these obligations have been entered 'with regard' to investments, they may have been entered with persons or entities other than foreign investors themselves, so that an undertaking by the host State with a subsidiary such as CNA is not in principle excluded.[638]

Other tribunals have similarly extended the effect of umbrella clauses to contracts of local subsidiaries of the foreign investors.[639]

In another group of cases, tribunals decided that a successful invocation of the umbrella clause required a contract directly with the foreign investor and not with its local subsidiary.[640] In *Azurix v Argentina*,[641] a concession agreement had been concluded between a province of Argentina and the subsidiary of Azurix ABA. The Tribunal recalled that Azurix and the respondent had no contractual relationship: the obligations undertaken in the concession contract were undertaken by the province, not Argentina, in favour of ABA, not Azurix.[642] The Tribunal said:

> there is no undertaking to be honored by Argentina to Azurix other than the obligations under the BIT. Even if for argument's sake, it would be possible under Article II(2)(c) [the umbrella clause] to hold Argentina responsible for the alleged breaches of the Concession Agreement by the Province, it was ABA and not Azurix which was the party to this Agreement.[643]

In *CMS v Argentina*, the claimant was a minority shareholder in a local company TGN. The Tribunal had allowed the application of the umbrella clause with respect to a licence obtained by TGN.[644] In proceedings for the Award's annulment, the ad hoc Committee noted that under Argentinean law the obligations of Argentina under the licence were obligations to TGN, not to CMS.[645] The Committee

[638] At para 297. See also para 98.

[639] *CMS v Argentina*, Award, 12 May 2005, paras 296–303; *Enron v Argentina*, Award, 22 May 2007, paras 269–277. The ad hoc Committee declined to annul this part of the Award: Decision on Annulment, 30 July 2010, paras 317–346; *Sempra v Argentina*, Award, 28 September 2007, paras 308–314; *Duke Energy v Ecuador*, Award, 18 August 2008, paras 314–325; *Supervisión v Costa Rica*, Award, 18 January 2017, para 287.

[640] *Siemens v Argentina*, Award, 6 February 2007, paras 204–206; *BG Group v Argentina*, Final Award, 24 December 2007, paras 206–215, 361–366; *El Paso v Argentina*, Award, 31 October 2011, paras 531–538; *Burlington v Ecuador*, Decision on Liability, 14 December 2012, paras 212–220; *WNC v Czech Republic*, Award, 22 February 2017, paras 317, 322–341.

[641] *Azurix v Argentina*, Award, 14 July 2006.

[642] At para 52.

[643] At para 384.

[644] *CMS v Argentina*, Award, 12 May 2005, paras 296–303.

[645] *CMS v Argentina*, Decision on Annulment, 25 September 2007.

annulled the part of the Award dealing with the umbrella clause for failure to state reasons. In the Committee's view it was 'quite unclear how the Tribunal arrived at its conclusion that CMS could enforce the obligations of Argentina to TGN.'[646]

(e) Umbrella clauses and unilateral undertakings

The discussion of umbrella clauses usually centres on contracts. States may, however, assume obligations not only by way of contracts but also through unilateral acts such as legislation or executive action.[647] Case law indicates that umbrella clauses are not restricted to contractual obligations but are capable of protecting obligations of the host State assumed unilaterally.[648]

Tribunals have recognized, in principle, that umbrella clauses in which States undertake to observe obligations with regard to investments cover unilateral undertakings.[649] *LG&E v Argentina*[650] involved an umbrella clause referring to the observance of 'any obligation it may have entered into with regard to investments'.[651] The case concerned the abrogation of rights granted to investors under a Gas Law and its implementing regulations. The Tribunal found that this legislation contained 'obligations' in the sense of the umbrella clause:

> These laws and regulations became obligations within the meaning of Article II(2)(c), by virtue of targeting foreign investors and applying specifically to their investments, that gave rise to liability under the umbrella clause.[652]

Some tribunals have read limitations into the clauses based on the specific wording of umbrella clauses. A reference to obligations with regard to 'specific investments' was seen to exclude general legal obligations arising from legislative measures.[653] Other tribunals found that the words 'entered into' in an umbrella clause could

[646] At para 96.

[647] WM Reisman and MH Arsanjani, 'The Question of Unilateral Governmental Statements as Applicable Law in Investment Disputes' (2004) 19 *ICSID Rev* 328.

[648] MC Gritón Salias, 'Do Umbrella Clauses Apply to Unilateral Undertakings?' in C Binder et al (eds) *International Investment Law for the 21st Century* (2009) 490.

[649] *SGS v Pakistan*, Decision on Jurisdiction, 6 August 2003, para 166; *Enron v Argentina*, Award, 22 May 2007, paras 269–277 and Decision on Annulment, 30 July 2010, paras 317–346; *Noble Energy v Ecuador*, Decision on Jurisdiction, 5 March 2008, paras 154–157; *Plama v Bulgaria*, Award, 27 August 2008, paras 185–187; *Al-Bahloul v Tajikistan*, Partial Award on Jurisdiction and Liability, 2 September 2009, para 257; *Khan v Mongolia*, Decision on Jurisdiction, 25 July 2012, para 438; *Micula v Romania*, Award, 11 December 2013, para 415; *OI European v Venezuela*, Award, 10 March 2015, para 589; *Greentech v Italy*, Final Award, 23 December 2018, para 466.

[650] *LG&E v Argentina*, Decision on Liability, 3 October 2006, paras 169–175.

[651] Argentina–United States BIT (1991) Article II(2)(c).

[652] At para 175.

[653] *SGS v Philippines*, Decision on Jurisdiction, 29 January 2004, para 121.

only be read as restricting the clause to contractual undertakings.[654] In *BayWa v Spain*,[655] the Tribunal interpreted the words 'any obligation it has entered into' in Article 10(1) of the Energy Charter Treaty and said:

> In the Tribunal's view, the umbrella clause in the last sentence of Article 10.1 of the ECT only applies to obligations specifically entered into by the host State with the investor or the investment. The paradigm case is an obligation under an investment contract duly entered into. By contrast the Tribunal does not accept that obligations arising under the general law, including legislation, of the host State, fall within the scope of the clause. When enacting legislation, the State establishes binding rules of conduct, but it does not make specific promises to each person entitled to claim under the law, nor does it enter into obligations to specific investors or their investments even when these entities are numbered among the beneficiaries of the law. A general law is not a promise.[656]

7. Effective means

ADDITIONAL READING: OM Garibaldi, 'Effective Means to Assert Claims and Enforce Rights' in M Kinnear et al (eds) *Building International Investment Law* (2015) 359; AP Karreman and K Dharmananda, 'Time to Reassess Remedies for Delays Breaching "Effective Means"' (2015) 30 *ICSID Rev* 118; HE Kjos, 'Domestic Courts under Scrutiny' in M Kanetake and A Nollkaemper (eds) *The Rule of Law at the National and International Levels* (2016) 353, 371; B Demirkol, *Judicial Acts and Investment Treaty Arbitration* (2018).

Some investment protection treaties contain an explicit obligation to provide effective means to assert claims and enforce rights. This standard is similar to human rights treaty clauses providing for a right to an effective remedy for human rights violations.[657] The standard was introduced into BITs in 1983 by the United States to

[654] *Noble Ventures v Romania*, Award, 12 October 2005, para 51; *CMS v Argentina*, Decision on Annulment, 25 September 2007, para 95 a) and b); *Continental Casualty v Argentina*, Award, 5 September 2008, paras 297–303; *Mobil v Argentina*, Decision on Jurisdiction and Liability, 10 April 2013, paras 1010–1013; *Oxus v Uzbekistan*, Final Award, 17 December 2015, paras 368–371; *Isolux v Spain*, Award, 12 July 2016, para 769; *Novenergia II v Spain*, Final Award, 15 February 2018, para 715; *Greentech v Spain*, Final Award, 14 November 2018, para 413; *RREEF v Spain*, Decision on Responsibility and the Principles of Quantum, 30 November 2018, paras 283–285; *Cube v Spain*, Decision on Jurisdiction, 19 February 2019, paras 452–454; *9REN v Spain*, Award, 31 May 2019, paras 342–346; *Belenergia v Italy*, Award, 6 August 2019, paras 612–619; *Stadtwerke München v Spain*, Award, 2 December 2019, paras 379–384; *RWE v Spain*, Decision on Jurisdiction, Liability and Certain Issues of Quantum, 30 December 2019; *Eskosol v Italy*, Award, 4 September 2020, para 462.

[655] *BayWa v Spain*, Decision on Jurisdiction, Liability and Directions of Quantum, 2 December 2019.

[656] At para 442.

[657] International Covenant on Civil and Political Rights Article 2(3); European Convention on Human Rights Article 13; American Convention on Human Rights Article 25; African Charter on Human and Peoples' Rights Article 7.

address a lack of clarity in customary international law.[658] The ECT and a relatively small number of BITs[659] contain the standard. Article 10(12) of the ECT provides in this regard:

> Each Contracting Party shall ensure that its domestic law provides effective means for the assertion of claims and the enforcement of rights with respect to Investments, investment agreements, and investment authorizations.

A provision of this type imposes a positive obligation on the State to provide effective judicial remedies before the host State's courts.[660]

The relative paucity of treaties containing a separate clause addressing adequate judicial protection for asserting claims and enforcing rights explains why there are only few cases dealing with such a provision.[661]

In *AMTO v Ukraine*,[662] the Tribunal found that the 'effective means standard' in Article 10(12) of the ECT established a specific requirement for the legislator to provide for effective means to assert claims and enforce rights. Legislative failures affecting these rights could be measured against this standard:

> In Article 10(12) of the ECT there is a specific obligation to ensure that domestic law provides an effective means for the assertion of claims and the enforcement of rights. Legislative failures affecting the administration of justice in cases under the ECT can therefore be measured against the express standard established by Article 10(12).[663]

[658] KJ Vandevelde, *U.S. International Investment Agreements* (2009) 411.

[659] See eg Article II (6), 1984 US Model BIT; Article II (7), Egypt–United States BIT (1986) and Protocol; Article II (7), Poland–United States BIT (1990) and Protocol; Article II (8), Turkey–United States BIT (1985) and Protocol; Article II (6), Sri Lanka–United States BIT (1991) and Protocol; Article II (6), Romania–United States BIT (1992) and Protocol; Article II (6), Moldova–United States BIT (1993) and Protocol; Article II (6), Kazakhstan–United States BIT (1992); Article II (7), Estonia–United States BIT (1994); Article II (6), Czech and Slovak Federal Republic–United States BIT (1991) and Protocol; Article 2 (4), Bahrain–United States BIT (1999); Article 4 (1), US–Viet Nam Trade Relations Agreement (2000); Article 2 (10), Czech Republic–United Arab Emirates BIT (1994); Protocol, 2 (d), Italy–Lithuania BIT (1994); Article 2 (3), Algeria–Finland BIT (2005); Article 2 (5), Kazakhstan–Sweden BIT (2004); Article 2 (8), Korea–Kuwait BIT (2004); Article 2 (10), Ukraine–United Arab Emirates BIT (2003).

[660] *Chevron v Ecuador I*, Partial Award on the Merits, 30 March 2010, para 248; *Apotex v United States*, Award, 25 August 2014, paras 9.66–9.70.

[661] *Petrobart v Kyrgyzstan*, Arbitral Award, 29 March 2005, p 77; *AMTO v Ukraine*, Final Award, 26 March 2008, paras 75–92; *Duke Energy v Ecuador*, Award, 18 August 2008, paras 390–403; *Chevron v Ecuador I*, Partial Award on the Merits, 30 March 2010, paras 241–275, 321–332; *White Industries v India*, Final Award, 30 November 2011, paras 11.1.1–11.4.20; *H&H v Egypt*, Award, 6 May 2014, paras 400–406; *Tatneft v Ukraine*, Award on the Merits, 29 July 2014, paras 350–361, 431–442; *Apotex v United States*, Award, 25 August 2014, paras 9.53, 9.66–9.70; *Gavazzi v Romania*, Decision on Jurisdiction Admissibility and Liability, 21 April 2015, paras 259–266; *Charanne v Spain*, Award, 21 January 2016, paras 468–474.

[662] *AMTO v Ukraine*, Final Award, 26 March 2008.

[663] At para 75.

Furthermore, the Tribunal set out certain quality requirements for the legislation that provides redress:

> There must be legislation for the recognition and enforcement of property and contractual rights. This legislation must be made in accordance with the constitution, and be publicly available. An effective means of the assertion of claims and the enforcement of rights also requires secondary rules of procedure so that the principles and objectives of the legislation can be translated by the investor into effective action in the domestic tribunals.[664]

The *AMTO* Tribunal added that the effective means standard required the State to create an effective system of enforcement but did not require the State to ensure that individual failures of that system do not occur.[665]

In *Chevron v Ecuador I*,[666] the claimant argued, on the basis of extensive evidence, that Ecuadorian courts had delayed local proceedings with the result that the case had been dormant for 14 years.[667] The Tribunal examined the issue in the light of the treaty-based requirement to provide 'effective means of asserting claims and enforcing rights'. The Tribunal found that this provision was to be understood as *lex specialis* vis-à-vis the rule on denial of justice,[668] even though the close link between the two standards was obvious. The treaty clause covered claims for undue delay, for interference by the government with the judicial process, but also manifestly unjust decisions.[669] Several factors had to be taken into account to evaluate the existence of undue delay: the complexity of the case, the behaviour of the litigants involved, the significance of the interests at stake, and the behaviour of the courts themselves.[670] Applying these criteria to the facts of the case, the Tribunal had no difficulty to find a violation of the clause.[671] Moreover, the Tribunal found that the clause, being different from the rule on denial of justice, did not require exhaustion of local remedies.[672]

The Tribunal in *White Industries v India*[673] confirmed the finding of the *Chevron I* Tribunal that 'the "effective means" standard is *lex specialis* and is a distinct and potentially less demanding test, in comparison to denial of justice in customary international law'.[674] The Tribunal denied a denial of justice but still found that the effective means standard had been violated as a result of the undue length of

664 At para 87.
665 At para 88. See also *H&H v Egypt*, Award, 6 May 2014, para 400.
666 *Chevron v Ecuador I*, Partial Award on the Merits, 30 March 2010.
667 At paras 171 et seq.
668 At paras 242, 275. On denial of justice see VIII.1(g)ee above.
669 At para 248.
670 At para 250.
671 At paras 252–274.
672 At paras 268, 321–332.
673 *White Industries v India*, Final Award, 30 November 2011.
674 At para 11.3.2(a).

domestic court proceedings. The Tribunal found the duration of the national proceedings overall to be 'certainly unsatisfactory',[675] but found that it did not show bad faith and did not amount to 'particularly serious shortcoming' or egregious conduct that 'shocks or at least surprises, a sense of judicial proprietary'. Therefore, the delay did not amount to a denial of justice.[676] One of the proceedings, however, in particular a failure of India's Supreme Court to decide an appeal for over five years, triggered a violation of the effective means standard.[677] In this respect, the approach differs from that of the *AMTO* Tribunal which had found that, under the effective means standard, a State does not have to ensure that individual failures do not occur in a system that in principle provides for an effective framework.[678]

In *Charanne v Spain*,[679] the claimant argued that the unavailability of a contentious-administrative claim against a Royal Decree-Law was a violation of the effective means standard in the ECT. The Tribunal, relying on *Chevron* and *White Industries*, described the standard as follows:

> The standard of effective mechanisms as foreseen in Article 10(12) of the ECT requires States to provide a legal framework that guarantees effective remedies to investors for realization and protection of their investments. To verify whether such requirements are met, tribunals must examine the legal system in question as a whole. The standard, however, does not impose any obligation on States regarding the way in which it organizes its judicial system. It is sufficient that an adequate system of laws and institutions is established and that it functions effectively.[680]

The Tribunal found that other means to contest the Royal Decree-Law were available to the claimant and dismissed the claim.[681]

In sum, tribunals deciding on violations of the effective means standard have used typical fair trial requirements as we find them in a denial of justice analysis and the FET standard or under human rights treaties. They assessed whether there was access to the courts, whether there was undue interference by the executive, whether there were undue delays in court proceedings and whether an investor was able to present its case properly.

[675] At paras 10.4.22.
[676] At paras 10.4.23–10.4.24.
[677] At para 11.4.19.
[678] *AMTO v Ukraine*, Final Award, 26 March 2008, para 88.
[679] *Charanne v Spain*, Award, 21 January 2016.
[680] At para 470. Footnotes omitted.
[681] At paras 471–474.

8. Transfer of funds

ADDITIONAL READING: A Kolo and T Wälde, 'Capital Transfer Restrictions under Modern Investment Treaties' in A Reinisch (ed) *Standards of Investment Protection* (2008) 205; M Waibel, 'BIT by BIT–The Silent Liberalisation of the Capital Account' in C Binder et al (eds) *International Investment Law for the 21st Century* (2009) 497; R Dolzer, 'Transfer of Funds' in M Giovanoli et al (eds) *International Monetary and Financial Law* (2010) 533; A Kolo, 'Transfer of Funds' in SW Schill (ed) *International Investment Law and Comparative Public Law* (2010) 345; A de Luca, 'Transfer Provisions of BITs in Times of Financial Crisis' (2013) 23 *Italian YBIL* 113; C Kern, 'Transfer of Funds' in M Bungenberg et al (eds) *International Investment Law* (2015) 870; A Reinisch and C Schreuer, *International Protection of Investments* (2020) 970.

Conditions for the transfer of funds by investors into the host State and out of the host State are of key concern for both the investor and the host State. The investor will typically need to import funds into the host State to start the investment or to expand its business. Repatriation of capital, including profits, into the home country or a third country will often be the major business purpose of the investment. In the words of *Continental Casualty v Argentina*, the right of transfer 'is fundamental to the freedom to make a foreign investment and an essential element of the promotional role of BITs'.[682]

The host State will want to administer its currency and its foreign reserves. Large currency transfers into the country and out of the country need to be monitored and controlled to protect national policies. Experience has shown that sudden short-term capital inflows, and especially capital flight, may lead to instability in the domestic financial markets.

Thus, the interests of the foreign investor and those of the host State in the permissibility of foreign transfers will often diverge, and investment treaties typically cover this subject. Separate types of regulations are found in the IMF's Articles of Agreement, in rules adopted in the OECD, and in the GATT regime.[683]

The modalities of regulation in the treaties vary considerably, and no single pattern is dominant. Monetary and financial policies, the volume of the domestic capital market, historical experience, and simple bargaining power of the parties will influence the outcome of the treaty negotiations.

[682] *Continental Casualty v Argentina*, Award, 5 September 2008, para 239.

[683] On the overlap with BIT's and the legal consequences see R Dolzer, 'Transfer of Funds' in M Giovanoli et al (eds) *International Monetary and Financial Law* (2010) 533.

(a) Monetary sovereignty

All treaty schemes are negotiated against the background of the host State's 'monetary sovereignty'. This means that the host State has 'the exclusive right to determine its own monetary unit, to give the unit legal meaning, to fix the exchange rate and to regulate, restrict or prohibit the conversion and transfer of foreign exchange'.[684] The rules of the IMF, which have been accepted in principle by 184 States, do not allow restrictions by the member States on so-called current transactions.[685] This leaves them the power to regulate the inflow and outflow of 'capital transactions' as opposed to 'current transactions'.[686]

The rules on transfer in investment treaties deal with the investor's right to make transfers, the types of payment covered by this right, convertibility and exchange rates, and limitations on the freedom of transfer.[687] In relation to the applicable IMF Rules, the Tribunal in *Continental Casualty v Argentina* properly considered that the BIT provisions on transfer are more liberal and will have to be considered as *lex specialis*.[688]

The Tribunal in *Rusoro v Venezuela*[689] expressly acknowledged the monetary sovereignty enjoyed by States. Venezuela required that residents must acquire foreign currency via its Central Bank, must sell a high percentage of foreign currency to the Central Bank and must accept the exchange rate determined by the Central Bank. The Tribunal found that this 'stringent exchange control mechanism' imposed by Venezuela did not violate the obligations under the transfer provision of the Canada–Venezuela BIT.[690]

684 R Dolzer and M Stevens, *Bilateral Investment Treaties* (1995) 85.

685 Article VIII of the IMF's Articles of Agreement states: 'Section 2. Avoidance of restrictions on current payments: (a) Subject to the provisions of Article VII, Section 3(b) and Article XIV, Section 2, no member shall, without the approval of the Fund, impose restrictions on the making of payments and transfers for current international transactions. (b) Exchange contracts which involve the currency of any member and which are contrary to the exchange control regulations of that member maintained or imposed consistently with this Agreement shall be unenforceable in the territories of any member. In addition, members may, by mutual accord, cooperate in measures for the purpose of making the exchange control regulations of either member more effective, provided that such measures and regulations are consistent with this Agreement.'

686 Article XXX(d) of the IMF's Articles of Agreement defines payments for current transactions in the following terms: 'Payments for current transactions means payments which are not for the purpose of transferring capital, and includes, without limitation: (1) all payments due in connection with foreign trade, other current business, including services, and normal short-term banking and credit facilities; (2) payments due as interest on loans and as net income from other investments; (3) payments of moderate amount for amortization of loans or for depreciation of direct investments; and (4) moderate remittances for family living expenses. The Fund may, after consultation with the members concerned, determine whether certain specific transactions are to be considered current transactions or capital transactions.'

687 Measures by the host State that affect the opportunity to earn profits do not violate the provision on the right of transfer. See *Biwater Gauff v Tanzania*, Award, 24 July 2008, para 735.

688 *Continental Casualty v Argentina*, Award, 5 September 2008, paras 243–244.

689 *Rusoro v Venezuela*, Award, 22 August 2016.

690 At para 578.

Free transfer clauses are aimed at protecting the investor against restrictions on the movement of capital and exchange control imposed by the host State. They do not protect the investor against the retention of funds by business partners.[691]

(b) Types of covered transfers

Treaty practice varies concerning the types of transfers that are protected. The right to transfer is sometimes limited to certain types of transfers. Under many treaties, the relevant rules guarantee the right of free transfer 'of payments resulting from investment activities', or they permit all transfers 'related to an investment' or 'in connection with an investment'.[692] In other treaties, the right to make transfers is not generalized. Types of payment covered by transfer clauses are often indicated in specific categories, sometimes in an exhaustive manner, sometimes in an illustrative manner. Such categories may refer to profits, interest, dividends, other current income, funds necessary to finance an investment, proceeds of liquidation, payments under a contract, management fees, royalties, or other items. Often, returns, loan payments, liquidation proceeds, or payments from licences and royalties are guaranteed free transfer, whereas qualifications of this right may be found for the transfer of salaries.

The types of transfer covered by the transfer clause in the Argentina–US BIT of 1991 were under consideration in *Continental Casualty v Argentina*.[693] The Tribunal ruled that 'transfers ... essential for, or typical to the making, controlling, maintenance, disposition of investments' were covered. On the other hand, a mere 'change of type, location and currency of part of an investor's existing investment, namely a part of the freely disposable funds, held short term at its banks' was not covered.[694] The Tribunal decided that the transfers at issue, short-term dollar placements held by the investor's subsidiary that it wanted to take out of Argentina, were not covered.[695]

By contrast, the Tribunal in *Karkey v Pakistan*[696] surprisingly decided that the BIT's transfer clause embraced all investments contained in its broad asset-based investment definition and, therefore, also covered detained vessels. Therefore, it found that the detention constituted a violation of the transfer provision.

In *Achmea v Slovakia*,[697] a ban on profits imposed by the host State stipulated that all profits from health insurance had to be used for healthcare purposes.[698]

691 *White Industries v India*, Final Award, 30 November 2011, para 13.2.3; *MNSS v Montenegro*, Award, 4 May 2016, para 366.

692 R Dolzer and M Stevens, *Bilateral Investment Treaties* (1995) 87.

693 *Continental Casualty v Argentina*, Award, 5 September 2008.

694 At paras 240–241.

695 At paras 241–245.

696 *Karkey v Pakistan*, Award, 22 August 2017, paras 654–655.

697 *Achmea v Slovakia*, Final Award, 7 December 2012.

698 At para 96.

The Tribunal found that the 'ban on profits was inconsistent with the respondent's obligations' under the transfer provision of the BIT. However, the Tribunal did not analyse the claim further since it considered it covered by the violation of the FET provision.[699]

In *Rusoro v Venezuela*, the Tribunal found that gold was a commodity, not a currency, and that, therefore, its sale was not protected by the free transfer obligation under the BIT.[700]

In *von Pezold v Zimbabwe*,[701] the Tribunal found a breach of the free transfer obligation of the BIT when the respondent refused to release foreign currency to allow the claimant's estate to repay loans.[702] It held that further breaches of the standard had occurred when the respondent forced the claimants to exchange US currency for Zimbabwean dollars and failed to release US dollars earned through the sale of tobacco.[703]

In *Ryan v Poland*, the rejection of management fees as tax deductible costs in tax proceedings did not violate the free transfer provision of the BIT. The Tribunal decided 'that the tax proceedings were initiated and the decisions issued after the Management Fees had already been paid, collected and—in fact—transferred' and had therefore not prevented the free transfer of funds.[704]

In *Valores Mundiales v Venezuela*,[705] the Tribunal found that the payments covered by the free transfer clause of the Spain–Venezuela BIT include accrued investment income, compensation for expropriation, and the sums necessary for the maintenance and development of the investment, including those for the acquisition of raw or auxiliary materials or for the substitution of capital goods.[706] The Tribunal held that:

> (i) Venezuela has failed to comply with its obligation to *guarantee* Claimants the unrestricted transfer of this payment related to their investments; (ii) it has also failed to *permit* the transfer to be made without delay in the convertible currency decided by Claimants and at the exchange rate applicable on the day of the transfers; (iii) it has failed to *facilitate* procedures for effecting this transfer without delay or restrictions.[707]

[699] At para 286. For a similar approach see *AES v Kazakhstan*, Award, 1 November 2013, paras 423–427.
[700] *Rusoro v Venezuela*, Award, 22 August 2016, para 574.
[701] *von Pezold v Zimbabwe*, Award, 28 July 2015.
[702] At para 608.
[703] At para 609.
[704] *Ryan v Poland*, Award, 24 November 2015, para 507.
[705] *Valores Mundiales v Venezuela*, Award, 25 July 2017.
[706] At para 635.
[707] At para 639. Italics original.

(c) Inward and outward transfers

A major difference between treaties relates to the question whether the right to transfer funds concerns only the transfer out of the host country or whether it also covers inward transfers. Most treaties cover both directions, but some treaties only address the duty of the host State to guarantee the right to transfer investments and returns abroad, thus referring only to outward payments. If transfers are allowed in general terms, such as 'in relation to investments', both directions of transfer are covered.

(d) Transfers in accordance with host State law

Practically no treaty grants an absolute right to investors to make transfers. Some treaties state that the rights guaranteed to the investor exist only 'subject to the laws' of the host State. For the investor, such a restriction substantially reduces the value of the right to transfer, especially since the national laws of the host State may be revised in the future as the host State deems appropriate. If the transfer of funds is subject to certain procedures, it is the investor's responsibility to comply with these and to obtain the necessary authorizations.[708]

(e) Currencies, exchange rates, and delay

Most treaties state that the investor has the right to carry out the transfer in a freely convertible currency, that the transfer takes place at the official rate of exchange of the host State on the date of the transfer, and that the transfer will be authorized 'without delay', 'without undue delay', or that the procedures are carried out 'expeditiously'.[709]

The Tribunal in *OI European v Venezuela*[710] dealt with the exchange rate and the time element. The system established by Venezuela allowed for a choice between an official favourable exchange rate, where the transfer depends on an authorization and the availability of foreign currencies, or an immediate conversion at the free market rate. The Tribunal found that this exchange control system was compatible with the BIT.[711] It said:

708 *Metalpar v Argentina*, Award on the Merits, 6 June 2008, paras 176–179.

709 Some treaties provide for a specific time limit: *Valores Mundiales v Venezuela*, Award, 25 July 2017, para 639.

710 *OI European v Venezuela*, Award, 10 March 2015.

711 At paras 623–627.

> [the BIT] allows the State to create restrictions or delays for justified cause. The introduction of exchange control systems is part of the economic and financial sovereignty of the States, and does not constitute an 'undue restriction' for purposes of the BIT.[712]

(f) Restrictions

Today, a liberalization of financial markets is considered advantageous for the investor and for the host State. But the experience of host States during periods of financial disorder indicates that the government may need the power to place restrictions on the right to transfer.

Three approaches can be found in treaty practice to allow such restrictions.[713] Some treaties are based on the view that the short-term withdrawal of funds by the investor is undesirable under all circumstances and therefore only allow transfer out of the host country one year after the capital has entered the territory. A second approach is to place restrictions on the right to transfer during periods of severe balance-of-payments crises, external financial difficulties, or other exceptional circumstances affecting monetary policies or the exchange rate. A third approach more recently favoured by Canada, the United States, and Japan, specifically concerns the right to restrict the freedom to provide financial services during extraordinary periods, preserving the right of the host and the home State to maintain 'the safety, soundness, integrity or financial responsibility of financial institutions'.[714] Clauses of this kind will be especially important in the context of treaties that cover the right to provide financial services. However, this approach may in the future also receive more attention in all treaties covering the right to transfer funds.

[712] At para 624.

[713] UNCTAD, *Bilateral Investment Treaties 1995–2006: Trends in Investment Rulemaking* (2007) 62 et seq.

[714] See Article 20 (Financial Services) of the 2004 and 2012 US Model BITs: '1. Notwithstanding any other provision of this Treaty, a Party shall not be prevented from adopting or maintaining measures relating to financial services for prudential reasons, including for the protection of investors, depositors, policy holders, or persons to whom a fiduciary duty is owed by a financial services supplier, or to ensure the integrity and stability of the financial system. It is understood that the term 'prudential reasons' includes the maintenance of the safety, soundness, integrity, or financial responsibility of individual financial institutions ...'.

On the NAFTA Rules, see *Fireman's Fund v Mexico*, Award, 17 July 2006, para 156 et seq.

IX
Emergency Situations and Armed Conflicts

ADDITIONAL READING: C Schreuer, 'The protection of investments in armed conflicts' in F Baetens (ed) *Investment Law within International law—Integrationist Perspectives* (2013) 3; GI Hernández, 'The interaction between investment law and the law of armed conflict in the interpretation of full protection and security clauses' in F Baetens (ed) *Investment Law within International law—Integrationist Perspectives* (2013) 21; M Lawry-White, 'International Investment Arbitration in a *Jus Post Bellum* Framework' (2015) 16 *JWIT*, 633; M Paparinskis, 'Circumstances Precluding Wrongfulness in International Investment Law' (2016) 31 *ICSID Rev* 484; F Pérez-Aznar, 'Investment Protection in Exceptional Situations' (2017) 32 *ICSID Rev* 696; K Fach Gómez et al (eds) *International Investment Law and the Law of Armed Conflict* (2019); J Zrilič, *The Protection of Foreign Investment in Armed Conflict* (2019).

1. Competing policies

The legal rules applicable to extraordinary events and periods of economic and social disorder are of direct interest both to the host State and to the foreign investor. The host State and the investor, however, take different perspectives. The host State's concern is to retain sufficient legal flexibility to deal with extraordinary situations. It will argue that security concerns must take precedence over investor interests. The position of the investor will be that one of the purposes of the legal framework protecting investments is to provide stability. Investors should not lose their protection during turbulent periods when they need it most. Moreover, effective protection of investments in times of unrest will signal stability and the rule of law to prospective investors.

The relevant international rules are contained in customary international law codified by the International Law Commission. In addition, treaties for the protection of foreign investments contain relevant provisions. These international rules operate independently of domestic provisions and measures dealing with a state of emergency and similar conditions.[1]

[1] *Funnekotter v Zimbabwe*, Award, 22 April 2009, para 103; *Sempra v Argentina*, Award, 28 September 2007, para 257; *von Pezold v Zimbabwe*, Award, 28 July 2015, para 624.

2. Effects of violence under traditional international law

Damage to aliens during periods of violence and the host State's duty under customary international law to protect their property have long preoccupied arbitral tribunals. Many of the cases were decided before 1930 and concerned the consequences of unrest in Central and Latin American countries upon foreign property. The basic picture emerging from these cases is summarized in the principle of non-responsibility of the host State for extraordinary events of social strife and disorder which lead to physical action against the assets of foreign investors. However, this principle is qualified by the host State's duty to exercise due diligence, that is, to use the police and the military forces to protect the interests of the alien to the extent feasible and practicable under the circumstances, before, while, and after the event unfolds.[2] A claimant has the burden of proving that the host State was negligent.

3. The ILC Articles on State Responsibility

Situations beyond the host State's control are addressed in the ILC Articles on Responsibility of States for Internationally Wrongful Acts (ARSIWA) under the headings '*force majeure*' (Article 23), 'distress' (Article 24), and 'necessity' (Article 25). It is widely accepted that the ARSIWA reflect customary international law.[3]

The common element of these concepts is that they allow a State to act in a manner that is not in conformity with existing obligations of customary law or treaties. By their very nature, these concepts are of an exceptional character in the general setting of the international legal order and must be strictly limited.

The concepts of necessity and of *force majeure* are listed in the ARSIWA among the circumstances precluding wrongfulness. Both have played important parts in the practice of investment tribunals.

[2] *Ziat, Ben Kiran*, 29 December 1924, 2 RIAA 730; *Spanish Zone of Morocco Claim*, 1 May 1925, 2 RIAA, 615, 642; *Pinson v Mexico*, 19 October 1928, 5 RIAA 327, 419; see also the *Diplomatic and Consular Staff in Teheran* (*United States v Iran*), Judgment, 24 May 1980, ICJ Reports (1980) 3, paras 58–61 where Iran failed to control militant groups and approved of their acts. Generally, I Brownlie, *Principles of Public International Law* (7th edn 2008) 466.

[3] See *Legal Consequences of the Construction of a Wall in the Occupied Palestinian Territory*, Advisory Opinion, 9 July 2004, ICJ Reports (2004) 136, para 140; *Gabčikovo-Nagymaros Project* (*Hungary v Slovakia*), Judgment, 25 September 1997, ICJ Reports (1997) 7, 63, para 102. This view is shared by investment tribunals: *Biwater Gauff v Tanzania*, Award, 24 July 2008, para 773; *Rumeli v Kazakhstan*, Award, 29 July 2008, paras 576–580; *Chevron v Ecuador I*, Interim Award, 1 December 2008, para 118; *Hamester v Ghana*, Award, 18 June 2010, para 171; *Tulip v Turkey*, Award, 10 March 2014, para 281; *Quiborax v Bolivia*, Award, 16 September 2015, para 555; *Crystallex v Venezuela*, Award, 4 April 2016, para 848; *Almås v Poland*, Award, 27 June 2016, para 206; *Masdar v Spain*, Award, 16 May 2018, para 167; *Gavrilović v Croatia*, Award, 26 July 2018, para 779.

(a) Necessity

Necessity is not defined in Article 25 of the ARSIWA but is described by way of identifying its limits:

1. Necessity may not be invoked by a State as a ground for precluding the wrongfulness of an act not in conformity with an international obligation of that State unless the act:
   (a) is the only means for the State to safeguard an essential interest against a grave and imminent peril; and
   (b) does not seriously impair an essential interest of the State or States towards which the obligation exists, or of the international community as a whole.
2. In any case, necessity may not be invoked by a State as a ground for precluding wrongfulness if:
   (a) the international obligation in question excludes the possibility of invoking necessity; or
   (b) the State has contributed to the situation of necessity.

In tribunal practice, the decisive questions were usually whether the measures taken were the only means to deal with the situation and whether the State had contributed to the situation of necessity.[4]

Since the rule dealing with necessity is an exception to existing international obligations, tribunals have construed it narrowly. In the absence of a clause allowing for self-judgment, they have refused to rely solely on the judgment of the host country.[5]

In *CMS v Argentina*,[6] the respondent had pleaded economic necessity, but the Tribunal found that the conditions for the application of this concept were not met:

[4] *Sempra v Argentina*, Award, 28 September 2007, paras 347, 350, 353–354; *National Grid v Argentina*, Award, 3 November 2008, paras 258–262; *Suez and Vivendi v Argentina*, Decision on Liability, 30 July 2010, paras 260, 263–265; *Total v Argentina*, Decision on Liability, 27 December 2010, paras 220–223, 345, 484; *Impregilo v Argentina*, Award, 21 June 2011, paras 351–353, 356–359; *EDF v Argentina*, Award, 11 June 2012, paras 1172–1176.

[5] *Gabčikovo-Nagymaros Project* (*Hungary v Slovakia*), Judgment, 25 September 1997, ICJ Reports (1997) 7, 63, para 51; *CMS v Argentina*, Award, 12 May 2005, para 317; *LG&E v Argentina*, Decision on Liability, 3 October 2006, paras 207–214; *Sempra v Argentina*, Award, 28 September 2007, para 345; *BG Group v Argentina*, Final Award, 27 December 2007, paras 410; *National Grid v Argentina*, Award, 3 November 2008, para 257; *Suez and Vivendi v Argentina*, Decision on Liability, 30 July 2010, paras 235–243; *Impregilo v Argentina*, Award, 21 June 2011, paras 344–345; *EDF v Argentina*, Award, 11 June 2012, para 1171.

[6] *CMS v Argentina*, Award, 12 May 2005.

the Tribunal is persuaded that the situation was difficult enough to justify the government taking action to prevent a worsening of the situation and the danger of total economic collapse.[7]

A different issue, however, is whether the measures adopted were 'the only way' for the State to safeguard the interests. This is indeed debatable... The International Law Commission's comment to the effect that the plea of necessity is 'excluded if there are other (otherwise lawful) means available, even if they may be more costly or less convenient,' is persuasive in assisting this Tribunal in concluding that the measures adopted were not the only steps available.[8]

The second limit is the requirement for the State not to have contributed to the situation of necessity... The issue, however, is whether the contribution to the crisis by Argentina has or has not been sufficiently substantial. The Tribunal, when reviewing the circumstances of the present dispute, must conclude that this was the case... the Tribunal observes that government policies and their shortcomings significantly contributed to the crisis and the emergency and while exogenous factors did fuel additional difficulties they do not exempt the Respondent from its responsibility in the matter.[9]

Therefore, the Tribunal considered that an economic crisis may give rise to a plea of necessity in principle. But it found that two requirements for a finding of necessity were not met in the particular case: the measures taken by Argentina were not the only way to cope with the situation and Argentina itself had contributed to the situation.[10]

The Tribunal in *LG&E v Argentina*[11] adopted a different view of the facts and accepted the respondent's plea of necessity for a limited period. This finding was based on the security clause[12] of the US–Argentina BIT supported by an analysis of Article 25 of the ARSIWA. The Tribunal said:

[7] At para 322.

[8] At paras 323–324.

[9] At paras 328–329; *Enron v Argentina*, Award, 22 May 2007, paras 294 et seq and *Sempra v Argentina*, Award, 28 September 2007, paras 333 et seq, essentially based their decisions on the reasoning of *CMS v Argentina*. In the context of its financial crisis, Argentina argued that its measures were necessary to protect the human rights of its citizens. However, the Tribunals saw no conflict between the rights of foreign investors and human rights of nationals; see eg *Suez and Vivendi v Argentina*, Decision on Liability, 30 July 2010, para 262; *Urbaser v Argentina*, Award, 8 December 2016, para 720.

[10] In the same sense: *Total v Argentina*, Decision on Liability, 27 December 2010, paras 220–224, 345, 482–484; *Impregilo v Argentina*, Award, 21 June 2011, paras 344–359.

[11] *LG&E v Argentina*, Decision on Liability, 3 October 2006. For a discussion of the differences between the *CMS* and *LG&E* rulings, see A Reinisch, 'Necessity in International Investment Arbitration—An Unnecessary Split of Opinions in Recent ICSID Cases? Comments on *CMS v Argentina* and *LG&E v Argentina*' (2007) 8 *JWIT* 191.

[12] See IX.4(b)*cc* below.

> In the judgment of the Tribunal, from 1 December 2001 until 26 April 2003, Argentina was in a period of crisis during which it was necessary to enact measures to maintain public order and protect its essential security interests.[13]
>
> Evidence has been put before the Tribunal that the conditions as of December 2001 constituted the highest degree of public disorder and threatened Argentina's essential security interests. This was not merely a period of 'economic problems' or 'business cycle fluctuation' as Claimants described… Extremely severe crises in the economic, political and social sectors reached their apex and converged in December 2001, threatening total collapse of the Government and the Argentine State.[14]
>
> A State may have several responses at its disposal to maintain public order or protect its essential security interests. In this sense, it is recognized that Argentina's suspension of the calculation of tariffs in U.S. dollars and the PPI adjustment of tariffs was a legitimate way of protecting its social and economic system.[15]

Both the *CMS* and the *LG&E* decisions assumed that the situation in Argentina affected, or possibly affected, an essential interest within the meaning of Article 25 of the ARSIWA.[16] But, contrary to the *CMS* ruling, the Tribunal in *LG&E* accepted that the measures adopted by Argentina had been the 'only means' available. In addition, the arbitrators in *LG&E* found that Argentina had not substantially contributed to the state of emergency.[17] Consequently, in the view of the Tribunal, Argentina was exempted from liability under the security clause of the Argentina–US BIT, as well as under general international law,[18] for the period between December 2001 and April 2003.

If the conditions for the existence of necessity are met, the further question arises whether the host State must resume performance of its obligations as soon as the situation of emergency ceases to exist and whether it has to compensate the foreign investor for the damage that arose from the suspension of its duties.[19] In *CMS v Argentina*, the Tribunal found that '[e]ven if the plea of necessity were accepted, compliance with the obligation would reemerge as soon as the circumstance precluding wrongfulness no longer existed'[20] and that it was the duty of the Tribunal

[13] At para 226.
[14] At para 231.
[15] At para 239.
[16] See paras 319 of *CMS* and paras 251–257 of *LG&E*.
[17] See *LG&E* at para 257: 'There is no serious evidence in the record that Argentina contributed to the crisis resulting in the state of necessity.'
[18] At para 258. See also: *Urbaser v Argentina*, Award, 8 December 2016, paras 717–718.
[19] See Article 27 of ARSIWA: 'The invocation of a circumstance precluding wrongfulness in accordance with this Chapter is without prejudice to: (a) compliance with the obligation in question, if and to the extent that the circumstances precluding wrongfulness no longer exists; (b) the question of compensation for any material loss caused by the act in question.'
See also *Gabčikovo-Nagymaros Project* (*Hungary v Slovakia*), Judgment, 25 September 1997, ICJ Reports (1997) 7, 63, paras 48, 101; *EDF v Argentina*, Award, 11 June 2012, paras 1177–1180.
[20] *CMS v Argentina*, Award, 12 May 2005, para 382.

to determine the compensation due.[21] In *LG&E v Argentina*, however, the Tribunal explicitly excluded the measures adopted by Argentina during the period of necessity from the calculation of damages, arguing that the damage suffered during the state of necessity should be borne by the investor. In the view of the Tribunal, Argentina could only be held liable for those measures it had adopted before and after the state of necessity.[22]

Since the decisions on the Argentine financial crisis, there have been several cases involving insurgencies[23] and civil war in which a state of necessity was invoked by host States. *Unión Fenosa v Egypt*[24] dealt with a shortfall of supply of gas to the claimant's gas liquefaction plant. Egypt argued that the events of the Arab Spring posed a threat to the basic functioning of the State and that the prioritization of its domestic needs was the only way to maintain public order and stability.[25] The Tribunal found that a shortage in gas supply had occurred before and after the Arab Spring and that this was caused by insufficient policies in the energy sector.[26] Since Egypt did not cut the gas supply proportionally to other consumers, the Tribunal also denied the 'only way' criterion:

> the non-supply of gas to the Plant was not attributable to the Egyptian revolution or social unrest; nor was it begun or maintained as the only way to safeguard the Respondent's essential interest against a grave and imminent peril, within the meaning of Article 25 of the ILC Articles.[27]

In *von Pezold v Zimbabwe*, the respondent attempted to defend controversial land reform policies by a state of necessity. Zimbabwe argued that the State had entered into a severe political and economic crisis threatening the survival of the State.[28] The Tribunal recognized that Zimbabwe faced challenging times but that the interest at stake was merely the political survival of the incumbent government. Thus, there was neither an essential interest[29] nor a grave and imminent peril for purposes of Article 25(1)(a) ARSIWA.[30] Zimbabwe argued that the objective of the land redistribution policies was to address colonial injustices. The Tribunal accepted that positive discriminatory measures to correct colonial wrongs may be

[21] At paras 383–394.

[22] *LG&E v Argentina*, Decision on Liability, 3 October 2006, paras 260–266; see also: *Urbaser v Argentina*, Award, 8 December 2016, para 719.

[23] *von Pezold v Zimbabwe*, Award, 28 July 2015, paras 610–668; *South American Silver v Bolivia*, Award, 22 November 2018, paras 611–621.

[24] *Unión Fenosa v Egypt*, Award, 31 August 2018, Part VIII.

[25] At paras 8.5–8.21.

[26] At para 8.44.

[27] At para 8.48.

[28] *von Pezold v Zimbabwe*, Award, 28 July 2015, paras 610–616.

[29] At paras 631–632.

[30] At paras 636–637.

justifiable. However, the Tribunal found Zimbabwe's approach too extreme and therefore in breach of the *erga omnes* obligation not to discriminate:

> This breach of an obligation *erga omnes* by Zimbabwe, through the implementation of the FTLRP and associated policies, was an impairment to the international community as a whole and ILC Article 25(1)(b) precludes a defence of necessity.[31]

(b) *Force majeure*

If a State finds itself in a situation that makes it impossible to perform an obligation, the principle of *force majeure* may apply. Article 23 of the ARSIWA, expresses the rule as follows:

> 1. The wrongfulness of an act of a State not in conformity with an international obligation of that State is precluded if the act is due to *force majeure*, that is the occurrence of an irresistible force or of an unforeseen event, beyond the control of the State, making it materially impossible in the circumstances to perform the obligation.
> 2. Paragraph 1 does not apply if:
>   (a) the situation of *force majeure* is due, either alone or in combination with other factors, to the conduct of the State invoking it; or
>   (b) the State has assumed the risk of that situation occurring.

Although the principle of *force majeure* may be viewed as a general principle of law,[32] this does not mean that only one version of the principle exists in practice. Various versions have been included in oil and gas contracts[33] and the interpretation of a contractual *force majeure* clause will turn primarily on the specific language of the clause.[34] A *force majeure* clause in a contract may provide for a consultation period[35] or limit its scope to non-discriminatory application.[36]

It is generally accepted that for the existence of *force majeure* it is not sufficient that performance becomes more difficult. Lack of funds, insolvency, or other forms of political and economic crises will not amount to *force majeure*.[37]

[31] At para 657. FTLRP: Fast Track Land Reform Programme.

[32] J Crawford, *The International Law Commission's Articles on State Responsibility* (2002) 173.

[33] R Dolzer, *Petroleum Contracts and International Law* (2018) 128–132.

[34] In *Strabag v Libya*, Award, 29 June 2020, paras 813, 821–830, 836–856, the Tribunal was confronted with different *force majeure* clauses in several construction contracts.

[35] *General Dynamics v Libya*, Final Award, 5 January 2016, para 338.

[36] *Unión Fenosa v Egypt*, Award, 31 August 2018, para 9.76.

[37] *Greentech v Italy*, Final Award, 23 December 2018, para 451.

Autopista v Venezuela[38] concerned the government's failure to adjust bridge tolls, as agreed with the investor, after violent public protests. In consequence, the funding of the construction costs became impossible. Venezuela invoked *force majeure*. The Tribunal found that three conditions must be fulfilled for a valid *force majeure* excuse: impossibility, unforeseeability, and non-attributability. The Tribunal found that Venezuela bore the burden of proof for the existence of these conditions. On the facts, the Tribunal found that the magnitude of the public protests and hence the impossibility of raising the toll was foreseeable. Therefore, it rejected the argument of *force majeure*.[39]

4. Treaty law

(a) Emergencies and armed conflicts in the law of treaties

The Vienna Convention on the Law of Treaties (VCLT) offers the doctrines of supervening impossibility of performance (Article 61) and of fundamental change of circumstances (Article 62) to deal with extraordinary developments such as emergencies and armed conflict. These two doctrines have a high threshold for their application.

Impossibility to perform a treaty under Article 61 of the VCLT would require the disappearance or destruction of an object indispensable for the treaty's performance. A strict interpretation of the term 'object' in the sense of a physical object would drastically reduce the use of impossibility of performance in the context of investment law. A more flexible interpretation that would also look at the disappearance of the objectives or the means for the treaty's performance, might lead to a different result. An example for impossibility of performance would be the impossibility to guarantee the free transfer of payments in times of war.

As for fundamental change of circumstances under Article 62 of the VCLT or *rebus sic stantibus*, the requirements are also difficult to meet. Not only would the continued existence of the circumstances have to constitute an essential basis of the parties' consent. The change would also have to transform the extent of the obligations radically. The existence of peace as an essential basis of consent to an investment treaty is difficult to argue, especially if the treaty contains provisions dealing with armed conflict. The second condition, the radical transformation of the obligations' extent, is also problematic. In the *Fisheries Jurisdiction* case, the

38 *Autopista v Venezuela*, Award, 23 September 2003.

39 At paras 106–119. The Tribunal added obiter remarks on the criteria of impossibility, and non-attributability at paras 120–129.

International Court of Justice (ICJ) required that the remaining performance was 'essentially different from that originally undertaken'.[40]

Moreover, any use of the doctrines of impossibility of performance and fundamental change of circumstances would be subject to the procedural requirements of the VCLT (Articles 65–68) for the termination or suspension of treaties. Therefore, the doctrines of supervening impossibility of performance and of fundamental change of circumstances under the law of treaties are available, in principle, to States in times of armed conflict. But the requirements for their application are difficult to meet.

Article 73 of the VCLT states that the Convention does not prejudge any question that may arise from the outbreak of hostilities between States. Therefore, any rules governing the effects of armed conflict on treaties continue to apply.

In 2011, the ILC presented Draft Articles on the effects of armed conflicts on treaties.[41] The Draft Articles contain a presumption of continuity of treaties: the existence of an armed conflict does not *ipso facto* terminate or suspend the operation of treaties (Article 3). The Draft Articles refer to certain factors that indicate whether a treaty is susceptible to termination, withdrawal, or suspension. These include the nature of the treaty and the characteristics of the armed conflict (Article 6). In addition, '[w]here a treaty itself contains provisions on its operation in situations of armed conflict, those provisions shall apply' (Article 4). As set out below, some investment treaties do indeed refer to situations of armed conflict and other forms of violence.

The Draft Articles on the effects of armed conflict also refer to treaties that, by their subject matter, implicate that they continue to operate, in whole or in part, during armed conflict (Article 7). A list of treaties annexed to that provision includes '[t]reaties of friendship commerce and navigation and agreements concerning private rights'.[42] In its Commentary, the ILC speaks of 'treaties of FCN and analogous agreements concerning private rights, including bilateral investment treaties'.[43] This would speak in favour of the continued application of bilateral investment treaties (BITs) during armed conflicts.

Under the Draft Articles, any termination or suspension of a treaty in times of armed conflict would not operate *ipso facto* but would be subject to procedural requirements. An intention by a State Party to terminate or suspend a treaty requires notification. A State Party thus affected may object. This would trigger formal

[40] *Fisheries Jurisdiction* (*Germany v Iceland*), Judgment, 2 February 1973, ICJ Reports (1973) 49, para 43. See also *Gabčíkovo-Nagymaros Project* (*Hungary v Slovakia*), Judgment, 25 September 1997, ICJ Reports (1997) 7, para 104. But see the CJEU in *Racke GmbH and Co v Hauptzollamt Mainz*, C-162/96, Judgment, 16 June 1998, para 56.

[41] Adopted by the International Law Commission at its sixty-third session in 2011 and submitted to the General Assembly as a part of the Commission's report covering the work of that session (A/66/10). *Yearbook of the International Law Commission*, vol II, Part Two (2011).

[42] Annex to Article 7, lit (e).

[43] Commentary 48 to Annex to Article 7.

dispute settlement procedures (Article 9). Even where suspension or termination does take place, the treaty may contain clauses that are separable (Article 11).

Therefore, to the extent that the ILC Draft Articles on the effects of armed conflict represent the law governing the effects of armed conflict on treaties, they tend to support the principle of the continued applicability of investment treaties.

(b) Treaty provisions dealing with emergencies and armed conflicts

Many treaties contain specific provisions dealing with the protection of investments in emergency situations. Of the standards of protection typically contained in investment treaties, the guarantee of full protection and security (FPS) is the most important one in situations of armed conflict and other forms of violence.[44] The FPS standard involves a duty of the State to refrain and a duty to protect. The duty to refrain involves the obligation of the host State to exercise restraint in the use of armed force. The duty to protect includes the obligation to defend the investment against violence by non-State actors.[45] These non-State actors may be rebels or insurgents engaged in a struggle against the government or private groups engaged in violent action against the investment.

Some treaties for the protection of investments offer provisions specifically tailored to emergency situations and armed conflicts. These are compensation for losses clauses, extended war clauses, and security clauses.

aa. Compensation for losses clauses

Many bilateral investment treaties contain clauses providing for national treatment and most-favoured-nation (MFN) treatment in relation to any measures taken by host States in reaction to war or to other forms of armed conflict, state of emergency, revolution, insurrection, civil disturbance, or similar events. The measures concerned would be restitution, indemnification, compensation, or other settlement that the States may take. These clauses are usually referred to as compensation-for-losses clauses. A typical clause of this kind is Article 5 of the Libya–Turkey BIT of 2009 which reads:

> Investors of either Contracting Party whose investments suffer losses in the territory of the other Contracting Party owing to war, insurrection, civil disturbance or other similar events shall be accorded by such other Contracting Party treatment no less favourable than that accorded to its own investors or to investors

[44] See VIII.2 above.

[45] *Biwater Gauff v Tanzania*, Award, 24 July 2008, para 730.

> of any third country, whichever is the most favourable treatment, as regards any measures it adopts in relation to such losses.

Clauses of this type do not create absolute rights to restitution, indemnification, compensation, or other settlement. All they do is to promise non-discrimination in comparison with host State nationals or nationals of third countries in case there is a program of indemnification. Therefore, their effect depends on measures taken by the host State in relation to these investors.

Many BITs contain clauses of this type. Multilateral treaties, such as the North American Free Trade Agreement (NAFTA) (Article 1105(2)), the United States–Mexico–Canada Agreement (USMCA) (Article 14.7(1)), and the Energy Charter Treaty (ECT) (Article 12(1)) also contain the obligation to grant non-discriminatory treatment with respect to measures adopted relating to losses suffered owing to armed conflict or civil strife.

In a series of cases against Argentina, the respondent relied on the compensation-for-losses clauses in the respective BITs. Argentina claimed the existence of an economic national emergency and argued that the compensation-for-losses clause constituted a *lex specialis* governing emergency situations exempting it from the BITs' other substantive obligations, notably FPS. The tribunals have consistently rejected this argument finding that the compensation-for-losses clauses did not displace the BITs' other protections but were additional to them.[46] In two cases against Zimbabwe, tribunals reached the same conclusion.[47]

In the context of its civil war, Libya similarly argued that a compensation for losses clause serves as *lex specials* to other treaty protection standards, resulting in a substantial limitation of protection. In *Cengiz v Libya*,[48] the Tribunal held that the compensation for losses clause did not replace the FPS standard but created an additional and independent obligation.[49] The Tribunal said:

> The FPS standard only provides limited protection to a foreign investor; the protection is only triggered if the host State directly causes harm to the investment or fails to meet a standard of due diligence. The State may provide an increased level of protection to its own investors, or to investors of a third country; in such

[46] *CMS v Argentina*, Award, 12 May 2005, para 375; *Enron v Argentina*, Award, 22 May 2007, paras 320–321; *BG Group v Argentina*, Final Award, 24 December 2007, para 382; *National Grid v Argentina*, Award, 3 November 2008, para 253; *Suez and Vivendi v Argentina*, Decision on Liability, 30 July 2010, paras 270–271; *Total v Argentina*, Decision on Liability, 27 December 2010, para 229; *EDF v Argentina*, Award, 11 June 2012, paras 1153–1160; *Impregilo v Argentina*, Award, 21 June 2011, paras 336–343; *El Paso v Argentina*, Award, 31 October 2011, paras 559–560.

[47] *Funnekotter v Zimbabwe*, Award, 22 April 2009, para 104; *von Pezold v Zimbabwe*, Award, 28 July 2015, paras 588–599.

[48] *Cengiz v Libya*, Final Award, 7 November 2018, para 351.

[49] At paras 350–370.

case Article 5 comes into operation, and such heightened standard must also be applied to Turkish (or Libyan) investors.[50]

bb. Extended war clauses

Some treaties contain extended war clauses. These also relate to war or to other armed conflict, state of emergency, revolution, insurrection, civil disturbance, or similar events, and typically include the non-discrimination provision of the compensation for losses clauses. But they go one step further in that they also contain absolute obligations. Under these clauses, losses suffered by investors at the hand of the host State's forces or authorities through requisitioning or through destruction not required by the necessities of the situation are treated in analogy to expropriation. In other words, such acts require compensation that is prompt, adequate and effective. Article 12 of the ECT is an example of such an extended war clause. After offering a compensation for losses clause in paragraph (1), it adds:

> (2) Without prejudice to paragraph (1), an Investor of a Contracting Party which, in any of the situations referred to in that paragraph, suffers a loss in the Area of another Contracting Party resulting from
> (a) requisitioning of its Investment or part thereof by the latter's forces or authorities; or
> (b) destruction of its Investment or part thereof by the latter's forces or authorities, which was not required by the necessity of the situation,
> shall be accorded restitution or compensation which in either case shall be prompt, adequate and effective.

Under an extended war clause, compensation is due only if the adverse act was caused by government forces or authorities and not by rebel forces. The duty to make restitution or pay compensation in the case of requisitioning does not hinge on military necessity: even if the requisitioning was mandated by military necessity, restitution or compensation is still due. By contrast, in the case of destruction, restitution or compensation would be due only if the forces acted in excess of military necessity. In other words, collateral damage arising from military action that is lawful under the *jus in bello* need not be compensated. Unlike the compensation-for-losses clauses, extended war clauses grant absolute rights. They reflect the principles of the laws of war on the protection of private property as codified in the Hague and Geneva Conventions.

[50] At para 361. To the same effect: *Strabag v Libya*, Award, 29 June 2020, paras 221–225. *Öztaş v Libya*, Final Award, 14 June 2018, para 167 reached a contrary decision but the question had not been argued before the Tribunal.

Although extended war clauses offer far-reaching rights, their practical relevance is limited. Only a minority of investment treaties contain clauses of this kind. In addition, they impose a high burden of proof upon investors wishing to rely on them.

AAPL v Sri Lanka,[51] involved the application of the extended war clause in Article 4(2) of the United Kingdom–Sri Lanka BIT to anti-insurgent operations that had led to the investment's destruction. The Tribunal held that the investor bore the burden of proving that the government forces and not the rebels had caused the destruction, that the destruction occurred out of combat, and that there was no military necessity for the destruction.[52] The Tribunal found that the claimant had been unable to bear this heavy burden of proof and dismissed the claim based on the extended war clause.[53]

In *AMT v Zaire*,[54] looting and destruction of the investment had taken place at the hands of elements of the armed forces in uniform involving the use of army weapons. In interpreting the extended war clause in Article IV 2(b) of the US–Zaire BIT, the Tribunal reached the conclusion that the soldiers in uniform did not, in fact, represent the country's armed forces since they had acted individually and not in any organized manner. Therefore, the destruction was caused by separate individuals and not by the forces.[55]

In *Strabag v Libya*,[56] the Tribunal applied Article 5 of the Austria–Libya BIT containing an extended war clause. The case involved both requisitioning and destruction of the investor's property. The claimant alleged that, in the course of the civil war, a significant quantity of its property had been requisitioned by Libyan government forces and not returned.[57] The Tribunal, although placing the burden of proof on the investor, awarded compensation for lost equipment based on the evidence before it.[58] The attribution of responsibility for destruction posed a particular challenge due to the chaotic circumstances of the civil war. The Tribunal found that several actors contributed to the destruction and said:

> The Tribunal observes in this regard that a portion of the loss at issue in this claim was inflicted by rebel or NATO forces; another portion involved losses due to looting by civilians and thefts by Al Hani's own employees; and a third portion resulted from actions by Libyan military personnel in non-combat situations. The Tribunal accordingly determines that approximately one-third of the claimed

[51] *AAPL v Sri Lanka*, Final Award, 27 June 1990.
[52] At para 58.
[53] At paras 59–64.
[54] *AMT v Zaire*, Award, 21 February 1997.
[55] At paras 7.02–7.15.
[56] *Strabag v Libya*, Award, 29 June 2020.
[57] At para 214.
[58] At paras 257–263, 270–271.

> losses are attributable to the actions by State forces not involving military necessity, actions for which Respondent is liable pursuant to Article 5(2)(b) of the Treaty.[59]

cc. Security clauses

Some investment treaties contain clauses that reserve far-reaching discretion to States in times of emergency and armed conflict. Under these non-precluded measures clauses, States may use essential security interests as a defence to justify action that is otherwise prohibited. These clauses have the potential to offset the entire range of protections in investment treaties including the FPS standard.

Article XI of the BIT between Argentina and the United States provides:

> This Treaty shall not preclude the application by either Party of measures necessary for the maintenance of public order, the fulfilment of its obligations with respect to the maintenance or restoration of international peace or security, or the Protection of its own essential security interests.

The conditions for the application of such a security exception are relatively easy to meet. The Article speaks of public order and of essential security interests. This would cover not only international or civil wars but also terrorism and armed rebellion. The reference to 'the maintenance or restoration of international peace or security' echoes Article 39 of the UN Charter. Therefore, action in pursuance of Security Council resolutions under Chapter VII of the Charter may also be covered by this exception. The potential danger to the rights of investors posed by security exceptions of this kind is considerable.

Security clauses show some variations. Some security clauses, like the one in the US–Argentina BIT, simply refer to 'measures necessary' for the protection of essential security interests. This means that the invocation of these clauses remains subject to the scrutiny of tribunals. Other clauses are self-judging. This means, the State taking the measures reserves the right to decide which measures it considers necessary. It is accepted in international practice that the self-judging nature of a clause must be stated expressly. It cannot be implied.[60] The self-judging

[59] At para 298; see also paras 320–321.

[60] *Military and Paramilitary Activities in and against Nicaragua* (*Nicaragua v United States*), Judgment, 27 June 1986, ICJ Reports (1986) 14, paras 222, 282; *Gabčíkovo-Nagymaros Project* (*Hungary v Slovakia*), Judgment, 25 September 1997, ICJ Reports (1997) 7, paras 51–52; *Oil Platforms* (*Iran v United States*) Judgment, 6 November 2003, ICJ Reports (2003) 161, para 43; *CMS v Argentina*, Award, 12 May 2005, paras 370–374; *Enron v Argentina*, Award, 22 May 2007, para 336; *LG&E v Argentina*, Decision on Liability, 3 October 2006, para 213; *Sempra v Argentina*, Award, 28 September 2007, para 383; *El Paso v Argentina*, Award, 31 October 2011, paras 563–610; *Mobil v Argentina*, Decision on Jurisdiction and Liability, 10 April 2013, paras 1030–1056; *Devas v India*, Award on Jurisdiction and Merits, 25 July 2016, paras 218–220.

nature is usually expressed by the words 'that it considers necessary'. The ECT (Article 24(3)), the NAFTA (Article 2102), the USMCA (Article 32.2.), and the Comprehensive Economic and Trade Agreement (CETA) (Article 28.6) contain self-judging security clauses. The current US Model BIT and recent BITs of the United States also contain clauses of this type.

A self-judging security clause gives the State far-reaching freedom of action. The only limiting factors to the State's discretion are the principles of good faith and the prohibition of abuse of right, but only a minority of treaties contain security clauses, and an even smaller number is self-judging.

The security clause in Article 24(3) of the ECT shows some special features. It provides:

> (3) The provisions of this Treaty other than those referred to in paragraph (1) shall not be construed to prevent any Contracting Party from taking any measure which it considers necessary:
> (a) for the protection of its essential security interests including those
> (i) relating to the supply of Energy Materials and Products to a military establishment; or
> (ii) taken in time of war, armed conflict or other emergency in international relations;
> (b) relating to the implementation of national policies respecting the non-proliferation of nuclear weapons or other nuclear explosive devices or needed to fulfil its obligations under the Treaty on the Non-Proliferation of Nuclear Weapons, the Nuclear Suppliers Guidelines, and other international nuclear non-proliferation obligations or understandings; or
> (c) for the maintenance of public order.

Therefore, the ECT's security clause is self-judging in that it refers to 'any measure which it [ie the State] considers necessary'. However, it relates only to international armed conflicts. It refers to measures 'taken in time of war, armed conflict or other emergency in international relations'. This excludes non-international armed conflicts from its scope.

The ECT's security clause also contains a savings clause with respect to certain standards of protection. Specifically, it exempts the articles dealing with expropriation (Article 13) and with the extended war clause (Article 12). In other words, requisitioning as well as destruction beyond the necessity of war remains compensable. This would seem to be a logical solution. It does not make sense to have a treaty provide specific protection in times of armed conflict only to have the entire treaty defeated by a far-reaching security clause which gives the State unlimited discretion.

The role of customary law in the interpretation of a security clause played a prominent role in cases involving Article XI of the Argentina–US BIT. These cases did not involve armed force but arose in the wake of Argentina's economic crisis around 2002 and the resulting government measures. The question was whether Article XI incorporated the customary law rule on necessity or should be considered as an autonomous standard. The point led to conflicting decisions by different tribunals and annulment committees.

The Tribunal in *CMS v Argentina* held that Article XI was to be interpreted in a manner which reflects the customary standard of necessity.[61] The *CMS* ad hoc Committee[62] disagreed and found that Article XI was a free-standing provision which is not the same as the necessity rule under customary international law as codified in Article 25 of the ARSIWA.[63] The ad hoc Committee held that Article XI was a threshold requirement: if it applies, the BIT's substantive provisions do not apply.[64] Nevertheless, the ad hoc Committee did not annul the Award on this ground. Subsequent tribunals and ad hoc committees have grappled with the issue of the relationship of security clauses and the rule on necessity in Article 25 of the ARSIWA without reaching a uniform answer.[65]

In some cases, the respondent invoked security clauses in situations not involving a public emergency or armed conflict. *Devas v India*[66] arose from the cancellation of an agreement to lease space segment capacity of satellites. India relied on the security clause in the Mauritius–India BIT[67] to defend national security interests, arguing that it needed the capacities for military purposes. The Tribunal found that the words 'directed to' in the security clause signified a lower threshold than 'necessary'.[68] It noted, however, that the action must be directed not at any security interest but at an 'essential security interest'.[69] Despite the characterization of the security clause as non-self-judging, the Tribunal granted India a wide margin of appreciation:

61 *CMS v Argentina*, Award, 12 May 2005, paras 322–358.

62 *CMS v Argentina*, Decision on Annulment, 25 September 2007.

63 At para 130.

64 At paras 128–136.

65 *Continental Casualty v Argentina*, Award, 5 September 2008, paras 160–236, Decision on Annulment, 16 September 2011, paras 114–132; *Sempra v Argentina*, Decision on Annulment, 29 June 2010, paras 192–219; *Enron v Argentina*, Decision on Annulment, 30 July 2010, paras 400–405; *El Paso v Argentina*, Award, 31 October 2011, paras 552–555; *Mobil v Argentina*, Decision on Jurisdiction and Liability, 10 April 2013, paras 1024–1028; *Devas v India*, Award on Jurisdiction and Merits, 25 July 2016, paras 256, 293–294; *Deutsche Telekom v India*, Interim Award, 13 December 2017, paras 225–229.

66 *Devas v India*, Award on Jurisdiction and Merits, 25 July 2016.

67 Article 11(3) Mauritius–India BIT: 'The provision of the Agreement shall not in any way limit the right of either Contracting Party to apply prohibitions or restrictions of any kind or take any other action which is *directed to* the protection of its essential security interests, or to the protection of public health or the prevention of diseases in pests and animals or plants.' Emphasis added.

68 At paras 233–243.

69 At paras 235, 243.

> An arbitral tribunal may not sit in judgment on national security matters as on any other factual dispute arising between an investor and a State. National security issues relate to the existential core of a state. An investor who wishes to challenge a State decision in that respect faces a heavy burden of proof, such as bad faith, absence of authority or application to measures that do not relate to essential security interests.[70]

The Tribunal concluded that the spectrum reservation for military purposes was 'directed to the protection of its essential security interests'.[71] Nevertheless, it found that India had allocated 40 per cent of the capacities to other sectors and held India liable accordingly.[72]

Deutsche Telekom v India,[73] involved similar facts but a differently worded security clause in the Germany–India BIT.[74] Under that provision, measures to safeguard essential security interests are allowed 'to the extent necessary'. The Tribunal accepted that in matters of essential security interests 'a degree of deference is owed to a State's assessment'.[75] The Tribunal said:

> To assess the necessity of the measures to safeguard the state's essential security interests, the Tribunal will thus determine whether the measure was principally targeted to protect the essential security interests at stake and was objectively required in order to achieve that protection, taking into account whether the state had reasonable alternatives, less in conflict or more compliant with its international obligations.[76]

The Tribunal emphasized that the security clause in the BIT with Germany, referring to 'the extent necessary', implied a more stringent requirement than under the India–Mauritius BIT and found that India's measures did not meet this standard.[77]

70 At para 245.
71 At para 354.
72 At para 373.
73 *Deutsche Telekom v India*, Interim Award, 13 December 2017.
74 Art 12 Germany–India BIT: 'Nothing in this Agreement shall prevent either Contracting Party from applying prohibitions or restrictions *to the extent necessary* for the protection of its essential security interests, or for the prevention of diseases and pests in animals or plants.' Emphasis added.
75 At para 235.
76 At para 239.
77 At para 288.

X
Attribution

ADDITIONAL READING: J Crawford, *The International Law Commission's Articles on State Responsibility* (2002); J Crawford, 'Investment Arbitration and the ILC Articles on State Responsibility' (2010) 25 *ICSID Rev* 134; L Schicho, 'Attribution and State Entities' (2011) 12 *JWIT* 283; J Crawford, *State Responsibility—The General Part* (2013); J Crawford and P Mertenskötter, 'The Use of the ILC's Attribution Rules in Investment Arbitration' in M Kinnear et al (eds) *Building International Investment Law* (2015) 27; S Olleson, 'Attribution in Investment Treaty Arbitration' (2016) 31 *ICSID Rev* 457; C Kovács, *Attribution in International Investment Law* (2018); G Petrochilos, 'Attribution' in K Yannaca-Small (ed) *Arbitration under International Investment Agreements* (2018) 14.01; C de Stefano, *Attribution in International Law and Arbitration* (2020).

1. Sources and principles

Attribution is the process whereby international law determines that a particular conduct is to be regarded as activity of a State which is capable of leading to State responsibility.[1] This area of customary international law was the object of extensive efforts at codification by the International Law Commission (ILC). After 40 years, this work culminated in the adoption of the Articles on Responsibility of States for Internationally Wrongful Acts (ARSIWA) in 2001.[2] Ever since their adoption there have been plans for a diplomatic conference with a view to conclude a convention on State responsibility.

The ARSIWA are accepted as reflecting the customary international law on matters of State responsibility. Therefore, tribunals generally treat them as binding.[3] Although the ARSIWA are designed primarily for the relations between States, their rules on attribution apply also to the relations between a State and a non-State entity such as an investor.[4]

[1] J Crawford, State Responsibility—The General Part (2013) 113.

[2] UN Doc A/56/10, Yearbook of the International Law Commission, 2001, vol II, Part Two. UN General Assembly Resolution 56/83 commended the ARSIWA to the attention of Governments. Since their adoption, the common designation as 'Draft Articles' is technically incorrect.

[3] *Hamester v Ghana*, Award, 18 June 2010, para 171; *Tulip v Turkey*, Award, 10 March 2014, para 281; *Almås v Poland*, Award, 27 June 2016, para 206; *Gavrilović v Croatia*, Award, 26 July 2018, para 779.

[4] See ARSIWA, General Commentary (5), Article 28, Commentary (3). See also *Flemingo v Poland*, Award, 12 August 2016, para 420; *Masdar v Spain*, Award, 16 May 2018, para 167.

As the name of the Articles on Responsibility of States for Internationally Wrongful Acts indicates, they cover conduct by States that is unlawful under international law. The rules on attribution in the ARSIWA are not general rules of representation and do not address the power of an entity to enter into agreements or undertake unilateral commitments on behalf of a State.[5] The Tribunal in *Devas v India*[6] described the limits of the ARSIWA in the following terms:

> ILC Articles 4, 5 and 8 do not provide general rules of attribution meaning that any act can be attributed to the State if the requirement of structure, function or control is met. The scope of these provisions is, rather, limited to conduct which constitutes a violation of international law, and should not be confused with rules on agency as they exist under private law.[7]

Nor do the ILC Articles apply to instances of simple breaches of contract. The distinction between a breach of international law and a breach of contract for purposes of attribution has been recognized by tribunals.[8] In *Impregilo v Pakistan*,[9] the Tribunal said:

> a clear distinction exists between the responsibility of a State for the conduct of an entity that violates international law (e.g. a breach of Treaty), and the responsibility of a State for the conduct of an entity that breaches a municipal law contract (i.e. Impregilo's Contract Claims). As noted by the *ad hoc* Committee in its decision on annulment in *Compañia de Aguas del Aconquija and Vivendi Universal v. Argentine Republic*, the international law rules on State responsibility and attribution apply to the former, but not the latter.[10]

Some treaties offer special rules on attribution. For instance, the Energy Charter Treaty (ECT) contains its own rules on attribution in Articles 22 and 23. The ARSIWA give precedence to these treaty provisions where they represent a *lex specialis*.[11] Tribunals have applied special rules on attribution where appropriate.[12]

[5] See J Crawford, 'Investment Arbitration and the ILC Articles on State Responsibility' (2010) *25* ICSID Rev 134.

[6] *Devas v India*, Award on Jurisdiction and Merits, 25 July 2016.

[7] At para 276.

[8] *Vivendi v Argentina*, Decision on Annulment, 3 July 2002, para 96; *Salini v Jordan*, Decision on Jurisdiction, 29 November 2004, para 157.

[9] *Impregilo v Pakistan*, Decision on Jurisdiction, 22 April 2005.

[10] At para 210.

[11] ARSIWA Article 55: '*Lex specialis* These articles do not apply where and to the extent that the conditions for the existence of an internationally wrongful act or the content or implementation of the international responsibility of a State are governed by special rules of international law.'

[12] *Genin v Estonia*, Award, 25 June 2001, para 327; *Ulysseas v Ecuador*, Final Award, 12 June 2012, paras 124–143; *Al Tamimi v Oman*, Award, 3 November 2015, para 321.

Attribution follows three basic principles:

(1) Structural attribution: actions of organs of States are attributed to the State. Under this principle attribution is based on the status of the acting entity. This principle is reflected in ARSIWA Article 4.
(2) Functional attribution: even without the status of an organ, the acts of an entity will be attributed to the State if the entity is acting in the exercise of governmental authority. This principle is reflected in ARSIWA Article 5.
(3) Control-based attribution: even without the status of an organ the actions of a person or entity will be attributed to the State if they take place under the direction and control of the State. This principle is reflected in ARSIWA Article 8.

In some decisions, especially those rendered before the adoption of the ARSIWA or shortly thereafter, tribunals have not applied these principles separately but have combined the criteria of structure, function, and control.[13] These decisions have been criticized by authors who have stressed the need for a differentiated and separate application of the rules on attribution.[14]

The three principles represent distinct grounds for attribution calling for different tests and should hence be kept apart. It is not permissible to amalgamate the characteristics of these principles into a blend of connecting points ultimately leading to attribution. More recent tribunal practice, set out below, has overwhelmingly recognized the discrete nature of the three principles of attribution and has applied them accordingly.

2. Organs, provinces, and municipalities

The ARSIWA deal with the attribution of the conduct of State organs in the following terms:

Article 4 Conduct of organs of a State

1. The conduct of any State organ shall be considered an act of that State under international law, whether the organ exercises legislative, executive, judicial or any other functions, whatever position it holds in the organization of the State,

[13] *Noble Ventures v Romania*, Award, 12 October 2005, paras 69–86; *MCI v Ecuador*, Award, 31 July 2007, para 225; *Deutsche Bank v Sri Lanka*, Award, 31 October 2012, para 405; *Ampal-American v Egypt*, Decision on Liability and Heads of Loss, 21 February 2017, paras 137–147.

[14] C Kovács, *Attribution in International Investment Law* (2018) 72, 214; C de Stefano, *Attribution in International Law and Arbitration* (2020) 121.

and whatever its character as an organ of the central government or of a territorial unit of the State.

2. An organ includes any person or entity which has that status in accordance with the internal law of the State.

(a) State organs

The ILC's Commentary (6) to ARSIWA Article 4 states:

> (6) Thus, the reference to a State organ in article 4 is intended in the most general sense. It is not limited to the organs of the central government, to officials at a high level or to persons with responsibility for the external relations of the State. It extends to organs of government of whatever kind or classification, exercising whatever functions, and at whatever level in the hierarchy, including those at provincial or even local level. No distinction is made for this purpose between legislative, executive, or judicial organs.

Therefore, the concept of 'organs' relates to the normal structure of the contemporary State. The ARSIWA are based upon the model of a hierarchical State, whether centralized or decentralized, operating with legislative, executive, and judicial organs, in which the structure and functions of these organs are determined by law.

Tribunals have held that actions by a variety of State organs were attributable to the State.[15] These included action by a government minister,[16] by the armed forces and police,[17] by the State treasury,[18] by the legislature,[19] and by the courts.[20] On the other hand, tribunals have refused to find that actions by private persons were attributable to the State.[21]

[15] *Rusoro v Venezuela*, Award, 22 August 2016, para 523.

[16] *Texaco v Libya*, Preliminary Award, 27 November 1975, para 23; *Zelena v Serbia*, Award, 9 November 2018, para 194.

[17] *Amco v Indonesia*, Award, 20 November 1984, paras 155, 170–172; *AAPL v Sri Lanka*, Award, 27 June 1990; *Busta v Czech Republic*, Award, 10 March 2017, para 400.

[18] *Eureko v Poland*, Partial Award, 19 August 2005, paras 115–134.

[19] *Nykomb v Latvia*, Award, 16 December 2003, sec 4.2; *Paushok v Mongolia*, Award on Jurisdiction and Liability, 28 April 2011, paras 298–299.

[20] *Azinian v Mexico*, Award, 1 November 1999, paras 97–103; *Loewen v United States*, Decision on Jurisdiction, 5 January 2001, paras 47–60; *Saipem v Bangladesh*, Award, 30 June 2009, paras 188–190; *RosInvest v Russian Federation*, Final Award, 12 September 2010, paras 602–603; *Gavrilović v Croatia*, Award, 25 July 2018, paras 795–804.

[21] *Tradex v Albania*, Award, 29 April 1999, paras 136, 147, 165, 169, 175, 198; *Tatneft v Ukraine*, Award, 29 July 2014, paras 514–516; *United Utilities v Estonia*, Award, 21 June 2019, paras 916–918.

(b) Provinces and municipalities

The same principles of attribution apply to the acts of territorial units of States, such as provinces and municipalities. Some treaties for the protection of investments specifically state that they apply to the political subdivisions of the parties.[22] The ECT in Article 23(1) contains a provision on the observance of the treaty by sub-national authorities:

> Each Contracting Party is fully responsible under this Treaty for the observance of all provisions of the Treaty, and shall take such reasonable measures as may be available to it to ensure such observance by regional and local governments and authorities within its Area.

This provision restates rather than amends the traditional rule of attribution.

Investment tribunals have consistently applied the rule that the central government is responsible for the acts of its territorial units. The Tribunal in *Vivendi v Argentina I*[23] said in this respect:

> it is well established that actions of a political subdivision of federal state, such as the Province of Tucumán in the federal state of the Argentine Republic, are attributable to the central government. It is equally clear that the internal constitutional structure of a country can not alter these obligations.[24]

Tribunals have applied this rule to provinces,[25] constituent states,[26] and municipalities.[27]

(c) The role of domestic law

The second paragraph of Article 4 of the ARSIWA underlines that the status of an organ depends primarily on the State's internal law. The ILC's Commentary states in this respect:

[22] Argentina–US BIT Article XIII: 'This Treaty shall apply to the political subdivisions of the Parties.'
[23] *Vivendi v Argentina*, Award, 21 November 2000.
[24] At para 49. Footnotes omitted. In the same sense: *ADF v United States*, Award, 9 January 2003, para 166.
[25] *Enron v Argentina*, Decision on Jurisdiction, 14 January 2004, para 32; *Suez and InterAgua v Argentina*, Decision on Liability, 30 July 2010, para 120; *Casinos Austria v Argentina*, Decision on Jurisdiction, 29 June 2018, para 288. See also the case of *Heirs of the Duc de Guise*, XIII RIAA, 150, 161, 15 September 1951, in which the Franco-Italian Conciliation Commission held that the Italian State was responsible for the conduct of Sicily even though Sicily enjoyed a status of autonomy in Italian law.
[26] *Grand River v United States*, Decision on Jurisdiction, 20 July 2006, para 1.
[27] *Metalclad v Mexico*, Award, 30 August 2000, para 73; *Mondev v United States*, Award, 11 October 2002, para 67; *Tokios Tokelės v Ukraine*, Decision on Jurisdiction, 29 April 2004, para 102.

> In determining what constitutes an organ of a State for the purposes of responsibility, the internal law and practice of each State are of prime importance. The structure of the State and the functions of its organs are not, in general, governed by international law. It is a matter for each State to decide how its administration is to be structured and which functions are to be assumed by government.[28]

Therefore, an inquiry into whether an entity is an organ of the State will normally start with an examination of its status under domestic law. If the domestic law endows it with the status of an organ the answer is clear. If it does not, the presumption is that it is not an organ.

In *Jan de Nul v Egypt*,[29] the Tribunal examined whether the Suez Canal Authority (SCA) was a State organ by looking at its status under Egyptian domestic law. The Tribunal found that under Egyptian law SCA was not classified as a State organ and that structurally it was not part of the Egyptian State.[30] The Tribunal said:

> An organ is part of the central or decentralized structure of the State, which means that it is a person or entity which is part of the legislative, executive, or judicial powers. To determine whether an entity is a State organ, one must first look to domestic law.[31]

Other tribunals too have relied on the law of the State concerned to determine whether an entity was a State organ.[32]

(d) Legal personality

If an entity has legal personality it will not normally be regarded as an organ of the State. An entity's capacity to own property, to sue and be sued and to perform transactions on its own behalf is difficult to reconcile with the status of a State organ.[33] Such an entity would be an actor in its own right rather than an instrument for the action of the State.

In *Bayindir v Pakistan*,[34] the Tribunal had to decide whether the National Highway Authority (NHA), a public corporation responsible for the planning,

28 ARSIWA Part One, Chapter II, Introductory Commentary (6).

29 *Jan de Nul v Egypt*, Award, 6 November 2008.

30 At para 161.

31 At para 160.

32 *Hamester v Ghana*, Award, 18 June 2010, paras 183–184; *Tulip v Turkey*, Award, 10 March 2014, para 288; *Almås v Poland*, Award, 27 June 2016, para 209.

33 C Kovács, *Attribution in International Investment Law* (2018) 80, 84. On the exceptional nature of lifting the corporate veil in cases of fraud and evasion see also the ICJ in *Barcelona Traction Light and Power Company Ltd (Belgium v Spain)*, Judgment, 5 February 1970, ICJ Reports (1970) 3, paras 56–58.

34 *Bayindir v Pakistan*, Award, 27 August 2009.

development, operation, and maintenance of Pakistan's highways, was a State organ for purposes of attribution. The Tribunal accepted Pakistan's argument that NHA's distinct legal personality ruled out the possibility that it was a State organ. The Tribunal said:

> Because of its separate legal status, the Tribunal discards the possibility of treating NHA as a State organ under Article 4 of the ILC Articles... Given that—as already indicated above—NHA is a separate legal entity and that the acts in question are those of NHA as a party to the Contract, the Tribunal considers that there are no grounds for attribution by virtue of Article 4.[35]

Other tribunals have similarly relied on an entity's legal personality to determine that it was not a State organ.[36]

(e) State ownership

Ownership of an entity by a state, does not convert that entity into a State organ.[37] The Tribunal in *Waste Management v Mexico II*[38] said in this respect:

> The mere fact that a separate entity is majority-owned or substantially controlled by the state does not make it *ipso facto* an organ of the state.[39]

(f) *De facto* organs

Paragraph 2 of Article 4 of the ARSIWA provides that the concept of an 'organ' includes any person or entity having that status under the State's internal law. This leaves open the possibility that in addition to *de jure* organs, which have that status under domestic law, there may additionally be *de facto* organs, which are not so designated by law.[40]

[35] At para 119.

[36] *EDF v Romania*, Award, 8 October 2009, para 190; *Hamester v Ghana*, Award, 18 June 2010, paras 185, 188; *Tulip v Turkey*, Award, 10 March 2014, para 289; *H&H v Egypt*, Award, 6 May 2014, para 387; *Almås v Poland*, Award, 27 June 2016, paras 208–209; *Ortiz v Algeria*, Award, 29 April 2020, paras 170, 174, 182.

[37] J Crawford, *State Responsibility—The General Part* (2013) 118; C Kovács, *Attribution in International Investment Law* (2018) 84.

[38] *Waste Management v Mexico II*, Award, 30 April 2004.

[39] At para 75. See also *Tulip v Turkey*, Award, 10 March 2014, para 289.

[40] ARSIWA Article 4, Commentary (11).

The concept of *de facto* organs has been developed by the International Court of Justice in the context of irregular military forces.[41] In international investment law, the phenomenon of *de facto* organs is possible but would be exceptional.[42] In several cases tribunals have rejected the classification of entities as *de facto* State organs.[43]

The decisive features of a *de facto* State organ would be the performance of core governmental functions, direct day-to-day subordination to the central government, and lack of all operational autonomy. On the other hand, conduct of commercial transactions on the entity's own account, possession of bank accounts in the entity's own name, and the holding of property in the entity's name would be incompatible with the status of a *de facto* organ.

In *Staur Eiendom v Latvia*,[44] the Tribunal, after finding that SJSC Airport was not a *de jure* State organ under Latvian law, proceeded to examine whether it could be regarded as a *de facto* State organ. The Tribunal found that the appointment and replacement of Board members by the State, oversight rights and other links with the State were insufficient to overcome the presumption of separateness from the State. The Tribunal found no evidence that the entity's day-to-day governance decisions were directed by the Ministry of Transport.[45] The Tribunal added that the fact that the entity's activities were in the national interest did not mean it had to be treated as a State organ. It said:

> Nor in the Tribunal's view, consistent with the position followed in the cases of *Almås v. Poland, Jan de Nul v. Egypt* and *Hamester v. Ghana*, is an SOE required to be treated as a State organ merely because certain of its activities may be regarded as important to the national interest, particularly where, as here, the SOE's activities are primarily of a commercial nature ... What matters is the degree to which an SOE's actions are directly controlled by the State.[46]

[41] *Military and Paramilitary Activities in and against Nicaragua (Nicaragua v United States of America)* Merits, Judgment, 27 June 1986, ICJ Reports (1986) 14, paras 109–110; *Application of the Convention on the Prevention and Punishment of the Crime of Genocide (Bosnia and Herzegovina v Serbia and Montenegro)*, Judgment, 26 February 2007, ICJ Reports (2007) 43, paras 392–393.

[42] J Crawford, *State Responsibility – The General Part* (2013) 124.

[43] *Hamester v Ghana*, Award, 18 June 2010, para 187; *Almås v Poland*, Award, 27 June 2016, paras 207–213; *Ortiz v Algeria*, Award, 29 April 2020, paras 159–188.

[44] *Staur Eiendom v Latvia*, Award, 28 February 2020.

[45] At paras 312–336.

[46] At para 335. Footnotes omitted.

(g) Excess of authority

Acts of a State's organs will be attributed to that State even if they are contrary to law and even if they are in violation of instructions. Put differently, a State cannot plead that the actions of its organs were *ultra vires*. The ARSIWA say in this respect:

> **Article 7 Excess of authority or contravention of instructions**
> The conduct of an organ of a State or of a person or entity empowered to exercise elements of the governmental authority shall be considered an act of the State under international law if the organ, person or entity acts in that capacity, even if it exceeds its authority or contravenes instructions.

This principle has been accepted in arbitral practice.[47] In *SPP v Egypt*,[48] the respondent contended that certain acts of Egyptian officials, upon which the claimants relied, were null and void because they were in conflict with the inalienable nature of the public domain and because they were not taken pursuant to the procedures prescribed by Egyptian law. The Tribunal rejected this argument and emphasized that the investor was entitled to rely on the official representations of the government:

> Whether legal under Egyptian law or not, the acts in question were the acts of Egyptian authorities, including the highest executive authority of the Government. These acts, which are now alleged to have been in violation of the Egyptian municipal legal system, created expectations protected by established principles of international law.[49]

In *Kardassopoulos v Georgia*,[50] the claimant had received several representations from the host State to the effect that a concession was valid and that its investment was in accordance with local law. Before the Tribunal, Georgia argued that the concessions had been awarded in breach of Georgian law and were void *ab initio*. The Tribunal, relying on Article 7 of the ARSIWA and on *SPP v Egypt*, ruled that the representations were attributable to Georgia, that the claimant had a corresponding legitimate expectation and that the host was estopped from arguing that the concession was void *ab initio*.[51]

[47] *OKO Pankki v Estonia*, Award, 19 November 2007, para 274; *Paushok v Mongolia*, Award on Jurisdiction and Liability, 28 April 2011, paras 603–608; *Deutsche Bank v Sri Lanka*, Award, 31 October 2012, paras 369–370, 407; *Arif v Moldova*, Award, 8 April 2013, para 539.
[48] *SPP v Egypt*, Award, 20 May 1992.
[49] At para 83.
[50] *Kardassopoulos v Georgia*, Decision on Jurisdiction, 6 July 2007.
[51] At paras 185–194.

3. Exercise of governmental authority

The ARSIWA deal with attribution based on function in the following terms:

> **Article 5 Conduct of persons or entities exercising elements of governmental authority**
> The conduct of a person or entity which is not an organ of the State under Article 4 but which is empowered by the law of that State to exercise elements of the governmental authority shall be considered an act of the State under international law, provided the person or entity is acting in that capacity in the particular instance.

Article 5 applies to entities that are not State organs. Therefore, the non-applicability of Article 4 is a condition precedent to the application of Article 5. Under Article 5, the exercise of governmental authority must have a foundation in the law of the State concerned. There can be no *de facto* exercise of governmental authority outside the State's legal system. Commentary (7) to ARSIWA Article 5 states accordingly:

> The internal law in question must specifically authorize the conduct as involving the exercise of public authority; it is not enough that it permits activity as part of the general regulation of the affairs of the community. It is accordingly a narrow category.

In addition, a general power to exercise governmental authority is not enough. Not every conduct of an entity that by State law is empowered to exercise elements of governmental authority is attributable to the State. The specific action, alleged to be unlawful, that is to be attributed to the State, must have been taken in the exercise of governmental authority.

(a) Governmental authority

Governmental authority is a function of a public character normally exercised by State organs. The conduct in question must concern governmental activity and not private or commercial activity. What is governmental depends, to a certain extent, on the particular society, its history, and traditions. Of importance is not just the content of the powers, but also the way they are conferred, the purposes for which they are to be exercised and the extent to which the entity is accountable to the government for their exercise.[52]

[52] ARSIWA Article 5, Commentaries (2), (5), and (6). See also J Crawford, *State Responsibility—The General Part* (2013) 129.

The distinction between *acta jure gestions* and *acta jure imperii* is well-known from the law of State immunity and may usefully be employed also in this context. It asks whether a course of action could have been taken by a private person or was reserved to the State. Another method is to ask whether the activity under scrutiny was governed by private law or by administrative (or even constitutional) law.[53]

In some cases, tribunals examining the conditions for the application of Article 5 ARSIWA reached the conclusion that the entity in question was not empowered to exercise elements of governmental authority.[54] In *Staur Eiendom v Latvia*,[55] the Tribunal found that there had been no delegation of governmental authority to SJSC Airport. There was no transfer of governmental powers in any legislation of Latvia. Nor was there any actual exercise of governmental powers such as acts of a regulatory nature. The fact that the airport had been classified as an object of national interest did not mean that it exercised elements of governmental authority. The Tribunal said:

> Although the Claimants have contended that SJSC Airport's powers have been bestowed upon it in order to advance 'classically sovereign purposes,' they have failed to demonstrate that SJSC Airport itself enjoys or is entitled to exercise any sovereign powers at all, such as acts of a regulatory nature or otherwise involving the use of the State's public prerogatives or *imperium*, *i.e.*, acts of '*puissance publique*.' In this regard, the Tribunal agrees with the Respondent that it does not follow simply from the Airport's classification as an 'object of national interest' that SJSC Airport has been empowered to exercise elements of governmental authority, in the absence of any showing that specific elements of governmental authority have, in fact, been conferred upon SJSC Airport.[56]

Therefore, as a first step under Article 5 ARSIWA, a tribunal will examine whether the entity has been endowed by law with the power to act in the exercise of governmental authority. If the entity does have the power, in principle, to act in the exercise of governmental authority, the tribunal will proceed to examine whether, in the particular instance, the entity acted in the exercise of governmental authority.

[53] For detailed discussion of the identification of governmental authority see C Kovács, *Attribution in International Investment Law* (2018) 132; C de Stefano, *Attribution in International Law and Arbitration* (2020) 158.

[54] *EDF v Romania*, Award, 8 October 2009, paras 169–170; *Tulip v Turkey*, Award, 10 March 2014, paras 292–300; *Tenaris v Venezuela I*, Award, 29 January 2016, paras 414–418.

[55] *Staur Eiendom v Latvia*, Award, 28 February 2020.

[56] At para 342.

(b) Exercise of governmental authority in the particular instance

Under Article 5 of the ARSIWA, in addition to the general power to exercise elements of the State's governmental authority, the entity must have acted in that capacity in the particular case. In some instances, tribunals found that there had, in fact, been an exercise of governmental authority.[57]

In *Maffezini v Spain*,[58] the Tribunal found that certain acts of a State entity, such as mistaken advice, had not been performed in the exercise of governmental authority.[59] By contrast, the Tribunal found that an irregular transfer of funds from the investor's personal account had been performed by the entity not in a commercial capacity but in the exercise of government functions.[60]

In other cases, tribunals found that the entity in question, although empowered to exercise governmental powers in principle, had not acted in that capacity in the particular instance.[61] In *Jan de Nul v Egypt*,[62] the Tribunal found that the SCA was empowered to exercise elements of governmental authority. It was empowered to issue decrees and to impose and collect charges. However, in contracting with the claimants for the dredging of the Suez Canal, 'the SCA acted like any contractor trying to achieve the best price for the services it was seeking'.[63] The fact that the contract resulted from a process of public procurement was not a sufficient element to establish that governmental authority was exercised. The Tribunal said:

> although the SCA is a public entity empowered to exercise elements of governmental authority, the acts of the SCA vis à vis the Claimants are not attributable to the Respondent in this arbitration on the basis of Article 5 of the ILC Articles, as they were not performed pursuant to the exercise of governmental authority.[64]

The dispute in *Bosh v Ukraine*,[65] concerned a contract between the investors and the National University of Kiev for the development and joint operation of facilities. The Tribunal found that the university was an entity that was empowered by the law of Ukraine to exercise certain elements of governmental authority. This

[57] *Toto v Lebanon*, Decision on Jurisdiction, 11 September 2009, paras 52, 60, 107–109; *Bosca v Lithuania*, Award, 17 May 2013, paras 127–128; *Crystallex v Venezuela*, Award, 4 April 2016, paras 692–707.

[58] *Maffezini v Spain*, Award, 13 November 2000.

[59] At paras 58–71.

[60] At paras 77–83.

[61] *Bayindir v Pakistan*, Award, 27 August 2009, paras 121–123; *Hamester v Ghana*, Award, 18 June 2010, paras 189–204, 231, 248, 250, 266, 284; *Ulysseas v Ecuador*, Final Award, 12 June 2012, paras 124–143; *Almås v Poland*, Award, 27 June 2016, paras 218–219, 251; *Ortiz v Algeria*, Award, 29 April 2020, paras 190–234.

[62] *Jan de Nul v Egypt*, Award, 6 November 2008.

[63] At para 169.

[64] At paras 170–171.

[65] *Bosh v Ukraine*, Award, 25 October 2012.

included the provision of higher education services and the management of State-owned property. The university's specific activity in relation to the investors was not, however, in the exercise of governmental authority but was private or commercial activity. Therefore, the contract's termination by the university was not attributable to Ukraine under Article 5 of the ARSIWA.[66]

Therefore, attribution under Article 5 requires an examination of the specific acts which are alleged to be in violation of international law. Only if these acts were performed in the exercise of the State's governmental authority can they be attributed to the State. If they were performed in the exercise of contractual powers or other form *jure gestionis*, they cannot be attributed under Article 5.

4. Instruction, direction, or control

The ARSIWA deal with attribution based on instruction, direction, or control in the following terms:

> **Article 8 Conduct directed or controlled by a State**
> The conduct of a person or group of persons shall be considered an act of a State under international law if the person or group of persons is in fact acting on the instructions of, or under the direction and control of, that State in carrying out the conduct.

This provision is not concerned with the status or function of the acting persons but only with their conduct. The acting persons may be individuals, juridical persons, or groups of persons without legal personality. Article 8 is concerned with control over conduct that is claimed to be in violation of international law.

(a) Effective and specific control

The Commentary (3) to ARSIWA Article 8 points out that what matters is the direction or control over the specific operation:

> Such conduct will be attributable to the State only if it directed or controlled the specific operation and the conduct complained of was an integral part of that operation.

66 At paras 177–178.

Therefore, in the words of Commentary (7), 'the instructions, direction or control must relate to the conduct which is said to have amounted to an internationally wrongful act'.

In the *Nicaragua* case,[67] the International Court of Justice found that a general situation of dependence and support did not amount to control for purposes of attribution. The Court explained that '[f]or this conduct [the activities of the contras] to give rise to legal responsibility of the United States, it would in principle have to be proved that that State had effective control of the military or paramilitary operations in the course of which the alleged violations were committed'.[68]

Although the Yugoslavia Tribunal in the *Tadic* case took a somewhat different position,[69] the International Court of Justice (ICJ) has since confirmed its position with regard to effective control in the *Genocide* case.[70] The ICJ specifically rejected the notion of 'overall control'. It stated that Article 8 of the ARSIWA would apply only:

> where an organ of the State gave the instructions or provided the direction pursuant to which the perpetrators of the wrongful act acted or where it exercised effective control over the action during which the wrong was committed.[71]

It follows that under Article 8 control must be specific and relate to every aspect of the alleged violation. General or overall State control over the entity is insufficient.[72]

Investment tribunals have adopted the test of effective control in relation to the specific conduct as developed by the ICJ.[73] In *Jan de Nul v Egypt*,[74] the Tribunal found that it saw no evidence of any specific instruction and that, hence, there was no attribution under Article 8:

> International jurisprudence is very demanding in order to attribute the act of a person or entity to a State, as it requires both a general control of the State over the person or entity and a specific control of the State over the act the attribution of which is at stake; this is known as the "effective control" test. There is no evidence

[67] *Military and Paramilitary Activities in and against Nicaragua (Nicaragua v United States of America)* Merits, Judgment, 27 June 1986, ICJ Reports (1986) 14.

[68] At para 115.

[69] Appeals Chamber of the International Tribunal for the Prosecution of Persons Responsible for Serious Violations of International Humanitarian Law Committed in the Territory of the Former Yugoslavia since 1991, *Prosecutor v Dusko Tadic*, Case No.: IT-94-1-A, Judgment, 15 July 1999, para 117.

[70] *Application of the Convention on the Prevention and Punishment of the Crime of Genocide (Bosnia and Herzegovina v Serbia and Montenegro)*, Judgment, 26 February 2007, ICJ Reports (2007) 43.

[71] At para 406.

[72] J Crawford, *State Responsibility – The General Part* (2013) 146.

[73] *Hamester v Ghana*, Award, 18 June 2010, paras 179, 267; *White Industries v India*, Final Award, 30 November 2011, paras 8.1.11–8.1.19; *Almås v Poland*, Award, 27 June 2016, paras 268–270; *Gavrilović v Croatia*, Award 26 July 2018, paras 828–829; *Marfin v Cyprus*, Award, 26 July 2018, paras 673–679; *Ortiz v Algeria*, Award, 29 April 2020, paras 242–260.

[74] *Jan de Nul v Egypt*, Award, 6 November 2008.

> on record of any instructions that the State would have given to the SCA in regard to the very specific acts and omissions of the SCA that are complained of in this arbitration. Accordingly, the Tribunal concludes that there can be no attribution of the acts of SCA to the Respondent under Article 8 of the ILC Articles.[75]

In other cases, tribunals applying the test of effective control found that there had been instructions, direction, or control.[76] In *Bayindir v Pakistan*,[77] the Tribunal, applying Article 8 of the ARSIWA, concluded upon an examination of the facts that:

> each specific act allegedly in breach of the Treaty was a direct consequence of the decision of the NHA to terminate the Contract, which decision received express clearance from the Pakistani Government.[78]

Therefore, NHA's conduct was attributable under Article 8.

(b) Degree of control

The instruction, direction, or control required by Article 8 ARSIWA must be binding or imperative. A mere encouragement or recommendation is not enough.

In *von Pezold v Zimbabwe*,[79] the claimants' farms had been occupied by 'settlers'. The Tribunal found that encouragement was insufficient for purposes of Article 8:

> While there is ample evidence of Government involvement and encouragement, the Tribunal is not persuaded that the acts of the invaders were based on a direct order or under the direct control of the Government when they initially invaded the Claimants' properties. Rather, the Government appears to have encouraged (and endorsed) the action once it had begun. Encouragement would not meet the test set out in Article 8.[80]

(c) Ownership and control

The control exercised by the State for purposes of Article 8 ARSIWA differs from the type of control exercised by shareholding.[81] In other contexts, such as Article

[75] At para 173. Footnote omitted.
[76] *EDF v Romania*, Award, 8 October 2009, paras 201–208; *Deutsche Bank v Sri Lanka*, Award, 31 October 2012, para 405(c).
[77] *Bayindir v Pakistan*, Award, 27 August 2009.
[78] At para 125.
[79] *von Pezold v Zimbabwe*, Award, 28 July 2015.
[80] At para 448. See also *Ortiz v Algeria*, Award, 29 April 2020, para 242.
[81] J Crawford, *State Responsibility—The General Part* (2013) 162.

25(2)(b) of the ICSID Convention, majority or sole ownership of a company typically amounts to control in a corporate law sense. Article 8 ARSIWA refers to a different type of control. For purposes of attribution, a degree of public or governmental control is necessary that goes beyond shareholder control.[82] The owner's power to appoint managers is irrelevant to control for purposes of Article 8.[83]

Tribunals have held that majority ownership or shareholding by the State of a company is insufficient for attribution under Article 8.[84] In *Marfin v Cyprus*,[85] the Tribunal confirmed the distinction between control through ownership and State control. It said:

> [T]he mere ownership of shares in Laiki by the Cypriot Government, along with the powers that this ownership entails, does not establish attribution under ILC Article 8. Claimants remain bound by the obligation to demonstrate that the challenged conduct was carried out under the instructions, direction or control of Cyprus.[86]

82 ARSIWA Article 8, Commentary (6). See also C Kovács, *Attribution in International Investment Law* (2018) 226; C de Stefano, *Attribution in International Law and Arbitration* (2020) 176.

83 *White Industries v India*, Final Award, 30 November 2011, para 8.1.6.

84 *Tulip v Turkey*, Award, 10 March 2014, paras 306–307, 309.

85 *Marfin v Cyprus*, Award, 26 July 2018.

86 At para 691.

XI
Political Risk Insurance

ADDITIONAL READING: P Bekker and A Ogawa, 'The Impact of Bilateral Investment Treaty (BIT) Proliferation on Demand for Investment Insurance' in (2013) 28 *ICSID Rev* 314; R Ginsburg, 'Political Risk Insurance and Bilateral Investment Treaties' (2013) 14 *JWIT* 943; J Webb Yackee, 'Political Risk and International Investment Law' (2014) 24 *Duke J Comp & Int L* 477; K Hober and J Fellenbaum, 'Political Risk Insurance and Investment Treaty Protection', in M Bungenberg et al (eds) *International Investment Law* (2015) 1517; M Kantor, 'Comparing Political Risk Insurance and Investment Treaty Arbitration' (2015) 6 *TDM*; C Peinhardt and T Allee, 'Political Risk Insurance as Dispute Resolution' (2016) 7 *JIDS* 205; H Sun and C Liu, 'Political Risk Insurance' in B Legum (ed) *The Investment Treaty Arbitration Review*, 3rd edn (2018) 216.

1. History and purpose

The risk for the investor inherent in major investment projects has led to the evolution of a market for investment insurance. The first phase of insurance programmes commenced in the 1950s and was entirely dominated by insurers run by national governments, which sought to promote the outgoing investments of their nationals.[1] In the early 1970s, private insurers entered the market, beginning with Lloyd's in London and the American International Group (AIG) in New York. In 1985 the member States of the World Bank decided to establish an international organization, the Multilateral Investment Guarantee Agency (MIGA) for the same purpose. The creation of the MIGA was prompted, according to its Preamble, by the recognition 'that the flow of foreign investment to developing countries would be facilitated and further encouraged by alleviating concerns related to non-commercial risks'. The Inter Arab Development Bank is charged primarily with underwriting investment insurance on the regional level.[2]

The purpose of national insurance programmes is tied to the promotion of the national economy. Often, protection is granted only to national companies and

[1] In the United States, the Agency for International Development carried out the task until the Overseas Private Investment Corporation (OPIC) took over in 1971. In 2019 it was replaced by the US International Development Finance Corporation (DFC).

[2] See I Shihata, 'Regional Investment Insurance Projects' (1972) 6 *J World Trade Law* 185.

their projects in countries friendly to the investor's home country. Covered risks are usually expropriation, non-convertibility of currency, and political violence.[3]

2. Different types of insurance

Some national programmes are subsidized, while others purport to act without a burden to the taxpayer. Private companies entered the investment insurance market on the assumption of higher efficiency and an acceptable margin of profit. In its original context and design, the private programmes emerged as extensions of traditional forms of marine insurance.

Private insurers seek to diversify their own risk by schemes of mutual cooperation with other companies and also by leveraging their operations by reliance on reinsurers. They have the advantage, vis-à-vis the public sector, of being able to tailor their products to the needs of the individual company insured. They can price and accept or reject risk based on commercial considerations and are able to act speedily and flexibly. According to an agreement among private insurers (Waterborne Agreement), they exclude nuclear risks, but will otherwise underwrite war risks on a controlled basis as part of a political risk account and now routinely insure against terrorism, although this risk is often supported by government-backed reinsurance. Private insurers do not in practice cover the risk of currency devaluation or depreciation.

The strongest difference between private and public insurers concerns the time horizon of the insurance offered: whereas the public sector has been prepared to offer coverage for up to 20 years, private companies typically limit their risk by offering protection for shorter periods. While some private market political risk insurers offer coverage for up to 15 years, others limit themselves to much shorter periods, sometimes only for three years, subject to renewal.

The existence, side by side, of these actors presents a unique panorama of competitive and complementary services by the private sector, national governmental agencies, and by international actors. Expectations held previously that the activities of the private sector might obviate or crowd out the need for the service of public institutions have turned out to be unrealistic. Some government agencies seek to cooperate with the private sector and not just compete with it. The result is often coinsurance and reinsurance.

To some extent, the governmental insurance programmes reflect foreign policy goals of the government especially as regards eligibility of projects. Also, major types of investment risks have remained so difficult to assess in mathematical terms or so risk prone that the private insurers have decided not to cover them. Thus,

[3] The DFC offers insurance against losses due to currency inconvertibility, government interference, and political violence including terrorism.

national insurance agencies work in a hybrid manner, reflecting principles of prudent private risk management but also governmental characteristics. In Germany, governmental insurance will only be granted for investments in countries that have concluded a bilateral investment treaty (BIT) with Germany or in which a similar degree of legal security exists.

As to the competition between the domestic insurers, private and public, and MIGA, they differ in their willingness to accept various types of risks and offer different rates for different packages of insurance. Altogether, overlapping elements exist among the policies and activities of the different insurers, and the divergences are explained by the different goals and institutional settings. The various existing regimes diverge in part in regard to the types of investment covered. Exports will be covered by MIGA if they contribute significantly to a specific investment.[4] MIGA is only prepared to insure an investment that satisfies its understanding of economic soundness and has received host country approval.[5] The rules of MIGA do not, however, require specific standards of protection of foreign investment in the host country. This is because MIGA only insures risk in 'MIGA member' countries where there is a bilateral agreement between MIGA and the host government.

3. Subrogation

It is the general practice of government insurers to conclude agreements with host countries that provide for subrogation. This means that the investor's rights against the host country are assigned to the insurer upon payment under the insurance contract. Some countries, such as Germany, include clauses to this effect in BITs,[6] whereas others, such as the United States, conclude specific agreements for this purpose.

Payment to the investor under an insurance will not release the host State from its liability towards the investor. In *Hochtief v Argentina*, the respondent objected to the admissibility of the claims on the ground that the German political risk insurance had agreed to pay claimants under a political risk insurance policy that covered the losses that were the substance of the claims in this case. Argentina argued

[4] 'Commentary on the Convention Establishing the Multilateral Investment Guarantee Agency' (1986) 1 *ICSID Rev* 193, 201.

[5] MIGA Convention Articles 12(d)(e) and 15.

[6] See eg Argentina–Germany BIT Article 6: 'If either Contracting Party makes payments to its nationals or companies under a guarantee it has assumed in respect of an investment in the territory of the other Contracting Party, the latter Contracting Party shall, without prejudice to the rights of the former Contracting Party under article 9, recognize the assignment, whether under a law or pursuant to a legal transaction, of any right or claim from such national or company to the former Contracting Party. The latter Contracting Party shall also recognize the reasons for and extent of the subrogation of the former Contracting Party to any such right or claim which that Contracting Party shall be entitled to assert to the same extent as its predecessor in title. As regards the transfer of payments by virtue of such assignment, article 5 shall apply *mutatis mutandis*.'

that Germany was now subrogated to the rights of Hochtief so that claimant could no longer pursue its claim. The Tribunal rejected this objection on the basis that Article 6 of the Argentina–Germany BIT allows for subrogation and obliges the respondent State to recognize and admit such a transfer of rights once it has been made but does not bring about the transfer.[7]

A related dispute in *Hochtief* concerned the question whether the amount received from the German political risk insurance policy should be deducted from the damages due to the investor because of a violation of the fair and equitable treatment (FET) provision in the Argentina–Germany BIT. The Tribunal decided that the insurance payment should not be deducted from the amount due to claimant:

> The Tribunal decides that the insurance payment . . . should not be deducted from the amount due to Claimant. The insurance payment is a benefit which Claimant arranged on its own behalf, and for which it paid. It does not reduce the losses caused by Respondent's actions in breach of the BIT: it is an arrangement that had been made by Claimant with a third party in order to provide a hedge against potential losses. The Tribunal does not consider that any principle of international law requires that such an arrangement, to which Respondent was not a party, should reduce Respondent's liability.[8]

4. Risks covered

The risks covered by political risk insurance are similar but not identical with those addressed in BITs. All schemes provide for protection against direct and indirect expropriation, and some government insurers and most private insurers also cover cases of business interruption. Beyond the protection of assets, most programmes offer protection against non-compliance with contracts. The risks of currency inconvertibility and restrictions on currency transfer are also covered. Risks of war and civil disturbance are generally covered. However, fair and equitable treatment is not covered by most schemes.

Many insurance policies are limited in scope. Most policies will reimburse only for net invested capital and not for market value.[9] Like more recent investment protection treaties, the MIGA Convention[10] specifically provides that no loss is covered arising from 'non-discriminatory measures of general application which governments normally take for the purpose of regulating economic activity in their territories'. Most government insurers and the larger private sector underwriters

[7] *Hochtief v Argentina*, Decision on Liability, 29 December 2014, paras 185, 186.
[8] At paras 308, 309.
[9] M Kantor, 'Comparing Political Risk Insurance and Investment Treaty Arbitration' (2015) 6 *TDM*.
[10] MIGA Convention Article 11(a)(ii).

will not cover projects that violate international environmental standards, create unreasonable health risks, or fail to respect human rights, in particular workers' rights.

Repudiation or breach of contracts will be covered by MIGA if the holder of the guarantee does not have access to a judicial and arbitral forum or the decision of such a forum is not rendered within a reasonable period as defined by MIGA, or such a decision cannot be enforced.[11] Non-payment of an obligation under an arbitral award may constitute an expropriation as understood in international law and as covered by an insurance contract, even if the host country considers that it is not able to pay the amount due under the arbitral award.[12]

5. Disputes between investors and insurers

Disputes have arisen between insured investors and the insurer when the two sides have disagreed on the interpretation or application of the insurance contract. Typically, such disputes are resolved through arbitration provided for in the insurance contracts. Often, the resulting decisions deal with legal issues that appear similar to those that come up in the relationship between the host State and the investor in the context of a BIT. For instance, the investor may claim that its treatment by the host State amounts to an indirect expropriation as covered by an insurance contract.

In some disputes, tribunals set up under insurance contracts have addressed legal issues of expropriation, currency inconvertibility, breaches of contract, the consequences of political violence, and attribution. Some of these decisions have been relied upon in disputes between investors and States.[13] The authority of arbitral awards rendered under insurance contracts for disputes between States and foreign investors will depend, not least, on whether the provisions in insurance contracts and the standards of protection in treaties and customary international law are the same.

[11] MIGA Convention Article 11(a)(iii).

[12] See eg *MidAmerican Energy Holdings Company v OPIC*, citing the *Restatement (Third) of Foreign Relations Law* (1999), § 712, comment h and the Harvard Draft Convention on the International Responsibility of States for Injuries to Aliens; an excerpt of the case is reproduced in D Bishop et al, *Foreign Investment Disputes* (2005) 563 et seq. But see also the position that non-payment of debts will not amount to an expropriation. See VII.2 above.

[13] The Award in *Revere Copper v OPIC*, Award, 24 August 1978, (1980) 56 ILR 258, is often cited in the context of defining an indirect expropriation.

XII
Settling Investment Disputes

ADDITIONAL READING: A Broches, 'The Convention on the Settlement of Investment Disputes between States and Nationals of Other States' (1972–II) 136 *Recueil* 331; M Hirsch, *The Arbitration Mechanism of the International Centre for the Settlement of Investment Disputes* (1993); J Paulsson, 'Arbitration without Privity' (1995) 10 *ICSID Rev* 232; L Reed et al, *Guide to ICSID Arbitration* 2nd edn (2010); M Waibel et al (eds), *The Backlash against Investment Arbitration* (2010); AM Steingruber, *Consent in International Arbitration* (2012); HE Kjos, *Applicable Law in Investor–State Arbitration* (2013); N Maurer, *The Empire Trap: The Rise and Fall of U.S. Intervention to Protect American Property Overseas 1893–2013* (2013); RD Bishop et al (eds), *Foreign Investment Disputes: Cases, Materials and Commentary*, 2nd edn (2014); JE Kalicki and A Joubin-Bret (eds), *Reshaping the Investor–State Dispute Settlement System: Journeys for the 21st Century* (2015); M Kinnear et al (eds), *Building International Investment Law* (2015); NJ Calamita, 'The Challenge of Establishing a Multilateral Investment Tribunal at ICSID' (2017) 32 *ICSID Rev* 611; J Commission and R Moloo, *Procedural Issues in International Investment Arbitration* (2018); F Fontanelli, *Jurisdiction and Admissibility in Investment Arbitration* (2018); E Gaillard and Y Banifatemi (eds), *Jurisdiction in Investment Treaty Arbitration* (2018); K Hobér, *Investment Treaty Arbitration* (2018); J Fouret et al (eds), *The ICSID Convention, Regulations and Rules* (2019); A Parra, *ICSID: An Introduction to the Convention and Centre* (2020); Y Radi, *Rules and Practices of International Investment Law and Arbitration* (2020); SW Schill et al (eds), *Schreuer's Commentary on the ICSID Convention*, 3rd edn (2022).

1. State v State disputes

(a) Diplomatic protection

Under traditional international law investors did not have direct access to international remedies to pursue claims against foreign States for violations of their rights. They depended on diplomatic protection by their home States. A State exercising diplomatic protection espouses the claim of its national against another State and pursues it in its own name. The Permanent Court of International Justice (PCIJ) explained diplomatic protection in the *Mavrommatis Palestine Concessions* case:

> It is an elementary principle of international law that a State is entitled to protect its subjects, when injured by acts contrary to international law committed by another State, from whom they have been unable to obtain satisfaction through the ordinary channels. By taking up the case of one of its subjects and by resorting to diplomatic action or international judicial proceedings on his behalf, a State is in reality asserting its own rights—its right to ensure, in the person of its subjects, respect for the rules of international law.[1]

In 2006 the International Law Commission adopted Draft articles on Diplomatic Protection.[2]

Diplomatic protection is subject to several conditions. The investor, whether it is an individual or a corporation, must be a national of the protecting State. This bond of nationality must have existed continuously from the time of the injury until the claim is presented or, according to some, until the claim is settled. In addition, the investor must have exhausted the local remedies in the State that has allegedly committed the violation.[3]

The usefulness of diplomatic protection is limited. Under international law, the investor has no right to diplomatic protection but depends on the political discretion of its government. The government may refuse to take up the claim, it may discontinue diplomatic protection at any time, and it may even waive the national's claim or agree to a reduced settlement. In other words, the investor is never in control of the process. As the International Court of Justice (ICJ) said in the *Barcelona Traction Case*:

> 79. The State must be viewed as the sole judge to decide whether its protection will be granted, to what extent it is granted, and when it will cease. It retains in this respect a discretionary power the exercise of which may be determined by considerations of a political or other nature, unrelated to the particular case. Since the claim of the State is not identical with that of the individual or corporate person whose cause is espoused, the State enjoys complete freedom of action.[4]

Diplomatic protection on behalf of investors also carries important disadvantages to the States concerned.[5] It can seriously disrupt their international relations, leading to protracted disputes. Weaker countries resent pressure from stronger

[1] *Mavrommatis Palestine Concessions Case (Greece v United Kingdom)*, Judgment, 30 August 1924, PCIJ Series A, No 2, p 12.

[2] See Official Records of the General Assembly, Sixty-first Session, Supplement No 10 (A/61/10). The General Assembly took note of the Draft articles in Resolution 61/35.

[3] CF Amerasinghe, *Diplomatic Protection* (2008).

[4] *Barcelona Traction, Light and Power Co., Ltd. (Belgium v Spain)*, Judgment, 5 February 1970, ICJ Reports (1970) 3, para 79.

[5] I Shihata, 'Towards a Greater Depoliticization of Investment Disputes: The Roles of ICSID and MIGA' in I Shihata, *The World Bank in a Changing World* (1991) 309.

counties whether it is exerted bilaterally or in multilateral fora such as international lending institutions. Diplomatic protection in investment disputes by capital exporting countries against developing countries has been a frequent source of irritation for the latter.

Some countries have gone as far as challenging the permissibility of diplomatic protection. Under the so-called Calvo Doctrine, Latin American countries have sought to exclude any special rights for foreigners.[6] This has led them to reject diplomatic protection as an undesirable or even impermissible interference in their internal affairs or to limit it to cases of denial of justice. However, so-called Calvo clauses in national legislation, including constitutions, cannot effectively protect a State against the exercise of diplomatic protection. Only the investor's home State can decline to exercise it or waive it.

If the investor's State of nationality decides to exercise diplomatic protection, the primary method of dispute settlement is negotiation. If negotiations prove fruitless, the protecting State may resort to international adjudication, including the ICJ. Examples of cases involving the protection of investors brought to the ICJ are the *Barcelona Traction* case and the *ELSI* case.[7] Diplomatic protection may also lead to arbitration between the two States.[8] Nearly all BITs contain arbitration clauses for the settlement of disputes arising from their application between the Contracting States, although they have been used sparingly. These arbitration clauses are often supplemented by provisions that require consultations and negotiations.

Alternatively, States may resort to unfriendly measures or countermeasures (reprisals). This right is limited by the prohibition of the use of force contained in the Charter of the United Nations. Therefore, armed force against a host State is no longer a permissible means to protect the rights of foreign investors. In the past, action by States on behalf of their nationals in investment disputes has repeatedly led to the use of force.[9]

The right to exercise diplomatic protection may be curtailed by treaty provisions. The Convention on the Settlement of Investment Disputes between States and Nationals of Other States (ICSID Convention) provides in Article 27(1) that, where consent to investor–State arbitration under the Convention exists, a Contracting State may not give diplomatic protection or bring an international claim. However, under Article 27(2) this does not exclude informal diplomatic exchanges for the sole purpose of facilitating a settlement of the dispute. In the course of the Convention's drafting, the exclusion of diplomatic protection was explained,

[6] See D Shea, *The Calvo Clause* (1955).

[7] *Case concerning the Elettronica Sicula SpA (ELSI) (US v Italy)*, Judgment, 20 July 1989, ICJ Reports (1989) 15.

[8] See eg the *Martini Case*, Award, 3 May 1930, 2 RIAA 974; *Canevaro Case*, Award, 3 May 1912, 11 RIAA 397; *Italy v Cuba*, Award, 15 January 2008.

[9] See U Kriebaum, 'Evaluating Social Benefits and Costs of Investment Treaties: Depoliticization of Investment Disputes' (2018) 33 *ICSID Review* 14.

inter alia, in terms of the removal of the dispute from the realm of politics and diplomacy into the realm of law.[10] The guarantee against diplomatic protection may constitute an incentive for host States to consent to investor–State arbitration. Any violation of the prohibition to exercise diplomatic protection under Article 27(1) of the ICSID Convention would not affect the jurisdiction of the ICSID tribunal.[11]

Even under the ICSID Convention, the right to diplomatic protection will exist in favour of an investor who has prevailed in investor–State arbitration if the host State fails to comply with the award.[12] Diplomatic protection to secure the compliance with awards has not played a major practical role.

As described below, in many cases investors are granted direct access to effective means of international dispute settlement. In consequence, investment disputes between States have become rare. In many situations investors no longer depend on diplomatic protection by their home States.

The rules of international law developed in the context of diplomatic protection are not applicable where a case is governed by a treaty that grants direct rights to investors. The ICJ has acknowledged that its decisions, given in the context of diplomatic protection based on customary international law, do not apply in the framework of international investment law which is dominated by treaties.[13] The ILC's Draft articles on Diplomatic Protection also proclaim their inapplicability to investment protection.[14] Investment tribunals have recognized the limited relevance of the customary rules governing diplomatic protection for the interpretation of treaties providing for the protection of investors.[15] This applies in particular to rules on the exhaustion of local remedies,[16] the nationality of investors,[17] and shareholder rights.[18]

[10] History of the Convention, Vol II, Part 1, pp 242, 273, 303, 372, 464.

[11] *Banro American v DR Congo*, Award, 1 September 2000, paras 18, 19; *Autopista v Venezuela*, Decision on Jurisdiction, 27 September 2001, paras 75, 140.

[12] See XII.16 below.

[13] *Barcelona Traction, Light and Power Co, Ltd (Belgium v Spain)*, Judgment, 5 February 1970, ICJ Reports (1970) 3, paras 89–90; *Diallo case (Guinea v Democratic Republic of Congo)*, Judgment, 24 May 2007, ICJ Reports (2007) 582, paras 88–90.

[14] Article 17 Special rules of international law: 'The present draft articles do not apply to the extent that they are inconsistent with special rules of international law, such as treaty provisions for the protection of investments.' See also the ILC's Commentary to Article 17.

[15] *AES v Argentina*, Decision on Jurisdiction, 26 April 2005, para 99; *Sempra v Argentina*, Decision on Jurisdiction, 11 May 2005, paras 150–153; *Merrill & Ring v Canada*, Award, 31 March 2010, para 205.

[16] *MNSS v Montenegro*, Award, 4 May 2016, para 216; *Valores Mundiales v Venezuela*, Award, 25 July 2017, para 576.

[17] *Siag v Egypt*, Decision on Jurisdiction, 11 April 2007, paras 198; *Yukos Universal v Russian Federation*, Interim Award on Jurisdiction and Admissibility, 30 November 2009, para 551; *Fakes v Turkey*, Award, 14 July 2010, para 69; *KT Asia v Kazakhstan*, Award, 17 October 2013, para 128.

[18] *von Pezold v Zimbabwe*, Award, 28 July 2015, paras 319–320, 326.

(b) Disputes between States

Apart from the espousal of a particular investor's claim, a dispute may arise between States simply in consequence of a general violation of international law, particularly of a treaty protecting investments.

Article 64 of the ICSID Convention provides that a dispute between parties to the Convention concerning its interpretation or application is to be referred to the ICJ unless it can be settled by negotiation or the States concerned agree on another method of settlement. The context of this provision and its drafting history make it clear that this procedure is not to be used to interfere in investor–State dispute settlement proceedings.[19] No case was ever brought to the ICJ under Article 64.

BITs typically contain two clauses on dispute settlement: one offers arbitration between the host State and the investor. Another provides for arbitration between the contracting parties to the treaty. During the ICSID Convention's drafting there seemed to be consensus that inter-State arbitration should neither interfere in investor–State cases nor affect the finality of ICSID awards.[20]

In *Lucchetti v Peru*, the investor had initiated arbitration against the host State under a bilateral investment treaty (BIT). Thereupon Peru initiated inter-State arbitration proceedings under the BIT against Chile, the investor's home State, and sought a suspension of the investor–State proceedings. Peru argued that interpretative priority should be given to the State–State proceedings. The Tribunal in the investor–State proceedings declined Peru's request for the suspension of proceedings.[21] Peru did not subsequently pursue the inter-State proceedings.

In *Italy v Cuba*,[22] a case brought under the BIT between the two countries, Italy relied on the clause for the settlement of disputes between the two contracting States. Italy presented two types of claims: one category was based on the diplomatic protection of its nationals, the other concerned Italy's own rights under the BIT. The Tribunal held that the exhaustion of local remedies was required for the claims based on diplomatic protection but not for Italy's pursuit of its own rights. The claims failed for a variety of jurisdictional and merits-related reasons.

In *Ecuador v United States*, Ecuador took the view that a tribunal deciding a dispute between a US investor and Ecuador,[23] had erred in its interpretation of the US–Ecuador BIT. The United States, emphasized the goal of depoliticizing disputes through arbitration and declined to take a position on the BIT's correct interpretation. Under these circumstances, the Tribunal found that there was no dispute between the parties over which it could exercise jurisdiction.[24]

19 See especially the Report of the Executive Directors on the Convention, para 45.
20 See History of the Convention, Vol. II, pp 65–66, 273–274, 349–350,433–435, 527–528, 576–577.
21 *Lucchetti v Peru*, Award, 7 February 2005, paras 7, 9.
22 *Italy v Cuba*, Final Award, 15 January 2008.
23 *Chevron v Ecuador I*, Partial Award on the Merits, 30 March 2010.
24 *Ecuador v United States*, Award, 29 September 2012, paras 187–228.

2. The limited usefulness of domestic courts

In the absence of an agreement to the contrary, an investment dispute between a State and a foreign investor would normally have to be settled by the host State's courts. Conflict of laws rules will normally point to these courts since the dispute is likely to have the closest connection to the State in which the investment is made.

From the investor's perspective, this is not an attractive solution. Rightly or wrongly, the investor will fear a lack of impartiality from the courts of the State against whom it wishes to pursue its claim. In many countries an independent judiciary cannot be taken for granted and executive interventions in court proceedings or a sense of judicial loyalty to the forum State are likely to influence the outcome of proceedings. This is particularly so where large amounts of money are involved.

Not infrequently, legislation is the cause of complaints by investors. Domestic courts will often be bound to apply the local law even if it is at odds with international legal rules protecting the rights of investors. In some countries the relevant treaties may not even be part of the domestic legal order. At times, domestic courts are the perpetrators of the alleged violation of investor rights.[25] Even where courts decide in the investor's favour, the executive may ignore their decisions.[26] In all these situations domestic courts cannot offer an effective remedy to foreign investors.

The courts of the investor's home country and of third States are usually not a viable alternative. In most cases they lack jurisdiction over investments taking place in another State. An agreement on forum selection for investment disputes in a State other than the host State is unlikely to be acceptable for the latter. The only exception is loan contracts which are often subject to the jurisdiction and the law of a major financial centre.

An additional obstacle to using domestic courts outside the host State would be rules on State immunity. Host States dealing with foreign investors will frequently act in the exercise of sovereign powers (*jure imperii*) rather than in a commercial capacity (*jure gestionis*). Therefore, even in countries which follow a doctrine of restrictive immunity, lawsuits against foreign States arising from investment disputes are likely to fail.[27] An explicit waiver of immunity is possible but will be difficult to obtain.

In addition to sovereign immunity, other judicial doctrines are likely to stand in the way of lawsuits in domestic courts. The act-of-State doctrine enjoins courts

[25] *Saipem v Bangladesh*, Award, 30 June 2009, para 170; *Sistem Mühendislik v Kyrgyzstan*, Award, 9 September 2009, para 128; *ATA v Jordan*, Award, 18 May 2010, paras 121–128; *Deutsche Bank v Sri Lanka*, Award, 31 October 2012, paras 474–480.

[26] *Siag v Egypt*, Award, 1 June 2009, paras 436, 448, 453–456; *Meerapfel v Central African Republic*, Award, 12 May 2011, paras 327–328; *Olin v Libya*, Final Award, 25 May 2018, paras 162–163.

[27] See *SGS v Pakistan*, Decision on Jurisdiction, 6 August 2003, paras 20–25 for a description of proceedings before the courts of Switzerland.

from examining the legality of official acts of foreign States in their own territory. For instance, the US Supreme Court has stated that it would not examine the validity of a taking of property by a foreign government in its territory even if its illegality under international law is alleged.[28] Further obstacles to lawsuits against host States in domestic courts of other States would be related doctrines of non-justiciability, political questions, and lack of a close connection to the local legal system.[29]

Enforcement of foreign arbitral awards is reasonably efficient[30] but enforcement of foreign judgments is often impossible.

It is mainly for these reasons that alternative methods have been created for the settlement of disputes between States and foreign investors. They consist primarily of granting the foreign investor direct access to arbitration with the host State.

3. Settlement of investor–State disputes by arbitration and conciliation

The gaps left by the traditional methods of dispute settlement (diplomatic protection and action in domestic courts) have led to the idea of offering investors direct access to effective international procedures, especially arbitration. This carries advantages for the investor, the host State as well as for the investor's home State. The advantage for the investor is obvious: it gains access to an effective international remedy. The advantage to the host State is twofold: by offering an international procedure for dispute settlement it improves its investment climate and is likely to attract more foreign investment. In addition, by consenting to international arbitration the host State shields itself against other processes, notably diplomatic protection, and the negative consequences this may entail. The investor's home State gains flexibility in its foreign policy choices and is freed of domestic pressure to pursue its nationals' interests.[31]

Arbitration is usually more efficient than litigation through regular courts. It offers the parties the opportunity to select arbitrators who enjoy their confidence and who have the necessary expertise in the field. Moreover, the private nature of arbitration, assuring the confidentiality of proceedings, is often valued by parties to major economic development projects. But confidentiality has also come under attack leading to calls for more transparency.[32]

[28] *Banco Nacional de Cuba v Sabbatino*, 376 U.S. 398, 3 ILM 381 (1964).

[29] *Chilean Copper Case*, Landgericht Hamburg, 22 January 1973, 13 March 1974, (1973) 12 ILM 251, (1974) 13 ILM 1115.

[30] (New York) Convention on the Recognition and Enforcement of Foreign Arbitral Awards, 10 June 1958; ICSID Convention, Article 54.

[31] For the political dynamics surrounding diplomatic protection see N Maurer, *The Empire Trap: The Rise and Fall of U.S. Intervention to Protect American Property Overseas 1893–2013* (2013).

[32] See XII.11(j) below.

In the vast majority of cases, the method chosen for the international settlement of investor–State disputes is arbitration. A second method is conciliation. Conciliation is flexible and relatively informal. It is designed to assist the parties in reaching an agreed settlement. It takes place before a conciliation commission that examines the facts and prepares a report that suggests a solution but is not binding on the parties. The ICSID Convention treats conciliation and arbitration as equivalent alternatives,[33] but conciliation is rarely used whereas arbitration is resorted to frequently.[34] The reason is evidently that conciliation leaves the final word with the disputing parties. Occasionally, a conciliation procedure is a necessary prerequisite for arbitration.

Some dispute settlement clauses offer both arbitration and conciliation by either mentioning both or by referring to the ICSID Convention without further specification. In a situation of this kind, the choice between the two methods is with the party initiating proceedings. In *SPP v Egypt*,[35] jurisdiction was based on domestic legislation which provided for the settlement of disputes 'within the framework of the [ICSID] Convention'. Egypt argued that this phrase was insufficient to express consent to arbitration since it did not refer expressly to arbitration. The Tribunal rejected this argument:

> Nowhere ... does the [ICSID] Convention say that consent to the Centre's jurisdiction must specify whether the consent is for purposes of arbitration or conciliation. Once consent has been given 'to the jurisdiction of the Centre', the Convention and its implementing regulations afford the means for making the choice between the two methods of dispute settlement. The Convention leaves that choice to the party instituting the proceedings.[36]

In contrast to conciliation, arbitration is more formal and adversarial. Most importantly, it leads to a binding decision based on law. This is the reason why claimants prefer arbitration over conciliation. In most cases it seems wiser to direct the necessary effort and expense to proceedings that lead to a binding decision.

The existence of an effective system of dispute settlement is likely to have an effect even without its actual use. The mere availability of an effective remedy will influence the behaviour of parties to potential disputes. It is likely to have a restraining influence on investors as well as on host States. Both sides will try to avoid actions that might involve them in arbitration that they are likely to lose. In addition, the parties' willingness to settle a dispute amicably will be strengthened by the existence of an arbitration clause.

[33] The ICSID Convention deals with conciliation in Articles 28–35.

[34] By mid-2020 ICSID had registered only twelve requests for conciliation. By contrast, at that time ICSID had registered 776 requests for arbitration.

[35] *SPP v Egypt*, Decision on Jurisdiction II, 14 April 1988.

[36] At para 102.

Investment arbitration uses a mechanism originally developed for the settlement of commercial disputes between private parties. The main characteristics of commercial disputes are often also present in investor–State arbitrations. But the application of international law rules governing the conduct of the State means that investor–State arbitration has its own distinctive features. In some respects, investment arbitration performs the function of judicial review of administrative acts.[37] This situation finds expression in the fact that States have negotiated the ICSID Convention as a distinct set of rules for investment disputes. At the same time mechanisms that have been devised primarily for classical commercial disputes between two private entities are also used for the settlement of investment disputes.

4. Arbitration institutions and regimes

Arbitration between a host State and a foreign investor may take place in the framework of a variety of institutions or rules. If arbitration is not supported by a particular arbitration institution, it is referred to as ad hoc arbitration. Ad hoc arbitration requires an arbitration agreement that regulates a number of issues. These include selection of arbitrators, applicable law and a large number of procedural questions. Some institutions, like the United Nations Commission on International Trade Law (UNCITRAL), have developed standard rules that may be incorporated into the parties' agreement.

(a) ICSID

The majority of investment cases are brought under the Convention on the Settlement of Investment Disputes between States and Nationals of Other States.[38] The Convention was drafted in the framework of the World Bank, was adopted on 18 March 1965 in Washington and entered into force on 14 October 1966. It created the International Centre for Settlement of Investment Disputes (ICSID, 'the Centre'), which is why the Convention is commonly referred to as the ICSID Convention. Sometimes it is also referred to as the Washington Convention. By early 2021, 155 States were parties to the Convention.[39]

The aim of the ICSID Convention, as expressed in its Preamble, is to promote economic development through the creation of a favourable investment climate.

[37] SW Schill (ed), *International Investment Law and Comparative Public Law* (2010).

[38] 575 UNTS159; (1965) 4 ILM 524.

[39] Three States have terminated their participation by denouncing the ICSID Convention in accordance with its Article 71: Bolivia on 2 May 2007; Ecuador on 6 July 2009; and Venezuela on 24 January 2012. Ecuador rejoined the ICSID Convention on 4 August 2021.

ICSID provides a system of dispute settlement that is designed exclusively for investor–State disputes. It offers standard clauses for the use of the parties, detailed rules of procedure and institutional support.[40] The institutional support extends not only to the selection of arbitrators but also to the conduct of arbitration proceedings: for instance, each tribunal is assisted by a legal secretary who is a staff member of ICSID; venues for hearings are arranged by ICSID; and all financial arrangements surrounding the arbitration are administered by ICSID. The Secretary-General of ICSID exercises a screening power over requests for arbitration and will refuse to register a request that is manifestly outside ICSID's jurisdiction.[41]

The jurisdiction of ICSID requires an investment dispute of a legal nature between a State party to the Convention and a national of another State that is also a party to the Convention. In addition, the two parties to the dispute (the host State and the investor) must have consented to ICSID's jurisdiction.[42] Participation in the ICSID Convention is not sufficient to establish jurisdiction since it does not amount to consent to jurisdiction.[43]

Proceedings under the ICSID Convention are self-contained. This means that they are not subject to the intervention of any outside bodies. In particular, domestic courts have no power to stay, to compel or to otherwise influence ICSID proceedings. Nor do domestic courts have the power to set aside or otherwise review ICSID awards.

ICSID proceedings are not threatened by the non-cooperation of a party. If one of the parties should fail to act, the proceedings will not be stalled. The Convention provides a watertight system against the frustration of proceedings by a recalcitrant party: arbitrators not appointed by the parties will be appointed by the Centre;[44] the decision on whether there is jurisdiction in a particular case is with the tribunal;[45] non-submission of memorials or non-appearance at hearings by a party will not stall the proceedings;[46] and non-cooperation by a party will not affect the award's binding force and enforceability.

[40] For a concise overview see L Reed, J Paulsson, and N Blackaby, *Guide to ICSID Arbitration*, 2nd edn (2010). For a more detailed exposition see SW Schill et al (eds), *Schreuer's Commentary on the ICSID Convention*, 3rd edn (2022).

[41] See XII.11(b) below.

[42] The ICSID Convention, Article 25(1), provides in relevant part:

> The jurisdiction of the Centre shall extend to any legal dispute arising directly out of an investment, between a Contracting State (or any constituent subdivision or agency of a Contracting State designated to the Centre by that State) and a national of another Contracting State, which the parties to the dispute consent in writing to submit to the Centre.

[43] ICSID Convention, Preamble, para 7:

> Declaring that no Contracting State shall by the mere fact of its ratification, acceptance or approval of this Convention and without its consent be deemed to be under any obligation to submit any particular dispute to conciliation or arbitration ....

[44] ICSID Convention Article 38.

[45] ICSID Convention Article 41.

[46] ICSID Convention Article 45.

ICSID Awards are binding and final and not subject to review except under the narrow conditions provided by the Convention itself (Arts 49–52). Non-compliance with an award by a State would be a breach of the Convention and would lead to a revival of the right to diplomatic protection by the investor's State of nationality (Arts 53 and 27). The Convention provides its own system of enforcement: awards are recognized as final in all States parties to the Convention. Pecuniary obligations arising from awards are to be enforced in the same way as final judgements of the local courts in all States parties to the Convention (Article 54).

ICSID had a slow start. The Convention entered into force in 1966 but the first case was not registered before 1972. The 1970ies and 1980ies saw steady but only intermittent action; one or two cases per year were typical for that period. Since the mid-1990s there has been a dramatic increase in activity. In 1996 the Secretary-General registered three new cases. During calendar year 2020 the Secretary-General registered 54 new cases. In April 2021, 295 cases were pending.[47]

(b) ICSID Additional Facility

In 1978, the Administrative Council of ICSID created the Additional Facility.[48] It is open to parties that submit to its jurisdiction in certain cases that are outside ICSID's jurisdiction. The most important situation involves cases in which only one side is either a party to the ICSID Convention or a national of a party to the ICSID Convention. Additional categories include cases which do not directly arise from an investment and fact-finding.[49]

The practical relevance of the Additional Facility lies in cases where either the host State or the investor's home State is not a party to the ICSID Convention.

[47] For detailed information look for the latest issue of: The ICSID Caseload Statistics.

[48] For detailed treatment of the Additional Facility see A Broches, 'The "Additional Facility" of the International Centre for Settlement of Investment Disputes (ICSID)' (1979) 4 *Yearbook Commercial Arbitration* 373; P Toriello, 'The Additional Facility of the International Centre for Settlement of Investment Disputes' (1978–79) 4 *Italian Yearbook of International Law* 59; A Parra, *The History of ICSID*, 2nd edn (2017) 128–137, 193–202; SW Schill et al (eds), *Schreuer's Commentary on the ICSID Convention*, 3rd edn (2022) Article 25, paras 12–19, 480–496, 513–518, 614–615.

[49] Article 2 of the Additional Facility Rules provides:

The Secretariat of the Centre is hereby authorized to administer, subject to and in accordance with these Rules, proceedings between a State (or a constituent subdivision or agency of a State) and a national of another State, falling within the following categories:

(a) conciliation and arbitration proceedings for the settlement of legal disputes arising directly out of an investment which are not within the jurisdiction of the Centre because either the State party to the dispute or the State whose national is a party to the dispute is not a Contracting State;

(b) conciliation and arbitration proceedings for the settlement of legal disputes which are not within the jurisdiction of the Centre because they do not arise directly out of an investment, provided that either the State party to the dispute or the State whose national is a party to the dispute is a Contracting State; and

(c) fact-finding proceedings.

This was especially important in the context of the NAFTA[50] since during most of the period of NAFTA's existence only the United States had ratified the ICSID Convention but Canada and Mexico had not. Many cases under the NAFTA were conducted under the Additional Facility.

Additional Facility Proceedings receive institutional support from ICSID in a similar way as proceedings under the ICSID Convention. Arbitration under the Additional Facility is not, however, governed by the ICSID Convention but by separate Additional Facility Rules. This means that the ICSID Convention's provisions on the recognition and enforcement of awards are not applicable to awards rendered under the Additional Facility. Rather, the Convention on the Recognition and Enforcement of Foreign Arbitral Awards of 1958 (the New York Convention) applies. Also, awards rendered under the Additional Facility, unlike ICSID awards, are not exempt from the scrutiny and setting aside of competent national courts.[51]

(c) Non-ICSID investment arbitration

ICSID has become the main forum for the settlement of disputes between a foreign investor and the host State. However, ICSID is not the only institution for foreign investment arbitration. Not all States are parties to the ICSID Convention. Moreover, it is not unusual that BITs leave the investor with a choice between ICSID and other types of arbitration. Despite clear differences between classical commercial arbitration and investment arbitration, institutions dealing primarily with commercial arbitration such as the International Chamber of Commerce (ICC) or the London Court of International Arbitration (LCIA), do not exclude investor–State arbitration. This applies also to the Arbitration Centres in Stockholm, Frankfurt, Vienna, Cairo, Kuala Lumpur, Singapore, and Hong Kong, or the China International Economic and Trade Arbitration Commission (CIETAC). These arbitrations are conducted either under the respective institutions' own arbitration rules or under the UNCITRAL Arbitration Rules or under the ICC Arbitration Rules.

As to the procedural law applicable in fora other than ICSID, the clear tendency is to reduce or eliminate the role of the domestic arbitration law at the place of arbitration and instead to develop and apply rules designed specifically for international proceedings. However, in non-ICSID proceedings, the law of the place of arbitration determines the extent to which local courts can intervene in arbitral proceedings and the applicable procedural law.

[50] The North American Free Trade Agreement (NAFTA), (1993) 32 ILM 289, 605, was a trilateral treaty between Canada, Mexico, and the United States that existed between 1994 and 2020.

[51] See eg *Mexico v Metalclad*, Judicial Review, Supreme Court of British Columbia, 2 May 2001, 5 ICSID Reports 236.

All procedures have in common that the parties can control the composition of the tribunal and the law applicable in the proceedings. Other common elements include the competence of tribunals to decide on their own competence,[52] the tribunal's power to determine the rules of procedure in the absence of a choice by the parties,[53] and the principle of confidentiality.[54] Basic procedural requirements are set forth in broad terms. For instance, the ICC Rules state that a tribunal 'shall act fairly and impartially and ensure that each party has a reasonable opportunity to present its case'.[55] Some variations exist in regard to document production, the taking of evidence, ethical standards for arbitrators and counsel, and the cost structure.

aa. The International Chamber of Commerce

The most established international arbitral institution is the ICC, with its seat in Paris. It has been in existence since 1923. Its current rules date from 2017 as amended in 2021. Its most distinctive feature is the administrative assistance and guidance provided by the so-called International Court of Arbitration. Despite its name, this is an administrative body made up of representatives from different countries. Similar to the 'Permanent Court of Arbitration',[56] the ICC Court provides technical assistance and a list of arbitrators but will not itself render a judgment or award. The Court will appoint the arbitrator(s) unless the parties agree otherwise.

A special feature in ICC proceedings is the 'Terms of Reference' which the arbitrators will usually draw up once they receive the files of the case from the ICC Secretariat.[57] Generally speaking, these Terms provide for a short characterization of the case, including a summary of the claims and, especially, a list of the issues to be decided. While these Terms are helpful for the parties and the tribunal in their focus on the relevant issues, the Terms reflect the impression of the tribunal at an early stage, and the issues may evolve substantially during the proceedings.

Another peculiar feature concerns the manner in which an ICC tribunal reaches its final award. Once the tribunal has agreed on a draft, this document is forwarded to the ICC Court of Arbitration, and the Court will check the formal side, ensuring that all relevant matters are covered and that there are no obvious mathematical errors or misprints in the draft.[58] However, responsibility for the final substance of the award remains with the tribunal and not with the Court.

52 UNCITRAL Rules Article 23 section 1; ICC Rules, Article 6 sections 3 and 5.

53 UNCITRAL Rules Article 17; ICC Rules, Article 19.

54 UNCITRAL Rules Article 28 section 3; ICC Rules, Article 22 section 3.

55 ICC Rules Article 22 section 4; see also UNCITRAL Rules Article 17 section 1 ('parties are treated with equality and ... at an appropriate stage of the proceedings each party is given a reasonable opportunity of presenting its case').

56 See XII.4(c)ee below.

57 ICC Rules Article 23.

58 ICC Rules Article 34.

bb. The London Court of International Arbitration

The LCIA has existed since 1981, following the previous London Chamber of Arbitration established in 1892. Regardless of the nationalities of the parties, the London Court is designed to deal with disputes arising out of commercial transactions, including investor–State disputes. The 'Arbitration Court' includes practitioners from all the major trading countries. The current Rules entered into force in October 2020. If requested, the Court will also apply the UNCITRAL Rules or act as an appointing authority.

cc. The UNCITRAL Rules

The UNCITRAL Rules of Arbitration 1976 (revised in 2010),[59] differ fundamentally from the previously described settings. They are rules only and they do not establish a machinery to administer proceedings in a particular case. It is up to the parties to provide an administrative framework for a case, and they may create an ad hoc tribunal anywhere in the world.[60] Alternatively, the UNCITRAL Rules may be applied by an existing institution such as ICSID[61] or the LCIA.[62] In some cases proceedings under the UNCITRAL Rules are administered by the Permanent Court of Arbitration (PCA).[63]

The UNCITRAL Rules are considered to reflect a modern, universally established set of international arbitration rules. They essentially address all matters that may arise in international proceedings, from the notice of arbitration to the appointment of arbitrators, interim measures, the rules governing the proceedings, and the form and effect of an award including the decision on costs.

UNCITRAL has also influenced the development of international arbitration by way of a proposal for national legislation called the UNCITRAL Model Law on International Commercial Arbitration (1985, amended 2006) and a corresponding proposal on international conciliation (2002). The Model Law is not binding, but individual States may adopt it by incorporating it into their domestic law. The useful UNCITRAL Notes on Organizing Arbitral Proceedings (2016) list and describe issues which will come up in international arbitrations. The 19 points cover matters such as decision-making, agreement on rules, language, place of arbitration, form of communications, confidentiality, evidence, and rules on hearings and on the award.

59 A 2013 version incorporates the UNCITRAL Rules on Transparency for Treaty-based Investor–State Arbitration.

60 See eg *CME v Czech Republic*, Final Award, 14 March 2003; *Lauder v Czech Republic*, Final Award, 3 September 2001.

61 See eg *Aven v Costa Rica*, Final Award, 18 September 2018.

62 See eg *Occidental Exploration v Ecuador*, Final Award, 1 July 2004.

63 See eg *Chevron v Ecuador I*, Final Award, 31 August 2011.

dd. The Iran–United States Claims Tribunal

Starting with the Jay Treaty in 1794 between Great Britain and the United States, States have often set up arbitral tribunals and mixed commissions[64] in order to resolve claims arising out of specific wars, revolutions, civil strife or other major events affecting foreign nationals. The Iran–United States Claims Tribunal was established in 1981 by the Algiers Declaration for the resolution of claims of both US and Iranian nationals and companies arising out of events of the Iranian revolution. The Algiers Declaration described the law applicable as 'such choice of law rules and principles of commercial and international law as the Tribunal determines to be applicable, taking into account relevant usages of trade, contract provisions and changed circumstances'.

Since its inception, the Tribunal, which is seated in The Hague, has addressed general issues of international law relating to foreign investment, such as matters of expropriation, State responsibility, nationality, and international arbitral procedure.

The jurisprudence of the Tribunal has made valuable contributions to the clarification and evolution of international law in general and investment law in particular. Its decisions are often cited by other tribunals and commentators. This is a remarkable achievement by a machinery set up to deal effectively with sensitive legal matters arising between two States with radically different political and legal values.

The Tribunal has decided over 3,900 cases but has still not concluded its work after almost 40 years. The Tribunal has resolved the claims by nationals of one State Party against the other State Party and certain claims between the State Parties. The remaining cases involve large and complex claims between the States Parties.

ee. The Permanent Court of Arbitration

The PCA was initially established in 1899 by the Hague Peace Conference which adopted the Convention on Pacific Settlement of International Disputes. In 1907 the Second Peace Conference decided to retain the Court. The PCA has its seat in The Hague.

The PCA is not, strictly speaking, a court. It only administers or facilitates arbitration, conciliation, and fact-finding. The parties to proceedings may be States, private parties, and international organizations. The PCA may address disputes both under public international law and private international law. Cases pertaining to foreign investment also fall within its wide range of activities.[65] The PCA's Secretariat, the International Bureau, may register a case, provide legal support to

[64] R Dolzer 'Mixed Claims Commissions' in R Wolfrum (ed) *Max-Planck-Encyclopedia of Public International Law*, vol VII (2012) 295.

[65] See eg *Saluka v Czech Republik*, Partial Award, 17 March 2006; *Frontier Petroleum v Czech Republic*, Final Award, 12 November 2010; *Almås v Poland*, Award, 27 June 2016; *Doutremepuich v Mauritius*, Award on Jurisdiction, 23 August 2019.

tribunals, process documents and conduct communications between parties, as well as provide legal research and organize meetings and hearings. The Bureau also maintains a list of arbitrators who may be chosen by the parties to a dispute.

The Secretary General of the Bureau may serve as appointing authority in UNCITRAL arbitrations or may be requested to designate an appointing authority and may rule on the challenge of an arbitrator.

The PCA Arbitration Rules of 2012 are a consolidation of prior sets of PCA procedural rules and include the Optional Rules for Arbitrating Disputes between Two Parties of Which Only One is a State (1993). Annexed are model arbitration clauses for use in connection with the PCA Arbitration Rules, which parties may consider inserting in treaties, contracts, or other agreements.

5. Investment disputes

The existence of a legal dispute concerning an investment is a jurisdictional requirement in investment arbitration. If proceedings are to be conducted under the ICSID Convention, the test is that there is a 'legal dispute arising directly out of an investment' (Article 25(1)). Each of these elements, the existence of a dispute, the legal nature of the dispute, the directness of the dispute and the existence of an investment may raise jurisdictional questions.

(a) The dispute

The International Court of Justice has defined a dispute as 'a disagreement on a point of law or fact, a conflict of legal views or interests between parties'.[66] In another case the ICJ referred to 'a situation in which the two sides held clearly opposite views concerning the question of the performance or non-performance of certain treaty obligations'.[67] The Tribunal in *Texaco v Libya* referred to a 'present divergence of interests and opposition of legal views'.[68] ICSID tribunals have adopted similar definitions of 'disputes'.[69]

[66] See *Case concerning East Timor (Portugal v Australia)*, Judgment, 30 June 1995, ICJ Reports (1995) 90, paras 21–22 and the references to earlier cases cited there.

[67] *Interpretation of the Peace Treaties with Bulgaria, Hungary and Romania*, Advisory Opinion, 30 March 1950 (first phase), ICJ Reports (1950) 65, 74; see also *Case Concerning Certain Property (Liechtenstein v Germany)*, Judgment, 10 February 2005, ICJ Reports (2005) 6, paras 20–27.

[68] *Texaco v Libya*, Preliminary Award, 27 November 1975, 53 ILR 389, 416.

[69] *AGIP v Congo*, Award, 30 November 1979, 1 ICSID Reports 306, paras 38–42; *Maffezini v Spain*, Decision on Jurisdiction, 25 January 2000, paras 93–98; *Tokios Tokelės v Ukraine*, Decision on Jurisdiction, 29 April 2004, paras 106, 107; *Lucchetti v Peru*, Award, 7 February 2005, para 48; *Impregilo v Pakistan*, Decision on Jurisdiction, 22 April 2005, paras 302, 303; *El Paso v Argentina*, Decision on Jurisdiction, 27 April 2006, para 61; *Suez and InterAgua v Argentina*, Decision on Jurisdiction, 16 May 2006, para 29; *Helnan v Egypt*, Decision on Jurisdiction, 17 October 2006, para 52; *AMTO v Ukraine*, Final Award, 26 March 2008, paras 49–54; *Pey Casado v Chile*, Award, 8 May 2008, paras 440–447; *ATA*

The existence of a dispute requires a minimum of communication between the parties. The matter must have been taken up with the other party which must have either positively opposed the claimant's position or must have failed to respond.[70] This does not apply if acceptance of the claimant's position cannot reasonably be expected, for instance in case of legislative measures which leave no room for flexibility.

The disagreement between the parties must also have some practical relevance for their relationship and must not be purely theoretical. The dispute must go beyond general grievances and must be susceptible of being stated in terms of a concrete claim.[71]

The dispute must exist when proceedings are started.[72] This follows from the general principle of adjudication that jurisdiction will be determined by reference to the date of institution of proceedings. Some BITs state that they shall not apply to disputes that have arisen before the BIT's entry into force. But the time of a dispute is not identical with the time of the events leading to the dispute. Typically, the incriminated acts will have occurred at some time before the dispute. Therefore, the exclusion of disputes occurring before a certain date cannot be read as excluding jurisdiction over events occurring before that date. A dispute requires the development of the events to a degree where a difference of legal positions becomes apparent and communication between the parties demonstrates that difference.[73]

(b) The legal nature of the dispute

Disputes are legal if they 'concern the existence or scope of a legal right or obligation, or the nature or extent of the reparation to be made for breach of a legal obligation'.[74] Respondents have sometimes argued that the tribunal lacked jurisdiction because the dispute before it was not legal but rather of a political or economic nature. Tribunals have invariably rejected these arguments since the claims had been presented in legal terms.

In *Suez and InterAguas v Argentina* the Tribunal found that the claimant had made legal claims. It said:

v Jordan, Award, 18 May 2010, paras 98–109, 115–120; *Burlington v Ecuador*, Decision on Jurisdiction, 2 June 2010, paras 254–340; *Teinver v Argentina*, Decision on Jurisdiction, 21 December 2012, para 119; *Lao Holdings v Laos*, Decision on Jurisdiction, 21 February 2014, paras 120–121; *Crystallex v Venezuela*, Award, 4 April 2016, para 447; *EuroGas v Slovakia*, Award, 18 August 2017, para 437.

70 *Valores Mundiales v Venezuela*, Award, 25 July 2017, para 231.

71 *Maffezini v Spain*, Decision on Jurisdiction, 25 January 2000, para 94; *Tokios Tokelės v Ukraine*, Decision on Jurisdiction, 29 April 2004, para 106; *AES v Argentina*, Decision on Jurisdiction, 26 April 2005, para 43; *Ecuador v United States*, Award, 29 September 2012, paras 198–207.

72 *Siemens v Argentina*, Decision on Jurisdiction, 3 August 2004, para 161.

73 See II.2(b) above.

74 Report of the Executive Directors to the ICSID Convention, para 26.

> A legal dispute, in the ordinary meaning of the term, is a disagreement about legal rights or obligations... In the present case, the Claimants clearly base their case on legal rights which they allege have been granted to them under the bilateral investment treaties that Argentina has concluded with France and Spain. In their written pleadings and oral arguments, the Claimants have consistently presented their case in legal terms... the dispute as presented by the Claimants is legal in nature.[75]

Political elements in a dispute do not affect its legal nature. In *CSOB v Slovakia*, the respondent stressed the dispute's political background and its close link with the dissolution of the former Czech and Slovak Federal Republic. The Tribunal found that this did not affect the dispute's legal nature:

> While it is true that investment disputes to which a State is a party frequently have political elements or involve governmental actions, such disputes do not lose their legal character as long as they concern legal rights or obligations or the consequences of their breach.[76]

Other tribunals have adopted similar descriptions of legal disputes and have rejected attempts to contest their jurisdiction on the ground that the disputes before them were political or economic.[77] It follows from the practice of tribunals that the legal nature of a dispute is determined by the way the claimant presents its claim. If the claim is couched in terms of violation of legal rights, is based on legal arguments, and seeks legal remedies, there is a legal dispute.

(c) The directness of the dispute in relation to the investment

Under Article 25(1) of the ICSID Convention, the dispute must arise directly out of an investment. The element of directness applies to the dispute in relation to the

[75] *Suez and InterAgua v Argentina*, Decision on Jurisdiction, 16 May 2006, paras 34–37.

[76] *CSOB v Slovakia*, Decision on Jurisdiction, 24 May 1999, para 61.

[77] See *Maffezini v Spain*, Decision on Jurisdiction, 25 January 2000, paras 94–98; *Gas Natural v Argentina*, Decision on Jurisdiction, 17 June 2005, paras 20–23; *Camuzzi v Argentina*, Decision on Jurisdiction, 11 May 2005, paras 54–55; *AES v Argentina*, Decision on Jurisdiction, 26 April 2005, paras 40–47; *Sempra v Argentina*, Decision on Jurisdiction, 11 May 2005, paras 67–68; *Continental Casualty v Argentina*, Decision on Jurisdiction, 22 February 2006, paras 66–69; *El Paso v Argentina*, Decision on Jurisdiction, 27 April 2006, paras 47–62; *Jan de Nul v Egypt*, Decision on Jurisdiction, 16 June 2006, para 74; *National Grid v Argentina*, Decision on Jurisdiction, 20 June 2006, paras 142–143, 160; *Pan American v Argentina*, Decision on Preliminary Objections, 27 July 2006, paras 71–91; *Saipem v Bangladesh*, Decision on Jurisdiction, 21 March 2007, paras 93–97; *Noble Energy v Ecuador*, Decision on Jurisdiction, 5 March 2008, paras 121–123; *Perenco v Ecuador*, Decision on Jurisdiction, 30 June 2011, paras 132–147; *von Pezold v Zimbabwe*, Award, 28 July 2015, paras 183–191; *Magyar Farming v Hungary*, Award, 13 November 2019, paras 277–279; *Interocean v Nigeria*, Award, 6 October 2020, paras 109–110.

investment. It does not relate to the investment as such. In *Fedax v Venezuela*, the respondent argued that the disputed transaction, debt instruments issued by the Republic of Venezuela, was not a 'direct foreign investment' and therefore could not qualify as an investment under the ICSID Convention. The Tribunal rejected this argument. It pointed out that

> jurisdiction can exist even in respect of investments that are not direct, so long as the dispute arises directly from such transaction.[78]

Tribunals have held consistently that investments can be made indirectly, that is, through intermediate companies.[79]

Tribunals have found that the dispute must have a reasonably close connexion to the investment.[80] The Tribunal in *Metalpar v Argentina* described this requirement in the following terms:

> there must be an immediate 'cause-and-effect' relationship between the acts of the host State and the effects of such acts on the protected investments; a first-hand causal link must be established between the investment and the events of the receiving State that cause it to be affected. This does not mean, however, that the measures adopted by the State must be directed specifically against the investment. It is enough that an immediate link can be established (as opposed to a remote one) between the effects on the investment and the acts that cause them.[81]

An investment operation often consists of a series of individual transactions and legal relationships. They may include financing, the acquisition of property, construction, the lease of land, purchase of various goods, marketing of produced goods, activities to comply with the regulatory framework, the payment of taxes, etc. Some of these activities are merely ancillary or peripheral to the investment although in economic terms, these transactions are all more or less linked to the investment. To answer the question whether disputes relating to these activities arise directly out of the investment, tribunals have developed the doctrine of the unity of the investment.[82]

In several cases, Argentina argued that the measures it had taken were of a general nature, were designed to serve the national welfare and were not specifically

[78] *Fedax v Venezuela*, Decision on Jurisdiction, 11 July 1997, para 24. See also *Siemens v Argentina*, Decision on Jurisdiction, 3 August 2004, para 150.

[79] *CMS v Argentina*, Decision on Jurisdiction, 17 July 2003, paras 66, 68; *Siemens v Argentina*, Decision on Jurisdiction, 3 August 2004, para 150. See also IV.9 above.

[80] *Tokios Tokelės v Ukraine*, Decision on Jurisdiction, 29 April 2004, paras 87–93; *Burimi v Albania*, Award, 29 May 2013, paras 142–146; *Bridgestone v Panama*, Decision on Expedited Objections, 13 December 2017, para 238.

[81] *Metalpar v Argentina*, Decision on Jurisdiction, 27 April 2006, para 95.

[82] See IV.5 above

directed at the particular investor's operation. Therefore, in Argentina's view, the dispute about these measures did not arise directly out of the investment. The Tribunal in *CMS v Argentina* did not accept this argument. It said:

> the Tribunal concludes on this point that it does not have jurisdiction over measures of general economic policy adopted by the Republic of Argentina and cannot pass judgment on whether they are right or wrong. The Tribunal also concludes, however, that it has jurisdiction to examine whether specific measures affecting the Claimant's investment or measures of general economic policy having a direct bearing on such investment have been adopted in violation of legally binding commitments made to the investor in treaties, legislation or contracts.[83]

Other tribunals have followed this line of argument.[84] It follows that a host State cannot rely on the general policy nature of measures taken by it if these measures had a concrete effect on the investment and violated specific commitments and obligations. These commitments may arise from legislation, a contract, or a treaty.[85]

(d) The investment

The existence of an investment is a cornerstone of the jurisdiction of investment tribunals. Yet, the ICSID Convention offers no definition of the term 'investment'. Investment protection treaties as well as investment legislation offer a variety of definitions.

Other issues that arise in connexion with the concept of an investment include the unity of the investment, indirect investments, the legality of investments, the origin of the invested funds, and the requirement that the investment take place in the host State's territory. The relevant issues are discussed above in Chapter IV on 'Investments'.[86]

83 *CMS v Argentina*, Decision on Jurisdiction, 17 July 2003, para 33.

84 *LG&E v Argentina*, Decision on Jurisdiction, 30 April 2004, para 67; *AES v Argentina*, Decision on Jurisdiction, 26 April 2005, paras 56–57; *Sempra v Argentina*, Decision on Jurisdiction, 11 May 2005, para 71; *Camuzzi v Argentina*, Decision on Jurisdiction, 11 May 2005, paras 56 et seq; *Gas Natural v Argentina*, Decision on Jurisdiction, 17 June 2005, paras 37–40; *Continental Casualty v Argentina*, Decision on Jurisdiction, 22 February 2006, paras 71–74; *Suez and InterAgua v Argentina*, Decision on Jurisdiction, 16 May 2006, paras 27–30; *El Paso v Argentina*, Decision on Jurisdiction, 27 April 2006, paras 89–100; *National Grid v Argentina*, Decision on Jurisdiction, 20 June 2006, paras 123–141; *Pan American v Argentina*, Decision on Preliminary Objections, 27 July 2006, paras 55–70; *Daimler v Argentina*, Award, 22 August 2012, paras 100–104.

85 See also VII.3(h) above.

86 See IV above.

6. The parties to investment disputes

Investment arbitration is mixed in the sense that it involves a sovereign State (the host State) on one side and a private foreign investor on the other.

(a) The host State

In investment arbitration, the host State is nearly always the respondent. Cases in which the host State acts as claimant are rare.[87] In most situations, host States can assert their position vis-à-vis foreign investors through their legislative and executive powers under domestic law. Investment protection treaties typically grant access to international arbitration to foreign investors but not to host States. The ICSID Convention is neutral on the respective position of host States and investors.[88]

Under the ICSID Convention, jurisdiction extends to Contracting States, parties to the ICSID Convention. Mere signatories are not Contracting States. Whether a particular State has ratified the Convention is evident from the List of Contracting States and Other Signatories of the Convention maintained by ICSID and available on its website.[89] The status as a Contracting State may be terminated by a written notice whereby the State denounces the Convention. Such a denunciation becomes effective after six months and does not affect perfected consent to the jurisdiction of the Centre given prior to the denunciation.[90]

The status of a Contracting State cannot be obtained through State succession.[91] New States must join the ICSID Convention as parties and are not able to derive their status as a Contracting State from their predecessor State. This practice was followed after the dissolution of Czechoslovakia, with the Czech and the Slovak Republics joining ICSID as new Contracting States. After the dissolution of the Socialist Federal Republic of Yugoslavia, Slovenia, Bosnia and Herzegovina, Croatia, and North Macedonia, and later Serbia and Montenegro acceded as new Contracting States to the Convention. Following the secessions of Timor-Leste,

[87] For cases initiated by the host State or an agency of the host State, see *East Kalimantan v PT Kaltim Prima Coal*, Award on Jurisdiction, 28 December 2009, paras 173–174; *Gabon v Société Serete*, Order Taking Note of the Discontinuance of the Proceedings, 27 February 1978; *TANESCO v IPTL*, Final Award, 12 July 2001 para 13; *Peru v Caravelí*, Procedural Order Taking Note of the Discontinuance of the Proceeding, 26 December 2013.

[88] The ICSID Convention Article 25 speaks of a legal dispute 'between a Contracting State (or any constituent subdivision or agency of a Contracting State designated to the Centre by that State) and a national of another Contracting State'. Under Article 36 a request for arbitration may be submitted by '[a]ny Contracting State or any national of a Contracting State'.

[89] List of Contracting States and other Signatories of the Convention ICSID/3.

[90] Articles 71 and 72 of the ICSID Convention.

[91] J Tams, 'State Succession to Investment Treaties' (2016) 31 *ICSID Rev* 314; P Dumberry, *A Guide to State Succession in International Investment Law* (2018).

Kosovo, and South Sudan, these new States followed the same procedure and became new Contracting States.

The critical time for the status of a State as an ICSID Contracting State is the date of the registration of the request for arbitration by the Secretary-General of ICSID. A State may give its consent to submit to the Centre's jurisdiction before becoming a Contracting State. But this consent becomes effective only once the State satisfies the requirements of a Contracting State.[92] A State that is not a Contracting State of the Convention is not subject to ICSID's jurisdiction even if it has given its consent to jurisdiction.

The host State may deal with foreign investors either through a central State organ such as a government ministry or through a separate entity. This may be a territorial entity such as a province or municipality. It may also be a specialized government agency such as an investment board or a privatization agency. Acts in violation of international law may be attributed to the central government even if they were committed by a sub-entity of the host State. Under the international law of State responsibility, the State is responsible for all its organs including those of a territorial unit as well as for State entities exercising elements of governmental authority.[93]

The ICSID Convention contains a provision that makes it possible for a sub-entity of the host State to appear in proceedings. Article 25, after referring to the Contracting State, adds in parentheses 'or any constituent subdivision or agency of a Contracting State designated to the Centre [ie ICSID] by that State'. This clause opens the possibility for such entities, by means of a designation by a Contracting State, to become party to ICSID proceedings.

The term 'constituent subdivisions' includes any territorial entity below the level of the State such as a province, a state or a municipality. The term 'agency' refers to an entity of the host State. Designations of constituent subdivisions or agencies serve procedural convenience, but do not affect questions of State responsibility. The State entity's party status is independent of the issue of the attribution of its actions to the State and solely depends on a valid designation pursuant to Article 25(1).[94]

The Convention requires that the constituent subdivision or agency be designated to ICSID. Designation assures an investor that the particular agency or entity with which it is dealing has been properly authorized by the State. Nevertheless, Article 25(3) of the ICSID Convention requires additionally that the constituent subdivision or agency's consent to ICSID's jurisdiction be approved by the State to which it belongs. ICSID keeps a public register of designated subdivisions and

[92] *Amco v Indonesia*, Decision on Jurisdiction, 25 September 1983, para 34; *LETCO v Liberia*, Decision on Jurisdiction, 24 October 1984, 2 ICSID Reports 351; *Cable TV v St Kitts and Nevis*, Award, 13 January 1997, para 4.09; *Generation Ukraine v Ukraine*, Award, 16 September 2003, paras 12.4–12.6.

[93] See Chapter X above.

[94] *Vivendi v Argentina*, Award, 21 November 2000, paras 41, 46, 51.

agencies of States.[95] Only relatively few countries have made designations under this provision. Constituent subdivisions or agencies have played a limited role in ICSID practice.[96]

In *Cable Television v St. Kitts and Nevis*,[97] the claimant had entered into a contract with the Nevis Island Administration (NIA) containing consent to ICSID arbitration. The Tribunal found that the NIA was a constituent subdivision of the Federation of St. Kitts & Nevis, a sovereign State, and a party to the ICSID Convention. But NIA had not been designated to ICSID as a constituent subdivision or agency in accordance with Article 25(1) of the ICSID Convention. Nor had its consent been approved by the Federation in accordance with Article 25(3). In turn, the Federation was not a party to the contract containing consent to ICSID's jurisdiction. The Tribunal found that it had no jurisdiction.[98]

(b) The investor

The role of investors is discussed in more detail above in Chapter III on 'Investor'.[99] In most instances, investors are juridical persons ie corporations. At times, also individuals appear as claimants in investment arbitration.[100]

Investment arbitration is designed for the protection of private investors. The ICSID Convention's Preamble speaks specifically of the role of private international investment. This would indicate that the investor must be a private individual or corporation. But State-owned corporations and State entities will be accepted as investors if they act in a private commercial capacity.[101]

In *CSOB v Slovakia*, the respondent contested the Tribunal's competence arguing that the claimant, a bank, was a State agency of the Czech Republic rather than an independent commercial entity and that it was discharging essentially governmental activities. The Tribunal rejected this contention. It held that access to arbitration did not depend upon whether or not the company was partially or

95 Designations by Contracting States Regarding Constituent Subdivisions or Agencies (ICSID/8-C).

96 See *TANESCO v IPTL*, Award, 12 July 2001, para 13; *Noble Energy v Ecuador*, Decision on Jurisdiction, 5 March 2008, para 63; *East Kalimantan v PT Kaltim Prima Coal*, Award on Jurisdiction, 28 December 2009, paras 186–202; *Cambodia Power v Cambodia*, Decision on Jurisdiction, 22 March 2011, paras 215–259; *Niko Resources v Bangladesh*, Decision on Jurisdiction, 19 August 2013, paras 257–348.

97 *Cable Television v St. Kitts and Nevis*, Award, 13 January 1997.

98 See also *Hamester v Ghana*, Award, 18 June 2010, paras 27, 62, where the Secretary-General of ICSID refused to register a Request for Arbitration against an undesignated State agency.

99 See III above.

100 See eg *Azinian v Mexico*; *Feldman v Mexico*; *Goetz v Burundi*; *Gruslin v Malaysia*; *Maffezini v Spain*; *Olguín v Paraguay*; *Soufraki v UAE*; *Doutremepuich v Mauritius*.

101 *CDC v Seychelles*, Award, 17 December 2003, paras 6, 19, 34; *Flughafen Zürich v Venezuela*, Award, 18 November 2014, paras 262–286; *Beijing Urban Construction v Yemen*, Decision on Jurisdiction, 31 May 2017, paras 31–44; *Masdar v Spain*, Award, 16 May 2018, paras 144(i), 145, 155, 169–173; *Stadtwerke München v Spain*, Award, 2 December 2019, paras 133, 134.

wholly owned by the Government. The decisive test was whether the company was discharging essentially governmental functions. CSOB's banking activities had to be judged by their nature and not by their purpose and were hence commercial.[102]

It has always been beyond doubt that arbitral proceedings are open to more than one claimant in one and the same case. The practice under the ICSID Convention shows numerous proceedings with more than one party on the claimants' side.[103]

In *Abaclat v Argentina*,[104] a group of more than 180,000 Italian bondholders, later reduced to about 60,000, instituted arbitration proceedings against Argentina for failing to honour government bonds. The Tribunal noted that this was not a class action since each investor had individually consented to the arbitration. Argentina's offer of consent, given through its BIT with Italy, included claims presented by multiple claimants in a single proceeding. The Tribunal, alluding to the fact that the BIT's definition of investment covered bonds, said:

> where the BIT covers investments which are susceptible of involving a high number of investors, and where such investments require a collective relief in order to provide effective protection to such investment, it would be contrary to the purpose of the BIT, and to the spirit of ICSID, to require in addition to the consent to ICSID arbitration in general, a supplementary express consent to the form of such arbitration.[105]

The Tribunal also rejected Argentina's objections to the admissibility of the proceeding. Any adaptations of the standard procedure under the ICSID Convention that may become necessary were within the Tribunal's powers. The claims were sufficiently homogeneous for the claimants to be treated as a group and to justify a simplification of the procedure.

Sometimes claimants start separate proceedings that are closely related because they arise from the same set of facts. Some investment treaties,[106] foresee the

[102] *CSOB v Slovakia*, Decision on Jurisdiction, 24 May 1999, paras 15–27. See also *Rumeli v Kazakhstan*, Award, 29 July 2008, paras 325–328: the Tribunal found that the extent of any control over claimants by the Turkish Government and the possibility that the proceeds of any award might be remitted to the Turkish Treasury did not deprive the claimants of their status as commercial entities.

[103] *Goetz v Burundi*, Award, 10 February 1999, paras 84–89; *Champion Trading v Egypt*, Decision on Jurisdiction, 21 October 2003, para 1; *Foresti v South Africa*, Award, 4 August 2010, para 1; *Ambiente Ufficio v Argentina*, Decision on Jurisdiction and Admissibility, 8 February 2013, paras 126–172; *Alemanni v Argentina*, Decision on Jurisdiction and Admissibility, 17 November 2014, paras 270–272, 287–295, 321–325; *von Pezold v Zimbabwe*, Award, 28 July 2015, para 9; *Spence v Costa Rica*, Interim Award, 25 October 2016, para 1; *Valores Mundiales v Venezuela*, Award, 25 July 2017, para 2; *Marfin v Cyprus*, Award, 26 July 2018, paras 2–20; *Adamakopoulos v Cyprus*, Decision on Jurisdiction, 7 February 2020, paras 188, 197–261.

[104] *Abaclat v Argentina*, Decision on Jurisdiction, 4 August 2011, paras 216, 294–298, 480–492, 506–551.

[105] At para 518.

[106] NAFTA Article 1126; USMCA Article 14.D.12.

consolidation of closely related proceedings.[107] Consolidation of separate proceedings may also simply be based on an agreement of the parties.[108] Exceptionally, claims arising from the same overall transaction between the same parties but subject to several jurisdictional instruments may call for consolidation: one and the same case may involve several investment protection treaties and may be conducted under more than one set of procedural rules.[109] Another possible method to coordinate separate claims that are closely related because they arise from related facts consists in the creation of tribunals that are formally separate but identically composed.[110]

(c) The investor's nationality

The investor's nationality has a number of procedural and jurisdictional consequences.[111] In order to gain access to dispute settlement under the ICSID Convention, there is a positive as well as a negative nationality requirement: an investor is required to be a 'national of another Contracting State', of a State that is a party to the ICSID Convention. Also, the investor must not be a national of the host State (Article 25).

If the investor relies on a jurisdictional clause in a treaty, it must also have the nationality of one of the States parties to that treaty. In the case of arbitration based on a BIT, the host State must be one of the parties to the BIT and the investor must demonstrate that it is a national of the other party to the BIT.

In the case of natural persons (individuals) the nationality of the Contracting State to the ICSID Convention must exist at two separate dates: an individual investor has to be a national of a Contracting State at the time the parties' consent to submit to ICSID's jurisdiction and also on the date the request for arbitration or conciliation is registered by ICSID. In addition, the individual investor must not be a national of the host State on either of these dates. A loss of nationality after the

[107] See *Canfor v United States, Tembec v United States, Terminal Forest Products v United States*, Order of the Consolidation Tribunal, 7 September 2005; *Corn Products v Mexico, Archer Daniels Midland v Mexico*, Order of the Consolidation Tribunal, 20 May 2005.

[108] *Pan American v Argentina*, Decision on Preliminary Objections, 27 July 2006, paras 1–4, 7; *Unglaube v Costa Rica*, Award, 16 May 2012, paras 8, 13, 14, 27; *Churchill Mining and Planet Mining v Indonesia*, Award, 6 December 2016, paras 2–7.

[109] See *Suez and Vivendi v Argentina* (ICSID) and *AWG v Argentina* (UNCITRAL), Decision on Jurisdiction, 3 August 2006, paras 1–4, 7; *Noble Energy v Ecuador*, Decision on Jurisdiction, 5 March 2008, paras 186–207.

[110] See *Alcoa Minerals v Jamaica, Kaiser Bauxite v Jamaica* and *Reynolds v Jamaica*; *Camuzzi v Argentina*, Decision on Jurisdiction, 11 May 2005, para 4 and *Sempra v Argentina*, Decision on Jurisdiction, 11 May 2005, para 5; *Salini v Morocco*, Decision on Jurisdiction, 16 July 2001 and *RFCC v Morocco*, Decision on Jurisdiction, 16 July 2001; *von Pezold v Zimbabwe*, Award, 28 July 2015, paras 5–8.

[111] More generally on the nationality of investors see III.2 and III.3 above.

date of the request's registration does not affect the tribunal's jurisdiction *ratione personae*.[112]

An individual's nationality is determined primarily by the domestic legislation of the State whose nationality is claimed. A certificate of nationality is strong evidence but not conclusive proof of nationality.

An investor's nationality must be determined objectively irrespective of an agreement between the host State and the investor. An agreement between a host State and an investor may specifically indicate the investor's nationality. Such an agreement creates a presumption but is not conclusive. In particular, it cannot create a nationality that does not objectively exist.

Investors who hold the nationality of the host State are barred from bringing claims before the Centre. The purpose of ICSID is to encourage the settlement of disputes that involve States and foreign investors. This will apply also to investors with dual nationality if one of the two nationalities is that of the host State even if it is not the effective one.

A claimant bears the burden of proving its nationality. The burden to prove that the claimant has the nationality of the host State falls on the respondent.[113]

A juridical person (company) must have the nationality of a State Party to the ICSID Convention only on the day the parties consented to submit to ICSID's jurisdiction. Juridical persons will normally qualify as nationals of Contracting States through their place of incorporation or seat of business.

A juridical person may, however, possess the host State's nationality and still qualify as a national of another Contracting State under an exception contained in Article 25(2)(b).[114] The prevalence of investment arbitration based on treaties has led to a decline in importance of this possibility for locally incorporated companies that are under foreign control to institute ICSID arbitration. Many of these treaties include shareholding or participation in companies in their definitions of investment. This allows the foreign shareholders in the locally incorporated company to pursue the claim internationally.[115]

(d) The significance of the Additional Facility

As set out above, under Article 25(1) of the ICSID Convention the host State and the investor's State of nationality must be Contracting States. If one or the other of

[112] *Kim v Uzbekistan*, Decision on Jurisdiction, 8 March 2017, para 223.

[113] *Ambiente Ufficio v Argentina*, Decision on Jurisdiction and Admissibility, 8 February 2013, para 312.

[114] For more detailed treatment of the application of Article 25(2)(b) of the ICSID Convention see Chapter III.4.

[115] For more detailed treatment see IV.9(b) above.

these States is not a party to the Convention, the requirements *ratione personae* are not fulfilled and there is no jurisdiction.

If only one of the two States is a party to the ICSID Convention, the Additional Facility[116] offers a method of dispute settlement. The Additional Facility enables a non-Contracting State or a national of a non-Contracting State to the ICSID Convention to participate in dispute settlement proceedings administered by ICSID. If both States are parties to the Convention, the parties must use the procedure under the Convention and may not use the Additional Facility. Also, there must be a separate submission to dispute settlement under the Additional Facility.

7. Consent to investment arbitration

Consent to arbitration by the host State and by the investor is an indispensable requirement for a tribunal's jurisdiction. Treaties play an important role but cannot, by themselves, establish jurisdiction. Both parties, the host State and the investor, must have expressed their consent.

In practice, consent is given in one of three ways: first, a consent clause may be included in a direct agreement between the parties. Dispute settlement clauses providing for investor–State arbitration are common in contracts between States and foreign investors.

A second technique to give consent to arbitration is a provision in the national legislation of the host State. Such a provision offers arbitration to foreign investors in general terms. Many capital importing countries have adopted such provisions. The mere existence of such a provision in national legislation will not suffice, but the investor may accept the offer in writing at any time while the legislation is in effect. The acceptance may also be made simply by instituting proceedings.

The third, most frequently used method to give consent to arbitration is through a treaty between the host State and the investor's State of nationality. Most BITs contain clauses offering arbitration to the nationals of one State party to the treaty against the other State party to the treaty. The same method is employed by a number of regional multilateral treaties such as the Energy Charter Treaty (ECT). Offers of consent contained in treaties must also be perfected by an acceptance on the part of the investor.

In some cases, claimants relied on several instruments to establish consent. Jurisdiction was said to exist on the basis of a contract and legislation,[117] on

[116] See XII.4(b) above.

[117] *Lighthouse v Timor-Leste*, Award, 22 December 2017, paras 1, 114.

the basis of a contract as well as on a treaty,[118] on the basis of legislation and a treaty,[119] or on more than one treaty.[120]

(a) Consent by direct agreement

An agreement between the parties recording consent to arbitration may be achieved through a compromissory clause in an investment agreement between the host State and the investor submitting future disputes arising from the investment operation to arbitration.[121] It is equally possible to submit a dispute that has already arisen between the parties through consent expressed in a *compromis*. Therefore, consent may be given with respect to existing or future disputes.[122]

The agreement on consent between the parties need not be recorded in a single instrument. An investment application made by the investor may provide for arbitration. If the application is approved by the competent authority of the host State, there is consent to arbitration by both parties.[123]

An agreement between the parties may record their consent to arbitration by reference to another legal instrument. Reference to a BIT that never entered into force,[124] submission to domestic law that provides for arbitration[125] and even a reference to standard terms and conditions that contain an arbitration clause,[126] may amount to contractual consent.

[118] *Noble Energy v Ecuador*, Decision on Jurisdiction, 5 March 2008, paras 22, 23, 150, 178; *Duke Energy v Ecuador*, Award, 18 August 2008, paras 99, 102, 111–189; *Lemire v Ukraine*, Decision on Jurisdiction and Liability, 14 January 2010, para 60; *Millicom v Senegal*, Decision on Jurisdiction, 16 July 2010, para 26.

[119] *Sistem Mühendislik v Kyrgyzstan*, Decision on Jurisdiction, 13 September 2007, paras 57, 99–131; *Rumeli v Kazakhstan*, Award, 29 July 2008, paras 162, 165, 220–222; *Mobil v Venezuela*, Decision on Jurisdiction, 10 June 2010, para 24; *Pac Rim v El Salvador*, Decision on Preliminary Objections, 2 August 2010, paras 21–23, 242, 253; *CEMEX v Venezuela*, Decision on Jurisdiction, 30 December 2010, para 59; *Khan Resources v Mongolia*, Decision on Jurisdiction, 25 July 2012, paras 3, 69–71; *Burimi v Albania*, Award, 29 May 2013, paras 92, 94–95; *ConocoPhillips v Venezuela*, Decision on Jurisdiction and the Merits, 3 September 2013, paras 1, 11, 222.

[120] *Poštová banka v Greece*, Award, 9 April 2015, para 1; *von Pezold v Zimbabwe*, Award, 28 July 2015, para 1; *Tenaris v Venezuela I*, Award, 29 January 2016, para 7; *Ampal-American v Egypt*, Decision on Jurisdiction, 1 February 2016, para 4; *Churchill Mining and Planet Mining v Indonesia*, Award, 6 December 2016, para 2; *Adamakopoulos v Cyprus*, Decision on Jurisdiction, 7 February 2020, paras 1, 213, 218–219, 270.

[121] See also V.3 above. ICSID has developed a set of Model Clauses to facilitate the drafting of consent clauses in investment contracts. See ICSID Model Clauses, Doc. ICSID/5/Rev 2 of 1993. Reproduced in 4 ICSID Reports 357.

[122] Agreements to submit existing disputes to arbitration are rare. But see *MINE v Guinea*, Award, 6 January 1988, 4 ICSID Reports 61, 67; *Santa Elena v Costa Rica*, Award, 17 February 2000, para 26.

[123] *Amco v Indonesia*, Decision on Jurisdiction, 25 September 1983, paras 10, 25. See also *Planet Mining v Indonesia*, Decision on Jurisdiction, 24 February 2014, paras 11–18, 199–217.

[124] *CSOB v Slovakia*, Decision on Jurisdiction, 24 May 1999, paras 49–55.

[125] *Inceysa v El Salvador*, Award, 2 August 2006, para 331.

[126] *Lighthouse v Timor-Leste*, Award, 22 December 2017, paras 9, 16, 144, 228–282.

The parties are free to delimit their consent to arbitration by defining it in general terms, by excluding certain types of disputes or by listing the questions they are submitting to arbitration. In practice, broad inclusive consent clauses are the norm. Consent clauses contained in investment agreements typically refer to 'any dispute' or to 'all disputes' under the respective agreements.[127]

Investment operations sometimes involve complex arrangements expressed in several successive agreements. Arbitration clauses may be contained in some of these agreements but not in others. The question arises whether the consent to arbitration extends to the entire operation or is confined to the specific agreements containing the arbitration clauses.

Tribunals have generally taken a broad view of expressions of consent of this kind. The arbitration clauses were not applied narrowly to the specific document containing them but were read in the context of the parties' overall relationship. The interrelated contracts were seen as representing the legal framework for one investment operation. Therefore, arbitration clauses contained in some, though not all, of the different contracts were interpreted as applying to the entire operation.[128]

In *Duke Energy v Peru*, the investor had concluded several successive contracts with Peru in relation to the same investment. Only one of the contracts contained a clause whereby the parties consented to ICSID arbitration. The Tribunal applied the principle of the 'unity of the investment'.[129] At the same time it held that the claimant would have to substantiate its claims by reference to the contract containing the arbitration clause. The other contracts would be taken into consideration for the purpose of interpreting and applying that contract.[130]

(b) Consent through host State legislation

The host State may offer consent to arbitration to foreign investors in general terms. However, not every reference to investment arbitration in national legislation amounts to consent to jurisdiction. Therefore, the respective provisions in national laws must be studied carefully.

Some national investment laws provide unequivocally for dispute settlement by international arbitration. For instance, Article 8(2) of the Albanian Law on Foreign Investment of 1993 states in part:

[127] *World Duty Free v Kenya*, Award, 4 October 2006, para 6.

[128] See *Holiday Inns v Morocco*, Decision on Jurisdiction, 12 May 1974. The case is unpublished but described by P Lalive, 'The First "World Bank" Arbitration (Holiday Inns *v* Morocco)—Some Legal Problems' (1980) 51 *BYIL* 123, 156–159; *Klöckner v Cameroon*, Award, 21 October 1983, 2 ICSID Reports 9, 13, 65–69; *SOABI v Senegal*, Decision on Jurisdiction, 1 August 1984, paras 47–58, Award, 25 February 1988, paras 4.01–4.52.

[129] See IV.5 above.

[130] *Duke Energy v Peru*, Decision on Jurisdiction, 1 February 2006, paras 119–134; Decision on Annulment, 1 March 2011, paras 145–160.

> the foreign investor may submit the dispute for resolution and the Republic of Albania hereby consents to the submission thereof, to the International Centre for Settlement of Investment Disputes.[131]

Other provisions are less explicit but still indicate that they express the State's consent to international arbitration. National laws may state that 'the investors may submit' the dispute to, or that the dispute 'shall be settled' by international arbitration.[132]

Other references in national legislation to investment arbitration do not amount to consent. Some provisions make it clear that further action by the host State is required to establish consent.[133] This would be the case where the law in question provides that the parties 'may agree' to settle investment disputes through arbitration.[134]

Some provisions are unclear and have led to disputes as to whether the host State has given its consent.[135] The Venezuelan Investment Law of 1999 contained Article 22 which, translated to English, reads:

> Disputes arising between an international investor whose country of origin has in effect with Venezuela a treaty or agreement on the promotion and protection of investments, or disputes to which are applicable the provision of the Convention Establishing the Multilateral Investment Guarantee Agency (OMGI–MIGA) or the Convention on the Settlement of Investment Disputes between States and Nationals of other States (ICSID), shall be submitted to international arbitration according to the terms of the respective treaty or agreement, if it so provides, without prejudice to the possibility of using, if appropriate, the dispute resolution means provided for under the Venezuelan legislation in effect.

In *Mobil v Venezuela*, the claimants sought to rely on this clause to establish ICSID's jurisdiction. The Tribunal undertook a detailed analysis of this text. It noted that the provision contrasted with clear expressions of consent in some of Venezuela's BITs. The Tribunal reached the conclusion that an intention of Venezuela to offer consent to ICSID's jurisdiction on the basis of this ambiguous clause could

[131] See *Tradex v Albania*, Decision on Jurisdiction, 24 December 1996, 5 ICSID Reports 47, 54.

[132] *Zhinvali v Georgia*, Award, 24 January 2003, paras 337–342; *Lighthouse v Timor-Leste*, Award, 22 December 2017, paras 283–334.

[133] *PNG Sustainable Development v Papua New Guinea*, Award, 5 May 2015, para 286.

[134] *Biwater Gauff v Tanzania*, Award, 24 July 2008, paras 326–337; *Metal-Tech v Uzbekistan*, Award, 4 October 2013, paras 381–388; *MNSS v Montenegro*, Award, 4 May 2016, paras 166–167; *Besserglik v Mozambique*, Award, 28 October 2019, paras 397–417.

[135] See *SPP v Egypt*, Decision on Jurisdiction I, 27 November 1985, paras 70–78; Decision on Jurisdiction II, 14 April 1988, paras 53–117.

not be established.[136] Other tribunals interpreting Article 22 of the Venezuelan Investment Law reached the same result.[137]

A legislative provision containing consent to arbitration is merely an offer by the State to investors. To perfect an arbitration agreement the investor must accept that offer. The investor may accept the offer simply by instituting arbitration.[138] The host State may repeal its offer at any time unilaterally until the investor has accepted it. Therefore, an investor is well advised to accept the offer of consent to arbitration through a written communication as early as possible.[139]

The investor's acceptance of consent can be given only to the extent of the offer made in the legislation. But it is entirely possible for the investor's acceptance to be narrower than the offer and to extend only to certain matters or only to a particular investment operation.

Some offers of consent to arbitration in national laws are quite broad and refer to disputes concerning foreign investment in general terms.[140] Others delimit the questions covered by consent clauses. Some laws offer consent only for disputes that relate to an expropriation.[141] Other references to international arbitration relate only to the application and interpretation of the piece of legislation in question.[142]

The host State's offer of consent contained in its legislation may be subject to certain conditions, time limits, or formalities. In some investment laws, consent is linked to the process of obtaining an investment authorization.[143] Other investment laws require that the investor must accept the offer of consent to arbitration within certain time limits.

(c) Consent through bilateral treaties

Most investment arbitration cases are based on jurisdiction established through bilateral treaties. These are typically BITs. Free trade agreements (FTAs) may also

136 *Mobil v Venezuela*, Decision on Jurisdiction, 10 June 2010, paras 67–140. The Tribunal found that it had jurisdiction on the basis of the BIT between The Netherlands and Venezuela, at paras 142–206.

137 *CEMEX v Venezuela*, Decision on Jurisdiction, 30 December 2010, paras 63–139; *Brandes v Venezuela*, Award, 2 August 2011, paras 79–118; *Tidewater v Venezuela*, Decision on Jurisdiction, 8 February 2013, paras 103–141; *OPIC Karimum v Venezuela*, Award, 28 May 2013, paras 100–108, 165–179; *ConocoPhillips v Venezuela*, Decision on Jurisdiction and the Merits, 3 September 2013, para 259; *Highbury v Venezuela*, Award, 26 September 2013, paras 237–241; *Venoklim v Venezuela*, Award, 3 April 2015, paras 81–113.

138 *Tradex v Albania*, Decision on Jurisdiction, 24 December 1996, 5 ICSID Reports 47, 63; *Zhinvali v Georgia*, Award, 24 January 2003, para 342.

139 *SPP v Egypt*, Decision on Jurisdiction I, 27 November 1985, para 40. See also *ABCI Investments v Tunisia*, Decision on Jurisdiction, 18 February 2011, paras 89–134.

140 *Inceysa v El Salvador*, Award, 2 August 2006, para 331.

141 *Tradex v Albania*, Award, 29 April 1999, paras 92, 132, 203–205.

142 *SPP v Egypt*, Decision on Jurisdiction I, 27 November 1985, para 70.

143 *Lighthouse v Timor-Leste*, Award, 22 December 2017, paras 310–334.

contain clauses providing for arbitration between States and investors. The States parties to these treaties offer consent to arbitration to nationals of the other contracting party. Mutual consent is perfected through the acceptance of that offer by an eligible investor.

Treaties can provide a basis for consent to arbitration only if they are in force at the relevant time. In some cases, tribunals found that a treaty invoked by claimant was not in force.[144]

The vast majority of BITs contain clauses referring to investment arbitration.[145] Most investor–State dispute settlement clauses in BITs offer unequivocal consent to arbitration. This will be the case where the treaty states that each Contracting Party 'hereby consents' or where the dispute 'shall be submitted' to arbitration.[146]

Not all references to investor/State arbitration in bilateral treaties necessarily constitute binding offers of consent by the host State. Some clauses referring to arbitration are phrased in terms of an undertaking by the host State to give consent in the future. For instance, the States may promise to accede to a demand by an investor to submit to arbitration by stating that the host State 'shall consent' to arbitration in case of a dispute.[147] In *Millicom v Senegal*, the Netherlands–Senegal BIT provided that the State concerned '*devra consentir*' ('shall assent') to a dispute's submission to ICSID arbitration. Senegal objected on the ground that this did not amount to consent but that under this formula the State retained a discretionary power to give or withhold consent. The Tribunal rejected this objection and found that the treaty provision amounted to 'a unilateral offer and a commitment by Senegal to submit itself to ICSID jurisdiction'.[148]

Some references to arbitration in BITs merely provide that the host State will give sympathetic consideration to a request for dispute settlement through arbitration. A clause of this kind does not amount to consent by the host State. Also, some BITs merely envisage a future agreement between the host State and the investor containing consent to arbitration.

Many dispute settlement clauses in BITs offer several alternatives. These may include the domestic courts of the host State, procedures agreed to by the parties to the dispute, ICSID arbitration, ICC arbitration, and ad hoc arbitration often under the UNCITRAL rules. The precise legal effect of such clauses depends upon their wording. Some of these composite settlement clauses require a subsequent

[144] *Tradex v Albania*, Decision on Jurisdiction, 24 December 1996, 5 ICSID Reports 47, 58; *CSOB v Slovakia*, Decision on Jurisdiction, 24 May 1999, paras 37–47; *Besserglik v Mozambique*, Award, 28 October 2019, paras 325–396.

[145] See R Dolzer and M Stevens, *Bilateral Investment Treaties* (1995) 129 et seq; KJ Vandevelde, *Bilateral Investment Treaties* (2010) 433 et seq.

[146] The first case brought successfully on the basis of a clause of this kind was *AAPL v Sri Lanka*, Award, 27 June 1990, para 2.

[147] See Article 10(2) of the Japan–Pakistan BIT of 1998.

[148] *Millicom v Senegal*, Decision on Jurisdiction, 16 July 2010, paras 56, 61–66. See also *Churchill Mining v Indonesia*, Decision on Jurisdiction, 24 February 2014, paras 154–231. But see *Planet Mining v Indonesia*, Decision on Jurisdiction, 24 February 2014, paras 153–198.

agreement by the disputing parties to select one of these procedures. Others contain the State's advance consent to all of them, thereby giving the party that initiates arbitration a choice. Some BITs offering several methods of settlement specifically state that the choice among them is with the investor.

A provision on consent to arbitration in a BIT is merely an offer by the respective States that requires acceptance by the other party. That offer may be accepted by a national of the other State party to the BIT.

It is established practice that an investor may accept an offer of consent contained in a treaty by instituting arbitration proceedings.[149] In *Abaclat v Argentina*, the Tribunal said:

> Within the context of BIT-based arbitration, it is widely admitted that an arbitration clause contained in a BIT and providing for ICSID arbitration constitutes a valid written offer for ICSID arbitration by the relevant State. ... Such an offer of consent may be validly accepted by an investor through the initiation of ICSID proceedings.[150]

Acceptance of an offer of consent contained in a BIT is possible not only by way of instituting proceedings. The investor may express its consent in writing at any time during the BIT's validity even before a dispute arises. In the case of arbitration clauses contained in treaties, a withdrawal of an offer of consent before its acceptance would be more difficult than in the case of national legislation. An offer of arbitration in a treaty remains valid notwithstanding an attempt to terminate it unless there is a basis for the termination under the law of treaties.

After the *Achmea* Judgment of the Court of Justice of the European Union (CJEU),[151] respondent States as well as the EU Commission have taken the position that consent to arbitration under treaties between EU Member States has become inapplicable. They argued that these treaties have become inapplicable by virtue of subsequent incompatible provisions of EU law, since these provisions have superseded the arbitration provisions of these BITs and the ECT by virtue of

[149] *Generation Ukraine v Ukraine*, Award, 16 September 2003, paras 12.2, 12.3; *Saipem v Bangladesh*, Decision on Jurisdiction, 21 March 2007, para 74; *Kardassopoulos v Georgia*, Decision on Jurisdiction, 6 July 2007, para 118; *Tokios Tokelės v Ukraine*, Award, 26 July 2007, para 104; *Toto v Lebanon*, Decision on Jurisdiction, 11 September 2009, para 94; *SGS v Paraguay*, Decision on Jurisdiction, 12 February 2010, para 70; *Millicom v Senegal*, Decision on Jurisdiction, 16 July 2010, paras 56–66; *Urbaser v Argentina*, Decision on Jurisdiction, 19 December 2012, para 47; *Ambiente Ufficio v Argentina*, Decision on Jurisdiction and Admissibility, 8 February 2013, para 208; *Agility v Pakistan*, Decision on Jurisdiction, 27 February 2013, paras 157–162; *E energija v Latvia*, Award, 22 December 2017, para 502.

[150] *Abaclat v Argentina*, Decision on Jurisdiction and Admissibility, 4 August 2011, para 258.

[151] *Slovak Republic v Achmea*, Judgment, 6 March 2018, Case C-284/16. The CJEU found that investment arbitration pursuant to a treaty between Member States of the European Union was incompatible with Articles 267 and 344 of the TFEU. See also Declaration of the Representatives of the Governments of the Member States, of 15 January 2019 on the Legal Consequences of the Judgment of the Court of Justice in *Achmea* and on Investment Protection in the European Union.

Articles 30[152] and 59[153] of the Vienna Convention on the Law of Treaties (VCLT). Tribunals have rejected these arguments holding, *inter alia*, that the relevant provisions of EU law were not later in time,[154] that the provisions of EU law and the arbitration provisions in the BITs and the ECT did not address the same subject-matter,[155] and that the two sets of provisions were not incompatible.[156] The Tribunal in *UP and C.D v Hungary*, said:

> The BIT and the TFEU do not relate to the same subject matter, and this renders Art. 59(1)(b) of the VCLT (implicit termination of an earlier treaty by a subsequent one) and Art. 30(3) of the VCLT (inapplicability of incompatible provisions in the earlier treaty) inapplicable. The lex posterior rule of Art. 30 of the VCLT does not apply because neither requirement—(1) the existence of a fundamental incompatibility between provisions of two successively ratified treaties, or (2) that the two rules in conflict have the same subject matter—is fulfilled. Respondent has failed to demonstrate that a fundamental or material incompatibility exists between Art. 9(2) of the BIT and the TFEU.[157]

Nevertheless, early acceptance of an offer of arbitration in a treaty is advisable. Once consent is perfected through the acceptance of the offer contained in the treaty, it remains in existence even if the States parties to the BIT agree to amend or terminate the treaty.[158] In some cases, investors have accepted offers of consent contained in BITs prior to the institution of proceedings.[159]

[152] Article 30 VCLT: '*Application of successive treaties relating to the same subject matter* 3. When all the parties to the earlier treaty are parties also to the later treaty but the earlier treaty is not terminated or suspended in operation under article 59, the earlier treaty applies only to the extent that its provisions are compatible with those of the later treaty.'

[153] Article 59(1)(b) VCLT: '*Termination or suspension of the operation of a treaty implied by conclusion of a later treaty*: 1. A treaty shall be considered as terminated if all the parties to it conclude a later treaty relating to the same subject matter and: ... (b) the provisions of the later treaty are so far incompatible with those of the earlier one that the two treaties are not capable of being applied at the same time.'

[154] *Vattenfall v Germany II*, Decision on the *Achmea* Issue, 31 August 2018, para 218.

[155] *Marfin v Cyprus*, Award, 26 July 2018, paras 583–595; *NextEra v Spain*, Decision on Jurisdiction, Liability and Quantum Principles, 12 March 2019, para 352; *Eskosol v Italy*, Decision on Italy's Request for Immediate Termination, 7 May 2019, paras 127–147; *OperaFund v Spain*, Award, 6 September 2019, para 383; *BayWa v Spain*, Decision on Jurisdiction and Liability, 2 December 2019, paras 272–273; *Micula v Romania II*, Award, 5 March 2020, paras 273–281.

[156] *Electrabel v Hungary*, Decision on Jurisdiction, Applicable Law and Liability, 30 November 2012, para 4.191; *Blusun v Italy*, Award, 27 December 2016, paras 229–303; *United Utilities v Estonia*, Award, 21 June 2019, paras 544–566; *Belenergia v Italy*, Award, 6 August 2019, paras 320–321.

[157] *UP and C.D v Hungary*, Award, 9 October 2018, para 218.

[158] See 'Agreement for the termination of Bilateral Investment Treaties between the Member States of the European Union'. The agreement was concluded among 23 Member States of the EU on 5 May 2020 and entered into force on 29 August 2020.

[159] *ADC v Hungary*, Award, 2 October 2006, para 363; *Wintershall v Argentina*, Award, 8 December 2008, para 10; *Abaclat v Argentina*, Decision on Jurisdiction and Admissibility, 4 August 2011, para 446; *Saint-Gobain v Venezuela*, Decision on Liability and the Principles of Quantum, 30 December 2016, paras 359, 360.

(d) Consent through multilateral treaties

Some multilateral treaties also offer consent to arbitration. The ICSID Convention is not one of these treaties. The Convention offers a detailed framework for the settlement of investment dispute but requires separate consent by the host State and by the foreign investor. The last paragraph of the Preamble to the Convention makes this quite clear by saying:

> no Contracting State shall by the mere fact of its ratification, acceptance or approval of this Convention and without its consent be deemed to be under any obligation to submit any particular dispute to conciliation or arbitration, . . .

By contrast, some regional treaties do offer consent to arbitration. The ECT provides consent to investment arbitration in Article 26(3)(a):

> each Contracting Party hereby gives its unconditional consent to the submission of a dispute to international arbitration or conciliation in accordance with the provisions of this Article.

Under the ECT the investor may submit the dispute to arbitration under the ICSID Convention, the ICSID Additional Facility Rules, the UNCITRAL Arbitration Rules, or under the Arbitration Institute of the Stockholm Chamber of Commerce.[160] The institution of proceedings constitutes the investor's acceptance of the offer of consent.[161]

Articles 1120 and 1122 of the NAFTA[162] provided consent to arbitration under the ICSID Convention, under the ICSID Additional Facility Rules or under the UNCITRAL Arbitration Rules. The NAFTA was replaced by the United States–Mexico–Canada Agreement (USMCA) on 1 July 2020. But NAFTA's Chapter 11, dealing with investments including investment arbitration, remains available to investors from all three countries should they choose to use it, for three years after that date.

The USMCA provides for the settlement of investment disputes between the United States or Mexico and investors of the respective other country.[163] Under the USMCA, the means of dispute settlement are ICSID arbitration, Additional Facility arbitration, UNCITRAL arbitration, or any other form of arbitration

160 Article 26(4) ECT.

161 *AMTO v Ukraine*, Final Award, 26 March 2008, paras 44–47.

162 The North American Free Trade Agreement (NAFTA), (1993) 32 ILM 289, 605, was a trilateral treaty between Canada, Mexico, and the United States that existed from 1994 to 2020.

163 USMCA Annex 14-D. Canada does not participate in this dispute settlement mechanism. Investment disputes between Canada and Mexico are subject to the investor–State arbitration provisions of the CPTPP.

agreed to by the parties. The claimant must consent in writing to arbitration and must waive any right to initiate or continue proceedings in respect of the measure alleged to constitute the breach before any court or administrative tribunal under the law of either State.

The Comprehensive and Progressive Agreement for Trans-Pacific Partnership (CPTPP)[164] contains Chapter 9 dealing with investment. Section B of that Chapter addresses investor–State dispute settlement. Article 9.19 provides for submission of a claim to arbitration under the ICSID Convention, the Additional Facility, and the UNCITRAL Rules.

The Central American Free Trade Agreement (CAFTA) of 2004 comprises the United States and five Central American countries. An FTA of the same year added the Dominican Republic (DR–CAFTA). Chapter 10 Section B of the DR–CAFTA provides for submission, at the investor's choice, to ICSID, Additional Facility, and UNCITRAL arbitration.

Other regional treaties providing for investment arbitration include the Treaty on the Eurasian Economic Union, the Eurasian Investment Agreement, the Association of Southeast Asian Nations (ASEAN), the Agreement for the Promotion and Protection of Investments, the Agreement on Promotion, Protection and Guarantee of Investments Among Member States of the Organisation of the Islamic Conference (OIC), the Organisation for the Harmonisation of Business Law in Africa (OHADA), and the Economic Community of West African States (ECOWAS).

(e) The irrevocability of consent

The binding and irrevocable nature of consent to arbitration is a manifestation of the maxim *pacta sunt servanda*. The principle applies not only where the consent is expressed in a direct agreement between the host State and the investor but also where an offer of consent is contained in national legislation or in a treaty. The irrevocability of consent operates only after the consent has been perfected. A mere offer of consent to arbitrate may be withdrawn at any time unless, of course, it is irrevocable by its own terms. In the case of national legislation and treaty clauses providing for arbitration, the investor must have accepted the consent in writing to make it irrevocable.

The irrevocability of consent applies only to unilateral attempts at withdrawal. The parties may terminate their consent by mutual agreement either before or after the institution of proceedings.

[164] On 30 December 2018, the CPTPP entered into force among the first six countries to ratify the agreement: Canada, Australia, Japan, Mexico, New Zealand, and Singapore. On 14 January 2019, the CPTPP entered into force for Vietnam.

Under the ICSID Convention, the irrevocability of consent is reflected in the Preamble[165] as well as in Article 25(1):

> When the parties have given their consent, no party may withdraw its consent unilaterally.

Under Article 71 of the ICSID Convention, a Contracting State may denounce the Convention at six months' notice. Since participation by the host State and the investor's State of nationality are conditions for the validity of consent, the termination of either State's participation in the Convention could vitiate consent. Article 72 blocks this indirect way of withdrawing consent by providing that the Convention's denunciation shall not affect the rights and obligations arising out of consent given before receipt of the notice of denunciation.[166]

If a direct agreement between the host State and the investor containing an arbitration clause is alleged to be invalid or is terminated, it could be argued that the arbitration clause is also invalidated or ceases to operate. But a unilateral invocation of invalidity or termination of the agreement cannot defeat the consent clause. Any other result would be contrary to the prohibition of unilateral withdrawal of consent. To this end, international arbitral practice has developed the doctrine of the severability or separability of the arbitration agreement.[167] Under this doctrine, the agreement providing for arbitration assumes a separate existence, which is autonomous and legally independent of the agreement containing it.[168]

In *Millicom v Senegal*, the respondent had terminated the Concession containing the ICSID arbitration clause. The Tribunal rejected the contention that the Concession's termination had extinguished the arbitration clause. It said:

> it is undisputed that an arbitration clause is autonomous and that the end of a contract in which it is incorporated does not eliminate its effects; on the contrary, the arbitration which is agreed to therein also covers the principle and effects of the end of the contract. To admit the contrary would amount to depriving

[165] ICSID Convention, Preamble: '*Recognizing* that mutual consent by the parties to submit such disputes to conciliation or to arbitration through such facilities constitutes a binding agreement which requires in particular that due consideration be given to any recommendation of conciliators, and that any arbitral award be complied with.' See also Report of the Executive Directors on the [ICSID] Convention, para 23: '[c]onsent to jurisdiction ... once given cannot be withdrawn unilaterally (Article 25(1))'.

[166] *Fábrica de Vidrios v Venezuela*, Award, 13 November 2017, para 277.

[167] See SM Schwebel, *International Arbitration: Three Salient Problems* (1987) 1–60. Article 45(1) of the Arbitration (Additional Facility) Rules expressly provides for the separability of the arbitration agreement from the underlying contract.

[168] See ICC Rules of Arbitration (2021) Article 6(9); UNCITRAL Arbitration Rules (2013) Article 23(1); UNCITRAL Model Law on International Commercial Arbitration (1985, amended 2006) Article 16(1); Institut de Droit International (IDI), 'Resolution on Arbitration between States, State Enterprises or State Entities, and Foreign Enterprises' (1989) 63 Ann IDI 324, 326, Article 3(a).

> it of an important part of its practical effect since it would suffice for a party to abandon a contract in order to escape from it. This reasoning must apply also to the Concession.[169]

A host State is free to change its investment legislation, including the provision concerning consent to arbitration. An offer of consent contained in national legislation that has not been taken up by the investor will lapse when the legislation is repealed. Once the investor has accepted the offer in writing, while the legislation was still in force, the consent agreed to by the parties becomes insulated from the validity of the legislation containing the offer and assumes a contractual existence independent of the legislative instrument that helped to bring it about. Therefore, repeal of investment legislation will not have the effect of a withdrawal of consent if the investor has accepted the offer during the legislation's lifetime.[170]

Consent based on treaties, once perfected by its acceptance by the investor, becomes irrevocable and hence insulated from attempts by the host State to terminate the treaty. BITs and multilateral international instruments providing for consent to arbitration are more difficult to terminate or amend than national legislation. However, some States have terminated some or all of their BITs.

In *CSOB v Slovakia*, the Tribunal found that the BIT had never entered into force despite the fact, that it was published in Slovakia's Official Gazette together with a notice announcing its entry into force. After the institution of ICSID proceedings, Slovakia published a corrective notice in its Official Gazette asserting the BIT's invalidity. The Tribunal confirmed that a unilateral withdrawal of consent by the host State is not possible and said:

> In this connection, it should be noted that if the Notice were to be held to constitute a valid offer by the Slovak State to submit to international arbitration, the corrective notice published by the Slovak Ministry of Foreign Affairs in the Official Gazette on November 20, 1997, asserting the invalidity of the BIT, would be of no avail to Respondent, since Claimant accepted the offer in the Request for Arbitration filed prior to the publication of the corrective notice.[171]

Many BITs may be terminated unilaterally subject to 'sunset clauses.' Under these clauses, the BIT will continue to apply for a certain period to investments made before its termination. The Italy–Romania BIT entered into force in 1995 and was terminated in 2010. It contained a sunset clause providing for its continued application for five years for investments made before its termination. In *Gavazzi*

[169] *Millicom v Senegal*, Decision on Jurisdiction, 16 July 2010, para 91. See also *Duke Energy v Peru*, Decision on Annulment, 1 March 2011, paras 125–144.

[170] *Rumeli v Kazakhstan*, Award, 29 July 2008, paras 165, 220–222, 308, 332–336. But see *Ruby Roz v Kazakhstan*, Award on Jurisdiction, 1 August 2013, para 156.

[171] *CSOB v Slovakia*, Decision on Jurisdiction, 24 May 1999, para 45.

v Romania, ICSID received the Request for Arbitration on 2 August 2012. The Tribunal proceeded to exercise jurisdiction based on the BIT without a discussion of its termination.[172]

Respondent States as well as the European Commission have argued that, after the *Achmea* judgment of the CJEU[173] and of a Declaration of EU Member States on the legal consequences of that judgment,[174] consent to arbitration under treaties with other EU Member States had become inapplicable. Claimants have successfully argued that perfected consent was irrevocable under the ICSID Convention and not subject to withdrawal by way of a novel interpretation of EU law.[175]

Tribunals have consistently rejected the '*Achmea* objection', *inter alia*, by relying on the impossibility of a unilateral withdrawal of consent under Article 25(1). The Tribunal in *Magyar Farming v Hungary* said to this effect:

> the Claimants accepted the BIT's offer to arbitrate prior to its purported termination. Pursuant to Article 25 of the ICSID Convention, '[w]hen the parties [i.e. the investor and the State] have given their consent, no party may withdraw its consent unilaterally.' . . Thus, the consent to arbitrate, in the sense of a meeting of the minds, which is perfected by the investor's acceptance of the State's offer to arbitrate expressed in the BIT would not be retroactively invalidated by a subsequent termination of the BIT.[176]

(f) The scope of consent

The parties to an agreement containing an arbitration clause are free to circumscribe their consent by defining it in general terms, by excluding certain types of disputes or by listing the questions they are submitting to arbitration. In practice, broad inclusive consent clauses, covering any dispute that may arise in connection with the agreement containing the clause, are the norm. Consent clauses contained in investment agreements typically refer to 'any dispute' or to 'all disputes' under the respective agreements.

Offers of consent to investment arbitration in national investment legislation may cover disputes between the foreign investor and the host State in general terms,

172 *Gavazzi v Romania*, Decision on Jurisdiction, Admissibility and Liability, 21 April 2015.

173 *Slovak Republic v Achmea*, CJEU, Judgment, 6 March 2018, Case C-284/16.

174 Declaration of the Representatives of the Governments of the Member States, of 15 January 2019 on the Legal Consequences of the Judgment of the Court of Justice in *Achmea* and on Investment Protection in the European Union.

175 *UP and C.D v Hungary*, Award, 9 October 2018, paras 211, 221, 227–229; *United Utilities v Estonia*, Award, 21 June 2019, para 492; *InfraRed v Spain*, Award, 2 August 2019, para 227; *OperaFund v Spain*, Award, 6 September 2019, paras 355, 367.

176 *Magyar Farming v Hungary*, Award, 13 November 2019, paras 213–214. See also *Marfin v Cyprus*, Award, 26 July 2018, paras 592–593; *Eskosol v Italy*, Decision on Italy's Request for Immediate Termination, 7 May 2019, para 226.

for instance by referring to 'disputes between a foreign investor and a government body'.[177] Some offers are narrower and relate to the application and interpretation of the piece of legislation offering consent.[178] Some national laws circumscribe the issues that are subject to arbitration even more narrowly by limiting it to certain matters such as expropriation.

In *Tradex v Albania* the consent to arbitration expressed in the Albanian Law on Foreign Investment was limited in the following terms:

> if the dispute arises out of or relates to expropriation, compensation for expropriation, or discrimination and also for the transfers in accordance with Article 7....[179]

After a detailed examination of the facts, the Tribunal found that the claimant had not been able to prove that an expropriation had occurred.[180]

The scope of consent to arbitration offered in treaties also varies considerably. Many BITs in their consent clauses contain phrases such as 'all disputes concerning investments' or 'any legal dispute concerning an investment'. These provisions do not restrict a tribunal's jurisdiction to claims arising from the treaty's substantive standards. By their own terms, these consent clauses encompass disputes that go beyond the interpretation and application of the treaty itself and include claims that arise from a contract in connection with the investment or from customary international law.

In *Vivendi v Argentina*,[181] Article 8 of the BIT between France and Argentina, applicable in that case, offered consent for '[a]ny dispute relating to investments'. In its discussion of the BIT's fork in the road clause, the ad hoc Committee said:

> Article 8 deals generally with disputes 'relating to investments made under this Agreement between one Contracting Party and an investor of the other Contracting Party'... Article 8 does not use a narrower formulation, requiring that the investor's claim allege a breach of the BIT itself. Read literally, the requirements for arbitral jurisdiction in Article 8 do not necessitate that the Claimant allege a breach of the BIT itself: it is sufficient that the dispute relate to an investment made under the BIT. This may be contrasted, for example, with Article 11 of the BIT [dealing with State/State dispute settlement], which refers to disputes 'concerning the interpretation or application of this Agreement' ....[182]

177 *Zhinvali v Georgia*, Award, 24 January 2003, para 329.
178 *SPP v Egypt*, Decision on Jurisdiction I, 27 November 1985, para 70.
179 *Tradex v Albania*, Decision on Jurisdiction, 24 December 1996, 5 ICSID Reports 47, 54–55.
180 *Tradex v Albania*, Award, 29 April 1999, paras 132–205.
181 *Vivendi v Argentina*, Decision on Annulment, 3 July 2002.
182 At para 55.

Other tribunals have taken the same position.[183]

The Tribunal in *SGS v Pakistan* decided otherwise. Article 9 of the applicable BIT between Switzerland and Pakistan referred to 'disputes with respect to investments'. The Tribunal found that the phrase was merely descriptive of the factual subject matter of the disputes and did not relate to the legal basis of the claims or cause of action asserted in the claims. The Tribunal said: 'from that description alone, without more, we believe that no implication necessarily arises that both BIT and purely contract claims are intended to be covered by the Contracting Parties in Article 9'. Therefore, the Tribunal held that it did not have jurisdiction with respect to contract claims which did not also constitute breaches of the substantive standards of the BIT.[184]

Other tribunals have distanced themselves from that decision.[185] However, some tribunals, without analysing the matter, seem to operate under the unfounded perception that they are restricted to treaty claims regardless of the wording of a BIT's jurisdiction clause.[186]

Other treaty clauses offering consent to arbitration do not refer to investment disputes in general terms but circumscribe the types of disputes that may be submitted to arbitration. A provision that is typical for United States BITs is contained in Article VII of the Argentina–US BIT of 1991. It offers consent for investment disputes which are defined as follows:

> a dispute between a Party and a national or company of the other Party arising out of or relating to (a) an investment agreement between that Party and such national or company; (b) an investment authorization granted by that Party's foreign investment authority (if any such authorization exists) to such national or company; or (c) an alleged breach of any right conferred or created by this Treaty with respect to an investment.

Other treaties restrict consent to disputes involving the respective treaty's substantive provisions. Tribunals operating under these restrictive clauses have found

[183] *Salini v Morocco*, Decision on Jurisdiction, 16 July 2001, para 61; *SGS v Philippines*, Decision on Jurisdiction, 29 January 2004, paras 131–135, 169(3); *Tokios Tokelės v Ukraine*, Decision on Jurisdiction, 29 April 2004, para 52, fn 42; *Impregilo v Pakistan*, Decision on Jurisdiction, 22 April 2005, paras 57, 82, 102, 188; *Siemens v Argentina*, Award, 6 February 2007, para 205; *Parkerings v Lithuania*, Award, 11 September 2007, paras 261–266; *Chevron v Ecuador I*, Interim Award, 1 December 2008, paras 203, 209–211; *SGS v Paraguay*, Decision on Jurisdiction, 12 February 2010, paras 129, 183–184; *Alpha v Ukraine*, Award, 8 November 2010, para 243; *Philip Morris v Uruguay*, Decision on Jurisdiction, 2 July 2013, paras 107, 109; *Metal-Tech v Uzbekistan*, Award, 4 October 2013, para 378.

[184] *SGS v Pakistan*, Decision on Jurisdiction, 6 August 2003, para 161.

[185] *SGS v Philippines*, Decision on Jurisdiction, 29 January 2004, paras 133–135; *Tokios Tokelės v Ukraine*, Decision on Jurisdiction, 29 April 2004, para 52, fn 42. See also the discussion in *Salini v Jordan*, Decision on Jurisdiction, 29 November 2004, paras 97–101.

[186] *Urbaser v Argentina*, Decision on Jurisdiction, 19 December 2012, para 254; *Kim v Uzbekistan*, Decision on Jurisdiction, 8 March 2017, paras 162–164; *E energija v Latvia*, Award, 22 December 2017, paras 498, 846, 853; *CMC v Mozambique*, Award, 24 October 2019, paras 219–222, 473.

that they could only apply the substantive standards contained in these treaties.[187] Under Article 26(1) of the ECT the scope of the consent is limited to disputes 'which concern an alleged breach of an obligation ... under Part III [of the ECT]'.[188]

In *Iberdrola v Guatemala*, the Guatemala–Spain BIT provided for jurisdiction 'concerning matters governed by this Agreement'.[189] The Tribunal contrasted this limited jurisdictional clause with comprehensive clauses contained in other treaties:

> the Treaty contrasts with other bilateral investment treaties signed by Guatemala and by Spain, which extend arbitral jurisdiction to 'any dispute', 'every dispute', 'the disputes', 'the differences' or 'every class of disputes or of differences' as regards the extent of protection. The language of the Treaty is restricted ... which means that the Republic of Guatemala did not give general consent to submit any kind of dispute or difference related to investments made in its territory to arbitration, but only those related to violations of substantive provisions of the treaty itself.[190]

An umbrella clause in the BIT should extend the jurisdiction of tribunals to violations of contracts even if the consent to arbitration was restricted to claims arising from breaches of the treaty.[191] If it is true that under the operation of an umbrella clause, violations of a contract relating to the investment become treaty violations, it follows that even a provision in a BIT merely offering consent to arbitration for violations of the BIT extends to contract violations covered by the umbrella clause.

In some treaties the subject-matter of consent to arbitration is even more narrowly confined. Consent is given only for disputes concerning specific standards. Typical examples for narrow clauses of this kind are expressions of consent that are limited to disputes relating to expropriations[192] or to the amount of compensation for expropriations.[193] For instance, the Italy–Bangladesh BIT provides in Article 9 for the submission to arbitration, including to ICSID, of:

> [a]ny dispute arising between a Contracting Party and the investors of the other, relating to compensation for expropriation, nationalization, requisition or similar measures including disputes relating to the amount of the relevant payments ...

[187] *Suez and Vivendi v Argentina*, Decision on Liability, 30 July 2010, para 63; *Roussalis v Romania*, Award, 7 December 2011, paras 43, 679–683.

[188] *Kardassopoulos v Georgia*, Decision on Jurisdiction, 6 July 2007, paras 249–251.

[189] *Iberdrola v Guatemala*, Award, 17 August 2012, paras 296–310.

[190] At para 306 (footnotes omitted).

[191] On umbrella clauses see VIII.6 above.

[192] *Saipem v Bangladesh*, Decision on Jurisdiction, 21 March 2007, paras 116, 129–133 and Award, 30 June 2009, paras 120–132.

[193] *Telenor v Hungary*, Award, 13 September 2006, paras 18(2), 25, 57, 81–83; *ADC v Hungary*, Award, 2 October 2006, paras 12, 445; *Tza Yap Shum v Peru*, Decision on Jurisdiction and Competence, 19 June 2009, paras 129–188.

Tribunals have held that clauses of this kind restricted their jurisdiction to claims based on expropriation to the exclusion of other standards of protection.[194] However, some tribunals have held that clauses referring to compensation for expropriation extend to the question of the existence of an expropriation.[195]

The USMCA limits consent to claims for violations of certain standards guaranteed by the Agreement. These are national treatment, most-favoured-nation (MFN) treatment, and expropriation and compensation (except with respect to indirect expropriation).[196]

(g) The interpretation of consent

Where consent to arbitration is based on a treaty it would seem obvious to apply principles of treaty interpretation.[197] Reliance on domestic law principles of interpretation appears attractive where consent is based on a clause in domestic legislation. But it must be kept in mind that the perfected consent is neither a treaty nor simply a provision of domestic law, but an agreement between the host State and the foreign investor.

Tribunals have held that questions of jurisdiction, including consent, are not subject to the law applicable to the merits of the case. Rather, questions of jurisdiction are governed by their own system which is defined by the instruments determining jurisdiction.[198] In the words of the Tribunal in *CMS v Argentina*:

> Article 42 [of the ICSID Convention][199] is mainly designed for the resolution of disputes on the merits and, as such, it is in principle independent from the decision on jurisdiction, governed solely by Article 25 of the [ICSID] Convention and those other provisions of the consent instrument which might be applicable, in the instant case the Treaty provisions.[200]

[194] *Telenor v Hungary*, Award, 13 September 2006, paras 18(2), 25, 57, 81–83; *Saipem v Bangladesh*, Decision on Jurisdiction, 21 March 2007, paras 70, 129–133; *Emmis v Hungary*, Award, 16 April 2014, paras 142–145; *Vigotop v Hungary*, Award, 1 October 2014, para 634; *WNC v Czech Republic*, Award, 22 February 2017, paras 362–364.

[195] *Tza Yap Shum v Peru*, Decision on Jurisdiction and Competence, 19 June 2009, paras 129–188; *Beijing Urban Construction v Yemen*, Decision on Jurisdiction, 31 May 2017, paras 50, 59–69, 74–108.

[196] Annex 14-D, Article 14.D.3.1. USMCA.

[197] For a general discussion of treaty interpretation in the context of investment law see II.1. above.

[198] *Azurix v Argentina*, Decision on Jurisdiction, 8 December 2003, paras 48–50; *Enron v Argentina*, Decision on Jurisdiction, 14 January 2004, para 38; *Siemens v Argentina*, Decision on Jurisdiction, 3 August 2004, paras 29–31; *Camuzzi v Argentina*, Decision on Jurisdiction, 11 May 2005, paras 15–17, 57; *AES v Argentina*, Decision on Jurisdiction, 26 April 2005, paras 34–39; *Jan de Nul v Egypt*, Decision on Jurisdiction, 16 June 2006, paras 65–68.

[199] Article 42 of the ICSID Convention deals with the law applicable to the dispute.

[200] *CMS v Argentina*, Decision on Jurisdiction, 17 July 2003, para 88.

Tribunal practice varies in its emphasis on domestic and on international law. Some of this variation is due to the different ways in which consent is expressed by way of contracts, on the basis of legislation, or on the basis of treaties. This leads to a methodological mix involving treaty interpretation, statutory interpretation, and general principles of contract law.

In *CSOB v Slovakia*, consent to arbitration was based on a contract between the parties that referred to a BIT. Although the BIT had never entered into force, the Tribunal concluded that the parties by referring to the BIT had intended to incorporate the arbitration clause in the BIT into their contract. With respect to the interpretation of the consent agreement, the Tribunal had no doubt that it was governed by international law:

> The question of whether the parties have effectively expressed their consent to ICSID jurisdiction is not to be answered by reference to national law. It is governed by international law as set out in Article 25(1) of the ICSID Convention.[201]

The host State's domestic law will be relevant to jurisdiction if the consent to arbitration is based on a provision in its legislation.[202] But from the perspective of international law, the offer of consent in domestic legislation is a unilateral act that may have to be interpreted accordingly.[203] In cases involving consent by way of domestic legislation, tribunals have grappled with the relative emphasis to be given to domestic law and international law.[204]

In *Mobil v Venezuela*, the claimant relied on an ambiguous clause in Venezuela's Investment Law that referred to the ICSID Convention.[205] The Tribunal said:

> Legislation and more generally unilateral acts by which a State consents to ICSID jurisdiction must be considered as standing offers to foreign investors under the ICSID Convention. Those unilateral acts must accordingly be interpreted according to the ICSID Convention itself and to the rules of international law governing unilateral declarations of States.[206]

201 *CSOB v Slovakia*, Decision on Jurisdiction, 24 May 1999, para 35.

202 *SPP v Egypt*, Decision on Jurisdiction II, 14 April 1988, paras 55–61; *Inceysa v El Salvador*, Award, 2 August 2006, paras 131, 222–264; *Zhinvali v Georgia*, Award, 24 January 2003, paras 229, 339–340.

203 See ILC, 'Guiding Principles Applicable to Unilateral Declarations of States Capable of Creating Legal Obligations' (2006) UN Doc A/CN.4/L.703; WM Reisman and MH Arsanjani, 'The Question of Unilateral Governmental Statements as Applicable Law in Investment Disputes' (2004) 19 *ICSID Rev* 328.

204 *CEMEX v Venezuela*, Decision on Jurisdiction, 30 December 2010, paras 67–139; *Brandes v Venezuela*, Award, 2 August 2011, paras 36, 81; *OPIC Karimun v Venezuela*, Award, 28 May 2013, paras 70–76; *ConocoPhillips v Venezuela*, Decision on Jurisdiction and the Merits, 3 September 2013, para 255; *Tidewater v Venezuela*, Decision on Jurisdiction, 8 February 2013, paras 75–141; *PNG Sustainable Development v Papua New Guinea*, Award, 5 May 2015, paras 264–265; *Pac Rim v El Salvador*, Decision on Jurisdiction, 1 June 2012, paras 5.32–5.33; Award, 14 October 2016, para 5.71; *Lighthouse v Timor-Leste*, Award, 22 December 2017, paras 149–153.

205 See XII.7(b) above.

206 *Mobil v Venezuela*, Decision on Jurisdiction, 10 June 2010, para 85.

Where consent is based on a treaty, tribunals have applied principles of treaty interpretation.[207] But the arbitration clause in a treaty is only the first step towards agreed consent. The consent, once accepted by the investor, is neither a treaty nor simply a contract under domestic law, but an agreement between the host State and the investor based on a treaty.

In some cases, the respondents argued that an expression of consent to arbitration should be construed restrictively. Most tribunals have rejected this argument. Some tribunals seemed to be leaning more towards an extensive interpretation of consent clauses.[208] The majority of tribunals have subscribed to a balanced approach that accepts neither a restrictive nor an expansive approach to the interpretation of consent clauses.[209]

In *SPP v Egypt*, the argument of the restrictive interpretation of jurisdictional instruments was raised in relation to an arbitration clause in national legislation. The Tribunal found that there was no presumption of jurisdiction and that jurisdiction only existed insofar as consent thereto had been given by the parties. Equally, there was no presumption against the conferment of jurisdiction with respect to a sovereign State. After referring to several international judgements and awards, the Tribunal said:

> Thus, jurisdictional instruments are to be interpreted neither restrictively nor expansively, but rather objectively and in good faith, and jurisdiction will be found to exist if—but only if—the force of the arguments militating in favor of it is preponderant.[210]

[207] *Fedax v Venezuela*, Decision on Jurisdiction, 11 July 1997, para 20; *Vestey v Venezuela*, Award, 15 April 2016, paras 114–115.

[208] *SGS v Philippines*, Decision on Jurisdiction, 29 January 2004, para 116; *Eureko v Poland*, Partial Award, 19 August 2005, para 248; *Tradex v Albania*, Decision on Jurisdiction, 24 December 1996, para 68; *Millicom v Senegal*, Decision on Jurisdiction, 16 July 2010, para 98.

[209] *Amco v Indonesia*, Decision on Jurisdiction, 25 September 1983, paras 12–24; *SOABI v Senegal*, Award, 25 February 1988, paras 4.08–4.10; *Cable TV v St. Kitts and Nevis*, Award, 13 January 1997, para 6.27; *CSOB v Slovakia*, Decision on Jurisdiction, 24 May 1999, para 34; *Ethyl v Canada*, Award on Jurisdiction, 24 June 1998, para 55; *Loewen v United States*, Decision on Competence and Jurisdiction, 5 January 2001, para 51; *Methanex v United States*, Preliminary Award on Jurisdiction, 7 August 2002, paras 103–105; *Mondev v United States*, Award, 11 October 2002, paras 42–43; *Aguas del Tunari v Bolivia*, Decision on Jurisdiction, 21 October 2005, para 91; *El Paso v Argentina*, Decision on Jurisdiction, 27 April 2006, paras 68–70; *Suez and InterAgua v Argentina*, Decision on Jurisdiction, 16 May 2006, paras 59, 64; *Pan American v Argentina*, Decision on Preliminary Objections, 27 July 2006, paras 97–99; *Duke Energy v Ecuador*, Award, 18 August 2008, paras 129–130; *Austrian Airlines v Slovakia*, Final Award, 9 October 2009, paras 119–121; *Mobil v Venezuela*, Decision on Jurisdiction, 10 June 2010, paras 112–119; *CEMEX v Venezuela*, Decision on Jurisdiction, 30 December 2010, paras 104–114; *National Gas v Egypt*, Award, 3 April 2014, para 119; *PNG Sustainable Development v Papua New Guinea*, Award, 5 May 2015, paras 253–255; *Lighthouse v Timor-Leste*, Award, 22 December 2017, para 148.

[210] *SPP v Egypt*, Decision on Jurisdiction II, 14 April 1988, para 63.

8. Conditions for the institution of proceedings

(a) Waiting periods for amicable settlement

Many BITs contain the condition that a negotiated settlement must be attempted before resort can be had to investment arbitration. This requirement is subject to certain time limits ranging from three to twelve months. A typical waiting period under BITs would be six months. Similarly, Article 26(2) of the ECT will offer consent to arbitration if the dispute cannot be settled within three months from the date on which either party requested an amicable settlement. National legislation offering consent to arbitration may similarly provide for waiting periods.[211]

The reaction of tribunals to these provisions requiring an attempt at amicable settlement before the institution of arbitration has not been uniform.[212] In the majority of cases, the tribunals found that the claimants had complied with these waiting periods before proceeding to arbitration.[213]

In other cases, the tribunals found that non-compliance with the waiting periods did not affect their jurisdiction. Some tribunals found that the non-observance of the waiting period was inconsequential since further negotiations would have been pointless.[214] Some tribunals found that waiting periods for amicable settlement were merely procedural and not a condition for jurisdiction.[215]

In *Biwater Gauff v Tanzania*, the UK–Tanzania BIT provided for a six-month period for settlement. There had been attempts to resolve the dispute, but the six-month period had not yet elapsed when the Request for Arbitration was filed. The Tribunal held that this did not preclude it from proceeding. It said:

[211] *Tradex v Albania*, Decision on Jurisdiction, 24 December 1996, 5 ICSID Reports pp 47, 60–61.

[212] For practice of the International Court of Justice on mandatory settlement periods see *Military and Paramilitary Activities in and against Nicaragua (Nicaragua v United States)*, Judgment (Jurisdiction and Admissibility), 26 November 1984, ICJ Reports (1984) 392, paras 81–83, and *Case Concerning Application of the International Convention on the Elimination of all forms of Racial Discrimination (Georgia v Russian Federation)*, Judgment, 1 April 2011, ICJ Reports (2011) 70, paras 115–184.

[213] See eg *Arif v Moldova*, Award, 8 April 2013, paras 336–342; *Marfin v Cyprus*, Award, 26 July 2018, para 637; *Cortec Mining v Kenya*, Award, 22 October 2018, para 282.

[214] *Ethyl v Canada*, Award on Jurisdiction, 24 June 1998, paras 76–84; *SGS v Pakistan*, Decision on Jurisdiction, 6 August 2003, para 184; *LESI-DIPENTA v Algeria*, Award, 10 January 2005, para 32(iv); *Teinver v Argentina*, Decision on Jurisdiction, 21 December 2012, paras 126–129; *Ambiente Ufficio v Argentina*, Decision on Jurisdiction and Admissibility, 8 February 2013, para 582; *Philip Morris v Uruguay*, Decision on Jurisdiction, 2 July 2013, paras 228–229; *Alemanni v Argentina*, Decision on Jurisdiction and Admissibility, 17 November 2014, paras 301–317; *Casinos Austria v Argentina*, Decision on Jurisdiction, 29 June 2018, paras 284, 311–313.

[215] *Wena Hotels v Egypt*, Decision on Jurisdiction, 29 June 1999, 6 ICSID Reports 74, 82 and 87; *Lauder v Czech Republic*, Final Award, 3 September 2001, para 187; *SGS v Pakistan*, Decision on Jurisdiction, 6 August 2003, para 184; *Bayindir v Pakistan*, Decision on Jurisdiction, 14 November 2005, paras 88–103; *Abaclat v Argentina*, Decision on Jurisdiction and Admissibility, 4 August 2011, para 564; *Casinos Austria v Argentina*, Decision on Jurisdiction, 29 June 2018, para 280.

> this six-month period is procedural and directory in nature, rather than jurisdictional and mandatory. Its underlying purpose is to facilitate opportunities for amicable settlement. Its purpose is not to impede or obstruct arbitration proceedings, where such settlement is not possible. Non-compliance with the six month period, therefore, does not preclude this Arbitral Tribunal from proceeding. If it did so, the provision would have curious effects, including:
> —preventing the prosecution of a claim, and forcing the claimant to do nothing until six months have elapsed, even where further negotiations are obviously futile, or settlement obviously impossible for any reason;
> —forcing the claimant to recommence an arbitration started too soon, even if the six month period has elapsed by the time the Arbitral Tribunal considers the matter.[216]

Some tribunals have found that waiting periods need not necessarily be complied with prior to initiating proceedings but can be fulfilled before the tribunal makes a decision on its jurisdiction.[217]

Other tribunals have reached a different conclusion.[218] In *Burlington v Ecuador*, the BIT between Ecuador and the United States provided for consultation and negotiation in case of a dispute. ICSID arbitration would become available six months after the dispute had arisen. The Tribunal found that the claimant had only informed the respondent of the dispute with its submission of the dispute to ICSID arbitration. It followed that the claim was inadmissible:

> by imposing upon investors an obligation to voice their disagreement at least six months prior to the submission of an investment dispute to arbitration, the Treaty effectively accords host States the right to be informed about the dispute at least six months before it is submitted to arbitration. The purpose of this right is to grant the host State an *opportunity* to redress the problem before the investor submits the dispute to arbitration. In this case, Claimant has deprived the host State of that opportunity. That suffices to defeat jurisdiction.[219]

It would seem, that the decisive question is whether there was a promising opportunity for a settlement. There will be little point in declining jurisdiction and

[216] *Biwater Gauff v Tanzania*, Award, 24 July 2008, paras 338–350 at 343.

[217] *Western NIS v Ukraine*, Order, 16 March 2006; *Casinos Austria v Argentina*, Decision on Jurisdiction, 29 June 2018, paras 279–281, 312.

[218] *Goetz v Burundi*, Award, 10 February 1999, paras 90–93; *Enron v Argentina*, Decision on Jurisdiction, 14 January 2004, para 88; *Wintershall v Argentina*, Award, 8 December 2008, paras 133–157; *Murphy v Ecuador I*, Award on Jurisdiction, 15 December 2010, paras 90–157; *Tulip v Turkey*, Decision on Jurisdiction, 5 March 2013, paras 55–72; *Supervisión y Control v Costa Rica*, Award, 18 January 2017, paras 336–348, 351.

[219] *Burlington v Ecuador*, Decision on Jurisdiction, 2 June 2010, para 315. Italics original.

sending the parties back to the negotiating table if negotiations are obviously futile. Even if the institution of arbitration was premature, the waiting period will often have expired by the time the tribunal is ready to make its decision on jurisdiction. Under these circumstances, declining jurisdiction and compelling the claimant to start the proceedings anew would be uneconomical. An alternative way to deal with non-compliance with a waiting period is a suspension of proceedings to allow additional time for negotiations if these appear promising.

(b) The requirement to resort to domestic courts

Under traditional international law, before an international claim on behalf of an investor may be put forward in international proceedings, the investor must have exhausted the domestic remedies offered by the host State's legal system. But it is well established that, where there is consent to investor–State arbitration, there is generally no need to exhaust local remedies. One of the purposes of investor–State arbitration is to avoid the vagaries of proceedings in the host State's courts. Article 26 of the ICSID Convention specifically excludes the requirement to exhaust remedies 'unless otherwise stated'.[220] ICSID[221] and non-ICSID tribunals[222] have confirmed that the claimants were entitled to institute international arbitration directly without first exhausting the remedies offered by local courts.

It is open to a host State to make the exhaustion of local remedies a condition of its consent to arbitration. In fact, some BITs offering consent require the exhaustion of local remedies. But clauses of this kind are rare and are found mostly in older BITs. In the absence of such a proviso, the investor does not need to exhaust local remedies before starting an international arbitration. The Tribunal in *Generation Ukraine v Ukraine* said:

> 13.4 The first sentence of Article 26 secures the exclusivity of a reference to ICSID arbitration vis-à-vis any other remedy. A logical consequence of this exclusivity is the waiver by Contracting States to the ICSID Convention of the remedies rule,

[220] Article 26 of the ICSID Convention:

> Consent of the parties to arbitration under this Convention shall, unless otherwise stated, be deemed consent to such arbitration to the exclusion of any other remedy. A Contracting State may require the exhaustion of local administrative or judicial remedies as a condition of its consent to arbitration under this Convention.

[221] *Amco v Indonesia*, Decision on Annulment, 16 May 1986, para 63; *Lanco v Argentina*, Decision on Jurisdiction, 8 December 1998, para 39; *IBM v Ecuador*, Decision on Jurisdiction and Competence, 22 December 2003, paras 77–84; *AES v Argentina*, Decision on Jurisdiction, 26 April 2005, paras 69–70; *Saipem v Bangladesh*, Award, 30 June 2009, paras 174–184.

[222] *CME v Czech Republic*, Final Award, 14 March 2003, para 412; *Yaung Chi Oo v Myanmar*, Award, 31 March 2003, para 40; *Nykomb v Latvia*, Award, 16 December 2003, sec 2.4. But see *Loewen v United States*, Award, 26 June 2003, paras 142–217.

> so that the investor is not compelled to pursue remedies in the respondent State's domestic courts or tribunals before the institution of ICSID proceedings. This waiver is implicit in the second sentence of Article 26, which nevertheless allows Contracting States to reserve its right to insist upon the prior exhaustion of local remedies as a condition of its consent.[223]

In some cases, tribunals have required an attempt to obtain redress in domestic courts, not as a matter of jurisdiction or admissibility but as part of the evidence that the relevant standard of international law had indeed been violated. The Tribunal in *Waste Management* has described this phenomenon in the following terms: 'in this context the notion of exhaustion of local remedies is incorporated into the substantive standard and is not only a procedural prerequisite to an international claim'.[224]

In a similar vein, the Tribunal in *Generation Ukraine v Ukraine* said:

> the failure to seek redress from national authorities disqualifies the international claim, not because there is a requirement of *exhaustion* of local remedies but because the very reality of conduct tantamount to expropriation is doubtful in the absence of a *reasonable*—not necessarily exhaustive—effort by the investor to obtain correction.[225]

Therefore, under this theory an attempt to seek redress in the domestic courts would be required to demonstrate that a substantive standard, such as protection against uncompensated expropriation or fair and equitable treatment, has indeed been violated.

This theory has been criticized severely. In *Helnan v Egypt*, the Tribunal relied on the above passage from *Generation Ukraine*. It found that the claimant's failure to challenge a key ministerial decision in the Egyptian administrative courts meant that there was no violation of the BIT's standards of protection.[226] This finding was subsequently annulled. The ad hoc Committee said:

> A requirement to pursue local court remedies would have the effect of disentitling a claimant from pursuing its direct treaty claim for failure by the executive to afford fair and equitable treatment, even where the decision was taken at the highest

[223] *Generation Ukraine v Ukraine*, Award, 16 September 2003, para 13.4.

[224] *Waste Management v Mexico II*, Award, 30 April 2004, para 97. Footnote omitted.

[225] *Generation Ukraine v Ukraine*, Award, 16 September 2003, para 20.30. Italics original. See also *EnCana v Ecuador*, Award, 3 February 2006, para 194.

[226] *Helnan v Egypt*, Award, 3 July 2008, para 148.

> level of government within the host State... Such a consequence would be contrary to the express provisions of Article 26, ...[227]

Some BITs provide that an investor, before bringing a dispute before an international tribunal, must seek its resolution before the host State's domestic courts for a certain period of time, often eighteen months. The investor may proceed to international arbitration if the domestic proceedings do not result in the dispute's settlement during that period or if the dispute persists after the domestic decision. For instance, the Argentina–Germany BIT provides in Article 10(2) that any investment dispute shall first be submitted to the host State's competent tribunals. The provision continues:

> (3) The dispute may be submitted to an international arbitration tribunal in any of the following circumstances:
>
> (a) at the request of one of the parties to the dispute if no decision on the merits of the claim has been rendered after the expiration of a period of eighteen months from the date in which the court proceedings referred to in para. 2 of this Article have been initiated, or if such decision has been rendered, but the dispute between the parties persist;

Tribunals have held that this was not an application of the exhaustion of local remedies rule.[228] The usefulness of such a requirement is questionable. It creates a considerable burden to the party seeking arbitration with little chance of advancing the settlement of the dispute. A substantive decision by the domestic courts in a complex investment dispute is unlikely within eighteen months, certainly if one includes the possibility of appeals. Even if such a decision should have been rendered, the dispute is likely to persist if the investor is dissatisfied with the decision's outcome. Therefore, arbitration remains an option after the expiry of the period of eighteen months. It follows that the most likely effect of a clause of this kind is delay and additional cost, since it is unlikely that the dispute will be resolved before the domestic courts within that time frame. One tribunal called a provision of this kind 'nonsensical from a practical point of view'.[229]

In some cases, tribunals found the requirement to submit the dispute to domestic courts for a certain period not to be jurisdictional but procedural. Therefore, it could be handled with some flexibility[230] and could be complied with subsequent

[227] *Helnan v Egypt*, Decision on Annulment, 14 June 2010, paras 43–57 at para 53. See also U Kriebaum, 'Local Remedies and the Standards for the Protection of Foreign Investment' in C Binder et al (eds) *International Investment Law for the 21st Century* (2009) 417.

[228] *Maffezini v Spain*, Decision on Jurisdiction, 25 January 2000, para 28; *Siemens v Argentina*, Decision on Jurisdiction, 3 August 2004, para 104; *Gas Natural v Argentina*, Decision on Jurisdiction, 17 June 2005, para 30.

[229] *Plama v Bulgaria*, Decision on Jurisdiction, 8 February 2005, para 224.

[230] *Telefónica v Argentina*, Decision on Jurisdiction, 25 May 2006, paras 91–93; *TSA Spectrum v Argentina*, Award, 19 December 2008, paras 98–113; *Teinver v Argentina*, Decision on Jurisdiction, 12

to the initiation of ICSID arbitration but before the decision on jurisdiction is taken.[231] Other tribunals have insisted on the requirement's jurisdictional nature and its strict application.[232]

In some cases, tribunals decided that there was no need to comply with directions contained in treaties to resort to domestic courts prior to the institution of arbitration proceedings since this would have been futile and would not have served any useful purpose.[233]

Investors were often able to avoid the application of such a rule by invoking MFN clauses which allowed them to rely on other BITs of the host State that did not contain that requirement.[234]

Where investors had sought relief in domestic courts before resorting to international arbitration, tribunals found that it did not matter whether that relief had been sought under domestic law or international law. Therefore, tribunals did not require that the cause of action before them and before the domestic courts was the same.[235]

(c) The fork in the road

Another way in which BITs sometimes refer to domestic courts is a so-called fork in the road provision. Such a clause provides that the investor must choose between litigation in the host State's domestic courts and international arbitration and that the choice, once made, is final. For instance, Article 8(2) of the Argentina–France BIT provides:

December 2012, para 135; *Philip Morris v Uruguay*, Decision on Jurisdiction, 2 July 2013, paras 98–150; *İçkale v Turkmenistan*, Award, 8 March 2016, paras 195–263.

[231] *Casinos Austria v Argentina*, Decision on Jurisdiction, 29 June 2018, paras 315–328, 337.

[232] *Maffezini v Spain*, Decision on Jurisdiction, 25 January 2000, paras 24–37; *Wintershall v Argentina*, Award, 8 December 2008, paras 114–157; *Impregilo v Argentina*, Award, 21 June 2011, paras 79–91; *Daimler v Argentina*, Award, 22 August 2012, paras 160–281; *Kiliç v Turkmenistan*, Award, 2 July 2013, paras 6.1.4–6.4.2.

[233] *Abaclat v Argentina*, Decision on Jurisdiction and Admissibility, 4 August 2011, paras 585–591; *Urbaser v Argentina*, Decision on Jurisdiction, 19 December 2012, paras 106–202; *Ambiente Ufficio v Argentina*, Decision on Jurisdiction and Admissibility, 8 February 2013, para 620; *Alemanni v Argentina*, Decision on Jurisdiction and Admissibility, 17 November 2014, paras 302–317.

[234] *Maffezini v Spain*, Decision on Jurisdiction, 25 January 2000, paras 54–64; *Siemens v Argentina*, Decision on Jurisdiction, 3 August 2004, paras 32–110; *Gas Natural v Argentina*, Decision on Jurisdiction, 17 June 2005, paras 24–49; *Suez and Interagua v Argentina*, Decision on Jurisdiction, 16 May 2006, paras 52–66; *National Grid v Argentina*, Decision on Jurisdiction, 20 June 2006, paras 80–93; *Suez and Vivendi v Argentina*, Decision on Jurisdiction, 3 August 2006, paras 52–68. But see *Wintershall v Argentina*, Award, 8 December 2008, paras 158–197.

[235] *Teinver v Argentina*, Decision on Jurisdiction, 21 December 2012, paras 132–133; *Philip Morris v Uruguay*, Decision on Jurisdiction, 2 July 2013, para 113; *Dede v Romania*, Award, 5 September 2013, paras 247, 250–253; *İçkale v Turkmenistan*, Award, 8 March 2016, paras 262–263; *Salini Impregilo v Argentina*, Decision on Jurisdiction, 23 February 2018, paras 115–140; *Casinos Austria v Argentina*, Decision on Jurisdiction, 29 June 2018, paras 296–305.

> Once an investor has submitted the dispute either to the jurisdictions of the Contracting Party involved or to international arbitration, the choice of one or the other of these procedures shall be final.

Similarly, under the ECT consent of the States Parties listed in Annex ID does not apply where the investor has previously submitted the dispute to the host State's courts.[236]

Investors or their subsidiaries are often drawn into local legal disputes of one sort or another. However, not every appearance before a court or tribunal of the host State will constitute a choice under a fork in the road provision. While such disputes may relate in some way to the investment, they are not necessarily identical to the dispute before the international tribunal. The appearance before a domestic court does not necessarily reflect a choice that would preclude international arbitration.

Tribunals have held that the loss of access to international arbitration under a fork in the road clause applies only if the 'triple identity test' is satisfied, that is, if the same dispute involving the same cause of action, the same object and the same parties has been submitted to the domestic courts of the host State.[237]

In *Yukos Universal v Russian Federation*,[238] the claimant argued that an objection based on a fork in the road provision must be based on a prior proceeding that satisfies the 'triple identity' test. The Tribunal said:

> there is ample authority for the application of a 'triple identity' test in the context of a 'fork-in-the-road' provision. To that extent, there is no question that the various Russian court proceedings and applications to the European Court of Human Rights cited by Respondent fail to trigger the 'fork-in-the-road provision' of the ECT.[239]

Tribunals have held that domestic proceedings related to proceedings before the international tribunal but dealing with a different basis of claim or cause of action did not constitute the choice foreseen by a fork in the road provision.[240] They also

[236] See Article 26(3)(b)(i) of the ECT.

[237] *Lauder v Czech Republic*, Final Award, 3 September 2001, paras 156–166; *CMS v Argentina*, Decision on Jurisdiction, 17 July 2003, paras 77–82; *Azurix v Argentina*, Decision on Jurisdiction, 8 December 2003, paras 37–41, 86–92; *Enron v Argentina*, Decision on Jurisdiction, 14 January 2004, paras 95–98; *Occidental Exploration v Ecuador*, Award, 1 July 2004, paras 37–63; *LG&E v Argentina*, Decision on Jurisdiction, 30 April 2004, paras 75–76; *Pan American v Argentina*, Decision on Preliminary Objections, 27 July 2006, paras 155–157; *Toto v Lebanon*, Decision on Jurisdiction, 11 September 2009, paras 203–217; *Pey Casado v Chile*, Award, 8 May 2008, paras 467–498; *Khan Resources v Mongolia*, Decision on Jurisdiction, 25 July 2012, paras 390–400.

[238] *Yukos Universal v Russian Federation*, Interim Award on Jurisdiction and Admissibility, 30 November 2009, paras 587–600; Final Award, 18 July 2014, paras 1256–1272.

[239] Interim Award, para 598.

[240] *Vivendi v Argentina*, Award, 21 November 2000, para 55; *Genin v Estonia*, Award, 25 June 2001, paras 321, 331–332; *Middle East Cement v Egypt*, Award, 12 April 2002, para 70–73.

held that only an identity of object in the domestic and international proceedings would trigger a fork in the road provision.[241] If there was no identity of the parties in the domestic and international proceedings the fork in the road did not apply.[242]

In a smaller group of cases tribunals found that fork in the road clauses, represented an obstacle to their jurisdiction since claimants had submitted their disputes with the respondent State to the domestic courts. In these cases, the tribunals did not apply the triple identity test but looked at the fundamental basis of the claim.[243]

(d) Waiver clauses

Some treaties providing for consent to arbitration require that the investor waive the right to initiate or continue dispute settlement procedures before domestic courts with respect to the same measures. Examples for clauses of this type are Article 1121(1) of the NAFTA, Article 14.D.5(1)(e) of the USMCA, and Article 10.18(2) of the DR–CAFTA. Tribunals have to assess the sufficiency of waivers under these treaties.[244]

In *Waste Management v Mexico*, the Tribunal found that the claimant's waiver did not satisfy Article 1121 of NAFTA. A waiver under Article 1121 could not be limited to claims specifically made under the NAFTA itself, but had to cover any claim concerning a measure that was in dispute, even if the basis of the claim was purely domestic. Therefore, the Tribunal declined jurisdiction.[245] The claimant resubmitted the same claim to arbitration accompanied by an amended waiver. The second Tribunal decided that the first Tribunal's dismissal on jurisdictional grounds did not preclude the resubmission,[246] and proceeded to give an Award on the merits.[247]

[241] *Olguín v Paraguay*, Decision on Jurisdiction, 8 August 2000, para 30; *Total v Argentina*, Decision on Liability, 27 December 2010, para 443; *Mobil v Argentina*, Decision on Jurisdiction and Liability, 10 April 2013, paras 139–146.

[242] *Champion Trading v Egypt*, Decision on Jurisdiction, 21 October 2003, sec 3.4.3; *LG&E v Argentina*, Decision on Jurisdiction, 30 April 2004, paras 19, 75; *Charanne v Spain*, Final Award, 21 January 2016, para 408; *Greentech v Italy*, Final Award, 23 December 2018, paras 195–205.

[243] *Pantechniki v Albania*, Award, 30 July 2009, para 51 et seq; *H&H v Egypt*, Award, 6 May 2014, paras 366–378; *Supervisión y Control v Costa Rica*, Award, 18 January 2017, paras 294–318.

[244] *Thunderbird v Mexico*, Award, 26 January 2006, paras 111–118; *Railroad Development v Guatemala*, Decision on Jurisdiction, 17 November 2008, paras 43–76; *Pac Rim v El Salvador*, Decision on Preliminary Objections, 2 August 2010, paras 173–188, 239–243, 250–253; *Commerce Group v El Salvador*, Award, 14 March 2011, paras 69–128; *Vannessa v Venezuela*, Award, 16 January 2013, para 229; *Corona v Dominican Republic*, Award, 31 May 2016, paras 10, 266–268; *Supervisión y Control v Costa Rica*, Award, 18 January 2017, paras 6, 133–146, 292–300; *Salini Impregilo v Argentina*, Decision on Jurisdiction, 23 February 2018, paras 141–149; *Casinos Austria v Argentina*, Decision on Jurisdiction, 29 June 2018, paras 329–335, 339.

[245] *Waste Management v Mexico I*, Award, 2 June 2000.

[246] *Waste Management v Mexico II*, Decision on Preliminary Objection Concerning the Previous Proceedings, 26 June 2002.

[247] *Waste Management v Mexico II*, Award, 30 April 2004. See also *B-Mex v Mexico*, Partial Award, 19 July 2019, paras 43–44.

9. MFN clauses and dispute settlement

An MFN clause contained in a treaty will extend the better treatment granted to a third State or its nationals to a beneficiary of the treaty.[248] Most BITs and some other treaties for the protection of investment[249] contain MFN clauses. This has led to the question whether these clauses apply only to the treaty's substantive clauses or also to its provisions on dispute settlement.[250]

(a) The wording of MFN clauses

The extent to which MFN clauses apply depends primarily upon their exact wording. Most MFN clauses are worded in general terms and typically just refer to the treatment of investments. But some MFN clauses indicate whether they cover dispute settlement.[251]

MFN clauses in British BITs typically specify the articles to which MFN treatment is to apply. In *Garanti Koza v Turkmenistan*, the United Kingdom–Turkmenistan BIT specified that its MFN clause applied to Articles 1–11. Since Article 8 of the BIT, dealing with investor–State arbitration, was among the listed Articles, the Tribunal found that the claimant, as a UK investor, was entitled by the MFN provision to avail itself of the more favourable dispute settlement provision contained in the Switzerland–Turkmenistan BIT.[252]

In *Beijing Urban Construction v Yemen*, Article 3 of the China–Yemen BIT contained an MFN clause that related to 'treatment accorded to investors of the other Contracting Party *in its territory*'.[253] The Tribunal rejected the application of this MFN clause to jurisdiction. The words 'in its territory' suggested the clause's application to substantive rights and not to international arbitration, which is not an activity inherently linked to the host State's territory.[254]

[248] Generally on MFN clauses see VIII.5 above.

[249] NAFTA Article 1103; USMCA Article 14.5; ECT Article 10(7).

[250] Some tribunals have cast doubt on the validity of this distinction. See *RosInvest v Russian Federation*, Award on Jurisdiction, 5 October 2007, paras 131–132; *Renta 4 v Russian Federation*, Award on Preliminary Objections, 20 March 2009, paras 99–100.

[251] The UK Model BIT confirms 'for the avoidance of doubt' that MFN treatment applies to a list of Articles that include the settlement of investor–State disputes. The BIT between Austria and Kazakhstan in Article 3(3) specifically includes dispute settlement in its MFN clause.

[252] *Garanti Koza v Turkmenistan*, Decision on Jurisdiction, 3 July 2013, paras 39–96. In the same sense, *Krederi v Ukraine*, Award, 2 July 2018, paras 283–343.

[253] Emphasis added.

[254] *Beijing Urban Construction v Yemen*, Decision on Jurisdiction, 31 May 2017, paras 110–121.

(b) MFN treatment and conditions for the institution of proceedings

The cases discussing the applicability of MFN clauses to conditions for the institution of proceedings, typically concerned the requirement to use domestic courts for a certain period of time before resorting to arbitration.

In *Maffezini v Spain*,[255] the consent clause in the Argentina–Spain BIT required resort to the host State's domestic courts for 18 months before the institution of arbitration. That BIT contained the following MFN clause: 'In all matters subject to this Agreement, this treatment shall not be less favorable than that extended by each Party to the investments made in its territory by investors of a third country.'

On the basis of that clause, the Argentinean claimant relied on the Chile–Spain BIT which does not contain the requirement to try the host State's courts for 18 months. The Tribunal undertook a detailed analysis of the applicability of MFN clauses to dispute settlement arrangements[256] and concluded:

> the most favored nation clause included in the Argentine–Spain BIT embraces the dispute settlement provisions of this treaty... the Tribunal concludes that Claimant had the right to submit the instant dispute to arbitration without first accessing the Spanish courts.[257]

At the same time, the *Maffezini* Tribunal warned against exaggerated expectations attached to the operation of MFN clauses and distinguished between the legitimate extension of rights and benefits and disruptive treaty-shopping. In particular, the MFN clause should not override public policy considerations that the contracting parties had in mind as fundamental conditions for their acceptance of the agreement.[258]

Subsequent decisions dealing with the application of MFN clauses to the requirement to seek a settlement in domestic courts for 18 months have adopted the same solution. The tribunals confirmed that the claimants were entitled to rely on the MFN clause in the applicable treaty to invoke the more favourable dispute settlement clause of another treaty that did not contain the 18-month rule.[259] These

[255] *Maffezini v Spain*, Decision on Jurisdiction, 25 January 2000.

[256] At paras 38–64.

[257] At para 64.

[258] At paras 62– 63.

[259] *Siemens v Argentina*, Decision on Jurisdiction, 3 August 2004, paras 32–110; *Gas Natural v Argentina*, Decision on Jurisdiction, 17 June 2005, paras 24–31, 41–49; *Suez and Interagua v Argentina*, Decision on Jurisdiction, 16 May 2006, paras 52–66; *Suez and Vivendi v Argentina*, Decision on Jurisdiction, 3 August 2006, paras 52–68 (confirmed in Decision on Annulment, 5 May 2017, paras 220–261); *Telefónica v Argentina*, Decision on Jurisdiction, 25 May 2006, paras 91–114; *National Grid v Argentina*, Decision on Jurisdiction, 20 June 2006, paras 53–94; *Impregilo v Argentina*, Award, 21 June 2011, paras 51–109; *Hochtief v Argentina*, Decision on Jurisdiction, 24 October 2011, paras 56–99; *Teinver v Argentina*, Decision on Jurisdiction, 21 December 2012, paras 137–186.

tribunals expressed their conviction that arbitration was an important part of the protection of foreign investors and that MFN clauses should apply to dispute settlement. For instance, the Tribunal in *Gas Natural v Argentina* said:

> assurance of independent international arbitration is an important—perhaps the most important—element in investor protection. Unless it appears clearly that the state parties to a BIT or the parties to a particular investment agreement settled on a different method for resolution of disputes that may arise, most-favored-nation provisions in BITs should be understood to be applicable to dispute settlement.[260]

However, practice on the application of MFN clauses to overcome procedural hurdles to arbitration is not uniform. In another group of cases, tribunals were more restrictive and refused to apply MFN clauses to overcome the requirement to first seek a remedy in domestic courts for a certain period of time.[261] In these decisions, tribunals relied on the central role of consent in international adjudication, on the *ejusdem generis* principle, on the Parties' presumed intention, as well as on the separability of dispute settlement clauses.

(c) MFN treatment and consent

In some cases, claimants invoked MFN clauses not to avoid procedural obstacles to the institution of proceedings but to overcome shortcomings in respondents' consent and to create a jurisdiction that was otherwise absent. In these cases, tribunals have overwhelmingly rejected reliance on MFN clauses.

In *Plama v Bulgaria*, the Tribunal found that it had jurisdiction on the basis of Article 26 of the ECT.[262] The claimant had additionally attempted to base the Tribunal's jurisdiction on the Bulgaria–Cyprus BIT. That BIT provides for investor–State arbitration only in very limited terms but it does contain an MFN clause that refers to 'treatment which is no less favourable'. The claimant sought to use that MFN clause to avail itself of the Bulgaria–Finland BIT which did provide for investor–State arbitration in broad terms. Therefore, the reliance on the MFN clause was not directed at overcoming a procedural obstacle but was an attempt to create a jurisdiction that would not have existed otherwise.

The Tribunal rejected this attempt stating that any intention to incorporate dispute settlement provisions from another treaty, by way of an MFN clause, would have to be expressed clearly and unambiguously. It said:

[260] *Gas Natural v Argentina*, Decision on Jurisdiction, 17 June 2005, para 49.

[261] *Wintershall v Argentina*, Award, 8 December 2008, paras 158–197; *Daimler v Argentina*, Award, 22 August 2012, paras 160–281; *Kiliç v Turkmenistan*, Award, 2 July 2013, paras 7.1.1–7.9.1; *H&H v Egypt*, Award, 6 May 2014, paras 356–358.

[262] *Plama v Bulgaria*, Decision on Jurisdiction, 8 February 2005, para 179.

> an MFN provision in a basic treaty does not incorporate by reference dispute settlement provisions in whole or in part set forth in another treaty, unless the MFN provision in the basic treaty leaves no doubt that the Contracting Parties intended to incorporate them.[263]

In *Telenor v Hungary*[264] the clause in the BIT between Hungary and Norway, offering consent to investor–State arbitration, was limited to the compensation or other consequences of expropriation. The claimant sought to rely on the MFN clause in the BIT to benefit from wider dispute resolution provisions in BITs between Hungary and other countries. The Tribunal endorsed the solution adopted in *Plama*. It found that the term 'treatment' contained in the MFN clause referred to substantive but not to procedural rights. Deciding otherwise would lead to undesirable treaty-shopping creating uncertainty and instability. Also, the jurisdiction of an arbitral tribunal as determined by a BIT was not to be inferentially extended by an MFN clause seeing that Hungary and Norway had made a deliberate choice to limit arbitration.[265] The Tribunal said:

> The Tribunal therefore concludes that in the present case the MFN clause cannot be used to extend the Tribunal's jurisdiction to categories of claim other than expropriation, for this would subvert the common intention of Hungary and Norway in entering into the BIT in question.[266]

In other cases too tribunals have rejected the reliance on MFN clauses to create or expand jurisdiction that did not exist under the basic treaty.[267]

Here too, however, practice is not uniform. A smaller number of tribunals have allowed the use of MFN clauses also to matters of jurisdiction to supplement consent.[268] In *RosInvest v Russian Federation*,[269] the UK–Russia BIT offered consent to jurisdiction over the amount of compensation in case of an expropriation. Based on an MFN clause in that treaty, the Tribunal applied a dispute settlement provision in the Denmark–Russia BIT which covered any dispute in connection with

263 At para 223.

264 *Telenor v Hungary*, Award, 13 September 2006.

265 At paras 90–97.

266 At para 100.

267 *Salini v Jordan*, Decision on Jurisdiction, 29 November 2004, paras 102–119; *Berschader v Russian Federation*, Award, 21 April 2006, paras 159–208; *Tza Yap Shum v Peru*, Decision on Jurisdiction and Competence, 19 June 2009, paras 189–220; *Austrian Airlines v Slovakia*, Final Award, 9 October 2009, paras 109–140; *Accession Mezzanine v Hungary*, Decision on Respondent's Objection under Rule 41(5), 16 January 2013, paras 73–74; *Ansung Housing v China*, Award, 9 March 2017, paras 123–141; *Menzies v Senegal*, Award, 5 August 2016, paras 132–145; *A11Y v Czech Republic*, Decision on Jurisdiction, 9 February 2017, paras 92–108; *Doutremepuich v Mauritius*, Award on Jurisdiction, 23 August 2019, paras 188–236; *Itisaluna v Iraq*, Award, 3 April 2020, paras 192–225.

268 See also *UP and C.D v Hungary*, Decision on Jurisdiction, 3 March 2016, paras 159–222.

269 *RosInvest v Russian Federation*, Award on Jurisdiction, October 2007, paras 124–139.

an investment. The Tribunal noted that the very character of an MFN clause is that protection not accepted in one treaty is widened by transferring the protection accorded in another treaty.[270] But the Tribunal's conclusion was limited to finding that the MFN clause enabled it to decide whether there had, in fact, been a valid expropriation.

The cases in which tribunals relied on MFN clauses may be distinguishable on factual grounds from those cases in which they did not. Most of the cases in which the tribunals accepted the applicability of the MFN clauses to dispute settlement concerned procedural obstacles. Most of the cases in which the effect of the MFN clauses was denied concerned attempts to extend consent to issues not covered by the arbitration clauses in the basic treaties. But not all cases fit this distinction. In addition, there is substantial contradiction in the reasoning of the tribunals. Both groups of tribunals made broad statements as to the applicability, or otherwise, of MFN clauses to dispute settlement in general. These broad statements are impossible to reconcile.[271]

The widespread disagreement on this point is underlined by carefully drafted dissenting opinions to decisions dealing with MFN clauses and dispute settlement. This applies both to decisions permitting the use of MFN clauses in connection with dispute settlement[272] and to decisions disallowing their use.[273]

The acceptance of MFN clauses for purposes of attracting substantive standards from other treaties[274] but their rejection when it comes to dispute settlement leads to a paradoxical situation. The importation of additional substantive standards of protection by way of an MFN clause inevitably has effects on the jurisdiction of tribunals. This is particularly evident where the jurisdiction of a tribunal is limited to violations of the treaty. For instance, if the basic treaty does not contain an umbrella clause or a guarantee of fair and equitable treatment, the applicability of these standards by way of an MFN clause will also widen the jurisdiction of a tribunal. The effect is that certain jurisdictional limitations in clauses dealing with dispute settlement can be overcome with the help of an MFN clause while others cannot.

The CETA and other treaties negotiated by the EU exclude not only investor–State dispute settlement procedures but also more favourable substantive obligations in other treaties from the effect of MFN clauses.[275]

[270] At para 131.

[271] See S Schill, '*Maffezini v. Plama:* Reflections on the Jurisprudential Schism in the Application of Most-Favored-Nation Clauses to Matters of Dispute Settlement' in M Kinnear et al (eds) *Building International Investment Law* (2016) 251.

[272] *Impregilo v Argentina*, Award, 21 June 2011, paras 51–109 (Diss Op B Stern); *Hochtief v Argentina*, Decision on Jurisdiction, 24 October 2011 (Diss Op C Thomas); *Garanti Koza v Turkmenistan*, Decision on Jurisdiction, 3 July 2013 (Diss Op L Boisson de Chazounes).

[273] *Renta4 v Russian Federation*, Award on Preliminary Objections, 20 March 2009, paras 68–120 (Sep Op C Brower); *Austrian Airlines v Slovakia*, Final Award, 9 October 2009, paras 109–140 (Sep Op C Brower); *A11Y v Czech Republic*, Decision on Jurisdiction, 9 February 2017, para 108 (Decl S Alexandrov).

[274] See VIII.5(e) above.

[275] CETA Article 8.7.

(d) Cherry picking

Another open question is the effect of a successful invocation of an MFN clause. Does the MFN clause attract only those provisions of the third-party treaty that are beneficial to the party invoking it? Or does it lead to the substitution of the relevant provision in the basic treaty by the provision in the third-party treaty including those aspects that are less beneficial? For instance, if the MFN clause is used to avoid a requirement to resort to domestic courts for a certain period of time, would a fork in the road clause in the third-party treaty, that is not contained in the basic treaty, become applicable?

The Tribunal in *Siemens v Argentina* took the view that the party invoking the MFN clause could pick and chose. It said:

> a benefit by the operation of an MFN clause does not carry with it the acceptance of all the terms of the treaty which provides for such benefit whether or not they are considered beneficial to the party making the claim;[276] ... its application will be related only to the benefits that the treaty of reference may grant and to the extent that benefits are perceived to be such.[277]

The Tribunal in *Hochtief v Argentina* reached a different result. It found that the claimant could not use an MFN clause to avoid the requirement to litigate in domestic courts for 18 months without at the same time being subject to a fork in the road provision in the third-party treaty. The Tribunal said: 'The MFN provision does not permit the selective picking of components from each set of conditions, so as to manufacture a synthetic set of conditions to which <u>no</u> State's nationals would be entitled.'[278]

10. Treaty claims and contract claims

(a) The selection of domestic courts in contracts

Contracts between host States and foreign investors frequently contain forum selection clauses that refer disputes arising from the application of these contracts to the host States' domestic courts. When disputes in connection with the

[276] *Siemens v Argentina*, Decision on Jurisdiction, 3 August 2004, para 109.

[277] At para 120. See also *RosInvest v Russian Federation*, Final Award, 12 September 2010, paras 269–271; *Garanti Koza v Turkmenistan*, Decision on the Objection to Jurisdiction for Lack of Consent, 3 July 2013, para 76.

[278] *Hochtief v Argentina*, Decision on Jurisdiction, 24 October 2011, para 98. Underlining original. See also *ICS v Argentina I*, Award on Jurisdiction, 10 February 2012, para 320; *Daimler v Argentina*, Award, 22 August 2012, paras 244–250.

investments arose, investors would invoke the provisions of treaties, usually BITs, granting them access to international arbitration. In turn, the host States would rely on the forum selection clauses in the contracts arguing that the investors had waived their right to international arbitration.

The arbitral tribunals confronted with these arguments have taken a differentiated attitude.[279] *Vivendi v Argentina I*,[280] involved a concession contract between the French investor and a province of Argentina. The contract contained a forum selection that referred disputes arising from the contract to the jurisdiction of the province's courts. The investor, seeking to bring its claim before an international tribunal rather than before a domestic court, relied on the BIT between Argentina and France to establish the jurisdiction of ICSID. Argentina challenged the ICSID Tribunal's jurisdiction by relying on the forum selection clause in the Concession Contract.

The ICSID Tribunal distinguished between claims based on the BIT and claims based on the Concession Contract. The forum selection clause in the Concession Contract did not affect the claimant's right to go to international arbitration to pursue violations of the BIT.[281] Nevertheless, the Tribunal found that all claims were closely linked to the performance of the Concession Contract and that it was impossible to separate the two types of claims. Therefore, resort to ICSID arbitration should be open to claimants only after they had failed in the pursuit of their claims before the domestic courts. The Tribunal added that the need to resort to domestic courts was not based on a requirement to exhaust local remedies but was based on the Concession Contract's forum selection clause.[282]

The Award was partly annulled.[283] The ad hoc Committee, which had to decide on the request for annulment of the Award, found that the Tribunal had manifestly exceeded its powers by not examining the merits of some of the claims before it. The Committee ruled that a particular investment dispute may at the same time involve issues of the interpretation and application of a treaty and of a contract.[284] On the relation between breach of treaty and breach of contract, the ad hoc Committee pointed out that these related to independent standards:

> A state may breach a treaty without breaching a contract, and *vice versa*... whether there has been a breach of the BIT and whether there has been a breach of contract are different questions... the existence of an exclusive jurisdiction clause in a

[279] In some cases, tribunals denied the existence of a forum selection seeing that the domestic courts had jurisdiction anyway under domestic law and that this jurisdiction was not subject to agreement or waiver: *LANCO v Argentina*, Decision on Jurisdiction, 8 December 1998, para 26; *Salini v Morocco*, Decision on Jurisdiction, 16 July 2001, paras 25–27.

[280] *Vivendi v Argentina*, Award, 21 November 2000.

[281] At paras 53–54.

[282] At paras 77–81.

[283] *Vivendi v Argentina*, Decision on Annulment, 3 July 2002.

[284] At paras 60, 72, 76.

> contract between the claimant and the respondent state or one of its subdivisions cannot operate as a bar to the application of the treaty standard... A state cannot rely on an exclusive jurisdiction clause in a contract to avoid the characterisation of its conduct as internationally unlawful under a treaty.[285]

The Decision on Annulment in *Vivendi* established the principle that a forum selection clause in a contract pointing to domestic courts will not oust the jurisdiction of an international tribunal based on a treaty. The decisive reason is that contract claims and treaty claims have different legal bases. Practice has since followed the distinction between contract claims, which are subject to contractual forum selection clauses, and treaty claims which are unaffected by such clauses. Under this practice the treaty-based jurisdiction of international arbitral tribunals to decide on violations of these treaties is not affected by domestic forum selection clauses in contracts. The contractual selection of domestic courts is restricted to violations of the respective contracts.[286]

For instance, in *AES v Argentina*, the jurisdiction of the international Tribunal was based on an offer of consent, accepted by the investor, in the BIT between Argentina and the United States. Argentina relied on forum selection clauses contained in concession contracts and objected to ICSID's jurisdiction. The Tribunal rejected Argentina's argument. It said:

> the Entities concerned have consented to a forum selection clause electing Administrative Argentine law and exclusive jurisdiction of Argentine administrative tribunals in the concession contracts and related documents. But this

[285] At paras 95–96, 101, 103.

[286] *CMS v Argentina*, Decision on Jurisdiction, 17 July 2003, paras 70–76; *SGS v Pakistan*, Decision on Jurisdiction, 6 August 2003, paras 43–74, 147–173; *Azurix v Argentina*, Decision on Jurisdiction, 8 December 2003, paras 26–36, 75–79; *Enron v Argentina*, Decision on Jurisdiction, 14 January 2004, paras 89–94; *SGS v Philippines*, Decision on Jurisdiction, 29 January 2004, paras 136–155,160–163; *LG&E v Argentina*, Decision on Jurisdiction, 30 April 2004, paras 58–62; *Siemens v Argentina*, Decision on Jurisdiction, 3 August 2004, paras 174–183; *Salini v Jordan*, Decision on Jurisdiction, 29 November 2004, paras 92–96; *Impregilo v Pakistan*, Decision on Jurisdiction, 22 April 2005, paras 286–289; *Camuzzi v Argentina*, Decision on Jurisdiction, 11 May 2005, paras 105–119; *Sempra v Argentina*, Decision on Jurisdiction, 11 May 2005, paras 116–128; *Eureko v Poland*, Partial Award, 19 August 2005, paras 81, 89, 92–114; *Aguas del Tunari v Bolivia*, Decision on Jurisdiction, 21 October 2005, paras 94–123; *Bayindir v Pakistan*, Decision on Jurisdiction, 14 November 2005, paras 139–167; *Suez and InterAgua v Argentina*, Decision on Jurisdiction, 16 May 2006, paras 41–45; *National Grid v Argentina*, Decision on Jurisdiction, 20 June 2006, paras 167–170; *Inceysa v El Salvador*, Award, 2 August 2006, paras 43, 212–217; *Total v Argentina*, Decision on Jurisdiction, 25 August 2006, paras 82–85; *Fraport v Philippines I*, Award, 16 August 2007, paras 388–391; *Vivendi v Argentina*, Resubmitted Case: Award, 20 August 2007, paras 7.3.1–7.3.11.; *Helnan v Egypt*, Award, 3 July 2008, paras 102–103; *TSA Spectrum v Argentina*, Award, 19 December 2008, paras 42–66; *Enron v Argentina*, Decision on Annulment, 30 July 2010, paras 128–150; *Abaclat v Argentina*, Decision on Jurisdiction and Admissibility, 4 August 2011, paras 498–499; *Impregilo v Argentina*, Award, 21 June 2011, paras 141–189; *Crystallex v Venezuela* Award, 4 April 2016, paras 471–484, 686–708; *MNSS v Montenegro*, Award, 4 May 2016, paras 148–159; *Casinos Austria v Argentina*, Decision on Jurisdiction, 29 June 2018, paras 214–222; *ESPF v Italy*, Award, 14 September 2020, paras 358–377.

> exclusivity only plays within the Argentinean legal order, for matters in relation with the execution of these concession contracts. They do not preclude AES from exercising its rights as resulting, within the international legal order from two international treaties, namely the US–Argentina BIT and the ICSID Convention.
> 94. In other terms, the present Tribunal has jurisdiction over any alleged breach by Argentina of its obligations under the US–Argentina BIT.[287]

Umbrella clauses will convert contract breaches into treaty breaches, although this point is not undisputed.[288] Some tribunals have held that a forum selection clause in a contract constitutes a waiver of treaty-based jurisdiction over contract claims and that such claims could not be submitted to investor–State arbitration, including by virtue of the operation of the umbrella clause, either because the tribunal lacks jurisdiction[289] or because the claims are inadmissible.[290]

(b) Jurisdiction of international tribunals over contract claims

The distinction between contract claims and treaty claims has appeared in many investment arbitrations.[291] In disputes before tribunals established under treaties, the question arises whether jurisdiction is limited to claims arising from violations of the treaty's substantive standards or extends to alleged violations of contracts. It is incorrect to assume that the jurisdiction of a treaty-based tribunal is necessarily restricted to violations of the treaty's substantive provisions. An investment

[287] *AES v Argentina*, Decision on Jurisdiction, 26 April 2005, paras 93–94.

[288] See VIII.6 above.

[289] *Toto v Lebanon*, Decision on Jurisdiction, 11 September 2009, paras 187–202; *MNSS v Montenegro*, Award, 4 May 2016, paras 148–165, 308–310.

[290] *SGS v Philippines*, Decision on Jurisdiction, 29 January 2004, paras 113–155; *BIVAC v Paraguay*, Decision on Jurisdiction, 29 May 2009, paras 143–159; *Bosh v Ukraine*, Award, 25 October 2012, paras 242–259. But see: *SGS v Paraguay*, Decision on Jurisdiction, 12 February 2010, paras 172–180.

[291] *El Paso v Argentina*, Decision on Jurisdiction, 27 April 2006, paras 63–65; *Jan de Nul v Egypt*, Decision on Jurisdiction, 16 June 2006, paras 79–82; *LESI & ASTALDI v Algeria*, Decision on Jurisdiction, 12 July 2006, para 84; *Telenor v Hungary*, Award, 13 September 2006, paras 32, 50, 47(1), 50; *Saipem v Bangladesh*, Decision on Jurisdiction, 21 March 2007, paras 139–142; *Parkerings v Lithuania*, Award, 11 September 2007, paras 257, 260–266, 289, 317, 345; *BG Group v Argentina*, Final Award, 24 December 2007, paras 177–185; *Helnan v Egypt*, Award, 3 July 2008, paras 102, 107; Decision on Annulment, 14 June 2010, paras 58–66; *Biwater Gauff v Tanzania*, Award, 24 July 2008, paras 468–475; *Rumeli v Kazakhstan*, Award, 29 July 2008, para 330; *Bayindir v Pakistan*, Award, 27 August 2009, paras 133–139, 197, 367–375; *Toto v Lebanon*, Decision on Jurisdiction, 11 September 2009, paras 95–130; *Burlington v Ecuador*, Decision on Jurisdiction, 2 June 2010, paras 76–81; *Hamester v Ghana*, Award, 18 June 2010, paras 325–331; *Daimler v Argentina*, Award, 22 August 2012, paras 54–64; *Tenaris v Venezuela I*, Award, 29 January 2016, paras 300–312; *Ampal-American v Egypt*, Decision on Jurisdiction, 1 February 2016, paras 249–257; *İçkale v Turkmenistan*, Award, 8 March 2016, paras 306–310; *Saint-Gobain v Venezuela*, Decision on Liability and the Principles of Quantum, 30 December 2016, paras 369–373; *Beijing Urban Construction v Yemen*, Decision on Jurisdiction, 31 May 2017, paras 139–146.

tribunal may well have jurisdiction over contract claims. This may be a consequence of broadly worded jurisdiction clauses covering all types of investment disputes.[292]

The scope of jurisdiction, as determined by treaty clauses providing for consent to arbitration, varies.[293] Under some treaties, jurisdiction for investor–State disputes is limited to disputes arising out of the interpretation and application of the treaty's substantive standards. For instance, under Article 26(1) of the ECT, the scope of the consent is limited to disputes 'which concern an alleged breach of an obligation ... under Part III [of the ECT]'.[294]

By contrast, many BITs, in their consent clauses, contain phrases such as 'all disputes concerning investments' or 'any legal dispute concerning an investment'. These provisions do not restrict a tribunal's jurisdiction to claims arising from alleged violations of the BITs' substantive standards. By their own terms, these consent clauses encompass disputes that go beyond the interpretation and application of the BIT itself and include disputes that arise from a contract and other rules of law in connection with the investment.[295]

Therefore, a tribunal, whose jurisdiction derives from an offer of consent in a treaty, is not necessarily restricted to applying the substantive protections of that treaty. If the clause circumscribing its jurisdiction is sufficiently broad to cover bases of claims that include contracts, the tribunal is authorized to entertain claims based on contract.[296]

In *Metal-Tech v Uzbekistan*, the Tribunal said:

> Article 8 of the Treaty contains the consent of the Contracting Parties to submit to ICSID any 'any legal dispute ... concerning an investment of the latter in the territory of the former.' Article 8 is thus a broad dispute resolution clause not limited to claims arising under the standards of protection of the BIT.[297]

[292] See C Schreuer, 'Jurisdiction and Applicable Law in Investment Treaty Arbitration' (2014) 1 *MJDR* 1, 6.

[293] See also XII.7(f) above.

[294] Similarly, under Article 1116 of the NAFTA the scope of the consent to arbitration was limited to claims arising from alleged breaches of the NAFTA itself.

[295] *Salini v Morocco*, Decision on Jurisdiction, 16 July 2001, para 61; *Tokios Tokelės v Ukraine*, Decision on Jurisdiction, 29 April 2004, para 52, note 42; *Siemens v Argentina*, Award, 6 February 2007, para 205. See also the discussions in *Salini v Jordan*, Decision on Jurisdiction, 29 November 2004, paras 97–101; *Bayindir v Pakistan*, Decision on Jurisdiction, 15 November 2005, paras 57, 82, 102, 188; *Vivendi v Argentina*, Decision on Annulment, 3 July 2002, para 55; *Parkerings v Lithuania*, Award, 11 September 2007, paras 261–266; *MCI v Ecuador*, Decision on Annulment, 19 October 2009, paras 71–72; *SGS v Paraguay*, Decision on Jurisdiction, 12 February 2010, paras 129, 183–184; *Alpha v Ukraine*, Award, 8 November 2010, para 243; *Philip Morris v Uruguay*, Decision on Jurisdiction, 2 July 2013, paras 107, 109. *Contra*: *SGS v Pakistan*, Decision on Jurisdiction, 6 August 2003, para 161.

[296] See S Alexandrov, 'Breaches of Contract and Breaches of Treaty' (2004) 5 *JWIT* 555, 572; AM Steingruber, *Consent in International Arbitration* (2012) 299–302.

[297] *Metal-Tech v Uzbekistan*, Award, 4 October 2013, para 378.

(c) Distinguishing treaty claims from contract claims

In many cases, the need remains to distinguish treaty claims from contract claims. The distinction between contract claims and treaty claims is a recurrent feature in many investment arbitrations.[298] The respondent's objection that the case only involves contract claims and the claimant's insistence on its treaty rights have become routine arguments in these cases.[299]

A clear-cut separation between treaty claims and contract claims is often difficult and hinges on the facts of each case. A particular course of action by the host State may well constitute a breach of contract as well as a violation of international law. The two categories are not mutually exclusive. Rather, two different standards must be applied to determine whether one or the other or both have been violated.

Tribunals have found that the nature of a claim as treaty or contract based, depended on how claimants presented their case. Therefore, for purposes of jurisdiction, the characterization of the claims must be undertaken primarily by reference

[298] *Vivendi v Argentina*, Award, 21 November 2000, paras 53, 54; Decision on Annulment, 3 July 2002, paras 4160, 95, 96, 101–112; *CMS v Argentina*, Decision on Jurisdiction, 17 July 2003, 70–76; *SGS v Pakistan*, Decision on Jurisdiction, 6 August 2003, 43, 44, 48–74, 147–173; *Azurix v Argentina*, Decision on Jurisdiction, 8 December 2003, paras 26, 79; *Enron v Argentina*, Decision on Jurisdiction, 14 January 2004, para 91; *IBM v Ecuador*, Decision on Jurisdiction and Competence, 22 December 2003, paras 50–70; *LG&E v Argentina*, Decision on Jurisdiction, 30 April 2004, paras 58–62; *Siemens v Argentina*, Decision on Jurisdiction, 3 August 2004, paras 174–183; *Salini v Jordan*, Decision on Jurisdiction, 29 November 2004, paras 92–96; *Impregilo v Pakistan*, Decision on Jurisdiction, 22 April 2005, paras 219, 258, 286–289; *AES v Argentina*, Decision on Jurisdiction, 26 April 2005, paras 90–99; *Camuzzi v Argentina*, Decision on Jurisdiction, 11 May 2005, paras 105–119; *Sempra v Argentina*, Decision on Jurisdiction, 11 May 2005, paras 95–101; *Aguas del Tunari v Bolivia*, Decision on Jurisdiction, 21 October 2005, paras 94–123; *Suez and InterAgua v Argentina*, Decision on Jurisdiction, 16 May 2006, paras 41–45; *National Grid v Argentina*, Decision on Jurisdiction, 20 June 2006, paras 167–170; *Vivendi v Argentina*, Resubmitted Case: Award, 20 August 2007, paras 7.3.1.–7.3.11.; *TSA Spectrum v Argentina*, Award, 19 December 2008, para 58; *Gemplus v Mexico*, Award, 16 June 2010, paras 6–22, 6–25, 8–26; *Malicorp v Egypt*, Award, 7 February 2011, para 103; *Abaclat v Argentina*, Decision on Jurisdiction and Admissibility, 4 August 2011, paras 302–332; *Philip Morris v Uruguay*, Decision on Jurisdiction, 2 July 2013, paras 107–113; *Tulip v Turkey*, Award, 10 March 2014, paras 329–365; *Venezuela Holdings v Venezuela*, Award, 9 October 2014, para 254; *İçkale v Turkmenistan*, Award, 8 March 2016, paras 306–310; *Saint-Gobain v Venezuela*, Decision on Liability and the Principles of Quantum, 30 December 2016, paras 369–373; *Supervisión y Control v Costa Rica*, Award, 18 January 2017, paras 278–279; *Karkey v Pakistan*, Award, 22 August 2017, paras 562–563; *CMC v Mozambique*, Award, 24 October 2019, paras 219–222.

[299] *El Paso v Argentina*, Decision on Jurisdiction, 27 April 2006, paras 63–65; *Telefónica v Argentina*, Decision on Jurisdiction, 25 May 2006, paras 21–22; *Jan de Nul v Egypt*, Decision on Jurisdiction, 16 June 2006, paras 79–82; *LESI & ASTALDI v Algeria*, Decision on Jurisdiction, 12 July 2006, para 84; *Telenor v Hungary*, Award, 13 September 2006, paras 32, 47(1), 50; *Saipem v Bangladesh*, Decision on Jurisdiction, 21 March 2007, paras 139–142; *Parkerings v Lithuania*, Award, 11 September 2007, paras 257, 260–266, 289, 317, 345; *BG Group v Argentina*, Final Award, 24 December 2007, paras 177–185; *Helnan v Egypt*, Award, 3 July 2008, paras 102, 107; *Biwater Gauff v Tanzania*, Award, 24 July 2008, paras 468–475; *Rumeli v Kazakhstan*, Award, 29 July 2008, para 330; *Bayindir v Pakistan*, Award, 27 August 2009, paras 133–139, 197, 367–375; *Toto v Lebanon*, Decision on Jurisdiction, 11 September 2009, paras 95–130; *Burlington v Ecuador*, Decision on Jurisdiction, 2 June 2010, paras 76–81; *Helnan v Egypt*, Decision on Annulment, 14 June 2010, paras 58–66; *Beijing Urban Construction v Yemen*, Decision on Jurisdiction, 31 May 2017, paras 139–145; *Unión Fenosa v Egypt*, Award, 31 August 2018, para 9.55; *ICS v Argentina II*, Award on Jurisdiction, 8 July 2019, paras 319–321, 324.

to the claimant's pleadings. It follows that whether for purposes of jurisdiction a dispute arises from a contract or from the treaty depends on how the claims are put forward by the claimant.[300]

In *Saipem v Bangladesh*, the respondent had submitted that the claim was in reality a contractual claim dressed up as a treaty claim. The Tribunal rejected this contention and said:

> In the Tribunal's view, the essence of Saipem's case is that the courts of Bangladesh acted in violation of the New York Convention and in an 'illegal, arbitrary and idiosyncratic' manner amounting to a violation of the protection afforded to foreign investors under Article 5 of the BIT. Saipem does not request relief under the Contract; it does not raise contract claims over which the Tribunal would have no jurisdiction.[301]

The fact that claims are closely related to a contract does not disqualify them as treaty claims. The Tribunal in *BG Group v Argentina* said in this respect:

> The fact that claims under a treaty may relate to underlying rights set out in domestic law, or in a concession, license or contract is not, in and of itself, an impediment to adjudication in the treaty forum. . . .[302]

In some cases, the tribunals did not restrict themselves to looking at the claims as presented by the claimants but examined whether the treaty claims put forward by them were plausible.[303] In *Crystallex v Venezuela*, the Tribunal was not content with accepting the treaty claims as formulated by the claimant. It said:

300 *Vivendi v Argentina*, Award, 21 November 2000, para 53 and Decision on Annulment, 3 July 2002, para 74; *SGS v Pakistan*, Decision on Jurisdiction, 6 August 2003, paras 144–145; *Azurix v Argentina*, Decision on Jurisdiction, 8 December 2003, para 76; *Siemens v Argentina*, Decision on Jurisdiction, 3 August 2004, para 180; *Camuzzi v Argentina*, Decision on Jurisdiction, 11 May 2005, paras 83–90; *Telefónica v Argentina*, Decision on Jurisdiction, 25 May 2006, para 87; *Rumeli v Kazakhstan*, Award, 29 July 2008, para 330; *SGS v Paraguay*, Decision on Jurisdiction, 12 February 2010, para 137; *Daimler v Argentina*, Award, 22 August 2012, para 62; *Tenaris v Venezuela I*, Award, 29 January 2016, paras 300–312; *Ampal-American v Egypt*, Decision on Jurisdiction, 1 February 2016, paras 249–257.

301 *Saipem v Bangladesh*, Decision on Jurisdiction, 21 March 2007, para 141.

302 *BG Group v Argentina*, Final Award, 24 December 2007, para 181.

303 *Azinian v Mexico*, Award, 1 November 1999, paras 86–92; *UPS v Canada*, Award on Jurisdiction, 22 November 2002, paras 33–37; *SGS v Philippines*, Decision on Jurisdiction, 29 January 2004, paras 26, 72, 83, 96(e), 157, 160–164, 169(5); *PSEG v Turkey*, Decision on Jurisdiction, 4 June 2004, paras 63–65; *Occidental Exploration v Ecuador*, Final Award, 1 July 2004, paras 47, 80, 89, 92; *Joy Mining v Egypt*, Award on Jurisdiction, 6 August 2004, paras 29, 30, 78; *Salini v Jordan*, Decision on Jurisdiction, 29 November 2004, paras 131–151; *Impregilo v Pakistan*, Decision on Jurisdiction, 22 April 2005, paras 237–254; *Bayindir v Pakistan*, Decision on Jurisdiction, 14 November 2005, paras 185–247; *RSM v Grenada II*, Award, 10 December 2010, paras 7.3.6–7.3.7; *Glencore v Colombia*, Award, 27 August 2019, paras 1036–1038.

> The Tribunal's starting point will be the Claimant's prayers for relief and the formulation of its claims, as it is for a claimant to file its claim and thus define the nature of the claim that it submits before a tribunal. However, it would of course not be sufficient for a claimant to simply label contract breaches as treaty breaches to avoid the jurisdictional hurdles present in a BIT. The Tribunal's jurisdictional inquiry is a matter of objective determination, and the Tribunal would in case of pure 'labeling' be at liberty and have the duty to re-characterize the alleged breaches.[304]

The separate treatment of contract claims and treaty claims leads to situations where the claimant may be compelled to pursue part of its claim through national and another part through international procedures. This has undesirable consequences. The need to dissect cases into contract claims and treaty claims to be dealt with by separate fora requires claim splitting and has the potential of leading to parallel proceedings. This is uneconomical and contrary to the goal of reaching final and comprehensive resolutions of disputes.

11. Procedure

(a) Arbitration rules

Arbitration requires a comprehensive body of procedural rules. In investment arbitration the most commonly applied set of rules are those provided for in the ICSID Convention and in the ICSID Arbitration Rules. In addition, ICSID offers a set of Institution Rules as well as Administrative and Financial Regulations. The Regulations and Rules are adopted by ICSID's Administrative Council. An amendment of the ICSID Rules and Regulations came into effect on 10 April 2006. At the time of writing these Rules and Regulations are in the process of being replaced by a new set of Rules and Regulations.

Article 44 of the ICSID Convention provides that arbitration proceedings are to be conducted in accordance with the Convention and, except as the parties otherwise agree, in accordance with the Arbitration Rules in effect on the date on which the parties consented to arbitration. This means that after the adoption of a new set of Rules, the previous ones will continue to apply for some time.

The parties may agree on a modification of the Arbitration Rules, but certain international minimum standards of fair procedure must be observed by the parties when agreeing on procedural issues. These standards would include such principles as the tribunal's obligation to hear both sides (*audiatur et altera pars*), each

[304] *Crystallex v Venezuela*, Award, 4 April 2016, para 475.

party's right to be informed of the other side's arguments and equal treatment of the parties.[305]

Procedural questions are typically discussed and agreed upon between the parties and the tribunal at the tribunal's first session. The agreements on procedure are almost invariably recorded in the form of the tribunal's Procedural Order No 1. Any question of procedure not covered by the Convention, the Arbitration Rules or an agreement is to be decided by the tribunal usually in the form of procedural orders.

ICSID proceedings are self-contained and denationalized; that is, they are independent of any national law including the law of the tribunal's seat. Domestic courts do not have the power to intervene.

Non-ICSID arbitration is governed by other sets of rules. Proceedings under the Additional Facility are subject to the Arbitration (Additional Facility) Rules. Proceedings under the auspices of other arbitration institutions are subject to the respective rules provided by these institutions.[306] For ad hoc arbitration, the parties frequently select the UNCITRAL Arbitration Rules.[307] Non-ICSID proceedings are not insulated from national law. For the sake of convenience, this Chapter focuses on ICSID procedure.

(b) Institution of proceedings

ICSID proceedings are initiated by a request for arbitration directed to the Secretary-General of ICSID.[308] The request may be submitted by either the investor or the host State. In practice, the investor is nearly always the claimant. The request must be drafted in one of ICSID's official languages (English, French, and Spanish). A non-refundable lodging fee of USD25,000 is due with the request. After the tribunal's constitution, an administrative fee of USD42,000 is payable per year.

The request for arbitration must contain information concerning the dispute, the parties and the jurisdictional requirements, including the basis of consent.[309] The Secretary-General will register the request unless she finds that the dispute is manifestly outside the Centre's jurisdiction.[310] Registration is often preceded by correspondence with both parties and a call by ICSID for further clarifications. Once the request is registered, the Secretary-General will notify the parties in writing.

305 *MINE v Guinea*, Decision on Annulment, 14 December 1989, para 5.06.

306 See XII.4(c) above.

307 The original UNCITRAL Arbitration Rules were adopted in 1976, (1976) 15 ILM 701. A revised version was adopted by UN General Assembly resolution 65/22 in 2010. In 2013, a new Article 1, para 4 was added dealing with transparency.

308 ICSID Convention Article 36(1).

309 ICSID Convention Article 36(2); Institution Rule 2.

310 ICSID Convention Article 36(3).

A decision by the Secretary-General to register a request for arbitration does not bind the tribunal in its determination of jurisdiction. A respondent remains free to raise jurisdictional objections and a tribunal remains free to accept or decline jurisdiction.

A decision by the Secretary-General not to register a request for arbitration is final and not subject to any form of review, but a party may at any time submit a new request based on the same claim.[311] A new request would have to follow the same procedure including the payment of the lodging fee.

(c) Constitution and composition of the tribunal

Tribunals are nearly always composed of three arbitrators. Sole arbitrators are relatively rare. Under the standard procedure for the appointment of arbitrators at ICSID, each party appoints one arbitrator and the third, who is the tribunal's president, is appointed by agreement of the parties.[312] A different mode of appointment may be agreed by the parties.[313] Sometimes the two party-appointed arbitrators are charged with the appointment of the tribunal's president.

If the tribunal is not constituted after 90 days, either party may request the Chairman of the Administrative Council[314] to make any outstanding appointments.[315] In doing so, the Chairman will consult with the parties as far as possible. The purpose of this provision is to avoid a stalemate if one party is uncooperative. The Chairman is bound to make this appointment from the Panel of Arbitrators kept by ICSID.[316] Arbitrators thus appointed must not be nationals of the State party to the dispute or co-nationals of the investor party to the dispute.

In the case of party-appointed arbitrators, national arbitrators are also excluded.[317] But this prohibition would not apply if each individual member of the tribunal is appointed by agreement of the parties. The idea behind this rule is to guarantee maximum objectivity of the arbitrators.

There are no rules on the nationality of arbitrators not related to the two parties. Also, there is no requirement that the arbitrators represent different forms of civilization or different legal systems. Nor is there a rule requiring arbitrators on a

311 *Accession Mezzanine v Hungary*, Decision on Jurisdiction, 8 August 2013, paras 7–8.

312 ICSID Convention Article 37(2)(b).

313 ICSID Arbitration Rule 2.

314 Under Article 5 of the Convention the President of the International Bank for Reconstruction and Development is *ex officio* Chairman of ICSID's Administrative Council.

315 ICSID Convention Article 38.

316 ICSID Convention Article 40(1). Articles 12 to 16 of the Convention establish a Panel of Arbitrators to be maintained by the Centre.

317 This effect is achieved through Article 39 and Arbitration Rule 1(3).

tribunal to be of different nationalities.[318] There has been some concern about the insufficient representation of arbitrators from developing countries[319] although this situation is improving.

Arbitrators must be of high moral character, have recognized competence in the fields of law, commerce, industry, or finance and may be relied upon to exercise independent judgment.[320] In addition, arbitrators must be independent of the parties. Each arbitrator must sign a declaration providing details of any relationships with the parties.[321] Arbitrators have a continuing obligation to notify any relationship or relevant circumstance that may arise during the arbitral proceedings. A conflict of interest is a bar to the appointment and may lead to the arbitrator's disqualification.

Once a tribunal is constituted its composition is fixed and can only change under limited circumstances. In case of the death, incapacity, or resignation of an arbitrator the resulting vacancy will be filled by the same method that was applied for the original appointment.[322]

A party may propose the disqualification of an arbitrator on the ground that the arbitrator manifestly lacks the qualities required for his or her appointment.[323] The decision on a proposal to disqualify is made by the unchallenged members of the tribunal. If the unchallenged members do not agree the decision is made by the Chairman of the Administrative Council who also decides if a sole arbitrator or a majority of the arbitrators is challenged.[324]

Proposals for disqualification typically involve allegations of a conflict of interest or other lack of independent judgment,[325] although non-compliance with the nationality requirements under the Convention is another possible ground.[326]

[318] Some tribunals were composed, by agreement of the parties, of three arbitrators who all had the nationality of the respondent State. See *IBM v Ecuador*, Decision on Jurisdiction and Competence, 22 December 2003, para 4.

[319] AK Bjorklund et al, 'The Diversity Deficit in International Investment Arbitration' (2020) 21 *JWIT* 410.

[320] ICSID Convention Articles 14(1) and 40(2).

[321] ICSID Arbitration Rule 6(2).

[322] ICSID Convention Article 56(1); Arbitration Rule 8. Exceptionally under Article 56(3) in the case of a resignation by a party-appointed arbitrator without the consent of the tribunal, the resulting vacancy is to be filled by the Chairman. See *ConocoPhillips v Venezuela*, Decision on the Proposal to Disqualify a Majority of the Tribunal, 1 July 2015.

[323] ICSID Convention Article 57.

[324] ICSID Convention Article 58; Arbitration Rule 9. See *Abaclat v Argentina*, Decision on Challenge, 21 December 2011.

[325] *Amco v Indonesia*, Decision on the Proposal to Disqualify an Arbitrator, 24 June 1982; *Generation Ukraine v Ukraine*, Award, 16 September 2003, paras 4.8–4.18; *Salini v Jordan*, Award, 31 January 2006, paras 5, 9; *Siemens v Argentina*, Award, 6 February 2007, paras 31, 35–38; *Saipem v Bangladesh*, Decision on Proposal for Disqualification, 11 October 2005 (unpublished) and Decision on Jurisdiction, 21 March 2007, para 47; *Total v Argentina*, Decision on Argentine Republic's Proposal to Disqualify Ms Teresa Cheng, 26 August 2015; *Fábrica de Vidrios v Venezuela*, Reasoned Decision on the Proposal to Disqualify L Yves Fortier, QC, 28 March 2016.

[326] *Olguín v Paraguay*, Decision on Jurisdiction, 8 August 2000, paras 12–13; Award, 26 July 2001, paras 15–16.

Some cases involved 'issue conflicts', that is, situations in which an arbitrator can be perceived as having prejudged a legal or factual issue.[327] A position taken by an arbitrator in academic writings will not, as a rule, lead to a successful challenge.[328] Similarly, prior adverse rulings in the same case will not be accepted as evidence of a lack of independence or impartiality.[329]

In *Blue Bank v Venezuela*, the Chairman distinguished between impartiality and independence. He decided that the relevant test was not actual proof of bias, but the appearance of bias or dependence, assessed from an objective point of view. The Decision said:

> Impartiality refers to the absence of bias or predisposition towards a party. Independence is characterized by the absence of external control. Independence and impartiality both '*protect parties against arbitrators being influenced by factors other than those related to the merits of the case*.' Articles 57 and 14(1) of the ICSID Convention do not require proof of actual dependence or bias; rather it is sufficient to establish the appearance of dependence or bias.
>
> The applicable legal standard is an '*objective standard based on a reasonable evaluation of the evidence by a third party*.' As a consequence, the subjective belief of the party requesting the disqualification is not enough to satisfy the requirements of the Convention.[330]

Following the *Blue Bank* decision, the same legal standard was applied in other cases.[331]

Decisions on challenges of arbitrators often refer to the non-binding International Bar Association (IBA) Guidelines on Conflict of Interest in International Arbitration.[332] At the time of writing, ICSID and the UNCITRAL

[327] *Caratube and Hourani v Kazakhstan*, Decision on the Proposal for Disqualification of Mr Bruno Boesch, 20 March 2014.

[328] *Urbaser v Argentina*, Decision on the Claimant's Proposal to Disqualify Prof Campbell McLachlan, 12 August 2010.

[329] *Abaclat v Argentina*, Decision on the Proposal to Disqualify a Majority of the Tribunal, 4 February 2014, para 80; *Quiborax v Bolivia*, Award, 16 September 2015, para 42; *Vattenfall v Germany II*, Recommendation Pursuant to the Request by ICSID on the Respondent's Proposal to Disqualify All Members of the Arbitral Tribunal, 4 March 2019, paras 64–78.

[330] *Blue Bank v Venezuela*, Decision on the Parties' Proposals to Disqualify a Majority of the Tribunal, 12 November 2013, paras 59–60. Italics original. Footnotes omitted.

[331] *Caratube and Hourani v Kazakhstan*, Decision on the Proposal for Disqualification of Mr Bruno Boesch, 20 March 2014, paras 54–57; *İçkale v Turkmenistan*, Decision on Claimant's Proposal to Disqualify Prof Philippe Sands, 11 July 2014, para 117; *Interocean v Nigeria*, Decision on the Proposal to Disqualify All Members of the Tribunal, 3 October 2017, paras 68–69; *Kruck v Spain*, Decision on the Proposal to Disqualify Mr Gary B Born, 16 March 2018, para 50; *KS and TLS v Spain*, Decision on the Proposal to Disqualify Prof Gary Born, 30 April 2018, paras 39–45; *Vattenfall v Germany II*, Recommendation Pursuant to the Request by ICSID on the Respondent's Proposal to Disqualify All Members of the Arbitral Tribunal, 4 March 2019, paras 47–50; *PNB Banka v Latvia*, Decision on the Proposals to Disqualify Messrs James Spiegelman, Peter Tomka and John M Townsend, 16 June 2020, paras 152–160.

[332] IBA Guidelines on Conflicts of Interest in International Arbitration (adopted 23 October 2014).

are working on a Code of Conduct for Adjudicators in Investor–State Dispute Settlement. The Code of Conduct is intended to apply to all 'adjudicators' in investor–State cases, that is, arbitrators, members of annulment committees, members of an appeal mechanism, or judges on a bilateral or multilateral standing mechanism.[333] Once it will be finalized, the Code may become binding through incorporation into investment treaties and arbitral rules.

(d) Provisional measures

Under the ICSID Convention, the tribunal has the possibility to take provisional measures.[334] The purpose of provisional measures is to induce behaviour by the parties that is conducive to a successful conduct of the proceedings. Provisional measures must be taken at a time when the outcome of a dispute is still uncertain. In fact, provisional measures are often requested before the tribunal has made a decision on jurisdiction. Therefore, the tribunal must strike a balance between the urgency of a request for provisional measures and the need not to prejudge the case. Tribunals have held that they have the power to take provisional measures on the basis of their prima facie evaluation of jurisdiction and that this is without prejudice to a subsequent determination of jurisdiction.[335]

The guiding principles for the indication of provisional measures are necessity and urgency.[336] For instance, it may be necessary to induce the parties to cooperate in the proceedings and to furnish all relevant evidence; it may be necessary to take early measures to secure compliance with an eventual award; it may be necessary to stop the parties from resorting to self-help or seeking relief through other remedies; and it may be necessary to prevent a general aggravation of the situation through unilateral action.

The requirement of urgency means that provisional measures will only be appropriate if the question cannot await the outcome of the award on the merits. The

333 See Draft Code of Conduct for Adjudicators in Investor–State Dispute Settlement (1 May 2020).

334 ICSID Convention Article 47; Arbitration Rule 39. Under Arbitration Rule 39(6) provisional measures by domestic courts are possible in ICSID proceedings only in the unlikely case that the parties have so agreed in their consent agreement.

335 *Pey Casado v Chile*, Decision on Provisional Measures, 25 September 2001, paras 5–14; *SGS v Pakistan*, Procedural Order No 2, 16 October 2002, 8 ICSID Reports 388, at p 391/92; *Azurix v Argentina*, Decision on Provisional Measures, 6 August 2003, paras 29–31; *Biwater Gauff v Tanzania*, Procedural Order No 1, 31 March 2006, paras 32, 47, 70; *Occidental Petroleum v Ecuador*, Decision on Provisional Measures, 17 August 2007, para 55; *Perenco v Ecuador*, Decision on Provisional Measures, 8 May 2009 para 43; *Caratube and Hourani v Kazakhstan*, Decision on Provisional Measures, 4 December 2014, paras 107, 108.

336 *Saipem v Bangladesh*, Decision on Jurisdiction and Recommendation on Provisional Measures, 21 March 2007, paras 174, 182, 185; *Valle Verde v Venezuela*, Decision on Provisional Measures, 25 January 2016, para 86; *Interocean v Nigeria*, Procedural Order No 6, 1 February 2017, para 26.

Tribunal in *Azurix v Argentina* related the probability of prejudice to the requirement of urgency as follows:

> Given that the purpose of the measures is to preserve the rights of the parties, the urgency is related to the imminent possibility that the rights of a party be prejudiced before the tribunal has rendered its award.[337]

Parties to proceedings have requested provisional measures in various situations. In some cases, tribunals have used provisional measures to secure access to evidence that was essential to the case.[338] Another situation involved requests for orders to desist from action that would further aggravate the dispute.[339]

In other cases, parties have requested provisional measures directing a party to post financial guarantees to secure recovery of the cost of the proceedings. Initially, tribunals were reluctant to grant this remedy.[340] The first ICSID tribunal that ordered the payment of security for costs is the Tribunal in *RSM v St Lucia*.[341] Subsequent tribunals have confirmed their power to order security for cost[342] and, occasionally, have done so.[343]

The most important category of provisional measures involved requests to order the termination or suspension of related domestic proceedings.[344] In *SGS v*

[337] *Azurix v Argentina*, Decision on Provisional Measures, 6 August 2003, para 33. See also *Occidental Petroleum v Ecuador*, Decision on Provisional Measures, 17 August 2007, para 59.

[338] *AGIP v Congo*, Award, 30 November 1979, paras 7–9; *Vacuum Salt v Ghana*, Decision on Provisional Measures, 14 June 1993; Award, 16 February 1994, paras 13–22; *Biwater Gauff v Tanzania*, Procedural Order No 1, 31 March 2006, paras 16, 20, 45–46, 56, 77–81, 84–88; *Railroad Development v Guatemala*, Decision on Provisional Measures, 15 October 2008; *Fakes v Turkey*, Award, 14 July 2010, para 13.

[339] *Amco v Indonesia*, Decision on Provisional Measures, 9 December 1983; *CSOB v Slovakia*, Procedural Order No 3, 5 November 1998; *Pey Casado v Chile*, Decision on Provisional Measures, 25 September 2001, paras 67–74; *World Duty Free v Kenya*, Award, 4 October 2006, para 16; *EDF v Romania*, Procedural Order No. 2, 30 May 2008; *Burlington v Ecuador*, Procedural Order No 1, 29 June 2009, para 60; *Gabriel Resources v Romania*, Decision on Second Request for Provisional Measures, 22 November 2016, paras 68–70.

[340] *Maffezini v Spain*, Procedural Order No 2, 28 October 1999; *Pey Casado v Chile*, Decision on Provisional Measures, 25 September 2001, paras 78–89; *Bayindir v Pakistan*, Award, 27 August 2009, para 55; *Cementownia v Turkey*, Award, 17 September 2009, paras 34, 36; *Anderson v Costa Rica*, Award, 19 May 2010, para 9; *Hamester v Ghana*, Award, 18 June 2010, paras 15, 17.

[341] *RSM v St Lucia*, Decision on Security for Costs, 13 August 2014.

[342] *EuroGas v Slovakia*, Decision on Provisional Measures, 23 June 2015; *Transglobal v Panama*, Decision on Provisional Measures relating to Security for Costs, 21 January 2016; *Lighthouse v Timor-Leste*, Procedural Order No 2, 13 February 2016; *Interocean v Nigeria*, Procedural Order No 6, 1 February 2017.

[343] *Manuel García Armas v Venezuela*, Award on Jurisdiction, 13 December 2019, paras 91–126, 751; *Herzig v Turkmenistan*, Decision on Security for Costs, 27 January 2020. In *Adamakopoulos v Cyprus*, Decision on Jurisdiction, 7 February 2020, paras 264–266, 342 (iii), the Tribunal took the initiative to invite the respondent to make an application for security for costs.

[344] *MINE v Guinea*, Award, 6 January 1988, 4 ICSID Reports 61, at pp 69, 77; *Vacuum Salt v Ghana*, Decision on Provisional Measures, 14 June 1993; Award, 16 February 1994, paras 13–22; *CSOB v Slovakia*, Procedural Order No 2, 9 September 1998, Procedural Order No 3, 5 November 1998, Procedural Order No 4, 11 January 1999, Procedural Order No 5, 1 March 2000; *TANESCO v IPTL*, Award, 12 July 2001, paras 26, 29; *Pey Casado v Chile*, Decision on Provisional Measures, 25 September 2001, paras 28–66; *Azurix v Argentina*, Decision on Provisional Measures, 6 August 2003; *Tokios Tokelės*

Pakistan, the Supreme Court of Pakistan had granted a motion by the respondent that the claimant be permanently enjoined from taking any steps to participate in the ICSID proceedings. The claimant requested provisional measures from the ICSID tribunal. One request was to the effect that the respondent should immediately withdraw from all proceedings in the courts of Pakistan relating in any way to the ICSID arbitration and cause these proceedings to be discontinued.

The Tribunal noted that under Article 41 of the ICSID Convention the tribunal is the judge of its own competence. It pointed out that the Supreme Court judgment, although final under the law of Pakistan, did not bind the Tribunal as a matter of international law. The Tribunal said:

> The right to seek access to international adjudication must be respected and cannot be constrained by an order of a national court. Nor can a State plead its internal law in defence of an act that is inconsistent with its international obligations. Otherwise, a Contracting State could impede access to ICSID arbitration by operation of its own law.[345]

In addition, the Tribunal asked Pakistan to ensure that no action be taken in respect of contempt proceedings.

The wording and drafting history of the ICSID Convention would suggest that a decision for provisional measures under Article 47 is not binding but merely a recommendation.[346] In *Maffezini v Spain*, the Tribunal compared the word 'recommend', used in connection with provisional measures, to the word 'order' used elsewhere in the Arbitration Rules. It said:

> The Tribunal does not believe that the parties to the Convention meant to create a substantial difference in the effect of these two words. The Tribunal's authority to rule on provisional measures is no less binding than that of a final award.

v Ukraine, Decision on Jurisdiction, 29 April 2004, paras 11, 12; *Bayindir v Pakistan*, Decision on Jurisdiction, 14 November 2005, para 46; Award, 27 August 2009, paras 52–66, 487, 488; *Duke Energy v Peru*, Decision on Jurisdiction, 1 February 2006, paras 15–18; *Saipem v Bangladesh*, Decision on Jurisdiction, 21 March 2007, paras 162–185; *Plama v Bulgaria*, Award, 27 August 2008, paras 23–26; *Burlington v Ecuador*, Decision on Jurisdiction, 2 June 2010, paras 65–75; *Millicom v Senegal*, Decision on Jurisdiction, 16 July 2010, paras 29–31, 33–35, 37; *ATA v Jordan*, Decision on Interpretation, 7 March 2011, paras 10–12, 46; *Lao Holdings v Laos*, Decision on Provisional Measures, 17 September 2013, para 30, Ruling on Motion to Amend Provisional Measures Order, 30 May 2014, paras 1, 25, 26, 35; *Alghanim v Jordan*, Procedural Order No 2, 24 November 2014, paras 68, 94, 103; *Hydro v Albania*, Order on Provisional Measures, 3 March 2016; *Nova Group v Romania*, Procedural Order No 7, 29 March 2017, paras 226–365.

345 *SGS v Pakistan*, Procedural Order No 2, 16 October 2002.

346 Article 47: 'the Tribunal may ... recommend any provisional measures'. By contrast, under Article 41 of its Statute, the International Court of Justice may 'indicate' provisional measures. Under Article 290 of the United Nations Convention on the Law of the Sea the court or tribunal may 'prescribe' provisional measures.

> Accordingly, for the purposes of this Order, the Tribunal deems the word 'recommend' to be of equivalent value as the word 'order.'[347]

Tribunals have since followed *Maffezini* and have held that decisions on provisional measures are binding upon the parties.[348] Apart from the question of binding force, non-compliance with provisional measures will be taken into account by the tribunal when making the award.[349]

(e) Expedited procedure

Under ICSID Arbitration Rule 41(5), introduced in 2006, a party may within 30 days of the tribunal's constitution object that the claim is manifestly without merit:

> Unless the parties have agreed to another expedited procedure for making preliminary objections, a party may, no later than 30 days after the constitution of the Tribunal, and in any event before the first session of the Tribunal, file an objection that a claim is manifestly without legal merit. The party shall specify as precisely as possible the basis for the objection. The Tribunal, after giving the parties the opportunity to present their observations on the objection, shall, at its first session or promptly thereafter, notify the parties of its decision on the objection. The decision of the Tribunal shall be without prejudice to the right of a party to file an objection pursuant to paragraph (1) or to object, in the course of the proceeding, that a claim lacks legal merit.[350]

Arbitration Rule 41(5) gives the tribunal the possibility to dismiss an evidently unmeritorious case expeditiously and at an early stage. But it is possible that a tribunal

[347] *Maffezini v Spain*, Procedural Order No 2, 28 October 1999, para 9.

[348] *Pey Casado v Chile*, Decision on Provisional Measures, 25 September 2001, paras 17–23; *Tokios Tokelės v Ukraine*, Procedural Order No. 1, 1 July 2003, para 4; *Biwater Gauff v Tanzania*, Procedural Order No. 1, 31 March 2006, paras 87–88, 97–98, 104–106; *Occidental Petroleum v Ecuador*, Decision on Provisional Measures, 17 August 2007, para 58; *Perenco v Ecuador*, Decision on Provisional Measures, 8 May 2009, paras 67–76; *Tethyan Copper v Pakistan*, Decision on Provisional Measures, 13 December 2012, para 120; *PNG Sustainable Development v Papua New Guinea*, Decision on Provisional Measures, 21 January 2015, para 102; *United Utilities v Estonia*, Decision on Provisional Measures, 12 May 2016, para 109; *RSM v St Lucia*, Decision on Annulment, 29 April 2019, paras 170–176. But see: *Caratube v Kazakhstan*, Decision on Provisional Measures, 31 July 2009, paras 67, 72.

[349] *AGIP v Congo*, Award, 30 November 1979, para 42; *Quiborax v Bolivia*, Award, 16 September 2015, paras 576–583.

[350] The Arbitration (Additional Facility) Rules offer a parallel provision in Article 45(6). Some investment protection treaties offer their own expedited procedures: DR-CAFTA, 5 August 2004, Arts. 10.20.4 and 10.20.5; CPTPP, 8 March 2018, Article 9.23.4; CETA, 30 October 2016, provisionally applied since 21 September 2017, [2017] OJ L 11/23, Article 8.23; EU–Vietnam Investment Protection Agreement, adopted 17 October 2018, not yet in force, chapter 3, section B, sub-section 5, Article 3.44; EU–Mexico Global Agreement (text as of April 2018) Article 17.

disposes of one of several claims by way of a summary decision under Arbitration Rule 41(5), while proceeding with other claims.[351]

The procedure under this provision is considerably accelerated. The summary procedure must be initiated within 30 days of the tribunal's constitution and before its first session. The tribunal's decision is to be made at its first session or promptly thereafter. The tribunal must, however, give the parties the opportunity to present their observations on the objection.

For an objection under Rule 41(5) to be successful the lack of merit must be manifest. The Tribunal in *Trans-Global v Jordan* found that the ordinary meaning of the word 'manifestly' required the respondent to 'establish its objection clearly and obviously, with relative ease and despatch'.[352]

The Secretary-General's screening power before registering a request for arbitration under Article 36(3) is restricted to jurisdiction and does not extend to the merits. The summary procedure under Rule 41(5) fills this gap but is not limited to challenges on the merits. It can also be used to dispute jurisdiction. The Tribunal in *Brandes v Venezuela* said:

> There exist no objective reasons why the intent not to burden the parties with a possibly long and costly proceeding when dealing with such unmeritorious claims should be limited to an evaluation of the merits of the case and should not also englobe an examination of the jurisdictional basis on which the tribunal's powers to decide the case rest.[353]

Other tribunals have followed *Brandes* on this point.[354] At the same time, there appears to be agreement that the objection must be based on a question of law and not of fact.[355]

[351] *Trans-Global v Jordan*, Decision on Respondent's Objection under Rule 41(5), 12 May 2008 (Partial); *Accession Mezzanine v Hungary*, Decision on Respondent's Objections under ICSID Arbitration Rule 41(5), 16 January 2013 (Partial); *Emmis v Hungary*, Decision on Respondent's Objections Under ICSID Arbitration Rule 41(5), 11 March 2013 (Partial).

[352] *Trans-Global v Jordan*, Decision under Arbitration Rule 41(5), 12 May 2008, para 88; *Brandes v Venezuela*, Decision on the Respondent's Objection Under Rule 41(5), 2 February 2009, para 63; *Global Trading v Ukraine*, Award, 1 December 2010, para 35; *RSM v Grenada II*, Award, 10 December 2010, para 6.1.2; *PNG Sustainable Development v Papua New Guinea*, Decision on the Respondent's Objections Under Rule 41(5), 28 October 2014, para 89; *MOL v Croatia*, Decision on Respondent's Application Under ICSID Arbitration Rule 41(5), 2 December 2014, para 45; *Álvarez v Panama*, Decision on Respondent's Preliminary Objections pursuant to Rule 41(5), 4 April 2016, para 80; *Lion v Mexico*, Decision on the Respondent's Preliminary Objections under Article 45(6) of the ICSID Arbitration Additional Facility Rules, 12 December 2016, para 67; *Ansung Housing v China*, Award, 9 March 2017, para 70.

[353] *Brandes v Venezuela*, Decision under Arbitration Rule 41(5), 2 February 2009, para 52.

[354] *Global Trading v Ukraine*, Award, 1 December 2010, paras 30–31; *RSM v Grenada*, Award, 10 December 2010, para 6.1.1; *Elsamex v Honduras*, Decision on Claimant's Preliminary Objection on Annulment, 7 January 2014, paras 93–96; *PNG Sustainable Development v Papua New Guinea*, Decision on the Respondent's Objections Under Rule 41(5), 28 October 2014, para 91; *Lion v Mexico*, Decision on the Respondent's Preliminary Objections under Article 45(6) of the ICSID Arbitration Additional Facility Rules, 12 December 2016, para 75; *Almasryia v Kuwait*, Award on the Respondent's Application under Rule 41(5), 1 November 2019, para 48.

[355] *Trans-Global v Jordan*, Decision under Arbitration Rule 41(5), 12 May 2008, para 97; *Brandes v Venezuela*, Decision under Arbitration Rule 41(5), 2 February 2009, paras 56–61; *Global Trading*

In *Global Trading v Ukraine*, the Tribunal found that the activities underlying the dispute 'are pure commercial transactions that cannot on any interpretation be considered to constitute "investments" within the meaning of Article 25 of the ICSID Convention'.[356] It therefore held that the claims put forward were manifestly without legal merit under Rule 41(5) and rendered an award to this effect.

Despite its summary nature the expedited procedure requires that both parties be properly heard both in writing and orally. A decision upholding an objection results in an award which, under Article 48(3) of the ICSID Convention, must deal with every question submitted to the tribunal and must contain a full statement of reasons.

(f) Written and oral procedure

Procedural questions are typically addressed at the tribunal's first session with the parties. The questions include representation of the parties, the place and language of proceedings, the number and sequence of the pleadings, a calendar with time limits for the submission of pleadings and the date of hearings, records of hearings, and production of evidence. Most awards contain a detailed description of the procedure.

Most proceedings involve a written phase followed by an oral one.[357] The written procedure consists of the request for arbitration and communications relating to it as well as of the parties' pleadings. The pleadings are opened by a memorial of the claimant followed by a counter-memorial of the respondent. In most cases there is another round of written exchanges termed reply and rejoinder. A memorial must contain a statement of the facts, a statement of the law and the party's submissions. A counter-memorial also must address the facts and legal arguments and make submissions.[358] A submission is a suggestion to the tribunal that it take a particular decision. In addition, the parties often submit voluminous supporting documentation. Pleadings should relate closely to the other party's last previous pleading.

An objection by respondent to the tribunal's jurisdiction, is to be submitted not later than at the time the counter-memorial is due. Upon receiving an objection to jurisdiction, the tribunal may decide to suspend the proceedings on the merits. The proceedings are then bifurcated, that is, the jurisdictional question is heard

v Ukraine, Award, 1 December 2010, para 31; *RSM v Grenada II*, Award, 10 December 2010, para 6.1.1; *MOL v Croatia*, Decision on Respondent's Application Under ICSID Arbitration Rule 41(5), 2 December 2014, para 44.

356 *Global Trading v Ukraine*, Award, 1 December 2010, para 57.
357 Exceptionally, the parties may dispense with a hearing if they so agree.
358 ICSID Arbitration Rule 31.

first, followed, if the tribunal finds that it has jurisdiction, by a resumption of the proceedings on the merits. Alternatively, the tribunal may decide to join the jurisdictional question to the merits.[359]

In making decisions on whether or not to bifurcate, tribunals have considered whether the jurisdictional objection is substantial, whether the objection to jurisdiction if granted results in a material reduction of the proceedings at the next phase, and whether the jurisdictional issue is closely intertwined with the merits.[360]

If the tribunal decides that the dispute is not within the jurisdiction of the Centre or outside its competence, or that all claims are manifestly without legal merit, it will render an award to that effect[361] and the proceedings are closed. Otherwise, the tribunal will resume the proceedings on the merits.

The oral phase consists of a hearing in the presence of the tribunal, its officers, and the parties and their representatives. In addition to the parties, the tribunal may hear witnesses and experts. It is important that the parties be given full and equal opportunity to be heard. Most hearings are closed to the public.[362] Portions of hearings, or entire hearings, may be conducted online, using video-conferencing technology. It has become standard practice for tribunals to permit the filing of post-hearing submissions.

The two phases of the procedure, written and oral, also apply to incidental or subsidiary parts of the proceedings. These are proceedings relating to objections to jurisdiction, to provisional measures, to ancillary claims, to reopened proceedings, to supplementation and rectification, to interpretation, to revision, and to annulment.

The evidence presented by the parties to the tribunal consists of documents, witness testimony, and expert opinions.[363] The tribunal has discretion in deciding on the relevance,[364] credibility,[365] and admissibility[366] of evidence. The tribunal may call upon the parties to produce further evidence.[367] In some cases, tribunals have issued orders for the production of documents, normally upon the request of a

[359] ICSID Convention Article 41; Arbitration Rule 41.

[360] *Glamis Gold v United States*, Procedural Order No 2 (Revised), 31 May 2005, para 12(c); *Standard Chartered Bank v TANESCO*, Procedural Order No 5, 29 May 2012, paras 19–23; *Emmis v Hungary*, Decision on Bifurcation, 13 June 2013, paras 47–56; *Gavrilović v Croatia*, Decision on Bifurcation, 21 January 2015, para 93; *Global Telecom v Canada*, Procedural Order No 2: Decision on Bifurcation, 14 December 2017, paras 102–107; *Eco Oro v Colombia*, Procedural Order No 2, 28 June 2018, paras 52–60.

[361] ICSID Arbitration Rule 41(6).

[362] On transparency see XII.11(j) below.

[363] ICSID Arbitration Rules 33–35.

[364] *Aguas del Tunari v Bolivia*, Decision on Jurisdiction, 21 October 2005, para 25.

[365] See *ADC v Hungary*, Award, 2 October 2006, paras 250–257; *Fraport v Philippines I*, Award, 16 August 2007, paras 328–329; *Rumeli v Kazakhstan*, Award, 29 July 2008, paras 442–448; *Rompetrol v Romania*, Award, 6 May 2013, paras 221–224, 243–244.

[366] *Methanex v United States*, Award, 3 August 2005, II, I, paras 1–60; *EDF v Romania*, Procedural Order No 3, 29 August 2008, para 38; *Rompetrol v Romania*, Award, 6 May 2013, para 181.

[367] ICSID Convention Article 43(a).

party, but occasionally also upon their own initiative.[368] The tribunals have developed criteria for the materiality, relevance and specificity of evidence.[369]

(g) Default

Default—that is, non-participation of an uncooperative party—will not stall the proceedings. If one party fails to present its case, the other party may request the tribunal to proceed and render an award. Before doing so, the tribunal will give the non-appearing party another chance to cooperate. The appearing party's assertions will not be accepted just because the other party does not cooperate and hence does not contest them. Rather, the tribunal must examine all questions and decide whether the appearing party's submissions are well-founded in fact and in law.[370]

Default by a party puts an extra burden on the tribunal but also on the cooperating party. The tribunal must examine the cooperating party's submissions on its own motion. The cooperating party may be called upon to prove assertions which might otherwise be accepted as uncontested. Default has only occurred in relatively few cases.[371] In some cases, the respondent States did not cooperate initially but appeared at a later stage of the proceedings.[372]

(h) Settlement and discontinuance

The parties may at any time agree to settle or otherwise discontinue the case. A settlement may be incorporated into an award if the parties so request and

368 *Fraport v Philippines I*, Award, 16 August 2007, paras 383, 400, 401; *Metal-Tech v Uzbekistan*, Award, 4 October 2013, paras 240–241.

369 *Pope & Talbot v Canada*, Ruling on Claim of Crown Privilege, 6 September 2000, 7 ICSID Reports 99; *UPS v Canada*, Tribunal Decision Relating to Canada's Claim of Cabinet Privilege, 8 October 2004; *CSOB v Slovakia*, Award, 29 December 2004, para 9; *Noble Ventures v Romania*, Award, 12 October 2005, paras 19–20; *Aguas del Tunari v Bolivia*, Decision on Jurisdiction, 21 October 2005, paras 24–28, 324–327; *Duke Energy v Peru*, Decision on Jurisdiction, 1 February 2006, para 19; *Biwater Gauff v Tanzania*, Procedural Order N° 2, 24 May 2006; *Azurix v Argentina*, Award, 14 July 2006, paras 22–27, 29, 31; *ADC v Hungary*, Award, 2 October 2006, paras 30, 33–37; *Champion Trading v Egypt*, Decision on Jurisdiction, 21 October 2003, paras 15, 17–23; *Bayindir v Pakistan*, Procedural Order No 4, Document Production, 27 November 2006; *Venezuela Holdings v Venezuela*, Decision on Annulment, 9 March 2017, para 127.

370 ICSID Convention Article 45; Arbitration Rules 34(3), 42.

371 *Kaiser Bauxite v Jamaica*, Decision on Jurisdiction and Competence, 6 July 1975, 1 ICSID Reports 299, paras 5–10; *LETCO v Liberia*, Award, 31 March 1986, 2 ICSID Reports 346, at pp 354–357; *Goetz v Burundi*, Decision, 2 September 1998, 6 ICSID Reports 5, paras 33–57.

372 *Benvenuti & Bonfant v Congo*, Award, 8 August 1980, 1 ICSID Reports 335, paras 1.7–1.12, 1.17–1.34; *AMT v Zaire*, Award, 21 February 1997, (1997) 36 ILM 1536, 5 ICSID Reports 14, paras 2.01–3.01.

submit their settlement in writing.[373] The ICSID Convention's provisions on recognition and enforcement of awards are applicable to such an award.

Alternatively, a party may unilaterally request a discontinuance of the proceedings, which the tribunal will grant if the other party does not object.[374] Discontinuance need not relate to the entire case but may concern certain claims only.[375] A partial discontinuance also occurs where one or several of the original claimants withdraw from the case.[376]

In addition, the proceedings will be discontinued if both parties fail to take any steps during six consecutive months.[377] Proceedings will also be discontinued in case of non-payment of the advances to ICSID to cover the costs of proceedings.[378]

A high percentage of cases are settled or otherwise discontinued at some stage of the proceedings.

(i) The award

After the pleadings of the parties are completed, the tribunal deliberates on the award. Only the members of the tribunal take part in the deliberations and their substance remains secret.[379]

Awards are rendered in writing and are signed by the members of the tribunal. Most awards are rendered unanimously, but majority decisions are possible.[380] A member of the tribunal may attach a dissenting opinion or a declaration.

An award must deal with every question submitted to the tribunal and contain a full statement of reasons. Under the ICSID Convention an award finally disposes of all questions before the tribunal. A failure to deal with all questions or serious

[373] ICSID Arbitration Rule 43. See *Trans-Global v Jordan*, Consent Award, 8 April 2009; *TCW v Dominican Republic*, Consent Award, 16 July 2009; *Azpetrol v Azerbaijan*, Award, 9 September 2009, paras 67–105; *Vattenfall v Germany I*, Award, 11 March 2011; *Saint-Gobain v Venezuela*, Award, 3 November 2017, para 52.

[374] ICSID Arbitration Rule 44. *Foresti v South Africa*, Award, 4 August 2010, paras 79–82.

[375] *Burlington v Ecuador*, Decision on Liability, 14 December 2012, para 93.

[376] *Suez and Vivendi v Argentina*, Decision on Liability, 30 July 2010, paras 14–16; *Suez and InterAgua v Argentina*, Decision on Liability, 30 July 2010, paras 16–19; *Abaclat v Argentina*, Decision on Jurisdiction and Admissibility, 4 August 2011, paras 613–639; *Ambiente Ufficio v Argentina*, Decision on Jurisdiction and Admissibility, 8 February 2013, paras 334–346; *Alemanni v Argentina*, Decision on Jurisdiction and Admissibility, 17 November 2014, paras 14–26, 327–337.

[377] ICSID Arbitration Rule 45. *Mobil & Murphy v Canada*, Decision on Liability and on Principles of Quantum, 22 May 2012, paras 9–11.

[378] ICSID Administrative and Financial Regulation 14(3)(d). *Quadrant Pacific v Costa Rica*, Order taking note of Discontinuance, 27 October 2010; *RSM v Grenada I*, Order of the Committee Discontinuing the Proceeding and Decision on Costs, 28 April 2011; *Commerce Group v El Salvador*, Order of the Committee Discontinuing the Proceeding and Decision on Costs, 28 Aug 2013; *Ambiente Ufficio v Argentina*, Order of Discontinuance of the Proceeding, 28 May 2015.

[379] ICSID Arbitration Rule 15.

[380] ICSID Arbitration Rule 16(1) provides that all decisions of the tribunal may be rendered by majority vote.

shortcomings in the reasoning may lead to a charge of excess of powers or failure to state the reasons, both of which are grounds for annulment.[381]

The award is dispatched promptly to the parties. The date of the award is not the date of signature by the arbitrators but the date of dispatch to the parties.[383] This is important for the exact determination of the time limits for any post-award remedies.[384]

Sometimes tribunals issue decisions on jurisdiction and liability leaving the determination of the quantum of damages for a subsequent decision. If this is the case, the last decision is the award which incorporates the earlier decisions by reference.[382]

Awards are final and binding. They are subject to review only under limited circumstances.[385] The binding force of awards is limited to the parties. It does not extend to other cases before different tribunals and does not create binding precedents. Tribunals have emphasized on many occasions that they are not bound by previous decisions. At the same time, they have also stated that they will take due account of previous cases when making their own decisions.[386] In actual fact, parties routinely rely on earlier decisions of other international tribunals and of international courts. Tribunals frequently refer to and rely on earlier decisions.

(j) Transparency

Confidentiality is traditionally considered one of the major advantages of commercial arbitration between private parties. Arbitration rules, other than ICSID, sometimes provide specifically that awards may not be published without the parties' consent.[387] But in investment arbitration, the presence of issues of public interest has led to demands for openness and transparency.

The Secretary-General of ICSID is under an obligation to publish information about the existence and progress of pending cases.[388] This is achieved primarily through the Centre's website.

Most hearings are closed to the public. In principle, only the members of the tribunal, officers of the tribunal, the parties and their representatives, and witnesses while giving testimony may attend. The tribunal may, unless a party objects and after consultation with the Secretary-General of ICSID, allow other persons

[381] See XII.15(b)bb and XII.15(b)ee below.
[382] *Lemire v Ukraine*, Decision on Annulment, 8 July 2013, para 196.
[383] ICSID Convention Article 49(1).
[384] See XII.15(b) below.
[385] See XII.15 below.
[386] See II.1(e) above.
[387] See UNCITRAL Arbitration Rules 2010, Article 34(5).
[388] ICSID Administrative and Financial Regulations 22 and 23.

to attend all or part of the hearings.[389] Some investment treaties provide that investor–State arbitration hearings shall be open to the public. In some cases, the parties agree to the streaming of a hearing.

Awards are not published automatically. ICSID will publish awards only with the consent of both parties.[390] Since 2006 ICSID is under an obligation to publish excerpts of the legal reasoning of each award.[391] The parties are free to release awards and other decisions for publication unless it is otherwise agreed. Most ICSID awards have been published in one way or another but there are some awards and other decisions that have remained unpublished. Non-ICSID awards are published sporadically. Some awards are published in redacted form, that is, portions of the text and footnotes are deleted.[392]

The parties are not prohibited from publishing their pleadings and other documents relating to pending arbitration proceedings. But they may come to an understanding to refrain from doing so.[393] The parties are also free to agree on a total or partial publication of documents relating to a proceeding.[394]

The 2014 UNCITRAL Rules on Transparency in Treaty-based Investor–State Arbitration[395] require the publication of party submissions as well as decisions and awards of the tribunal in UNCITRAL proceedings pursuant to treaties concluded on or after 1 April 2014.[396] The United Nations Convention on Transparency in Treaty-based Investor–State Arbitration of 2014 (the Mauritius Convention)[397] extends the scope of application of the UNCITRAL Transparency Rules to all investor–State arbitrations arising under treaties between Mauritius Convention-contracting States concluded prior to 1 April 2014, irrespective of the applicable arbitration rules. Recent investment arbitration agreements incorporate the UNCITRAL Transparency Rules, either by expressly stating that they shall apply, or by including transparency-related provisions modelled on these Rules.

389 ICSID Arbitration Rule 32.

390 ICSID Convention Article 48(5).

391 ICSID Arbitration Rule 48(4).

392 *Fireman's Fund v Mexico*, Award, 17 July 2006, paras 222–225; *Marfin v Cyprus*, Award, 26 July 2018.

393 For detailed discussion see *Biwater Gauff v Tanzania*, Procedural Order No. 3, 29 September 2006 and Procedural Order No. 5, 2 February 2007. See also *World Duty Free v Kenya*, Award, 4 October 2006, para 16; *Ipek v Turkey*, Procedural Order No 13, 13 March 2020.

394 See *Malaysian Historical Salvors v Malaysia*, Award, 17 May 2007, para 32; *BSG Resources v Guinea*, Procedural Order No 2, 17 September 2015.

395 Adopted by United Nations General Assembly Resolution 68/109 on 16 December 2013.

396 UNCITRAL Transparency Rules Article 3(1).

397 In force 18 October 2017. By 1 September 2021, the Mauritius Convention had been ratified by nine States: Australia, Benin, Bolivia, Cameroon, Canada, Gambia, Iraq, Mauritius, and Switzerland.

(k) *Amicus curiae* participation

In some cases, ICSID tribunals have permitted the submission of *amicus curiae* briefs by non-disputing parties.[398] Under a procedure introduced in 2006, an ICSID tribunal may, after consulting the parties, allow an entity that is not a party, to file a written submission regarding a matter within the scope of the dispute.[399] Tribunals have allowed applications for *amicus curiae* interventions in some cases[400] and rejected them in other cases.[401]

The EU Commission has applied for permission to make submissions as a non-disputing party in numerous proceedings involving BITs between Member States and the ECT, both before[402] and after[403] the European Court's judgment in *Achmea*.[404] In many of these cases, tribunals allowed the Commission's *amicus curiae* submissions.[405] In other cases, tribunals denied permission.[406] In some of these, the tribunals had required an undertaking to guarantee the resulting additional costs which the EU Commission declined to give.[407]

Non-ICSID tribunals operating in the framework of NAFTA under the UNCITRAL Rules, have at times allowed third parties to make written submissions.[408] In October 2003 the NAFTA Free Trade Commission issued a statement regarding the participation of non-disputing parties.[409]

The UNCITRAL Transparency Rules foresee *amicus curiae* participation as well as the participation of a non-disputing State that is a party to the relevant treaty. They provide that the tribunal may permit 'a person that is not a disputing party, and not a non-disputing Party to the treaty ... to file a written submission with the arbitral tribunal regarding a matter within the scope of the dispute'.[410] They

398 *Suez and Vivendi v Argentina*, Order in Response to a Petition for Transparency and Participation as *Amicus Curiae*, 19 May 2005; *Methanex v United States*, Award, 3 August 2005, II, C, paras 26–30; *Aguas del Tunari v Bolivia*, Decision on Jurisdiction, 21 October 2005, paras 15–18, Appendix III; *Aguas Provinciales v Argentina*, Order in Response to a Petition for Participation as *Amicus Curiae*, 17 March 2006.

399 ICSID Arbitration Rule 37(2).

400 *Biwater Gauff v Tanzania*, Award, 24 July 2008, paras 356–392.

401 *von Pezold v Zimbabwe*, Procedural Order No 2, 26 June 2012. The Tribunal rejected an application for intervention as *amicus curiae* for lack of the applicants' independence and lack of relevance of the proposed testimony.

402 *Micula v Romania I*, Award, 11 December 2013, paras 23, 25, 27–30.

403 *Magyar Farming v Hungary*, Award, 13 November 2019.

404 *Slovakia v Achmea*, Judgment, 6 March 2018, Case C-284/16. See XII.7(c) and (e) above.

405 *Adamakopoulos v Cyprus*, Decision on Jurisdiction, 7 February 2020, paras 28, 40, 42–44, 139–149.

406 *BayWa v Spain*, Decision on Jurisdiction, Liability and Directions on Quantum, 2 December 2019, paras 16–18, 30–31, 52–54.

407 *Watkins v Spain*, Award, 21 January 2020, paras 30–40.

408 *Methanex v United States*, Decision on *Amici Curiae*, 15 January 2001; *UPS v Canada*, Decision of the Tribunal on Petitions for Intervention and Participation as *Amici Curiae*, 17 October 2001.

409 NAFTA Free Trade Commission Statement on Non-Disputing Party Participation, 7 October 2003, (2005) 44 ILM 796.

410 UNCITRAL Transparency Rules Article 4.

also provide for the possibility that a non-disputing State that is a party to the treaty under which the claim is brought makes a submission.[411] The Mauritius Convention extends the application of these provisions to claims brought under investment treaties that pre-date 1 April 2014.

12. Applicable law

Foreign investments are subject to international as well as national rules. There is a considerable body of substantive international law protecting foreign investors.[412] It consists of treaty law, contained mostly in BITs, but also multilateral treaties such as the ECT. But there is also a good deal of customary international law that remains relevant. This customary international law includes various aspects of State responsibility and such issues as denial of justice, the law on expropriation, and rules relating to the nationality of individuals and corporations.

Investments typically are complex operations involving numerous transactions of different kinds. Many of these transactions will take place under the local law. These transactions will have their closest connection to the host State's law. The relevant legislation relates to commercial law, company law, administrative law, labour law, tax law, foreign exchange regulations, real estate law, and many other areas of the host State's legal system. At the same time, the application of international law gives the investor assurance that the international standards for the treatment of foreign investors will be observed.

(a) Choice of law

The parties to the dispute, that is the host State and the investor, may agree on the governing law.[413] Some contracts governing investments simply refer to the host State's domestic law.[414] The choice of the law of the investor's home country or of the law of a third State is rare but not unheard of.[415] In the majority of cases, clauses

[411] UNCITRAL Transparency Rules Article 5.

[412] See also I.2 above.

[413] See also V.2 above.

[414] *Attorney-General v Mobil Oil NZ Ltd.*, New Zealand, High Court, 1 July 1987, 4 ICSID Reports 117, p 123; *MINE v Guinea*, Decision on Annulment, 22 December 1989, para 6.31; *Perenco v Ecuador*, Decision on Remaining Issues of Jurisdiction and on Liability, 12 September 2014, para 318.

[415] *SPP v Egypt*, Award, 20 May 1992, para 225 (The choice of English law to the exclusion of Egyptian law turned out to be decisive for the computation of interest); *CDC v Seychelles*, Award, 17 December 2003, para 43; *World Duty Free v Kenya*, Award, 4 October 2006, paras 158–159; *Azpetrol v Azerbaijan*, Award, 8 September 2009, paras 49–65.

on applicable law in contracts between States and foreign investors include international law as well as host State law.[416]

Some treaties and other international documents providing for arbitration refer to the parties' agreement on choice of law.[417] Some of the relevant treaties contain their own choice of law clauses in case there is no agreement on applicable law between the parties. Article 42 of the ICSID Convention refers primarily to any agreement on choice of law that the parties may have reached. In the absence of such an agreement, it provides for the application of the host State's law and international law:

> Article 42
> (1) The Tribunal shall decide a dispute in accordance with such rules of law as may be agreed by the parties. In the absence of such agreement, the Tribunal shall apply the law of the Contracting State party to the dispute (including its rules on the conflict of laws) and such rules of international law as may be applicable.

The Arbitration Rules of the ICSID Additional Facility provide in Article 54 that a tribunal shall apply the rules of law designated by the parties. In the absence of a designation, the tribunal shall apply the law determined by the conflict of laws rules which it considers applicable and such rules of international law as the tribunal considers applicable. The UNCITRAL Rules (Article 35(1)) and the ICC Rules (Article 21(1)) state that a tribunal will apply the law designated by the parties. If there is no choice of law clause, the UNCITRAL Rules refer to 'the law which it determines to be appropriate' and to 'any usage of trade applicable to the transaction' which the tribunal shall take into account (Article 35 (3)). For ICC proceedings, its Rules provide in such a case that the tribunal 'shall apply the rules of law which it determines to be appropriate' (Article 21(1)) and that the tribunal 'shall take account of the provisions of the contract, if any, between the parties and of any relevant trade usages' (Article 21(2)).

Many treaty provisions that offer investor–State arbitration, such as the ECT and some BITs, also contain provisions on applicable law. By taking up the offer of arbitration, the investor also accepts the choice of law clause contained in the treaty's dispute settlement provision. In this way the treaty's provision on applicable law becomes part of the arbitration agreement between the host State and the foreign

[416] See already the Deeds of Concession concluded between Libya and two American companies between 1955 and 1968 in *Texaco v Libya*, Award, 19 January 1977, 53 ILR 389, 404. See also *LIAMCO v Libya*, Award, 12 April 1977, 62 ILR 141, 172; *British Petroleum v Libya*, Award (Merits), 10 October 1973, 53 ILR 297, 303; *AGIP v Congo*, Award, 30 November 1979, para 18; *Kaiser Bauxite v Jamaica*, Decision on Jurisdiction and Competence, 6 July 1975, para 12; *CSOB v Slovakia*, Award, 29 December 2004, paras 58–63; *Duke Energy v Ecuador*, Award, 18 August 2008, paras 190–197.

[417] Article 42 ICSID Convention; Article 54 of the ICSID Additional Facility Rules; Article 35 of the UNCITRAL Arbitration Rules.

investor. In other words, the clause on applicable law in the treaty becomes a choice of law agreed by the parties to the arbitration.[418]

Some clauses in treaties governing the applicable law in investment disputes refer exclusively to international law.[419] For instance, the ECT provides:

> Article 26 Settlement of disputes between an investor and a Contracting Party
> (6) A tribunal established under paragraph (4) shall decide the issues in dispute in accordance with this Treaty and applicable rules and principles of international law.

Similarly, some BITs refer to international law including the substantive rules of the BIT itself.[420]

Other provisions on applicable law in BITs, combine the host State's domestic law with international law. A frequently used formula lists (a) the host State's law, (b) the BIT itself as well as other treaties, (c) any contract relating to the investment, and (d) general international law. In *Goetz v Burundi*[421] the relevant Belgium–Burundi BIT contained a provision on applicable law of this type. The Tribunal found that it had to apply a combination of domestic law and international law. The Tribunal made the following general statement:

> a complementary relationship must be allowed to prevail. That the Tribunal must apply Burundian law is beyond doubt, since this last is also cited in the first place by the relevant provision of the Belgium–Burundi investment treaty. As regards international law, its application is obligatory for two reasons. First, because, according to the indications furnished to the Tribunal by the claimants, Burundian law seems to incorporate international law and thus to render it directly applicable; ... Furthermore, because the Republic of Burundi is bound by the international law obligations which it freely assumed under the Treaty for the protection of investments ....[422]

The Tribunal then stated that an application of international law and of domestic law might lead to different results. The Tribunal first undertook an analysis of the dispute from the perspective of the law of Burundi. This analysis led to the conclusion that under the law of Burundi the actions in question were legal. The Tribunal then examined the same issue from the perspective of international law,

[418] *Goetz v Burundi*, Award, 10 February 1999, para 94; *Siemens v Argentina*, Award, 6 February 2007, para 76; *Suez and Vivendi v Argentina*, Decision on Liability, 30 July 2010, paras 59–63; *EDF v Argentina*, Award, 11 June 2012, para 181; *Gold Reserve v Venezuela*, Award, 22 September 2014, para 533; *Rusoro v Venezuela*, Award, 22 August 2016, paras 347–349.

[419] NAFTA Article 1131.

[420] *Kardassopoulos v Georgia*, Decision on Jurisdiction, 6 July 2007, para 146.

[421] *Goetz v Burundi*, Award, 10 February 1999.

[422] At paras 95, 98.

in particular in light of the BIT. This examination led to the result that the legality of the measures taken by Burundi depended on the payment of an adequate and effective compensation which was still outstanding.[423]

In the absence of a choice of law expressed in the document providing for consent, the tribunals have sometimes perceived an agreement on the applicable law in the pleadings before them.[424] In *AAPL v Sri Lanka*, jurisdiction was based on the BIT between Sri Lanka and the United Kingdom. This BIT did not contain a provision on applicable law. The Tribunal found that by arguing their case on the basis of the BIT, the parties had expressed their choice of the BIT as the applicable law.[425] The Tribunal went on to state that the BIT was not a closed legal system but had to be seen in a wider juridical context. This wider juridical context as well as the parties' submissions led it to apply customary international law as well as domestic law.[426]

Other tribunals too have held that the choice of a BIT implied a choice of international law in general.[427]

Some tribunals have found that in cases involving disputes under BITs not containing a choice of law clause, the primary source of law had to be the BIT itself and other rules of international law.[428] In *Addiko v Croatia*, the Tribunal held that an investor implicitly consents to the applicable law in case of investment treaty arbitration. It believed that the acceptance of the offer to arbitrate in the BIT would also implicitly bring about a choice of the treaty and international law as applicable law, even in the absence of an explicit choice of law clause.[429]

In other cases, tribunals did not accept an implicit choice of law through reliance on a BIT that does not contain an applicable law clause. Rather, they found that they had to turn to the default provision in Article 42(1) of the ICSID Convention and apply host State law as well as applicable rules of international law.[430]

[423] At paras 100–133.

[424] *Gardella v Côte d'Ivoire*, Award, 29 August 1977, para 4.3.; *SOABI v Senegal*, Award, 25 February 1988, para 5.02.; *Wena Hotels v Egypt*, Award, 8 December 2000, para 79.

[425] *AAPL v Sri Lanka*, Final Award, 27 June 1990, para 20.

[426] At paras 18–24.

[427] *Middle East Cement v Egypt*, Award, 12 April 2002, paras 86–87; *MTD v Chile*, Award, 25 May 2004, paras 87, 112, 204; *CSOB v Slovakia*, Award, 29 December 2004, paras 61–63.

[428] *Wena Hotels v Egypt*, Award, 8 December 2000, paras 78–79; *MTD v Chile*, Award, 25 May 2004, paras 87, 112, 204; *ADC v Hungary*, Award, 2 October 2006, paras 288–291; *LG&E v Argentina*, Decision on Liability, 3 October 2006, paras 85, 97–98; *Saipem v Bangladesh*, Award, 30 June 2009, para 99; *Bayindir v Pakistan*, Award, 27 August 2009, paras 109–110; *Azurix v Argentina*, Decision on Annulment, 1 September 2009, paras 146–147; *Alpha v Ukraine*, Award, 8 November 2010, paras 228–233.

[429] *Addiko v Croatia*, Decision on Croatia's Jurisdictional Objection Related to the Alleged Incompatibility of the BIT with the EU Acquis, 12 June 2020, para 260.

[430] *LG&E v Argentina*, Decision on Liability, 3 October 2006, para 85; *MCI v Ecuador*, Award, 31 July 2007, paras 214–217; *Metal-Tech v Uzbekistan*, Award, 4 October 2013, para 119; *Perenco v Ecuador*, Decision on Remaining Issues of Jurisdiction and on Liability, 12 September 2014, paras 532–534; *Quiborax v Bolivia*, Award, 16 September 2015, paras 90–91; *E energija v Latvia*, Award, 22 December 2017, para 792; *Gosling v Mauritius*, Award, 18 February 2020, para 88.

The Tribunal in *Magyar Farming v Hungary*, rejected claimant's assertion that, in the absence of an explicit choice of law, only international law would apply to the merits since the claims were based on the BIT:

> ICSID jurisprudence supports the approach that, when the disputing parties have made no express choice-of-law, such choice cannot be implied from the mere fact that the claims arise under an international treaty... Therefore, in the absence of a choice-of-law provision in the BIT, or elsewhere for that matter, the default rule of the second sentence of Article 42(1) of the ICSID Convention applies.[431]

(b) Host State law and international law

In most cases the applicable substantive law in investment arbitration combines international law and host State law. This is so whether or not the parties have made a choice of law that combines international law with host State law. Most agreements on choice of law whether in contracts or through treaties, refer to host State law as well as international law. In the absence of an agreement on the governing law, Article 42 of the ICSID Convention provides that the tribunal apply host State law and applicable rules of international law.

In the majority of cases, tribunals have, in fact, applied both systems of law.[432] In some cases the tribunals were simply content to find that both systems of law reached the same result.[433]

In many cases, tribunals applied host State law and international law without much attention to their relationship.[434] In *Maffezini v Spain*,[435] the BIT required the Tribunal to apply treaties, including the BIT, host State law, and general principles of international law.[436] The subject-matter of the dispute was the construction of a chemical plant. The Tribunal did not engage in a theoretical discussion

431 *Magyar Farming v Hungary*, Award, 13 November 2019, paras 25, 26 (referring to *Perenco v Ecuador*, Decision on Remaining Issues of Jurisdiction and on Liability, 12 September 2014, paras 532–533, where the Tribunal applied the second sentence of Article 42(1) ICSID Convention, and *Burlington v Ecuador*, Decision on Liability, 14 December 2012, para 178).

432 *Amco v Indonesia*, Award, 20 November 1984, para 148; *Genin v Estonia*, Award, 25 June 2001, para 350; *MCI v Ecuador*, Award, 31 July 2007, para 217; *Perenco v Ecuador*, Decision on Remaining Issues of Jurisdiction and on Liability, 12 September 2014, paras 532–534; *Quiborax v Bolivia*, Award, 16 September 2015, paras 90, 91; *Burlington v Ecuador*, Decision on Counterclaims, 7 February 2017, para 74; *Magyar Farming v Hungary*, Award, 13 November 2019, paras 25–27; *Gosling v Mauritius*, Award, 18 February 2020, paras 87–88.

433 *Gardella v Côte d'Ivoire*, Award, 29 August 1977, para 4.3; *Benvenuti & Bonfant v Congo*, Award, 8 August 1980, para 4.64; *Klöckner v Cameroon*, Award, 21 October 1983, 2 ICSID Reports 9, 63; *Amco v Indonesia*, Award, 20 November 1984, paras 147–148, 188, 201, 245–250, 265–268, 281; *Duke Energy v Peru*, Award, 18 August 2008, paras 144–161; *Aguaytia v Peru*, Award, 11 December 2008, paras 71–74.

434 *BG Group v Argentina*, Final Award, 24 December 2007, paras 89–103; *National Grid v Argentina*, Award, 3 November 2008, paras 81–90.

435 *Maffezini v Spain*, Award, 13 November 2000.

436 Argentina–Spain BIT Article 10(5).

on applicable law. It applied international law to some questions and host State law to other questions before it. For instance, on the issue of whether Spain was responsible for the actions of a State entity the Tribunal relied on the international law of State responsibility and on Spanish administrative law. Having reached an affirmative reply on attribution, it then applied the BIT. On the issue of an environmental impact assessment the Tribunal applied international law, Spanish legislation, a European Community directive, and the BIT. To the question of whether a contract had been perfected between the investor and the State entity, the Tribunal applied the Spanish Civil Code and the Spanish Commercial Code together with authoritative commentaries. On the issue of a statute of limitation under Spanish legislation, the Tribunal found that it did not apply to claims filed under the ICSID Convention.[437]

A widely held theory on the relationship of international law to host State law under the second sentence of Article 42(1) was the doctrine of the supplemental and corrective function of international law vis-à-vis domestic law.[438] The ad hoc Committee in *Amco v Indonesia* described this doctrine as follows:

> Article 42(1) of the Convention authorizes an ICSID tribunal to apply rules of international law only to fill up lacunae in the applicable domestic law and to ensure precedence to international law norms where the rules of the applicable domestic law are in collision with such norms.[439]

It is questionable whether this doctrine accurately reflects reality. Tribunals have given international law more than a mere ancillary or subsidiary role. The Tribunal in the resubmitted case of *Amco v Indonesia* called this a distinction without a difference:

> This Tribunal notes that Article 42(1) refers to the application of host-state law and international law. If there are no relevant host-state laws on a particular matter, a search must be made for the relevant international laws. And, where there are applicable host-state laws, they must be checked against international laws, which will prevail in case of conflict. Thus international law is fully applicable and to classify its role as 'only' 'supplemental and corrective' seems a distinction without a difference.[440]

[437] At paras 47–57, 67–71, 77, 83, 89–90, 92–93.

[438] *Klöckner v Cameroon*, Decision on Annulment, 3 May 1985, para 69; *LETCO v Liberia*, Award, 31 March 1986, 2 ICSID Reports 343, 358–359; *SPP v Egypt*, Award, 20 May 1992, para 84; *Autopista v Venezuela*, Award, 23 September 2003, paras 101–105; *Caratube and Hourani v Kazakhstan*, Award, 27 September 2017, para 290.

[439] *Amco v Indonesia*, Decision on Annulment, 16 May 1986, para 20.

[440] *Amco v Indonesia*, Resubmitted Case: Award, 5 June 1990, para 40.

Gaillard and Banifatemi have shown convincingly that under the residual rule of Article 42(1) of the ICSID Convention both legal systems, international law and host State law, have equal positions.[441] It is left to the tribunals to identify the various issues before them to which international law or host State law is to apply.[442] In *CMS v Argentina* the Tribunal said:

> there is here a close interaction between the legislation and the regulations governing the gas privatization, the License and international law, as embodied both in the Treaty and in customary international law. All of these rules are inseparable and will, to the extent justified, be applied by the Tribunal.[443]

In *Occidental Exploration v Ecuador* the arbitration was conducted under the UNCITRAL Rules of 1976. The Tribunal listed a mix of sources of law under host State law and under international law:

> The dispute in the present case is related to various sources of applicable law. It is first related to the Contract … it is next related to Ecuadorian tax legislation; this is followed by specific Decisions adopted by the Andean Community and issues that arise under the law of the WTO. In particular the dispute is related to the rights and obligations of the parties under the Treaty [ie the US–Ecuador BIT] and international law.[444]

It is only where there is a conflict between the host State's law and international law that a tribunal must make a decision on precedence. Where there is a contradiction between the two, international law will prevail.[445]

441 E Gaillard and Y Banifatemi, 'The Meaning of "and" in Article 42(1), Second Sentence, of the Washington Convention: The Role of International Law in the ICSID Choice of Law Process' (2003) 18 *ICSID Rev* 375, 403–411.

442 *Quiborax v Bolivia*, Award, 16 September 2015, para 91; *Magyar Farming v Hungary*, Award, 13 November 2019, para 26.

443 *CMS v Argentina*, Award, 12 May 2005, para 117. See also *Wena Hotels v Egypt*, Decision on Annulment, 28 January 2002, paras 37–40; *Azurix v Argentina*, Award, 14 July 2006, para 67; *LG&E v Argentina*, Decision on Liability, 3 October 2006, paras 82–99; *Enron v Argentina*, Award, 22 May 2007, paras 203–209; *Tokios Tokelės v Ukraine*, Award, 26 July 2007, paras 138–145; *Sempra v Argentina*, Award, 28 September 2007, paras 231–240.

444 *Occidental Exploration v Ecuador*, Final Award, 1 July 2004, para 93. See also *Eastern Sugar v Czech Republic*, Partial Award, 27 March 2007, paras 191–197.

445 *Santa Elena v Costa Rica*, Award, 17 February 2000, paras 28, 35, 37, 40, 60–68; *Maffezini v Spain*, Award, 13 November 2000, paras 92, 93; *Wena Hotels v Egypt*, Award, 8 December 2000, para 107; *LG&E v Argentina*, Decision on Liability, 3 October 2006, para 94; *MCI v Ecuador*, Award, 31 July 2007, para 218; *ConocoPhillips v Venezuela*, Award, 8 March 2019, para 88.

The Tribunal in *LG&E v Argentina* emphasized that ultimately international law is controlling: 'International law overrides domestic law when there is a contradiction since a State cannot justify non-compliance of its international obligations by asserting the provisions of its domestic law.'[446]

When applying international law, tribunals have at times applied treaties outside the area of investment law such as the New York Convention,[447] treaties protecting human rights,[448] or the United Nations Convention against Corruption.[449] Tribunals have also applied customary international law, including principles of State responsibility,[450] the principle of respect for acquired rights,[451] and the standard of compensation for wrongful acts.[452] General principles of law,[453] including good faith,[454] estoppel,[455] and unjust enrichment,[456] were also applied by tribunals.

With respect to European law, tribunal practice is divided on whether it is part of domestic and/or international law,[457] and whether it is to be applied to a case as part of the applicable law or to be treated as a fact.[458]

[446] *LG&E v Argentina*, Decision on Liability, 3 October 2006, para 94. See also *Santa Elena v Costa Rica*, Award, 17 February 2000, paras 64–65; *Duke Energy v Peru*, Decision on Jurisdiction, 1 February 2006, para 162.

[447] United Nations Convention on the Recognition and Enforcement of Foreign Arbitral Awards: *Bayindir v Pakistan*, Decision on Jurisdiction, 14 November 2005, paras 174–179; *Saipem v Bangladesh*, Award, 30 June 2009, paras 163–170; *ATA v Jordan*, Award, 18 May 2010, paras 124 and 128.

[448] *Toto v Lebanon*, Decision on Jurisdiction, 11 September 2009, paras 158–160; *Al Warraq v Indonesia*, Final Award, 15 December 2014, paras 518–522, 556–605.

[449] *World Duty Free v Kenya*, Award, 4 October 2006, para 145.

[450] *Jan de Nul v Egypt*, Decision on Jurisdiction, 16 June 2006, para 89; *Almås v Poland*, Award, 27 June 2016, paras 207–272; *Staur Eiendom v Latvia*, Award, 28 February 2020, paras 312–354.

[451] *Amco v Indonesia*, Award, 20 November 1984, para 248(v); *Magyar Farming v Hungary*, Award, 13 November 2019, paras 343–348.

[452] *Burlington v Ecuador*, Decision on Reconsideration and Award, 7 February 2017, paras 177, 574; *Caratube and Hourani v Kazakhstan*, Award, 27 September 2017 paras 1072–1091; *Watkins v Spain*, Award, 21 January 2020, para 677.

[453] See generally *Inceysa v El Salvador*, Award, 2 August 2006, paras 226–227.

[454] *Plama v Bulgaria*, Decision on Jurisdiction, 8 February 2005, para 147; *Vigotop v Hungary*, Award, 1 October 2014, paras 585–586; *Poštová banka v Greece*, Award, 9 April 2015, para 284.

[455] *Quiborax v Bolivia*, Decision on Jurisdiction, 27 September 2012, paras 257–258; *Urbaser v Argentina*, Decision on Jurisdiction, 19 December 2012, para 109; *Minnotte v Poland*, Award, 16 May 2014, para 211.

[456] *Amco v Indonesia*, Resubmitted Case: Award, 5 June 1990, paras 154–156; *Saluka v Czech Republic*, Partial Award, 17 March 2006, para 449; *Inceysa v El Salvador*, Award, 2 August 2006, paras 253–254.

[457] *Electrabel v Hungary*, Decision on Jurisdiction, Applicable Law and Liability, 30 November 2012, paras 4.112–4.129; *Vattenfall v Germany II*, Decision on the *Achmea* Issue, 31 August 2018, paras 140–150; *Eskosol v Italy*, Decision on Italy's Request for Immediate Termination, 7 May 2019, paras 112–123, 173–174; *Landesbank Baden-Württemberg v Spain*, Decision on the Intra-EU Jurisdictional Objection, 25 February 2019, para 158; *Hydro Energy v Spain*, Decision on Jurisdiction, Liability and Directions on Quantum, 9 March 2020, para 494.

[458] *AES v Hungary*, Award, 23 September 2010, para 7.6.12; *Micula v Romania I*, Final Award, 11 December 2013, para 328.

(c) Special issues of applicable law

Most of the rules on applicable law, like Article 42 of the ICSID Convention, relate to the law to be applied to the merits of a dispute. Some other important aspects that can arise in an investment dispute are not, however, regulated by these general rules on the governing law.

The law governing procedure is governed by the procedural framework chosen by the parties. In ICSID arbitration this is the Convention and the rules adopted under it.[459]

Jurisdiction is governed by the instruments establishing jurisdiction which may involve elements of international law as well as domestic law.[460] Under the ICSID Convention, Article 42 does not apply to matters of jurisdiction.[461]

The nationality of individuals[462] is determined primarily by the law of the State whose nationality is claimed.[463] The nationality of juridical persons[464] is determined by the criteria of incorporation or seat of the company in question subject to pertinent agreements, treaties, and legislation.[465]

Questions relating to the legal personality, status and capacity of a foreign corporate investor are governed by the domestic law applicable to corporate bodies (*lex societatis*), most often the law of the company's State of incorporation.[466]

Tribunals have held that the *jus standi* of claimants, especially of minority shareholders, was governed not by domestic law but by the ICSID Convention and the relevant BIT.[467]

To establish the existence and scope of rights, especially property rights, which the investor claims, host State will be relevant.[468]

[459] See XII.11 above.

[460] See XII.7(g) above.

[461] *Vattenfall v Germany II*, Decision on the *Achmea* Issue, 31 August 2018, paras 118–119; *Landesbank Baden-Württemberg v Spain*, Decision on the Intra-EU Jurisdictional Objection, 25 February 2019, para 161; *Hydro Energy v Spain*, Decision on Jurisdiction, Liability and Directions on Quantum, 9 March 2020, para 502.

[462] See also III.2 above.

[463] *Champion Trading v Egypt*, Decision on Jurisdiction, 21 October 2003, sec 3.4.1; *Soufraki v UAE*, Award, 7 July 2004, para 55; *Siag v Egypt*, Decision on Jurisdiction, 11 April 2007, paras 195–201; *Micula v Romania I*, Decision on Jurisdiction, 24 September 2008, paras 86, 101.

[464] See also III.3 above.

[465] *AES v Argentina*, Decision on Jurisdiction, 26 April 2005, para 78.

[466] *LESI & ASTALDI v Algeria*, Decision on Jurisdiction, 12 July 2006, para 93(i); *Noble Energy v Ecuador*, Decision on Jurisdiction, 5 March 2008, paras 87–89; *Amco v Indonesia*, Resubmitted Case: Decision on Jurisdiction, 10 May 1988, 1 ICSID Reports 561–562; *Scimitar v Bangladesh*, Award, 4 May 1994, paras 26–29. But see: *Abaclat v Argentina*, Decision on Jurisdiction and Admissibility, 4 August 2011, paras 413–421.

[467] *Pan American v Argentina*, Decision on Preliminary Objections, 27 July 2006, para 217; *CMS v Argentina*, Decision on Jurisdiction, 17 July 2003, para 42, Decision on Annulment, 25 September 2007, para 68.

[468] *Suez and Vivendi v Argentina*, Decision on Liability, 30 July 2010, para 151; *Alpha v Ukraine*, Award, 8 November 2010, para 347; *Total v Argentina*, Decision on Liability, 27 December 2010, para 39; *Emmis v Hungary*, Award, 16 April 2014, para 48; *Libananco v Turkey*, Award, 2 September 2011, paras 112–113, 385 ff; *Quiborax v Bolivia*, Decision on Jurisdiction, 27 September 2012, paras 52, 115 et

13. Remedies

(a) Satisfaction and restitution

Under the international law of State responsibility reparation for a wrongful act takes the forms of restitution, compensation, or satisfaction.[469] In investment arbitration the remedy usually consists of monetary compensation. Satisfaction plays a subordinate role in investment law although obtaining a declaration of illegality may be an important factor motivating a claimant in some cases. In *Rompetrol v Romania*, the Tribunal found that 'the claim to declaratory relief retained an independent existence of its own irrespective of the question of consequential loss or damage'.[470] In some cases tribunals have granted requests for declaratory relief independently of an award of damages.[471]

Restitution in kind or specific performance is ordered infrequently.[472] This is not due to any inherent limitation upon tribunals but the consequence of the situations in which most disputes arise and the way the claims are put forward. In some cases, tribunals did in fact order restitution[473] or affirmed their power to do so.[474]

In *von Pezold v Zimbabwe*, the claimants' farms had been seized by 'settlers' with the encouragement of the government. The Tribunal found in favour of restitution in combination with damages:

> the Tribunal finds that restitution of the Zimbabwean Properties expropriated in 2005, including attached Water Permits, should be ordered in favor of the Claimants. While this Section of the Award has focused on restitution in kind, the Tribunal considers that it is further necessary to award compensation for

seq; *Philipp Morris v Uruguay*, Award, 8 July 2016, paras 177, 178; *Gavrilović v Croatia*, Award, 26 July 2018, para 432; *Italba v Uruguay*, Award, 22 March 2019, para 213; *Almasryia v Kuwait*, Award under Rule 41(5), 1 November 2019, paras 53–58.

[469] Articles on Responsibility of States for Internationally Wrongful Acts adopted by the International Law Commission (ILC) in 2001, Article 34. J Crawford, *The International Law Commission's Articles on State Responsibility* (2002) 211.

[470] *Rompetrol v Romania*, Award, 6 May 2013, para 294.

[471] *Biwater Gauff v Tanzania*, Award, 24 July 2008, paras 465–467, 807; *Europe Cement v Turkey*, Award, 13 August 2009, paras 146–148, 176, 181; *Bosca v Lithuania*, Award, 17 May 2013, paras 201–303; *Glencore v Colombia*, Award, 27 August 2019, paras 1104, 1663.

[472] See C Schreuer, 'Non-Pecuniary Remedies in ICSID Arbitration' (2004) 20 *Arbitr Int* 325.

[473] *Martini Case (Italy v Venezuela)*, Award, 3 May 1930, (1931) 25 *AJIL* 554, at p 585; *Texaco v Libya*, Award on the Merits, 19 January 1977, 53 ILR 389, at pp 497–511; *Goetz v Burundi*, Award, 2 September 1998 and 10 February 1999, paras 132–133; *Semos v Mali*, Award, 25 February 2003, 10 ICSID Reports p 116 at p 129; *Enron v Argentina*, Decision on Jurisdiction, 14 January 2004, paras 76–79; *ADC v Hungary*, Award, 2 October 2006, para 523; *Siemens v Argentina*, Award, 6 February 2007, para 403(5); *ATA v Jordan*, Award, 18 May 2010, paras 129–132; *Arif v Moldova*, Award, 8 April 2013, paras 559–572.

[474] *Nykomb v Latvia*, Award, 16 December 2003, sec. 5.1; *Micula v Romania I*, Decision on Jurisdiction and Admissibility, 24 September 2008, paras 158–168.

> the losses incurred by the Claimants due to, inter alia, land damage and losses to productivity.[475]

In other cases, tribunals declined to order restitution as involving a disproportionate burden to the State concerned[476] or as interfering with the State's sovereignty.[477]

(b) Damages for an illegal act

If an illegal act has been committed, the guiding principle is that reparation must, as far as possible, restore the situation that would have existed had the illegal act not been committed.[478] In the *Chorzow Factory Case*, the PCIJ expressed this principle in the following words:

> The essential principle contained in the actual notion of an illegal act—a principle which seems to be established by international practice and in particular by the decisions of arbitral tribunals—is that reparation must, as far as possible, wipe out all the consequences of the illegal act and re-establish the situation which would, in all probability, have existed if that act had not been committed.[479]

Under this principle, damages for a violation of international law should reflect the damage actually suffered by the victim. In other words, the victim's current situation will be compared with the one that would have prevailed had the act not been committed.[480] Punitive or moral damages will not be granted[481] unless there are exceptional circumstances.[482] This subjective method includes any consequential damage but also incidental benefits arising as a consequence of the illegal act. The Tribunal in *Petrobart v Kyrgyzstan* said:

[475] *von Pezold v Zimbabwe*, Award, 28 July 2015, para 744. See also paras 670–743, 1020.

[476] Article 35 of the ILC's Articles on State Responsibility.

[477] *LG&E v Argentina*, Award, 25 July 2007, paras 84–87; *Occidental Petroleum v Ecuador*, Decision on Provisional Measures, 17 August 2007, paras 66–86; *Antin v Spain*, Award, 15 June 2018, 631–637; *Masdar v Spain*, Award, 16 May 2018, paras 553–563.

[478] Articles 31, 36 of the ILC's Articles on State Responsibility.

[479] *Factory at Chorzów*, Merits, 13 September 1928, PCIJ, Series A, No 17, p 47.

[480] *SolEs Badajoz v Spain*, Award, 31 July 2019, paras 475–477, 487–489; *OperaFund v Spain*, Award, 6 September 2019, paras 684–687.

[481] *Siag v Egypt*, Award, 1 June 2009, paras 544–548; *Europe Cement v Turkey*, Award, 13 August 2009, paras 177–181; *Cementownia v Turkey*, Award, 17 September 2009, paras 164–172; *Lemire v Ukraine*, Decision on Jurisdiction and Liability, 14 January 2010, paras 426–486; *Rompetrol v Romania*, Award, 6 May 2013, paras 289–293; *ST-AD v Bulgaria*, Award on Jurisdiction, 18 July 2013, para 430.

[482] *Desert Line v Yemen*, Award, 6 February 2008, paras 284–291.

> in so far as it appears that Petrobart has suffered damage as a result of the Republic's breaches of the Treaty, Petrobart shall so far as possible be placed financially in the position in which it would have found itself, had the breaches not occurred.[483]

The calculation of monetary reparation can be a complex undertaking, often requiring the involvement of valuation experts.[484] One method to calculate damages is to look at the replacement value of property that has been taken or destroyed. This presupposes that the assets in question are actually replaceable. Another method is to look at the actual losses, that is, the amount invested as well as costs and expenses incurred by the investor.[485] Tribunals have developed a variety of valuation methods.[486]

If the illegal act results in deprivation of income, damages may have to include lost profits.[487] Lost profits will be awarded only if they are not speculative, that is, in cases where the investment has a record of profitability or there are other clear indicators of future profits.[488] Also a risk element has to be factored into any calculation of future profits. In addition, care must be taken to avoid double counting. This may occur if actual expenses are combined with expected future profits.

Tribunals have also taken negligent behaviour by the investors into account when calculating damages due to them.[489] In *MTD v Chile* the Tribunal found that the investors had made decisions that unnecessarily increased their risks and for which they bore responsibility. It followed that the damages due were to be appropriately reduced:

[483] *Petrobart v Kyrgyzstan*, Award, 29 March 2005, pp 77–78. See also *MTD v Chile*, Award, 25 May 2004, para 238.

[484] For a concise overview see I Marboe, 'Compensation and Damages in International Law, The Limits of "Fair Market Value"' (2006) 7 *JWIT* 723.

[485] *Metalclad v Mexico*, Award, 30 August 2000, para 122; *Azurix v Argentina*, Award, 14 July 2006, para 425.

[486] *Kardassopoulos v Georgia*, Award, 3 March 2010, paras 594–639; *Khan Resources v Mongolia*, Award on the Merits, 2 March 2015, paras 390–421; *von Pezold v Zimbabwe*, Award, 28 July 2015, paras 801–896; *Crystallex v Venezuela*, Award, 4 April 2016, paras 886–918; *Rusoro v Venezuela*, Award, 22 August 2016, paras 646–822.

[487] *Amco v Indonesia*, Resubmitted Case: Award, 5 June 1990, paras 163–284; *LETCO v Liberia*, Award, 31 March 1986, 2 ICSID Reports 346, at pp 373–377; *Crystallex v Venezuela*, Award, 4 April 2016, paras 872–885.

[488] *AAPL v Sri Lanka*, Award, 27 June 1990, paras 105–108; *SPP v Egypt*, Award, 20 May 1992, paras 186–189; *Metalclad v Mexico*, Award, 30 August 2000, paras 120–122; *Wena Hotels v Egypt*, Award, 8 December 2000, paras 123–124; *SD Myers v Canada*, Award on Damages, 21 October 2002, paras 173 et seq; *Tecmed v Mexico*, Award, 29 May 2003, para 186; *Autopista v Venezuela*, Award, 23 September 2003, paras 351–365; *PSEG v Turkey*, Award, 19 January 2007, paras 310–315; *LG&E v Argentina*, Award, 25 July 2007, paras 88–91; *Micula v Romania I*, Award, 11 December 2013, paras 990–1118.

[489] Article 39 of the ILC's Articles on State Responsibility. See *Cargill v Poland*, Final Award, 29 February 2008, paras 663–670; *Bear Creek Mining v Peru*, Award, 30 November 2017, paras 565–569, 662–668.

> The Tribunal considers therefore that the Claimants should bear part of the damages suffered and the Tribunal estimates that share to be 50% after deduction of the residual value of their investment ....[490]

In addition, tribunals have found that investors are under an obligation to mitigate their losses and any failure to do so would lead to an appropriate reduction of damages.[491] In *Yukos v Russian Federation*, the Tribunal said:

> the legal concept of contributory fault must not be confused with the investor's duty to mitigate its losses. There are cases where the claimant's damages were reduced because the tribunal found that it failed to take some reasonable steps to minimize its losses. In such cases, 'the injured party must be held responsible for its own contribution to the loss.'[492]

Events subsequent to the illegal act may affect the damage caused and can be taken into account.[493] All information available at the time of the award should be reflected in the calculation; this may include consequential damage or a diminution of damage. A subsequent increase in the value of the investment will also be relevant. In cases of unlawful expropriation tribunals have found that the claimant may select either the date of the expropriation or the date of the award for purposes of valuation.[494] In *ADC v Hungary* the Tribunal after noting that the value of the investment had risen very considerably after the date of the illegal expropriation said:

> the application of the *Chorzów Factory* standard requires that the date of valuation should be the date of the Award and not the date of expropriation, since this is what is necessary to put the Claimants in the same position as if the expropriation had not been committed.[495]

(c) Compensation for expropriation

The calculation of compensation for a lawful expropriation follows different standards.[496] Compensation is one of the requirements for a legal expropriation together

490 *MTD v Chile*, Award, 25 May 2004, para 243. See also *Azurix v Argentina*, Award, 14 July 2006, paras 425–429.

491 *EDF v Argentina*, Award, 11 June 2012, paras 1302–1317; *Unión Fenosa v Egypt*, Award, 31 August 2018, paras 10.124–10.132; *Magyar Farming v Hungary*, Award, 13 November 2019, paras 421–428.

492 *Yukos v Russian Federation*, Final Award, 18 July 2014, para 1603, see also para 1776.

493 *Siemens v Argentina*, Award, 6 February 2007, paras 352, 353, 360; *Kardassopoulos v Georgia*, Award, 3 March 2010, para 514; *OperaFund v Spain*, Award, 6 September 2019, para 683.

494 *Yukos v Russian Federation*, Final Award, 18 July 2014, paras 1759–1769.

495 *ADC v Hungary*, Award, 2 October 2006, para 497.

496 For decisions clearly distinguishing between compensation for expropriation and damages for an illegal act see: *Nykomb v Latvia*, Award, 16 December 2003, sec 5.1; *MTD v Chile*, Award, 25 May

with a public purpose, non-discrimination, and a fair procedure.[497] Most BITs and other treaties for the protection of investments contain this requirement.[498] These treaties often refer to 'adequate' or 'appropriate' compensation. The World Bank Guidelines on the Treatment of Foreign Direct Investment state that

> Compensation will be deemed 'adequate' if it is based on the fair market value of the taken asset as such value is determined immediately before the time at which the taking occurred or the decision to take the asset became publicly known.[499]

Many of the treaties dealing with compensation for expropriation also refer to the expropriated investment's fair market value.[500] For instance, the Argentina–US BIT provides:

> Compensation shall be equivalent to the fair market value of the expropriated investment immediately before the expropriatory action was taken or became known, whichever is earlier . . . .[501]

Tribunals have frequently relied on the fair market value as the appropriate standard for compensation.[502]

Whereas damages for an illegal act look at the victim's subjective position, compensation for expropriation, as expressed in the investment's fair market value, is an objective standard that looks at the amount that a willing buyer would normally pay to a willing seller in a free transaction, at arm's length. On the other hand, a market value will often be a fiction, especially where a market for large and complex investments does not exist. Therefore, market value is determined often on the basis of future prospects or earning capacity of the investment.

The most frequently used method for determining market value is the discounted cash flow (DCF) method which looks at the projected likely income created by the investment in the future. The underlying assumption is that this is the standard for the price that a hypothetical buyer would be willing to pay. Under this method an estimate is made of cash flows that may be expected in the future. To

2004, para 238; *ADC v Hungary*, Award, 2 October 2006, para 481, 483; *Siemens v Argentina*, Award, 6 February 2007, paras 349–352; *LG&E v Argentina*, Award, 25 July 2007, paras 29–58; *Magyar Farming v Hungary*, Award, 13 November 2019, paras 368–372.

497 See VII.4 above.
498 ECT Article 13.
499 Guideline IV (3), (1992) 31 ILM 1379, 1382.
500 ECT Article 13 (1).
501 Argentina–US BIT Article IV (1).
502 *Biloune v Ghana*, Award on Jurisdiction and Liability, 27 October 1989, 95 ILR 184, at p 211; *SPP v Egypt*, Award, 20 May 1992, para 197; *Santa Elena v Costa Rica*, Award, 17 February 2000, para 70; *Rusoro v Venezuela*, Award, 22 August 2016, paras 398–410; *Saint-Gobain v Venezuela*, Decision on Liability and the Principles of Quantum, 30 December 2016, paras 627–851.

calculate the present value of future cash flows, a discount factor has to be applied in order to take account of the time value of money and of risk. Past data are relevant but not necessarily decisive for the determination of future prospects. Other 'value drivers' may also be indicative of future cash flows. Risk may be influenced by macroeconomic factors or political crises but also by the specific risk borne by the investment.

If the investment has not yet produced income or is unlikely to produce further income in the future, the appropriate method for valuation may be the liquidation value. This is the price at which the remaining assets could be sold under conditions of liquidation. This method usually yields a much lower value than valuation on the basis of a going concern.

The valuation date in the case of a lawful expropriations should be the date immediately before the fact of the expropriation became publicly known.[503] This is designed to avoid an influence of the impending expropriation on the investment's market value.

(d) Interest

An award of damages or compensation normally includes interest.[504] Interest is a sum paid or payable as compensation for the temporary withholding of money. If the investor had to take out a loan as a consequence of the deprivation, interest is designed to cover the cost of the loan. If no loan was taken, interest may reflect the lost earning capacity of the money in question.

Interest is due from the date at which the principal amount was due. In the case of damages this is normally the date of the wrongful act.[505] In *AAPL v Sri Lanka* the Tribunal stated that:

> the case-law elaborated by international arbitral tribunals strongly suggests that in assessing the liability due for losses incurred the interest becomes an integral part of the compensation itself, and should run consequently from the date when the State's international responsibility became engaged....[506]

In case of compensation for an expropriation, interest is due normally from the date of the expropriation. That date may be difficult to determine with indirect or

[503] *Venezuela Holdings v Venezuela*, Award, 9 October 2014, para 307; *Tidewater v Venezuela*, Award, 13 March 2015, paras 159–163.

[504] Generally, see JY Gotanda, 'Awarding Interest in International Arbitration' (1996) 90 *AJIL* 40.

[505] In some cases, this date may be difficult to determine. *PSEG v Turkey*, Award, 19 January 2007, paras 349–351.

[506] *AAPL v Sri Lanka*, Award, 27 June 1990, para 114. See also *SPP v Egypt*, Award, 20 May 1992, para 234; *Metalclad v Mexico*, Award, 30 August 2000, para 128.

creeping expropriations. The appropriate date will be the day when the investor definitely lost control over the investment.[507]

The rate of interest may be calculated on the basis of the legal interest rate in an applicable legal system or some inter-bank rate such as LIBOR or EURIBOR.[508]

The practice of tribunals shows a clear trend towards compounding interest, that is, interest is capitalized at certain intervals and will then itself bear interest. While some tribunals have declined to award compound interest,[509] the majority of recent decisions accepts it.[510]

14. Costs

The costs of major investment arbitrations can be considerable and may run into millions of dollars.[511] The costs consist of three elements: the charges for the use of the facilities and expenses of ICSID[512] or any other arbitration institution, the fees and expenses of the arbitrators,[513] and the expenses incurred by the parties in connection with the proceedings. Of these three categories, the third, consisting mainly of the costs for legal representation, is typically by far the largest.

The ICSID Convention in Article 61(2) leaves it to the tribunal's discretion by whom these costs are to be paid, unless the parties agree otherwise. Other arbitration rules may provide differently. For instance, the UNCITRAL Arbitration Rules state that the costs of arbitration shall in principle be borne by the unsuccessful party.[514] But in a particular case, both parties may be partly successful.

The practice of tribunals on the attribution of costs is not uniform. In many cases the tribunals found that the fees and expenses of the Centre and of the arbitrators were to be shared equally and that each party had to bear its own expenses.[515] In *Eskosol v Italy* the Tribunal said:

[507] *Vestey v Venezuela*, Award, 15 April 2016, paras 253–254; *Spence v Costa Rica*, Interim Award, 25 October 2016, paras 259–264; *Saint-Gobain v Venezuela*, Decision on Liability and the Principles of Quantum, 30 December 2016, paras 440–456, 467–478.

[508] *Gavrilović v Croatia*, Award, 26 July 2018, para 1295; *UP and C.D v Hungary*, Award, 9 October 2018, para 599; *Greentech v Italy*, Award, 23 December 2018, para 577.

[509] *CME v Czech Republic*, Final Award, 14 March 2003, paras 642–647; *Autopista v Venezuela*, Award, 23 September 2003, paras 393–397; *Strabag v Libya*, Award, 29 June 2020, paras 962–963.

[510] *Valores Mundiales v Venezuela*, Award 25 July 2017, paras 821–822; *Bear Creek Mining v Peru*, Award, 30 November 2017, para 715; *Magyar Farming v Hungary*, Award, 13 November 2019, para 432.

[511] As of 2018, the average cost of an investment treaty arbitration was roughly US$ 11 million. US$ 10 million for the parties' combined legal costs and US$ 1 million costs for the tribunal and administrative costs. See SD Franck, *Arbitration Costs* (2019) 209–210.

[512] The details are set out in ICSID's Administrative and Financial Regulations as well as in a Schedule of Fees.

[513] See ICSID Schedule of Fees, para 3.

[514] UNCITRAL Arbitration Rules Article 42 (1).

[515] *Vacuum Salt v Ghana*, Award, 16 February 1994, paras 56–60; *World Duty Free v Kenya*, Award, 4 October 2006, paras 189–191; *RSM v Grenada I*, Award, 13 March 2009, paras 487–499; *RosInvest v Russian Federation*, Final Award, 12 September 2010, para 701; *AES v Hungary*, Award, 23 September 2010, para 15.3.3; *Brandes v Venezuela*, Award, 2 August 2011, para 120.

> considering that both Parties prevailed to some significant extent, the Tribunal concludes that each Party should bear 50% of the costs of the arbitration, and should continue to bear its own direct costs incurred in connection with the proceeding.[516]

In some cases, the tribunals awarded costs as a sanction for improper conduct of one of the parties. This was the case where they found that the claim had been frivolous or fraudulent or that there had been dilatory or otherwise improper conduct.[517] In *Churchill Mining v Indonesia*, the Tribunal held that the claimants were to pay the costs of the proceedings and the bulk of the costs incurred by respondent. The Tribunal's reason was as follows:

> this is a case where investors started two arbitrations on the basis of a large number of documents that turned out to be forged and revealed a large scale fraudulent scheme.[518]

In *Lighthouse v Timor-Leste*, the Tribunal noted that the claimants had raised additional arguments and filed new evidence just before the hearing. In light of this, and on an overall assessment of the course and outcome of the proceeding, the Tribunal concluded that the claimants were to bear the entirety of the ICSID arbitration costs and the reasonable legal costs of the respondent.[519]

More recently, tribunals have shown a growing tendency to adopt the principle that costs follow the event. An award of costs against the losing party may be total or, more frequently, may cover a certain part of the overall costs in proportion to the parties' relative success.[520] In *ADC v Hungary*, the claimant prevailed with its claim for illegal expropriation and other BIT violations. On the issue of costs, the Tribunal said:

> ... it can be seen from previous awards that ICSID arbitrators do in practice award costs in favour of the successful party and sometimes in large sums ... In the

516 *Eskosol v Italy*, Award, 4 September 2020, para 494.

517 *LETCO v Liberia*, Award, 31 March 1986, 2 ICSID Reports 370, at p 378; *Generation Ukraine v Ukraine*, Award, 16 September 2003, para 24.2; *Plama v Bulgaria*, Award, 27 August 2008, paras 321–322; *Phoenix v Czech Republic*, Award, 15 April 2009, paras 151–152; *Europe Cement v Turkey*, Award, 13 August 2009, paras 185–186; *Cementownia v Turkey*, Award, 17 September 2009, paras 177–178; *Fakes v Turkey*, Award, 14 July 2010, paras 153–154.

518 *Churchill Mining v Indonesia*, Award, 6 December 2016, para 549.

519 *Lighthouse v Timor-Leste*, Award, 22 December 2017, paras 344–345.

520 *Inceysa v El Salvador*, Award, 2 August 2006, para 338; *Telenor v Hungary*, Award, 13 September 2006, paras 104–108; *Champion Trading v Egypt*, Award, 27 October 2006, paras 165–178; *PSEG v Turkey*, Award, 19 January 2007, paras 352–353; *Alpha v Ukraine*, Award, 8 November 2010, para 516; *RSM v Grenada II*, Award, 10 December 2010, paras 8.3.4–8.3.6; *AFT v Slovakia*, Award, 5 March 2011, paras 260–270; *Flughafen Zürich v Venezuela*, Award, 18 November 2014, para 989; *Almasryia v Kuwait*, Award under Rule 41(5), 1 November 2019, paras 63, 65.

> present case, the Tribunal can find no reason to depart from the starting point that the successful party should receive reimbursement from the unsuccessful party... Were the Claimants not to be reimbursed their costs ... it could not be said that they were being made whole.[521]

In some cases, tribunals found that the costs claimed by successful respondents were excessive and declined to accept them for purposes of their cost calculations.[522]

Security for costs[523] to guarantee a cost award against claimant has been granted sparingly.[524] Tribunals have acknowledged their power to make decisions to this effect[525] but have reserved it for exceptional circumstances.

Some proceedings are financed by third-party funders. The purpose is to enable impecunious investors to pursue claims or to transfer the risk of litigation to a third party. Some tribunals have found that third-party funding did not affect their cost decisions.[526] Other tribunals have taken third-party funding into consideration.[527] Some tribunals have required the disclosure of third-party funding arrangements.[528]

15. Review of awards

Awards are final and not subject to any appeals procedures.[529] It is only under very limited circumstances that a review of awards is possible. Two potentially conflicting principles are at work in the process of review of a judicial decision: the principle of finality and the principle of correctness. Finality serves the purpose

[521] *ADC v Hungary*, Award, 2 October 2006, paras 531, 533.

[522] *Charanne v Spain*, Final Award, 21 January 2016, paras 563–564; *Cortec v Kenya*, Award, 22 October 2018, paras 400–401; *Interocean v Nigeria*, Award, 6 October 2020, paras 384–387.

[523] See also above XII.11(d).

[524] *RSM v St Lucia*, Decision on Saint Lucia's Request for Security for Costs, 13 August 2014; *Manuel García Armas v Venezuela*, Award on Jurisdiction, 13 December 2019, paras 91–126, 751; *Herzig v Turkmenistan*, Decision on Security for Costs, 27 January 2020. In *Adamakopoulos v Cyprus*, Decision on Jurisdiction, 7 February 2020, paras 264–266, 342 (iii), the Tribunal took the initiative to invite the respondent to make an application for security for costs.

[525] *Libananco v Turkey*, Decision on Preliminary Issues, 23 June 2008, para 57; *RSM v Grenada II*, Decision on Application for Security for Costs, 14 October 2010; *Burimi v Albania*, Provisional Measures Concerning Security for Costs, 3 May 2012, para 28; *Commerce Group v El Salvador*, Annulment Proceeding: Decision on El Salvador's Application for Security for Costs, 20 September 2012.

[526] *Kardassopoulos v Georgia*, Award, 3 March 2010, paras 691–692; *RSM v Grenada I*, Order of the Committee Discontinuing the Proceedings and Decision on Costs, 28 April 2011, para 68; *ATA v Jordan*, Annulment Proceeding: Order Taking Note of the Discontinuance of the Proceeding, 11 July 2011, para 34.

[527] *Renta 4 v Russian Federation*, Award, 20 July 2012, para 223; *Axos v Kosovo*, Award, 3 May 2018, para 270.

[528] *Muhammet Çap v Turkmenistan*, Procedural Order No 3, 12 June 2015; *EuroGas v Slovakia*, Award, 18 August 2017, paras 105 c), 110.

[529] ICSID Convention Article 53.

of efficiency in terms of an expeditious and economical settlement of disputes. Correctness is an elusive goal that takes time and effort and may involve several layers of control, a phenomenon that is well known from appeals in domestic court procedure. In arbitration the principle of finality is traditionally given more weight than the principle of correctness.

There have been recurrent attempts to introduce an appeals procedure in investment arbitration. The assumption behind these plans is that it will promote the consistency and correctness of decisions. An initiative to that effect within ICSID, launched in 2004, was not pursued.[530] Since 2004 treaties of the United States foresee the creation of appeals mechanisms.[531] More recently, the European Union has taken up the idea. The CETA[532] foresees a bilateral appeals mechanism together with an undertaking to pursue plans for a multilateral appellate mechanism.[533] In the negotiations taking place in the framework of the UNCITRAL Working Group III, on Investor–State Dispute Settlement Reform, the establishment of an appellate mechanism is under consideration.[534]

(a) Review in non-ICSID arbitration

In non-ICSID arbitration, including arbitration under the Additional Facility, the normal way to challenge an award is through national courts. This is done in the courts of the country in which the tribunal had its seat or by the courts charged with the task of enforcing the award.

The New York Convention on the Recognition and Enforcement of Foreign Arbitral Awards of 1958[535] in its Article V lists several grounds on the basis of which recognition and enforcement of a non-national arbitral award may be refused at the request of a party. The UNCITRAL Model Law on International Commercial Arbitration of 1985 foresees a limited number of grounds for the setting aside or non-recognition of an international commercial award by a domestic court, which are based on Article V of the New York Convention.[536] In many countries, national arbitration laws include rules on the setting aside of arbitral awards that are modelled on the UNCITRAL Model Law.

[530] ICSID Working Paper, *Suggested Changes to the ICSID Rules and Regulations*, 12 May 2005, para 4.

[531] United State Model Bilateral Investment Treaty of 2012, Article 28(10).

[532] Comprehensive Economic and Trade Agreement (CETA) between Canada, the European Union and its member States, signed 30 October 2016, not in force. Parts of the treaty are provisionally applied since 21 September 2017.

[533] CETA Articles 8.28 and 8.29. See also EU–Singapore Investment Protection Agreement Article 3.10 (not yet in force); EU–Viet Nam Investment Protection Agreement Article 3.39 (not yet in force).

[534] UN General Assembly Doc A/CN.9/WG.III/WP.185.

[535] 330 UNTS 38 (1959).

[536] UNCITRAL Model Law, Articles 34 and 36, (1985) 24 ILM 1302, 1311–1313.

The most important grounds for the setting aside of awards under these laws are the invalidity of the arbitration agreement, lack of proper notice of the arbitration proceedings, a decision in the award beyond the scope of the submission to arbitration, improper composition of the tribunal, a subject-matter not capable of settlement by arbitration under the law of the State in question, and an award that is in conflict with the public policy of that State. Proceedings for the setting aside of awards in non-ICSID investment arbitration have taken place in several cases.[537]

(b) Annulment of awards under the ICSID Convention

ICSID awards are not subject to annulment or any other form of scrutiny by domestic courts. Rather, Article 52 of the ICSID Convention offers its own self-contained system for review. Under this procedure, an ad hoc committee may annul the award upon the request of a party. The ad hoc committee consists of three persons, appointed by the Chairman of ICSID's Administrative Council.[538] The Chairman in making these appointments is restricted to ICSID's Panel of Arbitrators. Therefore, States have a structural advantage over annulment proceedings in that they control the composition of the Panel of Arbitrators. The exclusion of nationals and co-nationals of the parties to the proceedings applies also for members of ad hoc committees.

The application for annulment must come from one of the parties to the arbitration and must be submitted within 120 days of the award's dispatch to the parties.[539] There is no *ex officio* annulment.

The application for annulment must state one or several grounds for annulment listed in Article 52(1) and the annullable features of the award. But the applicant may further develop its arguments subsequently.[540] A party may not amend its application for annulment in the course of the proceedings for annulment by adding points that were known to it, but which it failed to raise in the original application. An ad hoc committee is restricted to the grounds for annulment raised by the parties.

Only awards are subject to annulment. There is no annulment of other decisions, such as decisions upholding jurisdiction or decisions on provisional

537 *Mexico v Metalclad*, Judicial Review, Supreme Court of British Columbia, 2 May 2001, 5 ICSID Reports 236; *Rusoro v Venezuela*, Paris Court of Appeal, 29 January 2019; *Veteran Petroleum, Yukos Universal and Hulley Enterprises v Russian Federation*, Court of Appeal of The Hague, Judgment, 18 February 2020.

538 The President of the World Bank holds this office, *ex officio*.

539 ICSID Convention Articles 52(2) and 49(1).

540 *Wena Hotels v Egypt*, Decision on Annulment, 28 January 2002, para 19; *Soufraki v UAE*, Decision on Annulment, 5 June 2007, paras 33–36; *von Pezold v Zimbabwe*, Decision on Annulment, 21 November 2018, paras 288–297; *Pey Casado v Chile*, Resubmitted Case: Decision on Annulment, 8 January 2020, paras 729, 740, 750–751.

measures, except to the extent that they are subsequently incorporated into the award. A decision by a tribunal declining jurisdiction is an award and therefore subject to annulment.

Under Article 52(5) of the ICSID Convention the ad hoc committee may stay the enforcement of the award while annulment proceedings are pending.[541] Before the constitution of the ad hoc committee the stay will be automatic if it is requested in the application for annulment. Some ad hoc committees have required a bank guarantee or similar security from the award debtor for the eventual payment of the award as a condition for the stay of enforcement.[542] The guarantee will be operative if annulment is rejected and the award becomes enforceable. Other ad hoc committees have declined to order such a security.[543]

Annulment is different from an appeal. Annulment is concerned only with the legitimacy of the process of decision but not with its substantive correctness. Appeal is concerned with both. Appeal may result in the replacement of the decision by a new decision. Annulment merely removes the original decision without replacing it. Therefore, an ad hoc committee acting under the ICSID Convention does not have the power to render its own decision on the merits. ICSID ad hoc committees have stressed the distinction between annulment and appeal.[544]

The ad hoc Committee in *CDC v Seychelles* described the function of annulment in the following terms:

> This mechanism protecting against errors that threaten the fundamental fairness of the arbitral process (but not against incorrect decisions) arises from the ICSID Convention's drafters' desire that Awards be final and binding, which is an

[541] ICSID Arbitration Rule 54.

[542] *Amco v Indonesia*, Decision on Annulment, 16 May 1986, paras 8–9; *Amco v Indonesia*, Resubmitted Case: Interim Order No. 1, 2 March 1991, para 19; *Wena Hotels v Egypt*, Decision on Annulment, 28 January 2002, paras 5–6; *CDC v Seychelles*, Decision on Continued Stay, 14 July 2004, Decision on Annulment, 29 June 2005, para 16; *Repsol v Ecuador*, Decision on Annulment, 8 January 2007, paras 8, 12; *Vivendi v Argentina*, Resubmitted Case: Decision on Stay of Enforcement, 4 November 2008; *Sempra v Argentina*, Decision on Continued Stay of Enforcement, 5 March 2009 and Decision on Termination of Stay of Enforcement, 7 August 2009; *Unión Fenosa v Egypt*, Decision on Termination of Stay, 24 January 2020, para 2; *Perenco v Ecuador*, Decision on Continuation of Stay, 21 February 2020, paras 79–80.

[543] *MINE v Guinea*, Interim Order No. 1 on Guinea's Application for Stay of Enforcement of the Award, 12 August 1988, 4 *ICSID Reports* 111; *Mitchell v Congo*, Decision on the Stay of Enforcement, 30 November 2004; *MTD v Chile*, Decision on Continued Stay of Execution, 1 June 2005; *CMS v Argentina*, Decision on Continued Stay of Enforcement, 1 September 2006; *Azurix v Argentina*, Decision on Continued Stay of Enforcement, 28 December 2007; *Enron v Argentina*, Decision on Second Request to Lift Stay of Enforcement, 20 May 2009; *Rumeli v Kazakhstan*, Decision on Annulment, 25 March 2010, paras 10–24; *Pey Casado v Chile*, Decision on Stay of Enforcement, 5 May 2010; *Carnegie Minerals v Gambia*, Decision on Continued Stay of Enforcement, 18 October 2018, paras 50–52.

[544] *Klöckner v Cameroon*, Decision on Annulment, 3 May 1985, paras 83, 118, 120, 178; *Amco v Indonesia*, Decision on Annulment, 16 May 1986, paras 43, 110; *MINE v Guinea*, Decision on Annulment, 14 December 1989, paras 4.04, 5.08, 6.55; *Fraport v Philippines I*, Decision on Annulment, 23 December 2010, para 76; *Tulip v Turkey*, Decision on Annulment, 30 December 2015, paras 42, 44; *Standard Chartered Bank v TANESCO*, Decision on Annulment, 22 August 2018, para 63; *Pey Casado v Chile*, Resubmitted Case: Decision on Annulment, 8 January 2020, paras 205, 604, 683.

> expression of 'customary law based on the concepts of *pacta sunt servanda* and *res judicata*,' and is in keeping with the object and purpose of the Convention. Parties use ICSID arbitration (at least in part) because they wish a more efficient way of resolving disputes than is possible in a national court system with its various levels of trial and appeal, or even in non-ICSID Convention arbitrations (which may be subject to national courts' review under local laws and whose enforcement may also be subject to defenses available under, for example, the New York Convention).[545]

A decision by an ad hoc committee upholding a request for annulment for any of the grounds listed in Article 52(1) invalidates the original award. But it does not replace it with a new decision on the merits. Under Article 52(6) of the ICSID Convention, if the award is annulled the dispute can be submitted to a new tribunal at the request of either party.

Requests for partial annulment of awards are possible. If the award is partially annulled only the annulled portion of the award falls to be re-litigated while the unannulled part remains *res judicata*.[546]

Any determinations of fact and law made by the ad hoc committee are not binding on the tribunal hearing the resubmitted case. Only the annulment of the award but not the reasoning accompanying it is binding.[547] But the parties may not introduce new claims that they had not presented to the first tribunal in the resubmitted case.[548]

The grounds for annulment under the ICSID Convention are listed exhaustively in Article 52(1):

> (a) that the Tribunal was not properly constituted;
> (b) that the Tribunal has manifestly exceeded its powers;
> (c) that there was corruption on the part of a member of the Tribunal;
> (d) that there has been a serious departure from a fundamental rule of procedure; or
> (e) that the award has failed to state the reasons on which it is based.

Annulment is restricted to these five grounds. Any request for annulment must be brought under one or several of these grounds and the ad hoc committee may

545 *CDC v Seychelles*, Decision on Annulment, 29 June 2005, para 36, footnotes omitted.

546 ICSID Arbitration Rule 55(3). *Amco v Indonesia*, Resubmitted Case: Decision on Jurisdiction, 10 May 1988, 1 ICSID Reports 543 pp 545–561; *Vivendi v Argentina*, Resubmitted Case: Decision on Jurisdiction, 14 November 2005, paras 30–31; *Pey Casado v Chile*, Resubmitted Case: Award, 13 September 2016, paras 173–179; *TECO v Guatamala*, Resubmitted Case: Award, 13 May 2020, paras 66–140.

547 *Amco v Indonesia*, Resubmitted Case: Decision on Jurisdiction, 10 May 1988, 1 ICSID Reports 543, at p 552.

548 At pp 560–561, 566–567.

not annul on other grounds. Also, a party may not present in the annulment proceedings new arguments on fact or law that it failed to put forward in the original arbitral proceeding. Therefore, Article 52 of the ICSID Convention offers a review process that is limited to a few fundamental standards of a mostly procedural nature.

Under Article 52(3) of the ICSID Convention the ad hoc committee has the authority to annul the award. Therefore, an ad hoc committee has discretion and will not be under an obligation to annul even if it finds that there is a ground for annulment listed in Article 52(1). An ad hoc committee must decide whether the fault is grave enough to warrant annulment, especially whether it has made a material difference to the position of one of the parties.[549] The ad hoc Committee in *Vivendi* said:

> it appears to be established that an *ad hoc* committee has a certain measure of discretion as to whether to annul an award, even if an annullable error is found. Article 52 (3) provides that a committee 'shall have the authority to annul the award or any part thereof', and this has been interpreted as giving committees some flexibility in determining whether annulment is appropriate in the circumstances. Among other things, it is necessary for an *ad hoc* committee to consider the significance of the error relative to the legal rights of the parties.[550]

Only three of the grounds for annulment listed above have played a significant role in practice: excess of powers, serious departure from a fundamental rule of procedure, and failure to state reasons. Parties requesting annulment typically have claimed the presence of more than one of these defects justifying annulment.

aa. Improper constitution of tribunal

Applications for annulment on the ground that the tribunal was not properly constituted are rare. ICSID carefully supervises the constitution of tribunals, making improprieties unlikely. In the few recorded cases, applicants took issue with the modalities of the appointment of an arbitrator by ICSID,[551] with the modalities of challenges of arbitrators during the proceedings before the tribunal,[552] with alleged relationships of an arbitrator to one of the parties,[553] and with prior professional

549 *MINE v Guinea*, Decision on Annulment, 14 December 1989, paras 4.09–4.10; *Vivendi v Argentina*, Decision on Annulment, 3 July 2002, para 66; *CDC v Seychelles*, Decision on Annulment, 29 June 2005, paras 37, 65; *Tulip v Turkey*, Decision on Anulment, 30 December 2015, paras 45–47; But see the early decision to the contrary in *Klöckner v Cameroon*, Decision on Annulment, 3 May 1985, paras 80, 116, 151, 179.

550 *Vivendi v Argentina*, Decision on Annulment, 3 July 2002, para 66, footnote omitted. See also paras 63, 86.

551 *Carnegie Minerals v Gambia*, Decision on Annulment, 7 July 2020.

552 *Mobil v Argentina*, Decision on Annulment, 8 May 2019, para 44; *Pey Casado v Chile*, Resubmitted Case: Decision on Annulment, 8 January 2020, para 564.

553 *Suez and Vivendi v Argentina*, Decision on Annulment, 5 May 2017, paras 186–219.

contacts of an arbitrator with a quantum expert.[554] All but one application resting on this ground for annulment have failed.

bb. Excess of powers

An excess of powers occurs where the tribunal deviates from the parties' agreement to arbitrate. This will be the case if the tribunal made a decision on the merits although it did not have jurisdiction or if it exceeded its jurisdiction. Jurisdiction is determined by Article 25 of the ICSID Convention. The requirements listed there must be met, otherwise there is no jurisdiction. This will be the case if there was no legal dispute arising directly out of an investment. Similarly, if the nationality requirements under the ICSID Convention were not met there was no jurisdiction and a decision on the merits would be an excess of powers. Absence of a valid consent to arbitration would also mean that there is no jurisdiction and an award on the merits would be an excess of powers.

An excess of powers must be manifest to constitute a ground for annulment. Manifest means that the excess of powers must be obvious.[555] Some ad hoc committees have added that the excess of powers must also be serious:

> It seems to this Committee that a manifest excess of power implies that the excess of power should at once be textually obvious and substantively serious.[556]

In *Mitchell v Congo* the request for annulment argued that the Tribunal had committed a manifest excess of powers by assuming jurisdiction although the dispute had not arisen from an investment. The ad hoc Committee held that a contribution to the host State's economic development was an indispensable element of the concept of an investment under the ICSID Convention. The ad hoc Committee found that there was no indication that the claimant's business—a legal counselling firm—had made such a contribution. It followed for the ad hoc Committee that there was no investment in the sense of Article 25 of the ICSID Convention and that the Tribunal had consequently committed a manifest excess of powers by assuming jurisdiction.[557]

554 *Eiser v Spain*, Decision on Annulment, 11 June 2020, paras 156–229.

555 *Klöckner v Cameroon*, Decision on Annulment, 3 May 1985, 2 ICSID Reports 95, paras 17, 52(e); *Wena Hotels v Egypt*, Decision on Annulment, 28 January 2002, 6 ICSID Reports 129, para 25; *CDC v Seychelles*, Decision on Annulment, 29 June 2005, paras 41, 42; *Mitchell v Congo*, Decision on Annulment, 1 November 2006, para 20; *Repsol v Petroecuador*, Decision on Annulment, 8 January 2007, para 36; *Daimler v Argentina*, Decision on Annulment, 7 January 2015, para 187; *Standard Chartered Bank v TANESCO*, Decision on Annulment, 22 August 2018, para 222.

556 *Soufraki v UAE*, Decision on Annulment, 5 June 2007, para 40. See also: *Fraport v Philippines I*, Decision on Annulment, 23 December 2010, paras 39–45, 112; *SGS v Paraguay*, Decision on Annulment, 19 May 2014, para 122; *Kiliç v Turkmenistan*, Decision on Annulment, 14 July 2015, para 53.

557 *Mitchell v Congo*, Decision on Annulment, 1 November 2006, paras 23–48.

Failure to exercise an existing jurisdiction also constitutes an excess of powers.[558] In *Vivendi* the ad hoc Committee said:

> It is settled, and neither party disputes, that an ICSID tribunal commits an excess of powers not only if it exercises a jurisdiction which it does not have ... but also if it fails to exercise a jurisdiction which it possesses ....[559]

The Tribunal had not decided certain claims that were before it but had referred the claimants to the domestic courts. The ad hoc Committee found that the Tribunal had thereby committed an excess of powers:

> In the Committee's view, it is not open to an ICSID tribunal having jurisdiction under a BIT in respect of a claim based upon a substantive provision of that BIT, to dismiss the claim on the ground that it could or should have been dealt with by a national court... the Committee concludes that the Tribunal exceeded its powers in the sense of Article 52(1)(b), in that the Tribunal, having jurisdiction over the Tucumán claims, failed to decide those claims.[560]

Article 52(1) of the ICSID Convention does not, in express terms, provide for annulment for failure to apply the proper law. But the provisions on applicable law are an essential element of the parties' agreement to arbitrate. Therefore, the application of a law other than that agreed to by the parties may constitute an excess of powers and can be a valid ground for annulment. On the other hand, an error in the application of the proper law, even if it leads to an incorrect decision, is not a ground for annulment. Ad hoc committees, although recognizing this distinction in principle, have grappled with the dividing line between non-application and erroneous application of the proper law.[561]

In *Wena v Egypt*, the proper law was host State law and applicable rules of international law. In the annulment proceedings, Egypt argued that the Tribunal, by awarding interest at the rate of 9 per cent, compounded quarterly, had failed to

[558] *Soufraki v UAE*, Decision on Annulment, 5 June 2007, para 43; *Lucchetti v Peru*, Decision on Annulment, 5 September 2007, para 99.

[559] *Vivendi v Argentina*, Decision on Annulment, 3 July 2002, para 86.

[560] At paras 102, 115.

[561] *Klöckner v Cameroon*, Decision on Annulment, 3 May 1985 paras 59–61; *Amco v Indonesia*, Decision on Annulment, 16 May 1986, paras 21–28; *MINE v Guinea*, Decision on Annulment, 14 December 1989, paras 5.02–5.04; *Wena Hotels v Egypt*, Decision on Annulment, 28 January 2002, paras 26–53; *CDC v Seychelles*, Decision on Annulment, 29 June 2005, para 46; *Mitchell v Congo*, Decision on Annulment, 1 November 2006, paras 55–57; *MTD v Chile*, Decision on Annulment, 21 March 2007, paras 44–48, 58–77; *Soufraki v UAE*, Decision on Annulment, 5 June 2007, paras 85–102; *CMS v Argentina*, Decision on Annulment, 25 September 2007, paras 128–136; *Azurix v Argentina*, Decision on Annulment, 1 September 2009, paras 46–48, 131–177, 314–329; *Sempra v Argentina*, Decision on Annulment, 29 June 2010, paras 186–210; *Enron v Argentina*, Decision on Annulment, 30 July 2010, paras 218–220, 377–405; *Duke Energy v Peru*, Decision on Annulment, 1 March 2011, para 212.

apply the proper law since such a calculation of interest was contrary to Egyptian law. The ad hoc Committee rejected this argument. It found that under the BIT, compensation had to reflect the market value of the expropriated investment. This had to be read as including a determination of appropriate interest. The ad hoc Committee said:

> 53. The option the Tribunal took was in the view of this Committee within the Tribunal's power. International law and ICSID practice, unlike the Egyptian Civil Code, offer a variety of alternatives that are compatible with those objectives. These alternatives include the compounding of interest in some cases.[562]

In *Standard Chartered Bank v TANESCO*, the ad hoc Committee was faced with the allegation that the Tribunal had committed a manifest excess of powers by referring to English law and not applying Tanzanian law. The Committee reviewed the Tribunal's analysis and found that, whilst it had referred to English doctrine, this was in the context of applying the relevant provision of Tanzanian law, which was identical to English law. There was no application of English law as such, and no manifest excess of powers.[563]

cc. Corruption

Corruption would be improper conduct by an arbitrator induced by personal gain. Corruption of an arbitrator has never been successfully alleged. It was listed as one of several grounds for annulment in one case but was subsequently dropped.[564]

dd. Serious departure from a fundamental rule of procedure

Under the ICSID Convention, a violation of a rule of procedure would be a ground for annulment only if the departure from the rule was serious and the rule concerned was fundamental. The seriousness of the departure requires that it is more than minimal and that it must have had a material effect on a party. A minor and inconsequential breach of a rule of procedure is no ground for annulment. A rule is fundamental if its observation is necessary for the fairness of the proceedings.[565]

[562] *Wena Hotels v Egypt*, Decision on Annulment, 28 January 2002, para 53, footnote omitted.

[563] *Standard Chartered Bank v TANESCO*, Decision on Annulment, 22 August 2018, paras 301–302.

[564] *Vivendi v Argentina*, Resubmitted Case: Decision on Annulment, 10 August 2010, paras 2, 17.

[565] *Klöckner v Cameroon*, Decision on Annulment, 3 May 1985, paras 82bis–113; *MINE v Guinea*, Decision on Annulment, 14 December 1989, paras 5.05–5.06; *Wena Hotels v Egypt*, Decision on Annulment, 28 January 2002, paras 56–58; *CDC v Seychelles*, Decision on Annulment, 29 June 2005, paras 48, 49; *Azurix v Argentina*, Decision on Annulment, 1 September 2009, paras 49–52, 234; *Enron v Argentina*, Decision on Annulment, 30 July 2010, paras 70–71; *Libananco v Turkey*, Decision on Annulment, 22 May 2013, para 85; *Lemire v Ukraine*, Decision on Annulment, 8 July 2013, para 263; *Tulip v Turkey*, Decision on Annulment, 30 December 2015, para 71.

An example for a fundamental rule of procedure is the right to be heard.[566] In several cases involving the charge of a violation of the right to be heard, a party complained that the award was based on a theory that had not been discussed by the parties before the tribunal. The ad hoc committees have rejected the idea that the tribunals in drafting their awards are restricted to the arguments presented by the parties.[567] In *Klöckner v Cameroon* the ad hoc Committee said:

> arbitrators must be free to rely on arguments which strike them as the best ones, even if those arguments were not developed by the parties (although they could have been). Even if it is generally desirable for arbitrators to avoid basing their decision on an argument that has not been discussed by the parties, it obviously does not follow that they therefore commit a 'serious departure from a fundamental rule of procedure.'[568]

Other instances of invocations of fundamental rules of procedure concerned impartiality and equal treatment of the parties[569] and issues of evidence.[570]

A party that is aware of a violation of a rule of procedure by the tribunal must react immediately by stating its objection and by demanding compliance. Under Arbitration Rule 27,[571] failure to do so will be interpreted as a waiver to object at a later stage. If a party has failed to protest against a perceived procedural irregularity before the tribunal, it cannot subsequently claim in annulment proceedings that this irregularity constituted a serious departure from a fundamental rule of procedure.[572]

[566] *MINE v Guinea*, Decision on Annulment, 14 December 1989, para 5.06; *Amco v Indonesia*, Resubmitted Case: Decision on Annulment, 3 December 1992, paras 9.05–9.10; *Wena Hotels v Egypt*, Decision on Annulment, 28 January 2002, para 57; *Lucchetti v Peru*, Decision on Annulment, 5 September 2007, para 122; *Helnan v Egypt*, Decision on Annulment, 14 June 2010, para 38; *Fraport v Philippines I*, Decision on Annulment, 23 December 2010, paras 127–133, 144–247.

[567] *Wena Hotels v Egypt*, Decision on Annulment, 28 January 2002, paras 66–70; *Vivendi v Argentina*, Decision on Annulment, 3 July 2002, paras 82–85; *Caratube v Kazakhstan*, Decision on Annulment, 21 February 2014, paras 178–179; *Daimler v Argentina*, Decision on Annulment, 7 January 2015, para 295; *Tza Yap Shum v Peru*, Decision on Annulment, 12 February 2015, paras 131, 141.

[568] *Klöckner v Cameroon*, Decision on Annulment, 3 May 1985, para 91.

[569] *Klöckner v Cameroon*, Decision on Annulment, 3 May 1985, paras 93–113; *Amco v Indonesia*, Decision on Annulment, 16 May 1986, paras 30, 32, 36, 88, 122–123; *CDC v Seychelles*, Decision on Annulment, 29 June 2005, paras 51–55.

[570] *Azurix v Argentina*, Decision on Annulment, 1 September 2009, paras 207–239; *Malicorp v Egypt*, Decision on Annulment, 3 July 2013, paras 61, 96–105; *Tenaris v Venezuela II*, Decision on Annulment, 28 December 2018, paras 240–247.

[571] ICSID Arbitration Rule 27: 'A party which knows or should have known that a provision of the Administrative and Financial Regulations, of these Rules, of any other rules or agreement applicable to the proceeding, or of an order of the Tribunal has not been complied with and which fails to state promptly its objections thereto, shall be deemed—subject to Article 45 of the Convention—to have waived its right to object.'

[572] *Klöckner v Cameroon*, Decision on Annulment, 3 May 1985, para 88; *CDC v Seychelles*, Decision on Annulment, 29 June 2005, paras 51–53; *Fraport v Philippines I*, Decision on Annulment, 23 December 2010, paras 204–208, 233–234; *Lemire v Ukraine*, Decision on Annulment, 8 July 2013, paras 200–219, 272–274.

ee. Failure to state reasons

The purpose of a statement of reasons is to explain to the reader of the award, especially to the parties, how and why the tribunal reached its decision. Article 48(3) of the ICSID Convention provides that the award shall state the reasons upon which it is based. Therefore, a total absence of reasons is unlikely. Requests for annulment have, however, repeatedly alleged the absence of reasons on specific points. In addition, complaints were directed at insufficient and inadequate reasons, contradictory reasons, or a failure to deal with every question before the tribunal.

If reasons on a particular point are missing, an ad hoc committee may reconstruct missing reasons. Therefore, an award will not be annulled if the reasons for a decision, though not stated explicitly, are readily apparent to the ad hoc committee. Implicit reasoning is sufficient provided it can be inferred reasonably from the terms and conclusions of the award.[573]

Insufficiency and inadequacy of reasons has been invoked frequently. This is a particularly subjective criterion and ad hoc committees have stated that reasons had to be 'sufficiently relevant', 'appropriate', and should 'allow the parties to understand the Tribunal's decision'.[574] The ad hoc Committee in *Vivendi* said in this respect:

> annulment under Article 52(1)(e) should only occur in a clear case. This entails two conditions: first, the failure to state reasons must leave the decision on a particular point essentially lacking in any expressed rationale; and second, that point must itself be necessary to the tribunal's decision.[575]

[573] *Amco v Indonesia*, Decision on Annulment, 16 May 1986, para 58; *MINE v Guinea*, Decision on Annulment, 14 December 1989, paras 6.103–6.104; *Wena Hotels v Egypt*, Decision on Annulment, 28 January 2002, paras 81–83, 93, 98, 106; *Vivendi v Argentina*, Decision on Annulment, 3 July 2002, paras 87–91; *CDC v Seychelles*, Decision on Annulment, 29 June 2005, paras 81, 87; *Soufraki v UAE*, Decision on Annulment, 5 June 2007, para 24; *CMS v Argentina*, Decision on Annulment, 25 September 2007, paras 125–127; *Rumeli v Kazakhstan*, Decision on Annulment, 25 March 2010, paras 83, 138; *Vivendi v Argentina*, Resubmitted Case: Decision on Annulment, 10 August 2010, para 248; *Fraport v Philippines I*, Decision on Annulment, 23 December 2010, paras 264–266; *Tulip v Turkey*, Decision on Annulment, 30 December 2015, para 108; *Suez and Vivendi v Argentina*, Decision on Annulment, 5 May 2017, para 292.

[574] *Klöckner v Cameroon*, Decision on Annulment, 3 May 1985, paras 117–120; *Amco v Indonesia*, Decision on Annulment, 16 May 1986, paras 38–43; *MINE v Guinea*, Decision on Annulment, 14 December 1989, paras 5.08–5.09; *Wena Hotels v Egypt*, Decision on Annulment, 28 January 2002, paras 75–83; *CDC v Seychelles*, Decision on Annulment, 29 June 2005, paras 66–71, 75; *Mitchell v DR Congo*, Decision on Annulment, 1 November 2006, paras 21, 39–41, 46, 65; *Soufraki v UAE*, Decision on Annulment, 5 June 2007, paras 121–134; *Lucchetti v Peru*, Decision on Annulment, 5 September 2007, paras 126–130; *CMS v Argentina*, Decision on Annulment, 25 September 2007, paras 86–98, 125–127; *Fraport v Philippines I*, Decision on Annulment, 23 December 2010, paras 248–280; *Standard Chartered Bank v TANESCO*, Decision on Annulment, 22 August 2018, paras 617–619.

[575] *Vivendi v Argentina*, Decision on Annulment, 3 July 2002, para 65.

It is also accepted that contradictory reasons may amount to a failure to state reasons since they will not enable the reader to understand the tribunal's motives. Genuinely contradictory reasons would cancel each other out.[576]

The tribunal's obligation to deal with every question submitted to it is contained in Article 48(3) of the ICSID Convention. Failure to deal with every question is not listed as a separate ground for annulment, but ad hoc committees have found that it was covered by failure to state reasons.[577] But this obligation does not mean that the tribunal must address every single argument put forward by a party. Only a crucial or decisive argument would be a 'question' in this context.[578] A decisive argument, if accepted, would have affected the tribunal's decision.

(c) Supplementation and rectification under the ICSID Convention

Under Article 49(2) of the ICSID Convention, the tribunal may, upon the request of a party, decide any question it had omitted to decide in the award and shall rectify technical errors in the award.[579] This gives the tribunal the possibility to correct inadvertent omissions and minor technical errors. This remedy is not designed for substantive amendments of the award.[580] The request has to be made within 45 days.

[576] *Klöckner v Cameroon*, Decision on Annulment, 3 May 1985, para 116; *Amco v Indonesia*, Decision on Annulment, 16 May 1986, para 97; *MINE v Guinea*, Decision on Annulment, 14 December 1989, para 6.105; *Vivendi v Argentina*, Decision on Annulment, 3 July 2002, paras 64–65, 72; *CDC v Seychelles*, Decision on Annulment, 29 June 2005, paras 77–86; *Azurix v Argentina*, Decision on Annulment, 1 September 2009, paras 364–366; *Duke Energy v Peru*, Decision on Annulment, 1 March 2011, para 166; *Daimler v Argentina*, Decision on Annulment, 7 January 2015, para 77; *Tza Yap Shum v Peru*, Decision on Annulment, 12 February 2015, para 167; *Total v Argentina*, Decision on Annulment, 1 February 2016, para 268; *Venezuela Holdings v Venezuela*, Decision on Annulment, 9 March 2017, para 119.

[577] *Klöckner v Cameroon*, Decision on Annulment, 3 May 1985, para 115; *Amco v Indonesia*, Decision on Annulment, 16 May 1986, para 32; *MINE v Guinea*, Decision on Annulment, 14 December 1989, para 5.13; *Wena Hotels v Egypt*, Decision on Annulment, 28 January 2002, paras 102–110; *Azurix v Argentina*, Decision on Annulment, 1 September 2009, paras 240–246; *MCI v Ecuador*, Decision on Annulment, 19 October 2009, paras 66–69; *Rumeli v Kazakhstan*, Decision on Annulment, 25 March 2010, para 84; *Daimler v Argentina*, Decision on Annulment, 7 January 2015, paras 87–88.

[578] *AES v Hungary*, Decision on Annulment, 29 June 2012, paras 133, 135; *Dogan v Turkmenistan*, Decision on Annulment, 15 January 2016, paras 262–263.

[579] ICSID Arbitration Rule 49.

[580] *Railroad Development v Guatemala*, Decision on Supplementation and Rectification, 18 January 2013, paras 43, 47; *İçkale v Turkmenistan*, Decision on Supplementation and Rectification, 4 October 2016, paras 120–123, 152; *Gavazzi v Romania*, Decision on Rectification, 13 July 2017, para 55; *Pey Casado v Chile*, Resubmitted Case: Decision on Rectification, 6 October 2017, paras 49–50; *Watkins Holdings v Spain*, Decision on Rectification, 13 July 2020, paras 35–65.

(d) Interpretation under the ICSID Convention

In case of a dispute between the parties concerning the meaning or scope of an award either party may request an interpretation under Article 50 of the ICSID Convention.[581] There is no time limit for such a request. If possible, the original tribunal is to decide upon the request. If this is not possible a new tribunal will be constituted for this purpose. There is no time limit for an application requesting the interpretation. Once the interpretation has been given, the award will be binding as interpreted.

The request for interpretation must relate to an award and not to a preliminary decision such as a decision on jurisdiction.[582] The purpose of an interpretation is to clarify points that were decided in the award and not to decide new points.[583] In addition, the dispute on the award's interpretation must have some practical relevance to the award's implementation.[584] The Tribunal in *ATA v Jordan* summarized the function of a decision on interpretation as follows:

(1) there must be a dispute between the parties over 'the meaning or scope' of the award;
(2) the purpose of the application must be to obtain a true interpretation of the award, rather than to reopen the matter; and
(3) the requested interpretation 'must have some practical relevance to the Award's implementation'.[585]

(e) Revision under the ICSID Convention

If decisive new facts come to light after the award has been rendered a party may, in accordance with Article 51 of the ICSID Convention request the award's revision.[586] Revision under Article 51 is not available for decisions preliminary to awards such as decisions on jurisdiction or provisional measures.[587]

The new facts must have been unknown to the applicant at the time the award was rendered.[588] A request for revision must be made within 90 days of discovery of the new facts and within three years of the rendering of the award. If possible,

[581] ICSID Arbitration Rules 50 and 51.
[582] *Waste Management v Mexico II*, Award, 30 April 2004, paras 13–17.
[583] *Wena Hotels v Egypt*, Decision on Interpretation, 31 October 2005, paras 103–107, 127–131, 133, 138; *Minnotte v Poland*, Decision on Interpretation, 22 October 2014, para 12.
[584] *Wena Hotels v Egypt*, Decision on Interpretation, 31 October 2005, paras 81, 87.
[585] *ATA v Jordan*, Decision on Interpretation, 7 March 2011, para 35.
[586] Arbitration Rules 50 and 51.
[587] *Pac Rim v El Salvador*, Award, 14 October 2016, para 5.36.
[588] *RSM v Grenada II*, Award, 10 December 2010, paras 7.1.15–7.1.30; *Venezuela Holdings v Venezuela*, Decision on Revision, 12 June 2015, paras 3.1.1–3.1.23; *Tidewater v Venezuela*, Decision on Revision, 7 July 2015, paras 33–39.

the original tribunal is to decide upon the request. If this is not possible, a new tribunal will be constituted for this purpose.

The new facts must be capable of affecting the award decisively, that is, they would have led to a different decision had they been known to the tribunal.[589] The request for revision must come from one of the parties; the tribunal may not revise the award on its own initiative. The award will be binding as revised.

16. Enforcement of awards

Arbitral awards are binding upon the parties and create an obligation to comply with them. Except for the limited possibilities for review described in the preceding chapter, they are final. Article 53 of the ICSID Convention specifically provides for the binding nature and finality of awards. Article 53 of the ICSID Convention explicitly excludes an appeal against an award. This makes the introduction of an appeals procedure[590] in the ICSID context difficult or impossible. The issues decided in awards are also *res judicata*. This means that the parties may not relitigate them before another tribunal or in a domestic court.

The binding force of awards rendered on the basis of intra-EU BITs and the ECT has been questioned as being in conflict with EU law.[591] In particular, following the judgment of the European Court in *Slovakia v Achmea*,[592] respondent States as well as the EU Commission have argued that compliance with awards resulting from such arbitrations would be contrary to EU law.[593] Investment tribunals have held that any potential conflict between the ICSID Convention or investment treaties and EU law needs to be assessed according to the VCLT. Tribunals have denied both the existence of a conflict between the ICSID Convention or investment treaties and EU law[594] and, if a conflict existed, any supremacy of EU law over the

589 *Pey Casado v Chile*, Decision on Revision, 18 November 2009, para 50.

590 See above XII.15.

591 See also above XII.7(c) and (e).

592 *Slovak Republic v Achmea*, Court of Justice of the European Union, Judgment, 6 March 2018, Case C-284/16. The Court held that the investor–State dispute settlement provisions in the bilateral investment treaty (BIT) between two EU Member States were contrary to EU law.

593 *Masdar v Spain*, Award, 16 May 2018, paras 296–341; *Vattenfall v Germany II*, Decision on the *Achmea* Issue, 31 August 2018, paras 48–59; *Adamakopoulos v Cyprus*, Decision on Jurisdiction, 7 February 2020, paras 50–63; *Addiko Bank v Croatia*, Decision on Croatia's Jurisdictional Objection Related to the Alleged Incompatibility of the BIT with the *EU Acquis*, 12 June 2020, paras 62–65, 125–131, 136–143. See also Declaration of EU Member States of 15 January 2019 on the Legal Consequences of the *Achmea* Judgment and on Investment Protection (and Declaration of 5 EU Member States on 16 January 2019 as well as the separate Declaration of Hungary on 16 January 2019).

594 *EURAM v Slovakia*, Award on Jurisdiction, 22 October 2012, paras 184–185; *Magyar Farming v Hungary*, Award, 13 November 2019, paras 238–239; *Adamakopoulos v Cyprus*, Decision on Jurisdiction, 7 February 2020, paras 163–186.

Convention and investment treaties.[595] Therefore, respondents remained bound to honour awards.[596]

The enforcement of non-ICSID awards, including Additional Facility awards,[597] is subject to the national law of the place of enforcement and to the New York Convention.[598] Article V of that Convention lists the grounds on which recognition and enforcement may be refused. The most important of these grounds are the invalidity of the arbitration agreement, lack of proper notice of the arbitration proceedings, a decision in the award outside the submission to arbitration, improper composition of the tribunal, an award that is not yet binding or has been set aside, a subject-matter not capable of settlement by arbitration under the law of the State in which enforcement is sought, and an award that conflicts with the public policy of that State.

The regime for the enforcement of ICSID awards is different. Under Article 54 of the ICSID Convention awards are to be recognized as binding and their pecuniary obligations are to be enforced like final domestic judgments in all States parties to the Convention. Only awards are covered by this obligation.[599] Decisions preliminary to awards, such as decisions on jurisdiction, decisions recommending provisional measures,[600] and procedural orders are not awards. They are not by themselves subject to recognition and enforcement.

The obligation to recognize an award extends to any type of obligation under it. By contrast, the obligation to enforce is limited to the pecuniary obligations under the award.

Recognition and enforcement may be sought not only in the host State or in the investor's State of nationality, but in any State that is a party to the ICSID Convention. The prevailing party may select a State where enforcement seems most promising. An important element in this choice will be the availability of suitable assets.

The procedure for the enforcement of ICSID awards is governed by the law on the execution of judgments in each country. The Contracting States are to designate a competent court or authority for this purpose.[601] The party seeking

[595] *RREEF v Spain*, Decision on Jurisdiction, 6 June 2016, paras 75, 87; *Eskosol v Italy*, Decision on Termination Request and Intra-EU Objection, 7 May 2019, paras 76, 182. See, however, *Electrabel v Hungary*, Decision on Jurisdiction, Applicable Law and Liability, 30 November 2012, para 4.189.

[596] *Marfin v Cyprus*, Award, 26 July 2018, para 577–597; *UP and C.D v Hungary*, Award, 9 October 2018, paras 252–267; *OperaFund v Spain*, Award, 6 September 2019, para 387; *NextEra v Spain*, Decision on Stay of Enforcement, 6 April 2020, para 90.

[597] See eg *Crystallex v Venezuela*, Canada, Superior Court of Justice of Ontario, 20 July 2016.

[598] Convention on the Recognition and Enforcement of Foreign Arbitral Awards (1958), 330 UNTS 38; (1968) 7 ILM 1046.

[599] *Standard Chartered Bank v TANESCO*, Award, 12 September 2016, para 314; *Burlington v Ecuador*, Decision on Reconsideration and Award, 7 February 2017, para 88.

[600] *RSM v St Lucia*, Decision on Security for Costs, 13 August 2014, para 50 and Decision on Annulment, 29 April 2019, para 174.

[601] Designations of Courts or Other Authorities Competent for the Recognition and Enforcement of Awards Rendered Pursuant to the Convention (ICSID/8-E).

recognition and enforcement must furnish a copy of the award certified by the Secretary-General of ICSID. If a stay of enforcement is in force the duty to enforce is suspended. A stay of enforcement may be granted while proceedings for the interpretation, revision or annulment are in progress.

There is no review of ICSID awards by domestic courts in proceedings for their recognition and enforcement.[602] Therefore, the domestic court or authority may not examine whether the ICSID tribunal had jurisdiction, whether it adhered to the proper procedure or whether the award is substantively correct. It may not even examine whether the award is in conformity with the forum State's *ordre public* (public policy). The domestic court or authority is limited to verifying that the award is authentic.

In proceedings for the enforcement of the Award in *Micula v Romania*,[603] the English Court of Appeal said:

> [I]t would be inconsistent with Article 54 ICSID for a national court to refuse to enforce the pecuniary obligations imposed by an award on the ground that, had the award been an ordinary domestic judgment giving effect to it would be contrary to a provision of national law... [T]he analogy with a judgment of the High Court is limited to defining the force and effect of a registered award for the purpose of execution. It does not give the High Court power to refuse to enforce an award for a reason that would justify staying enforcement of an ordinary domestic judgment.[604]

Proceedings for the recognition and enforcement of ICSID awards may be initiated in several States simultaneously. This may be necessary to secure their *res judicata* effect. If enforcement is sought in more than one State, appropriate steps must be taken to prevent double or multiple recovery.

Under Article 55 of the ICSID Convention the obligation to enforce the pecuniary obligations arising from ICSID awards does not affect any immunity from execution that States enjoy. State immunity is regulated by customary international law. A number of States have passed legislation in this field.[605] A United Nations

[602] *Vivendi v Argentina*, Resubmitted Case: Decision on Continued Stay of Enforcement, 4 November 2008, para 36; *Electrabel v Hungary*, Decision on Jurisdiction, Applicable Law and Liability, 30 November 2012, para 3.50; *Elsamex v Honduras*, Decision on the Termination of the Stay of Enforcement, 11 March 2014, para 30.

[603] *Micula v Romania I*, Award, 11 December 2013.

[604] *Micula v Romania* [2018] EWCA Civ 1801 (27 July 2018) para 121. See also the decision of the Supreme Court in *Micula v Romania* [2020] UKSC 5, 19 February 2020.

[605] United States: Foreign Sovereign Immunities Act (FSIA) 1976, 28 USC §§ 1330, 1602–1611, (1976) 15 ILM 1388, as amended in 1988, (1989) 28 ILM 396 and in 1996/7, (1997) 36 ILM 759; United Kingdom: State Immunity Act (SIA) 1978, (1978) 17 ILM 1123; Australia: Foreign States Immunities Act 1985, (1986) 25 ILM 715.

Convention dealing with State immunity is not yet in force[606] but many of its provisions are regarded as reflecting customary international law.

For purposes of State immunity from execution a distinction is usually made between commercial and non-commercial property. Execution is permitted against commercial property of the State but not against property serving official or governmental functions. The exact dividing line between the two types of property is not always easy to draw.[607] Diplomatic property, including embassy accounts[608] as well as accounts held by national central banks[609] enjoy special protection from execution. A waiver of immunity from execution may be possible but will be difficult to obtain from a host State.[610] Occasionally, domestic rules on State immunity from execution place limits on the possibility to agree on waivers. In cases for the enforcement of awards against States, courts have refused to order execution into property that belonged State-owned entities rather than to the State.[611]

State immunity from execution is merely a procedural bar to the award's enforcement but does not affect the obligation of the State to comply with it. Therefore, a successful reliance on State immunity does not alter the fact that non-compliance with an award is a breach of the ICSID Convention. The ad hoc Committee in *MINE v Guinea* said in this respect:

> It should be clearly understood ... that State immunity may well afford a legal defense to forcible execution, but it provides neither argument nor excuse for failing to comply with an award. In fact, the issue of State immunity from forcible execution of an award will typically arise if the State party refuses to comply with its

[606] United Nations Convention on Jurisdictional Immunities of States and their Property, 2004, Adopted by the General Assembly of the United Nations on 2 December 2004. See General Assembly Resolution 59/38, annex, Official Records of the General Assembly, Fifty-ninth Session, Supplement No. 49 (A/59/49).

[607] *LETCO v Liberia*, District Court, SDNY, 5 September and 12 December 1986; *Benvenuti & Bonfant v Congo*, Tribunal de grande instance, Paris, 13 January 1981, Cour d'appel, Paris, 26 June 1981, 1 ICSID Reports 368; *SOABI v Senegal*, Cour d'appel, Paris, 5 December 1989, Cour de cassation, 11 June 1991; *Sedelmayer v Russian Federation*, German Federal Supreme Court (Bundesgerichtshof), Case No VII ZB 9/05, Order, 4 October 2005, para 20; *Russian Federation v Sedelmayer*, Swedish Supreme Court, Ö 170-10, 1 July 2011, paras 18–25; *Sistem Mühendislik v Kyrgyzstan*, Swiss Federal Tribunal, 5A 681/2011, Decision, 23 November 2011; *Eiser v Spain*, Federal Court of Australia, 24 February 2020, [2020] FCA 157, para 108.

[608] *LETCO v Liberia*, US District Court for the District of Columbia, 16 April 1987.

[609] *AIG v Kazakhstan (National Bank of Kazakhstan Intervening)*, High Court, Queen's Bench Division (Commercial Court), 20 October 2005, [2005] EWHC 2239 (Comm), 11 ICSID Reports 118.

[610] In *Eiser v Spain*, Federal Court of Australia, 24 February 2020, [2020] FCA 157, paras 181–182, the Court saw a waiver of immunity through participation in the ICSID Convention. The Court also distinguished enforcement from execution.

[611] *Benvenuti & Bonfant v Banque Commerciale Congolaise*, France, Cour de Cassation, 21 July 1987, 1 ICSID Reports 373, (1988) 115 *JDI* 108; *AIG v Kazakhstan (National Bank of Kazakhstan Intervening)*, High Court, Queen's Bench Division (Commercial Court), 20 October 2005, [2005] EWHC 2239 (Comm), 11 ICSID Reports 118; *Belokon v Kyrgyzstan*, Canada, Superior Court of Justice, Ontario, 11 July 2016, 2016 ONSC 4506, 16.

> treaty obligations. Non-compliance by a State constitutes a violation by that State of its international obligations and will attract its own sanctions.[612]

Under Article 27 of the ICSID Convention the right of diplomatic protection revives in case of non-compliance with an award. Therefore, diplomatic protection is an alternative and supplement to the judicial enforcement of awards under Article 54. In particular, diplomatic protection will be available if enforcement is unsuccessful because of the award debtor State's immunity from execution. But diplomatic protection may be exercised only by the aggrieved investor's State of nationality.

612 *MINE v Guinea*, Interim Order No 1 on Guinea's Application for Stay of Enforcement of the Award, 12 August 1988, para 25.

Index

For the benefit of digital users, indexed terms that span two pages (e.g., 52–53) may, on occasion, appear on only one of those pages.